Eleventh Edition

State and Local Government

Ann O'M. Bowman
Texas A&M University

Richard C. Kearney
North Carolina State University

With

Carmine P. F. Scavo
East Carolina University

Australia • Brazil • Canada • Mexico • Singapore • United Kingdom • United States

CENGAGE

State and Local Government,
Eleventh Edition
Ann O'M. Bowman
Richard C. Kearney
with Carmine P. F. Scavo

Senior Vice President, Higher Education
& Skills Product: Erin Joyner

Product Director: Laura Ross

Product Manager: Lauren Gerrish

Product Assistant: Martina Umunna

Content Manager: Manoj Kumar,
Lumina Datamatics, Inc.

Senior Digital Delivery Lead:
Dana Edmunds

Senior In-House Subject Matter Expert:
Emily Hickey

Senior Marketing Manager:
Valerie Hartman

Intellectual Property Analyst:
Deanna Ettinger

Intellectual Property Project Manager:
Carly Belcher

Production Service:
Lumina Datamatics, Inc.

Learning Designer: Erika Hayden

Senior Designer: Sarah Cole

Cover Image: iStock.com/Sean Pavone

For product information and technology assistance, contact us at
Cengage Customer & Sales Support, 1-800-354-9706 or
support.cengage.com.
For permission to use material from this text
or product, submit all requests online at
www.cengage.com/permissions.

Library of Congress Control Number: 2020920365

ISBN: 978-0-357-36740-7

Cengage
200 Pier 4 Boulevard
Boston, MA 02210
USA

Cengage is a leading provider of customized learning solutions
with employees residing in nearly 40 different countries and
sales in more than 125 countries around the world. Find your
local representative at **www.cengage.com**.

To learn more about Cengage platforms and services, register or
access your online learning solution, or purchase materials for
your course, visit **www.cengage.com**.

Printed at CLDPC, USA, 11-20

Contents

Preface

If someone had told us in 1990 that the first edition of *State and Local Government* would become what is now widely recognized as "the market leader" and followed eventually by an eleventh edition, we would have been doubtful. That first edition broke the mold of traditional state and local government texts by offering a positive, thematic approach to introducing government at the grass roots. We were gratified and delighted when the book quickly built up adoptions in research universities, four-year colleges, and community colleges across the United States. There are quite a few rival texts today, but we like to think that the competition makes ours better. We heartily thank our colleagues in the State Politics and Policy section and the Urban Politics section of the American Political Science Association for their ideas and comments on various editions of this book. And we thank as well, researchers too numerous to mention individually, for their insightful analyses that are published in scholarly journals and inform our latest edition.

When the preparations began on the eleventh edition of this book, the COVID-19 pandemic was just a speck on the horizon. Work proceeded as the virus's threat to state and local government grew. Hospitals were crowded with patients, schools closed, businesses suspended operations, tax revenue fell, public works projects were delayed—the list of effects goes on and on. In short, demand for public services increased dramatically but resources to meet those needs fell just as dramatically. At first it looked like the Great Recession all over again, but then things grew even worse. Unemployment in late spring 2020 rivaled rates in the Great Depression of the mid-1930s. By the summer of 2020, state legislatures, city councils, county commissions, local school boards and all other governmental bodies were beginning to cope with the fiscal impacts of the pandemic. But other issues are just as complicated as the fiscal ones. How could the 2020 elections be held so that public health was not endangered by in-person voting? How long could businesses be required to stay closed before permanent damage to the national economy occurred? How should state and local government enforce closure regulations against businesses that insist on remaining open? How can state legislature or city council or county commission sessions occur online if laws require in-person votes? Can state and local governments require individuals to wear masks in public or is this a civil liberties violation? How can schools operate effectively while maintaining social distancing and public health?

Despite the drumbeat of criticism of government and public officials in the mass media and by anti-government talk-show hosts, we like politics and public service, particularly at the state and local levels. We believe that government can be—and often is—a force for good in society. We do acknowledge some of the concerns voiced by critics of government. Yes, there continue to be inefficiencies; and sure, there are some politicians who, once elected, seem to forget the interests of the people back home, not to mention what their parents taught them. But by and large, state and local governments work well. On a daily basis, they tackle some of the toughest issues imaginable, designing and implementing creative and successful solutions to problems ranging from crime and corrections to education and the environment. And they do so with a remarkable diversity of approaches.

In the eleventh edition of our text, we again seek to capture the immediacy and vitality of state and local governments as they address the challenges facing the American people. A major goal is to foster continuing student interest and involvement in state and local politics, policy, and public service. Many of the students who read this text will work in state and local government. Some will run successfully for public office. All will deal with state and local governments throughout their lives. We want our readers to know that state and local governments are places where one person can still "do good," make a difference, and serve a cause. For students who go on to graduate study in political science, public administration, public policy, or related fields, states and localities are fertile fields for research. And for students taking this course because they "have to" and who purport to dislike politics and government, we invite them to keep an open mind as they explore the fascinating world of politics at the grass roots.

The Theme of *State and Local Government*

This book revolves around a central theme: the growing capacity and responsiveness of state and local government. Our theme is being sorely tested by the COVID-19 pandemic, but not found to be wanting. Despite their many challenges, state and local governments continue to be proactive, expanding their capacity to address effectively the myriad problems confronting their citizens. From Alabama to Wyoming, they are responsive to their rapidly changing environment and to the demands of the citizens.

Our confidence in these governments does not blind us, however, to the varying capabilities of the 50 states and some 90,000 units of local government. Some are better equipped to operate effectively than others. Many state and local governments benefit from talented leadership, a problem-solving focus, and an engaged citizenry. Others do not fare so well, and their performance disappoints. Rank partisanship divides many states as they become increasingly "Red" or "Blue." Still, as a group, states and localities are the driving forces—the prime movers—in the U.S. federal system. Even those jurisdictions perennially clustered at the lower end of various ratings scales have made quantum leaps in their capability and responsiveness.

Features of the Text

The themes of *State and Local Government* are supplemented by boxed features that provide compelling examples of nonnational governments in action. The boxes labeled "Controversies in States and Localities" highlight issues that may cause a jurisdiction to venture out on a limb, trying something new. The It's Your Turn boxes, which are new to this edition, present students with two sides to an issue and ask them to consider their own position.

The **Controversies in States and Localities** features are intended to generate debate and discussion among students. For example, state government responses to the COVID-19 crisis are featured in Chapter 2, participatory budgeting in Vallejo, California, is explored in Chapter 4, and the effort to get more third parties on state ballots is covered in Chapter 5. Utah's innovative website that engaged citizens in redrawing legislative districts is the focus in Chapter 6, governors with primarily private sector experience are examined in Chapter 7, and the proposal to split California into several states is the subject of Chapter 12's Controversies box. Chapter 16 looks at the issue of prison privatization, and mandatory drug testing for welfare applicants is considered in Chapter 17. Each of the Controversies in States and Localities now concludes with a series of critical thinking questions.

The **It's Your Turn** boxes engage students more directly, by asking them to take a side in a controversial issue. These issues include whether Washington D.C., should become the 51st state, whether state legislatures should be more professionalized, and whether a state should bail out its financially stressed local governments. Other It's Your Turn boxes ask students to consider the arguments for and against state governments providing tax incentives to the film industry for filming in their state, cities enacting plastic bag bans, states enforcing strict voter ID laws, and states legalizing marijuana.

Sincere effort has been invested in making this book accessible to the student. Each chapter opens with a series of **Learning Objectives** and closes with a **Chapter Recap** to help structure student learning. The Learning Objectives are also called out within each chapter, to help students make the connection between each learning objective and chapter content. We have included updated photographs to provide visual images that bring the world of state and local government to life for the reader. Maps, tables, and figures offer an engaging format to assist in the identification of patterns and trends in the data. Many of these graphics are new to or updated for the eleventh edition. As noted, boxes throughout the chapters showcase the innovative, the unusual, and the insightful in state and local politics. Lists of states appear in each chapter and facilitate comparisons across the states. **Key Terms** are boldfaced, defined in the margins, and listed at the end of each chapter. References to websites in the end-of-chapter list of **Internet Resources** encourage student curiosity, engagement, and individual research.

The Content of the Eleventh Edition

As in the first 10 editions, this book provides thorough and completely updated coverage of state and local institutions, processes, and policies. The chapters blend the findings from the latest political science and public policy research with issues and events from the real world. It is intended to be a core text.

In Chapter 1, we introduce the functions of nonnational governments and explore the theme of capacity and responsiveness. The growing diversity in the United States and the contemporary controversy dubbed "culture wars" are featured in the chapter. Federalism's central importance is highlighted in Chapter 2, which traces the twists and turns of the federal system, from the scribblings of the Framers to the Supreme Court's latest pronouncements on the Tenth and Eleventh amendments. The fundamental legal underpinnings of state governments—their constitutions—are discussed in Chapter 3. Chapter 4 explores citizen participation and elections (including the 2014 elections), focusing on the increased access of citizens and the expectations they have for government. Chapter 5, "Political Parties, Interest Groups, and Campaigns," gets at subnational politics—the fascinating real world of candidates, lobbyists, organizations, and money.

Coverage of the three branches of government—legislative, executive, and judicial—is updated and reflects the institutional changes each branch has undergone recently. The intent of Chapter 6 is to show how legislatures actually work. In addition, responses of state legislatures to the institutional challenge posed by term limits are explored. Governors are featured in Chapter 7, including those who have misbehaved in various ways, and the issue of gubernatorial power is emphasized. Chapter 8, "Public Administration: Budgeting and Service Delivery," offers updated coverage of privatization as a strategy for improving government and the delivery of public services, as well as new material on e-government and budget transparency. In Chapter 9, the policy-making role of judges, judicial federalism, judicial accountability, and judicial selection mechanisms are emphasized.

Local governments are not treated as afterthoughts in this book. Two chapters focus solely on localities: Chapter 10 is devoted to the multiple types and structures of local government and Chapter 11 to leadership and governance, including new leadership approaches of mayors and city councils. Subsequent chapters consider localities within the context of the states: Chapter 12 focuses on the political and practical issues linking the two levels—and the resultant tensions between them—and Chapter 13 emphasizes the growing interdependence of state and local financial systems. Chapter 12 specifically tackles the issue of land use and urban sprawl, including New Urbanism approaches. Chapter 13 offers a comprehensive synthesis of the principles and political economy of taxation and spending and an overview of the strategies used by state and local governments to cope with the aforementioned economic crash.

Five policy chapters illustrate the diverse postures of state and local governments in responding to change and citizen demands. The roles of states and localities are different in each policy area. Chapter 14 examines economic development initiatives in the context of interstate and interregional competition for jobs and business. Chapter 15 focuses on the ever-important topic of public education; it includes examples of many of the most recent education reform efforts, including school choice plans, No Child Left Behind, homeschooling, and charter schools. Criminal justice policy is the subject of Chapter 16. Crime statistics have been updated, as have some of the newest initiatives for community policing, law enforcement technology, and criminal data applications. Social welfare and health care policy are featured in Chapter 17. Welfare traps are identified, state programs aimed at plugging the gaping holes in the national health system are examined, and the effects of the Affordable Care Act ("Obamacare") are explained. Finally, Chapter 18 covers a wide range of environmental topics such as sustainability, waste management, hydraulic fracturing, and global climate change. Of special interest are some of the success stories in "greening" states and localities.

Resources for Instructors

Instructor Companion Web Site for *State and Local Government*, 11e
ISBN: 9780357367414

This Instructor Companion Website is an all-in-one multimedia online resource for class preparation, presentation, and testing. Accessible through Cengage.com/login with your faculty account, you will find available for download: book-specific Microsoft® PowerPoint® presentations; a Test Bank compatible with multiple learning management systems; and an Instructor Manual.

The Test Bank, offered in Blackboard, Moodle, Desire2Learn, Canvas, and Respondus formats, contains Learning Objective-specific multiple-choice, true/false, and essay questions for each chapter. Import the test bank into your learning management system to edit and manage questions and to create tests.

The Instructor's Manual contains chapter-specific learning objectives, an outline, key terms with definitions, and a chapter summary. Additionally, the Instructor's Manual features a critical thinking question, a lecture launching suggestion, and an in-class activity for each learning objective.

The Microsoft PowerPoint presentations are ready-to-use, visual outlines of each chapter. These presentations are easily customized for your lectures. Access the Instructor Companion Website at www.cengage.com/login.

IAC Cognero for *State and Local Government*, 11e ISBN: 9780357367452

Cengage Learning Testing Powered by Cognero® is a flexible online system that allows you to author, edit, and manage test bank content from multiple Cengage Learning solutions, create multiple test versions in an instant and deliver tests from your LMS, your classroom, or wherever you want. The test bank for *State and Local Government*, 11e contains Learning Objective-specific multiple-choice, true/false, and essay questions for each chapter.

Acknowledgments

First, we thank the reviewers of the eleventh edition, who provided us with many thoughtful observations and examples:

Jeff Dense, Eastern Oregon University
Tobias O. Vogt, University of Alabama in Huntsville
Tassi Dalton, East Tennessee State University
Troy Hinrichs, California State University, San Bernardino
Joshua Mitchell, University of Arkansas
William E. Kelly, Auburn University
Elaine Thompson, Blue Ridge Community College
Arlene Sanders, Delta State University

We have incorporated their suggestions into this edition whenever possible.

We also extend our appreciation to our partners at Cengage. Finally, Lauren Gerrish, Sheila Moran, Sarah Cole, Erika Hayden, Martina Umunna, Dana Edmunds, Emily Hickey, and Manoj Kumar contributed in many special ways to the final product, as usual.

A. O'M. B.
R. C. K.
C. P. F. S.

About the Author

Courtesy of Ann O'M. Bowman

Ann O'M. Bowman (Ph.D., University of Florida) is professor and holder of the Hazel Davis and Robert Kennedy Endowed Chair in the Bush School of Government and Public Service at Texas A&M University. She teaches courses in state and local politics and policy, intergovernmental relations, environmental policy and management, and public policy process. Her research interests revolve around questions of institutional change, policy adoption and implementation, and intergovernmental dynamics. She has published numerous books and articles on these topics over the years.

Courtesy of Richard C. Kearney

Richard C. Kearney (Ph.D., University of Oklahoma) is retired as professor of political science and public administration at North Carolina State University. His career also included lengthy teaching, research, and administrative responsibilities at East Carolina University, the University of Connecticut, and the University of South Carolina. His research interests include comparative state politics and policy, labor relations, and human resource management policy. He has published prolifically on these and related topics. He lives in Raleigh and Beaufort, NC.

Courtesy of Carmine P. F. Scavo

Carmine P. F. Scavo (Ph.D., University of Michigan) is emeritus professor of political science at East Carolina University where he has taught since 1985. He taught undergraduate and graduate courses in state and local government, intergovernmental relations, policy analysis, and methodology. His research interests include e-government, homeland security and disaster management, intergovernmental relations, and voting behavior. He has published a number of books and articles on these and other topics in his career.

1

State and Local Governments: New Directions

North Dakota Governor Doug Burgum delivers his 2019 State of the State address.

Learning Objectives

LO 1-1 To recognize the importance of state and local governments in contemporary America.

LO 1-2 To identify ways in which states and localities have increased their capacity.

LO 1-3 To recognize the challenges that states and localities confront on a daily basis.

LO 1-4 To recognize how changing public attitudes influence government behavior.

LO 1-5 To understand the changing demographic landscape in the United States.

With appropriate oratorical flourishes, the governor of North Dakota, Doug Burgum, delivered his 2019 State of the State message to the people of the Peace Garden State. Although parts of the speech were specific to North Dakota—references to the Fargo-Moorhead Area Diversion Project and the planned Theodore Roosevelt Presidential Library, for example—many of the themes resonated beyond the state's borders. Fiscal health, job creation, and educational improvement were topics in countless gubernatorial addresses throughout the country. Governor Burgum's tone was upbeat and determined as he referenced both North Dakota's past and its future: "This Sunday, January 6th, marks the 100th anniversary of the passing of Theodore Roosevelt. By immersing himself in the rugged, beautiful and untamed Badlands, he transformed himself into a bold and fearless leader—whose later actions transformed our nation and the world. As we stand at the cusp of this new era, let us seize this opportunity for North Dakota to transform our image of ourselves—to reach beyond any doubts and self-imposed limitations. Now is the time to dream bold dreams—to build those dreams—and to create lasting legacies."[1]

Spirited exhortations such as these were echoed in one state capitol after another in 2019, 2020, and 2021. In North Dakota and elsewhere, state and local governments are indeed tackling difficult problems and seeking innovative solutions to contemporary issues.

LO 1-1
To recognize the importance of state and local governments in contemporary America.

Studying State and Local Governments in the Twenty-First Century

The study of state and local governments has typically received short shrift in the survey of U.S. politics.[2] Scholars and journalists tend to focus on glamorous imperial presidents, a rancorous and gridlocked Congress, an independent and powerful Supreme Court, and the interactions of the three branches of national government in issues such as impeachment of a president. National and international issues capture the lion's share of media attention. Yet, state and local politics are fascinating precisely because they are up close and personal. True, a governor seldom gets involved in an international peace conference, and state legislatures rarely debate the global narcotics trade. But the actors and institutions of states and localities are directly involved in our day-to-day lives. Education, job growth, climate change, health care, and crime are among the many concerns of state and local governments. And these issues affect all of us. Table 1.1 provides a sample of new state laws that took effect in 2020, laws that touch our daily lives.

From Sewers to Science: The Functions of State and Local Governments

State and local governments are busy. They exist, in large measure, to make policy for and provide services to the public. This is no easy task. Nonnational governments must perform efficiently, effectively, and fairly; and they must do so with limited financial resources. An efficient government is one that maximizes the output (services) from a given input (resources). A government operates effectively if it accomplishes what it sets out to do. Another expectation is that government function fairly—that its services be delivered in an equitable manner. It is no wonder, then, that state and local governments constantly experiment with new programs and new systems for producing services, all the while seeking efficiency, effectiveness, and fairness. For instance, the recent massive restructuring of the Arkansas state government was intended, according to the governor, to set "Arkansas on the right course to better serve her citizens."[3] The quest for better functioning government never ends. A 2011 report found

Table 1.1 A Sample of New State Laws That Took Effect in 2020

STATE	DESCRIPTION OF THE LAW
Arizona	Mandates training for sixth- through twelfth-grade teachers on spotting the signs of student suicidal behavior.
California	Makes it illegal to discriminate in the workplace and schools based on an individual's natural hairstyle or hair texture. Protected hairstyles include Afros, braids, twists, cornrows, and dreadlocks.
Illinois	Legalizes sale and use of recreational marijuana for people 21 and older, making Illinois the eleventh state to do so.
Massachusetts	Automatically registers to vote an eligible resident when they get a driver's license or health insurance in the state.
New York	Allows state residents who were adopted to have unrestricted access to their birth certificates once they turn 18.
North Carolina	Creates a new felony—Death by Distribution—that targets drug dealers who contribute to a user's overdose death.
Ohio	Requires the teaching of cursive writing in first grade through fifth.
Oregon	Allows bicyclists to slow down rather than come to a complete stop at stop signs and traffic signals.
Texas	Requires employees of higher education institutions to report to university authorities sexual harassment, sexual assault, stalking, and date rape incidents committed against an employee or student.
Washington	Requires children to ride in booster seats in cars until they are at least four feet, nine inches tall. When practical, children must ride in the back seat until age 13.

Sources: Associated Press, "These New Laws Are Taking Effect in North Carolina," *Spectrum News*, www.spectrumlocalnews.com/nc/charlotte/news/2019/11/30/-raise-the-age--juvenile-initiative-in-nc -begins-in-december (December 1, 2019); Jon Campbell, "New Laws for New York in 2020: Boating Safety, Farmworker Rights, Minimum Wage and More," *Democrat & Chronicle*, www.democratandchronicle .com/story/news/politics/albany/2019/12/26/new-laws-ny-2020-cash-bail-reform-farmworker-rights-birth -certificate/2736813001/ (December 26, 2019); KHOU Staff, "These Are New Texas Laws Going into Effect This Week That You Need to Know About," www.khou.com/article/news/local/texas/new-texas-laws -january-1/285-e9606fd0-9541-41f4-b070-c7904ba401bd (January 3, 2020); Erin Robinson, "New Car Seat Laws Coming to Washington State in 2020," www.kxly.com/new-car-seat-laws-coming-to-washington -state-in-2020/ (December 24, 2019); Erica Stapleton, "Here Are Some Arizona Laws Taking Effect in 2020," www.12news.com/article/news/politics/here-are-some-arizona-laws-taking-effect-in-2020/75-6cee8394 -e2c0-46d7-8587-800d11bee54c (December 21, 2019); Matt Stout, "A Look at the New Mass. Laws that Will Affect You in 2020, *Boston Globe*, www.bostonglobe.com/metro/2020/01/01/new-year-brings-slightly-higher -wages-and-lower-taxes/sTHu9L7D73aSxs6K7WrTRO/story.html (January 1, 2020); Lorraine Swanson, "25 New Illinois Laws in 2020 That Could Impact Your Life," patch.com/illinois/across-il/25-new-illinois-laws-2020-could -change-your-life (January 2, 2020); Brandon Urey, "2020 Oregon Laws: Bicycle Stops and Plastic Bags," www .corvallisadvocate.com/2019/2020-oregon-laws-bicycle-stops-and-plastic-bags/ (December 29, 2019); and Phil Willon and Alexa Díaz, "California Becomes First State to Ban Discrimination Based on One's Natural Hair," *Los Angeles Times*, www.latimes.com/local/lanow/la-pol-ca-natural-hair-discrimination-bill-20190703-story.html (July 3, 2019).

that, over a three-year period, nearly half of the states had eliminated or consolidated numerous state departments, agencies, boards, and commissions in an effort to increase the efficiency and effectiveness of government.[4]

Innovation has become a buzzword for state and local government. Different groups, ranging from the Council of State Governments (CSG)[5]—a national nonpartisan nonprofit organization—to Bloomberg Philanthropies[6]—a nonprofit organization created by former New York City mayor and billionaire Michael Bloomberg—to Harvard University's Ash Center for Democratic Governance and Innovation[7]—an advocate for innovative approaches in state and local governing. Each of these groups has a somewhat different approach to innovation, but they share a common focus on issues such as alternative energy, infrastructure investment, workforce development, cybersecurity, international trade, and others. Although many of the innovations deal with public policies, some of the new ideas these organizations address are internal to government operations and are intended to make government function more effectively. These include the use of social media, the adoption of **evidence-based practices**, the analysis of data with geographic information system technology, and the use of logic models to achieve desired program results. The unifying characteristic among these innovations is governmental willingness to try something new. And good ideas travel; that is, they are often adopted by other states or localities. For example, after the city of Houston debuted a new web tool, "My Tax Dollars at Work," other cities followed suit. Using this tool, homeowners can quickly find out how much of their local property taxes go to various city departments such as public safety, trash and recycling pick up, parks and recreation services, land development, and city administration.

Our Approach

The argument of this book is that states and localities have the capacity to play central roles in the U.S. federal system. **Capacity** refers to a government's ability to respond effectively to change, to make decisions efficiently and responsibly, and to manage conflict.[8] Thus, capacity is tied to governmental capability and performance. In short, states and communities with more capacity work better than those with less capacity.

But what factors make one government more capable than another? Governmental institutions such as the bureaucracy matter. The fiscal resources of a **jurisdiction** and the quality of its leadership make a difference. Much of the research on capacity has focused on the administrative dimension of government performance, evaluating items such as financial management, information technology, human resources, and strategic planning. In a 2008 study of state government performance, the highest overall scores went to Utah, Virginia, and Washington (each state received an A–) and Delaware, Georgia, Michigan, Missouri, and Texas (with grades of B+).[9] Earlier evaluations of forty large counties showed that Fairfax, Virginia, and Maricopa, Arizona, had the best performance grades. Among thirty-five cities examined, Austin, Texas, and Phoenix, Arizona, were the leaders. Other factors being equal, we would expect high-scoring states, counties, and cities to produce "better" government than low-scoring jurisdictions.

A survey in Iowa showed another side to governance. When asked about the characteristics of good government, Iowans put trustworthiness, ethics, financial responsibility, and accountability at the top of the list.[10] Residents

evidence-based practices
Making decisions based on the best research findings available.

capacity
The ability of government to respond effectively to change, make decisions efficiently and responsibly, and manage conflict.

jurisdiction
The territorial range of government authority; "jurisdiction" is sometimes used as a synonym for "city" or "town."

of the Hawkeye State are not unusual; all of us want our institutions and leaders to govern honestly and wisely. As political scientist David Hedge reminds us, better government is found in jurisdictions that are responsible and democratic.[11] But states and localities face significant challenges as they govern. Complex, often contradictory forces test the most capable of governments. As we have seen recently, trends in the national economy play out at the subnational level. Problems in one jurisdiction can spill over into nearby communities. State and local governments need all the capacity they can muster and maybe even a little bit of luck to meet those challenges. Sometimes states and localities fall short. For instance, in 2017, a budget imbroglio between the Republican governor and the Democratic legislature in New Jersey led to the partial shutdown of state government—including state parks and beaches on the Jersey Shore—for the busy three-day Fourth of July holiday. Obviously, this was not one of the shining moments in the annals of state government. That the public often displays a little skepticism about governmental performance is not surprising.

Federalism, with its overlapping spheres of authority, provides the context for state and local action. Intervention by the national government in the affairs of a state or local government is defensible, even desirable in some cases. For example, the environmental problems of the 1960s and 1970s exceeded state and local governments' ability to handle them, so corrective action by the national government was generally welcomed. However, some federal actions are greeted less enthusiastically. The Real ID Act was enacted by Congress in 2005 to upgrade the security of state-issued driver's licenses and other forms of identification. Real ID requires states to maintain databases of the documents used to prove their residency. The act threatened to prohibit any IDs that did not meet federal security requirements from being used for federal purposes such as boarding commercial aircraft or accessing federal facilities. As of 2020, forty-eight of the fifty states have fully complied with Real ID requirements. Only Oklahoma and Oregon have not yet complied. For many years, some states either resisted implementation (e.g., Maine, Pennsylvania, South Carolina) or sought extensions to the federally mandated timetable (e.g., California, Kentucky, North Carolina). States cited costs and the possibility of data insecurity as reasons for early noncompliance. The federal government responded by extending the deadline for full implementation of Real ID requirements. In response to the COVID-19 pandemic, the latest federal action extends the deadline for enforcing Real ID provisions to October 1, 2021.[12]

Our approach takes into account intergovernmental relations (i.e., the relationships among the three levels of government)—particularly, the possibilities for cooperation and conflict. Jurisdictions (national, state, or local) possess policy-making authority over specific, but sometimes overlapping, territory. They confront innumerable situations in which boundaries blur, and they must work together to accomplish an objective. However, cooperation in some cases is countered by conflict in other instances. Each level of government tends to see problems from its own perspective and design solutions accordingly. In sum, both cooperation and conflict define the U.S. federal system.

federalism
A system of government in which powers are divided between a central (national) government and regional (state) governments.

LO 1-2
To identify ways in
which states and
localities have
increased their
capacity.

The Capacity of States and Localities

To appreciate where state and local governments are today, it is important to understand where they were just sixty to seventy years ago. With notable exceptions, states and their local governments in the 1950s and 1960s were havens of traditionalism and inactivity. As a result of tradition, inertia, and a general unwillingness to change the status quo, many states were characterized by unrepresentative legislatures, glad-handing governors, and a hodgepodge court system. Public policy tended to reflect the interests of the elite; delivery of services was frequently inefficient and ineffective. According to former North Carolina governor Terry Sanford, the states "had lost their confidence, and people their faith in the states."[13] No wonder that, by comparison, the federal government appeared to be the answer, regardless of the question. In fact, political scientist Luther Gulick proclaimed, "It is a matter of brutal record. The American State is finished. I do not predict that the states will go, but affirm that they have gone."[14]

Those days are as outmoded as a 1950s-era black-and-white television. States and their local governments have proved themselves capable of designing and implementing "an explosion of innovations and initiatives."[15] As a result, even many national leaders have embraced the roles of states and localities as laboratories for policy experimentation. California's sweeping new data privacy law that allows consumers to access the private data that companies maintain on them and to have that data deleted is indicative of this. As one commentator noted, "Since it's a lot more work to create a separate infrastructure just for California residents to opt out of the data collection industry, these requirements will transform the internet for everyone."[16]

The blossoming of state governments in the 1980s—their transformation from weak links in the federal chain to viable and progressive political units—resulted from several actions and circumstances, as discussed in the next section.[17] In turn, the resurgence of state governments has generated a host of positive outcomes. During the 1990s, states and localities honed their capacity and became **proactive** rather than reactive. They faced hard choices and creatively crafted new directions. A word of caution is necessary, however. The challenges of governance can be great, and not all states enjoy the same level of capacity. Furthermore, fiscal stresses such as those endured by state governments in the second decade of the twenty-first century sorely tested the ability of even the most capable states to function effectively.

How States and Localities Increased Their Capacity

Several factors contributed to the resurgence of the states. U.S. Supreme Court decisions in the 1960s on legislative apportionment made for more equitable representation; the extension of two-party competition in the 1970s to states formerly dominated by one party gave voters more choices. At the same time, states and localities expanded their lobbying presence in the nation's capital, exerting influence on the design and funding of intergovernmental programs.

proactive
An anticipatory condition, as opposed to a reactive one.

Most important, state governments quietly and methodically reformed themselves by modernizing their constitutions and restructuring their institutions. Since the 1970s, more than three-quarters of the states have ratified new constitutions or substantially amended existing ones. Formerly thought of as the "drag anchors of state programs" and as "protectors of special interests,"[18] these documents have been streamlined and made more workable. Even in states without wide-ranging constitutional reform, tinkering with constitutions is almost endless thanks to the amendment process. Nearly every state general election finds constitutional issues on the ballot.

States have also undertaken various internal adjustments intended to improve the operations of state governments.[19] Modernized constitutions and statutory changes have strengthened the powers of governors by increasing appointment and removal powers and by allowing longer terms, consecutive succession, larger staffs, enhanced budget authority, and the power to reorganize the executive branch. Throughout the country, state agencies are staffed by skilled administrators, and the bureaucracy itself is more and more demographically representative of the public. Annual rather than biennial sessions, more efficient rules and procedures, additional staff, and higher salaries have helped make reapportioned state legislatures more professional, capable, and effective. State judicial systems have also been the targets of reform; examples include the establishment of unified court systems, the hiring of court administrators, and the creation of additional layers of courts.

Increased Capacity and Improved Performance

The enhanced capacity enjoyed by state and local governments has generated a range of mostly positive results. The five factors discussed next reinforce the performance of states and localities.

Improved Revenue Systems Economic downturns and limits on taxing and spending have caused states to implement new revenue-raising strategies to maintain acceptable service levels. Some states also granted local governments more flexibility in their revenue systems. South Carolina, for example, now allows counties the option of providing property-tax relief to residents in exchange for increasing the local sales tax.

As a rule, state governments prefer to increase user charges, gasoline taxes, and so-called sin taxes on alcohol and tobacco, and only reluctantly do they raise sales and income taxes. Over time, revenue structures have been redesigned to make them more diversified and more equitable. State **rainy day funds**, legalized gambling through state-run lotteries and pari-mutuels, and extension of the sales tax to services are examples of diversification strategies. The seventeen states where alcohol is sold only in state-run stores are reviewing how they do business, making changes to increase sales and revenue, and considering privatizing alcohol sales, as Washington did in 2011.[20] Legalization and taxation of marijuana sales has added substantial amounts of revenue to state coffers.[21] Exemptions of food and medicine from consumer sales taxes and the enactment of property-tax breaks for poor and

rainy day funds
Money set aside when a state's finances are healthy for use when state revenues decline. Formally called "budget stabilization funds."

elderly people characterize efforts at tax equity. These revamped revenue structures helped states respond to and recover from the budget crises they confronted during the Great Recession of 2008–2011. The COVID-19 pandemic of 2020 has again sorely tested state government revenue systems by dramatically increasing expenditures on health, safety, and other services while reducing tax revenues.

States continue to tinker with their revenue-raising schemes. One successful foray into creative revenue raising has been the specialty license plate. Maryland, for example, has generated millions of dollars over the years with its "Treasure the Chesapeake" plate. Monies generated by the plates are earmarked for special programs—in this case, water quality monitoring and erosion control in the Chesapeake Bay. Nearly all states now offer specialty plates. In New York, for instance, owners can equip their cars, for an extra fee, with license plates honoring their favorite professional sports teams or NASCAR drivers. A brand-new approach to generating cash for states comes from the world of retail stores: the marketing of official gift cards. For example, both Kentucky and Ohio sell gift cards that can be used at state park locations for various park services and merchandise.

Another effort of enterprising localities is to sell merchandise. Los Angeles County has marketed coroner toe tags as key chains; Tucson hosts online auctions of surplus property. New York City, which loses thousands of street signs (Wall Street is especially popular) to souvenir-stealing tourists, now sells replicas. But the revenue generated by those actions is dwarfed by Chicago, which has sold (actually, leased for seventy-five years) its parking meter system to an investment bank for $1.16 billion. As these examples show, states and localities are willing to experiment when it comes to revenue enhancement.

Expanding the Scope of State Operations State governments have taken on new roles and added new functions. In some instances, states are filling in the gap left by the national government's de-emphasis of an activity; in other cases, states are venturing into uncharted terrain. It was states that designed the first family leave legislation to give workers time off to care for newborn babies and ailing relatives, the first "Three Strikes" laws that mandated long prison sentences for habitual offenders, and the first Amber Alert systems to broadcast information about abducted children. The federal government eventually followed suit with a national family leave act, a federal Three Strikes law, and a national Amber Alert system. In addition, states have taken the initiative in ongoing intergovernmental programs by creatively using programmatic authority and resources. Prior to federal welfare reform in the mid-1990s, several states had established workfare programs and imposed time limits on the receipt of welfare benefits, provisions that were at the center of the subsequent federal legislation.

States persist in expanding their scope of operations, whether it is California's venture into stem-cell research or Florida's strides into bioterror readiness. Hawaii has begun development of an extensive network of plug-in spots where electric cars can be recharged; New Mexico is a partner in a new commercial spaceport facility that it hopes will become the center for space tourism. Fifteen states (and the District of Columbia) currently have legalized marijuana for recreational, as opposed to medicinal, use (another states allow broadly interpreted medical use of marijuana). In short, states are embracing their role as policy innovators and experimenters in the U.S. federal system.

Local governments are also pushing the policy envelope. For instance, in 2012, San Francisco took a bold step when it launched its K2C program to provide college savings accounts to every kindergarten student in the city school district; Cuyahoga County, Ohio, followed suit the next year. In an effort to offer more transit options to the public, Tulsa, Oklahoma, became the first city in the United States to establish an automated bike-share system, with two dozen bikes at three solar-powered stations; New York City took a slightly different approach by creating a public-private partnership for its Citi Bike system. Las Vegas won awards for its use of Amazon's Alexa to provide information to tourists and residents through its My Vegas platform. Some cities have begun to address the problem of food deserts—the absence of grocery stores and fresh food in low-income neighborhoods—by incentivizing investment by food retailers and by supporting urban agriculture. Cities such as Tulsa, Birmingham, and New Orleans are attempting to use their local zoning codes to restrict convenience stores that don't offer fresh meat, fruits, and vegetables from locating in certain areas.[22] These examples make an important point: Local governments are not sitting idly by as problems emerge; instead they actively seek solutions.

Faster Diffusion of Innovations Among states, there have always been leaders and followers; the same is true for local governments. Now that states and localities have expanded their scope and are doing more policy making, they are looking more frequently to their neighbors and to similar places for advice, information, and models.[23] As a result, successful solutions spread from one jurisdiction to another. For example, Florida was the first state to create a way for consumers to stop telephone solicitations. By 1999, five more states had passed laws letting residents put their names on a "do-not-call" list for telemarketers. Seven additional states adopted similar legislation over the next two years before Congress enacted a national statute.[24]

Local-level innovations spread rapidly, too. Education and environmental protection offer many examples of this phenomenon. When Miami-Dade County, Florida, hired a private company to run a public elementary school, other school districts hoping to improve quality and cut costs quickly did the same. Initial experiments with privatization spawned other innovations such as charter schools. The issue of climate change began to be addressed at the local level in 2005, when the mayor of Seattle became the first local official to commit his city to a plan to reduce the emission of greenhouse gases. Within the last fourteen years, some 1,066 mayors of other U.S. cities

? It's Your Turn

Should Governments Have Innovation Offices?

In comparison to businesses and corporations that are often seen as engines of innovation, some folks see state and local governments as slow-moving and reactive entities. In an effort to change that perception and to make government more proactive, city governments from Austin to Pittsburgh are creating innovation offices. These offices are tasked with discovering new and more efficient ways for government to do its job.

PROS	CONS
Having an innovation office could help cities become leaders in discovering new ideas and approaches rather than followers of others' innovations.	Creating a new office in city government means that money will need to be spent on that office. That money has to come from somewhere, whether it is from new revenue or diverted spending.
Internally focused innovation offices can lead to cost savings and efficiency improvements in government.	There are no guarantees of cost savings. Generating cost savings depends on the capabilities of the people employed in the innovation office and their leadership . . . and maybe even some good luck.
Externally focused innovation offices can lead to new government services or better ways to provide existing services. These offices may also identify new partnership opportunities.	

have joined the climate change bandwagon.[25] In 1985, San Francisco enacted a city ordinance that forbade city officials from assisting federal immigration officers, thus becoming the first "sanctuary city." There are now some 500 cities that call themselves sanctuaries for immigration purposes, a designation that is highly controversial in local, state, and national politics. It is worth noting, of course, that the diffusion of new ideas depends in large part on their fit with local conditions and their effectiveness in addressing local problems.

Obviously, state and local governments learn from one another. Communication links, including social media such as Facebook and Twitter, have become extensive. A state might turn to nearby states when searching for policy solutions. Regional consultation and emulation are logical: Similar problems often beset jurisdictions in the same region, a program used in a neighboring state may be politically more acceptable than one from a distant state, and organizational affiliations bring state and local administrators together with their colleagues from nearby areas. However, research has shown that states also borrow ideas from peer states, that is, states that are like them in important ways such as ideological leaning or economic base.[26] In the search for solutions, states and localities are increasingly inclusive.

A group of governors holds a press conference in Washington, D.C., after meeting with former President Obama.

Interjurisdictional Cooperation Accompanying the accelerated flow of innovations has been an increase in interjurisdictional cooperation. States are choosing to confront and resolve their immediate problems jointly. A similar phenomenon has occurred at the local level with the creation of regional organizations to tackle area-wide problems collectively.

Interjurisdictional collaboration takes many forms, including informal consultations and agreements, interstate committees, legal contracts, reciprocal legislation, and interstate compacts. For example, all fifty states and the District of Columbia, Puerto Rico, and the U.S. Virgin Islands have a mutual agreement to aid one another when natural disasters such as hurricanes, earthquakes, and forest fires strike.

States often cooperate when it comes to consumer protection litigation. Five states—Mississippi, Minnesota, West Virginia, Florida, and Massachusetts—were among the first to band together to share information and design tactics in their lawsuits against tobacco companies in the mid-1990s; by 1998, thirty-seven other states had joined in the successful effort to recover the Medicaid costs of treating tobacco-related diseases.[27] In analogous fashion, states are suing opioid manufacturers over the costs associated with treating addiction. Oklahoma recently won its suit against the consumer product manufacturer Johnson & Johnson while similar lawsuits by twenty-five other states proceed against OxyContin® manufacturer Purdue Pharma.[28] Increased jurisdictional cooperation fosters a healthy climate for joint problem solving. In addition, when state and local governments solve their own problems, they protect their power and authority within the federal system. It appears that states are becoming more comfortable working with one another. The beginning of the twenty-first century was indeed historic: States were engaged in more cooperative interactions than ever before.[29]

Increased National-State Conflict An inevitable by-product of more capable state and local governments is intensified conflict with the national government. One source of this discord has been federal laws and grant requirements that supersede state policy; another is the movement of states onto the national government's turf. National-state conflict is primarily a cyclical phenomenon, but contention has increased in recent years. The issue of unfunded mandates—the costly requirements that federal legislation imposes on states and localities—has been particularly troublesome. In an effort to increase the visibility of the mandates issue, several national organizations of state and local officials sponsored a "National Unfunded Mandate Day" in the mid-1990s. Making a strong case against mandates, then-governor George Voinovich of Ohio stated, "Unfunded mandates devastate our budgets, inhibit flexibility and innovation in implementing new programs, pre-empt important state initiatives, and deprive states of their responsibility to set priorities."[30] Congress responded in 1995 by passing a mandate relief bill that requires cost-benefit analyses of proposed mandates; however, the law contains loopholes that have weakened its impact.

Some of the disputes pit a single state against the national government, as in Nevada's fight to block the U.S. Energy Department's plan to build a nuclear fuel waste storage facility at Yucca Mountain, 100 miles northwest of Las Vegas. Another example is the effort by Texas to continue its use of a flexible permitting process to regulate industrial air pollution, a process that has been challenged repeatedly by the U.S. Environmental Protection Agency (EPA). In other conflicts, the national government finds itself besieged by a coordinated, multistate effort, for example, when twelve states sued the U.S. EPA in 2014 over the regulation of carbon emissions from existing coal plants, or when twenty states challenged the federal Affordable Care Act in 2010.[31] Cities, counties, and states designating themselves as sanctuaries—forbidding law enforcement from cooperating with federal immigration officials in identifying or detaining those who may have arrived in the United States illegally—have created disputes between the federal government and state and local governments. In 2018, the U.S. Justice Department sued the state of California over three state "sanctuary" laws that the Justice Department alleges violate the U.S. Constitution, and President Donald Trump has attempted to block federal grants-in-aid funding from being awarded to state and local governments that fail to cooperate with U.S. immigration authorities.[32]

National-state conflicts are resolved (and sometimes intensified) by the federal judicial system. Cases dealing with alleged violations of the U.S. Constitution by state and local governments are heard in federal courts and decided by federal judges. Sometimes the rulings take the federal government into spheres long considered the purview of state and local governments. For instance, within the space of two days in 2009, Arizona both won and lost cases before the U.S. Supreme Court. The state was successful in its argument that state spending on language training for non-English-speaking students should not be subject to federal supervision, but it was unsuccessful in defending the actions of school officials who conducted a strip search of a middle-school student suspected of drug possession.

Challenges Facing State and Local Governments

LO 1-3
To recognize the challenges that states and localities confront on a daily basis.

Increased capacity does not mean that all state and local problems have been solved. A Gallup poll released in 2016 asked a sample of residents in each of the fifty states about their level of confidence in their state government to handle problems facing the state.[33] On average, 57 percent of a state's residents said that they had confidence in their state government. This level of confidence is respectable but certainly not stellar. Moreover, the average masks substantial variation across the states ranging from North Dakota's 81 percent to Illinois' 25 percent. A look at Table 1.2 shows that confidence in state government tends to be higher in less-populated states and in states located

Table 1.2 Confidence in State Government to Handle Problems

STATE	PERCENTAGE CONFIDENT	STATE	PERCENTAGE CONFIDENT
Alabama	48	Montana	72
Alaska	64	Nebraska	74
Arizona	49	Nevada	61
Arkansas	63	New Hampshire	68
California	54	New Jersey	41
Colorado	66	New Mexico	48
Connecticut	39	New York	46
Delaware	65	North Carolina	55
Florida	57	North Dakota	81
Georgia	59	Ohio	59
Hawaii	55	Oklahoma	60
Idaho	63	Oregon	55
Illinois	25	Pennsylvania	46
Indiana	55	Rhode Island	33
Iowa	68	South Carolina	59
Kansas	45	South Dakota	71
Kentucky	54	Tennessee	63
Louisiana	44	Texas	64
Maine	48	Utah	70
Maryland	56	Vermont	60
Massachusetts	66	Virginia	58
Michigan	48	Washington	54
Minnesota	69	West Virginia	51
Mississippi	55	Wisconsin	49
Missouri	50	Wyoming	76

Source: Jeffrey M. Jones, "Illinois Residents Least Confident in Their State Government," www.news.gallup.com/poll/189281/illinois-residents-least-confident-state-government.aspx (access December 17, 2019).

in the upper plains region, but undoubtedly other factors contribute to these poll numbers. The percentages serve as a reminder that even though states (and localities) have made many strides forward, there is plenty of room for improvement. Three tough challenges for nonnational governments include fiscal stress, interjurisdictional conflict, and political corruption.

Fiscal Stress The most intractable problem for states and localities involves money. State and local finances are vulnerable to cyclical peaks and troughs in the national economy as well as to occasional changes in public finance.

The national economic recession of 2008–2011 hit states and localities hard—very hard—and the impact on governmental budgets was significant. Connecticut governor Jodi Rell did not mince words when she said, "These are the worst financial times any of us can remember . . . let's face it, it's scary."[34]

The fiscal impact of the Great Recession was deep and prolonged, with four consecutive years in which states faced significant mismatches between revenues and spending. During that time, state lawmakers scrambled to close budget gaps that, according to estimates by the National Conference of State Legislatures, totaled $510.5 billion.[35] State rainy day funds grew precariously drier as legislators looked to them for short-term relief. In an effort to save money, some prisons were closed in Colorado, Kansas, Michigan, North Carolina, and Washington; in some states, funding for education was reduced, and cash assistance for low-income families was cut; in others, state agencies were **downsized** and employee wages were frozen. State leaders sought new revenues also: Income tax rates were increased in California, Hawaii, Illinois, and New York; sales tax increases were enacted in Arizona, California, and Massachusetts, among other states. Facing the largest deficit of any state, the governor of California battled with the legislature over several money-saving proposals, including "selling the Los Angeles Memorial Coliseum, San Quentin State Prison and other state property, eliminating welfare benefits for 500,000 families, terminating health coverage for nearly 1 million low-income children and closing 220 of the state's parks."[36]

Local governments felt the recessionary heat as well; Dallas, one of the country's largest cities, provides an example. To close a $190.2 million deficit in its budget, the city of Dallas made cuts in numerous city services, including street repairs, arts funding, library hours, and park maintenance; in addition, nearly 800 city employees lost their jobs.[37] The story was much the same in many other localities: reduce costs as painlessly as possible and, if necessary, increase fees. Some relief was forthcoming when Congress passed the $787 billion American Recovery and Reinvestment Act, informally known as the federal stimulus plan, but many states and communities felt the fiscal pinch well into 2012. Now, cash-strapped states and localities are confronting a "new normal" in which they are expected to provide public services with fewer dollars at their disposal.[38]

The COVID-19 pandemic provides another threat to state and local government. To slow the spread of the disease, governors and mayors ordered businesses to shut down operations. While this "flattening of the curve"

downsize
To reduce the size and cost of something, especially government.

resulted in reducing the daily number of new disease cases and so helped health care systems from becoming overloaded, it also resulted in much higher unemployment rates in March and April and concomitant reductions in sales, income, and in some places, property tax revenues. In response to this, Congress passed the Coronavirus Aid, Relief, and Economic Security (CARES) Act in March 2020. This act established a $150 billion Coronavirus Relief Fund to provide grants to help state and local governments cope with the unexpected additional expenses associated with the public health emergency. In addition, The Families First Coronavirus Response Act increased by $35 billion the federal funding share to the Medicaid program, the joint federal-state program that provides health insurance to lower income people. The actual financial impact of COVID-19 is expected to be much greater than the total of this federal assistance, meaning difficult budgetary decisions by state and local governments in 2020 and afterward.

Increased Interjurisdictional Conflict Tension is inherent in a federal system because each of the governmental entities has its own set of interests, as well as a share of the national interest. When one state's pursuit of its interests negatively affects another state, conflict occurs. Such conflict can become destructive, threatening the continuation of state resurgence. In essence, states end up wasting their energies and resources on counterproductive battles among themselves.

Interjurisdictional conflict is particularly common in two policy areas very dear to state and local governments: natural resources and economic development. States rich in natural resources want to use these resources in a manner that will yield the greatest return. Oil-producing states, for instance, levy severance taxes that raise the price of oil. And states with abundant water supplies resist efforts by arid states to tap into these supplies. The most serious disputes often occur among neighboring states. One illustration is the protracted dispute between California and six other western states over water allocations from the Colorado River, an issue made even more contentious since California experienced a drought for much of the 2010s. In short, the essential question revolves around a state's right to control a resource that occurs naturally and is highly desired by other states. Resource-poor states argue that resources are in fact national and should rightfully be shared among states.

In the area of economic development, conflict is extensive because all jurisdictions want healthy economies. Toward this end, states try to make themselves attractive to business and industry through tax breaks, regulatory relaxation, and even image creation. (The Controversies in States and Localities box explores how jurisdictions seek to reverse negative images and to **rebrand** themselves more positively.) Conflict arises when states get involved in bidding wars—that is, when an enterprise is so highly valued that actions taken by one state are matched and exceeded by another. The recent searches by Amazon—for a second headquarters facility in addition to Seattle—and Apple—for a new campus—pitted states and cities against each other in attempting to attract the 50,000 jobs to be created by Amazon

rebrand
An effort to change how a state or city is perceived by the public, to create a new image of a place.

and the 15,000 by Apple. States hungry to attract these facilities assembled packages of incentives such as below-cost land, tax concessions, and subsidized job training in their efforts to attract Amazon, Apple, and other large companies. Virginia reportedly granted Amazon more than $750 million in incentives to get the new headquarters facility located in Arlington.[39] Similar incentives were offered by many cities to attract Apple; eventually the company opted to locate in Austin, Texas, where incentives totaled less than $50 million.[40]

A particularly fascinating interjurisdictional contest involves the recurring rounds of U.S. military base closures and consolidations. Military bases are economic plums that no jurisdiction wants to lose. Thus, states mount public relations efforts to protect local bases and to grab jobs that will be lost in other states. Politics and lobbying are supposed to play no role in the Pentagon's decisions about which bases will remain open and which ones will close, but states prefer to hedge their bets. In the most recent round of base closings, Texas devoted $250 million to defending its bases, and Massachusetts allocated $410 million for its own bases. As one observer put it, "It is a war of all against all."[41] In 2017, President Trump asked Congress to authorize a new study of base closings, which would report its recommendations in 2021.

Political Corruption Corruption exists in government, which is no great surprise. Most political systems can tolerate the occasional corrupt official, but if corruption becomes commonplace, it undermines governmental capacity and destroys public trust. Public reaction ranges from cynicism and alienation (corruption as "politics as usual") to anger and action (corruption as a spur to reform). A survey found that the more extreme the corrupt act (a city clerk embezzling $100,000 versus a police officer accepting free food at a restaurant), the more harsh the public's judgment.[42] Even so, mitigating motives or circumstances tend to reduce the public's outrage (e.g., a public official taking a bribe but using the money to pay his sick child's hospital bills). But governmental scandals have been linked tentatively to another negative effect—a slowdown in economic growth. Research on states found that federal corruption convictions are associated with declines in job growth primarily because, from a business perspective, corruption creates uncertainty and inflates costs.[43]

States and localities have taken great precautions to reduce the amount of wrongdoing occurring in their midst. Government has much more **transparency** than it ever has before, with more openness and more rules. But the statutes and policies are only as good as the people whose behavior they regulate. Unfortunately, examples of corrupt behavior are not hard to find. For instance, in 2018, Dallas Mayor Pro Tem Dwaine Caraway pled guilty to federal bribery charges related to contracts he illegally steered to a local business operator, and, in 2019, John Green, who served as the elected sheriff of Philadelphia from 1988 to 2010, was convicted of bribery and other financial offenses he committed during his twenty-two years in office.

transparency
A characteristic of a government that is open and understandable, one in which officials are accountable to the public.

Controversies in States and Localities

Creating an Image, Rebranding a Place

What image best captures a state's essential being? Ohio, for example, calls itself the Buckeye State, but most Americans do not know what a buckeye is. (It is a shrub or tree of the horse chestnut family and it produces buckeye nuts. There are a lot of these trees in Ohio.) Consider New Hampshire, which stamps the motto "Live Free or Die" on its license plates. A few years ago, some legislators advocated replacing the uncompromising phrase with the word *scenic*, arguing that the state needed to project a more caring image. In other words, New Hampshire wanted to rebrand itself.

The North Dakota legislature took the image issue to new heights when it seriously entertained a resolution that would have dropped the word *North* from the state's name. The name *North Dakota* was said to summon images of "snowstorms, howling winds, and frigid temperatures." Simply going with *Dakota*, a word that means "friend" or "ally" in the Sioux language, would project a warmer image of the state, supporters claimed. (The state senate ultimately defeated the name-changing resolution.) Image and reputation are serious business: West Virginia's governor protested an Abercrombie & Fitch T-shirt that featured a map of the state and the phrase "It's all relative in West Virginia." Not exactly the image the state wanted to project, to be sure. An aide to the governor said, "It really hinders our ability to market the state." In response, the company decided to pull the shirt from its shelves.

Images are not trivial. They matter because they project and reflect public perceptions, which can be both accurate and inaccurate. They offer a shorthand understanding of a place, a slice of the whole. States and communities have become much more conscious of their images in recent years, and many have launched promotional campaigns to rebrand themselves with more positive images. Jersey City, New Jersey, which has been termed "unfashionable" by some, "scruffy" by others, recently developed a campaign to change people's perception of the city, and ideally, encourage them to consider the city as a place to live, visit, and start businesses. The city's new slogan is "Make It Yours," which is incorporated into an inventive logo and even has a social media presence with a hashtag, #JCMakeItYours. The total budget for the city's rebranding effort? $1.2 million.

Critical Thinking Questions

1. Every state has an image. Take a moment to think about your state, its culture, and its icons. What is your state's image? Has your state created a brand for itself? If it has, do you think that it is fitting, or can you think of a better brand for your state? If your state does not have a brand, what would be a good brand for it?

2. Corporations such as Coca-Cola, Apple, and Disney spend millions of dollars each year maintaining their brands. Should public money go toward states' creation and maintenance of brands for themselves?

3. Do you think that brands are effective in changing the perceptions of a state?

Sources: Dale Wetzel, "Dakotans Consider Dropping 'North' to Thaw State's Image," *The Missoulian* (June 25, 2001), p. B4; Tony Dokoupil, "Hillbilly No More? West Virginia's Image Makeover," *Newsweek*, www.newsweek.com/hillbilly-no-more-west-virginias-image-makeover-82641 (March 10, 2009); and Stuart Elliott, "A New Effort from a 'New' Jersey City Urges, 'Make It Yours,'" *New York Times*, www.nytimes.com/2014/10/06/business/media/a-new-effort-from-a-new-jersey-city-urges-make-it-yours.html?_r=0 (October 6, 2014).

A pair of economists researching corruption in the states asked statehouse reporters—folks who are familiar with the goings-on in the capitol—to assess the overall level of corruption in their state compared with other states.[44] At the top of the list was Rhode Island, followed by Louisiana and New Mexico. States at the bottom of the comparative corruption list included the Dakotas, Colorado, and Maine. Others have speculated that capital cities isolated from major population centers tend to breed more corruption. At the local level, data on the number of federal convictions for public corruption over a thirty-five-year period showed the Chicago metropolitan area to be the most corrupt in the nation.[45] Clearly, states and localities are not corruption-free; however, the amount of corruption is relatively low, given the vast number of public officials serving in nonnational levels of government. Still, even a whiff of scandal can undermine public confidence in government and sap governmental capacity.

The People: Designers and Consumers of Government

A book on state and local governments is not only about places and governments but also about people—the public and assorted officeholders—and the institutions they create, the processes in which they engage, and the policies they adopt. Thus, this volume contains chapters on institutions, such as legislatures, and on processes, such as elections; it also discusses policies, such as those pertaining to education. But in each case, *people* are the ultimate focus: A legislature is composed of lawmakers and staff members who deal with constituents; elections involve candidates, campaign workers, and voters (as well as nonvoters); and education essentially involves students, teachers, administrators, parents, and taxpayers. In short, the word *people* encompasses an array of individuals and roles in the political system.

Ethnic-Racial Composition

More than 330 million people live in the United States. Some can trace their heritage back to the *Mayflower*, whereas others look back only as far as a recent naturalization ceremony. Very few can claim indigenous (native) American ancestry. Instead, most Americans owe their nationality to some forebear who came here in search of a better life or—in the case of a significant minority, the descendants of slaves—to ancestors who made the journey to this country not out of choice but by force. The appeal of the United States to economic and political refugees from other countries continues, with people from Mexico, Central America, Asia, and eastern Africa among the most recent arrivals.

The United States is a nation of immigrants, and therefore ethnic richness and cultural diversity abound. Official U.S. Census figures for 2010 put the white population at 72 percent, the black population at 13 percent, the Latino population at 16 percent, the Asian population at 5 percent, and the American Indian and Alaska Native population at 1 percent.[46] (The numbers total more than 100 percent because of people who check multiple categories.) Approximately 38 million, or 13 percent, of the nation's population was born in another country, with 53 percent of the foreign born from Latin America and another 28 percent from Asia.[47] The 2020 census is expected to show the population of the United States increasing at a slower rate than previous decades. The minority population—especially those identifying with two or more racial or ethnic groups—will increase much more rapidly than will the white population. Whereas the white non-Latino population will increase by only 1 percent, the African American population will increase by 10 percent and the Latino population by 23 percent. More importantly, immigration—which has always been a major factor in the increase in racial and ethnic change in the United States—will be outstripped by natural increase (births). This will be particularly pronounced in Latino, African American, and multi-racial populations.[48]

One aspect of immigration—illegal immigration—is putting the words from the sonnet inscribed on the Statue of Liberty ("Give me your tired, your poor, your huddled masses") to a severe test. Although accurate numbers are hard to come by, one recent estimate by the U.S. Department of Homeland Security placed the number of undocumented immigrants at roughly 12 million, of which approximately 55 percent were from Mexico.[49] The issue of illegal immigration has divided the American public into two camps. One camp argues that people who are in the United States illegally receive public benefits, take scarce jobs, and pay little in taxes. This group favors legislative proposals that clamp down on illegal immigration by requiring verification of workers' legal status and restricting the issuance of drivers' licenses to U.S. citizens and legal immigrants. The other camp contends that undocumented workers actually contribute more in taxes than they consume in public services; moreover, they take on jobs that others do not want and therefore contribute to economic growth. This group tends to support legislation that includes a "path to citizenship" and the "DREAM Act," which makes high school graduates and those who have served honorably in the military eligible for citizenship, despite their illegal immigration status. Emblematic of these differing perspectives, five states explicitly prohibit unauthorized immigrant students from receiving in-state tuition at state colleges or universities whereas twenty states offer these benefits to them.

A 2010 Arizona law required immigrants to carry documents proving they were in the United States legally, and it gave local police broad power to question and arrest anyone suspected of being in the country illegally. Critics claimed that the law was discriminatory and would lead to ethnic profiling. Upon enactment, the law unleashed a flurry of demonstrations, both supportive and oppositional, initially in Arizona and eventually around the country. Some jurisdictions such as Los Angeles threatened to boycott the Grand Canyon State in retaliation for the law, whereas several other states rallied around Arizona. Similar laws were passed in 2011 in Alabama, Georgia, Indiana, South Carolina, and Utah. The federal government filed suit against the Arizona law, and in 2012 parts of the law were struck down by the U.S. Supreme Court, although the provision allowing police to investigate the immigration status of individuals who were stopped or arrested was sustained. Further action on immigration occurred at the federal level when President Obama issued a series of executive orders in 2012 implementing the Deferred Action for Childhood Arrivals program (DACA). Obama's executive orders intended to protect some undocumented immigrants from deportation. DACA allowed some who had been brought into the United States illegally when they were children to have deportation proceedings deferred for a renewable two-year period. President Trump reversed much of this in 2017, stating he want to phase out DACA unless Congress acted to pass the DREAM Act or similar legislation. Trump also encouraged U.S. Immigration and Customs Enforcement (ICE) to aggressively use the 287(g) Program to deputize state and local law enforcement officers in the enforcement of federal immigration law.[50] Trump's actions on DACA were challenged in federal court. In June 2020, the U.S. Supreme Court, while refusing to take a position on the overall legality of DACA, ruled that the manner by which the Trump administration sought to end the program was arbitrary and capricious. The Trump administration is seeking other ways to change or end the DACA program.[51]

Clearly, ethnicity and culture still matter, despite the image of America as a melting pot. Researchers have found that a state's racial and ethnic diversity goes a long way in explaining its politics and policies.[52] For example, racial diversity has been shown to have effects on education, welfare, and health policies in the states.[53] Looking toward the future, census projections for the year 2060 estimate a nation of approximately 417 million people, with the non-Latino white population dropping to less than 50 percent of the total, the African American population increasing slightly to 14 percent, the Latino population reaching 29 percent, and an Asian population of 12 percent.[54] If these population trends hold, state politics and policy in the mid-twenty-first century will be affected.

Population Growth and Migration

As a whole, the United States grew by almost 6 percent from 2010 to 2019. Disaggregating the data by state reveals several trends. Reflecting the pattern of the previous decade, high rates of growth occurred in the western and southern states; substantially slower growth rates characterized the Northeast and to a lesser extent, the Midwest. The South grew by 9.3 percent, the West by 8.7 percent, the Midwest by 2.0 percent, and the Northeast by 1.1 percent. (The map in Figure 1.1 displays the percentage change in each state's population from 2010 to 2019.) Among the states, Utah, Texas, Colorado, Nevada, and Florida continued to outpace the growth in other states, with rates of 15.5 percent, 14.9 percent, 14.1 percent, 14.0 percent, and 13.9 percent, respectively. The District of Columbia was another high-growth jurisdiction with a 16.6 percent increase. Four states—West Virginia, Illinois, Connecticut, and Vermont—lost population (3.3 percent, 1.3 percent, 0.4 percent, and 0.3 percent, respectively) during the ten-year period. Five states experienced extremely low rates of growth: Mississippi by 0.2 percent, New York by 0.3 percent, Rhode Island by 0.5 percent, Pennsylvania by 0.7 percent, and New Jersey by 0.9 percent. In terms of absolute increase from 2010 to 2019, the number of Texans rose by 3.7 million, Florida added 2.6 million, and California added 2.2 million new residents.[55]

For cities, the population trends for the four-year period are equally compelling. Higher rates of growth were much more prevalent in cities in the **Sunbelt** region than in cities of the **Frostbelt**. The growth leaders among large cities (defined as cities of 200,000 population or more) between 2010 and 2019 were Irvine, California, and Seattle, Washington. Both of these cities

Sunbelt
An unofficial region of the United States, generally consisting of the South and the West.

Frostbelt
An unofficial region of the United States, generally comprising the Northeast and the Midwest.

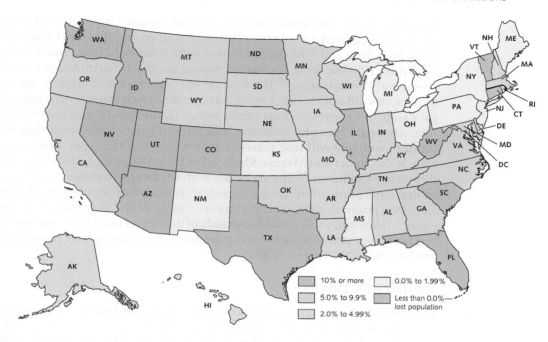

Figure 1.1 Percent Change in State Population, 2010–2019

Source: U.S. Census Bureau, "State Population Totals and Components of Change: 2010–2019," www.census.gov/data/tables /time-series/demo/popest/2010s-state-total.html (December 30, 2019).

experienced population increases of more than 30 percent. Seattle was the only non-Sunbelt city in the top ten fastest growing cities. At the other end of the spectrum are large, older industrialized cities of the Frostbelt like Detroit and Saint Louis that each lost more than 5 percent or Toledo that lost more than 4 percent.[56]

Migration—moving from one state to another—may be on the minds of many folks these days. A recent Gallup poll showed that, on average, 33 percent of a state's residents want to move to another state.[57] The question was phrased like this: "Regardless of whether you *will* move, if you had the opportunity, would you *like* to move to another state, or would you rather remain in your current state?" Illinois had the dubious distinction of landing at the top of the out-migration list: Half of the residents said they would leave the state if they had the opportunity. Connecticut and Nevada were close behind at 49 percent and 47 percent, respectively. At the other end of the spectrum were states like Montana, Hawaii, and Maine, where only 23 percent of the current residents would leave if they could.

Population changes carry economic and political consequences for state and local governments. As a general rule, power and influence follow population. A state's representation in the U.S. Congress and its votes in the Electoral College are at stake. As a result of the 2010 census, Texas picked up four seats in the U.S. House of Representatives, while Florida added two seats.

Six other states (Arizona, Georgia, Nevada, South Carolina, Utah, and Washington) gained a single seat. This means, of course, that other states lost seats. New York and Ohio each lost two seats, with eight other states losing one apiece (Illinois, Iowa, Louisiana, Massachusetts, Michigan, Missouri, New Jersey, and Pennsylvania).[58] The number of congressional districts in the rest of the states did not change. For the 2020 census, seven states most likely will gain seats in Congress—Texas (three seats); Florida (two); and North Carolina, Arizona, Colorado, Montana, and Oregon (one each). Meanwhile ten states most likely will lose seats—Alabama, Illinois, Michigan, Minnesota, New York, Ohio, Pennsylvania, Rhode Island, West Virginia, and—for the first time ever—California.[59] The stakes are high for local governments, too. As a central city's population size is eclipsed by its suburban population, a loss in the city's political clout typically occurs. Aware of the importance of "the count," many cities will spend thousands of dollars on media advertisements, text messages, and social networking websites encouraging their residents to mail in their 2020 Census forms.

Political Culture

One of the phrases that a new arrival in town may hear from long-time residents is "We don't do things that way here." **Political culture**—the attitudes, values, and beliefs that people hold toward government—is the conceptual equivalent of simply saying "It's *our* thing."[60] As developed by political scientist Daniel Elazar in the 1960s, the term refers to the way people think about their government and how the political system operates. Political culture is a soft concept—one that is difficult to measure—yet it has remained quite useful in explaining state politics and policy.

According to Elazar, the United States is an amalgam of three major political cultures, each of which has distinctive characteristics. In an **individualistic political culture**, politics is a kind of open marketplace in which people participate because of essentially private motivations. In a **moralistic political culture**, politics is an effort to establish a good and just society. Citizens are expected to be active in public affairs. In a **traditionalistic political culture**, politics functions to maintain the existing order, and political participation is confined to social elites. These differing conceptions about the purpose of government and the role of politics lead to different behaviors. Confronted with similar conditions, officials in an individualistic community would resist initiating a program unless public opinion demanded it; leaders in moralistic areas would adopt the new program, even without pressure, if they believed it to be in the public interest; and traditionalistic rulers would initiate the program only if they thought it would serve the interests of the governing elite.

Political culture is a factor in the differences (and similarities) in state policy. Research has found that moralistic states demonstrate the greatest tendency toward policy innovation, whereas traditionalistic states exhibit the least.[61] In economic development policy, for example, political culture has been shown to influence a state's willingness to offer tax breaks to businesses.[62] Other research has linked political culture to state environmental policy and successful state implementation of welfare reform.[63]

political culture
The attitudes, values, and beliefs that people hold toward government.

individualistic political culture
A set of attitudes, beliefs, and sentiments in which politics is thought of as a marketplace in which people compete to achieve private goals.

moralistic political culture
A set of attitudes, beliefs, and sentiments in which politics is viewed as an effort to establish a good and just society.

traditionalistic political culture
A set of attitudes, beliefs, and sentiments in which politics is viewed as a method of maintaining the existing order.

Today, few states are characterized by pure forms of these cultures. The mass media have had a homogenizing effect on cultural differences; migration has diversified cultural enclaves. This process of cultural erosion and synthesis has produced hybrid political cultures. For example, Florida, once considered a traditionalistic state, now has many areas in which an individualistic culture prevails and even a moralistic community or two. In an effort to extend Elazar's pioneering work, researcher Joel Lieske has used race, ethnicity, and religion to identify contemporary subcultures.[64] With counties as the building blocks and statistical analysis as the method, he identified eleven distinctive regional subcultures. A state like Ohio, which Elazar characterized as individualistic, becomes a mix of Germanic, rural/urban, global, and "heartland" counties in Lieske's formulation. Very few states are dominated by a single subculture, except perhaps Utah, by a Mormon subculture, and New Hampshire, Rhode Island, and Vermont, by an Anglo-French subculture.

Political culture is not the only explanation for why states do what they do, of course. Socioeconomic characteristics (income and education levels, for example) and political structural factors (the amount of competition between political parties) also contribute to states' and communities' actions. In fact, sorting out the cause-and-effect relationships among these variables is a daunting job. For example, why do some states pass more laws to regulate handguns than other states do? Emily Van Dunk's study found that several factors were important, although the crime rate and partisanship, surprisingly, were not among them.[65] States with nontraditional political cultures adopt more handgun regulations, as do states with more women in the legislature and those with populations that are more urbanized and nonwhite. In general, political factors, socioeconomic characteristics, and the particulars of a specific problem combine to produce government action.

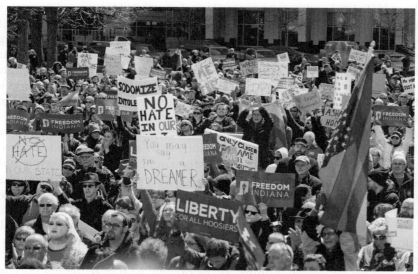

Protestors march to Indiana's state capitol after passage of the Religious Freedom Restoration Act in 2015.

Culture Wars

In 2004, when San Francisco's mayor ordered city clerks to remove all references to gender on local marriage license applications, it opened the door for same-sex marriages to take place in the city. As lesbian and gay activists and supporters celebrated, many politically conservative groups denounced the action and promised legal challenges and political repercussions for the mayor. This type of social conflict over morality issues is known informally as **culture wars**, or "morality politics." And these culture wars are defining the politics of many communities and states. Besides gay rights, battlegrounds in the culture wars include abortion, pornography, and prayer in schools.

These issues tend to involve deeply held values, sometimes connected to religion, and they are less about economics than are many political issues. According to political scientist Elaine Sharp, culture wars have several distinctive features.[66] Values are highly salient to people, eliciting passionate reactions; they mobilize people across different neighborhoods and racial and ethnic groups; and the ensuing political activism often takes unconventional forms, such as demonstrations. Recent research has confirmed the presence of wide disagreements in public opinion on fundamental values such as freedom, equality, individualism, and patriotism, among others.[67] Throughout the country, battle lines have been drawn over issues such as more restrictive abortion laws and displaying the Ten Commandments in public buildings. But the most volatile culture war during the past two decades involved same-sex marriage.

As of 2010, more than thirty-five states had Defense of Marriage Acts (DOMAs) in their statutes, defining marriage as between one man and one woman, but by 2015, same-sex marriage had been legalized in thirty-seven states. The explanation for the dramatic shift in public policy had a lot to do with pressure from gay and lesbian rights activists on state legislatures, and rulings by federal and state courts striking down DOMAs as a violation of the Fourteenth Amendment's equal-protection and due-process clauses.[68] In 2015, the U.S. Supreme Court ruled that states cannot ban same-sex marriage. Even as public attitudes became more supportive of same-sex marriage, many religious conservatives maintained their staunch opposition. The issue came to a head over whether state officials and private businesses can use their religious beliefs as a justification for refusing service to customers. In North Carolina, several civil magistrates—who are empowered to marry people in that state—refused to marry same-sex couples, citing a state law that allowed magistrates to refrain from officiating such marriages if they had "sincerely held religious objections."[69] Utah and Mississippi have similar laws, and the issue has arisen in Oregon, Kentucky, and other states.[70] Federal courts are considering the issue and it is likely the U.S. Supreme Court eventually will be required to decide the controversy.

The COVID-19 pandemic created its own culture war posing public health against personal freedom. Governors and mayors closed many businesses to reduce the spread of the disease, but these closures became controversial as they went on for several months. As the original goal of flattening the curve of new infections seemed to have been achieved, pressure grew on officials to reopen the economy. By May and June 2020, many businesses had reopened,

culture wars
Political conflicts that emerge from deeply held moral values.

but controversy surrounded sporting events, bars, health clubs, churches and similar venues where large numbers of people would gather in close contact. In several states, health club operators reopened their clubs in violation of governors' orders for them to remain closed. Local law enforcement officials were conflicted over enforcing policy on the one hand or supporting free enterprise on the other. North Carolina Governor Roy Cooper's orders to keep health clubs and gyms closed were challenged by the North Carolina General Assembly which passed legislation allowing them to open. Cooper vetoed the legislation; health club and gym operators filed suit to overturn the closure orders. The iconic symbol of the COVID culture war is perhaps the face mask. Some states and localities made wearing face masks mandatory while others advised people to wear masks when they went out in public. Many people wore masks as protection against infecting others with the coronavirus, while others refused to wear masks citing their individual rights to do so.

Linking Capacity to Results

State and local governments have strengthened their position in the American federal system. On a regular basis, they tackle some of the most pressing problems facing the country.[71] The interaction of three unique characteristics of our fifty-state system—diversity, competitiveness, and resiliency—both facilitates and complicates their task. Consider the *diversity* of the United States. States and their communities have different fiscal capacities and different voter preferences for public services and taxes. As a result, citizens and businesses are offered real choices in taxation and expenditure policies across different jurisdictions.

Diversity is tempered, however, by the natural *competitiveness* of a federal system. No state can afford to be too far out of line with the prevailing thinking on appropriate levels of taxes and expenditures because citizens and businesses may opt to relocate. In essence, each jurisdiction is competing with every other jurisdiction. Such competition over the price and performance of government stabilizes the federal system.

The third characteristic, *resiliency*, captures the ability of state governments to recover from adversity. This feature was certainly put to the test during the economic downturn of 2008–2011. The stresses of that period compelled states to retrench and rethink; the fresh policy ideas that resulted were successful in some instances, unsuccessful in others. But the larger point is that state governments squared their shoulders to meet the challenges head on. Resiliency is the key.

As one astute observer of the U.S. governmental scene has commented, "Over the past decade, without ever quite admitting it, we have ceased to rely on Congress (or the federal government, for that matter) to deal with our most serious public problems. . . . [T]he states have been accepting the challenge of dealing with problems that no other level of government is handling."[72] Return to the first page of this chapter and reread Governor Burgum's inspirational words. The twenty-first century began full of challenges, but states and their local governments are taking charge. In the final analysis, that is what increased capacity is all about: results.

Chapter Recap

- State and local governments are directly involved in our daily lives.

- The story of states and localities over the past two decades has been one of transformation. They have shed their backward ways, reformed their institutions, and emerged as capable and proactive.

- State resurgence is exemplified in improved revenue systems, the expanded scope of state operations, faster diffusion of innovations, more interjurisdictional cooperation, and increased national-state conflict.

- Several persistent challenges confront states and localities: fiscal stress, interjurisdictional competition, and political corruption.

- The United States is becoming more racially and ethnically diverse. Sunbelt states tend to outpace the rest of the nation with their population growth.

- An outbreak of culture wars is redefining the politics of some communities and states.

- As a whole, the states are diverse, competitive, and resilient. Their increased capacity to govern effectively was sorely tested in the first decade of the twenty-first century.

Key Terms

evidence-based practices *(p. 4)*
capacity *(p. 4)*
jurisdiction *(p. 4)*
federalism *(p. 5)*
proactive *(p. 6)*
rainy day funds *(p. 7)*
downsize *(p. 14)*

rebrand *(p. 15)*
transparency *(p. 16)*
Sunbelt *(p. 20)*
Frostbelt *(p. 20)*
political culture *(p. 22)*
individualistic political culture *(p. 22)*

moralistic political culture *(p. 22)*
traditionalistic political culture *(p. 22)*
culture wars *(p. 24)*

Internet Resources

Nearly all states use the URL suffix **gov** in their online addresses, such as **Ohio.gov** or **mt.gov**. Florida does something a little different with its URL: **www.myflorida.com**.

A website that offers a wealth of policy information about the states, along with links to multistate organizations, national organizations of state officials, and state-based think tanks is **www.stateline.org**, established by the Pew Center on the States. The Center's own website contains useful information on state policies and trends at **www.pewtrusts.org/en/topics/state-policy**.

Since 1933, the CSG has collected and disseminated information about state institutions, policies, and trends. Its website is **www.csg.org**.

At **www.census.gov**, the website of the U.S. Bureau of the Census, you can find historical, demographic data on states and localities.

The website for *State Politics and Policy Quarterly*, a scholarly journal that publishes research on important state-level questions, is **spa.sagepub.com**. Also, the journal *State and Local Government Review* contains the latest research on issues in the states and localities. Its URL is **slg.sagepub.com**.

2

Federalism and the States: Sorting Out Roles and Responsibilities

U.S. Border Patrol officer apprehends illegal child immigrant in Arizona.

Learning Objectives

LO 2-1 To describe the history and evolution of American federalism from the writings of the Framers and the growth of national power to the contemporary time.

LO 2-2 To recognize the changing balance of formal and informal power and responsibility between the national government and the states.

LO 2-3 To describe the principal models of federalism that attempt to explain the nature of federal–state–local relationships.

LO 2-4 To explain the complex nature and tools of intergovernmental financial relations.

LO 2-5 To recognize finances as a source of friction and conflict between the three levels of government.

A single broad and enduring issue in American federalism transcends all others: What is the proper balance of power and responsibility between the national government and the states? The debate over this profound question was first joined by the Founders in pre-constitutional days and argued between the Federalists and Anti-Federalists. It continues today in the halls of Congress, the federal courts, and the state and local governments, over issues ranging from the mundane to the profound. For instance, which level of government is responsible for addressing illegal immigration? And what should the respective responsibilities of federal, state, and local governments be?

Over the last twenty years, illegal immigration across the southwestern U.S. border has shifted from a composition of largely adult Mexican males to one with many more Central American families. In 2000, some 97 percent of the 1.6 million people apprehended trying the cross the border into the United States were single Mexican nationals. By 2019, 56 percent of the apprehensions were families, with people from Guatemala and Honduras outnumbering people from Mexico.[1] To detain families entering the United States illegally, the federal government has separated children from their parents because children and parents cannot be held together in the same detention facilities. This has resulted in a growing number of unaccompanied children requiring shelter, which the U.S. government initially filled by contracting with state and local governments that agreed to provide facilities for them. However, in opposition to federal immigration policies, a number of state and local governments have terminated their contracts and are urging local organizations to end their contracts as well. As a county commissioner in Texas put it, "the federal government made their bed with its policies, so let them sleep in it."[2]

States are contesting the boundaries of federalism through varied approaches—some highly restrictive, and others much less so. Florida, Tennessee, and eighteen other states offer in-state college tuition to undocumented immigrants, and most states avert their eyes from evidence of local businesses employing undocumented workers. Undocumented immigrants can be issued drivers' licenses in many states, and in Oregon and New York, they are eligible for health care benefits. Other states come down hard on undocumented immigrants. In Arizona, for example, they are denied all social services and aggressively pursued for arrest. At least seven states expressly prohibit them from receiving in-state tuition assistance; other states will not issue them drivers' licenses.[3]

When Arizona, Alabama, and other states enacted laws that placed severe legal restrictions on undocumented immigrants and their employers, the U.S. Justice Department secured court orders blocking parts of those laws. Provisions in the Arizona, for example, required immigrants to carry papers showing they were legally admitted into the United States, made it illegal for undocumented aliens to seek work without authorization, required state and local law enforcement officers to verify the immigration status of those they stopped or detained, and criminalized being in the United States without proper authorization. A founding principle of our country is the right of the national government to keep states from enacting laws that usurp its powers, and in these particular cases, the federal government referred to that principle when it asserted that a "state may not pursue policies that undermine federal law." The U.S. Supreme Court agreed, invalidating large parts of the Arizona state law in the 2010 case of *Arizona v. United States*.[4] Still, the current situation is a crazy quilt of state laws, some of which—as in Arizona or Alabama—require local law enforcement officials to verify arrestees' citizenship while others—as in California or Colorado—forbid local law enforcement from doing so.

Complex and highly politicized issues that Congress fears to act upon—like immigration control—tend to expose the soft underbelly of federalism. Every response is intergovernmentally complex, with respective roles and responsibilities that need to be sorted out, or ultimately resolved, by the U.S. Supreme Court. Emotional issues like illegal immigration have spawned a critical analysis of American federalism that has significant implications for all levels of government. These types of events and conflicts help define U.S. federalism and exhibit both its strengths and weaknesses. As a system for organizing government, federalism has important consequences that often affect our political and personal lives in ways both direct and hidden.

The Concept of Federalism

In a nation—a large group of people organized under a single, sovereign government and sharing historical, cultural, and other values—powers and responsibilities can be divided among different levels of government in three ways: through a unitary government, a confederation, or a federal system. To understand our federal system, we must know how it differs from the other forms of government.

Unitary, Confederate, and Federal Systems

The large majority of countries (more than 90 percent) have a **unitary system** of government, in which the central government may create or abolish regional or local governments as it sees fit. These subgovernments can exercise only those powers and responsibilities granted to them by the central government. In France, the United Kingdom, Chile, Japan, and many other countries with unitary systems, the central government is strong, and the regional or local jurisdictions are weak. In the United States, the states themselves function as unitary systems in their relationships with local governments.

A **confederation** is the opposite of a unitary system. In a confederation the central government is weak, and the regional governments are powerful. The regional jurisdictions establish a central government to deal with areas of mutual concern, such as national defense and a common currency, but they severely restrict the central government's authority in other areas. If they see fit, they may change or even abolish the central government. The United States began as a confederation, and the southern states formed a new confederacy following secession in 1861.

A **federal system** falls somewhere between the unitary and confederate forms in the method by which it divides powers among levels of government. It has a minimum of two governmental levels, each of which derives its powers directly from the people and can act directly on the people within its jurisdiction without permission from any other authority. Each level of government is supreme in the powers assigned to it, and each is protected by a constitution from being destroyed by the other. Thus, federalism divides the power and functions of government between a central government and a specified number of geographically defined regional jurisdictions. In effect, people hold dual citizenship, in the national government and in their regional government.

unitary system
One in which all government authority is derived from a central government.

confederation
A league of sovereign states in which a limited central government exercises few independent powers.

federal system
A means of dividing the power and functions of government between a central government and a specified number of geographically defined regional jurisdictions.

In the U.S. federal system, the regional governments are called states. In others, such as Canada, they are known as provinces. Altogether, there are approximately twenty federal systems in the world.

The Advantages and Disadvantages of Federalism

As it has evolved in the United States, federalism is a reasonably effective system of government. But, as immigration policy illustrates, it is not perfect, nor is it well suited to the circumstances of most other nations. Ironically, federalism's weaknesses are closely related to its strengths.

STRENGTHS	WEAKNESSES
1. *A federal system helps manage social and political conflict.* It broadly disperses political power within and among governments, enabling national, as well as regional and local, concerns to reach the central government. Many venues, or "democratic safety valves," exist for resolving conflicts before they reach the crisis stage.	1. *If such conflicts are not addressed satisfactorily, they can eventually lead to regional or ethnic conflict on a fearsome scale.*
2. *Federalism promotes administrative efficiency.* The wide variety of services demanded by citizens is delivered more efficiently without a large central bureaucracy. From public elementary education to garbage collection, the government closest to the problem seems to work best in adapting public programs to local needs.	2. *Federalism presents problems in coordinating action across governments and boundaries.* Picture trying to get 90,000 squawking and flapping chickens to move in the same direction at once. Confusion and deadly delays in responding to issues such as a disease pandemic and illegal immigration illustrate this point.
3. *Federalism encourages innovation.* States and localities can customize their policies to accommodate diverse demands and needs— and, indeed, such heterogeneity flourishes. New policies are constantly being tested by the more than 90,000 government "laboratories" that exist throughout the country, thus further encouraging experimentation and flexibility.	3. *Federalism's many points of involvement can encourage obstruction and delay and result in ineffective national government programs and priorities.* Duplication and confusion can be the result. Fifty sets of laws on banking and lending practices, firearms regulation, and medical marijuana can make crossing state lines an exercise in comparative public law.
4. *A federal system maximizes political participation in government.* Citizens have opportunities to participate at all three levels of government through elections, public hearings, and other means. The local and state governments fill almost one million offices in regular elections, serving as valuable political training camps for aspiring public leaders. The great majority of presidents and congressional representatives first wet their feet in state or local politics.	4. *Such broad participation encourages local biases inimical to national interests.* Problems in locating nuclear and hazardous waste disposal facilities readily illustrate this dilemma.

The History of U.S. Federalism

The men who met in Philadelphia during the hot summer of 1787 to draw up the U.S. Constitution were not wild-eyed optimists, nor were they revolutionaries. In fact, as we'll see in this section, they were consummate pragmatists whose beliefs shaped the new republic and created both the strengths and the weaknesses of our federal system.

Early History

The Framers of the Constitution held to the belief of English political philosopher Thomas Hobbes that human beings are contentious and selfish. Some of them openly disdained the masses. For example, Gouverneur Morris of New York declared of the American majority, "The mob begin to think and reason. Poor reptiles! . . . They bask in the sun, and ere noon they will bite, depend upon it."[5] Most of the Framers agreed that their goal in Philadelphia was to find a means of controlling lower forms of human behavior while still allowing citizens to have a voice in making the laws they were compelled to obey. The "philosopher of the Constitution," James Madison, formulated the problem in terms of factions— groups that pursue their own interests without concern for the interests of society as a whole. Political differences and self-interest, Madison felt, led to the formation of such factions, and the Framers' duty was to identify "constitutional devices that would force various interests to check and control one another."[6]

Three practical devices to control factions were placed in the U.S. Constitution. The first was a system of representative government in which citizens would elect individuals who would filter and refine the views of the masses. The second was the division of government into three branches (executive, legislative, and judicial). The legislative body was divided into two houses, each with a check on the activities of the other. Equal in power would be both a strong chief executive with the authority to veto legislative acts, and an independent judiciary. Third, the government was structured as a federal system, in which the most dangerous faction of all—a national majority— would be constrained by the sovereign states. Alternatively, insurrection in one state would be put down by the others, acting through the national government. Madison's ultimate hope was that the new Constitution would "check interest with interest, class with class, faction with faction, and one branch of government with another in a harmonious system of mutual frustration."[7]

Even though today there appears to be more frustration, factionalism, and fragmentation than harmony, Madison's dream did come true. The U.S. federal system is the longest-lived national constitutional government on earth. Its dimensions and activities are vastly different from what the Framers envisioned, but it remains a dynamic, adaptable, responsive, and usually effective system for conducting the affairs of government.

The Move Toward Federalism

The drive for independence from the British Crown by the thirteen American colonies was in large measure a reaction to "a history of repeated injuries and

LO 2-1
To describe the history and evolution of American federalism from the writings of the Framers and the growth of national power to the contemporary time.

usurpations" and "absolute tyranny" (according to the Declaration of Independence) under a British unitary system of government.

The immediate struggle for independence left little time to develop a consensus on the form of government best suited to the future needs of American society. Hence, the move toward federalism was gradual. The first independent government established in America was a confederation; thus, Americans tested two types of government—unitary and confederate—before deciding permanently on the third, federalism.

The Articles of Confederation

The Articles of Confederation During the War for Independence, the colonies, now called states, agreed to establish a confederation. A unicameral (one-house) Congress was created to exercise the authority of the new national government. Its powers were limited to the authority to wage war, make peace, enter into treaties and alliances, appoint and receive ambassadors, regulate Indian affairs, and create a postal system. The states held all powers not expressly granted to the Congress. The governing document was the Articles of Confederation (effective from 1776 to 1787).

The inherent weaknesses of the confederation quickly became apparent. The states had significant authority within their own borders, but the federal government was unable to carry out its basic responsibilities or honor its financial obligations because it did not have the power to force the states to pay their share of the bill. The lack of national authority to regulate either domestic or international commerce led to discriminatory trade practices by the states. Anarchy and even warfare between the fractious states were a very real concern.[8] Indeed, the key event that brought together representatives of the states to draft a constitution for a new type of government was Shays' Rebellion. Daniel Shays, a Revolutionary War officer, led an armed revolt of New England farmers who were fighting mad about debt and taxes. The weak central government had difficulty putting down the rebellion.

The Constitutional Convention

The Constitutional Convention How did the Framers create a long-lasting and successful system of government that seems to have the best features of both unitary and confederate forms? They were familiar with developments in political and theological federalism in Europe and the ancient world. They were aware of tribal confederations among the Native Americans and, most important, the Framers were well informed by their own colonial experience.[9] Truly, the Framers were learned individuals, well schooled in the theories of politics, and most of them did believe in designing a government that would serve the people and ensure justice. But above all they were pragmatists; they developed a practical compromise on the key issues of the day, including the proper role of the national government and the states. The reconciliation of the interests and powers of the states with the need for a strong national government, what Madison called a "middle ground," was purely an American invention. Today, the United States stands as the prototypical federal system. It is our most distinctive political contribution.

Delegates representing each of the states assembled at the constitutional convention. Here, the self-interests of the large states and the small states diverged. The large states supported the Virginia Plan, which proposed a strong central government spearheaded by a powerful bicameral Congress. Because representation in both chambers was to be based on population, larger states would be favored. The smaller states countered with the New Jersey Plan, which put forward a one-house legislature composed of an equal number of representatives from each state. There were other differences between the two plans, but the issue of state representation was paramount.

The New Jersey Plan was defeated by a vote of 7 to 3, but the smaller states refused to give in. Finally, Connecticut moved that the lower house (the House of Representatives) be based on the population of each state and the upper house (the Senate) be based on equal state membership. This Great Compromise was approved, ensuring that a faction of large states would not dominate the small ones.

The Framers reached another important set of compromises by specifying the powers of the new central government and the powers to be granted (and denied) to the states. The seventeen **enumerated (delegated) powers** were listed in the Constitution, along with state government powers and **concurrent powers** to be exercised by both the national and state governments. Figure 2.1 illustrates the constitutional distribution of powers.

enumerated (delegated) powers Those expressly given to the national government, primarily in Article I, Section 8, of the Constitution.

concurrent powers Those granted by the Constitution to both the national and the state governments.

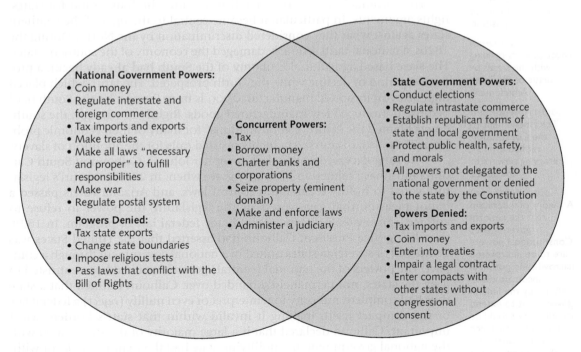

National Government Powers:
- Coin money
- Regulate interstate and foreign commerce
- Tax imports and exports
- Make treaties
- Make all laws "necessary and proper" to fulfill responsibilities
- Make war
- Regulate postal system

Powers Denied:
- Tax state exports
- Change state boundaries
- Impose religious tests
- Pass laws that conflict with the Bill of Rights

Concurrent Powers:
- Tax
- Borrow money
- Charter banks and corporations
- Seize property (eminent domain)
- Make and enforce laws
- Administer a judiciary

State Government Powers:
- Conduct elections
- Regulate intrastate commerce
- Establish republican forms of state and local government
- Protect public health, safety, and morals
- All powers not delegated to the national government or denied to the state by the Constitution

Powers Denied:
- Tax imports and exports
- Coin money
- Enter into treaties
- Impair a legal contract
- Enter compacts with other states without congressional consent

Figure 2.1 Constitutional Distribution of Powers

LO 2-2
To recognize the changing balance of formal and informal power and responsibility between the national government and the states.

nation-centered federalism
Theory holding that the national government is dominant over the states.

state-centered federalism
Theory holding that the national government represents a voluntary compact or agreement between the states, which retain a dominant position.

reserved powers
Those powers residing with the states by virtue of the Tenth Amendment.

Tenth Amendment
The amendment to the Constitution, ratified in 1791, reserving powers to the states.

compact theory
A theory of federalism that the national government's Constitutional powers are to be interpreted narrowly, and potential unconstitutional efforts by the federal government to extend its authority should be met with resistance by the states. This theory became the foundation for states' rights arguments.

State-Centered Federalism

The first decades under the new Constitution witnessed a clash between profoundly different views on governing. George Washington, John Adams, Alexander Hamilton, and their fellow Federalists favored national supremacy, or **nation-centered federalism**. Opposed to their idea were Thomas Jefferson and the Republicans, who preferred **state-centered federalism**. Much of the debate then, as today, concerned the meaning of the **reserved powers** clause of the **Tenth Amendment** to the Constitution. Ratified in 1791, the Tenth Amendment gave support to the states by openly acknowledging that "the powers not delegated to the United States by the Constitution, nor prohibited by it to the States, are reserved to the states respectively, or to the people." But in fact, the Tenth Amendment was an early omen of the eventual triumph of nation-centered federalism. As pointed out by constitutional scholar Walter Berns, if the states were intended to be the dominant federal actors, they would not have needed the Tenth Amendment to remind them.[10]

Those who defended the power of the states under the Constitution—that is, state-centered federalism—saw the Constitution as a *compact*, an agreement, among the sovereign states, which maintained their sovereignty, or the right of self-governance. The powers of the national government enumerated in the Constitution were to be interpreted narrowly, and the states were obliged to resist any unconstitutional efforts by the national government to extend its authority.[11]

This **compact theory** of federalism became the foundation for states' rights arguments. In particular, it became central to the fight of the southern states against what they considered discrimination by the North. During the 1820s, a national tariff seriously damaged the economy of the southern states. The slave-based agricultural economy of the South had already begun a protracted period of decline while the North prospered. The tariff, which placed high taxes on imported manufactured goods from Europe, hit the South hard because it produced few manufactured goods. Rightly or wrongly, the southerners blamed the "tariff of abominations" for many of their economic problems. They also, of course, staunchly resisted calls for the abolition of slavery.

The long-deceased political philosopher John C. Calhoun of South Carolina must have saluted in his musty grave when, in 2014, Missouri's legislature voted to nullify federal gun control laws, and Arizona voters passed a ballot measure that gave voters or the legislature the power to refuse to enforce, administer, or cooperate with any federal law or program. In 1828, then-living Vice President Calhoun had asserted that the United States was composed of sovereign states united in a national government through a compact. The powers of the national (central) government had been entrusted to it by the states, not permanently handed over. Calhoun claimed that a state thus had complete authority to reinterpret or even nullify (reject) a federal law or the compact itself, making it invalid within that state's borders. Most important, Calhoun declared that if a large majority of the states sided with the national government, the nullifying state had the right to *secede*, or withdraw from the Union. (Indeed, until the Civil War, when Americans referred to "my country," they usually meant their state—not the United States.)

In 1832, after an additional tariff was enacted by the national government, South Carolina nullified it. President Andrew Jackson and the Congress threatened military action to force the state to comply with the law, and Jackson even threatened to hang Calhoun, who by this time had resigned from the vice presidency.[12]

Ultimately, eleven southern states (led by South Carolina) did secede from the Union, at which point they formed the Confederate States of America. The long conflict between state sovereignty and national supremacy, and the question of slavery as well, was definitively resolved by five years of carnage in such places as Antietam, Shiloh, and Gettysburg, followed by the eventual readmittance of the renegade states to the Union. The Civil War, sometimes referred to in the South as The War Between the States, remains the single most violent episode in American history, resulting in more than 620,000 deaths (more than in all our other wars combined) and countless civilian tragedies.

The Growth of National Power Through the Constitution and the Judiciary

After the Civil War, a *nation-centered* concept of federalism evolved. For the most part, the national government has become the primary governing force, with the states and localities generally following its lead. Recently, the states have been inclined to act more independently, but their power vis-à-vis the national government has been eroded by the U.S. Supreme Court's interpretations of key sections of the Constitution.

The National Supremacy Clause Article III of the Constitution established the U.S. Supreme Court. The supremacy of national law and the Constitution is constitutionally grounded in the **national supremacy clause** (Article VI), which provides that the national laws and the Constitution are the supreme laws of the land. Later Supreme Court decisions established its role as arbiter of any legal disputes between the national government and the states.

The Necessary and Proper Clause The fourth chief justice of the United States, John Marshall, was the architect of the federal judiciary during his thirty-four years on the bench. Almost single-handedly, he made the judiciary a coequal branch of government. Several of his rulings laid the groundwork for the expansion of national governmental power. In the landmark case of *McCulloch v. Maryland* (1819), two issues were before the bench: the right of the national government to establish a national bank and the right of the state of Maryland to tax that bank, once it was established.[13] The secretary of the treasury, Alexander Hamilton, had proposed a bill that would allow Congress to charter such a bank for depositing national revenues and facilitating the borrowing of funds. Those who wanted to limit the power of the national government, such as James Madison and Thomas Jefferson, argued that the Constitution did not provide the government with the specific authority to charter and operate a national bank.

national supremacy clause
Article VI of the Constitution, which makes national laws superior to state laws.

The crux of the issue was how to interpret the **necessary and proper clause**. The final power delegated to Congress under Article I, Section 8, is the power "to make all laws which shall be *necessary and proper* for carrying into execution the foregoing powers, and all other powers vested by this Constitution in the Government of the United States" (emphasis added). Jefferson argued that *necessary* meant "indispensable," whereas Hamilton asserted that it merely meant "convenient." Hamilton argued that in addition to the enumerated powers, Congress possessed **implied powers**. In the case of the national bank, valid congressional action was implied through the powers of taxation, borrowing, and making currency found in Article I, Section 8.

Meanwhile, the state of Maryland had levied a tax on the new national bank, which was located within its borders, and the bank had refused to pay. The bank dispute was eventually heard by Chief Justice Marshall. Marshall was persuaded by the Hamiltonian point of view. Marshall pointed out that nowhere in the Constitution does it stipulate that the only powers that may be carried out are those expressly described in Article I, Section 8. Thus, he ruled that Congress had the implied power to establish the bank and that Maryland had no right to tax it. In one of the most widely quoted lines from a judicial opinion, Marshall wrote, "the power to tax involves the power to destroy," so Maryland could not tax or destroy an institution established by Congress. Significantly, *McCulloch v. Maryland* meant that the national government had an almost unlimited right to decide how to exercise its delegated powers. Over the years, Congress has enacted a great many laws that are only vaguely, if at all, associated with the enumerated powers and that stretch the phrase *necessary and proper* beyond its logical limits.

necessary and proper clause
Portion of Article I, Section 8, of the Constitution that authorizes Congress to enact all laws "necessary and proper" to carry out its responsibilities.

implied powers
Those that are not expressly granted by the Constitution but that are inferred from the enumerated powers.

commerce clause
Part of Article I, Section 8, of the U.S. Constitution, which gives Congress the power to regulate trade with foreign countries and among the states.

general welfare clause
The portion of Article I, Section 8, of the Constitution that allows the national government to tax and spend for the general welfare of the United States.

The Commerce Clause Another important ruling of the Marshall Court extended national power through an expansive interpretation of the **commerce clause** (often referred to as the interstate commerce clause) of Article I, Section 8. The commerce clause gives Congress the power "to regulate commerce with foreign nations, and among the several states, and with the Indian tribes." In *Gibbons v. Ogden* (1824),[14] two important questions were addressed by Marshall: What is commerce? And how broadly should Congress's power to regulate commerce be interpreted?

The United States was just developing a national economy as the Industrial Revolution expanded. National oversight was needed, along with regulation of emerging transportation networks and of state activities related to the passage of goods across state lines (interstate commerce). The immediate question was whether New York could grant a monopoly to run a steamship service between New York and New Jersey. What was Marshall's answer? No, it could not. He defined commerce broadly and held that Congress's power to regulate commerce applied not only to traffic across state boundaries but, in some cases, also to traffic of goods, merchandise, and people *within* a state. The Court further expanded the meaning of "commerce" in later rulings.

The General Welfare Clause The **general welfare clause** of Article I, Section 8, states that "the Congress shall have power to lay and collect taxes, duties, imposts, and excises to pay the debts and provide for the common defense and *general welfare* of the United States" (emphasis added). Before the Great Depression of the 1930s, it was believed that it was up to private charity and state and local governments to provide limited assistance to the poor. The Great Depression brought massive unemployment and poverty throughout the country and made necessary a major change in the national government's attitude. The states and localities were staggered by the tremendous loss of tax revenues and the persistent pleas to help poor and displaced persons obtain food and shelter. Franklin D. Roosevelt, who won the presidency in 1932, set in motion numerous New Deal programs that completely redefined federal responsibility for the general welfare. These programs, such as Social Security, propelled the national government into a position of dominance within the federal system and extended it into fields previously within the province of the states, the localities, and the private sector. The U.S. Supreme Court has always considered powers granted under the general welfare clause to be qualified rather than absolute; related to taxing power and not to the general legislative power.[15]

The Fourteenth Amendment   Ratified by the states in 1868, the **Fourteenth Amendment** had the effects of giving former slaves official status as citizens of the United States and of the state in which they lived, as well as setting a precondition for southern states to be readmitted to the Union. It included two other important principles as well: *due process* and *equal protection* under the law. The federal courts have used the Fourteenth Amendment to increase national power over the states in several critical fields, especially with regard to civil rights, criminal law, and election practices.

Before the ratification of the Fourteenth Amendment, the U.S. Supreme Court had taken the position that the Bill of Rights was applicable *only* to the national government and not to the states. In the case of *Barron v. Baltimore* (1833),[16] John Barron sued the city of Baltimore for depriving him of property by depositing so much sand near his wharf in Baltimore harbor that it made the wharf unusable. In Chief Justice Marshall's final case on the Supreme Court, he wrote that the Bill of Rights, "contain no expression indicating an intention to apply them to the State governments. This court cannot so apply them." The Fourteenth Amendment changed this by expressly making the due process and equal protection provisions of the Bill of Rights applicable to the states, and the U.S. Supreme Court has used the Fourteenth Amendment to incorporate other provisions of the Bill or Rights as applying to state governments. Examples include First Amendment rights to freedom of speech (*Gitlow v. New York*, 1925),[17] Second Amendment rights to firearm ownership (*McDonald v. City of Chicago*, 2010),[18] Fourth Amendment provisions on privacy (*Mapp v. Ohio*, 1961),[19] and a wide variety of others. However, the U.S. Supreme Court has never ruled that all the rights contained in the Bill of Rights are applicable to the states. For example, the Seventh Amendment's right to a jury trial in civil suits has expressly not been made applicable to the states by the U.S. Supreme Court, although many commentators have advocated that it should be.[20]

Fourteenth Amendment Enacted in 1868, this amendment contains citizenship rights, due process, and equal protection provisions that states must apply to all citizens.

Controversies in States and Localities

What Level of Government Should Take the Lead for Pandemic Threats?

The novel coronavirus, COVID-19, first appeared in Wuhan, China in late 2019. A month later, cases began appearing in Europe and then in February in the United States. COVID-19 is a disease related to Severe Acute Respiratory Syndrome (SARS) and Middle East Respiratory Syndrome (MERS) that infected many countries in 2004 and 2013, respectively. Like SARS and MERS, COVID-19 most likely migrated from animal hosts to humans, making it difficult or impossible for human immune systems to fight off early infections. COVID-19 seems to have a lower fatality rate than SARS or MERS, but it also is much more infectious. By spring 2020, COVID-19 had infected and killed more people worldwide than either SARS or MERS. Especially vulnerable to COVID-19 are older people; people with preexisting health conditions such as high blood pressure, diabetes, obesity; and people who are in close quarters such as nursing homes, jails and prisons, on cruise ships or naval vessels, and in densely populated urban areas.

COVID-19 first emerged in the United States in Seattle where several nursing homes were hard hit. Soon, New York City and other heavily populated urban areas became hotbeds with large numbers of infected residents. While the federal government was first briefed on COVID-19 in early January, it took some two months for it to recognize the threat of this illness and develop a national strategy to address the pandemic. In the meantime, governors in New York, Washington, Illinois, Florida, and other states, worried about what a flood of people needing hospitalization might do to their health care systems, began issuing shelter at home orders, banning public gatherings, and requiring many businesses to close their doors in order to slow the spread of the virus. Because of differential needs for items such as ventilators to support respiration for severely affected patients and protective gear like masks, face shields and medical gowns, some governors found themselves in bidding wars against other states in attempting to purchase equipment.

The Tenth Amendment of the U.S. Constitution recognizes the powers of the state governments. Traditionally, these included the "police powers" of health, education, and welfare. The Tenth Amendment states: "The powers not delegated to the United States by the Constitution, nor prohibited by it to the states, are reserved to the states respectively, or to the people." The seventeen "express powers" of the national government in the Constitution do not list anything about protecting the health and safety of the Citizens; this resides with the states though their "police powers." The U.S. Constitution contains two references to "the General Welfare," one occurring in the Preamble and the other in the Taxing and Spending Clause. The U.S. Supreme Court has held that these clauses are not a general grant of legislative power to the federal government.

The Trump administration and the Centers for Disease Control and Prevention issued national guidelines for voluntary isolation and monitoring of people exposed to COVID-19, but the national government lacks authority to do much more. States and their health departments can reject the federal guidelines and substitute their own. Especially problematic is control over the U.S. economy in a pandemic. After much of the economy was shut down by governors, President Trump and the Centers for Disease Control issued guidelines for reopening. Many state governors ignored those guidelines and began allowing some businesses to reopen in early May. Separate decisions by states could cause people to "venue-shop," hopping across state boundaries to go on vacation or for major shopping excursions. This would allow infections to spread widely from state to state. Health experts fear that too early action on reopening businesses would cause a new surge in COVID-19 infections as occurred in summer 2020.

Critical Thinking Questions

1. Which level of government should exercise primary responsibility for addressing a disease pandemic? Why?

2. Should the fifty states be permitted to determine such policy as they see fit, or should there—indeed can there—be a single, comprehensive national policy to handle such problems?

The Growth of National Power Through Congress

The U.S. Supreme Court has not been the only force behind nation-centered federalism; Congress has worked hand in hand with the judiciary. The commerce clause represents a good example. Given the simple authority to control or eliminate state barriers to trade across state lines, Congress now regulates commercial activities within a state's boundaries as well, as long as these activities purportedly have substantial national consequences (examples include banking, insurance, and the movement of goods). Congress has also used the authority of the commerce clause to expand national power into fields only vaguely related to commerce, such as protecting endangered species. The states have made literally hundreds of legal challenges to such exercise of the commerce power. Until recently, almost all of these were resolved by the U.S. Supreme Court in favor of the national government. But the court dramatically changed direction on June 28, 2012, when a 5-to-4 majority held that the Patient Protection and Affordable Care Act ("Obamacare") overstepped Congress's constitutional authority under the commerce clause by mandating that states extend Medicaid to hundreds of thousands of new recipients. Fourteen states had filed litigation challenging the constitutionality of the federal health care law. (The court revisited the law in 2015, ruling that the federal government could legally subsidize federally run health insurance exchanges.)

Taxing and Spending Power Probably the most controversial source of the rise in national power in recent years has been the use of the *taxing and spending power* by Congress to extend its influence over the state and local governments. Under Article I, Section 8, Congress holds the power to tax and spend to provide for the common defense and general welfare. But the **Sixteenth Amendment**, which grants Congress the power to tax the income of individuals and corporations, moved the center of financial power from the states to Washington, D.C. Through the income tax, the national government raises trillions of dollars. A portion of this money is sent to the states and localities through grants-in-aid. Congress insists on some sort of accountability in the way these funds are spent, and as a consequence, attaches various conditions to which the recipients must adhere if they are to receive the money. These conditions include requirements for recipient governments to match national grant dollars with some portion of state contributions. (The interstate highway program requires one state dollar for every ten federal dollars, for example.) Congress also imposes mandates and regulations directly related to the purposes of the individual grant, such as effectively forcing the states to adopt national policies on driver's licenses (noncomplying states face the loss of federal transportation dollars). At times, Congress has used crossover sanctions to coerce states into addressing national concerns. Crossover sanctions threaten loss of federal aid in one area for noncompliance in a different policy area. An early example of this is the 1984 requirement for all states to raise their minimum age for purchase of alcoholic beverages to 21. Noncomplying states risked losing 10 percent of their federal highway aid.

Sixteenth Amendment Enacted in 1913, this amendment grants the national government the power to levy income taxes.

Federal Preemption The national government has also seized power through the process known as **federal preemption**. The legal basis for preemption is Article VI of the Constitution, the national supremacy clause: Whenever a state law conflicts with a national law, the national law is dominant.

Congressional passage of a national law that supersedes existing state legislation is directly preemptive. The Real ID Act of 2005 is one such example. Another is evolving federal regulation of unmanned aviation vehicles (drones). Drones have been mentioned as potentially useful for all sorts of activities—scanning agricultural fields for pests, delivering goods to households, conducting hazardous inspections, and so on. As commercial use of drones has expanded, state and local governments have sought to regulate their use in order to preserve the privacy of individuals and safety of airspaces. In 1958, Congress gave the Federal Aviation Administration (FAA) the authority to regulate all aspects of aircraft (at that time meaning manned aircraft) in flight. Congress is now discussing directly preempting state and local statutes and putting unmanned aircraft under FAA regulation.[21]

Smothering (Then Resuscitating) the Tenth (and Eleventh) Amendments Actions by Congress and the federal courts have gradually undermined the Tenth Amendment, which reserves to the states all powers not specifically granted to the national government nor prohibited to the states. In fact, it is difficult to identify any field of state activity not intruded on by the national government today. Although the Tenth Amendment is a declaration of the original division of powers between nation and states under the Constitution, the configuration is hardly descriptive of American federalism today.

The U.S. Supreme Court has sent mixed messages on the relevance of the Tenth Amendment. A good example of the Court's fickle federalism involves the Fair Labor Standards Act (FLSA). Following forty years of case law that essentially relegated the Tenth Amendment to the basement of federalism, the Court surprisingly ruled in favor of state and local governments in the 1976 case of *National League of Cities v. Usery*. At issue was the constitutionality under the commerce clause of the 1974 amendments to the FLSA, which extended federal minimum wage and maximum hour requirements to state and local employees. In this case, the Court said that Congress did not have the constitutional right to impose wage and hour requirements on employees carrying out basic—or integral—functions, such as law enforcement or firefighting.[22]

But just nine years later, the Court reversed that decision in *Garcia v. San Antonio Metropolitan Transit Authority*. A spate of litigation had not been able to resolve the issue of just which state and local activities are "integral." So the Court overturned its findings in *Usery* and once again applied federal wage and hour laws to nonnational governments—in this specific instance, to a mass transit system run by the city of San Antonio.[23] What really offended the states was the written opinion of the Court, in which it excused itself from such future controversies involving state claims against congressional and

federal preemption The principle that national laws take precedence over state laws.

executive branch power exercised under the commerce clause. Now Congress alone, with little or no judicial oversight, would be allowed to determine, through the political process, how extensively it would intrude on what had previously been state and local prerogatives. One dissenting Supreme Court justice wrote that "all that stands between the remaining essentials of state sovereignty and Congress is the latter's underdeveloped capacity for self-restraint."[24] In the view of some critics, the states were relegated to the status of any other special interest group and the Tenth Amendment was irrelevant. Other critics more optimistically observed that the narrow 5-to-4 decision could be revisited by a more conservative Supreme Court at a later date.[25]

Sure enough, in 1995, the Court reaffirmed the Tenth Amendment in *United States v. Lopez* by recognizing a limit to Congress's power over interstate commerce. Ironically, this case also involved San Antonio, where a high-school student, Alfonso Lopez, was arrested for bringing a handgun to school. He was charged with violating the Gun Free School Zones Act of 1990, which banned the possession of a firearm within 1,000 feet of a school. The Court ruled in this instance that Congress had unconstitutionally extended its power to regulate commerce because there was no connection between the gun law and interstate commerce.[26]

The Court continued to recalibrate the scales of power in favor of the states in a series of rulings beginning in 1997. First, the Court upheld states' authority to incarcerate sexual predators in mental institutions after their criminal sentences had been served.[27] Next, the Court ruled that Congress offended "the very principle of separate state sovereignty" by requiring local police to conduct background checks on people who want to purchase handguns.[28] More recently, the Court affirmed the right of state and local governments to seize private land for commercial development[29] and the authority of states to grant tax breaks and other financial inducements to attract and keep businesses.[30] As noted above, the Court overturned the power of Congress to mandate that states extend Medicaid benefits to a new—and large—segment of their citizenry. And in 2018 the Court ruled that provisions of federal law forbidding states from allowing gambling on sports were unconstitutional, creating a new and thriving industry in many states.[31]

Recent rulings based on the Eleventh Amendment have revived the notion of the sovereign immunity of the states. According to this doctrine, which dates back to the Middle Ages, a king (the state) cannot be sued without his (its) consent (the Eleventh Amendment protects states from lawsuits by citizens of other states or foreign nations). U.S. Supreme Court decisions have upheld the sovereign immunity of the states from being sued in federal courts in cases involving lawsuits by Indian tribes[32] and discrimination against older or disabled employees.[33] The Court also protected the states against private complaints taken before federal agencies[34] while restricting the states' Eleventh Amendment immunity under the Americans with Disabilities Act.[35] And in its most recent Eleventh Amendment case, the Court ruled that California was immune from a civil lawsuit filed in Nevada, overturning forty years of legal precedence.[36]

Federalism and the Courts Today The Supreme Court under Chief Justice William Rehnquist (1986–2005) clearly and decisively positioned itself on the side of the states in most conflicts with the national government. However, the U.S. Supreme Court does not decide unilaterally in favor of the states in all cases, notwithstanding one justice's complaint that the majority has become "[a] mindless dragon that indiscriminately chews gaping holes in federal statutes." In many cases that involve federalism, there are other, sometimes more compelling issues that the Court chooses to prioritize. For example, the Court limited the authority of the states to regulate tobacco advertising,[37] ruled that federal laws trump state laws with respect to product liability claims and certain restrictions on voting,[38] and held that states cannot under federal law compel coal-burning power plants to reduce their greenhouse emissions.[39] In these and many other cases, business interests, ideology, and partisanship sometimes trump federalism.

During the Rehnquist Court, a large majority of the Court's decisions in federalism cases were by a fragile 5-to-4 margin. Two pro-state justices, William Rehnquist and Sandra Day O'Connor, left the bench in 2005. The federalism feelings of today's Chief Justice John Roberts are not clearly defined.[40] For instance, in deciding that corporations—like individuals—have free political speech rights, the Roberts Court effectively abrogated states' authority to limit corporate and nonprofit campaign contributions directly to or in the interests of candidates in state and local elections (overturning a Montana state law); struck down Arizona's and other states' voter registration laws; and held unanimously that Massachusetts' 35-foot abortion clinic protest buffer zone violated the First Amendment by limiting free speech.[41] Pivoting in a 2012 ruling on the Affordable Care Act ("Obamacare"), however, the Roberts Court held that the federal government cannot force the states to expand Medicaid funding or penalize them for not doing so.[42]

American federalism, by its nature, is ambiguous: It "was born in ambiguity, it institutionalizes ambiguity in our form of government, and changes in it tend to be ambiguous, too."[43] President Trump's two most recent Supreme Court appointments—Neil Gorsuch and Brett Kavanaugh—seemingly have much more state-oriented views on federalism, although their views have yet to be tested in court cases.[44] Both voted in the majority to make California immune from civil suits in the Eleventh Amendment case described above but have differed in their positions and votes on other recent federalism-related cases.[45] As one influential review of the current U.S. Supreme Court concluded, "The Court is now firmly more conservative, which is likely to amplify state and local government authority vis-à-vis the federal government in some areas, while curtailing it in others."[46]

Judicial intervention in the affairs of state and local governments has not rendered them mere administrative appendages or relics of the past. But federal intrusions into the affairs of state and local governments continue to be burdensome and unwelcome, and the states are pushing back through resisting intrusive federal laws and regulations.[47] The Tenth and Eleventh Amendments have been useful weapons for fending off federal encroachments on the power of state and local officials, but those weapons can be shattered by a single justice's change of heart or a new appointment to the bench.

Models of Federalism

Perceptions of the role of the states in the federal system have shifted from time to time throughout our history. Those who study the federal system have generally described these perceptions through various models or metaphors that attempt to present federalism's complexity in a form that is intuitively understandable. Such models have been used both to enhance understanding and, when opportunities arise, to pursue ideological and partisan objectives. One complete inventory uncovered 326 models of federalism,[48] but only the best-known ones are reviewed here to demonstrate that the U.S. federal system and people's perceptions of it change over time.

LO 2-3
To describe the principal models of federalism that attempt to explain the nature of federal–state–local relationships.

Dual Federalism (1787–1932)

The model of **dual federalism** holds that both the national and state governments are sovereign and that they are equal within their respective spheres of authority as set forth in the Constitution. The national government exercises those powers specifically designated to it, and the remainder are reserved for the states. The nation and the states are viewed as primarily competitive, not cooperative, in their relationships with one another. The metaphor is that of a layer cake, with two separate-colored layers, one on top of the other.

Dual federalism, which has its roots in the compact theory, dominated political thought for the first 145 years of U.S. federalism, although the Civil War and other events led to substantial modifications of the model.[49] Until 1860, the functions of the national government remained largely restricted to the delegated powers. Federal financial assistance to the states was extremely limited. The states had the dominant influence on the everyday lives of their citizens, acting almost unilaterally in areas such as elections, education, economic development, labor relations, and criminal and family law.[50] After the Civil War shattered secession and dealt the compact theory of state-centered federalism a death blow, the nation-centered view became paramount.

Cooperative Federalism (1933–1964)

The selection of a specific date for the demise of dual federalism is rather subjective, but a reasonable estimate is 1933, when Franklin D. Roosevelt became president. Roosevelt's New Deal buried dual federalism by expanding national authority over commerce, taxation, and the economy. The question of which level of government was constitutionally empowered to do what became much less important than the question of some level doing something to address the economic devastation affecting the country as a whole.

Cooperative federalism recognizes the sharing of responsibilities and financing by all levels of government. Beginning with the Great Depression, the national government increasingly worked with states and localities to provide jobs and social welfare, develop the nation's infrastructure, and promote economic development.

dual federalism
Model in which the responsibilities and activities of the national and state governments are separate and distinct.

cooperative federalism
A model of federalism that stresses the linkages and joint arrangements among the three levels of government.

The cooperative aspects of this era were measured in governmental finances. The national government spent huge amounts of money to alleviate the ravages of the Great Depression and to get the U.S. economic machinery back into gear. Total federal expenditures rose from 2.5 percent of the gross national product (GNP) in 1929 to 18.7 percent just thirty years later, far surpassing the growth in state and local spending during the same period. The number of federal grants-in-aid rose from twelve in 1932, with a value of $193 million, to twenty-six five years later, with a value of $2.66 billion. A substantial amount of the federal aid was sent directly to local governments, particularly counties and school districts. The variety of grant programs also expanded with funds now earmarked for maternal and child health, assistance for the elderly, fire control, treatment of venereal disease, public housing, road and bridge construction, and wildlife conservation.

Contemporary Variations on Cooperative Federalism (Since 1964)

The broad theme of cooperative federalism has many variations. All of them stress intergovernmental sharing. Among these variations are creative federalism and new federalism.

Creative federalism was devised by President Lyndon B. Johnson to promote his dream of a Great Society. Johnson sought to build the Great Society through a massive national government attack on the most serious problems facing the nation: poverty, crime, poor health care, and inadequate education, among others. The weapon for the attack was the federal grant-in-aid. More than 200 new grants were put into place during the five years of Johnson's presidency. Johnson's policy of vast government spending bypassed the states in distributing funds directly to cities and counties for many of the new programs, a major change. Understandably, the states did not appreciate losing influence over how localities could spend those national dollars.

New federalism is a model that has been employed with separate but related meanings during different presidencies. The new federalism initiated by President Richard Nixon was intended to restore power to the states and localities and to improve intergovernmental arrangements for delivering services. Among the major policy changes brought about by the Nixon administration were the establishment of ten regional councils to coordinate national program administration across the country and the greater flexibility granted to states and localities in terms of program spending and decision making.

Ronald Reagan's brand of new federalism, like Nixon's version, sought to give more power and program authority to states and localities, at least in theory. However, Reagan's main goal—to shrink the size of the national government—soon became obvious. Reagan's new federalism initiative won congressional approval to merge fifty-seven categorical grants into nine new block grants and to eliminate another sixty categorical grants. The states got more authority, but the funding for the new block grants decreased almost 25 percent from the previous year's allocation for the separate categorical grants.[51]

creative federalism
A model of cooperative federalism in which many new grants-in-aid, including direct national–local financial arrangements, were made.

new federalism
A model that represents a return of powers and responsibilities to the states.

Reagan and his congressional allies chipped away steadily at other grant programs in an effort to shrink the size of government and also terminated revenue sharing. Called *general revenue sharing* (GRS) when enacted during the Nixon administration, this program provided funds, with no strings attached, to state and general-purpose local governments (cities, counties, towns, and townships). It was discontinued largely because of the mounting national budget deficit and Congress's desire to exert greater control over, and to take more credit for, the way federal monies were spent. A new form of GRS, popularly known as the "stimulus plan," was adopted by Congress in 2009 to help bail out the states from the Great Recession. When these funds expired in 2011, most states' budgets suffered significantly.

In 1994, with the election of Republican majorities in the U.S. House and Senate and also the election of many new Republican governors, new federalism came back in style with impressive force. The new federalists, whose ranks included many Democrats, sought once again to sort out intergovernmental responsibilities. For the first time in recent memory, the states and localities were basically united and working together through a coalition of government interest groups, including the National Governors' Association and the National League of Cities, to design smaller, more efficient government with greater program and policy flexibility for the states and localities.

This planned delegating of power from the federal to state and local governments is termed **devolution**. The constellation of supporters for devolution is impressive. The governors, acting as individuals and through the National Governors' Association, found a sympathetic President Bill Clinton and congressional majority, and a U.S. Supreme Court inclined to rule in favor of state authority. Public opinion is generally in favor of greater state and local government authority, though it varies over time.[52] Public opinion polls consistently show that citizens believe the state and local governments do a better job than the national government in spending money and delivering services. Together, these powerful forces for devolution reversed more than a century of centralizing tendencies in U.S. federalism. This trend was so striking that it earned the moniker "devolution revolution."

Coercive federalism characterized the actions of the presidency of George W. Bush (2000–2008) and of Republican supporters in Congress, who preempted state authority over school testing systems and other aspects of public education, driver's license procedures, and right-to-die decisions; obstructed state laws that permit the medical use of marijuana; and imposed burdensome new homeland security requirements on the states; among other preemptive acts. The predominance of business interests in Washington, D.C., appeared to have deterred devolution through what one writer calls "the law of political physics—that for every flurry of state and local business regulations, there is an equal and opposite" effort by business to counter it in the nation's capital.[53] The centralizing tendencies of the "War on Terror" served as a convenient justification for other coercive actions by President Bush and congressional supporters,[54] including citizen surveillance, nationalization of the state national guards, and various mandates that pulled power into the White House. By 2008, state dissatisfaction had reached such a peak that

devolution
The delegating of power and programs from the federal government to state and local governments.

coercive federalism
A form of federalism in which the national government uses regulations, mandates, conditions, preemptions, and other actions to impose national priorities on the states.

governors from both political parties denounced the coercive federalism of Washington, D.C., and increasingly pushed back by roundly criticizing some actions, ignoring others, and litigating still others.[55]

With the economic crisis of 2008–2011, a mild version of coercive federalism lived on in the administration of President Barack Obama, on terms somewhat more acceptable to state and local governments. Obama's federalism tendencies were to mix coercion with collaboration, depending on the issue at hand.[56] This hybrid approach "mixed money, mandates and flexibility in new and distinctive ways."[57] For example, the American Recovery and Reinvestment Act, designed to inject money and jobs to stimulate the struggling economy, permitted flexibility to the states in how they spent the money, while mandating strong spending and accountability provisions. Yet the Obama approach to health care reform and climate change policy was highly centralized and unpalatable to many of the states. Thus, Obama federalism was more opportunistic than theory- or principle-driven.

The election of Donald Trump as president in 2016 promised a new era of federalism with many at the state and local level thinking that the federal government would be reduced in both scope and activity. However, it seems that the Trump administration has not sought a signature large federalism action but instead a series of smaller more focused actions concerning policies like the Affordable Care Act, Environmental Protection Agency rules on coal-fired power plants, and Department of Education rules on student loan collection companies. One observer has termed these actions "Jenga federalism" after the popular game where players pull wooden blocks out of a tower while trying not to bring the whole tower down.[58]

Perhaps the most appropriate metaphor today is "fragmented federalism."[59] Political polarization at all levels of government is producing highly diverse approaches to policy making, as witnessed in same-sex marriage, immigration, abortion, and drug policy. With the national government tied up in partisan and ideological knots since at least 2012, the states have enjoyed greater latitude in pursuing their own policy interests and inclinations. As one observer has noted, "As the American political system remains deeply polarized, minority parties are effectively using state governments as proxies for national political battles. . . . [T]he policy changes already taking place at the state level may have the most impact in shaping Americans' futures."[60]

Intergovernmental Relations

Whatever the current trend in federal–state–local relations, both cooperative and coercive activities are always in evidence. Relationships between the states and the American Indian tribes present an interesting example of the presence of both.

Tribal Governments

With the arrival of the Europeans, the estimated 7 to 10 million people who lived in what is now the United States soon were severely depleted by warfare, disease, and famine. Hundreds of treaties, statutes, and other agreements notwithstanding, American Indians were eventually deprived of their traditional lands and isolated on reservations. Today, some 5.1 million people identify themselves as American Indians, belonging to 573 federally recognized tribes, about one-third of whom continue to live on tribal reservations located primarily in the western portion of the United States. The Navajo Nation, for instance, has a population of more than 250,000 and covers some 17 million acres extending from northwest New Mexico to northeast Arizona and southeast Utah. At the other extreme of the tribal spectrum are the Mashantucket Pequots. Registering just thirty-five to forty members with "only the barest trace of Indian descent"[61] when officially recognized by the federal government in the 1990s, the Pequots today occupy about 1,250 acres in Connecticut. They operate Foxwoods Resort Casino— once the largest and most profitable gambling establishment in North America, though today threatened by nearby competition from both tribally owned and commercial casinos. On average, however, American Indians are the poorest and least healthy group in the United States.

Tribes are semi-sovereign nations exercising self-government on their reservations. They are under the general authority and supervision of Congress and are subject to the federal courts and the U.S. Bill of Rights, but their legal relationship with the states is complex. Tribal governments are permitted to regulate their internal affairs, hold elections, and enforce their own laws, codes, and constitutions under congressional supervision. States are generally prevented from taxing or regulating tribes or extending judicial power over them. Off the reservation, however, American Indians are, with some exceptions such as local hunting and fishing rights, subject to the same laws as any other state residents. They have the right to vote in tribal, federal, and state elections.

Recently, the tribes and the states have adopted a cooperative relationship[62] to pursue certain interests, such as fishing and hunting rights and regulation of reservation gaming. The highly lucrative gaming enterprises of some tribes have advanced tribal political interests and clout by providing financial resources to politicians and others. Many tribal governments have developed policy and lobbying expertise to advance gaming and other enterprise activities.[63] Occasionally, however, interactions among tribal governments, the state, and nearby local governments are testy. Some tribes seek to recover ancestral lands from present occupants. Actions concerning tribal land use may conflict with local zoning or state environmental policy. The tax-free sale of gasoline, alcohol, and tobacco products on the reservation diminishes state sales tax revenues. And tribes sometimes offer casino games that are prohibited under state law. When conflicts arise, states and tribal governments may sort out their differences through compacts. Otherwise, Congress may be asked to enter the fray.

In 2020, the U.S. Supreme Court weighed in on the status of tribal lands in Oklahoma. The case of McGirt v Oklahoma involved the conviction of Jimcy McGirt, a member of the Seminole Nation, in Oklahoma state court. McGirt argued that the offenses took place on the Creek Reservation in eastern Oklahoma and so the state could not try him. In a decision written by Justice Gorsuch, the Supreme Court agreed with McGirt. the court ruled the treaty the U.S. government signed with the Creek Nation in 1832 granting most of eastern Oklahoma to the Muscogee Creek was still in effect. Without express congressional action amending the treaty, some 3 million acres in Oklahoma, including parts of the city of Tulsa, thus remained "Indian Territory."[64]

Official federal recognition brings a tribe a number of benefits: recognized tribes are treated as sovereign nations and receive many government benefits. There are also some 200 tribes that are not recognized by the U.S. government. The issue of recognition often becomes politically sensitive. For example, the Lumbee in North Carolina have been seeking federal recognition for at least the last 100 years, but their efforts have been opposed by other American Indian tribes—in particular, the Eastern Band of the Cherokee. While much of the Cherokee opposition to full Lumbee recognition has to do with issues like the percentage of American Indian blood Lumbee tribal members actually carry, looming in the background are concerns about casino operation. The Cherokee casino in western North Carolina generates profits large enough to provide each tribal member payments of as much as $10,000 each year. Full recognition of the Lumbee could lead to the development of a competing casino on Lumbee land, threatening the profitability of the Cherokee casino.[65]

Meanwhile, the Caawba Nation secured federal approval to build a new casino in King's Mountain, NC – some 35 miles west of Charlotte. The Catawba Nation is based in South Carolina, where gambling is not legally allowed. The tribe thus sought federal approval to build the new casino in North Carolina. A lawsuit challenging the casino has been filed by the Cherokee who see the new casino as yet another competitor.[66]

Interstate Cooperation

Cooperation under the Constitution Four formal provisions exist for cooperation among the states:

1. *The full faith and credit clause* of the Constitution binds every citizen of every state to the laws and policies of other states. This means, among many other things, that a person who has a legitimate debt in North Dakota will be made to pay even if he moves to Montana. Crossing a state boundary does not alter a legal obligation. The courts have interpreted full faith and credit to apply to contracts, wills, divorces, and many other legalities.
2. *The interstate rendition clause* begins where the full faith and credit clause leaves off, covering persons convicted of criminal violations. Governors are required to extradite (return) fugitives to the state in which they were found guilty or are under indictment (although in certain cases they can and do refuse).
3. *The privileges and immunities clause* states that "the citizens of each state shall be entitled to all privileges and immunities of citizens in the several states." This clause was intended by the Framers to prevent any state from discriminating against citizens of another state who happen to be traveling or temporarily dwelling outside their own state's borders. Of course, states do discriminate against nonresidents in matters such as out-of-state tuition, hunting and fishing license fees, and residency requirements for voting. The U.S. Supreme Court has upheld these and other minor discrepancies, as long as the "fundamental rights" of nonresidents are not violated. The issue of same-sex marriage raised questions before a 2015 U.S. Supreme Court decision upheld the right of gay couples to wed in all states.

4. Finally, the *interstate compact clause* authorizes the states to negotiate compacts, which are binding agreements between two or more states that address important cross-boundary issues. Early interstate compacts were used to settle boundary disputes. About 175 of them are in effect today in various areas, including rights to interstate water resources, pest control, riverboat gambling, and education.[67]

Informal Cooperation Among the States Interstate cooperation can be facilitated through several informal methods. One example is the establishment of regional interstate commissions such as the Appalachian Regional Commission (ARC), which was created by federal law in 1965 to attack poverty in the states of Appalachia. Another example is found in the Mississippi Delta region, where several states adopted a ten-year economic development plan to help pull the area out of its own cycle of poverty.

In addition, states have developed uniform laws to help manage common problems ranging from child support to Medicaid cheating.[68] Interstate cooperation also occurs through information sharing among elected and appointed officials and the organizations to which they belong, such as the National Governors' Association and the National Conference of State Legislatures. It may take place in legal actions, as demonstrated by state attorneys general who unite to file class action lawsuits against various corporate malefactors and even federal agencies. Alternatively, one state may contract with another for a service, as Hawaii does with Arizona for health care. States have also marshaled their resources in cooperative efforts to reduce greenhouse emissions, establish common core curriculum education standards in their schools, and protect interstate fisheries.

But just as states may cooperate, they also compete for firms, tax revenues, tourists, and gamblers. Some of their fiercest conflicts are joined over water. Vital for human and farm animal consumption, fishing and shell fishing, fracking for oil and gas, industry, electric power generation, transportation, and many other critical uses, water has elicited interstate disputes since the earliest days of the Republic. Such conflicts have been settled in a variety of ways including memoranda of understanding, enactment of identical or similar laws, voluntary associations, and litigation before the U.S. Supreme Court.

But water wars continue to rage as population increases and drought occurs more frequently and persistently in some parts of the United States. Usually, states can resolve their concerns and differences rather informally. In more complex cases involving more than two disputants, the interstate compact is the method of choice.[69] Twenty-seven interstate compacts have been ratified by states and Congress to address water issues.[70] Recent examples include the Great Lakes Compact (eight states and two Canadian provinces) and the Colorado River Compact (seven states). But what if the states cannot reach an acceptable solution to water problems?

When the states cannot settle their own differences, the federal government becomes the final and binding arbitrator. Although Congress has the power to act through statute, the most likely venue is the federal courts. For instance, Georgia is at loggerheads with Tennessee over a water-related issue. The Georgia–Tennessee border was originally drawn in 1818 using primitive measuring devices later found to have placed the border 1.1 miles northward from where it should have been. The border should have been delineated up to the middle of the Tennessee River, thereby permitting the thirsty Peach State to extract water supplies from the river. Tennessee asserted that the "law of adverse possession" meant that the original boundary should remain the de facto border. Georgia disagreed. The state legislatures of Tennessee, North Carolina, and Georgia attempted to address this issue by establishing a commission to renegotiate the "true border"[71] while the case proceeds through federal courts, but Georgia Governor Brian Kemp's 2019 veto of the commission bill passed by the state legislature threw everything back into the hands of federal courts. Such water wars are illustrative of intergovernmental conflict that ignites local passions, and in some instances may provoke head scratching or ruffle feathers, such as in the case of California's ban of the sale of eggs from hens kept in tiny cages. Six egg-exporting states have challenged the "egg law" in federal courts. As Missouri's attorney general crowed, "If California legislators are permitted to mandate the size of chicken coops on Missouri farms, they may just as easily demand that Missouri soybeans be harvested by hand or that Missouri corn be transported by solar-powered trucks."[72] In January 2019, the U.S. Supreme Court refused to hear the case, leaving the issue in limbo.[73] Importantly, such conflicts demonstrate that federalism "lives" and indeed will always be a work in progress—a journey, not a destination.

Intergovernmental Financial Relations

LO 2-4
To explain the complex nature and tools of intergovernmental financial relations.

Revenues are the funds that governments have at their disposal. They are derived from taxes, fees and charges, and transfers from other levels of government. Expenditures are the ways in which governmental revenues are disbursed. Governments spend money to operate programs, build public facilities, and pay off debts.

The **grant-in-aid** is the primary mechanism for transferring money from the national to the state and local governments. The national government makes grants available for several reasons: to redistribute resources, to encourage policy experimentation, to establish minimum policy standards, and to achieve national goals. But grants are primarily designed to help meet the needs of state and local governments, including environmental protection, transportation, education, health care, and security. Federal grant outlays totaled nearly $750 billion in 2019.

grant-in-aid
An intergovernmental transfer of funds or other assets, subject to conditions.

categorical grant
A form of financial aid from one level of government to another to be used for a narrowly defined purpose.

block grant
A form of financial aid from one level of government to another for use in a broad, functional area.

Discretion of Recipients There are two major variations in grants: the amount of discretion (independence) the recipient has in determining how to spend the money and the conditions under which the grant is awarded. A **categorical grant** can be used by the recipient government only for a narrowly defined purpose, such as food stamps or Medicaid supplements.

Block grants are *broad-based grants*; that is, they can be used anywhere within a functional area such as transportation, energy efficiency, or health care. The difference between categorical and block grants is that the recipient government decides how block grants will be spent. For instance, when given a block grant, a local school system can decide whether the purchase of distance education technology is more important than buying microscopes for the science laboratory. Today there are some 1,274 grants in existence, including 21 block grants. By giving nonnational governments considerable flexibility in responding to pressing needs and preferred goals, these grant mechanisms assume that state and local governments can make fair and rational choices among competing claims.

Conditions for Grants Grants also vary in the manner in which they are allocated. A **formula grant** makes funding available automatically, based on state and local conditions such as poverty level or unemployment rate. A **project grant** is awarded to selected applicants based on the granting agency's assessment of the strength of competing proposals. Block grants are distributed on a formula basis; categorical grants can be either formula- or project-based.

Another factor also affects intergovernmental financial relations: the existence of *matching requirements*. Most federal grants require that the recipient government use its own resources to pay a certain percentage of program costs. This arrangement is designed to stimulate state and local spending on programs deemed to be in the national interest and to discourage participation in a program simply because money is available. For example, if a state government wants funding through the Boating Safety Financial Assistance program administered by the U.S. Department of Transportation, it must contribute 50 percent itself. Similarly, for a state government to participate in a wind energy demonstration project, a 50 percent match is required. In each case, the recipient government's commitment to boating safety or renewable energy is likely to be high because of the joint funding.

Federal Purse Strings

LO 2-5
To recognize finances as a source of friction and conflict between the three levels of government.

Federalism today turns less on theory and more on money. The distribution of intergovernmental monies and the conditions attached to them define the distribution of governmental power and authority. Federalism is a matter not only of which level of government will do what but also of which level will pay for it. Some have called this "fend-for-yourself" federalism, with each jurisdiction essentially on its own in a Darwinian struggle for financial survival.

The Importance of Federal Funds

Figure 2.2 provides a historical look at national grant-in-aid expenditures. The growing proportion of national dollars in the total expenditures of states and localities should be placed in the context of the fact that aid to states and localities consumes a relatively small share of the federal government's budget (only 4 percent of GDP). In 2009, for the first time in history, federal aid became the single largest source of total state and local revenues, as the national government pumped billions of dollars into state and local treasuries to stimulate the economy out of its prolonged slide.

The Washington-funded portion of state and local government expenditures has been around 31 percent recently, representing a critical source of financial support for major functions of nonnational governments

formula grant
A funding mechanism that automatically allocates monies based on conditions in the recipient government.

project grant
A competitive funding mechanism that awards monies based on the strength of an applicant government's proposal.

(see Figure 2.3). However, the funds are not spread evenly across the country (see Figure 2.4). Federal financial support represents 43.3 percent of Mississippi's general fund revenue, but only 18.6 percent of Virginia's.

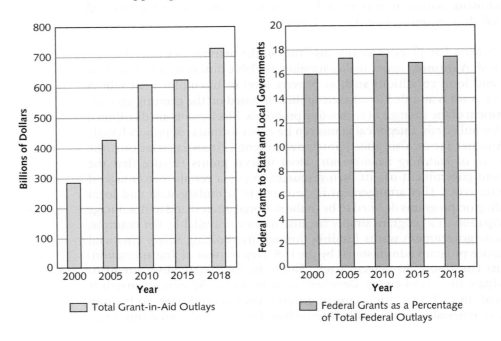

Figure 2.2 Historical Trends in Federal Grant-in-Aid Outlays

Source: Congressional Research Service, "Federal Grants to State and Local Governments: A Historical Perspective on Contemporary Issues," www.fas.org/sgp/crs/misc/R40638.pdf (May 22, 2019).

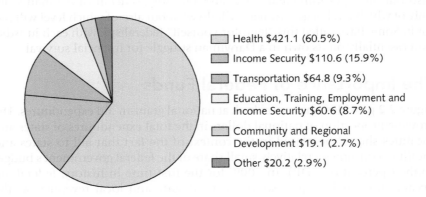

Figure 2.3 Federal Aid to State and Local Governments: Amounts and Percentages by Major Function 2018

Source: Congressional Research Service, "Federal Grants to State and Local Governments: A Historical Perspective on Contemporary Issues," www.fas.org/sgp/crs/misc/R40638.pdf (May 22, 2019).

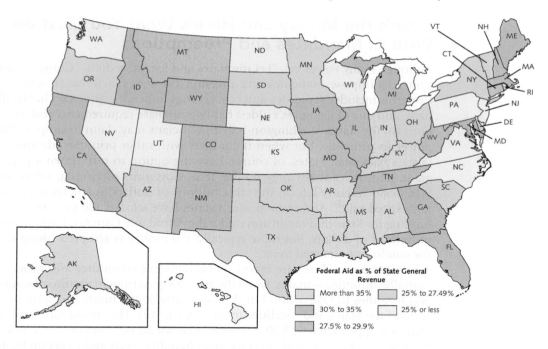

Figure 2.4 Federal Aid to State Governments in 2016

Source: U.S. Census Bureau, 2016 State and Local Government Finance Historical Datasets and Tables (www.census.gov/data/datasets/2016/econ/local/public-use-datasets.html).

These amounts shot up in 2009–2010 as a federal stimulus package injected additional billions into state and local coffers for quick pass-through for job creation, but then plummeted in 2011 when the spigot was turned down. By 2014, federal grant outlays began to creep up again, exceeding $660 billion in 2014 and reaching close to $750 billion by the end of 2019.[74]

In competition with forty-nine others, each state battles in Congress over its share of grant allocations, which are affected by factors such as military installations and other federal offices and facilities in the state. The states attempt to influence competitive project-grant awards, and they lobby Congress to adjust the weighting of certain factors in formula grants in their favor. State and local influence is wielded by their representatives sitting in Congress and through various actions by elected state and local officials and their Washington lobbyists.

National expenditures in nongrant forms also affect state and local economies substantially. In the nongrant category are payments to individuals (representing about 59 percent of total federal outlays today, up from 41 percent in 1980),[75] notably through the Social Security system; Medicare payments; purchases by the national government; and wages and salaries of federal employees, most of whom work outside of Washington, D.C. In this sense, federal expenditures emphasize people more than places, at the expense of other types of federal aid to states and localities.

Here's the Money and Here's What You Must do With It: Mandates and Preemptions

Although many voices cry, "Let the states and localities do it," Congress continues to impose mandates and preempt the states' actions. In addition, Congress includes set-asides and cost ceilings in block grants. Old habits die hard, and one of Congress's oldest habits is to place requirements and conditions on the states. Washington-based politicians may claim to support state power in principle, but when it conflicts with other priorities, devolution takes a back seat. States, of course, have the option to turn down a federal grant, and occasionally they do just that. Governors of Florida, Ohio, and Wisconsin recently left on the table billions of dollars in federal grants for high-speed rail.[76] And some thirteen states have refused 100 percent federal funding for Medicaid expansion under the Affordable Care Act, forgoing tens of billions of dollars. But more typically, the money is accepted, along with the conditions attached to it.

Federal mandates are especially burdensome when they are entirely or partially unfunded—that is, when the national government requires the states and localities to take action but does not provide the funds necessary to do so, and the states and localities must foot the bill. The Affordable Care Act imposed approximately $20 billion in new Medicaid costs on the states by requiring them to expand coverage and eligibility levels and to set up health insurance exchanges. More than half the states sued the federal government to block the law. Oppositional states heaved a sigh of relief when the 2012 U.S. Supreme Court decision freed them from the expansion of coverage, thus permitting them to forgo federal Medicaid dollars.

Mounting opposition to mandates without money finally convinced Congress to enact the Unfunded Mandate Reform Act of 1995 (UMRA), which provides that any bill imposing a mandate of more than $50 million (adjusted in 2017 to $78 million) on a state or local government must include a cost estimate. If passed, the legislation is supposed to include sufficient funds to pay for the mandate. Indications are that proposed laws containing unfunded mandates are facing tougher scrutiny in Congress than before and that Congress is taking a more consultative approach with state and local elected officials. However, UMRA is riddled with loopholes, and members of Congress still seize opportunities to revert to their mandating ways. Since UMRA was adopted, eighteen mandates have exceeded the cost threshold by billions of dollars.[77]

As noted earlier, *preemption* represents another intrusion of the national government into the state sphere. It takes two forms: *total* preemption, whereby the national government seizes all regulatory authority for a given function from states and localities; and *partial* preemption, whereby the national government establishes minimum national standards for state-implemented programs. Both forms prevent states from doing what they want. One example of a totally preemptive action is the Americans with Disabilities Act, which requires states and localities to make physical and occupational accommodation for disabled persons. A little-known but important federal preemption concerns railroad crossings, where federal law supersedes

federal mandate A requirement that a state or local government undertake a specific activity or provide a particular service as a condition of funding.

state and local laws on warning devices, speed of trains, loudness of train horns, and other matters.[78] Many partial preemptions involve environmental protection, whereby states may regulate pollution emissions as long as state standards are at least as stringent as those of the federal government. California has been especially active in setting automobile emission standards stricter than those required by the federal government. In 2019, the Trump Administration announced a rule that would forbid states from setting their own fuel economy or greenhouse gas pollution from motor vehicles. California and 22 other states have sued the federal government over this action.[79]

Thus, when mandates and preemptions are taken into consideration, a less positive picture of intergovernmental relations emerges. To the states and localities, it seems that the country has shifted from cooperative federalism to coercive federalism, or, in the words of former Governor Ben Nelson of Nebraska, demoted states from significant policy makers to branch managers "of a behemoth central government."[80] The result has been an escalation of federal–state conflict that is probably at the highest level since the Civil War.

The Future of Federalism

For the states and localities, national political gridlock has meant a golden opportunity to reverse more than a century of centralizing forces. They have taken up the slack in the federal system, busily innovating, developing, and implementing policies in a great variety of fields. Public opinion polls consistently show that there is greater trust in state and local governments than in the federal government.[81] As laboratories of democracy, state and local governments have designed and experimented with numerous policies that later have served as models for other states and for Congress. Research shows that the states actively learn from one another in a targeted and systematic way. For instance, states have recently pioneered policy initiatives on the opioid crisis, immigration control, stem-cell research, nanotechnology, and global climate change, among many other fields. Lobbyists who once focused their attentions on Washington, D.C., are now spending hundreds of millions of dollars to woo state legislators. Hordes of lobbyists representing the health care, insurance, and banking and finance industries and other special interests have been attracted to state capitals like fleas to a dog.

States are definitively not all on the same page. Political party polarization, one-party control of state governments, and basic policy beliefs have led to markedly diverse policy approaches. Groups of states have both legalized or banned medical marijuana, the death penalty, gun control, and abortion rights. It is as if politics abhors the policy vacuum that has been Congress and therefore flows into the states and localities. Recent state laws restricting abortions are a particularly good example of states diverging on policy. In 2019, nine states passed bills further restricting abortions while six states reduced abortion restrictions. The new restrictions passed in the states are being challenged in court and as of 2020, none had yet gone into effect. The sponsor of the Alabama law that includes the most restrictive abortion language in the nation said she introduced the bill in order to get the U.S. Supreme Court to reconsider its decisions legalizing abortions.[82]

Journalists and many citizens routinely refer "to 'the government' as if there were only one—the Big One."[83] But the United States is a nation of many governments, and Washington is not the best location for addressing all the nation's complex policy problems. Whereas centrally designing and implementing policies and programs can sometimes be the best approach, it can also result in wasteful and ineffective one-size-fits-all government. The trend in government, as well as in business, is to decentralize decision making to the lowest feasible level of the organization. For the U.S. federal system, that means shifting decision making to the states and localities and even, in some instances, to nonprofit organizations and citizens' groups.

At the very time that the state and local governments are most needed as policy leaders and problem solvers, powerful social and economic forces seriously threaten state and local governments' capability. The collapse of the financial and housing markets and the ensuing free-fall in the U.S. economy in 2008–2011 produced frightening revenue declines in nearly all the states, putting at risk children, the poor, and the infirm. Ranks of Medicaid recipients climbed, as did the homeless. Following expiration of the federal stimulus funds, record budget deficits and budget sequestration severely depressed federal funding for state and local grants-in-aid. Yet the problems of the poor, the long-term jobless, the homeless, and undocumented immigrants are great. And the growing disparity of wealth and income threatens our great reservoir of political and social stability: the middle class. The COVID pandemic has exacerbated these disparities and presented even greater threats to the American middle class.

For its part, the federal government provokes criticism for tying the hands of the states and localities with mandates, preemptions, and confused and conflicting policy directives. Most state and local governments *want* to become more creative, but they are also being *forced* to, so that they can figure out how to implement and pay for increasingly onerous federally mandated requirements. The result is an increasingly state and local policy world. But should it be? See the It's Your Turn feature.

Even homeland security, usually considered to be primarily a national government responsibility, actually calls for more—not less—intergovernmental cooperation. State and local governments play critical roles in all four key functions of homeland security: prevention, preparedness, response, and recovery. Local governments are first responders to any sort of domestic disaster, natural or human-caused, whereas states provide crisis management and emergency services while coordinating and steering recovery efforts.

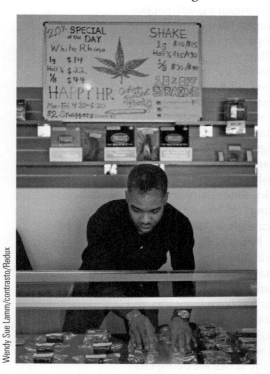

Wendy Sue Lamm/contrasto/Redux

Nigel Spicer arranges the bakery of marijuana brownies and treats at "Green Oasis" medical marijuana dispensary in Los Angeles.

? It's Your Turn

Should the States Legalize Marijuana?

The possession, cultivation, and use of marijuana for any purpose are prohibited under the federal Controlled Substances Act. An estimated 20 million Americans have been arrested, and many of them jailed for long periods of time, for marijuana offenses over the past fifty years. Millions of law enforcement, court, and prison dollars have been spent on marijuana offenses. Yet the herb is relatively easy to acquire and is widely available throughout the United States. Despite federal law, twenty-four states have legalized prescription-based medical consumption of marijuana, and fourteen states have decriminalized possession. Fifteen states (AK, AZ, CA, CO, IL, MA, ME, MI, MT, NJ, NV, OR, SD, VT, and WA) and the District of Columbia have legalized the recreational sale and use of marijuana.

PROS	CONS
The money now spent on enforcement and justice could be diverted to treatment and prevention programs.	Legalization could lead to higher use by teens and serve as a stepping-stone to more harmful drugs.
Marijuana arrests and prosecutions disproportionately target minorities.	Citizens in some localities vehemently oppose legalization in their communities.
A sales tax on marijuana is expected to bring in tens of millions of dollars in those states that have legalized it.	Medical studies have indicated that heavy marijuana use affects the young brain and causes memory problems.
Marijuana has been shown to ease symptoms of nausea from chemotherapy and other invasive treatments, control seizures, and to have other medical benefits.	Wider use of marijuana would lead to more impaired driving and endanger the public.
Marijuana is much less dangerous to health than alcohol, which is legal and regulated.	Traffickers could purchase marijuana in a legal state and sell it in a neighboring state that prohibits its sale and possession.
A majority of Americans (around 58 percent) now favor legalization, according to recent polls.	Marijuana remains illegal under federal law; a shift in congressional, presidential, or Justice Department sentiment could result in aggressive enforcement, throwing state policies into disarray.
Marijuana is widely available anyway on the street, much of it controlled by drug gangs. Legalization would take it out of the hands of criminals.	There are cases in which children have eaten marijuana cookies and other edibles mistakenly left within their grasp and become very ill.
	Colorado prices 1/8 ounce at $50 to $60, more than black market marijuana. A black market will continue to thrive even with legalization.

In homeland security, disaster response, and almost all other fields, what the states and localities are demanding is cooperative, consultative relationships and flexible or facilitative federalism, in which the national government helps them through selective funding for technical assistance—a federalism in which they are treated as partners in governance, not as just another self-absorbed interest group. It is something of a paradox that even as state and local governments have assumed the primary policymaking duties in the federal system, their influence with the national government has diminished. Many of their calls for national action, such as permitting state online sales taxes and adopting a coherent national immigration policy, have fallen on the deaf ears of a navel-gazing, unresponsive Congress and president.[84] As Andrew Romanoff, Colorado's former speaker of the house, put it, "We want the federal government to recognize that there are problems that are best solved at the state level. . . . Either give us the tools or remove the barriers so we can solve the problem. The worst thing the feds can do is say, It's your problem and we're going to make it harder for you to solve it."[85]

In fairness to the national government, remember that much federal intervention has been in response to state failures to govern effectively and fairly. Corruption, racial prejudice and exclusion, and rampant parochialism, among other shortcomings, have prompted presidential, congressional, and judicial interventions that have, on the whole, helped the states move to the much higher plane they inhabit today.

The question of the balance of power and responsibility in U.S. federalism is no less important now than it was when the representatives of the colonies met in Philadelphia's Independence Hall, first to draft the Articles of Confederation and later to design the Constitution. The focus of the debate has shifted, however, to a pragmatic interest in how the responsibility of governing should be sorted out among the three levels of government. As pointed out by an insightful observer of U.S. government, "[the] American federal system has never been static. It has changed radically over the years, as tides of centralization and decentralization have altered the balance of power and the allocation of functions among the different levels of government."[86]

Centripetal forces steadily pull things to the federal center. The fiscal crisis, continuing fears of terrorist attacks, foreign wars, health threats akin to the Ebola crisis, among other issues, encourage a centralizing direction, yet for many years, Congress has been deadlocked along partisan and ideological lines. American federalism tends to oscillate with national government policy activism—when Washington, D.C., wanes, the states wax. When national government policy activism is at a low level, the states step in to fill the gap.[87] The hope, then, is for a new era of cooperative federalism to supplant the coercive and fragmented federalism of previous years.

 # Chapter Recap

- U.S. federalism is an ongoing experiment in governance.

- A fundamental question is: What is the proper balance of power and responsibility between the national government and the states?

- Actions of the courts, Congress, and the executive branch have expanded powers of the national government.

- Over time, the trend has generally been in the direction of a stronger national government. Beginning in the early 1980s, however, there was a resurgence of the state and local governments as political and policy actors. States and localities continue to lead today.

- The power relationships among the three levels of government are described by various models, including dual and cooperative federalism. The operative model is cooperative federalism, under the variant known as new federalism, but intergovernmental

relations have become increasingly coercive and fragmented.

- A key concept in federalism is intergovernmental relations, particularly financial relationships among the three levels of government.

- The national government imposes certain controversial requirements on grants-in-aid, including mandates and preemptions.

Key Terms

unitary system *(p. 29)*
confederation *(p. 29)*
federal system *(p. 29)*
enumerated (delegated) powers *(p. 33)*
concurrent powers *(p. 33)*
nation-centered federalism *(p. 34)*
state-centered federalism *(p. 34)*
reserved powers *(p. 34)*
Tenth Amendment *(p. 34)*

compact theory *(p. 34)*
national supremacy clause *(p. 35)*
necessary and proper clause *(p. 36)*
implied powers *(p. 36)*
commerce clause *(p. 36)*
general welfare clause *(p. 36)*
Fourteenth Amendment *(p. 37)*
Sixteenth Amendment *(p. 39)*
federal preemption *(p. 40)*

dual federalism *(p. 43)*
cooperative federalism *(p. 43)*
creative federalism *(p. 44)*
new federalism *(p. 44)*
devolution *(p. 45)*
coercive federalism *(p. 45)*
grant-in-aid *(p. 50)*
categorical grant *(p. 50)*
block grant *(p. 50)*
formula grant *(p. 51)*
project grant *(p. 51)*
federal mandate *(p. 54)*

Internet Resources

Examples of unfunded mandates are found on a Heritage Foundation webpage at **www.regulation.org/states.html**.

Federalism decisions by the U.S. Supreme Court may be reviewed at the Council of State Governments' website at **www.statenews.org** or **www.csg.org**. For other sites with federalism content, see **www.governing.com** and **www.stateline.org**.

The leading scholarly journal on federalism is *Publius: The Journal of Federalism*, located at academic.oup.com/publius.

The website **www.census.gov** has comparative data on the states and localities, particularly state and local finances. It is not particularly user-friendly—you'll have to dig around for what you seek.

Information on tribal governments and politics may be acquired at **www.tribal-institute.org** and **www.narf.org**.

3

State Constitutions: The Fundamental Rules of State Government

The original copy of California's first constitution.

Sacramento Bee/ZUMA Press/Newscom

Learning Objectives

LO 3-1 To identify the origins, evolution, and purposes of state constitutions.

LO 3-2 To explain how state constitutions have evolved to meet the challenges of modern governance and how they have not.

LO 3-3 To comprehend the basic content of state constitutions and how they compare with the U.S. Constitution.

LO 3-4 To be able to describe the formal and informal methods for changing state constitutions.

State constitutions are alike in many important respects, but they are decidedly different in others. Consider recent public votes on state constitutional changes. Mississippi finally outlawed slavery by passing the Thirteenth Amendment to the U.S. Constitution. A "Right to Farm" amendment was approved in Missouri. Alabama voters, finding that Sharia (Islamic) law was a threat to legal processes in the Yellowhammer State, joined those of six other states in banning its use. Vermont became the seventh state to legalize assisted suicide for the terminally ill. These actions demonstrate that constitutions are, in their essence, political documents—products of state history, culture, events, economics, and, above all, the clash of interests.

The History and Development of the Fundamental Documents

LO 3-1
To identify the origins, evolution, and purposes of state constitutions.

All state constitutions both distribute and constrain political power among groups and regions. They set forth the basic framework and operating rules for government, allocate power to the three branches, establish the scope of state and local governmental authority, protect individual rights, and address various public policy concerns.[1] Constitutions represent the **fundamental law** of a state, superior to statutory law. They provide a set of rules for running state government, and those who master the regulations and procedures have a distinct advantage over novices. Everything that a state government does and represents is rooted in its constitution. Constitutions do not describe the full reality of a political system, but they do provide a window through which to perceive its reality. Only the federal Constitution and federal statutes take priority over state constitutions.

To most people, however, constitutional law still means the federal document. State constitutions are often neglected in secondary school and college history and even American government courses. Astonishingly, one national survey discovered that 51 percent of Americans were not aware that their state had its own constitution.[2] Yet state constitutions are distinctly different from the federal Constitution in their length, inclusion of policy concerns, and relative ease of amendment or revision.

In the U.S. system of *dual constitutionalism*, in which there are both national and state constitutions, the national government is supreme within the spheres of authority specifically delegated to it in the U.S. Constitution. Powers granted exclusively to the national government are denied to the states. But the national Constitution is incomplete. It leaves many key constitutional issues to the states, including local finance, public education, and the organization of state and local governments.[3] In theory, state constitutions are supreme for all matters not expressly within the national government's jurisdiction or preempted by federal constitutional or statutory law. In practice, however, congressional actions and federal court interpretations have expanded the powers of the national government and, in some cases, eroded the powers of the states. And in reality, many concurrent (shared) powers, such as taxing, spending, and protecting citizens' health and safety, are shared by all levels of government.

The earliest state constitutions were simple documents reflecting an agrarian economy, single-owner businesses, and horse-and-buggy transportation. As American society and the economy changed, the rules of state government also required transformation. Constitutional reform is a regular theme throughout the U.S. experiment in federalism. As a result, state constitutions "are a mine of instruction for the national history of democratic communities. They are distinctive in history, design, and underlying premises."[4]

Some reforms have reflected changing political fortunes. Newly powerful groups have pressed to revise the state constitution to reflect their interests, or one or another political party has gained control of state government and sought to solidify its power. Constitutional reforms have promoted widely

fundamental law
The basic legal and political document of a state; it prescribes the rules through which government operates.

different views of politics and the public interest. In more recent years, some state constitutional revisions have sought to make state government more effective and responsive to shifting social and economic forces. Other revisions have established individual rights such as privacy of personal information and the right to hunt and fish. The fact that constitutions are subject to change also recognizes that human judgment is fallible and human understanding imperfect.[5] Through constitutional reform, states can elevate their role as democratic laboratories and respond to the changing needs and opinions of citizens. This capacity for change is in sharp contrast to the seldom-amended federal Constitution.

LO 3-2
To explain how state constitutions have evolved to meet the challenges of modern governance and how they have not.

The Evolution of State Constitutions

When the states won their independence from Great Britain almost 240 years ago, there was no precedent for writing constitutions. A constitution for the Five Nations of the Iroquois called the Great Binding Law existed, but it was oral and not particularly appropriate for consideration by the people in the colonies.[6] The thirteen colonial charters provided the foundation for the new state constitutions. These were brief documents (around five pages each) that the British Crown had granted to trading companies and individuals to govern settlements in the new territories. As the settlements became full colonies, the charters were expanded to incorporate the "rights of Englishmen"—political and civil rights first enumerated by the Magna Carta in 1215. For territories too remote from their native country to be governed by its laws, these charters also laid down some basic principles of colonial government.[7]

In a sense, the existence of these documents helped fuel the fires of independence. In what was to become Connecticut, early settlers escaping the oppressive rule of the Massachusetts Bay Colony took matters of governance into their own hands. Under the leadership of Thomas Hooker, these ambitious farmers established an independent government free from references to the Crown. The Fundamental Orders of 1639 contended that "the choice of the public magistrates belongs unto the people by God's own allowance. The privilege of election belongs to the people . . . it is in their power, also, to set and limit the bounds and limitations of the power [of elected officials]."[8] Elements of the Fundamental Orders were later incorporated into Connecticut's Royal Charter. Years later, a representative of King James II was sent to take possession of the Royal Charter and unite the New England colonies under the Crown. In a night meeting, as the Charter was laid out on a table before the king's men, the candles suddenly were extinguished. When they were relighted, the document had disappeared. According to legend, a patriot had hidden the Charter in a nearby hollow tree, later to be known as the Charter Oak. Infuriated, the king's men dissolved the colony's government and imposed autocratic rule that lasted many years. But they never found the Royal Charter, which essentially governed Connecticut until the Constitution of 1818 was adopted.[9]

The First State Constitutions

In a May 1776 resolution, the Continental Congress instructed the thirteen colonies "to reorganize their governments solely on the basis of 'the authority of the people.'" This task, of critical importance, had never been achieved in human history. How would "the people" write the laws of their states?[10] Following the War of Independence, the former colonies turned their attention to this task, drafting their first constitutions in special revolutionary conventions or in legislative assemblies. Apparently without a sense of irony, the new states put their constitutions into effect immediately, without popular ratification (Massachusetts was an exception).

Making the first state constitutions was not a simple affair. Issues of political philosophy were debated. How would citizens' "natural rights" be defined and protected? How would the principle of popular sovereignty be addressed in words and in practice? Many practical questions had to be answered in constitutional conventions, including the structure of the new government, how and when elections would be held, and how land once owned by the Crown would be distributed.

Territorial integrity was not well defined. For example, in what is now known as Kentucky, people frustrated with Virginia's rule met in 1784 and petitioned the Congress for statehood. It took six years and nine constitutional conventions before Kentucky became a state. Complicating factors causing delay involved the "necessity of communicating across the mountains, the change from the Articles of Confederation to the Constitution of the United States, Indian attacks, [and] the revelation of a plot to have Kentucky secure independence and join Spain."[11]

Other Western territories were constituted as states under terms of the Northwest Ordinance of 1787, which established the principle that the United States would expand westward by drawing boundaries for and admitting new states, rather than simply extending the boundaries of existing states to the west. Each new state had to write its own constitution.

In content, most of these documents simply extended the colonial charters, removing references to the king and inserting a bill of rights. All the documents incorporated the principles of limited government: a weak executive branch, the separation of powers, checks and balances, a bill of rights to protect the people and their property from arbitrary government actions, and (except for Pennsylvania) a bicameral legislature.[12] The earliest constitutions were not truly democratic. Essentially, they called for government by an aristocracy. Office holding and voting, for instance, were restricted to white males of wealth and property.[13]

Only one of the thirteen original state constitutions, that of Massachusetts, survives (although it has been amended 120 times). It is the oldest functioning constitution in the world. Its longevity can be attributed in large part to the foresight of its drafter, John Adams, who grounded the document in extensive research of governments that took him all the way back to the ancients and the Magna Carta. Even after many amendments, the Massachusetts constitution reflects a composite of the wisdom of the foremost political philosophers of the eighteenth century: John Locke, Jean-Jacques Rousseau, and the Baron de Montesquieu.[14] In this enduring document, Massachusetts establishes itself as a commonwealth (from the words *common weal*, meaning "general well-being"), on the principle that its citizens have a right to protect and manage their collective interests. (Kentucky, Pennsylvania, and Virginia are also commonwealths.)[15] Rhode Island was established as "The State of Rhode Island and Providence Plantations."

Legislative Supremacy

The first state constitutions reflected the Framers' fear and distrust of the executive—a result of their experiences with the colonial governors. The governors were not all tyrants, but because they represented the British Crown and Parliament, they became a symbol of oppression to the colonists. As a result, the guiding principle of the new constitutional governments was **legislative supremacy**, and the legislatures were given overwhelming power at the expense of governors. Most governors were to be elected by the legislature, not the people, and were restricted to a single term of office. State judiciaries also were limited in authorized powers; judges, like governors, were to be elected by the legislature. The preeminence of legislative power was so great that an English observer, Lord James Bryce, was moved to remark: "The legislature . . . is so much the strongest force in the several states that we may almost call it the government and ignore all other authorities."[16]

The Growth of Executive Power

Disillusionment with the legislatures soon developed, spreading rapidly through the states during the early 1800s. There were many reasons for disenchantment, including the legislatures' failure to address problems caused by rapid population growth and the Industrial Revolution; the growing amount of legislation that favored private interests; and a mounting load of state indebtedness, which led nine states to default on their bonds in a single two-year period.

Gradually, the executive branch began to accumulate more power and stature through constitutional amendments that provided for popular election of governors, who were also given longer terms and the authority to veto legislative bills. The constitutions of those states admitted to the Union during the early 1800s established stronger executive powers at the outset.

As executive power grew, public confidence in state legislatures continued to erode. This trend was reflected in the process of constitutional revision. One delegate at Kentucky's 1890 constitutional convention proclaimed that "the principal, if not the sole purpose of this constitution which we are here to frame, is to restrain the legislature's will and restrict its authority."[17] Also affecting constitutional change were broader social and economic forces in the United States, such as the extension of suffrage and popular participation in government, the rise of a corporate economy, the Civil War and Reconstruction, the growth of industry and commerce, the process of urbanization, and a growing movement for government reform. States rapidly replaced and

legislative supremacy The legislature's dominance of the other two branches of government.

amended their constitutions from the early 1800s to 1920s in response to these forces and others. The decade immediately after the Civil War saw the highest level of constitutional activity in U.S. history, much of it in the southern states; between 1860 and 1870, twenty-seven constitutions were replaced or thoroughly revised as Confederate states ratified new documents after secession, then redrew the documents after Union victory to incorporate certain conditions of readmission to the United States.

Constitutional change after Reconstruction was driven by the Populist and Progressive reform movements. During the late 1800s, the Populists championed the causes of the "little man," including farmers and laborers. They sought to open the political process to the people through constitutional devices such as the initiative, the referendum, and the recall. The Progressives, who made their mark from 1890 to 1920, were kindred spirits whose favorite targets were concentrated wealth, inefficiencies in government, machine politics, corruption, and boss rule in the cities. Reformers in both groups successfully promoted constitutional reforms such as regulation of campaign spending and party activities, replacement of party conventions with direct primary elections, and selection of judges through nonpartisan elections.

Weaknesses of Constitutions Despite the numerous constitutional amendments and replacements enacted during the nineteenth and twentieth centuries, by 1950, the states were buffeted by a rising chorus criticizing their fundamental laws. Ironically, many states were victims of past constitutional change, which left them with documents that were extravagantly long, frustratingly inflexible, and distressingly detailed. In general, state constitutions now provided for a feeble executive branch because they limited the governor's administrative authority, permitted the popular election of numerous other executive branch officials, and organized the executive into a hodgepodge of semiautonomous agencies, boards, and commissions. State judiciaries remained uncoordinated and overly complex, whereas legislatures suffered from archaic structures and procedures. Statutory detail, outdated language, local amendments (those that apply only to designated local governments), and other problems contaminated the documents and straitjacketed state government.

Excessive Length

From the first constitutions, which averaged 5,000 words, state documents expanded into enormous tracts averaging 27,000 words by 1967. (The U.S. Constitution contains 8,700 words.) Some of this increase resulted from growing social and economic complexity and from a perceived need to be very specific about what the legislatures, and local governments, could and could not do.

Some constitutions became positively verbose. Georgia's contained around 583,500 words, surpassing Tolstoy's *War and Peace* in length. (The Peach State's constitution was replaced with a much briefer version in 1982.) Even today, the constitution of South Carolina limits local government indebtedness but lists seventeen pages of exceptions. Oklahoma's sets the flash point for kerosene at 115 degrees for purposes of illumination, and California's addresses a compelling issue of our time—the length of wrestling matches. A constitutional initiative in Florida prohibits "cruel and unusual confinement of pigs during pregnancy." The dubious prize for the most verbose constitution in the world today goes to Alabama's 402,852-word document. An estimated 70 percent of its 946 amendments apply to only one county, and provisions regulate garbage fees and the disposal of dead farm animals.[18] Table 3.1 provides an overview of the fifty state constitutions, including each one's length.

Table 3.1 State Constitutions, 2019

| STATE | NUMBER OF CONSTITUTIONS | EFFECTIVE DATE OF PRESENT CONSTITUTION | NUMBER OF AMENDMENTS | | |
			NUMBER OF WORDS	SUBMITTED TO VOTERS	ADOPTED
Alabama	6	Nov. 28, 1901	402,852	1,280	946
Alaska	1	Jan. 3, 1959	13,479	423	29
Arizona	1	Feb. 14, 1912	47,306	280	156
Arkansas	5	Oct. 30, 1874	59,120	208	108
California	2	July 4, 1879	76,930	909	538
Colorado	1	Aug. 1, 1876	84,239	355	164
Connecticut	4	Dec. 30, 1965	16,401	35	33
Delaware	4	June 10, 1897	25,445	not submitted to voters	150
Florida	6	Jan. 7, 1969	49,230	185	137
Georgia	10	July 1, 1983	41,684	107	83
Hawaii	1	Aug. 21, 1959	21,498	140	114
Idaho	1	July 3, 1890	24,626	214	126
Illinois	4	July 1, 1971	16,401	22	15
Indiana	2	Nov. 1, 1851	11,610	81	49
Iowa	2	Sept. 3, 1857	11,089	59	54
Kansas	1	Jan. 29, 1861	14,097	128	98
Kentucky	4	Sept. 28, 1891	27,234	76	42
Louisiana	11	Jan. 1, 1975	76,730	281	196
Maine	1	March 15, 1820	16,313	206	173
Maryland	4	Oct. 5, 1867	43,198	269	233
Massachusetts	1	Oct. 25, 1780	45,283	148	120
Michigan	4	Jan. 1, 1964	31,164	76	32
Minnesota	1	May 11, 1858	12,016	218	121

(continued)

Table 3.1 State Constitutions, 2019 (*continued*)

STATE	NUMBER OF CONSTITUTIONS	EFFECTIVE DATE OF PRESENT CONSTITUTION	NUMBER OF AMENDMENTS		
			NUMBER OF WORDS	SUBMITTED TO VOTERS	ADOPTED
Mississippi	4	Nov. 1, 1890	26,229	164	126
Missouri	4	March 30, 1945	84,924	193	126
Montana	2	July 1, 1973	12,790	58	32
Nebraska	2	Oct. 12, 1875	34,934	354	230
Nevada	1	Oct. 31, 1864	37,418	238	140
New Hampshire	2	June 2, 1784	13,238	291	147
New Jersey	3	Jan. 1, 1948	26,360	88	72
New Mexico	1	Jan. 6, 1912	33,198	306	172
New York	4	Jan. 1, 1895	49,360	305	229
North Carolina	3	July 1, 1971	17,177	51	41
North Dakota	1	Nov. 2, 1889	18,746	282	161
Ohio	2	Sept. 1, 1851	63,140	294	177
Oklahoma	1	Nov. 16, 1907	84,956	373	199
Oregon	1	Feb. 14, 1859	49,430	505	258
Pennsylvania	5	April 23, 1968	26,078	39	33
Rhode Island	2	Dec. 4, 1986	11,407	14	12
South Carolina	7	Jan. 1, 1896	27,421	690	500
South Dakota	1	Nov. 2, 1889	28,840	243	122
Tennessee	3	Feb. 23, 1870	13,960	66	43
Texas	5	Feb. 15, 1876	92,025	676	498
Utah	1	Jan. 4, 1896	20,700	178	122
Vermont	3	July 9, 1793	8,565	212	54
Virginia	6	July 1, 1971	22,570	60	52
Washington	1	Nov. 11, 1889	32,578	181	107
West Virginia	2	April 9, 1872	33,324	126	75
Wisconsin	1	May 29, 1848	15,102	197	147
Wyoming	1	July 10, 1890	26,349	130	101

Source: *Book of the States*, 2019, knowldegecenter.csg.org/kc/system/files/1.3.19.pdf [Table 1.3] (accessed December 23, 2019).

Not surprisingly, lengthy state constitutions tend to be plagued by contradictions and meaningless clauses, legal jargon, and redundancy. Some address problems that are no longer with us, such as the regulation of steamboats[19] or the need to teach livestock feeding in Oklahoma public schools. Some, such as Alabama's, are burdened by embarrassingly discriminating and illegal provisions (under U.S. constitutional law), including passages calling for segregated schools for black and white students and poll taxes. New Jersey's archaic wording uses terms like "bastardly" and provides that a woman forfeits her property rights to her husband if she has been "ravished" by another man *with* her consent.

Long-winded constitutions, such as those of Alabama, Oklahoma, and Colorado, fail to distinguish between the fundamental law and particularistic issues that properly should be decided by the state legislature.[20] Excessive detail invites litigation and then the courts must rule on conflicting provisions and challenges to constitutionality; hence, the courts are often burdened unnecessarily with decisions that should be made more appropriately by the legislature. Colorado's constitutional contradictions, for instance, led the speaker of the Colorado House to observe in 2008 that "We're one of the only states where the constitution requires simultaneous revenue reductions and spending increases."[21]

Once incorporated into a constitution, a decision becomes as close to permanent as anything can be in politics (though congressional or federal court review can overturn state constitutional provisions). In contrast to a statute, which can be changed by a simple legislative majority, constitutional change requires an extraordinary majority, usually two-thirds or three-fourths of the legislature, or a majority of the voting public. This requirement hampers the legislature's ability to confront problems quickly and makes policy change more difficult. Of course, enshrining a principle in the constitution can be a deliberate strategy to protect special interests. Too many amendments may also deprive local governments of needed flexibility to cope with their own problems. Indeed, excessive detail generates confusion, not only for legislatures and courts but also for the general public. It encourages political subterfuge to get around archaic or irrelevant provisions and breeds disrespect or even contempt for government.

State constitutions are political documents and, contrary to the admonitions of reformers, may sometimes be used to address some of the most controversial issues in politics, such as abortion rights, gun rights, and immigration policy. Many detailed provisions favor or protect special interests, including public utilities, farmers, timber and mining companies, oil and gas drillers, designated businesses, and many others.

There is enormous variance in the length of state constitutions (see Table 3.1). What accounts for such disparity? Studies by political scientists find, not surprisingly, that interest groups play an important role. In states with a single dominant political party, where legislative outcomes tend to be unpredictable because of dissension among members of the majority party, interest groups try to insulate their favorite agencies and programs from uncertainty by seeking protective provisions for them in the constitution.[22] Also, research indicates that long, detailed documents tend to become even longer because their very complexity encourages further amendment, until they finally become so cumbersome that political support develops for a simpler version. Finally, the easier it is to amend a constitution, the higher the amendment rate.[23]

Problems of Substance

In addition to the contradictions, anachronisms, wordiness, and grants of special privilege found in state constitutions, their *substance* has drawn criticism. Specific concerns voiced by reformers include the following:

- *The long ballot.* Because elected executive branch officials are not accountable to the governor for their jobs, the governor has little or no formal influence on their decisions and activities. Reformers who seek to maximize the governor's powers would restrict the executive branch ballot to only two elected leaders: the governor and the lieutenant governor.
- *A glut of executive boards and commissions.* Such entities were originally intended to expand opportunities for public participation in state government and to limit the powers of the governor. Today, they lead to fragmentation and a lack of policy coordination in the executive branch.
- *A swamp of local governments.* There are some 90,000 municipalities, counties, school districts, and special-purpose districts in the states. Sometimes they work at cross-purposes, and nearly always they suffer from overlapping responsibilities and an absence of coordination.
- *Restrictions on local government authority.* Localities in some states have to obtain explicit permission from the state legislature before providing a new service, tapping a new source of revenue, or exercising any other authority not specifically granted to them by the state.
- *Discriminatory treatment.* Constitutional language sometimes discriminates against African Americans, Latinos, immigrants, or gay people by denying them certain rights guaranteed to straight white males. (Although a few holdouts remain, most states have now adopted race- and gender-neutral language.)

Constitutional Reform

Shortly after World War I, problems of constitutional substance began to generate increasing commentary on the sorry condition of state constitutions. An important voice for constitutional reform was the National Municipal League, which developed a **Model State Constitution** in 1921, which is now in its sixth version.[24]

Another influential voice came in 1955 from the U.S. Advisory Commission on Intergovernmental Relations, popularly known as the Kestnbaum Commission. In its final report to the president, the commission stated that:

> the Constitution prepared by the Founding Fathers, with its broad grants of authority and avoidance of legislative detail, has withstood the test of time far better than the constitutions later adopted by the States. . . . The Commission believes that most states would benefit from a fundamental review of their constitutions to make sure that they provide for vigorous and responsible government, not forbid it.[25]

LO 3-3
To comprehend the basic content of state constitutions and how they compare with the U.S. Constitution.

Model State Constitution
An ideal of the structure and contents of a state constitution that emphasizes brevity and broad functions and responsibilities of government.

Thomas Jefferson believed that each generation has the right to choose for itself its own form of government. He suggested that a new constitution every nineteen or twenty years would be appropriate. Between 1960 and 1980, it seems that the states took his remarks to heart. Every state altered its fundamental law in some respect during this period, and new or substantially revised constitutions were put into operation in more than half the states. During the 1970s alone, ten states held conventions to consider changing or replacing their constitution. One such state was Louisiana, which set a record by adopting its eleventh constitution; Georgia is in second place with ten.

Two state constitutional traditions are evident today.[26] The newer **positive-law tradition** is represented by the detailed and lengthy documents of states such as Alabama, New York, and Texas. Detailed provisions tend to usurp the lawmaking powers of state legislatures by locking in rigid procedures and policies that typically favor strong political or economic interests. The original **higher-law tradition** is represented by the U.S. Constitution and the National Municipal League's Model State Constitution. It is embodied in brief documents that put forward basic and enduring framework principles and processes of government, recognizing that public policy choices are the proper responsibility of legislatures. Of course, no constitutional formula can be suitable for all the states because they differ too much in so many respects. The best constitutions strike a balance between the need for stability and the requirement for enough flexibility to deal with emerging problems. Today the higher-law tradition is in favor in those states whose constitutions have become briefer, more readable, and simple enough for the average citizen to understand. In others, however, conflicts between special interests are often resolved through constitutional change, particularly through citizen initiatives.

The Essential State Constitution

The Model State Constitution has twelve basic articles, which are embodied to a greater or lesser extent in the various state constitutions today. A brief description of each article and the ways in which its contents are changing follows.

Bill of Rights Individual rights and liberties were first protected in state constitutions. They closely resemble, and in some cases are identical to, those later delineated in the first eight amendments to the U.S. Constitution. Originally, the national Bill of Rights protected citizens only from actions by the U.S. government. State constitutions and courts were the principal guardians of civil liberties until the Supreme Court's interpretation of the Fourteenth Amendment extended the protective umbrella of the national courts over the states in 1925.[27] U.S. Supreme Court rulings also applied the U.S. Bill of Rights to the states, especially during the Warren Court beginning in 1953. Some states had failed to uphold their trust, particularly those that perpetuated the unequal treatment of women and minorities.

In the 1980s, however, activist states began to reassert guarantees of individual rights under state constitutions. At a minimum, all state constitutions must protect and guarantee those rights found in the U.S. Bill of Rights. But state constitutional provisions may guarantee additional or more extensive

positive-law tradition
A state constitutional tradition based on detailed provisions and procedure.

higher-law tradition
A state constitutional tradition based on basic and enduring principles that reach beyond statutory law.

rights to citizens. Twenty-two states now have equal rights amendments that guarantee sexual equality and prohibit sex-based discrimination. (But more than half the states once banned same-sex marriages.) The U.S. Constitution does not guarantee a right of privacy, but eleven states do guarantee it. And thirty-six states give constitutional rights to crime victims. Some constitutional provisions border on the exotic. Residents of New Hampshire hold the right to revolution, and all Massachusetts citizens enjoy freedom from excessive noise. Constitutions of Missouri and North Dakota guarantee the right to farm. To counter animal rights activists, twenty-two states have inserted the rights to hunt and fish into their constitutions. As just observed, constitutions are political documents reflecting state interests and culture; they bear the marks of the state's people, embodied in the fundamental law in response to a serious concern or issue of the time. (See Table 3.2 for other rights provisions.)

The major reason for the rebirth of state activism in protecting civil liberties and individual rights has been the conservatism of the U.S. Supreme Court. One commentator accused the Supreme Court of having abdicated its role as "keeper of the nation's conscience."[28] The states' powers to write and interpret their constitutions differently from the U.S. Constitution's provisions in the area of protecting civil rights and liberties has been upheld by the Supreme Court, as long as the state provisions have "adequate and independent" grounds.[29] Increasingly, civil rights and liberties cases are being filed by plaintiffs in state rather than federal courts, based on state bill of rights protections.

As we observed earlier, constitutions are "living" documents that evolve over time and bear the temporal imprints of the people of a state. Table 3.2 illustrates this point with a selection of constitutional quirks and oddities, many of them anachronisms.

Table 3.2 Excerpts from States Bills of Rights

Alabama	"The legislature may hereafter, by general law, provide for an indemnification program to peanut farmers for losses incurred as a result of *Aspergillus flavus* and freeze damage in peanuts."
Alaska	"Public schooling shall always be conducted in English."
Illinois	"The equal protection of the laws shall not be denied or abridged on account of sex by the State or its units of local government."
Montana	"Human dignity is inviolable."
New York	"The aid, care and support of the needy are public concerns and shall be provided by the state and by such of its subdivisions. . . ."
North Carolina	"Secret political societies shall not be tolerated."
Pennsylvania	"The people have a right to clean air, pure water, and to the preservation of the natural, scenic, historic and esthetic values of the environment. Pennsylvania's public natural resources are the common history of all the people, including generations yet to come. . . ."
Rhode Island	"The power of the state and its municipalities to regulate and control the use of land and waters in the furtherance of the preservation, regeneration, and restoration of the natural environment, and . . . of the rights of the people to enjoy and freely exercise the rights of fishery and the privileges of the shore . . . shall be liberally construed, and shall not be deemed a public use of private property."

Controversies in States and Localities

New States' Rights?

Lately, a revolt of the states has been witnessed. This "New States' Rights" is perhaps less a movement than an angry backlash against perceived overreaching by the federal government into state affairs at a time when economic problems have been building up. Its principals include Tea Party activists, political conservatives, and other "new states' righters."

Examples of the new revolt abound:

- South Dakota and Wyoming declared federal firearms regulation invalid for weapons made and used in their states.
- Utah enacted a law prohibiting the federal government from carrying out its Affordable Care Act ("Obamacare") without explicit legislative approval, asserted Utah's authority to seize federal land, and declared that the state can restrict federal law enforcement authority on federal lands within the state.
- Alaska filed suit against the federal government to overturn federal laws protecting polar bears and other endangered species so that oil and gas drilling could proceed more expeditiously.
- Twenty states have legalized medical marijuana, despite federal policy prohibiting it; eleven have legalized recreational possession, use, and sale of the substance.
- Several states, including Utah, introduced Repeal Amendments to the U.S. Constitution that

would grant states the power to veto any act of Congress they disagreed with if two-thirds of the states opposed the act.

- In response to Trump administration policies on separation of parents and children illegally entering the United States, seventeen states sued, attempting to derail the executive orders that implemented the policy.

Article VI of the U.S. Constitution, as interpreted by the courts, establishes the supremacy of federal law when it conflicts with state law. Yet the Tenth Amendment states that "powers not delegated to the United States by the Constitution . . . are reserved to the states respectively, or to the people." In instances of conflict or confusion, the U.S. Supreme Court has the final say.

Critical Thinking Questions

1. How genuine is the New States' Rights? Is it a legitimate response of states to federal inactions or intrusions? Or, is it simply political grandstanding by elected state officials?
2. How, if at all, *should* the states be able to act when the federal government refuses to move forward on a pressing problem or, alternatively, when the federal government acts in such a way that one or more states feel they must resist?

Power of the State This very brief article states simply that the powers enumerated in the constitution are not the only ones held by the state— that, indeed, the state has all powers not denied to it by the state or national constitutions.

Suffrage and Elections Voter registration and election procedures are provided for here. Extensions—and retractions—of voting rights and changes in election procedures have been made in response to U.S. Supreme Court decisions and to federal law. Some states have improved election administration; liberalized registration, voting, and office-holding requirements; and enhanced election technology and security. Other (Republican controlled) states have shortened early voting periods, imposed restrictive voter identification requirements, and taken other measures that supporters claim help to prevent voter fraud. Opponents assert that these restrictions are intended to discourage traditional Democratic voters (minorities and the young) from participating in elections.

The Legislative Branch This article sets forth the powers, procedures, and organizing principles of the legislature, including apportionment of state legislatures on the basis of one person, one vote. District lines must be redrawn every ten years after the national census has revealed population changes (most recently in 2011–2012). Nineteen states have placed term limits on their elected officials in this article.

Interestingly, the Model State Constitution originally recommended a unicameral (one house) legislature as a means to overcome complexity, delay, and confusion. In its most recent revision, the National Municipal League tacitly recognized the refusal of the states to follow this suggestion by providing recommendations appropriate only for a bicameral body. Only Nebraska has a single-house general assembly today. The bold—even radical—constitutional amendment for unicameralism was adopted by the voters of Nebraska in 1934 in a popular initiative. Why Nebraska? Apparently, several events were at least partly responsible for what Nebraskans have come to call "Unicam." For one thing, it was on the same statewide ballot with two other popular initiatives: repeal of Prohibition and approval of pari-mutuel horse racing. In addition, the bicameral body had been suffering increasing criticism for its apparent inability to conduct the state's business efficiently and effectively. But the key factor was the unrelenting preaching of the evils of bicameralism and the virtues of unicameralism by influential and popular U.S. Senator George W. Norris. Norris "wore out two sets of tires and two windshields" driving around on Nebraska's dusty back roads to make the case for Unicam.

Unicameralism has several virtues. It eliminates conference committees, which speeds up the legislative process and prevents the two houses from passing the buck to one another, each hoping the other will deal with the tough or complicated issues. The unicameral legislature can be small (it numbers forty-nine representatives in Nebraska, the smallest legislature among the states). And if the single body is nonpartisan, as in Nebraska, representatives may be more likely to focus on the important business of the state than on national issues of partisan significance.

Nebraska's Unicam gets high marks for efficiency, simplicity, and effectiveness. And it remains popular except for its nonpartisan feature. The major complaint is that nonpartisanship depresses voter interest and turnout in elections because voters do not have party identification as a voting cue.

The Executive Branch The powers and organization of the executive branch, which are outlined in this article, have seen many notable modifications. Governors have won line item vetoes, the authority to make appointments within the executive branch, and the ability to reorganize the state bureaucracy. A number of states have opted for team election of the governor and lieutenant governor.

The Judicial Branch Court organization and procedures are outlined here, along with the selection method for judges. Most states have unified their court systems under a single authority, usually the state Supreme Court. Many states now select judges through a merit plan rather than by gubernatorial appointment, legislative election, or popular election. The states have also established means to investigate charges against judges and to recommend discipline or removal from the bench when necessary.

Finance Taxation, debt, and expenditures for state and local governments are the subjects of this article. In many states, tax relief has been granted to senior citizens, veterans, and disabled people. In others, taxation and expenditure limitations have been added.

Local Government Here, the authority of municipalities, counties, and other local governments is recognized. Most states have increased local authority through home rule provisions, which give localities more discretion in providing services; some have extended local taxing authority. In addition, mechanisms for improved intergovernmental cooperation, such as consolidated city and county governments and regional districts to provide services, have been created.

Public Education On the basis of this article, the states establish and maintain free public schools for all children. Higher education institutions, including technical schools, colleges, and universities, are commonly established in this section.

Civil Service The Model State Constitution sets forth a *merit system* of personnel administration for state government, under which civil servants are to be hired, promoted, paid, evaluated, and retained on the basis of competence, fitness, and performance instead of political party affiliation or other such criteria.

Intergovernmental Relations Some states stipulate specific devices for cooperation among various state entities, among local jurisdictions, or between a state and its localities. They may detail methods for sharing in the provision of certain services, or they may list cost-sharing mechanisms such as local option sales taxes.

Constitutional Revision The methods for revising, amending, and replacing the constitution are described.

Constitutions Today In general, state constitutions today conform more closely to the higher-law tradition and the Model State Constitution than did those of the past. They are shorter, more concise, and simpler, and they contain fewer errors, anachronisms, and contradictions. The latest states to enter the Union, Alaska and Hawaii, have constitutional documents that follow the Model State Constitution quite closely.

However, work always remains to be done. Some state constitutions are still riddled with unnecessary details because new amendments have continually been added to the old documents, and obsolete provisions and other relics can still be found. But more important deficiencies exist in states whose constitutions inhibit the administrative and financial operations of state government and obstruct the ability to adapt to change. In some jurisdictions, the governor's formal powers remain weak; a plethora of boards and commissions makes any thought of executive management and coordination a pipe dream; local governments chafe under the tight leash of state authority; and many other problems persist. Constitutional revision must be an ongoing process if the states are to cope with the changing contours of American society and stay in the vanguard of innovation and change.

Methods for Constitutional Change

There are only two methods for altering the U.S. Constitution. The first is the constitutional convention, wherein delegates representing the states assemble to consider modifying or replacing the Constitution. Despite periodic calls for a national constitutional convention, only one has taken place—in Philadelphia, more than two and a quarter centuries ago. Two-thirds of the states must agree to call a convention; three-fourths are required to ratify any changes in the Constitution.

The second means of amending the U.S. Constitution is through congressional initiative, wherein Congress, by a two-thirds vote of both houses, agrees to send one or more proposed changes to the states. Again, three-fourths of the states must ratify the proposals.

Since 1787, more than 1,000 amendments have been submitted to the states by Congress. Only twenty-seven have been approved (the most recent one, in 1992, limits the ability of members of Congress to increase their pay), and the first ten of these were appended to the Constitution as a condition by several states for ratification. Note that neither method for amending the U.S. Constitution requires popular participation by voters, in sharp contrast to the citizen participation requirements for state constitutional change, as we shall see in the next section.

Informal Constitutional Change

In a letter to James Madison, Thomas Jefferson wrote the following: "The earth belongs to the living, and not to the dead. . . . Every constitution, then, and every law, naturally expires at the end of 19 years. If it be enforced longer, it is an act of force and not of right."[30] Though Jefferson's admonitions are not followed literally, the states do frequently alter their constitutions.

One informal and four formal methods for amending state constitutions exist. The informal route is **interpretation** of constitutional meaning by the state legislature, executive branch, courts, or attorneys general, or through usage and custom.[31] Governors issue executive orders; courts and attorneys general produce advisory opinions on meanings of specific provisions; state agencies make decisions and implement policy. The force of habit can be a

interpretation
An informal means of revising constitutions whereby members of the executive, legislative, or judicial branch apply constitutional principles and law to the everyday affairs of governing.

? It's Your Turn

Should Washington, DC Become the 51st State?

The residents of the District of Columbia demand the right to statehood. They make some compelling points and arguments. The District has its own license plates, prison system, and income tax. It has three electoral votes. But it has no U.S. senators and only a single, nonvoting member of the U.S. House of Representatives.

Though it granted the District some self-governing authority under a 1974 home rule charter, Congress retains full veto power over the District's legislative and financial affairs, including its budget. Congress has been known to overturn laws enacted by the District.

The U.S. Constitution (Article I, section 8) designates DC as the seat of the national government. The Framers believed that a separate district would not only prevent the state, whose territory included the national capital, from exerting powerful pressures on Congress but also prevent the national government from being dependent on any single state for services and security. It did not help that Congress, concerned about a near mutiny

of General Washington's army in 1783, had to flee the early capital of Philadelphia after Pennsylvania refused to protect it.

Several attempts have been made to gain DC statehood for the 68 square-mile District, including a proposed constitutional amendment that received approval by only sixteen of the necessary thirty-eight states. Congressional hearings on the issue have been held, the most recent one in October 2014. President Obama stated that he favored DC statehood, but he decided not to risk political capital promoting it in Congress. President Trump has been ambivalent on the issue, stating that he has a conflict of interest because he owns property in DC. Some have suggested sending the District back to its original home, the state of Maryland. In November 2016, voters in DC overwhelmingly approved an advisory referendum asking Congress to admit the district as the 51st state, and in March 2019 the U.S. House of Representatives passed HR 1 calling for DC statehood; the Senate has so far taken no action on this.

Globe Turner, LLC/Getty Images

PROS	CONS
The district's 711,500 population outnumbers that of Vermont and Wyoming.	Constitutional problems weigh heavily.
Residents pay billions in federal taxes each year; they serve on juries and in the armed forces.	The District has no meaningful agriculture or industry, except for tourism and, of course, government.
Residents say they are disrespected and treated like second-class citizens who are taxed without meaningful representation.	Its population is majority African American, two-thirds minority, and decidedly Democratic in its voting. Republicans are adamantly against statehood for the District.
	The District has been rocked by numerous high-level corruption scandals during recent decades, tarnishing the reputation of the District's elected officials.

powerful influence, specific constitutional provisions notwithstanding. It is a good bet that one or more antiquated or unrealistic constitutional provisions are ignored in every state. A common example is the requirement that all bills be read, in their entirety, three times in each house for enactment. Another is the list of requirements for holding political office, such as a belief in God.

State supreme courts play the most direct role in changing constitutions through interpretation. In large measure, a constitution is what the judges say it is in their decisions from the bench. Judicial interpretation of constitutions may be based on various standards, including strict attention to the express language of the document and to the original intent of the Framers or authors of amendments, deference to legislative enactments or executive actions, precedent, policy considerations, and individual rights. The power of the state supreme courts to review executive actions, legislative actions, and decisions of lower courts is known as **judicial review**. This power evolved in the states much as it did on the national level—through the courts' own insistence that they hold this authority. During recent years, as the U.S. Supreme Court has become more conservative and less activist in its interpretations of the law, some state courts have moved in the opposite direction and earned reputations as judicial activists. On occasion, federal courts strike down state constitutional law. For instance, federal courts have recently overturned constitutional amendments banning same-sex marriage and voting procedures.

We have already noted that state supreme courts have the authority to interpret and apply state guarantees of civil rights and liberties more broadly than the U.S. Supreme Court's interpretation of the Bill of Rights in the U.S. Constitution. For instance, the New Hampshire Supreme Court extended the right to privacy to household garbage, even when it is placed at the curb for collection. The U.S. Supreme Court does not review state court decisions that are clearly and properly based on state constitutional provisions.[32] In practice, however, state supreme courts are often guided by constitutional rulings of the

judicial review
The power of the U.S. Supreme Court or state supreme courts to declare unconstitutional actions of the executive and legislative branches, as well as decisions of lower courts.

U.S. Supreme Court and high courts in other states. Because courts apply similar constitutional language to many common issues, it is natural for them to share their experiences in legal problem solving.[33] Of course, the national courts are paramount under the U.S. Constitution and will strike down any serious constitutional contradictions between the nation and the states, but for more than two decades now, the U.S. Supreme Court has shown "a studied deference to the work of the state judiciaries."[34]

Formal Constitutional Change

The four formal procedures for constitutional change are legislative proposal, initiative, constitutional convention, and constitutional commission. All involve two basic steps: initiation and **ratification**. The state legislature, or in some cases the voters, propose (initiate) a constitutional change. Then the proposed amendment is submitted to the voters for approval (ratification).

Legislative Proposal **Legislative proposal** is the most common road to revision. More than 90 percent of all changes in state constitutions have come through this method, which is permitted in all fifty states.

The specifics of legislative proposal techniques vary, but most states require either two-thirds or three-fifths of the members of each house to approve a proposal before it is sent to the voters for ratification. Twelve states require two consecutive legislative sessions to consider and pass a proposed amendment. The procedure can become quite complicated. For instance, South Carolina's legislative proposal must be passed by two-thirds of the members of each house; then it is sent to the people during the next general election. If a majority of voters approve, the proposal returns to the next legislative session, in which a majority of legislators have to concur.

Almost all states accept a simple majority for voter ratification of a proposed revision. In New Hampshire, however, two-thirds of the voters must approve the proposal. Florida requires a 60 percent majority. And Tennessee requires approval by a majority of the number of citizens who cast a vote for governor. No voter approval of constitutional amendments is necessary in Delaware. A proposed amendment that passes by a two-thirds majority in two consecutive sessions of the state legislature is considered adopted.

Legislative proposal is probably best suited to a limited number of revisions that are relatively narrow in scope. The disadvantage to presenting a far-reaching amendment is that voters may not understand it, or they may distrust it. And a multitude of individual proposals threatens to overwhelm and confuse voters. Moreover, a patchwork of amendments can conflict with or overlap other constitutional provisions. This circumstance spawns additional revisions, which in turn lead to increased litigation in the state supreme court. Either strategy—a far-reaching proposal or a plentitude of amendments—is likely to go down in defeat at the polls.

Initiative Eighteen states permit their citizens to initiate and ratify changes in the constitution and thus bypass the legislature (see Table 3.3). Only five of these initiative states are east of the Mississippi River, thus reflecting the fact

ratification
The formal approval of a constitution or constitutional amendment by a majority of the voters of a state.

legislative proposal
The most common means of amending a state constitution, wherein the legislature proposes a revision, usually by a two-thirds majority.

Table 3.3 States Authorizing Constitutional Amendment by Citizen Initiative

STATE	YEAR ADOPTED	NUMBER OF SIGNATURES REQUIRED ON INITIATIVE PETITION
Arizona	1910	15 percent of total votes cast for all candidates for governor at last election
Arkansas	1909	10 percent of voters for governor at last election
California	1911	8 percent of total voters for all candidates for governor at last election
Colorado	1910	5 percent of total legal votes for all candidates for secretary of state at last general election
Florida	1972	8 percent of total votes cast in the state in the last presidential election
Illinois*	1970	8 percent of total votes cast for candidates for governor at last election
Massachusetts†	1918	3 percent of total votes cast in the last gubernatorial election
Michigan	1908	10 percent of total votes for all candidates at the gubernatorial election
Mississippi	1992	12 percent of total votes for all candidates for governor at last election
Missouri	1906	8 percent of legal voters for all candidates for governor at last election
Montana	1904	10 percent of qualified electors, the number of qualified electors to be determined by the number of votes cast for governor in the preceding general election
Nebraska	1912	10 percent of registered voters
Nevada	1904	10 percent of voters who voted in entire state in last general election
North Dakota	1914	4 percent of population of the state
Ohio	1912	10 percent of total number of electors who voted for governor in last election
Oklahoma	1907	15 percent of legal voters for state office receiving the highest number of voters at last general state election
Oregon	1902	8 percent of total votes for all candidates at last election, at which the governor was elected for a four-year term
South Dakota	1898	10 percent of total votes for governor in last election

*Only Article IV, the Legislature, may be amended by initiative petition.

†Before being submitted to the electorate for ratification, initiative measures must be approved at two sessions of a successively elected legislature by not less than one-fourth of all members elected, sitting in joint session.

Source: Copyright 2018 The Council of State Governments. Adapted with permission from *The Book of the States*. Reprinted by permission of The Council of State Governments.

that the initiative was a product of the Progressive reform movement of the early 1900s. Most of the territories admitted as states during this period chose to permit the **initiative** (known as "constitutional initiative" in some states). Twenty-three states also authorize the initiative for enacting statutory change.

The initiative is used much less often than legislative proposal in amending constitutions, although recently proposed initiatives have won more frequently on state ballots. The initiative is less successful than legislative proposal in terms of the percentage of amendments that are adopted by the voters. Less than half of all initiatives have been written into state constitutions in recent years.

The number of signatures needed for the initiative petition to be valid varies widely: Arizona requires 15 percent of total votes cast in the last gubernatorial election, whereas Massachusetts requires 3 percent (see Table 3.3).

initiative
A proposed law or constitutional amendment that is placed on the ballot by citizen petition.

Eight states specify that the petition signatures must be collected widely throughout the state as a means of ensuring that an initiative that favors one specific region does not become embodied in the constitution.

In general, a petition for constitutional amendment is sent to the office of the secretary of state for verification that the required number of registered voters have signed their names. Then the question is placed on a statewide ballot in the next general election. Ratification requires a majority vote of the people in most states.

It is usually easy enough to collect the required number of signatures to place a proposed amendment on a statewide ballot (for a fee, a firm will be happy to perform this service, and a surprising number of people will sign almost anything). But actual passage of the initiative is much more difficult once it receives a close public examination and opposing interests proclaim their objections. If the legislature is circumvented altogether and propositions are placed directly on the general-election ballot by citizens, the procedure is called a **direct initiative**. If a legislature participates by voting on the citizen proposal, as in Massachusetts and Mississippi, the procedure is known as an **indirect initiative**.

The initiative is useful in making limited changes to the state constitution and, in recent years, has addressed some controversial issues that state legislatures are hesitant to confront. Voters in several states have recently addressed abortion rights, immigration policy, property rights, school vouchers, the right to carry firearms, and bans on foreign (Sharia) law. A major advantage of the initiative is that the people's will can counter a despotic or inertia-ridden legislature. Another advantage is that this method appears to enhance citizen interest and participation in government.

However, the initiative can also be abused through signature fraud or by well-heeled special interests with selfish motives or social agendas who seek to gain privileges, and under crisis conditions it can result in ill-conceived, radical changes to the constitution. Indeed, the initiative can result in just the kind of excessive detail and poorly drafted verbiage that is so widely condemned by constitutional scholars and reformers. It can also make doing routine business extremely difficult. In Colorado, for example, an initiative appears to require simultaneous tax cuts and spending increases.

The perceived excesses of the initiative have recently spawned efforts to raise the threshold for voter approval. Ironically, in a constitutional referendum, Florida voters agreed to raise the bar for initiative approval from a simple majority passed by less than 60 percent of the vote, to 60 percent. Montana banned paid signature gatherers and restricted the time for signature acquisition to one year.[35]

Constitutional Convention Legislative proposals and initiatives are quite specific about the type of constitutional change that is sought. Only those questions that actually appear on the ballot are considered. By contrast, a **constitutional convention** assembles delegates who suggest revisions or even an entirely new document, then submit the proposed changes to the voters for ratification. The convention is especially well suited to consider far-reaching constitutional changes or a new fundamental law.

direct initiative A procedure by which the voters of a jurisdiction propose the passage of constitutional amendments, state laws, or local ordinances, bypassing the legislative body.

indirect initiative Similar to the direct initiative, except that the voter-initiated proposal must be submitted to the legislature before going on the ballot for voter approval.

constitutional convention An assembly of delegates chosen by popular election or appointed by the legislature or the governor to revise an existing constitution or to create a new one.

The convention is the oldest method for constitutional change in the states and is available in all fifty of them. The process begins when the electorate or the legislature decides to call for a constitutional convention. In fourteen states, the question of calling a convention must be regularly voted on by the electorate, but all convention calls have been routinely rejected since Rhode Island's won approval in 1986. Alaskans and Iowans hold an automatic convention call every ten years; in New York and Maryland, the convention issue is submitted to the voters every twenty years. Except in Delaware, where the legislature can take direct action, proposals emerging from the convention must be ratified by the voters before they become part of the constitution. Delegates to a convention are usually elected on a nonpartisan ballot by the voters from state house or senate districts.

Voter approval of convention proposals is problematic. If partisan, racial, regional, or other disagreements dominate media reports on the convention, voter approval is difficult to obtain. Greater likelihood of voter approval occurs when specific changes are considered.[36] As with the case of legislative proposals, people naturally tend to be skeptical of suggestions for sweeping, unsettling changes in the basic structures and procedures of government. Once a convention is approved and convened, delegates usually understand these dynamics and are sensitive to how their proposed changes may affect the general public.

Constitutional Commission Often called a *study commission*, the **constitutional commission** is usually established to examine the existing document and to recommend changes to the legislature or to the voters. Depending on the mandate, the constitutional commission may study the entire constitution with a view toward replacement or change, focus on one or more specific articles or provisions, or be given the freedom to decide its own scope of activity. Commission recommendations are only advisory, thus helping to account for this method's popularity with elected officials, who sometimes prefer to study a problem to death rather than engage it head on. Some or all of the recommendations may be submitted to the voters; others may be completely ignored. Only in Florida can a commission send its proposals directly to the voters.

Constitutional commissions operate from time to time in the states; the most recent ones were in Ohio and Florida. Utah's revision commission functions permanently. Service on a constitutional commission can be a thankless task because legislators sometimes ignore the commission's recommendations or employ them as a symbolic device for relieving political pressure. For example, the Ohio state legislature approved a modernization commission in 2011, giving it a ten-year charge to propose constitutional changes. But the 2017 Ohio state legislature ended the work of the commission after only six years. The modernization commission had proposed many changes to the Ohio constitution, but the state legislature did not take action on any of them. However, several of the commission's proposals, including changes to legislative redistricting, were adopted as a result of citizen initiatives.[37] When used properly and taken seriously, commissions can furnish high-quality research both inexpensively and relatively quickly.

constitutional commission
A meeting of appointed delegates established to study an existing constitution, or specific provisions, and to recommend proposed changes.

State Responsiveness and Constitutional Reform

Each state's constitution is designed specifically to meet the needs of that state. The rich history, economics, values, ideals, and political culture of the state are reflected in its constitutional language. Through their constitutions, the states experiment with different governmental institutions and processes. As Thomas Paine observed in 1791 in his essay entitled "The Rights of Man," "It is in the interest of all the states, that the constitution of each should be somewhat diversified from each other. We are a people founded upon experiments, and . . . have the happy opportunity of trying variety in order to discover the best."[38]

State constitutions were the original guardians of individual rights and liberties, with their own bills of rights preceding those of the U.S. Constitution by many years. They have generally resumed that responsibility during the past several decades. Yet, few tasks in government are more difficult than modernizing a constitution. As one writer on constitutional change observed, the process requires "sustained, dedicated, organized effort; vigorous, aggressive and imaginative leadership; bipartisan political support; education of the electorate on the issues; judicious selection of the means; and seemingly endless patience."[39] In the words of another constitutional scholar, "The advocate of constitutional reform in an American state should be endowed with the patience of Job and the sense of time of a geologist."[40] The solemn duty of framing the original state constitutions, which was so effectively discharged by our predecessors, is now vested in the continuous oversight of present and future generations.

The constitutional changes enacted in the states since the Kestnbaum Commission report have generally resulted in documents in the higher-law tradition, documents that "are shorter, more clearly written, modernized, less encumbered with restrictions, more basic in content and have more reasonable amending processes. They also establish improved governmental structures and contain substantive provisions assuring greater openness, accountability, and equity."[41] The states have made a great deal of progress in modernizing their governments. As state constitutional scholar Richard Leach has put it, "There are not many constitutional horrors left."[42]

Old-style constitutions were "the drag anchors of state programs, and permanent cloaks for the protection of special interests and points of view."[43] These constitutions held back progress and delayed the states' resurgence as lead players in the drama of U.S. federalism. Recent constitutional amendments have responded to, and indeed caused, profound changes in state government and politics. Problems persist, and future constitutional tinkering and replacements will be necessary—indeed, inevitable.

Chapter Recap

- The constitution is the fundamental law of a state, superior to statutory law.

- State constitutions evolved from the original colonial charters. Shifting from an original basis of legislative supremacy, they have gradually increased executive power.

- Some constitutions continue to suffer from excessive length and substantive problems.

- Constitutional reform has modernized the documents and made them conform more closely to present challenges of governance.

- Methods for changing constitutions include interpretation and judicial review, legislative proposal, initiative, constitutional convention, and constitutional commission.

Key Terms

fundamental law *(p. 61)*
legislative supremacy *(p. 64)*
Model State Constitution *(p. 69)*
positive-law tradition *(p. 70)*
higher-law tradition *(p. 70)*

interpretation *(p. 75)*
judicial review *(p. 77)*
ratification *(p. 78)*
legislative proposal *(p. 78)*
initiative *(p. 79)*
direct initiative *(p. 80)*

indirect initiative *(p. 80)*
constitutional convention *(p. 80)*
constitutional commission *(p. 81)*

Internet Resources

For full texts of state statutes and constitutions, see individual state websites (e.g., **www.colorado.gov**).

State constitutions can also be accessed through FindLaw at **www.findlaw.com/11stategov/indexconst.html** or **www.constitution.org**.

The Alaska constitution draws heavily on the Model State Constitution. It is located in the State of Alaska Documents Library at **www.ltgov.alaska.gov/information/alaskas-constitution/**.

For everything you want to know about Nebraska's Unicam, go to **www.nebraskalegislature.gov**. Live webcasts of Unicam may be viewed at **www.netnebraska.org/publicmedia/capitol.html**.

Another helpful site is the Center for State Constitutional Studies at **www.statecon.camden.rutgers.edu/**.

The most recent data on state constitutional change can be accessed at the Council of State Governments website: **www.csg.org**.

4

Citizen Participation and Elections: Engaging the Public in Government

Voters in Boise, Idaho, cast their ballots in a middle school gym.

Learning Objectives

LO 4-1 To recognize the various ways in which citizens can participate in government.

LO 4-2 To compare state differences in election administration, voter turnout, and election results.

LO 4-3 To differentiate primary election types, general elections, and nonpartisan elections.

LO 4-4 To identify the pros and cons of the mechanisms of direct democracy.

LO 4-5 To recognize the importance of the internet and social media in connecting the public with government.

LO 4-6 To identify the impact of volunteerism in states and localities.

The city of Takoma Park, Maryland, a suburb of Washington, D.C., made history in 2013 when it granted 16- and 17-year-olds the right to vote in city elections. Why take such an unprecedented step? Simple: City leaders believed that lowering the voting age would help local residents develop a lifelong habit of participation in government. Sure, there were naysayers who claimed that teenagers are too immature to handle the responsibility. But in the end, the desire to engage local teens in the most basic right of citizenship prevailed. After all, as one of the newly enfranchised high school students said, "We cultivate interest in democracy by giving people opportunities to participate."[1] Several other Maryland municipalities—Greenbelt, Hyattsville, and Riverdale Park—soon followed. And Berkeley, California, allows 16-year-olds to vote in school board elections. Legislation is currently pending in seven states and the District of Columbia—as well as in the U.S. House of Representatives—to lower the voting age to either 16 or 17.[2]

Participation

LO 4-1
To recognize the various ways in which citizens can participate in government.

Democracy assumes citizen **participation**—acting to influence government. In contemporary America, there is persistent evidence that citizens are not much interested in participation. We have grown accustomed to reports of low voter turnout and public hearings that few attend. In his influential book *Bowling Alone*, political scientist Robert Putnam documented this gradual disengagement of people from all sorts of community activities and organizations.[3]

On the surface, government works just fine with limited participation: The interests of the active become translated into public policy, and those who are inactive can be safely ignored because they do not vote.[4] If, however, some traditional nonvoters such as low-income, less-educated citizens went to the polls or engaged in other forms of political participation, then vote-seeking candidates would be forced to pay more attention to their interests, and public policy might be nudged in a different direction.[5] In this light, it is important to understand both why many people do participate and why others do not. This chapter addresses individual citizen involvement in government.

Why and How People Participate

In a representative democracy, voting is the most common form of participation. For many citizens, it is a matter of civic responsibility. It is a fundamental facet of citizenship—after all, it is called "the right to vote." Citizens go to the polls to elect the officials who will govern them. But there are other methods of participation. Consider the citizen who is unhappy because the property taxes on their home have increased substantially from one year to the next. What options are available to them besides voting against incumbent officeholders at the next election? As shown in Figure 4.1, they can either be active or passive; their actions can be either constructive or destructive. Basically, there are four potential responses: loyalty, voice, exit, and neglect.[6]

According to this formulation, voting is an example of *loyalty*, a passive but constructive response to government action. Specifically, this response reflects the irate taxpayer's underlying support for their community despite their displeasure with specific tax policies. An active constructive response is *voice*: The aggrieved property owner could contact officials, work in the campaign of a candidate who promises to lower tax assessments, or, assuming others in the community share their sentiments, participate in anti-tax groups and organize demonstrations. Research has shown that emotions, especially anger, can be a powerful stimulant to participation.[7] The Occupy Movement of 2011 and 2012, in which protestors camped out in tents in downtown areas to protest the growing economic inequality in the United States, is an example of exercising the voice option. The use of social media by Occupy protestors gave rise to the phrase **hashtag activism**.

Destructive responses (those that undermine the citizen-government relationship) are similarly passive or active. If the citizen simply shrugs and concludes that they can't fight city hall, they are exhibiting a response termed *neglect*. They have nearly given up on the community and do not participate.

participation
Actions through which ordinary members of a political system attempt to influence decisions.

hashtag activism
Using social media, especially Twitter to raise public awareness of an issue.

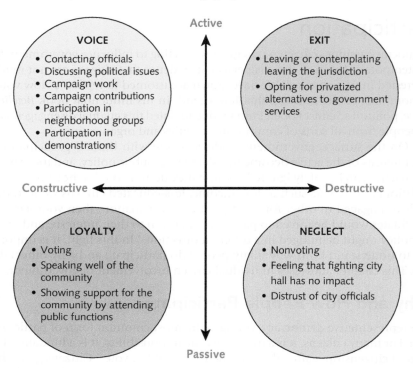

Figure 4.1 Possible Responses to Dissatisfaction in the Community

Source: From "The Organization of Political Space and Citizen Responses to Dissatisfaction in Urban Communities: An Integrated Model," William E. Lyons and David Lowery, *Journal of Politics* 48, no. 2 (1986): 321–45, Figure 1.

A more active version of giving up on a community is to *exit*—that is, to leave the community altogether (a response often referred to as "voting with your feet"). The unhappy citizen will relocate to a community that is more in line with their tax preferences.

Every citizen confronts these participatory options. Local residents' satisfaction with their city government tends to be a direct result of their experiences with city services and their perception of governmental responsiveness.[8] It is much healthier for the political system if citizens engage in the constructive responses, but some individuals are likely to conclude that constructive participation is of little value to them and opt for neglect or, in more extreme cases, exit.[9]

Nonparticipation

What motivates the citizens who choose neglect as their best option? One explanation for nonparticipation in politics is socioeconomic status. Individuals with lower levels of income and education tend to participate less than wealthier, more educated individuals do.[10] Tied closely to income and education levels is occupational status. Unskilled workers and hourly wage earners do not participate in politics to the same degree as white-collar workers and professionals. Individuals of lower socioeconomic status may not have the time, resources, or civic skills required to become actively involved in politics.

Other explanations for nonparticipation have included age (younger people have participated less than middle-aged individuals have), race (black people have participated less than white people have), and gender (women have participated less than men have). Of these factors, however, only age continues to affect political activity levels, and a newly eligible group of young voters undeniably appears in each election. African American political participation actually surpasses that of whites when socioeconomic status is taken into consideration,[11] and the gender gap in the types and levels of political participation has disappeared.[12] America's youth, however, remain less likely to frequent polling places. Turnout for 18- to 24-year-olds has bounced around in recent presidential elections, going from 41.9 percent in 2004 to 44.3 percent in 2008 then down to 38.0 percent in 2012 and back up to 43.6 percent in 2016. In each of these elections, however, the turnout of 18- to 24-year-olds was at least twenty percentage points lower than the turnout for those 65 and older.[13] Turnout for all groups tends to be lower in off-year elections than in presidential years, with youth turnout running around 20 percent in off-year elections in the 2000s. However, in 2018, youth turnout was estimated to be more than 30 percent for the first time in recent history.[14]

Another factor that exerts an independent effect on participation is where one lives. Big-city dwellers (those who live in places with a population of one million or more) are less likely than people in small communities (with fewer than 5,000 inhabitants) to participate in various civic activities, including contacting local officials, attending community meetings, and voting in local elections.[15]

When nonvoters are asked why they failed to participate in an election, the responses show that events in the potential voter's own life often play a major role. Also, a lack of enthusiasm for the candidates or the campaign issues contributes to nonvoting. Table 4.1 provides data from a survey conducted by the U.S Census Bureau into the reasons why people didn't vote in the 2016 presidential election. Although the top reason for nonvoting for both all voters and for young voters was that they didn't like the candidates or issues, a much larger percentage of young voters than older voters indicated they were not interested in the election, were too busy to vote, or were out of town on Election Day. A much lower percentage of younger voters than older voters gave illness or disability as a reason for nonvoting.

The explanation for nonparticipation does not rest solely with the individual. Institutional features—the way the political system is designed—may suppress participation. For example, local governments that have instituted nonpartisan elections, in which candidates run without political party affiliation, have removed an important mobilizing factor for voters. Voter turnout tends to be lower in these elections than in partisan contests. City council meetings scheduled at 10 a.m. put a tremendous strain on workers who must take time off from their jobs if they want to attend; consequently, attendance

Table 4.1 Reasons for Not Voting in 2016 Presidential Election

PERCENTAGE SAYING* ...	ALL VOTERS	18- TO 24-YEAR-OLD VOTERS	25 AND OLDER VOTERS
Did not like candidates or campaign issues	24.8	20.8	25.6
Not interested	15.4	17.3	15.1
Too busy, conflicting schedule	14.3	18.3	13.6
Illness or disability	11.7	2.7	13.4
Other reason (e.g., did not receive absentee ballot, did not know where to vote, lines too long at polling place)	11.1	10.8	11.2
Out of town on Election Day	7.9	13.2	6.9
Registration problems	4.4	5.5	4.2
Forgot to vote	3.9	4.7	2.7
Transportation problems	2.6	1.5	2.8
Inconvenient polling place	2.1	2.3	2.1

*Some 2.7 percent of all nonvoters surveyed declined to give a reason for not voting; 3.1 percent of 18- to 24-year-olds declined to give a reason; and 2.6 percent of 25 and older voters declined to give a reason.

Source: Calculated from U.S. Census Bureau, Current Population Survey, Table 10: Reasons for Not Voting, by Selected Characteristics: November 2016.

is low. And local governments in which it is difficult for citizens to contact the appropriate official with a service request or complaint are not doing much to facilitate participation. Features like these play an often-unrecognized role in dampening participation. Although participation in politics and government is often considered a civic duty, it is not a costless act, a point that economist Anthony Downs argued more than fifty years ago.[16] It is no wonder that some folks who are reasonably content with the actions of government decide that nonparticipation is a rational use of their time. These **free riders** receive the benefits of government, although they do not participate.

Nonparticipants typically have lower levels of interest in politics and tend to be weakly connected to their communities.[17] In many communities, the media have launched efforts to boost participation in civic life. Television stations convene forums and town meetings on the issues of the day, and local newspapers report the views of ordinary citizens on current events. Called public or civic journalism, the idea is to reconnect people with the democratic process and, in doing so, to make them active participants in public life. This is just one effort at restoring some of the **social capital** that Putnam found lacking in contemporary communities. In the language of Figure 4.1, greater social capital leads to more constructive forms of citizen participation.

free rider
A person who enjoys the benefit of a public good without bearing the cost.

social capital
A dense network of reciprocal social relations that promotes greater civic engagement.

The Struggle for the Right to Vote

State constitutions in the eighteenth and early nineteenth centuries entrusted only propertied white males with the vote. They did not encourage public involvement in government, and the eventual softening of restrictions on suffrage did not occur without a struggle. Restrictions based on property ownership and wealth were eventually dropped, but women, blacks, and Native Americans were still denied the right to vote.

In an effort to attract women to its rugged territory, Wyoming enfranchised women in 1869. The suffragists—women who were actively fighting for the right to vote—scored a victory when Colorado extended the vote to women in 1893. Gradually, other states began enfranchising women, and in 1920 the Nineteenth Amendment to the U.S. Constitution, forbidding states to deny the right to vote "on account of sex," was ratified.

Even after the Fifteenth Amendment (1870) extended the vote to blacks, some southern states clung defiantly to traditional ways that denied blacks and poor people their rights. Poll taxes, literacy tests, and white primaries were among the barriers erected by the segregationists. U.S. Supreme Court decisions such as *Smith v. Allwright* (1944), which outlawed white primaries, and federal actions such as the Civil Rights Act of 1964 and the Twenty-Fourth Amendment (1964), which made poll taxes unconstitutional, helped blacks gain access to the polls. But in some jurisdictions, informal methods designed to discourage participation by African Americans continued.

The **Voting Rights Act of 1965** (VRA) finally broke the back of the segregationists' efforts. Under its provisions, federal poll watchers and registrars were dispatched to particular counties to investigate voter discrimination. Counties covered under the Voting Rights Act (all of nine southern states and parts of seven other states) had to submit to the U.S. Department of Justice any changes in election laws, such as new precinct lines or new polling places, well in advance of the election. This was known as the *preclearance* provision. During the ensuing decades, Congress revised and extended the VRA several times. One of the most important modifications of the law was to substitute an effects test for the original intent test. In other words, if a governmental action has the effect of discouraging minority voting, whether intentionally or not, the action must be rejected. Civil rights activists welcomed this change because proving the intent of an action is much more difficult than demonstrating its effect. A dramatic change occurred in 2013 when the U.S. Supreme Court, arguing that times had changed, ruled that the formula used to determine which jurisdictions were covered under the VRA was flawed, thereby eliminating the preclearance requirement.[18]

Voting Patterns

Voter turnout is affected by several things. First, it varies according to the type of election. A presidential race usually attracts a higher proportion of eligible voters than a state or local election does. In 2020, with a presidential race under way, turnout was approximately 62 percent of the **voting-age population** (VAP); in 2018, when there was no presidential election on the ballot—but many governors' races—turnout was only 42 percent. Second, popular candidates running a close race seem to increase voter interest. When each candidate has a chance to win, voters sense that their vote will matter more than in a race with a sure winner. Third, not only partisan competition but also party ideology affects voter turnout.[19] When candidates take

Voting Rights Act of 1965
The law that effectively enfranchised racial minorities by giving the national government the power to decide whether individuals are qualified to vote and to intercede in state and local electoral operations when necessary.

voting-age population
Adults 18 years of age and older.

LO 4-2
To compare state differences in election administration, voter turnout, and election results.

distinctive ideological stances in competitive elections, the incentive for party-identifiers to vote increases. Finally, based on new research, it appears that media handwringing about low-voter turnout may have a quite unintended effect: rather than stimulating turnout, it may actually depress it.[20]

Nationally, voter registration stands at approximately 76 percent of the voting-age population. Not everyone who is of voting age is actually eligible to vote, however. Noncitizens cannot vote (although they can in school board elections in a few localities), and most states have laws barring the mentally incompetent and some convicted felons from participating. When the ineligible population was removed from consideration, turnout among the **voting-eligible population (VEP)** stood at approximately 50 percent in 2018 and 67 percent in 2020. The voting-age population for each state is reported by the U.S. Census; the voting-eligible population must be calculated from those census numbers. The difference between reported turnout for the voter-age population and voter-eligible population in the 2020 presidential election for the United States as a whole was about 4.7 percentage points. But that difference varied widely by state—it was 9.8 percentage points in California, 9.1 percentage points in Texas, and over 8.0 in New Jersey and Florida. At the other end of the spectrum, West Virginia, Montana and Maine had only about a one percentage point difference between VAP and VEP turnout.[21]

Registering to vote has gotten easier. Passage of the National Voter Registration Act in 1993 means that individuals can register to vote when they apply for a driver's license, welfare benefits, or unemployment compensation or when they register their automobile. Oregon has taken it a step further by automatically registering people using drivers' license data collected at the Department of Motor Vehicles. (There is an opt-out option.) States allow voters to register by mail, and more than twenty-five states, such as Indiana and Nevada, have taken another step by allowing online voter registration; any computer terminal with an internet connection can be a registration site. Washington has pioneered registration via Facebook in a bid to attract younger voters. And many states have moved the closing date for registration nearer to the actual date of the election, giving potential voters more time to register. This factor is important because campaigns tend to heighten the public's interest in the election.[22] Most states now close their registration books fewer than thirty days before an election, and seventeen states allow registration on Election Day.[23] Allowing voters to register on Election Day has been shown to be an important way to increase turnout.[24] North Dakota is the only state in the nation that does not require voter registration. Thirty-one states allow voters to declare a party affiliation when they register to vote; in the other nineteen states voters simply register without indicating a party preference.

voting-eligible population
The voting-age population excluding those who are noncitizens, and depending on a state's law, convicted felons or the mentally incompetent.

States can be differentiated according to voter turnout rates (see Figure 4.2 for VEP turnout levels in 2020). In 2020, nine states, led by Maine and Minnesota where turnout reached nearly 80 percent, had estimated turnout rates of more than 75 percent of those eligible. Garnering the dubious distinction of being the states with the lowest voter turnout in 2020 were Oklahoma (55.3 percent), Arkansas (56.1 percent), West Virginia (57 percent), Hawaii

? It's Your Turn

Voter ID Laws: Good or Bad Idea?

Voter ID laws, enacted in some thirty-five states since 2006, require voters to show a government-issued photo ID card at the polling place before voting.

These laws have caused much debate. What do you think?

PROS	CONS
Every fraudulent vote cast dilutes the integrity of all the other votes cast.	The occurrence of voter fraud is very low. Few instances of voter fraud that a voter ID law could have prevented have been reported since 2000.
Elections are the bedrock of democracy. Therefore, they deserve the highest protections that we can achieve.	Voter ID laws disproportionately affect older, poorer, and minority populations, and are therefore discriminatory.
Many other activities require providing identification, such as owning a firearm or driving a car. Voting should be no different.	Voting is one of the core rights that we have as citizens; therefore, the burden should be on the government to prove fraud rather than on the citizen to prove innocence.
Many states offer free state identification cards so there is no financial cost to the person who gets the card.	

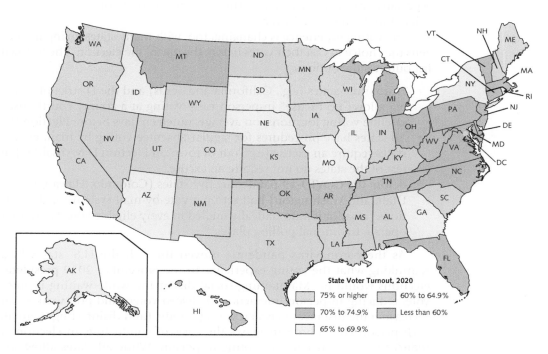

State Voter Turnout, 2020

- 75% or higher
- 70% to 74.9%
- 65% to 69.9%
- 60% to 64.9%
- Less than 60%

Figure 4.2 Estimated State Voter Turnout, 2020

Source: 2020 November General Election Turnout Rates, United States Elections Project, www.electproject.org/2020g (November 4, 2020).

(57.5 percent), and Tennessee (59.7 percent), and Mississipi (60.4 percent).[25] Nationally, estimated turnout in the 2020 presidential election was 66.4 percent of those eligible to vote—a figure that was higher than any presidential election since 1900. States with moralistic political cultures typically experience higher voter turnout than do states with traditionalistic political cultures. States with competitive political parties (as opposed to states where one party dominates) tend to have elections with a higher proportion of voters participating; each party needs to mobilize individuals who identify with it in order to win. When parties and other political organizations reach out to the public, participation in state politics increases.[26] Studies have shown that sending "remember to vote tomorrow" text messages can boost turnout; so can thanking voters for having voted in a previous election.[27]

States can affect turnout by the way in which they administer the registration and election processes. Is voting a convenient exercise, or is it an arduous task marked by long lines at the polling places, a requirement to show photo identification, and confusing ballots inside the voting booth? For instance, when Los Angeles County consolidated voting precincts and changed polling locations in an effort to cut administrative costs, turnout dropped by three percentage points.[28] Voter ID laws, enacted in several states, beginning with Indiana in 2006, require voters to show a government-issued photo ID card at the polling place. This has caused much debate: Supporters contend the laws will reduce fraud, whereas opponents expect the laws to reduce turnout, especially among poor voters.[29] The pros and cons of voter ID laws are considered in the It's Your Turn box.

The voting experience is changing, too, with many states giving their citizens the choice to cast their votes before the day of the election. The following list outlines the options:

- Thirty-nine states (e.g., California and Texas) and the District of Columbia allow "no-excuse" in-person early voting at a county courthouse or satellite voting locations, on average, nineteen days before Election Day.
- All states have procedures for regular absentee voting by mail; eighteen states require an excuse (e.g., out of town on Election Day, disabled), the rest of the states do not require an excuse.
- Before the COVID-19 pandemic, five states (Colorado, Hawaii, Oregon, Utah, and Washington) had set up a vote-by-mail system for their elections (a ballot is automatically mailed to every eligible voter) and do not operate traditional polling places.[30]

As the coronavirus pandemic moved through the U.S. states began rethinking what the voting experience in the November 2020 presidential elections would be. Maintaining social distancing while waiting in line to vote, reducing in-person interactions between voters and poll workers, and increasing the distances between voting booths (and disinfecting them after each person votes) both increases the costs of conducting an election and reduces the attractiveness of voting in person. While all states allow some form of absentee balloting by mail, proposals were actively being considered in many states to conduct all balloting by mail. In May 2020, Michigan and Nevada adopted vote-by-mail plans that resembled those already in use by the five states noted above. The main difference between the traditional absentee voting by mail and the new 100 percent mail balloting are:[31]

- In the traditional absentee vote-by-mail systems, the voter requests a ballot from the board of elections. In some states the voter must supply an excuse for why they will not be able to vote in person. The ballot is sent to the voter who fills it out and mails it back to the board of elections by Election Day. In sixteen states, the return mailing is prepaid; in the other thirty-four the voter must pay for postage. In some states the absentee ballot must be endorsed by one or more witnesses or the ballot must be signed by a notary.
- In the newer vote-by-mail systems, the local board of elections sends ballots (or in some states requests for absentee ballots) to the address at which voters are registered. The ballots contain a prepaid return envelope. The voter fills out the ballot and sends it back to the board of elections by Election Day.

Mailed-in ballots often require two envelopes. The marked ballot is sealed in the first un-addressed envelope which is then sealed in a second pre-addressed envelope. This allows the board of elections to record the voter as having voted without seeing who the person voted for. For states to make the transition to a complete vote-by-mail system in November 2020, decisions on implementation needed to be made in summer 2020.

Vote-by-mail is not noncontroversial. In the spring and summer of 2020, as various states began to consider moving to vote-by-mail systems for the November elections, concerns arose about ballot security, postal system adequacy, partisanship, and federalism.

Those worried about ballot security cite the example of a 2018 scandal in North Carolina's 9th Congressional District. In that election, mailed-in absentee ballots were apparently completed or collected by people other than the voters themselves. The results seemed so odd in several areas of the district that the election was not certified by the state Board of Elections which required a redo later in the year.

Concerns about the U.S. Postal Service's ability to handle election mail became an issue related to the financial deficit the Postal Service was running in 2020—$19.4 billion in the January–March quarter. The Postal Service asked Congress for a $75 billion dollar bailout to allow them to continue delivering mail past September when it would run short in operating funds, but congressional action had not occurred by summer 2020. Vermont Secretary of State Jim Condos was quoted on this, "Mid-election year is not the time to risk the dependability of the Postal Service."[32]

Last are the issues of federalism and partisanship. Republican leaders generally oppose vote-by-mail systems because they believe they favor Democrats. President Trump tweeted, "Republicans should vote very hard when it comes to statewide mail-in voting. Democrats are clamoring for it. Tremendous potential for voter fraud, and for whatever reason, doesn't work out well for Republicans."[33] Congress is split on the issue with the Democratic controlled House of Representatives willing to issue grants to states to make it easier for them to convert to all-mail voting and the Republican controlled Senate unwilling to take up the issue. Senate Majority Leader Mitch McConnell of Kentucky said, "The [House] bill . . . tries to use the virus as cover to implement sweeping changes to election laws that Democrats have wanted for years,"[34] and "The federal government is not going to take over how we do elections. They are done at the state and local level and every state is different. They're fully capable of doing that, as they have been for many years."[35] Meanwhile, President Trump threatened to withhold federal funds from Michigan and Nevada if they went ahead with their vote-by-mail programs, Interestingly, the secretary of state (responsible for election administration) in Michigan is a Democrat but that office is occupied by a Republican in Nevada.[36]

Does making voting easier really matter? The findings of research on conveniently located Election Day vote centers—alternatives to precinct-based polling places—suggest that it does, especially among people who tend to be infrequent voters.[37] Moreover, analysis of Oregon's vote-by-mail system showed that the turnout rate increased in some types of elections.[38] More voters are choosing to cast their ballots early, upward of 60 percent in some states. More than 39 million Americans voted early in the 2018 midterm elections, 2.3 million more than the 2014 midterm elections.[39] As more states loosen the restrictions on early voting, the notion of Election Day is gradually giving way to Election Season.

LO 4-3
To differentiate primary election types, general elections, and nonpartisan elections.

Elections

Elections are central to a representative democracy. Voters choose governors and legislators, and in most states, lieutenant governors, attorneys general, secretaries of state, and state treasurers. In some states, they also choose the heads of the agriculture and education departments, judges, and the public utility commissioners. At the local level, the list of elected officials includes mayors and council members, county commissioners, county judges, sheriffs, tax assessors, and school board members. If state and local governments are to function effectively, elections must provide talented, capable leaders. But elections are not just about outcomes; they are also about the process itself. Florida's troubles with ballot design, voting machines, and recount rules in the 2000 presidential election underscored the need for elections to be administered fairly and transparently.

Significant changes in election management and especially in voting technology have occurred during the past few years. Lever-operated voting machines and punch card devices have lost favor, whereas electronic voting machines and optical scan ballots are being used more widely. This is an important trend, because improvements in voting technology have been shown to lead to a significant decline in the number of "lost" or uncounted votes, which are referred to as **residual votes**.[40] Although electronic voting

residual votes
The number of uncounted, unmarked, or spoiled ballots in an election.

machines (akin to automatic teller machines) are becoming more popular, concerns over their accuracy and security remain. At issue is whether these systems should provide a VVPAT, or voter-verified paper audit trail, to supplement the record of the count in the electronic machine's memory.

Primaries

For a party to choose a nominee for the general-election ballot, potential candidates must be winnowed. In the pre-Jacksonian era, party nominees were chosen by a legislative caucus—that is, a conference of the party's legislators. Caucuses gave way to the mechanism of state party conventions, which were similar to national presidential nomination conventions but without most of the spectacle; popularly elected delegates from across a state convened to select the party's nominees. Then the Progressive movement made an effort to open up the nomination process and make it more democratic. Political parties adopted the **primary system**, whereby voters directly choose from among several candidates to select the party's nominees for the general election. The use of primaries has effectively diminished the organizational power of political parties.

Several states still allow for party conventions in particular instances, such as nominations for secretary of state and attorney general (Michigan) and selection of a slate of nominees by third parties (Kansas). Connecticut, the last state to adopt primaries, operates a unique challenge system whereby party nominees for various state offices are selected at a convention; but if a contest develops at the convention and a second candidate receives as much as 15 percent of the votes, the convention's nominee and the challenger square off in a primary.[41]

Primary Types Primaries can be divided into two types: closed and open. The only voters who can participate in a closed primary for a particular party are those who are registered in that party; an open primary does not require party registration. Even this basic distinction, however, lends itself to some variation. States differ, for example, in the ease with which voters can change party affiliation and participate in the closed primary of the other party. In nine **fully closed primary** states, a voter is a person who registered as a member of one party and can change that affiliation only well in advance of the primary election date. Registered Democrats vote in the Democratic Party primary; registered Republicans vote in the GOP primary. In another seven **partially closed primary** states, unaffiliated voters can vote in either the Democratic or Republican primary (but not in both!) along with party registrants if the parties choose to allow them to do so. Thirty states operate some variation on open primaries. Fifteen of those states operate **fully open primaries** in which voters choose in which primary they want to participate in the privacy of the voting booth. In the other fifteen open primary states, voters must publicly state in which party primary they intend to participate. These last fifteen states can be divided according to how easy or difficult they make it for voters to change their party affiliation or to vote in other parties'

primary system The electoral mechanism for selecting party nominees to compete in the general election.

fully closed primary A primary in which only voters registered in the party are allowed to participate.

partially closed primary A primary in which unaffiliated voters and registered party voters can participate.

fully open primary A primary in which all voters choose, in the privacy of the voting booth, which primary they participate in.

partially open primary A primary in which voters must publicly declare their voting choice in order to vote in that party's primary.

open to unaffiliated voters A primary in which unaffiliated voters can vote in whichever primary they want but voters registered with a party cannot vote in another party's primary.

primaries In the six states that operate **partially open primaries**, voters can choose which primary they want to vote in, but the choice must be made publicly or the choice is recorded as a party registration. In the last variation—primaries **open to unaffiliated voters**—voters in nine states who are registered with a party can only vote in that party's primary but unaffiliated voters can choose to vote in whichever primary they like.[42] Table 4.2 groups the states by the types of primaries they operate.

Louisiana and three other states do something completely different: they use a single primary for state and congressional races. Candidates, regardless of party affiliation, appear on the same ballot, and voters are free to choose from among them. If a candidate receives a majority of votes in the first round of voting, they are elected to office; if they do not, the top two vote-getters face each other in a **runoff election**. In 2010, California voters, dissatisfied with the level of partisan rancor in the Golden State, approved a constitutional amendment that provided a similar **top-two primary** system there, starting with the 2012 elections. Washington, which historically had allowed voters to cross over

Table 4.2 State Use of Different Types of Primary Elections

CLOSED		OPEN			
FULLY CLOSED	**PARTIALLY CLOSED**	**PARTIALLY OPEN**	**OPEN TO UNAFFILIATED VOTERS**	**FULLY OPEN**	**TOP-TWO**
Delaware	Alaska	Illinois	Arizona	Alabama	California
Florida	Connecticut	Indiana	Colorado	Arkansas	Louisiana
Kentucky	Idaho	Iowa	Kansas	Georgia	Nebraska
Maryland	North Carolina	Ohio	Maine	Hawaii	Washington
Nevada	Oklahoma	Tennessee	Massachusetts	Michigan	
New Mexico	South Dakota	Wyoming	New Hampshire	Minnesota	
New York	Utah		New Jersey	Mississippi	
Oregon			Rhode Island	Missouri	
Pennsylvania			West Virginia	Montana	
				North Dakota	
				South Carolina	
				Texas	
				Vermont	
				Virginia	
				Wisconsin	
(9)	(7)	(6)	(9)	(15)	(4)

Source: "State Primary Election Types: National Conference of State Legislatures," www.ncsl.org/research/elections-and-campaigns/primary-types.aspx (June 26, 2018).

from one party to another in a single election, adopted its own variation on the top-two primary scheme. Finally, Nebraska uses a top-two primary for its non-partisan legislative races. These top-two primaries sometimes result in general elections with two candidates of the same party running against each other. For example, in the May 2018 U.S. Senate top-two primary in California, incumbent Democratic Senator Dianne Feinstein finished first of six candidates on the ballot, but second place went to Democrat Kevin de León (nobody received a majority of the vote). So the two Democrats ran against each other in the November general election with Feinstein winning reelection.

One of the major reasons for the tremendous variation in types of primaries is state party concerns with exactly who gets to determine who represents the party on the general-election ballot. Closed primaries minimize the possibility that nonparty members participate in that choice. Open primaries give voters more choice to participate in whichever primary they find more interesting; for example, if there were one dominant Republican running in that party's primary, but several competitive Democrats were running, we might expect to see more voters choosing to vote in the Democratic primary rather than the Republican primary. Open primaries however lead to the possibility of raiding—Democrats crossing over to vote for a weak candidate in the Republican primary or vice versa. While there has been much speculation about the threat of raiding in open primaries, there is little empirical evidence that it actually has occurred.[43]

Primary Runoff Elections A runoff election is held in some states if none of the candidates for an office receives a majority of votes in the primary. Primary runoff elections are used by parties in eight states: Alabama, Arkansas, Georgia, Mississippi, North Carolina, Oklahoma, South Carolina, and Texas. (South Dakota uses primary runoffs but only in certain instances; Vermont uses a runoff if there is a tie in the original primary; Florida abolished primary runoffs in 2005, Kentucky in 2008. North Carolina calls its runoff a second primary, required if no candidate receives more than 40 percent of the vote in the first primary.) In the past, most of these states were one-party (Democratic) states, so the greatest amount of competition for an office occurred in the Democratic Party's primaries, in which as many as ten candidates might enter the race. When many candidates compete, it is quite probable that no one will receive a majority of the votes, so the top two vote-getters face each other in a runoff election. This process ensures that the party's nominee is preferred by a majority of the primary voters. For example, after U.S. Representative Walter Jones, Jr., passed away in early 2019, seventeen Republican candidates filed to run for his North Carolina Third Congressional District seat in the April special primary. The top vote-getter in that election, Greg Murphy, garnered some 22.5 percent of the vote while the second-place finisher, Joan Perry, received 15.4 percent; the other fifteen candidates split the remaining 62 percent of the vote. Murphy and Perry then ran against each other in a second primary in July with Murphy beating Perry 60 percent to 40 percent. Murphy went on to win the congressional seat by beating the Democratic candidate Allen Thomas in a September special election.

runoff election
A second election pitting the top two vote-getters from a first election in which no candidate received a majority of the votes cast.

top-two primary
A primary in which all candidates, regardless of party, appear on the ballot. If one candidate wins a majority, they are considered elected. If nobody wins a majority, a runoff election is held between the two top vote getters in the first primary.

Theoretically, the rationale for the runoff primary is majority rule. But political circumstances have changed since several southern states adopted the runoff primary system in the 1920s, and the Democratic Party no longer dominates the region. In fact, the two parties are competitive in some southern states, and in others the Republican Party has overtaken the Democrats. This raises an important question: Has the runoff primary outlived its usefulness? It is often difficult for a party to mobilize its voters for the second election, and voter participation in the runoff drops, on average, by one-third.[44] And they are costly to operate: Kentucky estimated the administrative cost of holding a statewide gubernatorial runoff primary to be approximately $5.4 million.[45] And, of course, a primary runoff campaign can be expensive for candidates themselves. One solution to this problem for parties might be the "ranked choice" or **instant runoff** that a few cities have begun using in their municipal elections. In an instant runoff, voters rank the primary candidates in their order of preference. If no candidate receives a majority of first choices, the candidate with the fewest of them is eliminated and voters who ranked the eliminated candidate first now have their ballots counted for their second choice. The process continues until one candidate has a majority; a runoff election is avoided.

In 2018, Maine became the first state to use ranked choice voting in congressional primaries and general elections. Maine also used ranked choice voting in both congressional and presidential primaries and general elections in 2020. Similar proposals for ranked choice voting were rejected by voters in Alaska and Massachusetts in 2020.

General Elections

Primaries culminate in the general election, through which winning candidates become officeholders. When the general election pits candidates of the two major parties against one another, the winner is the candidate who receives a majority of the votes cast. In a race in which more than two candidates compete (which occurs when an Independent or a third-party candidate enters a race), the winner may not receive a majority but instead receives a **plurality**. Seven states allow candidates to run under the label of more than one party, which is called **fusion**. In the 2018 New York governor's race, for instance, Andrew Cuomo was the candidate for governor of the Democratic, Working Families, Women's Equality, and Independence parties, whereas his major opponent, Marc Molinaro, was the candidate of the Republican, Conservative, and Reform parties.

Political parties have traditionally been active in general elections, mobilizing voters in support of their candidates. Their role has diminished over time, however, because general-election campaigns have become more candidate-centered and geared to the candidate's own organization. One new twist in the past two decades has been the emergence of legislative party caucuses as major factors in general elections. In large states with professionalized legislatures, the funds distributed to their party's nominees by legislative party caucuses run into the millions of dollars. In addition to funding,

instant runoff Voters use preference rankings to select candidates at a single election.

plurality The number of votes (though not necessarily a majority) cast for the winning candidate in an election with more than two candidates.

fusion A state election provision that allows candidates to run on more than one party ticket.

legislative party caucuses provide other types of election assistance, such as seminars on issues and campaign management, making these organizations powerful players in some states' politics.

Most states schedule their gubernatorial elections in off years, that is, in years in which no presidential election is held. Only eleven states normally elect governors during presidential election years (in 2016, twelve did, because Oregon held a special election to replace John Kitzhaber who resigned in February 2015); thirty-six states hold statewide races in even-numbered nonpresidential years, whereas five states (Kentucky, Louisiana, Mississippi, New Jersey, and Virginia) hold their gubernatorial elections in odd-numbered years. (The number sums to fifty-two because New Hampshire and Vermont limit elected governors to two-year terms, thereby holding gubernatorial elections in both off and on years.) Off-year elections prevent the presidential race from diverting attention from state races while minimizing the possible **coattail effect**, by which a presidential candidate can affect the fortunes of state candidates of the same party. By holding elections in off years, races for governor may serve instead as referenda on the sitting president's performance in office. Generally, however, the health of a state's economy tends to be a critical issue in guber-natorial elections.[46]

Recent State Elections

State elections in 2017 were limited to gubernatorial and legislative races in New Jersey and Virginia; Democrats won the governorship in both states. Only 220 state legislative seats were at stake in 2017. In New Jersey, Democrats continued to hold 60 percent of the seats in both chambers. In Virginia, Republicans lost fifteen seats but maintained control of the House of Delegates by fifty-one to forty-nine. One race in the Newport News, Virginia, area resulted in a dead heat. Both candidates received 11,608 votes. So, on January 10, 2018, according to Virginia state law, the election was decided when Republican David Yancey's name was randomly selected from a ceramic bowl containing his name and the name of Shelley Simonds, the Democratic candidate.[47]

The stakes were high in 2018, with thirty-six governors' seats, 6,073 state legislative seats in forty-six states, and 303 statewide executive branch offices up for election. In the governors' races, Republicans won twenty seats and Democrats sixteen, for a net Democratic gain of seven governorships. As of 2019, the partisan composition of America's governors was twenty-seven Republicans and twenty-three Democrats.

In state legislatures, the 2018 elections were favorable to the Democrats, with a net increase of some 308 seats. Of course, what really matters is how gains or losses play out at the state level. Before the 2018 elections, Republicans controlled sixty-five state legislative chambers and Democrats thirty-one (two were tied); after the 2018 elections, Republicans controlled sixty-one and Democrats thirty-seven.[48] (The total is ninety-eight chambers in forty-nine states because Nebraska's unicameral legislature is officially nonpartisan.)

coattail effect
The tendency of a winning (or losing) presidential candidate to carry state candidates of the same party into (or out of) office.

In 2019, four states held legislative elections; Republicans retained control of both houses of the state legislature in Louisiana and Mississippi; Democrats retained control of the lower house of state legislature. In Virginia Democrats took control of both houses of the state legislature for the first time since 1993. Three states also conducted gubernatorial elections. The Democratic governor of Louisiana was reelected; a Republican was also elected to replace the term-limited Republican governor of Mississippi. In Kentucky, the Democratic candidate for governor—Andy Beshear—beat the Republican incumbent—Matt Bevin—by about 5,000 votes out of some 1.4 million cast. After the 2019 elections, Republicans controlled fifty-nine state houses and Democrats thirty-nine; there were also twenty-six Republican governors and twenty-four Democratic governors.

In 2020, Republicans won eight governorships, Democrats three. Beginning 2021, there were twenty-seven Republican governors and twenty-three Democrats. Montana flipped from Democratic to Republican. Only two state houses flipped—the New Hampshire house and senate changed from Democratic to Republican majorities.

Nonpartisan Elections

A **nonpartisan election** removes the political party identification from the candidate in an effort to make campaigns and elections less partisan. Elections that have been made nonpartisan include those for many judicial offices and for many local-level positions. The special task of judges—adjudicating guilt or innocence, determining right and wrong—does not lend itself to partisan interpretation. The job of local governments—delivering public services—has also traditionally been considered nonideological. Nonpartisan local elections are likely to be found in municipalities and in school districts and special districts. Although approximately three-quarters of cities use nonpartisan elections, some regional variation exists in their usage. The prevalence of nonpartisanship is somewhat lower in the Northeast and Midwest than it is in western cities.[49]

Most studies have concluded that nonpartisanship depresses turnout in municipal elections that are held independent of state and national elections. The figures are not dramatic, but in what are already low-turnout elections, the difference can run as high as 10 percent of municipal voters.[50] Studies have shown that lower turnout results in lessened representation of Latinos and Asian Americans on city councils and in the mayor's office.[51] Nonpartisan elections seem to produce a city council that is somewhat well-to-do by socioeconomic standards and a greater number of officeholders who consider themselves Republicans.[52]

What does it take to get elected? In the absence of political parties, candidates are forced to create their own organizations to run for office. They raise and spend money (much of it their own), and they seek the support of business and citizen groups. Money matters, and according to studies of city elections in Atlanta and St. Louis, so do incumbency and newspaper endorsements.[53] In some communities, **slating groups** function as unofficial parties by recruiting candidates and financing their campaigns; citizens' groups can also be an important factor in local elections.[54]

nonpartisan election
An election without party labels.

slating groups
Nonpartisan political organizations that endorse and promote a slate of candidates.

Direct Democracy

What happens when the government does not respond to the messages that the people are sending? More and more frequently, the answer is to transform the messages into ballot propositions and let the citizens make their own laws. The **Initiative** is a proposed law or constitutional amendment that is placed on the ballot by citizen petition to be approved or rejected by popular vote. An initiative lets citizens enact their own laws, bypassing the state legislature. This mechanism for legislation by popular vote was one of several reforms of the Progressive era, which lasted roughly from 1890 to 1920.

Other Progressive reforms included the popular referendum and the recall. The **popular referendum** allows citizens to petition to vote on actions taken by legislative bodies. It provides a means by which the public can overturn a legislative enactment. (A popular referendum is different from a general **referendum**—a proposition put on the ballot by the legislature that requires voter approval before it can take effect. Constitutional amendments and bond issues are examples of general referenda.) The **recall** election, another citizen-initiated process, requires elected officials to stand for a vote on their removal before their term has expired. Recall provides the public with an opportunity to force an official out of office.

The key characteristic shared by initiative, popular referendum, and recall is that they are actions begun by citizens. The Progressives advocated these mechanisms to expand the role of citizens and to restrict the power of intermediary institutions such as legislatures, political parties, and elected officials. Their efforts were particularly successful in the western part of the United States, probably due to the difficulty of amending existing state constitutions in the East and to an elitist fear of the working class (namely, industrialized immigrants in the Northeast and rural black sharecroppers in the South). The newer western states, by contrast, were quite open, both procedurally and socially. In 1898, South Dakota became the first state to adopt the initiative process; the initiative was actually used for the first time in Oregon in 1902 when citizens successfully petitioned for ballot questions on mandatory political party primaries and local option liquor sales. Both of the initiatives were approved.

Today, twenty-four states allow the initiative for constitutional amendments, statutes, or both; Mississippi is the most recent addition, having adopted it in 1992. A few of the twenty-four states use the indirect initiative, which gives the legislature an opportunity to consider the proposed measure. If the legislature fails to act or if it rejects the measure, the proposal is put before the voters at the next election. Popular referendum is provided in twenty-three states, and recall of state officials is provided in nineteen, with Illinois voters the most recent to approve a recall provision in 2010. Table 4.3 compares the states on their direct democracy provisions.

LO 4-4
To identify the pros and cons of the mechanisms of direct democracy.

Initiative
A proposed law or constitutional amendment placed on the ballot by citizen petition.

popular referendum
A special type of referendum whereby citizens can petition to vote on actions taken by legislative bodies.

referendum
A procedure whereby a governing body submits proposed laws, constitutional amendments, or bond issues to the voters for ratification.

recall
A procedure that allows citizens to vote elected officials out of office before their terms have expired.

Table 4.3 Direct Democracy Provisions

STATE	INITIATIVE	POPULAR REFERENDUM	RECALL*
Alabama	No	No	Local
Alaska	Yes	Yes	Yes
Arizona	Yes	Yes	Yes
Arkansas	Yes	Yes	Local
California	Yes	Yes	Yes
Colorado	Yes	Yes	Yes
Connecticut	No	No	No
Delaware	No	No	No
Florida	Yes	No	Local
Georgia	No	No	Yes
Hawaii	No	No	No
Idaho	Yes	Yes	Yes
Illinois	Yes	No	Yes
Indiana	No	No	No
Iowa	No	No	No
Kansas	No	No	Yes
Kentucky	No	No	No
Louisiana	No	No	Yes
Maine	Yes	Yes	No
Maryland	No	Yes	No
Massachusetts	Yes	Yes	No
Michigan	Yes	Yes	Yes
Minnesota	No	No	Yes
Mississippi	Yes	No	No
Missouri	Yes	Yes	Local
Montana	Yes	Yes	Yes
Nebraska	Yes	Yes	Local
Nevada	Yes	Yes	Yes
New Hampshire	No	No	Local
New Jersey	No	No	Yes
New Mexico	No	Yes	Local
New York	No	No	No
North Carolina	No	No	No
North Dakota	Yes	Yes	Yes
Ohio	Yes	Yes	Local

(continued)

Table 4.3 Direct Democracy Provisions (*continued*)

STATE	INITIATIVE	POPULAR REFERENDUM	RECALL*
Oklahoma	Yes	Yes	No
Oregon	Yes	Yes	Yes
Pennsylvania	No	No	No
Rhode Island	No	No	State
South Carolina	No	No	No
South Dakota	Yes	Yes	Local
Tennessee	No	No	Local
Texas	No	No	No
Utah	Yes	Yes	No
Vermont	No	No	No
Virginia	No	No	No
Washington	Yes	Yes	Yes
West Virginia	No	No	Local
Wisconsin	No	No	Yes
Wyoming	Yes	Yes	Local

*"yes" means recall of state and local officials is allowed; "local" means that only certain types of local officials are subject to recall; "state" means only certain types of state officials are subject to recall; "no" signifies that no recall provisions exist.

Sources: "State by State List of Initiative and Referendum Provisions," Initiative & Referendum Institute, www.iandrinstitute.org/states.cfm (accessed January 28, 2019); "Recall of State Officials," National Conference of State Legislatures, www.ncsl.org/research/elections-and-campaigns/recall-of-state-officials.aspx (accessed January 28, 2019); "Recall of Local Officials," National Conference of State Legislatures, www .ncsl.org/research/elections-and-campaigns/recall-of-local-officials.aspx (accessed January 28, 2019).

The Initiative

The first step in the initiative process is the petition. A draft of the proposed law (or constitutional amendment) is circulated along with a petition for citizens to sign. The petition signature requirement varies by state but usually falls between 5 and 10 percent of the number of votes cast in the preceding statewide election. To ensure that a matter is of statewide concern and that signatures have been gathered beyond a single area, some states set geographic distributional requirements. In Montana, for example, signature requirements must be met in at least one-third of the legislative districts and in Nebraska in two-fifths of the counties. Signatures can be gathered by door-to-door canvassing, buttonholing people at shopping malls and sporting events, posting downloadable petition forms on the internet, and sending forms to a preselected list of likely signers.

The Popularity of Initiatives One of the most influential modern initiatives was California's Proposition 13 (1978), which rolled back property taxes in the state and spawned an immediate wave of tax-reduction propositions across the land. The increased popularity of initiatives has at least two explanations: (1) Some observers believe that wavering public confidence in government has led citizens to take matters into their own hands. The attitude seems to be that "if government can't be trusted to do the right thing, we'll do it ourselves." (2) New methods of signature collection have brought the initiative process within the reach of almost any well-financed group with a grievance or concern. An example from Massachusetts makes the point. When then-governor Paul Cellucci could not get the legislature to pass his tax-cut proposals, he took the issue straight to the voters in 2000. Using donations from supporters, he paid a company to collect sufficient signatures on petitions, and he got his issue on the ballot.[55] Massachusetts voters approved it.

Recent Initiatives If ballot questions are any indication of the public's mood, then the public has had quite an attitude lately. There were sixty-two initiatives on the ballot in 2018 (down a bit from the seventy-one in 2016 but up substantially from the numbers in 2010 to 2014); 52 percent of them passed, a slightly better passage rate than the average 41 percent.[56] Following is a sampling of the 2018 initiatives in particular states and the outcomes.

- Alaska: An initiative to establish new requirements on permits that might have impacts on salmon and steelhead habitats (failed)
- Arkansas: An initiative to raise the minimum wage incrementally to $11 an hour by 2021 (passed)
- Florida: An initiative to automatically restore the right to vote for people convicted of felonies, except those convicted of murder or sexual offense, upon completion of their sentence, parole, and probation (passed)
- Michigan: An initiative to legalize the recreational use of marijuana for people 21 years of age or older (passed)
- Washington: An initiative to raise the minimum age to purchase semiautomatic assault-type rifles from 18 to 21 (passed)

A number of initiatives appeared on the 2020 ballot. Some of these include increasing taxes on North Slope oil production in Alaska, expanding the power of local governments to control rents in California, reintroducing gray wolves on public lands in Colorado, and establishing a medical marijuana program in South Dakota.

Questions About the Initiative By resorting to initiatives, citizens can bypass (or, in the case of indirect initiatives, prod) an obstructive legislature. And initiatives can be positive or negative—that is, they can be used in the absence of legislative action or they can be used to repudiate actions taken by the legislature. But is the initiative process appropriate for resolving tough public problems? Seldom are issues so simple that a yes-or-no ballot question can adequately reflect appropriate options and alternatives. A legislative setting, by contrast, fosters the negotiation and compromise that are likely to produce workable solutions.

Is the public sufficiently informed to make intelligent choices or to avoid susceptibility to emotional appeals? Ballot questions are considered low-information elections: Facing little information or conflicting claims, voters respond to readily available cues that may be misleading or erroneous. One interesting experiment showed that putting different titles on the same ballot question—but keeping the wording of the proposal exactly the same—produced very different outcomes in terms of voting "yes" or "no" on that question.[57] Ballot questions are often complicated and confusingly worded. A 2017 study of twenty-seven ballot questions by the popular election-analysis website Ballotpedia concluded that it would take a person with a graduate degree to understand the language in the propositions.[58] For example, a 2018 initiative in Maine asked voters "Do you want to reject the parts of a new law that would delay the use of ranked-choice voting in the election of candidates for state or federal office until 2022, and then retain the method only if the constitution is amended by December 1, 2021, to allow ranked-choice voting for candidates in state elections?" A 2016 seventy-five-word Florida constitutional amendment on solar energy was so complicated that it required two experts on ballot language nearly an hour to figure out what it proposed to do.[59]

Initiatives seem to have positive effects on the electoral process by stimulating more participation, but do ballot initiatives place citizens in an adversarial relationship with their government? Research has found that voters with frequent exposure to ballot questions are more likely to vote, donate money to political campaigns, and feel more politically efficacious.[60] However, amid these salutary effects, ballot initiatives seem to place citizens at loggerheads with government and spur distrust of public officials.[61]

Legislators are of two minds when it comes to direct citizen involvement in policy making. On the one hand, having the public decide a controversial issue such as abortion or school prayer helps legislators out of tight spots. On the other hand, increased citizen lawmaking intrudes on the central function of the legislature and usurps legislative power. Given the popularity of initiatives, legislators must proceed cautiously with actions that would alter the initiative process. In 2014, California revised its initiative law to increase the transparency of initiative campaign contributions, provide more voter-friendly explanations of propositions, allow for legislative review modifications, and pre-identify flaws or errors in proposed initiative language. These changes were aimed at making the initiative process in California work better.[62] After all, citizens in states that have an initiative process value it. A survey of Oregon citizens found 81 percent agreeing with this statement: "Ballot initiatives enhance the democratic process in Oregon by allowing voters to decide important policy issues."[63]

Once an initiative is passed, the new law has to be implemented and, as research has shown, "under normal conditions, legislatures, bureaucrats, or other government officials will work to alter a winning initiative's impact on public policy."[64] Direct democracy enthusiasts should heed the words of political scientist Valentina Bali, who studied local compliance with a California initiative intended to dismantle bilingual education programs: ". . . the large number of constraints suggests that the final policy outcome of an initiative can be quite limited after the initiative's implementation."[65] Initiative sponsors have learned that if they want their initiative to have the desired impact, they have to keep the pressure on, even after the measure has been approved. A good example of this is the 2018 citizen initiated constitutional amendment in Florida to restore the voting rights of convicted felons. While the amendment passed with nearly 65 percent of the vote, Florida Governor Ron DeSantis said actual implementation would require action by the state legislature. In 2019, Governor DeSantis signed into law a bill requiring felons to complete all terms of their sentence including full payment of fines, restitution and other costs before their voting rights were restored.[66] Celebrities such as Michael Bloomberg and Lebron James contributed funds to help pay these fines, allowing up to 13,000 felons to vote in Florida in 2020.

The number and topics of many of the initiatives passed in the 2018 elections have caused some state legislators to reconsider the initiative process in their states. Beginning in 2016 but then accelerating in 2018 and 2019, state legislatures have debated several different measures changing how signatures on initiative petitions are collected, the timing for when initiatives can be submitted for placement on the ballot, and the percentage of the vote that initiatives must garner to be approved. For example, Michigan recently passed legislation requiring ballot initiative signatures to come from a larger geographic area of the state rather than from one or two congressional districts, and both Florida and Missouri are considering changing the threshold for adoption of ballot measures to 66 percent.[67]

The Recall

Recalls were once a little-used mechanism in state and local governments. Only nineteen states provide for recall of state officials, and in seven of them, judicial officers are exempt. City and county government charters, even in states without recall provisions, often include a process for recalling local elected officials. In fact, the first known recall was aimed at a Los Angeles city council member in 1904. Recalls have a much higher petition signature requirement than initiatives do; it is common to require a signature minimum of 25 percent of the votes cast in the last election for the office of the official sought to be recalled. Kansas, for example, requires a 40 percent minimum.

Recall efforts usually involve a public perception of official misconduct. On occasion, however, simply running afoul of citizen preferences is enough to trigger a recall, as former California governor Gray Davis discovered in 2003. Californians unhappy with Davis's leadership in resolving the state's budget crunch and its problems with energy deregulation, collected sufficient signatures (a total of 986,874) to force a recall election. Governor Davis was recalled from office by a 55 to 45 percent margin. What can only be described as "recall fever" hit Wisconsin as nine state senators (six Republicans and three Democrats) faced recall elections in 2011 as a result of controversy surrounding Governor Scott Walker's efforts to eliminate most collective bargaining for public employees. Two Republican senators who had supported the governor's proposal in the legislature were recalled from office. And, in 2012, as public discontent continued, recall elections were held for governor, lieutenant governor, and four Republican state senators in the Badger State. Except for one state senator, these officials survived their recall elections and continued in office.

The rationale for the recall process is straightforward: Public officials should be subject to continuous voter control. The power to recall elected officials is valued by the public. But it can be a costly process, not only for the groups organizing the recall petition process and for the candidates but also for state and local government. Wisconsin estimated the price tag for the nine state senate recall elections it held in 2011 at about $2.1 million, with the statewide gubernatorial recall election in 2012 costing taxpayers an estimated $13 million.[68] Initiatives and recalls have helped open up state and local governments to the public. Yet, ironically, increased citizen participation can also jam the machinery of government, thus making its operation more cumbersome. Advocates of greater citizen activism, however, would gladly trade a little efficiency to achieve their goals.

Citizen Access to Government

As we saw in Figure 4.1, citizens have opportunities to participate in government in many nonelectoral ways. Because state and local governments have undertaken extensive measures to open themselves to public scrutiny and stimulate public input, citizen access to government has been increased. Many of these measures are directly connected with the policy-making process. At a minimum, they enable government and the citizenry to exchange information, and thus they contribute to the growing capacity of state and local governments. At most, they may alter political power patterns and resource allocations. Participatory budgeting, the subject of the Controversies in States and Localities box, describes the efforts of one California city to engage its residents in determining which projects and activities should receive city funds.

Opening Up Government

Many of the accessibility measures adopted by state and local governments are the direct result of public demands that government be more accountable. Others have resulted from an official effort to involve the public in the ongoing work of government.

Open Meeting Laws Florida's 1967 Sunshine Law is credited with sparking a surge of interest in openness in government, and today **open meeting laws** are on the books in all fifty states. These laws do just what the name implies: They open meetings of government bodies to the public, or, in Florida's parlance, they bring government "into the sunshine." Open meeting laws apply to both the state and local levels and affect the executive branch as well as the legislative branch. Basic open meeting laws have been supplemented by additional requirements in many states. Advance public notice of meetings is required in all states; most keep minutes, levy penalties against officials who violate the law, and void actions taken in meetings held contrary to sunshine provisions.

Although some states might prefer to resist the sun's rays, the trend is toward more openness. But this is complicated by the fact that most states' sunshine laws were written for a world of paper-based records stored in metal filing cabinets. Colorado was one of the first states to make the archived e-mail files of the state's politicians open to the public. Now, forty states make governmental e-mails subject to their open-records laws, and twelve states treat text messages the same way.[69] Figure 4.3 lists states' transparency grades

open meeting laws
Statutes that open the meetings of government bodies to the public.

Controversies in States and Localities

Participatory Budgeting: Letting the Public Decide How to Spend Public Money

Vallejo, California, a city of 117,000 people near San Francisco, got serious about citizen participation when it adopted a participatory budgeting process for the 2013 budget cycle. Participatory budgeting (PB) directly involves residents in deciding how public funds should be spent. The process is far more participatory than simply showing up at a meeting or two and making the case for building a new library or hiring more firefighters. In PB, citizens decide the rules for the process and identify an array of spending ideas through a series of budget assemblies; a steering committee then winnows the ideas into a set of viable options and places them on a ballot for a vote.

In Vallejo, $3.2 million was made available for PB, which was a portion of the revenue generated by an increase in the sales tax. Of the 800 ideas initially generated, thirty-three of them made it to the ballot and, of them, twelve were funded. Any resident who was 16 or older could vote for as many as six projects; about 3,600 residents voted. The three projects receiving the most votes were pothole and street repair ($550,000), street light installation ($170,000), and park improvements ($621,500). Voters also approved funding the purchase of science, art, and math equipment for the schools; the development of community gardens; a series of grants to small businesses; installation of security cameras around the city; and renovations at a local Boys & Girls Club facility, among others.

In 2020, Vallejo was in its eighth year of PB. It has experienced a few bumps along the way. Some of the folks who have been involved in PB have found the process time-consuming and frustrating. And it can be difficult to draw other residents into the process, so participation has remained relatively low, even though the city has lowered the minimum age for participation to 14. Some members of the city council have become a bit skeptical of PB, contending that as the elected representatives of the public, they are ones who should be making spending decisions. Moreover, the amount of revenue to be allocated via the PB process has been reduced, thereby limiting its impact. Still, to PB's avid proponents in the city and beyond, it holds tremendous promise as a tool to spur civic engagement and restore public trust in government.

Critical Thinking Questions

1. Budget experts spend years in school to learn how to prepare a budget. Do citizens have adequate information to make budgeting decisions?

2. Vallejo committed $3.2 million to PB the first year that it was implemented, but has since dropped that figure to $1 million. How much of the budget should be subject to this process?

3. The city of Vallejo estimates that it costs $300,000 to administer the program. Do the administrative costs justify the increased citizen participation?

4. Cities like New York City, Chicago, San Francisco, and St. Louis have experimented with PB as a way to determine public spending preferences in some of their city council districts. Would PB work better on a less-than-citywide basis?

Sources: Alana Semuels, "The City That Gave Its Residents $3 Million," *The Atlantic*, www.theatlantic.com/business /archive/2014/11/the-city-that-gave-its-residents-3-million /382348/ (accessed January 29, 2019); John M. Kamensky, "When Citizens Decide How Public Money Is Spent," www.governing .com/blogs/bfc/col-neighborhood-participatory-budgeting -ibm-center-business-government-report.html (accessed January 29, 2019).

Chip Chipman/Bloomberg/Getty Images

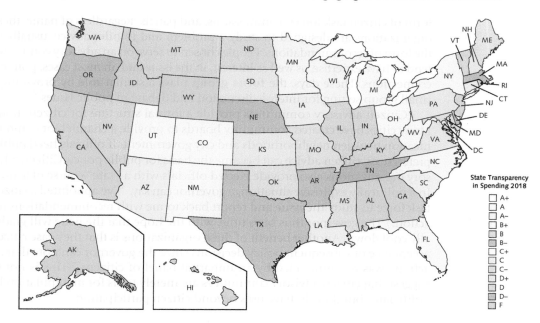

Figure 4.3 State Transparency in Spending Data

Source: U.S. PIRG, "Following the Money 2018: How the 50 States Rate in Providing Online Access to Government Spending Data," www
.uspirgedfund.org/sites/pirg/files/reports/FtM%20NATIONAL%20FINAL%20VERSION_0.pdf (April 2018).

from a study done by U.S. Public Interest Research Group.[70] The scores reflect
how well states do in providing online access to government spending data.
The states earning A's are performing substantially better at opening up
government to public scrutiny than the states with D's and F's.

Administrative Procedure Acts After state legislation is passed or a local
ordinance is adopted, an administrative agency typically is responsible for
implementation. This process involves the establishment of rules and
regulations and hence constitutes powerful responsibility. In practice, agencies
often have wide latitude in translating legislative intent into action. For
example, if a new state law creates annual automobile safety inspections, it is
the responsibility of the state's Department of Motor Vehicles to make it work.
Unless the law specifies the details, bureaucrats will determine the items to be
covered in the safety inspection, the location of inspection stations, and the
fee to be charged. These details are just as important as the original enactment.

To ensure public access to this critical rule-making process, states have
adopted **administrative procedure acts**, which require public notice of the
proposed rule and an opportunity for citizen comment. All states provide for
this "notification and comment" process, as it is known. These provisions
offer the public and various political actors a way to influence the content of
agency rules.[71] In addition, some states give citizens the right to petition an
administrative agency for an adjustment in the rules.

Advisory Committees Another arena for citizen participation that is popular
in states and especially local governments is the **advisory committee**, in the

**administrative
procedure acts**
Acts that standardize
administrative agency
operations as a means
of safeguarding clients
and the general public.

advisory committee
An organization
created by
government to
involve members of
the public in studying
and recommending
solutions to public
problems.

form of citizen task forces, commissions, and panels. Regardless of name, these organizations are designed to study a problem and to offer advice, usually in the form of recommendations. People chosen to serve on an advisory committee tend to have expertise, as well as interest, in the issue and, in most cases, political connections. These days, the **focus group** plays a similar role by providing a small group setting for intense discussion and debate of public issues.[72]

Citizen advisory committees provide a formal structure for citizen input. Many cities have created community boards to provide a channel for communication between neighborhoods and city government. If officials heed public preferences, citizen advice can become the basis for public policy. Citizen advisory organizations also provide elected officials with a "safe" course of action. In a politically explosive situation, a governor can say, "I've appointed a citizen task force to study the issue and report back to me with recommendations for action." The governor thus buys time, with the hope that the issue will gradually cool down. Another benefit of these organizations is that they ease citizen acceptance of subsequent policy decisions since the governor can note that an action "was recommended by an impartial panel of citizens." This is not to suggest that citizen advisory committees are merely tools for manipulation by politicians, but they do have uses beyond citizen participation.

E-Government

LO 4-5
To recognize the importance of the internet and social media in connecting the public with government.

The internet has brought state and local governments into citizens' homes in a way earlier technology could not. States and localities of all sizes have incorporated electronic communications into their daily operations. Websites abound and e-mails proliferate. State governments have created elaborate websites that link the user to vast databases and information resources. People can click on a city's homepage and find an array of useful information, such as the agenda for the next city council meeting, the minutes of previous council sessions, the city budget, the comprehensive plan, crime statistics, and the like. Some elected officials use blogs to stay in touch with their constituents— and to bypass conventional media. Facebook, Twitter, and YouTube offer more ways for politicians to connect with the public.

Now states and localities are expanding their use of the internet and social media in dealing with the public. It started with the downloading of public reports and generic forms and has moved into more highly individualized interaction such as filing taxes, applying for licenses and permits, and making service requests. Although some have touted the use of the internet in voting, worries over security and accuracy have slowed the move to the internet as a virtual polling place.

An example of a local jurisdiction that has embraced citizen participation through e-government is Tacoma, Washington, a city of 200,000 people with a territorial range of 63 square miles. On the city's official website, the first page features a box titled "Connect with Us," which features a social media icon that can be clicked on and opened from the webpage. That icon takes one to a listing of how the user can interact with various city departments and offices on Facebook, Twitter, Instagram, and so on. TV Tacoma lets people watch livestreamed and archived city council meetings, while the Newsroom option provides access to news releases and the city's media office. By clicking on "Contact Us," citizens can make service requests online, and even upload an attachment

focus group
A small group of individuals assembled to provide opinion and feedback about specific issues in government. Participants are often paid for their time.

such as a photo of a pothole on a neighborhood street or a broken bench at a city park. At Sign Up for Updates, people can sign up for e-mail updates about the latest events and alerts in the city. The intent of these "Connect with Us" options is to make it easier for Tacoma residents and businesses to interact with the city. The expectation is that this interaction will produce a more effective city government and a more engaged and satisfied public.

One of the major concerns as the push toward e-government grows is that the so-called technology have-nots will be left behind. Low-income Americans lag far behind middle- and upper-income groups in their access to the internet. This digital divide has led many communities to install personal computers in libraries, as well as in government information kiosks located in shopping malls and transit stations. Some rural areas have found it difficult to attract start-up businesses and related investment because high-speed internet is not available. To combat this, New York has created a $25 million fund to expand broadband internet access to rural and underserved urban areas of the Empire State. Other e-government concerns involve security and privacy.

Ransomware attacks, where a hacker encrypts files on a computer network and then demands financial payments to return access to those files, have increased dramatically in recent years. In just the first ten months of 2019, there were some 140 attacks on state and local governments and health care providers in the United States, up from sixty-five in all of 2018. Hackers demanded $76,000 from the city of Baltimore to return user access to city websites; the city refused and instead paid millions of dollars cleaning up the damage. The suburban Miami town of Riviera Beach has the dubious honor of paying a record $600,000 in bitcoin to regain access to their city computers.[73]

Volunteerism as Participation

Voluntary action is another constructive participatory activity unrelated to the ballot box. People and organizations donate their time and talents to supplement or even replace government activity. **Volunteerism** is a means of bringing fresh ideas and energy, whether physical or financial, into government while relieving some of the service burden. Washington created the first statewide volunteerism office in 1969, and within twenty years, all states had volunteer programs in place.

One highly visible example of volunteerism is the Adopt-a-Highway program, which is active in forty-nine states and Puerto Rico. The program grew out of a successful anti-littering effort in Texas, dubbed "Don't Mess with Texas." Over the past twenty years, the number of local businesses and civic clubs willing to pick up litter along designated stretches of state highways has skyrocketed. You have probably noticed the Adopt-a-Highway signs, with the names of volunteering groups listed underneath. The state saves money, the roadsides stay cleaner, and the volunteering groups have good feelings and free advertising to go along with their sore backs.

Successful volunteer programs like Adopt-a-Highway are emblematic of the concept of social capital, as mentioned earlier in this chapter. Stephen Knack's study showed a positive relationship between several indicators of social capital, especially the percentage of the public engaged in volunteerism, and state governmental quality.[74] States with a greater propensity toward

LO 4-6
To identify the impact of volunteerism in states and localities.

ransomware attack
A type of malicious computer hacking in which hackers encrypt files on a computer server or lock access to the system and then demand a ransom to return access.

volunteerism
A form of participation in which individuals or groups donate time or money to a public purpose.

volunteerism scored higher on several government performance measures, including financial management, capital management, and information technology.

Local governments use volunteers in various ways. Generally, volunteerism is most successful when citizens can develop the required job skills quickly or participate in activities they enjoy, such as library work, recreation programs, or fire protection. In addition to providing services to others, volunteers can be utilized for self-help; that is, they can engage in activities in which they are the primary beneficiaries. For example, some New York City neighborhoods take responsibility for the security and maintenance of nearby parks. Residential crime-watch programs are another variety of self-help. In both these instances, the volunteers and their neighborhoods benefit. Overall, studies show that volunteerism is especially successful in rural areas and small towns.[75]

Important supplements to government volunteer programs are those of the nonprofit sector. Members of local faith-based groups and civic organizations, for example, often volunteer their time in support of community improvement projects such as Habitat for Humanity, Meals on Wheels, and Sistercare. Nonprofit organizations often take leadership roles in disaster recovery, especially when government programs are either slow or inadequate to assist those suffering the effects of disaster. For example, Rebuilding Together Baton Rouge helped many residents in that city rebuild their flooded homes after they did not receive sufficient federal assistance in 2016. The internet has made it much easier for concerned individuals to contribute funding to nonprofits that assist people in recovering from disaster.[76]

The Effects of Citizen Participation

Consider again the four quadrants of Figure 4.1. Constructive participatory behaviors, whether active or passive, invigorate government. The capacity of state and local governments depends on several factors, one of which is citizen participation. Underlying this argument is the implicit but strongly held belief shared by most observers of democracies that an accessible, responsive government is a legitimate government. Some commentators held out hope that new media technologies such as cable television and the internet would stimulate interest in politics and move more people into the constructive quadrants. However, research indicates that this has not happened. Instead, politically interested individuals use these technologies to become better informed, whereas the politically uninterested opt for entertainment programming.[77]

An active public, one that chooses the *voice* option in Figure 4.1, has the potential to generate widespread change in a community. Public policy tends to reflect the interests of active citizens. The mobilization of lower-class voters, for instance, is linked to more generous state welfare policies.[78] The challenge for government is to incorporate citizen participation into ongoing operations. Some places are trying to do just that. One is Durham, North Carolina, which has posted a clever one-minute YouTube video inviting its residents to join the city council for coffee and conversation about the city's budget priorities.[79] Citizen involvement may not always be easy or efficient, but, in a democracy, it is the ultimate test of the legitimacy of that government.

Chapter Recap

- Citizen participation in the community can be active or passive and constructive or destructive. Local governments have devoted much time and energy to encouraging active, constructive participation among the citizenry.

- Voter turnout rates vary dramatically from one state to another, and the reasons have to do with the political culture of the state, the competitiveness of the political parties, and the way elections are administered.

- After the 2018 elections, twenty-seven gubernatorial offices were in Republican hands; twenty-three were held by Democrats.

- Almost half of the states have an initiative process, and in those that do, it has become an important tool for policy making.

- The use of recall has increased, led by efforts in Wisconsin to oust the governor, lieutenant governor, and thirteen state senators.

- e-government is on the rise, with states and localities adopting more and more high-tech ways of interacting with citizens. This trend holds tremendous potential for increasing citizen participation in government.

- Volunteerism is a way of bringing fresh ideas and energy into government and helps connect citizens to their communities.

- State and local governments continue to encourage their citizens in meaningful participation.

Key Terms

participation *(p. 85)*
hashtag activism *(p. 85)*
free rider *(p. 88)*
social capital *(p. 88)*
Voting Rights Act of 1965 *(p. 89)*
voting-age population *(p. 89)*
voting-eligible population *(p. 90)*
residual votes *(p. 94)*
primary system *(p. 95)*
fully closed primary *(p. 95)*
partially closed primary *(p. 95)*
fully open primary *(p. 95)*

partially open primary *(p. 96)*
open to unaffiliated voters *(p. 96)*
runoff election *(p. 96)*
top-two primary *(p. 96)*
instant runoff *(p. 98)*
plurality *(p. 98)*
fusion *(p. 98)*
coattail effect *(p. 99)*
nonpartisan election *(p. 100)*
slating groups *(p. 100)*
Initiative *(p. 101)*

popular referendum *(p. 101)*
referendum *(p. 101)*
recall *(p. 101)*
open meeting laws *(p. 107)*
administrative procedure acts *(p. 109)*
advisory committee *(p. 109)*
focus group *(p. 110)*
ransomware attack *(p. 111)*
volunteerism *(p. 111)*

Internet Resources

The website of the Federal Election Commission, **www.fec.gov**, contains information about U.S. elections, including laws, campaign financing, and results. To learn more about various state laws on elections, visit each state's home page or see the website of the National Association of Secretaries of State at **www.nass.org**.

The League of Women Voters, a well-respected organization that encourages informed and active participation of citizens in government, maintains a website at **www.lwv.org**.

MTV's Rock the Vote, an effort to boost political participation among young voters, is at **www.rockthevote.com**.

You can find just about anything you want to know about ballot measures at **www.iandrinstitute.org** and election results at **www.ballotpedia.org**.

5

Political Parties, Interest Groups, and Campaigns: Influencing Public Policy

A candidate for the state senate in Texas talks with potential voters at a restaurant in Houston.

Learning Objectives

LO 5-1 To describe the functions of political parties in state government.

LO 5-2 To analyze the evolution of political parties over time.

LO 5-3 To describe the roles of interest groups in states and localities.

LO 5-4 To differentiate interest groups according to their influence.

LO 5-5 To discuss the impact of lobbying in state politics.

LO 5-6 To critique the role of money in state political systems.

LO 5-7 To investigate the use of new campaign technologies.

LO 5-8 To compare state differences in the regulation of campaign finance.

Research tells us that, on average, Americans prefer to live near people whose political beliefs and ideology are similar to their own. But how can someone determine which area is most closely aligned with her ideology? Finding out how a neighborhood voted in a presidential election is a logical starting point, but then what? That's where consulting firms such as Clarity Campaign Labs come in. Clarity, which provides an array of services to political campaigns, has developed an algorithm that uses big data and your responses to a series of agree/disagree questions to identify the area (defined by postal zip code) that most fits your ideological profile. Answer seven questions on Clarity's "What Town Matches My Politics?" website about your partisanship; positions on abortion, climate change, taxes, and gun control; and preferences for urban living and religious practice, then select the state you live in and, voila, your ideological "best place" is identified.[1]

An interesting exercise to be sure, but the larger point is that big data, advanced analytics, and technology are changing the way political campaigns operate. Campaign strategists can design specifically targeted messages that resonate with potential voters in an area. Research on state legislative campaigns has shown that these approaches can be successful in increasing both candidate name recognition and voter turnout.[2] And it just goes to show that political campaigns aren't what they used to be.

Political Parties

LO 5-1
To describe the functions of political parties in state government.

The two major **political parties**, the Democratic Party and the Republican Party, offer slates of candidates to lead us. Candidates campaign hard for the high-profile jobs of governor, state legislator, mayor, and various other state and local positions. In some states, even candidates for judicial positions compete in partisan races. But party involvement in our system of government does not end on Election Day—the institutions of government themselves have a partisan tone. Legislatures are organized along party lines; governors offer Republican or Democratic agendas for their states; county commissioners of different ideological stripes fight over the package of services provided to their residents. Through the actions of their elected officials, political parties play a major role in the operation of government.

The Condition of Political Parties

The condition of contemporary American political parties has been described with words such as *decline*, *decay*, and *demise*. In some ways, the description is accurate, but, in other ways, it is overstated. True, fewer people consider themselves members of either of the two major political parties these days, whereas the number of people calling themselves independents is often as much as 40 percent of the electorate.[3] Furthermore, campaigns are increasingly candidate centered rather than party centered, and they rely on personal organizations and political consultants. But at the same time, the party organization has become more professionalized, taking on new tasks and playing new roles in politics and governance. Parties have more financial and technological resources at their disposal. Thus, to some observers, political parties are enjoying a period of revitalization and rejuvenation. Although the debate over the condition of political parties continues, it seems clear that they have undergone a transformation during the past thirty years and that they have proven to be quite adaptable.

American political parties are composed of three interacting parts: the party organization (party committees, party leaders, and activists), the party in government (candidates and officeholders), and the party in the electorate (citizens who identify with the party).[4] These parts interact to do many things, but among their central tasks are nominating and electing candidates, educating (some might say propagandizing) citizens, and, once in office, governing.

political parties
Organizations that nominate candidates to compete in elections and promote policy ideas.

ideology
Core beliefs about the nature and role of the political system.

Parties in the United States function as umbrella organizations that shelter loose coalitions of relatively like-minded individuals. In terms of **ideology**, Republicans tend to be more conservative, favoring a limited role for government; Democrats tend to be more liberal, preferring a more activist government. A general image for each party is discernible: The Republicans typically have been considered the party of big business; the Democrats, the party of workers. In foreign affairs, Republicans favor a more assertive U.S. policy than Democrats typically do. On many of the social issues of the day—gay rights, abortion, pornography, and prayer in schools—the two parties tend to take different positions. By 2020, approximately 31 percent of the voting-age public considered themselves Democrats, and 28 percent considered themselves to be Republicans. Some 37 percent considered themselves to be independent of either party.[5] Note, however, that typically about one-third to one-half of the independents lean toward one of the two major parties. (See Figure 5.1, which tracks party identification during the recent past.) These national percentages mask tremendous variation across jurisdictions: Washington, D.C., Hawaii, Rhode Island, and Massachusetts have substantially higher percentages of voters favoring the Democratic Party; Utah, Wyoming, and Idaho have significantly more Republicans.

The geographical distribution of partisan loyalties has produced some interesting patterns. The South, where conservative political attitudes predominate, has become a region of so-called "red" states—that is, states that vote Republican in presidential elections. Other red states are found in the plains region and the Rocky Mountain west. States that are more reliably Democratic in presidential elections—usually the Northeastern region, the Pacific Coast, and the upper Midwest—are designated "blue" states. (The labels "red" and "blue" have become the norm, originating from the color-coded maps used by television broadcasters to show election returns.) States with greater

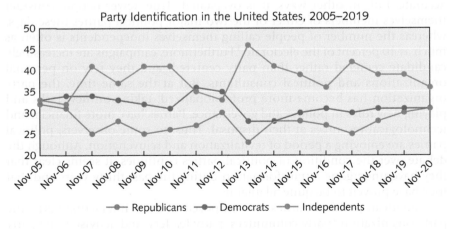

Figure 5.1 Party Identification in the United States, 2005–2019

Note: Poll data for 2005–2019 as of November each year.

Source: Gallup, "Party Affiliation," www.gallup.com/poll/15370/party-affiliation.aspx (accessed November 6, 2020).

partisan diversity have been called "purple" by some pollsters.[6] It is important not to overgeneralize from these colorful, but simple, descriptors of state-level partisanship. Within an individual state, various partisan configurations exist from one place to another, as research on presidential voting at the county level has shown.[7] Voters display a remarkable penchant for **ticket splitting**—that is, voting for a Democrat for one office and a Republican for another in the same election. In fact, many voters are fond of saying that they "vote for the person, not the party."

ticket splitting
Voting for candidates of different political parties in a general election.

Party Organization

LO 5-2
To analyze the evolution of political parties over time.

Political parties are decentralized organizations, with fifty state Republican parties and fifty state Democratic parties. Each state also has local party organizations, most typically at the county level. Although they interact, each of these units is autonomous, a situation that promotes independence but is not so helpful to party discipline. Specialized partisan groups, including the College Democrats, the Young Republicans, Democratic Women's Clubs, Black Republican Councils, and so on, have been accorded official recognition. Party organizations are further decentralized into precinct-level clusters, which bear the ultimate responsibility for turning out the party's voters on Election Day.[8] Figure 5.2 shows a typical state party organization.

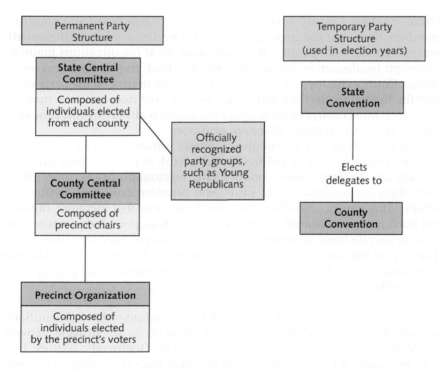

Figure 5.2 Typical State Party Organization
Most political party organizations look something like this.

State Parties State governments vary in how closely and vigorously they regulate political parties. In states with few laws, parties have more discretion in their organization and functions.[9] Regardless, each state party has a charter or bylaws to govern its operation. The decision-making body is the state committee, sometimes called a "central committee," which is headed by a chairperson and is composed of members elected in party primaries or at state party conventions. State party organizations differ in their organizational vitality and resources. In nonelection years, the parties operate with limited staff and revenue; in election years, however, their employment and their funds increase dramatically. Republican organizations generally outstrip Democratic ones in these measures of organizational strength.

State parties, officially at least, lead their party's push to capture statewide elected offices. Although they may formulate platforms and launch party-centered fundraising appeals, their value to candidates is in the services they provide.[10] In many states, parties host seminars for party nominees about campaigning effectively, they conduct research into the public's mood, and they advertise on behalf of their candidates. To a candidate, one of the most valuable services the state party can provide is access to its database of party voters.[11] Although partisan volunteers still canvass neighborhoods, knocking on doors and talking to would-be voters, these activities are increasingly supplemented by web-based and e-mail appeals for funds and votes.

Local Parties County party organizations are composed of committee members chosen at the precinct level. Local parties are less professionally organized than state parties. Although many local organizations maintain campaign headquarters during an election period, few operate year-round offices. County chairpersons report devoting a lot of time to the party in the months before an election, but otherwise the post does not take much of their time. Most chairpersons lead organizations without any full-time staff, and vacancies in precinct offices are common.

Local party workers are volunteers, whose primary reward is the satisfaction of being involved in politics. But the work is rarely glamorous. Party workers are the people who conduct voter registration drives, drop off the lawn signs for residents' front yards, and organize candidate forums. On behalf of the party's candidates, they distribute campaign literature, organize fundraising events, contact voters, and run newspaper advertisements. But what impact do these activities have on the campaign? State legislative candidates report that local parties are most beneficial when providing traditional grassroots services such as rounding up volunteer workers and getting voters to the polls on Election Day.[12]

Factions Political parties frequently develop factions—that is, identifiable subsets. These may be ideologically based, such as the struggle between moderates and progressives for control of state Democratic parties. They may be organized around particular political leaders, or they may reflect sectional divisions within a state. When factions endure, they make it difficult for a party to come together on behalf of candidates and in support of policy.[13] Persistent intraparty factions create electoral opportunities for the opposing party.

President Donald Trump's campaign for the presidency in 2016 brought a challenge to the Republican Party in many states. In 2016, much of the Republican leadership at the national, state, and local levels did not support nor overtly oppose Trump's presidential bid.[14] Early polls showed Democratic presidential candidate Hillary Clinton handily beating Donald Trump, so it was a surprise to most observers when Trump won the presidential election. During the presidential campaign, but even more so after the election, many Republicans came around to a position supporting the president, especially when he made it clear that he was willing to intercede in elections to support those who agreed with him.[15] One of the first tests of this was the 2017 U.S. Senate special election in Alabama. Jeff Sessions resigned from the Senate when he was appointed U.S. attorney general, and Governor Robert Bentley appointed Alabama Attorney General Luther Strange to fill the vacancy. In the Republican primary for a special election later in 2017, Trump supported Strange against Republican challenger Roy Moore, a well-known and controversial Alabama former judge who had become a leading advocate on extreme conservative issues. Moore handily beat Strange in the Republican primary. Trump then endorsed Moore one week before the special election to the U.S. Senate in November. In that election, Moore lost to Democrat Doug Jones; Jones becoming the first Democrat elected to statewide office in Alabama since 1992.[16]

The 2018 congressional and gubernatorial elections were widely considered to be a referendum on President Trump's performance in office. As one observer said, "A sitting president has never been as central an issue in a midterm election as Trump is in 2018,"[17] and as another noted, "President Trump would not have had it any other way."[18] Trump campaigned vigorously for Republican candidates, "putting him on the campaign trail more than his recent predecessors,"[19] in both Republican primaries and in the general election, much as he had been active in the Alabama election in 2017. Generally, Trump-endorsed candidates in congressional and gubernatorial *primaries* tended to win. Only in Wyoming, where Trump campaigned for gubernatorial candidate Foster Friess, did his efforts not succeed in a Republican primary election. In the 2018 *general elections*, however, President Trump's campaign efforts were less successful. A Brookings Institute analysis concluded that of the seventy-five U.S. House and Senate candidates directly endorsed by Trump in 2018, forty-two (55 percent) won their elections. When Trump was more heavily involved—for example, directly campaigning for candidates—his success rate was higher, with those candidates winning twenty-three of thirty-six races (64 percent).[20]

Likewise, the Democratic Party faced its own form of revolt in 2016, with the presidential candidacy of Vermont U.S. Senator Bernie Sanders. Sanders' political affiliation is officially listed as Independent, but he is closely aligned with the liberal wing of the Democratic Party. Sanders won twenty-two Democratic state primary elections or caucuses in 2016, including the early New Hampshire primary and primaries in the important midwestern states of

Indiana, Michigan, and Wisconsin. By the end of the primary season, Sanders was Hillary Clinton's sole remaining contestant for the presidential nomination, and, after he refused to concede the nomination to her, it took two ballots at the Democratic National Convention for Clinton to secure the nomination.

Clinton's loss to Donald Trump led to soul searching in the Democratic Party, with some saying the party needed to provide more of a left-leaning alternative to an increasingly conservative Republican Party. The 2018 election of self-avowed Democratic Socialists Alexandria Ocasio-Cortez in New York's Fourteenth Congressional District, Ilhan Omar in Minnesota's Fifth Congressional District, and Rashida Tlaib in Michigan's Thirteenth Congressional District suggested that the Sanders challenge to the Democratic Party establishment had some legs. In 2020, there were some ninety-seven U.S. House members of the Congressional Progressive Caucus, up from sixty-eight in 2014. Polls in 2019 and 2020 generally showed Sanders running second to former Vice President Joe Biden for the Democratic nomination for president, with Massachusetts Senator Elizabeth Warren, former New York City Mayor Michael Bloomberg, and former South Bend, Indiana, Mayor Pete Buttigieg rounding out the top five in national polls.[21] By summer of 2020, Biden had won a sufficient number of delegates to the national convention that his nomination was assured.

Both political parties have therefore shown themselves recently to be susceptible to "party crashers," outsiders who can run well in national nominating contests and who can succeed in winning offices at the state or local level. Recent research shows such outsider challengers have the potential for remaking U.S. political parties in a time when the electorate is polarized in its political positions.[22]

The Two-Party System

General elections in the United States are typically contests between candidates representing the two major political parties. Such has been the case for the past century and a half. The Democratic Party has been in existence since the 1830s, when it emerged from the Jacksonian wing of the Jeffersonian Party. The Republican Party, despite its label as the Grand Old Party, is newer; it developed out of the sectional conflict over slavery in the 1850s.

Why Just Two? There are numerous reasons for the persistence of two-party politics. Explanations that emphasize sectional dualism, such as East versus West or North versus South, have given way to those focusing on the structure of the electoral system. Parties compete in elections in which there can be only one winner. Most legislative races, for example, take place in single-member districts in which only the candidate with the most votes wins; there is no reward for finishing second or third. Hence, the development of radical or noncentrist parties that appeal to a small subset of the electorate is discouraged. In addition, laws regulating access to the ballot and receipt of public funds contribute to two-partyism by creating high start-up costs for third parties. Another plausible explanation has to do with tradition. Americans are accustomed to a political system composed of two parties, and that is how we understand politics. The institutionalization of the two-party system is reflected in these numbers: In 2019, of the nation's 7,333 state legislators (this number excludes Nebraska where legislators are elected in nonpartisan races), only thirty-five were not Democrats or Republicans—and twelve of the thirty-five were in the Vermont House of Representatives.[23]

Third Parties The assessment of former Alabama governor George Wallace that "there ain't a dime's worth of difference between Democrats and Republicans," although exaggerated, raises questions about the need for alternative parties. Third parties (also called nonmajor or minor parties) are a mostly unsuccessful but constant phenomenon in U.S. politics. The Greens, Libertarians, Progressives, and the Constitution Party are some examples of third parties currently active in some states. The two major parties may not differ substantially, but for the most part their positions reflect the public mood. Third parties suffer because the two established parties have vast reserves of money and resources at their disposal; new parties can rarely amass the finances or assemble the organization necessary to make significant inroads into the system. Moreover, as noted earlier, most states have erected barriers making it difficult for minor parties to get on the ballot; lawsuits challenging these barriers typically have been dismissed by the courts. (The Controversies in States and Localities box discusses efforts in some states to ease minor party access to the ballot.) Further, third parties typically receive scant attention from the news media, and, without it, their credibility wanes. Still, even with the odds stacked against them, many third parties contest elections because a campaign provides an opportunity to promote the party's policy positions.

Public interest in partisan alternatives may be increasing. One national survey reported that 57 percent of the electorate believed that there should be a third major political party.[24] Many indicated that their estrangement from the Democratic and Republican parties had reached the point that they would willingly affiliate with a third party that reflected their interests. Two third parties that have enjoyed some success in local races in recent times are the Libertarian Party, which celebrates individual rights, and the Green Party, which grew out of the environmental movement. By 2019, Libertarians held 299 elective offices in local jurisdictions in thirty-six states, with their numbers highest in New York and Pennsylvania. That same year, 161 Greens held local offices in nineteen states, including city council positions in cities such as Laredo, Texas, and Minneapolis, Minnesota.[25]

Interparty Competition

These days, most states exhibit meaningful two-party electoral competition. In other words, when you look at a general-election ballot, you will find both the Democrats and the Republicans offering credible candidates for state

Controversies in States and Localities

Opening Up the Ballot to More Parties

For many years, Pennsylvania had some of the most restrictive ballot access laws in the United States. In order to be automatically listed on the ballot, a political party had to have a membership of at least 15 percent of the registered voters in the state. All other parties who wanted to list candidates had to do so through petitions requiring 2 percent of the votes cast for the top stateside candidate in the last general election. The difference between these two methods meant that a Democrat or Republican running for the party's nomination for governor, for example, would only need 2,000 signatures to get his or her name on the ballot, whereas a third-party or Independent candidate might need as many as 21,000 signatures to get ballot access. Pennsylvania's ballot access law requiring a party of have a membership of 15 percent of the number of voters registered statewide was so restrictive that Republicans wouldn't make the ballot if the law were in effect in Rhode Island or Massachusetts, and Democrats wouldn't make the ballot if it were in effect in Idaho or Utah.

Tired of such restrictive ballot access laws, a group of individuals and organizations, including several third parties (Libertarian, Green, Constitution, and Reform, among others) formed an interest group in 2005 called the Pennsylvania Ballot Access Coalition (PABAC). The goal of the group was simple: to change the state's laws to make it easier for minor parties to get on the ballot. They argued that it would create more political competition and give voters more choices. PABAC worked on doing this legislatively for the last fifteen years. Eventually this went to federal court, and in 2018 the case was finally settled, reducing the number of signatures on third-party or Independent ballot petitions to 5,000.

Pennsylvania is not the only state in which the issue of ballot access for third parties has been on the agenda. Arkansas lowered the petition signature requirement for minor parties to 10,000 some ten years ago, but recently increased the number of signatures to 3 percent of the voters in the last gubernatorial election (which was more than 25,000 in 2020). In Arizona, a change in state law in 2015 made it more difficult for minor party candidates to get on the ballot, by redefining the signature requirements. Under the new law, a minor party candidate would need signatures of one-quarter of 1 percent of the party's registered voters *and* registered Independents in the district in which they were competing. That may not sound like a lot, but because many places in Arizona have a large number of Independents, the change had the effect of substantially increasing the signature requirements. As might be expected, these changes are being challenged in court.

Almost every state in the United States also has some variation on a "sore loser" law, which makes it illegal for a candidate who loses in a party primary to run as an Independent or third-party candidate in the general election. Researchers on such laws have concluded that they pressure nontraditional candidates to run for a major party nomination rather than running as an Independent or third-party candidate in a general election, potentially reducing competition and fostering party polarization.

Although ballot access for minor parties is on the agenda, the resolution of this issue is not necessarily automatic or uniform across the states. The issue certainly raises a series of interesting questions.

Critical Thinking Questions

1. Are there any representatives in your state's legislature who are neither Republican nor Democrat? If so, what party are they affiliated with? If not, do you think there should be?

2. Would having more parties on the ballot expand voter choice or make elections more difficult to navigate?

3. Opening the ballot to more parties could force more compromise and cooperation and perhaps more coalition-building among various parties in the legislature. But this would likely make it harder to pass bills that are more ideologically pure. Why would this be a good or a bad thing?

Sources: "Voter's Choice Act," Pennsylvania Ballot Access Coalition, www.paballotaccess.org/ (accessed January 8, 2020); Conor M. Dowling and Steve B. Lern, "Explaining Major and Third Party Candidate Entry in U.S. Gubernatorial Elections, 1980–2005," *State Politics and Policy Quarterly* 9 (Spring 2009): 1–23; FairVote, "The Worst Ballot Access Laws in the United States," www .fairvote.org (January 13, 2015); "Gov. Doug Ducey Signs Elections-Related Measures," www.azcapitoltimes.com/news/2015/04/14 /gov-doug-ducey-signs-elections-related-measures/ (April 14, 2015); Michael Kang and Barry Burden, "Sore Loser Laws in Presidential and Congressional Elections," in Robert Boatright (ed.) *Routledge Handbook of Primary Elections*, 1st Edition (New York: Routledge); Jonathan Lai, "Pennsylvania Just Made It Easier to Run as a Third-Party or Independent. Will People Do it?" *Philadelphia Inquirer*, www.inquirer.com/philly/news/pa-third-party-ballot-access -signature-requirements-20180209.html (February 9, 2018).

offices. The extension of interparty competition to states that had lacked it in the past is a healthy development in American politics. Citizens who are dissatisfied with the performance of the party in power have another choice. And there is an interesting twist to increased party competition and more choices for voters. Research has found that the amount of competition for legislative seats appears to be related to the policy outputs of the legislatures. States with higher levels of electoral competition tend to adopt more progressive policies than do states with less-competitive legislative elections.[26] Of course, the relative strength of the two parties helps explain partisan competition and legislative actions.

Patterns of Competition Another way of thinking about interparty competition is to examine which party controls the major policy-making institutions in the state: the governor's office and the state legislature. In the past, some states experienced long periods of institutional dominance by one party, but that trend has been on the decline for years. Although this is no longer true, there has been a great sorting of states into those that are more Democratic and those that are more Republican. Based on gubernatorial vote margins and legislative seats held, twenty states can be classified as two-party competitive, and no states fall into the "one-party" category.[27] Of the remaining thirty states, eleven are considered modified Democratic states (i.e., Democrats control more institutions more often); nineteen are modified Republican states. During the period 2012–2017, Hawaii was the closest to a one-party Democratic state; Wyoming was the closest to a one-party Republican state. However, even in these two states, the minority parties have rebranded themselves and are becoming more competitive.[28]

Generally, there is a link between the partisan composition of the electorate and partisan control of a state's institutions. For instance, in Utah in 2018, the Republican Party had a voter registration advantage over the Democratic Party of more than four to one. Not surprisingly, in the Utah legislature, Republicans outnumbered Democrats by a substantial margin, and a Republican occupied the governor's office. When the governorship and both legislative chambers are controlled by the same party, the result is **unified government**, or what the popular media calls a trifecta. But the electorate-institution relationship is not a simple one. Sometimes control of policy-making institutions is split between the two parties, and the result is called **divided government**. The patterns of partisan control in the states in 2021 are displayed in Figure 5.3. Thirty-nine states were characterized by unified government (twenty-four states in Republican hands, fifteen states controlled by the Democratic Party); eleven states experienced divided government. Nebraska's state legislature is officially nonpartisan, but its governor is a Republican.

Consequences of Competition Two-party competition has spread at a time when states are becoming the battleground for the resolution of difficult policy issues. Undoubtedly, as governors set their agendas and legislatures outline their preferences, cries of partisan politics will be heard.

unified government
Both houses of the legislature and the governor's office are controlled by the same party. Also called a trifecta.

divided government
One party controls the governor's office and the other party controls the legislature, or each party controls one legislative chamber.

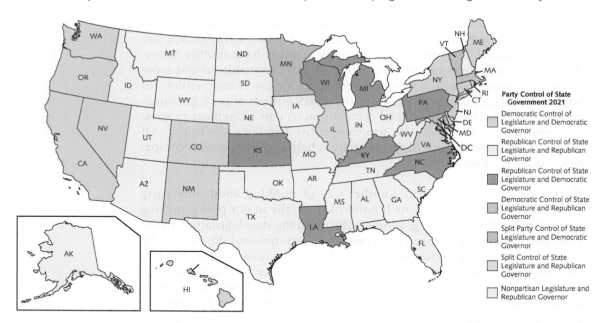

Figure 5.3 Party Control of State Government in 2021
Source: www.ballotpedia.org/State_government_trifectas (accessed November 6, 2020).

But in a positive sense, such cries symbolize the maturation of state institutions. Partisan politics will probably encourage a wider search for policy alternatives and result in innovative solutions.

In the view of many, two parties are better than one. Heated partisan competition turns a dull campaign into a lively contest, sparking citizen interest and increasing voter turnout. In governance, however, many believe that unified government is preferable to divided government. When competitive elections produce unified party control of government institutions, it is easier for the public to hold the party accountable for what it does—or does not do—while in office.

Is the Party Over?

Have political parties as we know them outlived their usefulness? Will they be cast aside as new forms of political organization and communication emerge? As some have argued, a more educated populace that can readily acquire political information via the internet is likely to be less reliant on party cues.[29] Today's generation is less loyal to political parties than its grandparents were and is not so likely to vote along party lines. As younger voters mature, will they continue to be hesitant to identify with a political party or will their partisan feelings become stronger as they age, as previous generations have done?[30] The trend toward **dealignment**, or weakening of individual partisan attachments, slowed for a period but has begun to pick up again. But, importantly, weakening partisan attachments may not determine weakened

dealignment
The weakening of an individual's attachment to political parties.

party voting. One recent study shows that when it comes to consistent voting for one party or the other, "what we traditionally consider to be unattached or inattentive voters . . . now appear more similar to past party stalwarts."[31] This is, at best, a mixed blessing for the two major parties; they may wind up with a fairly loyal group of voters who don't consider themselves as belonging to either of the parties.

The two major political parties are not sitting idly by as their role in the political system is challenged. Party organizations are making their operations more professional and have more money to spend and more staff to spend it. They are actively seeking to make their organizations more meaningful to younger voters, using various new technologies to engage the millennial generation. The past several years have seen the development of party-centered advertising campaigns, the embrace of new campaign technology, and a renewed commitment to get-out-the-vote drives.[32] Moreover, both parties are developing networks that connect party leaders across state boundaries. All in all, parties are doing their best to adapt to the changing environment.

Interest Groups

Interest groups have become powerful players in our democratic system. Joining a group is a way for individuals to communicate their preferences— their interests—to government. Interest groups attempt to influence governmental decisions and actions by pressuring decision-making bodies to, for example, put more guidance counselors in public schools, restrict coastal development, or strengthen state licensing of family therapists. Success is defined in terms of getting the group's preferences enacted—or blocking actions that are detrimental to the group's interests.

In considering the role of groups in the political system, we must remember that people join groups for reasons other than politics. For instance, a teacher may be a member of a politically active state education association because the group offers a tangible benefit such as low-cost life insurance, but he may not be interested in or may even disagree with some of the political positions taken by the organization. In general, then, motivations for group membership are individually determined.

Types of Interest Groups

Interest groups come in all types and sizes. If you were to visit the lobby of the state capitol when the legislature was in session, you might find the director of the state school boards association conversing with the chairperson of the education committee, or the lobbyist hired by the state hotel-motel association exchanging notes with the lobbyist for the state's restaurateurs. If a legislator were to venture into the lobby, they would probably receive at least a friendly greeting from the lobbyists and at most a serious heart-to-heart talk about the merits of a bill. You would be witnessing efforts to influence public policy. Interest groups want state government to enact policies that are in their interest or, conversely, not to enact policies at odds with their preferences.

LO 5-3
To describe the roles of interest groups in states and localities.

LO 5-4
To differentiate interest groups according to their influence.

interest groups
Organizations of like-minded individuals who desire to influence government.

The interests represented in the capitol lobby are as varied as the states themselves. One interest that is well represented and powerful is business. Whether a lobbyist represents a single large corporation or a consortium of businesses, when they talk, state legislators tend to listen. From the perspective of business groups (and other economically oriented groups), legislative actions can cost or save their members money. Thus, the chamber of commerce, industry groups, trade associations, financial institutions, and regulated utilities maintain a visible presence in the state capitol during the legislative session. Table 5.1 documents the influential nature of business interests at the state level. It is important to remember, however, that business interests are not monolithic; occasionally they may find themselves on opposite sides of a bill.

Other interests converge on the capitol. Representatives of labor, both established AFL-CIO unions and professional associations such as the state optometrists' group or sheriffs' association, frequent the hallways and committee meeting rooms to see that the legislature makes the "right" decision on the bills before it. For example, if a legislature is considering a bill to change the licensing procedures for optometrists, you could expect to find the optometrists' interest group immersed in the debate. Another employees' group—schoolteachers—has banded together to form one of the most effective state-level groups. In fact, as Table 5.1 indicates, schoolteachers' organizations are ranked among the most influential interest groups in thirty-one states. There have been only a few changes in these rankings since 2006–2007 when the data reported in Table 5.1 were compiled. "Some interests, such as gaming, contractors and developers, tourism and hospitals have made gains over the years, whereas others, such as state employees, banks and financial institutions, and the oil and gas industry, have seen the largest declines."[33]

Many other interest groups are active (but not necessarily influential) in state government, and a large number are ideological in nature. For some, their political activity is oriented toward some higher good, such as clean air or fairer tax systems or consumer protection. Members of these groups do not have a direct economic or professional interest in the outcome of a legislative decision. Instead, their lobbyists argue that the public as a whole benefits from their involvement in the legislative process. Consider PennPIRG, which describes itself as a nonprofit, nonpartisan watchdog group working on behalf of consumers, the environment, and responsive government in Pennsylvania. The group's motto, and that of other public interest research groups (PIRGs), is "Standing Up to Powerful Interests."

Interest Groups in the States

For the most part, interest group politics is defined by its state context. First of all, interest groups and political parties have evolving, multidimensional relationships. Typically, in states where political parties are weak, interest groups are stronger; where political parties are strong, interest groups tend to be weaker.[34] Strong parties provide leadership in the policy-making process, and interest groups function through them. In the absence of party leadership and organization, interest groups fill the void, becoming important recruiters of

Table 5.1 The Twenty Most Influential Interests in the States

RANK	INTEREST	NUMBER OF STATES IN WHICH THE INTEREST WAS SEEN AS MOST EFFECTIVE
1	General business organizations (chambers of commerce, etc.)	39
2	Schoolteachers' organizations (NEA and AFT)	31
3	Utility companies and associations (electric, gas, water, telephone/telecommunications)	28
4	Manufacturers (companies and associations)	25
5	Hospital/nursing home associations	24
6	Insurance: general and medical (companies and associations)	22
7	Physicians/state medical associations	21
8	Contractors/builders/developers	21
9	General local government organizations (municipal leagues, county organizations, elected officials)	18
10	Lawyers (predominately trial attorneys and state bar associations)	20
11	Realtors' associations	20
12	General farm organizations (state farm bureaus, etc.)	14
13	Bankers' associations	15
14	Universities and colleges (institutions and employees)	14
15	Traditional labor associations (predominantly the AFL-CIO)	15
16	Individual labor unions (Teamsters, UAW, etc.)	13
17	Gaming interests (racetracks, casinos, lotteries)	13
18	Individual banks and financial institutions	11
19	State agencies	10
20	Environmentalists	8

Note: Rank is determined by "Most Effective" plus additional information.

Source: Adapted from Anthony J. Nownes, Clive S. Thomas, and Ronald J. Hrebenar, "Interest Groups in the States," in Virginia Gray and Russell L. Hanson, eds., *Politics in the American States: A Comparative Approach* (Washington, D.C.: Congressional Quarterly Press, 2008), pp. 117–18.

candidates and financiers of campaigns; accordingly, they exert tremendous influence in policy making.

A second, related truth adds a developmental angle to interest group politics. As states diversify economically, their politics are less likely to be dominated by a single interest. Studies of state interest systems show that the number of groups has increased over time and the power of once-dominant economic interests has decreased.[35] As states increasingly become the arena in which important social and economic policy decisions are made, more and more groups go to statehouses hoping to find a receptive audience.

Techniques Used by Interest Groups

Interest groups want to have a good public image. It helps a group when its preferences can be equated with what is good for the state (or the community). Organizations use slogans like "What's good for the timber industry is good for Oregon" or "Schoolteachers have the interests of New York City at heart." Groups, then, invest resources in creating a positive image.

Being successful in the state capitol or at city hall involves more than a good public image, however. For example, interest groups have become effective at organizing networks that exert pressure on legislators. If a teacher pay-raise bill is in jeopardy in the senate, for instance, schoolteachers throughout the state may be asked by the education association to contact their senators to urge them to vote favorably on the legislation. To maximize their strength, groups with common interests often establish coalitions.

Sometimes related groups carve out their own niches to avoid direct competition for members and support.[36] For example, when gay and lesbian groups first became active in state politics, they tended to focus on narrow issues, such as ending prohibitions on same-sex marriages, rather than on broader concerns.[37] This type of targeting strategy allows more groups to flourish. To ensure that legislators will be receptive to their pressures, groups try to influence the outcome of elections by supporting candidates who reflect their interests. Interest groups also hire lobbyists who can effectively promote their causes.

Several factors affect the relative power of an interest group. In their work, Thomas, Hrebenar, and Nownes identify twelve characteristics that give some groups more political clout than others:

- The degree of necessity of group services and resources to public officials
- Whether the group's lobbying focus is primarily defensive or offensive
- The extent and strength of group opposition
- Potential for the group to enter into coalitions
- Group financial resources
- Size and geographical distribution of group membership
- Political cohesiveness of the membership
- Political, organizational, and managerial skill of group leaders
- Timing and the political climate
- Lobbyist-policymaker relations
- Legitimacy of the group and its demands—how these are perceived by the public and public officials
- Extent of group autonomy in political strategizing[38]

No single interest group is at the high end of all twelve of these characteristics all of the time. Many of the effective groups listed in Table 5.1, for example, possess quite a few of these factors. An indispensable group armed with ample resources, a cohesive membership, and skilled leaders, when the timing is right, can wield enormous influence in the state capitol. This is especially true when the group has taken a defensive posture—that is, when it wants to block proposed legislation. On the other hand, victory comes less easily to a group lacking these characteristics.

Lobbying

LO 5-5
To discuss the impact
of lobbying in state
politics.

Lobbying is the attempt to influence government decision makers. States have developed official definitions to determine who is a lobbyist and who is not. A common definition is "anyone receiving compensation to influence legislative action." A few states, such as Nevada, North Dakota, and Washington, require everyone who attempts to influence legislation to register as a lobbyist (even those who are not being paid), but most states exclude from this definition public officials, members of the media, and people who speak only before committees or boards.

As state government has expanded and taken on more functions, the number of interests represented in statehouses has exploded.[39] The increase in the number of lobbyists has a very simple but important cause: Interests that are affected by state government cannot afford to be without representation. On top of this, the political gridlock in Washington has convinced interest groups that the real action in public policy may be taking place in state capitals rather than in the national capital.[40] Many national interest groups—the National Rifle Association, Planned Parenthood, the American Association of Retired People, and hundreds of others—have state affiliates that lobby for changes in state laws that would benefit the causes they espouse or against state laws that might hurt their interests.

To win over legislators in their decision making, lobbyists need access, so they cultivate good relationships with lawmakers. In other words, they want connections; they want an "in." There are many ways of establishing connections, such as contributing to campaigns, gift giving (if allowed), and entertaining. For example, during the 2012 legislative session in Georgia, the Savannah Chamber of Commerce spent $88,000 to host a seafood festival for lawmakers.[41] After a 2013 law limited these kinds of expenditures in Georgia, lobbyists began organizing individual meals for legislators and staff in their offices. The Georgia Telecommunications Association, for example, hosted a breakfast for senior senators and their staff during the 2019 session in order to discuss with them expanding rural broadband services.[42]

Social lobbying—wining and dining legislators—still goes on, but it is being supplemented by another technique: the provision of information. Lawmakers want to know how a proposed bill might affect the different interests throughout the state and especially in their legislative districts and what it is expected to achieve. And lobbyists are only too happy to provide that information. Anthony Nownes, a noted researcher on interest groups and lobbying writes, "in most instances when a lobbyist lobbies, he provides information to the target of his lobbying effort in an attempt to convince the target that his position is correct on a given issue."[43] An analysis of the lobbying environment in three states—Colorado, Ohio, and West Virginia—identified the kinds of techniques that lobbyists rely on.[44] Table 5.2 lists the techniques that more than 75 percent of the 376 lobbyists surveyed said they used. Making contacts with key actors in the policy-making process—legislators, legislative and gubernatorial staff, and agency officials—is at the top of a lobbyist's to-do list. Moreover, a substantial 92 percent of the lobbyists

lobbying
The process by which groups and individuals attempt to influence policy makers.

Table 5.2 The Most Popular Techniques Used by Lobbyists

1	Meeting personally with state legislators
2	Meeting personally with state legislative staff
3	Entering into coalitions with other organizations
4	Helping to draft legislation
5	Meeting personally with executive agency personnel
6	Testifying at legislative committee hearings
7	Meeting personally with members of the governor's staff
8	Talking with people from the media
9	Inspiring letter-writing, telephone, or e-mail campaigns to state legislators
10	Submitting written testimony to legislative committees
11	Submitting written comments on proposed rules/regulations
12	Helping to draft regulations, rules, or guidelines

Source: Anthony J. Nownes and Krissy Walker DeAlejandro, "Lobbying in the New Millennium: Evidence of Continuity and Change in Three States," *State Politics and Policy Quarterly* 9 (Winter 2009): 429–55.

indicated that they helped draft legislation, which makes them key actors as well. Notice that lobbying is not confined to the legislative process. Lobbyists regularly attempt to shape the implementation of policies after they are enacted.

The influence of lobbyists specifically and of interest groups generally is a subject of much debate. The popular image is one of a wheeler-dealer lobbyist whose very presence in a committee hearing room can spell the fate of a bill. But, in fact, his will is done because the interests he represents are considered vital to the state, because he has assiduously laid the groundwork, and because legislators respect the forces he can mobilize if necessary. Few lobbyists cast this long a shadow, but in many states, some of the most effective lobbyists are former legislators themselves. They know how the policy-making system works, thus making them valuable to myriad interests.

A not-so-new tactic that is enjoying a resurgence is **grassroots lobbying**, in which groups use their members to communicate with legislators (translation: bombard with mail, e-mail, and telephone calls) on behalf of the group's issue. Grassroots lobbying is not just a technique for outsiders. Citizen groups, unions, religious/charitable groups, corporations, and trade and professional associations all use grassroots techniques.[45] Are they effective? While earlier studies generally concluded that "Grassroots lobbying by e-mail has a substantial influence on legislative voting behavior,"[46] more recent work has shown that now, "it costs much less to generate one additional e-mail message than before. In this environment, the volume of grassroots lobbying no longer signals the value of the information it contains."[47] Industry groups have become adept lately at simulating grassroots lobbying—what has become known as Astroturf lobbying. For example, groups with titles like Consumers for Cable Choice and Keep It Local NJ were actually financed by Verizon and

grassroots lobbying
Group mobilization of citizens to contact public officials on behalf of shared public policy views.

AT&T, who were looking for changes to laws that would allow telephone companies to offer cable services.[48]

LO 5-6
To critique the role of money in state political systems.

In most states, lobbyists are required to file reports indicating how and on whom they spent money. Concern that lobbyists would exert undue influence on the legislative process spurred states to beef up reporting requirements and to impose tougher penalties for their violation. Many states now require lobbyists to report their sources of income, total and categorized expenditures, the names of the individual officials who received their monies or gifts, and the legislation they supported or opposed.

Disclosure requirements offer one way of dealing with the problem of undue influence; another approach is to limit gifts from lobbyists to public officials. In Minnesota, a lobbyist is prohibited from giving a legislator any gift except a plaque, trinkets, or mementos of insignificant value. Virginia law was recently tightened to forbid state officials from receiving gifts that exceed $100 per year from lobbyists.[49] There is evidence that these laws produce the desired effect. In a fifty-state study, political scientist Joshua Ozymy found that when states increase the number of formal lobbying regulations, the influence of interest groups in the legislative process declines.[50] In a similar vein, recent research has shown that citizens' opinions receive greater consideration in states that regulate lobbyists more strictly.[51] In other words, in states with strict lobbying regulations, state policy conforms more closely to public opinion.

Political Action Committees Political action committees (PACs) have been a regular feature of state politics since the 1980s. Narrowly focused subsets of interest groups, PACs are political organizations that collect funds and distribute them to candidates. PACs serve as the campaign-financing arm of corporations, labor unions, trade associations, and even political parties. They grew out of long-standing federal laws that made it illegal for corporations and labor unions to contribute directly to a candidate. Barred from direct contributions, these organizations set up "political action" subsidiaries to allow them legal entry into campaign finance.

The impact of PACs on state politics is potentially far-reaching. Some Michigan legislators, for example, consider PACs a potentially dangerous influence on state politics because their money "buys a lot of access that others can't get."[52] And access usually means influence. Analysis of tobacco industry PACs suggests that their campaign contributions affected legislative behavior: "As legislators [in California, Colorado, Massachusetts, Pennsylvania, and Washington] received more tobacco industry campaign contributions . . . legislators were more likely to be pro-tobacco industry."[53] Similarly, in Florida, campaign contributions from teacher union PACs were shown to have influenced legislators' votes on a school vouchers bill.[54]

States have responded to the proliferation of PACs by increasing their regulation. In New Jersey, for instance, PACs are required to register and to provide information regarding their controlling interests. One likely possibility is that an independent interstate network of groups with money to spend could emerge as a real threat to political parties as a recruiter of candidates and a

political action committees (PACs) Organizations that raise and distribute campaign funds to candidates for elective office.

527 groups
Nonprofit, tax-exempt political organizations set up to accept contributions and make expenditures in campaigns, although not explicitly connected to candidates.

financier of campaigns. As a harbinger of tighter regulation of PACs, Alaska and Washington enacted laws that restrict contributions from out-of-state PACs. Most states have acted to limit PAC contributions, although the content of the laws varies. For example, Tennessee restricts the proportion of PAC contributions to 50 percent of a candidate's total contribution amount; Colorado allows "small donor" PACs to contribute more than "regular" PACs.[55] Some states such as Nevada ($5,000 per candidate per election campaign) and North Carolina ($5,400 per candidate per election campaign) have set absolute dollar amount ceilings on PAC contributions; others differentiate by office and set lower amounts for legislative races than for statewide campaigns. Rhode Island has an extremely low allowable contribution level ($1,000 per candidate per election year). Thirteen states (Alabama, Indiana, Iowa, Mississippi, Missouri, North Dakota, Oregon, Pennsylvania, South Dakota, Texas, Utah, Virginia, and Wyoming) have taken a completely different approach and allow unlimited contributions from PACs to candidates.

Table 5.3 lists the five highest-spending interest groups and PACs in Alabama, Iowa, and Texas during the 2017–2018 election cycle. It is important to remember that these figures are just a snapshot, but, even so, they show the variation across the three states in the types of big-spending interests and their spending patterns.

In addition to PACs, another type of political organization has sprung up: **527 groups** (named after the section of the Internal Revenue Code that defines this type of organization). These groups are not connected to candidates but spend money to influence the outcome of elections. For instance, in

Table 5.3 Big Spending Interest Groups and Political Action Committees in Three States, 2017 and 2018 Elections

ALABAMA		IOWA		TEXAS	
Five Highest Spending Groups	**Amount**	**Five Highest Spending Groups**	**Amount**	**Five Highest Spending Groups**	**Amount**
Business Council of Alabama	$2,416250	Iowa Republican Party	$9,297,035	Texans for Lawsuit Reform	$7,755,193
Retailers of Alabama PAC	$2,241,016	Iowa Democratic Party	$6,278,117	Texas Association of Realtors	$6,287,298
Alabama Education Association	$2,192,827	Republican Governors Association	$6,216,093	Empower Texas	$4,654990
Home Builders Association	$1,847,208	Service Employees International Union/ SEIU of Iowa	$1,796,550	Ted Cruz Victory Committee	$4,638,661
Alabama Farmers Federation	$1,697,327	Democratic Governors Association	$1,500,000	Rafael Edward (Ted) Cruz Campaign Committee	$3,866,789

Source: National Institute on Money in State Politics, "State Overviews," www.followthemoney.org/our-data/state-overviews/ (accessed January 12, 2020).

the 2018 gubernatorial election in Michigan, a 527 group called "A Stronger Michigan" (a group largely funded by the Democratic Governors Association) spent more than $8.5 million in independent expenditures to assist Democrat Gretchen Whitmer in beating Republican Bill Schuette. However, Schuette was not neglected by 527 groups. State Solutions, funded largely by the Republican Governors Association, spent $1.48 million on his behalf, while Americans for Prosperity, funded by the late conservative political activist David Koch, spent $1.8 million. In total, candidate organizations in this race spent about $10.8 million, but outside 527 groups spent more than twice that amount—$22.8 million.[56] The spending of 527 groups has gone up each election cycle from 2004 through 2018. Total state and local expenditures by 527 groups rose from $167.6 million in 2004 to $705.2 million in 2018.[57] Expenditures by 527 groups weaken a state's campaign finance laws. They skew spending upward and circumvent disclosure provisions.

Local-Level Interest Groups

Interest groups also function at the local level. Because so much of local government involves the delivery of services, local interest groups devote a great deal of their attention to administrative agencies and departments. Groups are involved in local elections and in community issues, to be sure, but much of their major focus is on the *actions* of government: policy implementation and service delivery. According to surveys of local officials in small cities, the two functional areas in which interest groups have the greatest influence are economic development and parks and recreation.[58]

As in states, business groups are influential in local government. Business-related interests, such as the local chamber of commerce, a downtown merchants association, and land developers, usually wield power in the community. These groups speak with a loud voice because business contributes both to the local tax base and to candidates for local offices. An increasingly important group at the local level is the neighborhood-based organization, which in some communities rivals business interests in influence. Other groups active at the local level include faith-based organizations, public employee unions, and ethnic minority groups.[59] Thus far, these groups have not achieved the degree of influence accorded business and neighborhood groups.

Neighborhood organizations deserve a closer look. Some have arisen out of issues that directly affect neighborhood residents—a nearby school that is scheduled to close, a wave of violent crime, a proposed freeway route that will destroy homes and businesses. Members of these groups devote much of their time to networking, to building relationships with policy makers, and to recruiting more individuals to their cause.[60] Others have been formed by government itself as a way of channeling citizen participation. In Los Angeles, for instance, the city established neighborhood councils in an effort to increase governmental responsiveness to local needs. In practice, these councils have been most active in opposing the city's land use and taxation decisions.[61]

Neighborhood groups, as well as others lacking a bankroll but possessing enthusiasm and dedication, may resort to tactics such as **direct action**, which might include protest marches at the county courthouse or standing in front of bulldozers clearing land for a new highway. Direct action is usually designed to attract attention to a cause, and it tends to be a last resort, a tactic employed when other efforts at influencing government policy have failed. A study of citizen groups in seven large cities found that 34 percent of the groups engaged in protests or demonstrations at least occasionally.[62]

After the killing of George Floyd by police officers in Minneapolis, a coalition of interest groups known collectively as Black Lives Matter dramatically grew in influence in major cities throughout the United States partly by engaging in mass protests against police mistreatment of minorities. Originally formed in 2013 in response to acquittal of George Zimmerman in the death of Trayvon Martin a year earlier, Black Lives Matter's community-based approach to organizing and its use of social media for mobilization greatly increased its presence and effectiveness in state and local policy making.[63] Another national political movement, Antifa, grew in prominence after the 2017 Unite the Right white supremacist rally in Charlottesville, Virginia. Antifa may have originated in Britain in 1936 when anti-fascist protestors violently stopped pro-fascist groups from marching through a London neighborhood.[64] The movement gained some prominence by staging demonstrations, some resulting in property destruction, during Donald Trump's inauguration in Washington, D.C. Antifa's possible role in looting and violence during the recent demonstrations against police actions has led President Trump to call for the group to be labeled as a domestic terrorism organization. Antifa's organization as an amorphous, virtually leadership organization would make enforcement of such designation difficult.[65]

Political Campaigns

Political parties and interest groups bump into each other all the time, especially in political campaigns. Like so many things these days, political campaigns aren't what they used to be. But despite changes in campaign styles and technologies, the goal remains the same: attracting enough voters to win the election. Figure 5.4 diagrams the voting configuration in a hypothetical election district. This district typically splits its vote evenly between Democrats and Republicans. Thus, in any given election, each party can count on about 25 percent of the vote (labeled the "base" in the diagram), with another 17 percent that is fairly likely to vote for the party's candidate (the "soft" partisan vote). That leaves about 16 percent of the vote up for grabs (the toss-up vote).[66] The toss-up vote and the soft partisan vote comprise what is typically referred to as the *swing vote*. Candidates target their energies on the swing vote, the size of which varies with the distribution of the partisan base vote. Keep in mind that most districts are not so evenly divided in their partisan loyalties.

direct action
A form of participation designed to draw attention to a cause.

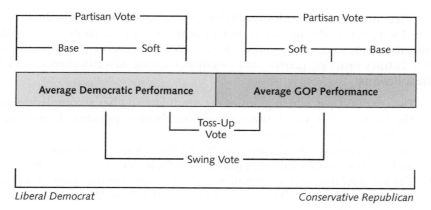

Figure 5.4 The Voting Configuration of a Hypothetical Election
District candidates rely on their partisan base and compete for the swing vote.

Source: Daniel M. Shea and Michael John Burton, *Campaign Craft: The Strategies, Tactics, and Art of Political Campaign Management* (Westport, CT: Praeger, 2001), p. 77.

A New Era of Campaigns

LO 5-7
To investigate the use of new campaign technologies.

Campaigns of the past conjure images of fiery oratory and county fairs. But campaigns orchestrated by rural courthouse gangs and urban ward bosses have given way to stylized video and electronic campaigning that relies on the mass media and political consultants. In the new era of campaigns, direct contact with potential voters still matters, of course. Candidates for state legislative seats, for example, devote time to door-to-door canvassing, neighborhood drop-ins, and public forums. New studies confirm the value of these types of contacts in mobilizing voter turnout, especially among folks who are considered "occasional voters."[67] Yet, more and more, candidates rely on direct mail and electronic media to deliver their messages, and on political consultants to help them craft their messages to targeted subsets of potential voters. The paragraph that opened this chapter makes precisely this point.

Using Old and New Media The mass media, especially television, are intrinsic aspects of modern statewide campaigns. Even candidates for legislative and local offices are increasingly using the mass media to transmit their messages. Campaigns can either buy their air time and newspaper space for advertising or get it free by arranging events that reporters are likely to cover. These events range from serious (a candidate's major policy statement) to gimmicky (a candidate climbing into the ring with a professional wrestler to demonstrate his "toughness"); either way, they are cleverly planned to capture media attention. A candidate seeking free media attention needs to create visual events, be quotable, and relentlessly attack opponents or targeted problems. Televised debates, common in campaigns for statewide office, offer another opportunity for free media time.

Free media time is seldom sufficient. Candidates, particularly those running for higher-level state offices and for positions in large cities, rely on paid advertisements to reach the public. Paid media advertisements seem to be of two distinct varieties: generic and negative. Generic advertisements include the following:

1. *The sainthood spot*, which glorifies the candidate and her accomplishments
2. *The testimonial*, in which other people (celebrities, average citizens) attest to the candidate's abilities
3. *The bumper-sticker policy spot*, which emphasizes the campaign's popular and noncontroversial themes (good schools, lower taxes, more jobs)
4. *The feel-good spot*, which identifies and capitalizes on the spirit of a place and its people (e.g., "Vermont's a special place" or "Nobody can do it better than Pennsylvania")[68]

Media advertising is important because it is frequently the only contact a potential voter has with a candidate. A candidate's personal characteristics and style—important considerations to an evaluating public—are easily transmitted via the airwaves. Experimental research on gubernatorial campaigns has shown that television advertising has a statistically significant effect on voter preferences.[69] Notably, however, the effects of these advertisements dissipate rapidly—sometimes within a week or two.

The internet has become a powerful campaign tool that can disseminate the candidate's message to far-flung audiences, mobilize potential supporters, and serve as a vehicle for attracting contributions. Nearly all major candidates for state and local offices routinely maintain campaign websites, some rudimentary, others much more elaborate. The current challenge is to design campaign websites that effectively scale down in size for smartphones and tablets, which are estimated to account for more than 60 percent of Americans' digital media time.[70] Several statewide candidates pioneered the use of campaign e-cards (the electronic equivalent of chain letters) so that supporters could contact people in their e-mail address books about the candidate. YouTube provides opportunities for candidates and for their opponents as videos of campaign high points—and low moments—make their way to the website. YouTube is easy to use, cost-effective for campaigns, and increasingly popular.

Social networking sites such as Facebook and Twitter generate tremendous potential fan bases for candidates and for raising money. As might be expected, the increased popularity of social media has led to some abuses and, in reaction, to efforts by government to address them. In 2010, Maryland was one of the first states to act, and, in 2013, California followed suit. The Golden State's Fair Political Practices Commission now requires anyone paid $500 or more by a campaign to provide social media content to report that activity to the state.[71] As with other media, campaign tweets, texts, and blogs must include an attribution such as "The author was paid by the Committee to Re-Elect Mayor Jane Doe in connection with this posting."

fake news
False news stories that appear to be true, typically spread on the internet.

The 2016 presidential campaign, with its accusations of foreign government and other group intervention, put political postings on social media in the spotlight. Social media **fake news** postings were widely disseminated in

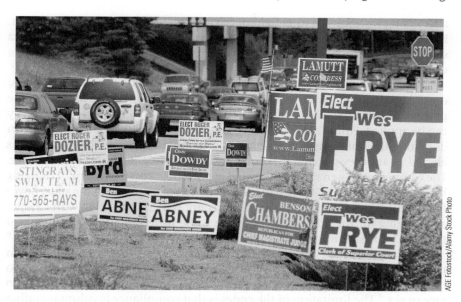

Empty lots along a busy road become crowded with campaign signs as the election nears.

the 2016 campaign; one conservative estimate showed the average American experienced between one and three stories from known fake news publishers in the one-month period before the November election.[72] After the election, social media platforms reacted differently to the threat of false news postings in the 2020 election cycle. Twitter announced a ban on all political ads, Google restricted the targeting of such ads, and Facebook said it would not police political ads for truthfulness at all.[73] Fake news has filtered down to state and local politics, but often it is difficult to tell what is fake and what is real. In Michigan, for example, dozens of what appeared to be local newspaper websites were found to be a network of outlets related to websites in Illinois and Maryland. The information published on these websites mixed legitimate news with advocacy in such a way that it was difficult for readers to tell one from the other. Rachel Davis Mersey, executive director of the Media Leadership Center at Northwestern University, said about this, "Any kind of politically slanted information which people think could be from a reputable news source really compromises the quality of discourse we have in this country. It's not fake news but it's not exactly what we want people to be consuming either."[74]

Negative Campaigning Negative campaign advertising comes in three flavors: fair, false, and deceptive. A fair ad might emphasize some embarrassing aspect of an opponent's voting record or some long-forgotten indiscretion. A false ad, as the label implies, contains untrue statements. More problematic are deceptive advertisements, which distort the truth about an opponent. The task for states is to regulate negative campaign advertising without violating free speech guarantees of the U.S. Constitution. False advertising that is done with actual malice can be prohibited by a state, but deceptive ads, replete with accusation and innuendo, are more difficult to regulate.[75]

Most states have enacted laws prohibiting false campaign statements; candidates who use false ads against their opponents can be fined. One of the problems with these laws is that the damage is done long before the remedy can be applied. Fining a candidate after the election is akin to latching the barn door after the horse has fled. In 2000, for example, Democrat Roy Cooper was elected as attorney general of North Carolina, beating Republican Dan Boyce. The Cooper campaign ran a negative ad against Boyce accusing him of charging high legal fees in a suit Boyce had filed on behalf of taxpayers in the state. Boyce filed suit against Cooper, but the case was not settled until 2014 with Cooper apologizing for the ad. Cooper went on to be reelected attorney general for three additional terms and then won election as governor in 2016 and 2020.[76]

Some states, such as California and Nevada, have adopted fair campaign practices codes. These codes typically contain broad guidelines such as "do not misrepresent the facts" or "do not make appeals to prejudice based on race or sex." The limitation of the codes is that compliance is voluntary rather than mandatory.

In addition to government action, many newspapers and websites report regularly on the content, presentation, and relative accuracy of campaign advertising. Ad watches or truth boxes, as they are often called, occasionally have led to the retraction or redesign of ads. Despite the efforts of government and the media, however, negative campaign advertising persists because many candidates believe that, if done cleverly, it can benefit their campaigns. Research by political scientist Ted Braden has confirmed that negative messages, accompanied by fear-evoking music and images, trigger strong reactions in viewers.[77] People may not like negative ads, but they certainly seem to remember them.

Political Consultants An occupational specialty that sprang up during the 1970s and 1980s is clearly here to stay: political consulting. Individuals with expertise in polling, direct mail, fundraising, advertising, and campaign management put their talents to work in political campaigns. These consultants form the core of the professional campaign management team assembled by candidates for state offices. They identify and target likely voters, both those who are already in the candidate's camp and need to be reminded to vote *and* those who can be persuaded to vote for the candidate. Consultants use survey research and focus groups to find out what the public is thinking. They carefully craft messages to appeal to specific voters, such as the elderly, homeowners, or environmentalists. Advertising on cable television, radio, and through direct mail are three popular means of getting a candidate's message to targeted segments of the voting public. In fact, research has found that much of the public actually prefers narrowcast messages, tailored to their interests.[78]

Any number of factors can influence the result of an election, such as the presence of an incumbent in a race and the amount of funds that a challenger has accumulated, but one significant factor is the ability to frame or define the issues during the campaign. Even in a quietly contested state legislative race, district residents are likely to receive mailings that state the candidates' issue positions, solicit funds, and perhaps comment unfavorably on the opposition. The candidate who has an effective political consultant to help set the campaign agenda and thereby put her opponent on the defensive is that much closer to victory. A study of legislative elections indicates that the use of campaign professionals is especially valuable to challengers who are hoping to unseat incumbents.[79]

Campaign Finance

To campaign for public office is to spend money—frequently a lot of money. For instance, in 2018, running for reelection in New York, Governor Andrew Cuomo spent nearly $35 million on his campaign, with half of that amount going to television advertising. The New York governor's race was not unique: Gubernatorial elections are multimillion dollar affairs these days. Table 5.4 lists the contributions received by gubernatorial candidates in ten states across the country in 2018. Variation across the states both in the total amounts and in the partisan shares is substantial.

Big spending is not confined to gubernatorial contests. Spending in legislative races is climbing, and fast. Consider 2018 data from two large states, New York and Texas, each with 150 seats in their lower legislative chamber. In New York, 336 candidates competed for the Assembly seats, raising a total of $21.7 million, or an average of just over $65,300 per candidate. In Texas,

LO 5-8
To compare state differences in the regulation of campaign finance.

Table 5.4 Contribution Totals for Gubernatorial Races by Party and State, 2018, Selected States

State	Contribution Total (All Gubernatorial Candidates)	Contributions to Democrats	Contributions to Republicans	Contributions to Third Parties/ Nonpartisan
Arkansas	$ 7,876,946	$ 669,231	$ 7,200,080	$ 7,635
Colorado	$ 28,943,362	$ 24,383,211	$ 4,558,224	$ 1,927
Florida	$ 38,030,714	$ 18,877,471	$19,083,547	$ 69,696
Illinois	$267,775,797	$176,346,769	$86,494,274	$4,934,754
Kansas	$ 10,042,846	$ 3,475,428	$ 4,094,580	$2,372,838
Massachusetts	$ 33,234,744	$ 2,688,757	$30,545,987	$ 0
Maryland	$ 23,238,624	$ 5,459,264	$17,773,094	$ 6,266
Pennsylvania	$ 56,686,387	$ 35,382,294	$21,195,142	$ 8,951
South Carolina	$ 11,145,773	$ 3,187,034	$ 7,958,739	$ 0
Wisconsin	$ 47,918,109	$ 11,337,086	$36,565,133	$ 15,890

Source: National Institute on Money in State Politics, "State Overviews," www.followthemoney.org/our-data/state-overviews/ (accessed January 14, 2020).

the 399 candidates for House seats spent a total of $90.3 million, which averages to approximately $226,300 per candidate.[80] It should be noted, however, that spending in some states is substantially less. For instance, in Arkansas, the average expenditure total for lower House seats was $37,000 in 2018; in Kansas, it was $24,000; and in Wyoming, it was $7,000.

Political science research has confirmed several long-standing truths about the costs of campaigning.[81] For instance, close elections cost more than elections in which one candidate is sure to win, because uncertainty regarding the outcome is a spur to spending. A candidate quickly learns that it is easier to get money from potential contributors when the polls show that they have a chance of winning. Also, elections that produce change—that is, in which an incumbent is unseated, or the out-of-office party gains the office—typically cost more. Taking on an existing officeholder is a risky strategy that drives up election costs. And an open race in which there is no incumbent represents an opportunity for the party out of office to capture the seat, thus triggering similar spending by the in-office party in an effort to protect the seat. It is no wonder that campaign costs are exploding. But there may be a side benefit to more campaign spending: an increase in voter turnout. Studies of state legislative elections revealed a link between expenditure levels and voter turnout.[82]

State Efforts at Campaign Reform Concerns over escalating costs and the influence of deep-pocketed special interests in campaigns have led reform groups such as Common Cause to call for changes, including (1) improve state laws to provide comprehensive and timely disclosure of campaign finances, (2) impose limitations on contributions by individuals and groups, (3) create a combined public-private financing mechanism for primaries and general elections, and (4) establish an independent commission to enforce tough sanctions on violators of campaign finance laws.

States have performed impressively on the first of these recommendations; in fact, all states have some sort of campaign financing reporting procedure. Most states make information on campaign contributions available online in a searchable database; many states provide similar access to campaign expenditure data. In response to the fourth recommendation, more than half of the states have established independent commissions, such as California's Fair Political Practices Commission, to oversee the conduct of campaigns, although these organizations have found it somewhat difficult to enforce the law and punish violators.

The other recommendations have proven more troublesome. States have grappled with the issue of costly campaigns but have made only modest progress in controlling costs. A 1976 decision by the U.S. Supreme Court in *Buckley v. Valeo* made these efforts more difficult; the Court ruled that governments cannot limit a person's right to spend money in order to spread their views about particular issues and candidates. In essence, then, candidates have unlimited power to spend their own money on their own behalf, and other individuals may spend to their hearts' content to promote their own opinions on election-related issues. The U.S. Supreme Court extended this logic to corporations and labor unions, ruling in 2010 in *Citizens United v. Federal Election Commission* that these entities have a constitutional right to advertise on issues and influence elections. A 2014 case, *McCutcheon v. Federal Election Commission,* pushed the logic even further by striking down limits on the total amount of money an individual can donate in a two-year period to candidates for federal offices and to political committees. In an earlier case involving a lawsuit from Colorado, the Court had decided that independent spending by political parties, so-called **soft money**, could not be limited, either. What the Court let stand, however, were state limits on an individual's contributions to candidates and parties; it also ruled that if a candidate accepts public funds, then they are bound by whatever limitations the state may impose. The 2002 Federal Bipartisan Campaign Reform Act, typically referred to as the McCain-Feingold law, aims at controlling the flow of soft money, but reports from recent election cycles suggest that loopholes remain.[83]

Amid the evolving web of federal court rulings, the states have tried to address campaign finance. Some states established specific limits on the amount of money that organizations and individuals can contribute to a political race. In New York, for example, corporations are limited to a contribution maximum of $5,000 per calendar year, and individuals (other than official candidates) are restricted to $47,100 in a gubernatorial election and to $11,800 and $4,700 in general elections for senate and house seats, respectively. Florida's approach is straightforward: Individuals (other than the candidate), corporations, labor unions, and PACs are allowed to contribute a maximum of $3,000 per candidate per election to statewide offices and $1,000 to legislative or judicial candidates. Some twenty-three states have gone even further by prohibiting direct contributions from corporations and labor unions. Washington state has a unique approach—banning contributions from corporations not doing business in the state. But a totally different philosophy pervades the politics of several states that continue to operate their election systems without any limitations on contributions. In Alabama, Nebraska, Oregon, Utah, and Virginia, organizations and individuals can contribute as much as they wish.[84]

States have also considered the other side of the campaign financing equation: expenditures. All states require candidates and political committees to file reports documenting the expenditure of campaign funds. A few states tried to impose limits on a candidate's total expenditures, but a 2006 U.S. Supreme Court ruling that Vermont's spending limits were too low to allow candidates to compete effectively has complicated that approach. Many have followed Hawaii's lead and set voluntary spending limits. Colorado, for example, adopted a nonbinding $3.4 million spending cap for gubernatorial candidates. Michigan takes a different approach: Publicly funded candidates (governor and lieutenant governor) are restricted to $2 million per election, with additional spending allowable in certain circumstances. Florida has a similar system in place for candidates receiving public funds.

Public Funding as a Solution

One-third of the states have adopted some sort of public funding of some campaigns, although in most of these states, public financing supplements the private contributions candidates receive. As a condition of accepting

soft money
Unregulated funds contributed to national political parties and nonparty political groups.

public money, whether it is a matching grant (as in Florida and Hawaii) or a fixed subsidy (as in Minnesota), candidates must abide by state-imposed spending limits. In states that have adopted a fully funded "clean elections" system of campaign finance (Arizona, Connecticut, Maine, and New Mexico), a candidate who wishes to participate must first demonstrate their viability by getting signatures on a petition and/or collecting a certain number of small dollar contributions. Once in the program, they may spend only public funds.[85] Not all elective offices are covered by public funding, however. For instance, Arizona's and Connecticut's programs cover statewide offices and the legislature, Maine's applies to the governor and the legislature, and New Mexico's affects the Public Regulation Commission and statewide judicial offices.

The public financing system is fairly easy to administer and is relatively transparent for citizens. In most of the public funding states, citizens can use their state income tax form to earmark a portion (a dollar or two) of their tax liability for the fund. A check-off system of this sort does not directly increase taxpayers' tax burden. (Iowa, Kentucky, and Utah are among the eight states in which a taxpayer can specify that a political party be the recipient of the check-off amount.) In a few states, the public fund is amassed through a voluntary surcharge, or additional tax (usually $1 or $5). In addition to check-offs and surcharges, some of the public-funding states, including Arkansas and Virginia, offer taxpayers a tax credit (usually a percentage of the contribution, up to a specific maximum) when they contribute to political campaigns. Another option is a state tax deduction for campaign contributions, an approach used in Oklahoma. In addition to taxpayer contributions, some states also allocate money from specific sources, such as Arizona's traffic and criminal fine surcharges.

Public campaign financing is supposed to rid the election process of some of its evils. Proponents argue that it will democratize the contribution process by freeing candidates from excessive reliance on special-interest money. Other possible advantages include expanding the pool of potential candidates, allowing candidates to compete on a more equal basis, and reducing the cost of campaigning. Not everyone has embraced public funding, however. Obviously, it represents a cost to taxpayers, and some contend that incumbents will benefit from limits on campaign spending and that nonserious candidates will be able to use public funds as their own personal treasury. In Arizona, in 2002, Janet Napolitano became the first governor to be elected with full public financing of her campaign. In the next election cycle, 60 percent of state legislative candidates ran with public money, and 93 percent of them were elected. Research on Arizona and Maine shows that clean elections programs deliver on the promise of increased competition.[86] A U.S. Supreme Court ruling in 2011, however, weakened some aspects of Arizona's law.[87]

By contributing to the fund, average citizens may feel that they have a greater stake in state elections. Although more research needs to be done, studies suggest that public financing produces at least some of the benefits its supporters claim. For instance, an analysis of gubernatorial campaigns indicated that the use of public funds by incumbents and challengers holds down overall spending. It also narrows the expenditure gap between them.[88]

? It's Your Turn

Should Political Spending in Campaigns Be Unrestricted by Government?

Money plays a significant role in today's political campaigns. States have struggled to reform and control the influence of money in campaigns.

PROS	CONS
Money is an essential part of campaigns. It allows candidates to convey their views to potential voters, thereby making candidates' positions more clear. Therefore, people should be able to spend as much as they like on candidates and on political issues.	Allowing money to flow unrestricted in political campaigns means that the wealthiest interests have the greatest opportunity to influence public policy.
Interest groups are aggregations of people who share similar views on certain issues. People have the right to express their opinions (the U.S. constitutional guarantee of freedom of speech), and expressing opinions often costs money. Consequently, interest group spending should be unrestricted, just so long as it is disclosed.	The government must protect both freedom and equality. However, to the vast majority of Americans, the "freedom" to contribute unlimited funds to a campaign is purely theoretical, as they often cannot spare *any* money to give to candidates. The government could, however, give some protection to their equality of input by limiting the amount of money in politics. In other words, contribution limits help level the playing field.
The current system of regulations is so complicated that it requires a fleet of accountants and lawyers to navigate it and a host of bureaucrats to administer it. Abolishing campaign finance laws would simplify the process and save the government money.	Allowing the unrestricted flow of private money into campaigns increases the likelihood of corruption and bribery.
Placing limits on campaign spending encourages the proliferation of PACs and 527 groups as a way to circumvent the limits. And these organizations are much more difficult for the public to monitor.	Limiting contributions lessens the likelihood of government capture by private economic interests.

Chapter Recap

- Even though voter loyalties have weakened, political parties have proved remarkably resilient and have taken on new roles in politics and governance.

- The Democratic Party can claim about 31 percent of the voting-age public for itself and the Republican Party around 28 percent. The rest of the electorate is considered Independents (although they might lean toward one of the major parties), with a small fraction affiliated with third parties.

- Interparty competition has increased over time. One result has been a rise in divided government in the states.

- Interest groups exert a powerful force in state government, with business lobbyists and teachers' groups the most influential in the majority of states.

- The state interest group system is changing: A more diverse set of interests lobbies at the statehouse; meanwhile, state governments have tightened their regulation of lobbyists.

- Groups are involved in local elections and in community issues, but their major focus is on the *actions* of government: policy implementation and service delivery.

- Campaigns for state office still involve door-to-door canvassing, neighborhood drop-ins, and public forums, but they increasingly use direct mail, various electronic media, and political consultants.

- Running for public office can be an expensive proposition. To try to level the playing field and diminish the role of private money, most states limit contributions, and some states provide public financing.

Key Terms

political parties *(p. 115)*
ideology *(p. 116)*
ticket splitting *(p. 117)*
unified government *(p. 123)*
divided government *(p. 123)*
dealignment *(p. 124)*

interest groups *(p. 125)*
lobbying *(p. 129)*
grassroots lobbying *(p. 130)*
political action committees
(PACs) *(p. 131)*
527 groups *(p. 132)*

direct action *(p. 134)*
fake news *(p. 136)*
soft money *(p. 141)*

Internet Resources

The major political parties have official websites: The Democratic Party is at **www.democrats.org**, and the Republican Party is at www.gop.com. At the state level, examples are Hawaii's website at **www .hawaiidemocrats.org** and Virginia's at **www .rpv.org**. An interesting state-level, third-party website, **www.cagreens.org**, is the site for the Green Party of California.

Common Cause has a website, **www.commoncause .org/states**, that tracks the activities of its thirty-five state offices and the progress of campaign finance reform.

A group devoted to cleaning up elections is Public Campaign. Its website is **www.publicampaign .org**. Another group with a reform focus is the Center for Public Integrity, at **www.publicintegrity .org**.

The National Institute on Money in State Politics provides an abundance of information on the subject at **www.followthemoney.org**.

To learn more about 527 groups, see **www .opensecrets.org/527s**.

Different perspectives are reflected in the websites of the American Civil Liberties Union, **www.aclu.org**, and the Christian Coalition, **www.cc.org**.

www.flchamber.com and **www.ilchamber.org** are the websites for the chambers of commerce for Florida and Illinois, respectively. Other state chambers use similar URLs.

The Texas State Teachers' Association, at **www.tsta .org**, is an example of a state school teachers' organization. A different but related perspective is provided by the Oregon PTA at **www .oregonpta.org**.

Other examples of state-level interest groups include the Mississippi Association of Realtors, at **msrealtors.org**, and the Arizona Hospital and Healthcare Association, at **www.azhha.org**.

6

State Legislatures: The People's Representatives

The New York senate in session in its historic chamber.

Learning Objectives

LO 6-1 To differentiate the three functions of legislatures.

LO 6-2 To examine the redistricting process and its consequences.

LO 6-3 To weigh the importance of informal norms amid formal rules in the legislative institution.

LO 6-4 To recognize the intricacies of the lawmaking process.

LO 6-5 To appraise the efforts to reform state legislatures.

LO 6-6 To discuss the impact of legislative term limits.

LO 6-7 To interpret the interaction of the legislative branch with the executive branch.

LO 6-8 To examine the link between legislatures and the public.

The start of a new legislative session is a time of celebration in state capitols around the country. Bouquets of flowers decorate the chamber as family members join legislators on the floor for the swearing-in ceremony. In Montana, opening day 2017 was even more special than usual. There, the nation's youngest state legislator, 18-year-old college freshman Jacob Bachmeier was sworn in as a member of the state's house of representatives. Representative Bachmeier beat incumbent Stephanie Hess in 2016 by a margin of 53 percent to 47 percent. Bachmeier's campaign manager was his high school classmate, Daniel Almas. In 2018, Bachmeier was reelected to a second term, winning nearly 60 percent of the vote, while also completing the first couple of years of his undergraduate degree at Montana State University. Just after he was first elected, Bachmeier described his typical day to a newspaper reporter: He "woke up at 5 a.m. to do homework. He decided not to seek reelection in 2020 citing work conflicts.[1]

LO 6-I
To differentiate the
three functions of
legislatures.

The Essence of Legislatures

The new year dawns quietly in Boise, Idaho, in Jefferson City, Missouri, and in Harrisburg, Pennsylvania, but it does not remain quiet for long: State legislators are set to converge on state capitols. Every January (or February or March in a few states; every other January in a few others), state legislatures reconvene in session to do the public's business. More than 7,000 legislators hammer out solutions to intricate and often intransigent public problems. They do so in an institution that is steeped in tradition and governed by layers of formal rules and informal norms.

Legislatures engage in three principal functions: *policy making, representation,* and *oversight.* The first, policy making, includes enacting laws and allocating funds. The third decade of the twenty-first century finds legislators debating issues such as health care, public education, criminal justice, and immigration. These deliberations resulted in the revision of old laws, the passage of new laws, and changes in spending, which is what policy making is all about. As legislative sessions moved into the summer of 2020, new issues of COVID-19 pandemic health and financial impacts and civil unrest in the wake of police shootings rose to the top of the policy agenda and may likely dominate policy discussions. Legislatures do not have sole control of the state policy-making function; governors, courts, and agencies also determine policy through executive orders, judicial decisions, and administrative regulations, respectively. But legislatures are the dominant policy-making institutions in state government. Table 6.1 lists the issues that attracted legislative attention in 2020.

Table 6.1 Popular Legislative Issues in 2020

ISSUE	WHAT IT'S ALL ABOUT
Abortion	Increasing or decreasing restrictions on abortions
Climate	Addressing rising sea levels in coastal states while coping with potential public indifference to such issues
Criminal Justice Reform	Reducing the high costs of incarceration; decriminalizing or reducing sentencing for some offenses; addressing bans on voting by felons
Election Security	Reducing the possibility that 2020 balloting might be hacked by foreign or domestic agents
Health Care	Deciding whether and how to expand Medicaid in the thirteen states that have not already done so; addressing rural health access issues
Highway Funding	Changing how highway construction and repair are funded from a per gallon tax on fuel to some other system
Housing	Addressing chronic homelessness and the increasing lack of affordable housing in many areas
Immigration	Addressing issues such as sanctuary laws for state and local jurisdictions, in-state tuition, and driver's licenses for immigrants
Net Neutrality	Deciding whether to require internet service providers to treat all web traffic equally or to allow metering of such traffic in response to changes in federal policy
Pensions	Ensuring there is funding for the growing number of retiring state and local government employees

Source: Alan Greenblatt, David Kidd, and Todd Newcombe, "The Biggest Issues to Watch in 2020," *Governing,* https://www.governing.com/next/The-Biggest-Issues-to-Watch-in-2020.html (January 13, 2020).

In their second function, legislators are expected to represent their constituents—the people who live in their districts—in two ways. At least in theory, they are expected to speak for their constituents in the legislative chamber—to do the will of the public in designing policy solutions. This is not easy. On quiet issues, a legislator seldom has much of a clue about public opinion. However, on noisy issues, constituents' will is rarely unanimous. Individuals and organized groups with different perspectives may write to or visit their legislator to urge them to vote a certain way on a pending bill. In another representative function, legislators act as their constituents' facilitators in state government. For example, they may help a citizen deal with an unresponsive state agency. This kind of constituency service (or **casework**, as it is often called) can be time-consuming, but it pays dividends at reelection time, because voters tend to look favorably on a legislator who has helped them.[2]

The third function, oversight, is different from the policy-making and representation functions. Concerned that the laws they passed and the funds they allocated frequently did not produce the intended effect, lawmakers began to pay more attention to the performance of the state bureaucracy. Legislatures have adopted several methods for checking on agency implementation and spending. The oversight role takes legislatures into the administrative realm of state government. Not surprisingly, agencies rarely welcome this scrutiny, although legislatures see it as a logical extension of their policy-making role.

Legislative Dynamics

State legislative bodies are typically referred to as the legislature, but their formal titles vary. In Colorado, it is the General Assembly that meets every year; in Massachusetts, the General Court; and in Oregon, the Legislative Assembly. The legislatures of forty-six states meet annually; in only four states (Montana, Nevada, North Dakota, and Texas) do they meet every other year. (Arkansas and Oregon had been among the biennial sessions group until 2008 and 2010, respectively, when voters approved a switch to annual legislative sessions.) The length of the legislative session varies widely. For example, the Utah General Assembly convened in Salt Lake City on January 28, 2019, and left town on March 14, 2019, for a total of forty-four calendar days in session. By contrast, in states like Michigan and New Jersey, legislative sessions run nearly year-round.

The length of a state's legislative session can be a sensitive issue. In 1997, the Nevada legislature met for 169 days—the longest, most expensive session in its history.[3] Nevadans showed their displeasure the following year when they passed a measure limiting future legislative sessions to 120 days. Voters in the Silver State apparently believed that it should not take more than four months—every two years—to conduct their state's business.

The Senate and the House

Forty-nine state legislatures are bicameral, that is, they have two houses or chambers, similar to those of the U.S. Congress. (The exception is Nebraska, which in 1934 established a nonpartisan unicameral legislature.) Bicameralism is a legacy

casework
Legislative assistance on behalf of constituents who have a problem or grievance with a state agency.

of the postcolonial era, in which an upper house represented the interests of the propertied class, and a lower house represented everyone else. Even after this distinction was eliminated, states stuck with the bicameral structure, ostensibly because of its contribution to the concept of checks and balances. It is much tougher to pass bills when they have to survive the scrutiny of two legislative houses. Having a bicameral structure, then, reinforces the status quo. Unicameralism might improve the efficiency of the legislature, but efficiency has never been a primary goal of the consensus-building deliberative process.

In the forty-nine bicameral states, the upper house is called the senate; the lower house is usually called the house of representatives. The average size of a state senate is forty members; houses typically average about 100 members. As with many aspects of state legislatures, chamber size varies substantially—from the Alaska senate, with twenty members, to the New Hampshire house, with 400 representatives. Chamber size seldom changes, but in 2003, a voter mandate forced Rhode Island to reduce the size of its 150-member legislature by one-fourth. Size matters in a legislature. Research has found that large and small chambers produce different patterns of interaction among their members.[4]

For senators, the term of office is usually four years; approximately one-quarter of the states use a two-year senate term. In many states, the election of senators is staggered. House members serve two-year terms, except in Alabama, Louisiana, Maryland, Mississippi, and North Dakota, where four-year terms prevail. The 2021 state legislative sessions found Republicans in control of both chambers in thirty states, the Democratic Party controlling both houses in nineteen states, with Nebraska's unicameral house being officially nonpartisan.

There are 7,383 state legislators in this country: 1,972 senators and 5,411 representatives. As of 2020, Democrats held 47 percent of the seats, Republicans held 52 percent, with the remainder being Independent or representatives of third parties. Men outnumbered women 71 to 29 percent. The legislatures of Nevada (52 percent) and Colorado (47 percent) had the highest percentage of female legislators. In 2012, Katrina Shealy was elected to the South Carolina state senate making it the last state legislative body to no longer be all male. Legislatures are becoming more racially and ethnically diverse. African Americans occupied 9 percent of all legislative seats; Latinos, 5 percent; Asian Americans, 1 percent; and Native Americans, 1 percent. These proportions of women and racial-ethnic minorities represent substantial increases relative to their near absence from most pre-1970s legislatures.[5] Increased diversity is important with respect to the representation function of a legislature. Research has found that constituents are less likely to communicate with legislators of a different race than they are with legislators of their same race.[6]

The average age of legislators is 56, but as the example that opened this chapter showed, an occasional "millennial" can be found amid the lawmakers. Legislators range in age from 19 to 94. In terms of occupations, business executives/managers (16 percent) and attorneys (14 percent) are the largest occupational categories. These two groups are followed by business owners (13 percent), full-time legislators (11 percent), retirees (8 percent), and educators (6 percent).[7]

Legislative Districts

LO 6-2
To examine the redistricting process and its consequences.

Legislators are elected from geographically based districts, with each district in a state containing approximately the same number of inhabitants. Most legislative districts are single-member districts (SMDs), that is, one legislator represents the district. In Nebraska, for instance, each member of the unicameral legislature represents 37,272 people, more or less. Dividing or apportioning a state into districts is an intensely political process that affects the balance of power in a state. In the 1960s, for example, Florida's legislative districts were drawn such that the less-populated panhandle area was overrepresented in the legislature at the expense of the heavily populated southern areas of the state. Therefore, despite Florida's rapid urbanization during that period, public policy continued to reflect the interests of a rurally based minority of the population.

Eight states, including Arizona and the Dakotas, continue to use **multimember districts (MMDs)** for the lower house of the state legislature; two states—Vermont and West Virginia—use MMDs for their state senates. (Usually, it is a two-member district, and the number of people residing in the MMD is approximately double that of an SMD.) There are two main types of MMDs. In the first type, all candidates compete against one another, and the two candidates with the most votes are elected. In the other type, candidates have to declare which of the district's two seats they are seeking. In both types, voters in the district vote in as many races as there are seats in the district. Once elected, the two legislators represent the entire MMD area. Is there any difference between legislators in MMDs and those in SMDs? The answer is a cautious yes, if research on the Arizona and Maryland legislatures can be extended to other states. Lawmakers in the MMD house of representatives tended to be more ideologically extreme than lawmakers in the SMD senate, while lawmakers elected from MMDs in Maryland tended to focus more on high-profile credit claiming activities than did lawmakers from SMDs.[8]

Malapportionment Unequal representation, or **malapportionment**, has characterized many legislative bodies. In the past, for example, some states allocated an equal number of senators to each county. (This system calls to mind the U.S. Senate, which has two senators per state.) Because counties vary in population size, some senators were representing ten or twenty times as many constituents as their colleagues were. New Jersey offered one of the most extreme cases. In 1962, one county contained 49,000 residents and another had 924,000, yet each county was allotted one senator, and each senator had one vote in the senate. This kind of imbalance meant that a small group of people had the same institutional power as a group that was nineteen times larger. Such disproportionate power is inherently at odds with representative democracy, in which each person's vote carries the same weight.

Until the 1960s, federal courts ignored the legislative malapportionment issue. It was not until 1962, in a Tennessee case in which the malapportionment was especially egregious (house district populations ranged from 2,340 to 42,298), that the courts stepped in. In *Baker v. Carr*, the U.S. Supreme Court ruled that the Fourteenth Amendment guarantee of equal protection applies

multimember districts (MMDs) Legislative districts containing more than one seat.

malapportionment Skewed legislative districts that violate the "one person, one vote" ideal.

to state legislative apportionment. With this decision as a wedge, the Court ruled that state houses should be apportioned on the basis of population. Two years later, in *Reynolds v. Sims* (1964), which extended the principle of equal representation to state senates, Chief Justice Earl Warren summed up the apportionment ideal by saying, "Legislators represent people, not trees or acres."[9] Accordingly, districts should reflect population equality: one person, one vote. In the aftermath of this decision, which overturned the apportionment practices of six states, a **reapportionment** fever swept the country, and district lines were redrawn in every state.

Reapportionment provided an immediate benefit to previously underrepresented urban areas, and increased urban representation led to a growing responsiveness in state legislatures to the problems and interests of cities and suburbs. Where reapportionment had a partisan effect, it generally benefitted Republicans in the South and Democrats in the North. Other impacts of reapportionment have included the election of younger, better-educated legislators and, especially in southern states, better representation of African Americans. All in all, reapportionment is widely credited with improving the representativeness of American state legislatures.

Redrawing District Lines State legislatures are redistricted at least every ten years following the U.S. Census. Redistricting allows population fluctuations—growth in some areas, decline in others—to be reflected in redrawn district lines. Twenty-six legislatures **redistrict** themselves; by contrast, thirteen states attempt to depoliticize the process by using impartial commissions to develop their redistricting plans.[10] In the remaining states, the redistricting task involves the legislature and either a commission or another political institution such as the governor (Maryland) or the state Supreme Court (Florida). A state's decision to use a less-politicized approach such as a commission often comes about after a well-publicized redistricting controversy that creates a climate for reform of the process.[11]

In states where the legislature redistricts itself (and the state's congressional districts), the party controlling the legislature controls the redistricting process. Therefore, district lines have traditionally been redrawn to protect incumbent legislators and to maximize the strength of the party in power. The art of drawing district lines creatively was popularized in Massachusetts in 1812, when a political cartoonist for the *Boston Gazette* dubbed one of Governor Elbridge Gerry's district creations a **gerrymander** because the district, carefully configured to reflect partisan objectives, was shaped like a salamander. Two hundred years later, gerrymandering has not disappeared and neither has the partisan politics surrounding the process. Republicans claim that the district lines drawn by Democrats disadvantage the GOP; when Republicans create the maps, it is the Democrats who cry "foul." Litigation often ensues. Clearly, the practice of redrawing district lines in response to population shifts is highly politicized, as a study of the Kansas legislature demonstrated.[12] The goal, of course, is to maintain and grow the partisan majority. Not surprisingly, gerrymandering makes it more difficult for true two-party competition to develop.

reapportionment
The reallocation of seats in a legislative assembly.

redistrict
The redrawing of legislative district lines to conform as closely as possible to the "one person, one vote" ideal.

gerrymander
The process of creatively designing a legislative district, usually to enhance the electoral fortunes of the party in power.

Amid the politics, redistricting has become a sophisticated operation in which statisticians and geographers use computer mapping to assist the legislature in designing an optimal districting scheme. (Check out Utah's efforts to engage the public in redistricting in the Controversies in States and Localities box.) Although "one person, one vote" is the official standard, some unofficial guidelines are also taken into consideration. Ideally, districts should be geographically compact and unbroken. Those who draw the lines pay close attention to traditional political boundaries such as counties and, as noted, to the fortunes of political parties and incumbents. As long as districts adhere fairly closely to the population-equality standard (if an MMD contains three seats, it must have three times the population of a SMD), federal courts tolerate the achievement of unofficial objectives. But redistricting does occasionally produce some oddly shaped districts resembling lobsters, spiders, and earmuffs. Dividing Montgomery County, Maryland, into legislative districts after the 2010 Census produced the shapes displayed in Figure 6.1.

Figure 6.1 State Legislative Districts in Montgomery County, Maryland, 2012

Controversies in States and Localities

Do-It-Yourself e-Redistricting

Redistricting is a controversial process, as the discussion in this chapter indicates. It is contentious and often becomes litigious. To the general public, it seems mysterious and opaque. Cognizant of this, the Utah legislature tried something different in 2011, when residents were encouraged to access map-drawing software on their home computers and try their hand at redistricting. More than 1,000 Utahans took a crack at carving the state's 82,170 square miles into four congressional districts, twenty-nine state senate districts, seventy-five state house districts, and fifteen state board of education districts. In each category, districts had to have substantial equality of population based on the 2010 census ($+/-$ 1 percent for congressional districts, $+/-$ 3.5 percent for the others), and be contiguous and reasonably compact. (Note that party considerations did not factor explicitly into the public's process. The legislative redistricting committee, made up of fourteen Republicans and five Democrats, paid more attention to the partisan impact when they drew their own maps.) Eventually, more than 400 plans were submitted by the citizenry to the redistricting committee for its review.

The reason for the state's outreach to the public was twofold: to engage the citizenry in the process to increase their understanding of it and, importantly, to increase their influence in it. Anyone who submitted a plan and attended a redistricting hearing could present arguments in favor of their plan. According to the chair of the redistricting committee, legislators actually moved district lines based on the logic offered by some of the map drawers. Once the process ended and official maps were adopted by the legislature, comments from participants were generally positive. One thing for certain, the online do-it-yourself map drawing experience generated a lively public conversation on redistricting. By the next round of redistricting after the 2020 census, expect to see most states following Utah's example.

Critical Thinking Questions

1. Are average citizens qualified to draw district boundaries? How can they gain the information that is required to make these decisions?

2. What components would be included in a computer program to produce unbiased district lines?

3. Should there be a political component to the districting process? Do politics serve a valid social function here?

Source: Mary Branham, "Technology Opens Redistricting Process," *Capitol Ideas*, https://www.csg.org/pubs/capitolideas /jan_feb_2012_regionPDFs/CIJanFeb2012SOUTH.pdf (January/ February, 2012): 40–41.

Legislatures have to pay attention to the effects of their redistricting schemes on the voting strength of racial minorities. In fact, amendments to the Voting Rights Act and subsequent court rulings instructed affected states to create districts in which racial minorities would have majority status. The intentional creation of majority minority districts more favorable to the election of African Americans had a partisan consequence. African Americans are more likely to be Democrats than Republicans; therefore, clustering black voters into specific districts diluted the potential Democratic vote of adjacent districts. This increased the likelihood that Republican candidates would win in those nearby districts. For instance, Florida drew thirteen heavily African American house districts, leaving the other 107 districts with fewer black voters. Some observers contended that this situation made it easier for Republicans to win sixty-five of those seats and thus control the house.[13]

The courts have not spoken with crystal clarity on the question of reapportionment. Yes, the racial composition of districts should be taken into account, but, no, racial considerations should not be the sole criterion. In its most recent rulings on gerrymandering, the U.S. Supreme Court ruled in a North Carolina case—*Rucho v. Common Cause* (2019)—that while it was "incompatible with democratic principles," partisan gerrymandering represented a political question that was beyond the scope of federal court jurisdiction, sending such issues back to the states for resolution.[14] As states gear up for redistricting after the 2020 U.S. Census, the strategy for line-drawers is "to determine the best way to waste the vote of the partisans of the other party."[15] Deals are made, interests are protected, and coalitions are built, all in an effort to craft an acceptable map, one that the legislature will adopt and the courts will uphold.

Compensation

Legislative compensation has increased handsomely in the past three decades, again with some notable exceptions. Before the modernization of legislatures, salary and *per diem* (a daily amount to cover legislators' expenses while staying in the state capital during the session) levels were set in the state constitution and thus were impossible to adjust without a constitutional amendment. The lifting of these limits in most states puts legislatures, as the policy-making branch of state government, in the curious position of setting their own compensation levels. Recognizing that this power is a double-edged sword (legislators can vote themselves pay raises, and the public can turn around and vote them out of office for doing so), almost half the states have established compensation commissions or advisory groups to make recommendations on legislative remuneration. Arizona carries it a step further, requiring that a commission-recommended pay raise for legislators be submitted to the voters for approval—or rejection.

As of 2019 annual salaries of legislators ranged from a low of $100 in New Hampshire to a high of $110,459 in California.[16] Other states at the top of the compensation list include New York ($110,000), Pennsylvania ($88,610), Michigan ($71,685), Massachusetts ($66,257), Illinois ($65,836), and Ohio ($63,007). Eleven states pay their lawmakers between $30,000 and $60,000 annually. Compare these figures with the more modest pay levels of legislators in states such as Idaho ($17,879), Georgia ($17,342), South Dakota ($11,379), Nebraska ($12,000), and Texas ($7,200). (These figures do not include *per diem*, which can increase overall compensation, depending on the state's rules for documenting expenses.)

As a general rule, states paying a more generous compensation typically demand more of a legislator's time than do low-paying states. And in most states, legislative leadership positions such as speaker of the house come with additional pay; in a few states, the chairs of major committees get a salary supplement. New Mexico legislators cannot be accused of seeking elective office for the money. There, legislators receive no salary. What is their financial reward for legislative service? One hundred sixty-one dollars per day for living expenses (increasing to $184 per day if the session goes past the end of February) while in Santa Fe during the session, plus a travel allowance.

Legislative pay is but a fraction of the cost of operating a legislature. Legislative staff salaries—all totaled, state legislatures employ around 33,000 professional staffers—consume a large chunk of institutional expenditures, as do building maintenance and technological improvements.

Leadership

Legislatures need leaders, both formal and informal. Each chamber usually has four formal leadership positions. In the senate, a president and a president pro tempore (who presides in the absence of the president) are in charge of the chamber; in the house, the comparable leaders are the speaker and the speaker pro tempore. These legislative officials are chosen by the members, who almost always vote along party lines. (In many states, the post of senate president is occupied by the lieutenant governor, but the role is ceremonial in most of these states.[17]) Both houses have two political party leadership positions: a majority leader and a minority leader.

The leaders are responsible for making the legislature, which is a relatively decentralized system, run smoothly and for seeing that it accomplishes its tasks. In a typical chamber, the presiding officer appoints committee members, names committee chairs, controls the activity on the floor, allocates office space and committee budgets, and (in some states) selects the majority leader and the holders of other majority-party posts. The actual influence of the leadership varies from one chamber to another. One study found that house speakers in West Virginia, New Hampshire, and Arizona enjoy the greatest power; whereas the Alaska, Hawaii, and Wyoming speakers possess the least power.[18] One factor that affects leaders' power is whether the positions are rotated or retained. Leaders who have the option of retaining their position can build power bases. In the case of rotation, however, one set of leaders is replaced with another on a regular basis, so the leaders are **lame ducks** when they assume the posts.

On average, today's leaders are different from the caricatured wheeler-dealers of the past. For one thing, in 2019, seventeen women were senate presidents or presidents pro tempore; seven women served as speakers of the house.[19] New Hampshire scored two historic firsts in 2009: the first state with a female majority in a legislative chamber (the senate: 54 percent women) and the first state to have women occupy both the house speakership and the senate presidency. More evidence that legislative leadership has changed comes from Colorado, where, in 2009, it became the first state in which African Americans led both chambers of the legislature at the same time, an accomplishment repeated in Nevada in 2017. Another indicator of change has less to do with diversity and more to do with process: Rank-and-file members of the legislature are not as reluctant as they used to be to challenge their leaders on both procedural and policy matters.

lame duck
An elected official who cannot serve beyond the current term of office.

Leadership in legislatures is linked to political parties. As noted, voting to fill leadership posts follows party lines. In chambers with even numbers of members, the possibility exists that election results might produce a tie (assuming the absence of Independents and third-party members in the chamber). For example, after the 2016 elections, the Connecticut senate had eighteen Democrats and eighteen Republicans. Democrats thought the Democratic lieutenant governor could break the tie, leading to Democratic control over the chamber. Republicans threatened to sue, which would have resulted

Lobbyists cluster in the Florida Capitol rotunda that connects (and separates) the house and senate sides of the building.

in a delay in organizing the senate for legislative work. The result—a compromise power-sharing arrangement in which a Democrat was elected president pro tempore of the senate, with a Republican ascending to the newly created position of Republican president pro tempore.[20]

As political parties become more competitive in the states, legislative behavior and decisions take on a more partisan cast, that is, the legislature becomes more "procedurally partisan."[21] There are Democratic and Republican sides of the chamber and Democratic and Republican positions on bills. Each party meets in a caucus to design its legislative strategy and generate camaraderie. In states where one political party continues to dominate, partisanship is less important; moreover, in one-party settings, the dominant party typically develops splits or factions at the expense of party unity. But when the outnumbered minority party begins to gain strength, the majority party usually becomes more cohesive.

In many states, legislative leaders have embraced a new function: fundraising. Leaders tap interest groups and lobbyists for money and divide it among their party's candidates for legislative seats. California has led the way, with multimillion-dollar **war chests**. In other states, the amount of money raised is not as great, but it has been growing and has become a significant source of campaign funding. Lobbyists find it difficult to say no to a request for funds from the leadership. The leaders allocate the funds to the neediest candidates—those in close races. If these candidates are victorious, their loyalty to party leaders pays legislative dividends.

The Committee System

The workhorse of the legislature is the committee. Under normal circumstances, a committee's primary function is to consider bills—that is, to hear testimony, perhaps amend the bills, and ultimately approve or reject them.

war chest
A stash of funds accumulated in advance of a campaign.

A committee's action on a bill precedes debate in the house or senate. Along with the leadership, committees provide a structure for organizing the process of making laws.

All legislative chambers are divided into committees, and most committees have created subcommittees. Committees can be of several types. A *standing committee* regularly considers legislation during the session. A *joint committee* is made up of members of both houses. Some joint committees are standing; others are temporary (sometimes called ad hoc or select committees) and are convened for a specific purpose, such as investigating a troubled agency or solving a particularly vexing public policy problem. A *conference committee* is a special type of joint committee that is assembled to iron out differences between house- and senate-passed versions of a bill. Most states use *interim committees* during the period when the legislature is not in session to get a head start on an upcoming session. The number of committees varies, but most senates and houses have standing committees on the issues listed in Table 6.2. Most of these committees, in turn, have professional staffs assigned to them.

A substantive standing committee tends to be made up of legislators who have expertise and interest in that committee's subject matter.[22] Thus, farmers would be assigned to the agriculture committee, teachers to the education committee, small-business owners to the commerce committee, lawyers to the judiciary committee, and so on. These legislators bring knowledge and commitment to their committee assignments; they also may bring a certain bias because they tend to function as advocates for their career interests. Note, too, that every chamber has at least one undesirable committee (usually defined as one whose substance is boring) to which few legislators want to be assigned.[23]

Table 6.2 Standing Committees of the Legislature

Both houses of state legislatures typically have standing committees dealing with these substantive issues:	
Agriculture	Government operations
Banking/financial institutions	Health
Business and commerce	Insurance
Communications	Judiciary and criminal justice
Education	Local affairs
Elections	Public employees
Energy	Rules
Environment and natural resources	Social/human services
Ethics	Transportation
In addition, both houses have standing committees that address the raising and allocating of state funds. These committees may have different names in different chambers:	
Appropriations	Finance and taxation
Ways and means	

The central concern of a standing committee is its floor success—getting the full chamber to accede to its recommendations on a bill. Several plausible explanations exist for a committee's floor success. A committee whose ideological composition is similar to that of the whole chamber is likely to be more successful than one whose members' views are at odds with the chamber. The leadership takes this situation into account when it makes committee assignments; thus, very few committees are ideological outliers.[24] Also, committees full of legislatively experienced members generally have more floor success than committees composed of legislative novices. And committees that have a reputation for being tough have more floor success with their bills than committees that pass everything that comes before them.

Legislative Behavior

LO 6-3
To weigh the importance of informal norms amid formal rules in the legislative institution.

Legislatures have their own dynamics, their own way of doing things. Senate and house rule books spell out what can and cannot be done in the same way that an organization's bylaws do. These rules matter, that is, they account for much of what happens in a given legislative chamber.[25] Legislatures are self-regulating institutions for the most part; it is especially important, therefore, that participants know what is expected of them. To make certain that the chamber's rules are understood, most legislatures conduct orientation sessions for new members.

Norms of the Institution

An understanding of the legislature involves not only knowledge of formal structures and written rules but also awareness of informal norms and unwritten policies. For example, nowhere in a state's legislative rules does it say that a freshman legislator is prohibited from playing a leadership role, but the unwritten rules of most legislatures place a premium on seniority. A primary rule of legislative bodies is that you must "go along to get along," a phrase that emphasizes teamwork and paying your dues. Legislators who are on opposite sides of a bill to regulate horse racing might find themselves on the same side of a bill outlawing the use of cell phones while operating a motor vehicle. Yesterday's opponent is today's partner. For this reason, no one can afford to make bitter enemies in the legislature and expect to flourish.

Those who aspire to rise from rank-and-file legislator to committee chairperson and perhaps to party leader or presiding officer find consensus-building skills quite useful. These skills come in handy because many norms are intended to reduce the potential for conflict in what is inherently a setting full of conflict. For instance, a freshman legislator is expected to defer to a senior colleague. Although an energetic new legislator might chafe under such a restriction, one day he will have gained seniority and will take comfort in the rule. Moreover, legislators are expected to honor commitments made to each other, thus encouraging reciprocity: "If you support me on my favorite bill, I will be with you on yours." A legislator cannot be too unyielding. Compromises, which are sometimes principled but more often political, are the backbone of the legislative process. Few bills are passed by both houses and sent to the governor in exactly the same form as when they were introduced.

Informal rules are designed to make the legislative process flow more smoothly. Legislators who cannot abide by the rules find it difficult to get along. They are subjected to not-so-subtle efforts at behavior modification, such as powerful social sanctions (ostracism and ridicule) and legislative punishment (the bottling up of their bill in committee or their assignment to an unpopular committee), actions that promote adherence to norms.

Legislative Cue Taking and Decision Making

Much has been written about how legislators make public policy decisions, and a number of explanations are plausible. Legislators may adopt the policy positions espoused by their political party. They may follow the dictates of their conscience—that is, do what they think is right. They may yield to the pressures of organized interest groups. They may be persuaded by the arguments of other legislators, such as a committee chairperson who is knowledgeable about the policy area or a trusted colleague who is considered to be savvy; or they may succumb to the entreaties of the governor, who has made a particular piece of legislation the focus of their administration. Of course, legislators may also attempt to respond to the wishes of their constituents. On a significant issue—one that has received substantial media attention—they are likely to be subjected to tremendous cross-pressures.

A legislator reflecting on his years in the Massachusetts house tells this revealing story. During one session, he voted yes on corporate tax break legislation that he was opposed to because the speaker of the house favored the bill and wanted him to vote yes. Why was the speaker's position so compelling? Because the legislator's favorite bill was due to be voted on later and he wanted the speaker's support on it.[26] Another remarkably candid assessment of how legislators make public policy decisions was offered by a freshman in the Tennessee House of Representatives. He identified two often unspoken but always present considerations: "Will it cost me votes back home?" and "Can an opponent use it against me [in the] next election?"[27] These pragmatic concerns intrude on the more idealistic notions of decision making. They also suggest a fairly cautious approach to bold policy initiatives.

Assuming that legislators are concerned about how a vote will be received back home, it seems logical that they would be particularly solicitous of public opinion. In actuality, state legislators frequently hold opinions at odds with those of their constituents. They occasionally misperceive what the public is thinking; at such times, it is difficult for them to act as mere **delegates** and simply fulfill the public's will. To improve the communications link, some lawmakers use mail questionnaires and interactive websites to poll constituents about their views; others hold town meetings at various places in the district to assess the public's mood.

delegate
A legislator who functions as a conduit for constituency opinion.

It is quite probable that first-term legislators feel more vulnerable to the wishes of the public than legislative veterans do. Hence, the new legislator devotes more time to determining what the people want, whereas the experienced legislator "knows" what they want (or perhaps knows what they need) and thus functions as a **trustee**—someone who follows their own best judgment. Because the vast majority of legislators are returned to office election after election, it appears that there is some validity to this argument. In fact, a study of lawmakers in eight states found that the members' personal opinions were consistently important in their decision choices.[28]

In the final analysis, the determining factor in how legislators make decisions depends on the issue itself. On one hand, "when legislators are deeply involved with an issue, they appear to be more concerned with policy consequences" than with constituency preferences.[29] In this situation, the legislators are focused on a goal other than reelection. On the other hand, if lawmakers are not particularly engaged in an issue that is important to their constituents, they will follow their constituents' preference. In that sense, they act as **politicos**, adjusting as the issues and cues change.

How a Bill Becomes Law (or Not)

LO 6-4
To recognize the intricacies of the lawmaking process.

A legislative bill starts as an idea and travels a long, complex path before it emerges as law. It is no wonder that of the 2,066 bills introduced in the Missouri legislature in 2018, only 111 had become law by the end of the regular session.[30] A legislative session has a rhythm to it. Minor bills and symbolic issues tend to be resolved early, whereas major, potentially divisive issues take a much longer time to wend their way through the legislative labyrinth. With the clock ticking at the end of the session, legislators try to broker compromises and build coalitions to get key bills passed.[31] The budget or appropriations bill typically generates several rounds of contentious debate among legislators. And if legislatures cannot get their work completed, they may end up back in the state capitol at a later date in a special session. In 2018, for example, twenty-eight special legislative sessions were called; some states held more than one extra session.

The lawmaking process has been described in many ways: a zoo, a circus, a marketplace. Perhaps the most apt description is a casino because there are winners and losers, the outcome is never final, and there is always a new game ahead.[32] Lawmaking is a dynamic and exciting process; it can be an arduous process as well. Ideas for bills are everywhere: with constituents, interest groups, and state agencies. Legislators may turn to other states for ideas or to their staffs. **Policy entrepreneurs**, people who are knowledgeable about certain issues and are willing to promote them, abound. Introducing a bill—"putting it in the hopper," in legislative parlance—is just the beginning. A bill can get sidetracked at many points, and even derailed altogether. Subcommittee and committee hearings may pose a challenge, and even if the committee does approve the bill, getting it scheduled for floor debate can be another

trustee
A legislator who votes according to their conscience and best judgment.

politico
A legislator who functions as either a delegate or a trustee, as circumstances dictate.

policy entrepreneurs
People who bring new ideas to a policy-making body.

hurdle. Assuming successful passage in the first chamber, a bill goes through the same steps in the second chamber. Even if it is successful there, a conference committee may be needed to resolve any differences between the two passed versions. And most legislatures impose deadlines for the completion of the various steps.

Clearly, a bill does not make it through the legislative process without a lot of effort and even a little luck. A bill's chances of passage rise as more legislators sign on as co-sponsors, and if the co-sponsors are legislative leaders, even better. Assignment of the bill to a favorable committee improves the likelihood that the bill will be scheduled for a hearing in a timely manner. Many bills get bottled up in committee and never receive a hearing. Strong support from key interest groups is a powerful advantage as is the emergence of only weak opposition to the bill. Sometimes bill passage is a matter of fortuitous timing. For example, a spectacular prison break from an overcrowded state penitentiary would help garner support for passage of a prison construction bill.

Controversial issues such as abortion raise the stakes. The former speaker of the Wisconsin Assembly, Tom Loftus, described abortion politics in his state as trench warfare in which compromise was almost impossible. Leadership on the issue came from legislators who felt strongly about the matter and who held safe seats. (In this instance, "safe" meant that taking a position was not likely to cost them too many votes or generate too many serious challengers when they ran for reelection.) As antiabortion bills were introduced, battle lines were drawn. According to the speaker:

> The pro-choice side, which included the Democratic leadership, tried to keep the bill bottled up in committee, and the pro-life side, through political pressure on the Republicans and conservative Democrats, tried to pull it out so the whole assembly could vote on it on the floor of the chamber. If the pro-life people could get the bill to the floor for a vote, they would win. To accomplish this end, they needed to gain supporters from the pivotal middle group of legislators, usually moderates of both parties from marginal districts.[33]

The powerful antiabortion group, Wisconsin Citizens Concerned for Life, pressured vulnerable legislators. These legislators were in a tough position because they knew "regardless of how you voted, you were going to make a slew of single-issue voters mad."[34] Their strategy became one of parliamentary maneuvering.

Even if a bill is successful in one chamber, potential hurdles await in the other chamber. Representatives and senators may see the same issue in very different terms. In Ohio, a few years back, everyone agreed that the state's system for funding public education needed reform. (The Ohio Supreme Court had found the state's school-funding system unconstitutional and had given the legislature one year to devise a new system.) But initial efforts derailed when the house and senate could not agree on a plan. The senate approved a funding package that would have increased the sales tax, provided debt financing, and allowed local school boards to propose property tax increases.[35] The house, dominated by Republicans who had signed an anti-tax pledge the preceding year, approved a bill that did not include tax hikes. Each chamber rejected the other's plan. Hammering out a compromise agreeable to both chambers took a long time, even with the court's order as a spur to action.

Once conference or concurrence committees resolve differences and agreement is secured in both chambers, then the bill is enrolled (certified and signed) and sent to the governor. The governor may do one of three things: (1) sign the act (once passed, a bill is called an *act*) into law, (2) veto it (in which case the legislature has a chance to have the last word by overriding the veto), or (3) take no action. If the governor does not take action and the session has ended, then in most states the act will become law without the governor's signature. Why not simply sign it if the act will become law anyway? Sometimes it is a matter of political symbolism for the governor. In approximately one-third of the states, if the governor does not sign or veto the act and the legislature has adjourned, the act dies (a circumstance called a *pocket veto*).

During its 2018 regular session, the Missouri General Assembly passed only about 5 percent of the bills that were introduced. Is this a sign of success or failure? Missouri's figures are lower than those of most states—20 to 25 percent is a common passage rate—but not necessarily a cause for alarm. Not all bills are good ones, and the inability to generate sufficient consensus among legislators may reflect that condition.

Legislative Reform and Capacity

During the 1970s, fundamental reforms occurred throughout the country as legislatures sought to increase their capacity and become more professional. And, even though these reforms have had a substantial impact, the institutional modernization process never really ends.

LO 6-5
To appraise the efforts to reform state legislatures.

The Ideal Legislature

In the late 1960s, the Citizens' Conference on State Legislatures (CCSL) studied legislative performance and identified five characteristics critical to legislative improvement.[36] Ideally, a legislature should be functional, accountable, informed, independent, and representative (FAIIR).

The *functional* legislature has almost unrestricted time to conduct its business. It is assisted by adequate staff and facilities and has effective rules and procedures that facilitate the flow of legislation. The *accountable* legislature's operations are open and comprehensible to the public. The *informed* legislature manages its workload through an effective committee structure, legislative activities between sessions, and a professional staff; it also conducts regular budgetary review of executive branch activities. The *independent* legislature runs its own affairs independently of the executive branch. It exercises oversight of agencies, regulates lobbyists, manages conflicts of interest, and provides adequate compensation for its members. Finally, the *representative* legislature has a diverse membership that effectively represents the social, economic, ethnic, and other characteristics of the state.

The fifty state legislatures were evaluated and scored by CCSL according to the FAIIR criteria. For the first time ever, the rankings offered a relatively scientific means of comparing one state legislature with another. Overall, the "best" state legislatures were found in California, New York, Illinois, Florida, and Wisconsin. The "worst," in the assessment of CCSL, were those in Alabama, Wyoming, Delaware, North Carolina, and Arkansas.

The CCSL report triggered extensive self-evaluation by legislatures around the country. Most states launched ambitious efforts to reform their legislatures. The results are readily apparent. In terms of the CCSL criteria, states have made tremendous strides in legislative institution building. The evidence of increased professionalism includes more staff support, higher legislative compensation, longer sessions, and better facilities. Many legislatures revamped their committee systems, altered their rules and procedures, and tightened their ethics regulations. The consequences of these actions are state legislatures that are far more FAIIR now than they were found to be in the late 1960s. The National Conference of State Legislatures sums it up this way: "Legislatures became more muscular, agile, intelligent, and independent than at any other time in American history."[37]

The Effects of Reform

Today's legislative institutions are different, but are they better? Although many observers would answer in the affirmative, the legislative reform picture is not unequivocally rosy. Political scientist Alan Rosenthal, who has closely observed legislative reform, warns that "the legislature's recent success in enhancing its capacity and improving its performance may place it in greater jeopardy than before."[38] Rosenthal's argument is that a constellation of demands pulls legislators away from the legislative core. That is, the new breed of legislators gets caught up in the demands of reelection, constituent service, interest groups, and political careerism and thus neglects institutional matters such as structure, procedure, staff, image, and community. The legislature as an institution suffers because it is not receiving the necessary care and attention from its members. For example, California's highly reformed legislature performed poorly in the early 2000s, mired in a period of bitter partisanship and gridlock. Some observers blame reform for some of the Golden State's legislative troubles.

Consider the idea of a citizen-legislator, one for whom service in the legislature is a part-time endeavor. Since the onset of reform, the proportion of legislators who are lawyers, business owners, or insurance or real estate executives has dropped, and the number of full-time legislators has risen. In states such as California and Pennsylvania, roughly three-quarters of lawmakers identify themselves as legislators with no other occupation. The critical issue is whether the decline of the citizen-legislator is a desirable aspect of modernization. Should a state legislature represent a broad spectrum of vocations, or should it be composed of career politicians? One perspective is this: "If I'm sick, I want professional help. I feel the same way about public affairs. I want legislators who are knowledgeable and professional."[39] Another view is represented by a

Michigan legislator who believes that his careerist colleagues have lost touch with their constituents: "When you spend all your time in Lansing, you're more influenced by the lobbyists than by your constituents."[40]

In effect, state legislatures are becoming more like the U.S. Congress.[41] In many states, legislators are staying in the legislature in record numbers. Modernization has made the institution more attractive to its members, so turnover rates are declining. But do we really want fifty mini-Congresses scattered across the land? Today's legislatures are more FAIIR than in the past, but reform has also brought greater professionalization of the legislative career, increased polarization of the legislative process, and more fragmentation of the legislative institution.[42] Figure 6.2 shows the pattern of "citizen" (fourteen states), "professional" (ten states), and "hybrid" (twenty-six states) state legislatures throughout the land. The categories are derived from an index developed by the National Conference of State Legislatures that reflects legislator salary and benefits, the time demands of legislative service, and the staff resources available to the legislature.[43] Lawmakers in the most professionalized legislatures are paid more, devote more time to the job, and have far greater staff resources at their disposal than their counterparts in citizen legislatures. States categorized as hybrids fall between professional and citizen on these characteristics. The It's Your Turn box takes up the issue of legislative professionalization.

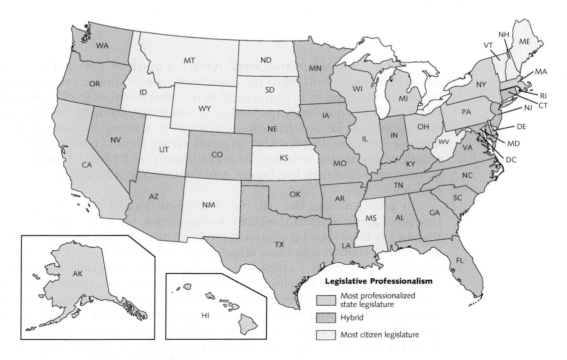

Figure 6.2 Legislative Professionalism

Source: National Conference of State Legislatures, "Full and Part-Time Legislatures," www.ncsl.org/research/about-state-legislatures/full-and-part-time-legislatures.aspx (accessed January 19, 2020).

? It's Your Turn

Should State Legislatures Be More Professionalized?

PROS	CONS
Employing more staff improves a legislature's ability to analyze legislation. This should result in more thoughtful, effective laws.	Legislators in professional legislatures spend more time in the state capitol and risk becoming "part of the system" and perhaps disconnecting from their constituents. In less-professional legislatures, lawmakers likely have regular jobs back home, and likely remain more connected to their communities.
By meeting more often and in longer sessions, legislatures have more time to tackle the state's problems. The pressure of a ticking time clock is lessened.	Professional legislatures are more expensive to operate due to larger staffs, longer terms, and higher salaries, and that's money that comes out of taxpayers' pockets.
Paying legislators a higher salary would likely make legislative races more competitive, thereby giving voters more choices.	Thomas Jefferson was an advocate of a citizen legislature. If it was good enough for Thomas Jefferson, it should be good enough for us today. It is important to keep legislators grounded in the communities they represent.
A professional legislature can work more effectively with the state's full-time governor.	

Change continues in state legislatures, but much of it is cloaked in an anti-reform guise. Term limits (discussed next) are, of course, a major component in the effort to limit the legislature. Other attempts to chip away at reform include Louisiana's approval of a constitutional amendment that, in even-numbered years, limits the legislature to a thirty-day session that addresses only fiscal issues. Also, as noted earlier, Nevada has trimmed the length of legislative sessions, whereas Illinois and Rhode Island have reduced the size of their legislatures. And California legislators have endured pay cuts.

To some analysts, the reforms of the past decades have produced a legislative monster. Richard Nathan, a veteran observer of the states, argues that the key to increased government productivity is the empowerment of the governor.[44] Nathan advocates term limits, unicameral legislative bodies, rotation of committee memberships, and reduction of legislative staff and sessions as a means of reining in the legislature vis-à-vis the governor. If adopted, Nathan's recommendations would undo thirty-five years of legislative reform. And the governor's political power would be significantly strengthened. This helps explain why, in 2007, Pennsylvania's governor Ed Rendell proposed a far-reaching plan to trim the size of the Keystone State's General Assembly, limit legislative terms, and change the redistricting process. As you might imagine, Governor Rendell's plan fell on deaf ears in the legislative branch.[45] The legislative-gubernatorial nexus is the subject of a later section of this chapter.

Term Limits

LO 6-6
To discuss the impact of legislative term limits.

In September 1990, Oklahoma voters took an action that sent state legislatures reeling. Oklahomans overwhelmingly approved a ballot measure limiting the tenure of state legislators and statewide officers. As it turned out, limiting terms was not just a Sooner thing. Within two months, voters in California and Colorado had followed suit. With a close defeat in Washington state slowing it only slightly, the term-limits movement swept the country. In Oregon, a group called LIMITS (Let Incumbents Mosey into the Sunset) grew out of a tax limitation organization. In Wisconsin, a coalition known as Badgers Back in Charge took up the cause of term limitation. And political activists of many stripes—populists, conservatives, and libertarians—found a home in the term-limitation movements in Florida, Michigan, and Texas.[46] In time, twenty-one states slapped limits on state legislative terms, although in six of these states, term limits were repealed by state courts or the legislature itself. All told, approximately one-fourth of state legislative seats are subject to term limits. The term-limits laws gradually bore the intended fruit: In any even-numbered election year, at least 100 state legislators are termed out of office. Table 6.3 compares the term-limit provisions of the states where

Table 6.3 Term Limits in the States

STATE	YEAR ADOPTED	SENATE	HOUSE	YEAR LAW TOOK EFFECT	REFERENDUM VOTE	BALLOT STATUS
Arizona	1992	8	8	2000	74 to 26	Initiative
Arkansas	1992	16	16	2000/1998	60 to 40	Initiative
California	1990	12	12	1998/1996	52 to 48	Initiative
Colorado	1990	8	8	1998	71 to 29	Initiative
Florida	1992	8	8	2000	77 to 23	Initiative
Louisiana	1995	12	12	2007	76 to 24	Referendum
Maine	1993	8	8	1996	67 to 33	Indirect Initiative
Michigan	1992	8	6	2002/1998	59 to 41	Initiative
Missouri	1992	8	8	2002	74 to 26	Initiative
Montana	1992	8	8	2000	67 to 33	Initiative
Nebraska	2000	8	—	2006	56 to 44	Initiative
Nevada	1994	12	12	2010	70 to 30	Initiative
Ohio	1992	8	8	2000	66 to 34	Initiative
Oklahoma	1990	12	12	2004	67 to 33	Initiative
South Dakota	1992	8	8	2000	63 to 37	Initiative

Note: In California and Oklahoma, a legislator may serve a total of twelve years in the legislature during their lifetime. The total time may be split between the two chambers or spent in its entirely in a single chamber. In Arkansas, a 2014 change extended the amount of time a legislator can serve to a total of sixteen years.

Sources: State Term Limits (2018), www.termlimits.org, and the National Conference of State Legislatures, "The Term-Limited States," www.ncsl.org/research/about-state-legislatures/chart-of-term-limits-states.aspx (March 13, 2015).

legislative term limits remain in force. Note that Nebraska voters had approved term limits three times prior to the 2000 initiative, but the courts had invalidated the measures.

In most states, the measures limit service in each chamber separately. In Maine, for example, a legislator is limited to eight years in the house and eight years in the senate. It is quite possible, then, that an individual could serve a total of sixteen years in the legislature under this plan. In a few states, the restriction is on total legislative service. In California and Oklahoma, for instance, the limitation is twelve years, whether in the house, the senate, or a combination of the two. Some term limits are for a lifetime (as in Arkansas and Nevada); others simply limit the number of consecutive terms (as in Ohio and South Dakota).

Limiting legislative terms captured the fancy of a public angry with entrenched politicians. The measure offers voters a chance to strike back at an institution that they perceive as self-serving and out of touch. But not everyone favors limiting legislative terms. Opponents offer several arguments against them. On a theoretical level, they argue that term limits rob voters of their fundamental right to choose their representatives. In a related vein, they contend that these measures unfairly disqualify a subset of the population—legislators—from seeking office. And, finally, opponents claim that term limits are unnecessary; that sufficient legislative turnover occurs without them.

Term limits were expected to produce several consequences:

- Ending the domination of a chamber by powerful, entrenched veteran legislators
- Increasing the proportion of first-term legislators in any given session
- Increasing representation by groups underrepresented in the legislature, especially women and minorities, because of the guarantee of open seats[47]
- Shifting power from the legislature to the governor and to lobbyists

Three of the four expected consequences have indeed come to pass. The exodus of veteran legislators and the influx of inexperienced members have some observers shaking their heads in dismay. For instance, twenty-five of Michigan's thirty-eight senators (66 percent) could not seek reelection in 2018 due to term limits. However, fourteen of the twenty-five term-limited senators were replaced with Michigan house members who ran and won senate seats. Not surprisingly, data from term-limit states reflect procedural difficulties, a slower-working institution, less deliberation in committees, and less complex legislation.[48] As for shifting power to other actors, consensus seems to exist among researchers that governors, agency heads, legislative staff, and interest groups have benefitted at the expense of the term-limited legislature.[49]

The expectation that term limits would produce greater representation of underrepresented groups has not been borne out, at least not yet. The number of women in term-limited legislatures has actually decreased slightly, and the increase in racial and ethnic minorities may be due more to their increased voting strength rather than to term limits.[50] Term-limit devotees who wanted to strike back at an out-of-touch institution would be surprised to learn that term-limited legislators actually become less beholden to their constituents.[51] Moreover, a recent study found that term-limited legislatures appear to be less able to develop effective fiscal policy for their states.[52] Furthermore, term limits have had partisan effects by removing more senior Democrats from office than Republicans.[53] In sum, limiting the terms of legislators has consequences beyond simply forcing incumbents out of office.

Despite these effects, term limits remain popular with the public.[54] In 2008, South Dakota legislators asked voters if they wanted to repeal legislative term limits; the answer was a resounding "no"—76 percent to 22 percent. But the term-limit movement has lost steam. As Table 6.3 indicates, citizen initiatives are the primary vehicle through which the term-limit question has been placed before the voters. And the issue has just about run the gamut of states that allow initiatives. (The Utah legislature imposed term limits on itself in 1994, but it had a change of heart and repealed the law in 2003.) Court challenges have undone legislative term limits in Massachusetts, Oregon, Washington, and Wyoming (see Table 6.4). In 2019, eight Michigan former state legislators—five Democrats and three Republicans—sued the state alleging that its "draconian" term limits violate their constitutional rights.[55] And in a surprising move, the Idaho legislature, bowing to an array of political pressures, repealed the term-limits law that was adopted via the initiative process in 1994.[56] Angry Idahoans gathered a sufficient number of signatures to place a question on the 2002 ballot asking whether the legislature's action should be upheld. After a heated campaign, the "Repeal the Repeal" question was defeated, thus ending term limits in Idaho before they took effect.

Support for legislative term limits comes from other quarters as well. Not surprisingly, governors often look fondly at legislative term limits. For instance, when campaigning for the governorship in 2014, Republican Bruce Rauner proposed an initiative that would have imposed an eight-year term limit on Illinois lawmakers. Despite getting substantially more signatures than required on initiative petitions, Illinois courts ruled the measure violated the state's constitution, thus the term-limits question was not put before the voters.

Table 6.4 Repeals of Legislative Term Limits

STATE	YEAR ADOPTED	YEAR REPEALED	REPEALED BY
Idaho	1994	2002	Legislature
Massachusetts	1994	1997	State Supreme Court
Oregon	1992	2002	State Supreme Court
Utah	1994	2003	Legislature
Washington	1992	1998	State Supreme Court
Wyoming	1992	2004	State Supreme Court

LO 6-7

To interpret the interaction of the legislative branch with the executive branch.

Relationship with the Executive Branch

Strong legislatures are charting a course for the twenty-first century. Strong governors are also attempting to lead states boldly in the same century. Do these institutions ever collide in their policy making? You bet they do. Conflict between the legislature and the governor is inevitable, but it is not necessarily destructive. It is inevitable because both governors and legislators think that they know what is best for the state. It is not necessarily destructive because, during the posturing, bargaining, and negotiating that produces a consensus, governors and legislators may actually arrive at an optimal solution.

Dealing with the Governor

The increased institutional strength of the legislature and its accompanying assertiveness have made for strained relations with a governor accustomed to being the political star. Institutional conflict is exacerbated under conditions of divided government, that is, when a legislature is controlled by one party and the governor is of the other party. The result of divided government is often gridlock, accompanied by finger pointing and blame gaming. As the former Republican governor of Mississippi, Haley Barbour, said to the Democratic-controlled legislature in his first State of the State address, "As Governor of Mississippi you have two choices . . . you can work with the Legislature, or you can fail. Well, I'm not into failure, so I look forward to working with each of you to make sure we all succeed."[57] As Governor Barbour quickly learned, that is much easier said than done.

A governor and a legislature controlled by the same party do not necessarily make for easy interbranch relations either. Especially in states where the two parties are competitive, legislators are expected to support the policy initiatives of their party's governor. Yet the governor's proposals may not mesh with individual legislators' attitudes, ambitions, and agendas. South Carolina offers an illustration. In May 2019, Republican governor Henry McMaster of South Carolina vetoed twenty-eight bills passed by the overwhelmingly Republican legislature. A month later, a special session of the legislature overrode twenty-five of those twenty-eight vetoes. Despite their partisan affinity, they saw these and many other issues very differently.

Sometimes governors who have previously served as legislators seem to have an easier time dealing with the lawmaking institution. For example, former governor Madeleine Kunin of Vermont assumed the office after three terms in the legislature and one term as lieutenant governor, "knowing the needs of legislators, the workings of the legislative process, the sensitivities of that process."[58] Usually about two-thirds of the governors have had legislative experience, although the proportion has recently declined.

Governors have a media advantage over deliberative bodies such as a legislature. The governor is the visible symbol of state government and, as a single individual, fits into a media world of thirty-second sound bites. By contrast, media images of the legislature often portray deal making, pork barrel politics, and general silliness. To be sure, those images can be quite accurate at times. "Gotcha" journalism, the term for media efforts to catch public officials in seemingly questionable situations, certainly complicates legislative life.

The legislature is not without its weapons. If the legislature can muster the votes, it can override a gubernatorial veto. In fact, new research shows that in states with term-limited legislatures, the incidence of veto overrides is actually higher than it is in states that do not limit legislative terms.[59] Legislatures have also enacted other measures designed to enhance their control and to reduce the governor's flexibility in budgetary matters. For example, some states now require the governor to obtain legislative approval of budget cutbacks in the event of a revenue shortfall. Professional legislatures with their longer sessions and higher-paid members can hold their own in budget battles with the governor.[60] Other states have limited the governor's power to initiate transfers of funds among executive branch agencies. These actions reflect the continuing evolution of legislative-executive relations.

Overseeing the Bureaucracy

Legislative involvement with the executive branch does not end with the governor. State legislatures are increasingly venturing into the world of state agencies and bureaucrats, with the attitude that after authorizing a program and allocating funds for it, they should check on what has happened to it. Legislative oversight involves four activities: policy and program evaluation, legislative review of administrative rules and regulations, sunset legislation, and review and control of federal funds received by the state.

Policy and Program Evaluation   Legislatures select auditors to keep an eye on state agencies and departments. (In a few states, auditors are independently elected officials.) Auditors are more than super accountants; their job is to evaluate the performance of state programs as to their efficiency and effectiveness, a task sometimes known as the *postaudit function*. Specifically, they conduct periodic performance audits to measure goal achievement and other indicators of progress in satisfying legislative intent, a process that has been credited with both saving money and improving program performance. Virginia's Joint Legislative Audit and Review Commission (JLARC) is regarded as a model for the rest of the country. Throughout its forty-year history, JLARC has conducted hundreds of evaluations of state programs and saved the state millions of dollars. The key to a useful auditing function is strong legislative support (even in the face of audits that turn up controversial findings) and, at the same time, a guarantee of a certain degree of independence from legislative interference.

Legislative Review of Administrative Rules   Forty-seven state legislatures conduct reviews of administrative rules and regulations, but they vary in their methods. They may assign the review function to a special committee (such as a rule review committee) or to a specific legislative agency, or they may incorporate the review function in the budgetary process. In this role, the legislature acts as a gatekeeper, striving to keep agency rules in line with legislative preferences.[61]

Legislative review is a mechanism through which administrative abuses of discretion can be corrected. Legislative bills frequently contain language to the effect that "the Department of Youth Services shall develop the necessary rules and regulations to implement the provisions of this act." Such language gives the agency wide latitude in establishing procedures and policies. The legislature wants to be certain that, in the process, the agency does not over-step its bounds or violate legislative intent. If it is found to have done so, then the legislature can overturn the offending rules and regulations through mod-ification, suspension, or veto—depending on the state.

This issue is a true gray area of legislative-executive relations, and court rulings at the national level have found the most powerful of these actions, the **legislative veto**, to be an unconstitutional violation of the separation of powers. There is some disagreement among the states on this issue. In the eleven or so states in which the legislative veto has been challenged, state courts have ruled against it in nine states and in favor in two states. For example, in 1997, the Missouri Supreme Court ruled that the legislature's rule-review process was an unconstitutional intrusion into the functions of the executive branch, whereas some seven years earlier the Idaho Supreme Court upheld the legislature's authority to veto administrative rules.[62] Leg-islatures continue to use the budgetary process to review (and sanction) agency behavior. Increasingly, legislatures are requiring state agencies to fur-nish extensive data to justify their budget requests, and they can use their appropriations power to indicate their displeasure with agency rules and regulations.

Sunset Legislation Half the states have established **sunset laws** that set automatic expiration dates for specified agencies and other organizational structures in the executive branch. An agency can be saved from termination only through an overt renewal action in the legislature. Review occurs any-where from every four years to every twelve years, depending on individual state statute, and is conducted by the standing committee that authorized the agency or by a committee established for sunset review purposes (such as a government operations committee). The reviews evaluate the agency's performance and its progress toward achieving its goals.

During the 1970s, sunset legislation was widely hailed as an effective tool for asserting legislative dominion over the executive branch, but more than thirty years' experience with the technique has produced mixed results, and some states have repealed their sunset laws. Agency reviews tend to be time-consuming and costly. And the process has become highly politicized in many states, involving not only agencies and legislators but also lobbyists. On the positive side, sunset reviews are said to increase agency compliance with legislative intent. Statistics show that, nationwide, only about 13 percent of the agencies reviewed are eventually terminated, thus making termination more of a threat than an objective reality.[63]

legislative veto
An action whereby the legislature overturns a state agency's rules or regulations.

sunset laws
Statutes that set automatic expiration dates for specified agencies and other organizations.

Review and Control of Federal Funds Since the early 1980s, legislatures have played a more active role in directing the flow of federal funds once they have reached the state. Before this time, the sheer magnitude of federal funds and their potential to upset legislatively established priorities caused great consternation among legislators. The executive branch controlled the disposition of these grant funds almost completely by designating the recipient agency and program. In some cases, federal money was used to fund programs that the state legislature did not support. Federal dollars were simply absorbed into the budget without debate and discussion, and legislators were cut out of the loop. By making federal fund disbursement part of the formal appropriations process, however, legislators have redesigned the loop.

If legislatures are to do a decent job in forecasting state priorities, some control of federal funds is necessary. In the face of reduced federal aid to states, it is critical for legislators to understand the role that federal dollars have played in program operation. When funding for a specific program dries up, it is the legislature's responsibility to decide whether to replace it with state money.

How effectively are legislatures overseeing state bureaucracies? As with so many questions, the answer depends on who is asked. From the perspective of legislators, their controls increase administrative accountability. A survey of legislators in eight states found legislative oversight committees, the postaudit function, and sunset laws to be among the most effective bureaucratic controls available.[64] Another effective device, and one that legislatures use in special circumstances, is legislative investigation of an agency, an administrator, or a program. But from the perspective of the governor, many forms of legislative oversight are simply meddling and, as such, they undermine the separation of powers.

Legislatures and Capacity

LO 6-8
To examine the link between legislatures and the public.

State legislatures are fascinating institutions. Although they share numerous traits, each maintains some unique characteristics. Houses and senates have different traditions and styles, even in the same state. And across states, the variation in legislative systems is notable. As Alan Rosenthal writes, "Legislatures are interwoven in the fabric of their states."[65] As institutions, legislatures are dynamic; amid the layers of traditions and rules, they change and evolve.

The demands placed on state legislatures are unrelenting. Challenges abound. The ability of a legislature to function effectively depends on institutional adaptation. The extensive modernization that almost all legislatures underwent in the 1970s is evidence of institutional renewal. Structural reforms and a new breed of legislator have altered state legislatures and made them more capable. How ironic then, with all their institutional improvement, legislatures continue to struggle with their public image. Figure 6.3 arrays the states on two dimensions: public approval of the institution and the degree

Figure 6.3 Legislative Approval Across the States

Source: Lilliard E. Richardson, Jr., David M. Konisky, and Jeffrey Milyo, "Public Approval of U.S. State Legislatures," *Legislative Studies Quarterly* 37 (February 2012): 99–116.

of legislative professionalism. As is evident, in the vast majority of states, public approval falls below the 50 percent mark. This is especially the case with the more professional legislatures. Research has found that it is among ideological conservatives that the negative relationship between professionalism and approval is greatest.[66]

Other stressors remain. Another real concern is that the legislatures of some states are being marginalized through a citizen-empowering mechanism, the initiative, and an institution-weakening provision, term limits. No wonder then that the National Conference of State Legislatures has encouraged its members to develop "a process that clarifies the current problems, what changes are needed, and how to put those remedies into place."[67] Perhaps a new and different era of legislative reform is upon us.

Chapter Recap

- The three principal functions of legislatures are policy making, representation, and oversight.

- Redistricting is a battleground for state legislatures because drawing district lines is a partisan process.

- Legislatures operate with their own formal and informal rules. Violations of institutional norms result in sanctions.

- The lawmaking process is a complex one, with multiple opportunities for delay and obstruction. Most bills never make it through; those that do seldom look like they did when they were introduced.

- Although legislatures perform more effectively than they used to, in 2020, fifteen states had term limits in effect. Term limits create open seats and thus increase competition for legislative seats. But when legislative terms are limited, other institutional actors, such as the governor, gain power.

- Legislators vie with governors in the policy-making process. Governors have the power to veto, but legislators have the power to override a gubernatorial veto. In addition, the legislature plays several oversight roles with regard to the bureaucracy.

- Legislative capacity has increased, but at the same time, legislatures risk becoming marginalized in states with the initiative process and term limits.

Key Terms

casework *(p. 147)*
multimember districts (MMDs) *(p. 149)*
malapportionment *(p. 149)*
reapportionment *(p. 150)*

redistrict *(p. 150)*
gerrymander *(p. 150)*
lame duck *(p. 154)*
war chest *(p. 155)*
delegate *(p. 158)*

trustee *(p. 159)*
politico *(p. 159)*
policy entrepreneurs *(p. 159)*
legislative veto *(p. 170)*
sunset laws *(p. 170)*

Internet Resources

To find out what's up in state legislatures, visit the website of the National Conference of State Legislatures at **www.ncsl.org**.

Most states have websites that allow citizens to follow the progress of legislation during the session. See, for example, the legislative sites for Iowa and West Virginia at **www.legis.iowa.gov** and **www.wvlegislature.gov**/, respectively.

The scholarly journal *Legislative Studies Quarterly* is a good source for research on legislatures at **www.onlinelibrary.wiley.com/ journal/19399162**.

The website **votesmart.org** tracks the performance of political leaders, including state legislators.

To learn about model state laws, see the National Conference of Commissioners on Uniform State Laws at **www.uniformlaws.org**.

An advocacy website, **www.termlimits.org**, provides up-to-date coverage of the term-limits issue.

An avowedly conservative organization that drafts model legislation on various topics and reviews legislative activities across the states maintains a website at **www.alec.org**.

7

Governors: Power, Politics, and Executive Leadership

New York Governor Andrew Cuomo.

Learning Objectives

LO 7-1 To describe the evolution in powers of the governor from postcolonial days to the present.

LO 7-2 To discuss the diverse roles of the governor.

LO 7-3 To appraise the dynamics of working with the legislature to enact policy.

LO 7-4 To explain the formal powers of the office today and how they are used.

LO 7-5 To analyze the informal powers of the office, their importance, and how they can enhance the formal powers.

LO 7-6 To explain the responsibilities of the other elective statewide executive branch offices.

Today's governors speak as voices of authority on important national policy issues. Although they do not always agree on what they want, the governors assert themselves as a righteous third force in U.S. politics, and speaking through the National Governors Association (NGA), other organizations, and the media, they have helped shape federal reform of welfare, education, and health care policies, and even lead the response to combating global warming. And while Congress feuds along partisan and ideological lines over virtually all issues of significance and many issues of no significance at all, the governors preach—and often practice—partisan peacemaking to reach common policy ground with their own legislatures to advance positive policy changes. The challenges of conciliation are complicated by a voting public with no stomach for raising taxes and tight state budgets, in which some three-quarters of expenditures are earmarked to education, Medicaid, and local government. Governors are further challenged by the divisive partisan politics that infect the national government and that are threatening to sicken the states.

The governors must make tough choices. Some bravely advance tax hikes despite the possible electoral consequences. Others impose brutal spending cuts on prisons, aid to the poor and helpless, and higher education. Their responsibilities are prodigious. But the governors' enhanced visibility and contributions in national politics and policy are a tribute to their policy-making capacity and responsiveness to common—and uncommon—problems affecting the citizens of their respective states. It also reflects the policy leadership of the states in the U.S. federal system.

The COVID-19 pandemic sorely tested gubernatorial powers. Governors took controversial actions under their constitutionally granted police powers. As the virus spread throughout the country in spring 2020, governors banned large gatherings, required many businesses to close, and shut school systems down, all in the interest of slowing the spread of the virus. Some of the most controversial actions governors took concerned religious gatherings. In ten states governors included religious gatherings in their bans on all public gatherings.[1] California Governor Gavin Newsom's order including religious gatherings in the ban on public gatherings was challenged in court by several churches citing the First Amendment's guarantee of free exercise of religion. In May 2020, the U.S. Supreme Court ruled that states could enforce social distancing and other restrictions on religious gatherings in the same manner as they restrict other gatherings when public health was threatened by these kinds of gatherings.[2]

A second major test of gubernatorial powers came in the wake of the killing of George Floyd by Minneapolis police officers in May 2020. Police officers restrained Floyd, a black man, by kneeling on his neck, cutting off his breathing and leading to his death. Two months earlier, Breonna Taylor, an emergency medical technician, was shot and killed by Louisville police officers who were executing a no-knock search warrant. Taylor's boyfriend, thinking the police officers were intruders, fired his handgun at the officers who returned fire. Demonstrations against these and other police actions against black people quickly began in Minneapolis and then spread rapidly to other cities throughout the country. Some of these demonstrations turned violent, resulting in damage to police stations, other public buildings, and commercial establishments. Urban police forces soon found themselves undermanned against large groups of demonstrators. Mayors prevailed on governors for assistance. Governors in at least 15 states activated National Guard units to assist local law enforcement in controlling increasingly unruly crowds. While most of the 5,000 National Guardsmen provided support to local law enforcement through such activities as traffic control and intelligence gathering, some troops were used in more active roles. In Louisville, National Guard troops and Louisville police officers returned fire against a group of demonstrators resulting in the death of one person. Kentucky Governor Andy Beshear asked the Kentucky State Police to open a fact-finding investigation into the incident. While governors activated National Guard units to protect lives and property against a relatively small number of violent protestors, they also issued statements supporting the rights of the larger number of protestors to exercise their First Amendment rights to protest. In a conference call with governors in early

June, President Trump warned against this middle ground and advised governors to take a stronger stance against violent demonstrators. "You have to dominate, if you don't dominate you're wasting your time. They're going to run over you, you're going to look like a bunch of jerks. . . . You've got to arrest people, you have to track people, you have to put them in jail for ten years and you'll never see this stuff again." Trump told the governors.[3]

While the immediate question in the demonstrations was the killings of black individuals by police officers, the more generalized concerns go much deeper into the nature of American culture and the recent national environment. First, while the death of George Floyd and Breonna Taylor were certainly tragedies, they were two of more than 1,000 such minority deaths from police actions since 2016.[4] The causes therefore go much deeper than the actions of one or more Minneapolis or Louisville police officers. Second, the COVID-19 pandemic affected racial and ethnic minorities much more than it affected whites. The Centers for Disease Control reported death rates from the virus for black people and Hispanics were almost twice as high as for whites or Asian Americans. Much of this disparity has to do with poverty and its effects on health—minorities suffer a much greater incidence of poverty-related health conditions such as heart disease, high blood pressure, and diabetes, all of which contribute greatly to more severe COVID-19 effects.[5] Third, minorities were also disproportionately affected by the closing of businesses during the pandemic. As one economist noted, "It's what always happens during disasters like this. Those with the least power and resources are hit first and hardest."[6] As of May 2020, some 12.4 percent of whites were unemployed while nearly 16.8 percent of black people and 17.6 percent of Latinos were unemployed. The 2.5 million jobs created in May represented a dramatic improvement to April's employment statistics but it was unclear whether this represented an economic turnaround, a temporary reprieve or even a data problem in the Bureau of Labor Statistics reporting.[7] Combining these underlying conditions with a focusing event such as the killing of George Floyd created an incendiary situation that governors were required to address immediately while attempting to develop long-term solutions. Solving these kinds of questions is emblematic of the job of the twenty-first century state governor.

LO 7-1
To describe the evolution in powers of the governor from postcolonial days to the present.

The Office of Governor

It has been said that the American governorship was conceived in mistrust and born in a straitjacket. Indeed, because the excesses of some colonial governors appointed by the English Crown resulted in strong dislike and distrust of executive power by the early American settlers, the first state constitutions concentrated political power in the legislative branch.

History of the Office

Early governors were typically elected by the legislature rather than by the voters, were restricted to a single one-year term of office and had little authority. Two states—Pennsylvania and Georgia—even established a plural (multi-member) executive. Slowly the governorships became stronger through longer terms, popular election, and the power to veto legislation, but power did not come easily. The movement for popular democracy during the Jacksonian era led to the election of other executive branch officials, and reaction to the excesses of Jacksonian democracy resulted in numerous independent boards and commissions in the executive branch. Although governors did gain some power, they were not able to exercise independent authority over these executive boards and commissions.

In the early 1900s, along with their efforts to democratize national politics and clean up the corrupt city political machines, Progressive reformers launched a campaign to reform state government. Their principal target was the weak executive branch. Efforts to improve the state executive branch continued throughout the twentieth and into the twenty-first century. The essential goal has been to increase the governor's powers to make them more commensurate with the increased duties and responsibilities of the office. As a result, constitutional and statutory changes have fortified the office of the chief executive, reorganized the executive branch, and streamlined the structure and processes of the bureaucracy. The capacity of governors and the executive branch to apply state resources to the solution of emerging problems has thus been greatly enhanced.[8] And, the governors have become prominent players in national policy making.

Today's Governors

Today, being governor is a high-pressure, physically demanding, and emotionally draining job. As one political scientist states, "Governors must possess many skills to be successful. They are expected to be adroit administrators, dexterous executives, expert judges of people, combative yet sensitive and inspiring politicians, decorous chiefs of state, shrewd party tacticians, and polished public relations managers."[9] The job is also hard on a governor's private life. It consumes an enormous number of waking hours at the expense of family activities; hobbies; and, in some cases, more significant moneymaking opportunities in law, consulting, or business.

Fortunately, governorships are attracting well-qualified chief executives, most of whom are a far cry from the figureheads of the eighteenth and nineteenth centuries and the stereotypical backslapping, cigar-smoking wheeler-dealers of the early twentieth century. Today's governors are better educated and better prepared for the job than their predecessors were. Many recent governors hold law or other advanced degrees. Most of today's governors paid their political dues in state legislatures, gaining an understanding of important issues confronting the state, a working familiarity with influential figures in government and the private sector, and a practical knowledge of the legislative process and other inner workings of state government. About 40 percent of governors in 2020 were elected state executive branch officials, including lieutenant governor and attorney general (AG), when they ran for governor. As Table 7.1 shows, there are ample opportunities for individuals interested in becoming governor to serve in statewide elected office. Two were serving in local elected positions and thirteen were in either in the U.S. House of Representatives or the state senate.

Table 7.1 Separately Elected State Officials

OFFICE	NUMBER OF STATES ELECTING OFFICIALS
Governor	50
Lieutenant governor	43
Attorney general	43
Treasurer	36
Secretary of state	35
Education (superintendent or board)	13
Auditor	24
Secretary of agriculture	12
Controller	10
Public utilities commissioner	6
Insurance commissioner	11
Land commissioner	5
Labor commissioner	4
Mines commissioner	1
Adjutant general (National Guard)	1

Source: Adapted from *The Book of the States 2019*, Table 4.10 and Ballotpedia.org.

Although previous elected experience is a tremendous advantage in winning a governorship, thirteen current governors came straight from the private sector, touting their business credentials. (See the Controversies in States and Localities box.) The attractiveness of the governorship is evident in the fact that eight of the current chief executives left a congressional seat to take statewide office. Why would someone desert the glamour of the nation's capital for the statehouse in Baton Rouge, Topeka, or Providence? For political power and the opportunity to make a difference in one's own state. Simply put, being a state chief executive is just more rewarding and more fun. It is, according to current and former governors, "the best job in politics."[10] As Rhode Island governor Gina Raimondo has said, "It's incomparable to any other job. . . . On any given day, you deal with public health, public safety, labor and training, schools, the economy. The breadth is huge."[11]

Although still predominantly white males, today's governors are more representative of population characteristics than former chief executives were. One Latino—Michelle Lujan Grisham of New Mexico (elected in 2019), one Native American—Kevin Stitt of Oklahoma (also elected in 2019), and one Asian American—David Ige of Hawaii (elected in 2014 and reelected in 2018) currently serve as governor. Three African Americans have served recently as governor: L. Douglas Wilder, Virginia (1990–1994); Deval Patrick, Massachusetts (2006–2015); and David Paterson (2009–2014) of New York. Gary Locke, the first Asian American governor not from Hawaii, was elected governor of Washington in 1996 and served until 2005. Bobby Jindal (2008–2016) was the first Indian American (Asian) governor in Louisiana, followed by Nikki Haley (2011–2017) in South Carolina. A substantial number of women have been elected to their state's top office. The first to be popularly elected was Mirium "Ma" Ferguson of Texas in 1924. She served two terms. Nine women were serving in their state's top office in 2019.

Getting There: Gubernatorial Campaigns

Without question, the governorship is an alluring office. Occasionally its luster attracts truly oddball candidates, such as Texas mystery writer, songwriter, and performer Kinky Friedman, who ran for governor in 2006. His progressive country band "Kinky Friedman and the Texas Jewboys" recorded various alternative hits in the 1970s, including "They Ain't Making Jews Like Jesus Anymore" and "We Reserve the Right to Refuse Service to You." While cracking jokes and one-liners ("I'll sign anything but bad legislation"), he also campaigned on serious issues, including election reform, education improvement, and legalization of marijuana. Friedman modeled his appeal after former professional wrestler Jesse Ventura who was elected governor of Minnesota in 1998, going so far as to hire Ventura's campaign manager to run his Texas campaign. Friedman has placed his name in the Democratic primary on three occasions, most recently in 2014 when he campaigned for agriculture commissioner.[12] The 2014 Republican primary in Idaho featured two rather conventional candidates: the incumbent governor Butch Otter and state senator Russell Fulcher. And then there were Harley Brown, a biker who campaigned in a motorcycle jacket and hat, and Walt Baves, "a long-bearded perennial candidate [who] simply read verses from the Bible."[13]

The lure of the governorship must be weighed against the financial costs. Campaigning for the office has become hugely expensive. Because candidates no longer rely on their political party to support them, they must continuously solicit great sums of money from donors to pay for campaign costs—political consultants, opinion polls, air travel, media advertisements, telephone banks, direct mailings, websites, and interactive video links.

Until recently, the most expensive governor's race was the 2010 election in California between Meg Whitman and Jerry Brown. Meg Whitman spent $144 million of her own money, and $178.5 million in total, compared to Brown who spent $36.5 million (but was aided with $26 million in outside group spending).[14] Official figures do not include in-kind donations, such as free transportation, door-to-door canvassing, telephones, and other contributions from supporters. Spending in the Illinois gubernatorial election in 2018 rivalled those California numbers. Democratic challenger J. B. Pritzker raised more than $176 million ($172 million from himself!), outspending incumbent Republican Bruce Rauner by a large margin. The total spent in the 2018 Illinois governor's race could top $285 million, making it the most expensive race on record.[15] While 2018 cost-per-vote basis figures are not yet available, races in 2016 ranged from $25.36 per vote in Missouri to $3.24 per vote in Delaware.[16]

Controversies in States and Localities

Is Private Sector Experience the Best Preparation for the Governorship?

Rhode Island governor Gina Raimondo addresses a crowd on a cold day in the Ocean State.

Historically, governors have previously served their states in the legislature or in other executive branch positions. Hands-on government experience is conventionally considered to be an important advantage for governors, as they presumably enter office with an understanding of the workings of the three branches of government and the state bureaucracy, and knowledge of key political actors. Such experience should help a new governor to successfully achieve their goals and exercise effective leadership.

But the 2018 and 2019 elections ushered into office twenty-one new governors (nineteen in the 2018 election and two in the 2019 election), eleven of whom had relatively little state government experience. Four invested most of their professional life in the private sector. Illinois governor J. B. Pritzker's family owns the Hyatt hotel chain and is one of the

wealthiest families in the United States. When he was inaugurated in 2019, he was listed as the wealthiest governor ever to have held office in the country. Ned Lamont, governor of Connecticut, was chief executive officer (CEO) of Campus Televideo, a company that provides television services to U.S. universities. Tennessee governor Bill Lee's family owns a 1,000-acre cattle farm in western Tennessee. His family later started a construction company where he served as CEO. On the other hand, Oklahoma governor Kevin Stitt, was born into a rather modest family; his father was a pastor in Norman. Stitt worked his way through Oklahoma State University by selling books door-to-door. In 2000, he started Gateway Mortgage with $1,000 and a computer, growing it into a nationwide mortgage company with a loan servicing portfolio of more than $16 billion. Despite their varied backgrounds and career stories, all four appealed to voters by presenting themselves as political outsiders who would draw from their business experience to run the state efficiently and effectively.

Critical Thinking Questions

1. What advantages does significant private sector experience bring to the office of governor? Should a business background produce better results than a political background?
2. What disadvantages might relative unfamiliarity with state government likely bring to the governorship in terms of attaining legislative priorities, working with state agencies (including some headed up by other elected officials), and avoiding legal problems with the courts?

Money has a profound influence on gubernatorial elections, but it isn't the only important factor. As one veteran of political campaigns has reflected, "Everyone knows that half the money spent in a political campaign is wasted. The trouble is that nobody knows which half."[17] Other factors are also important in candidate success, such as incumbency, the strength of the candidate's political party in the electorate, and prevailing levels of unemployment and other economic conditions.[18] High-profile candidates stand a solid chance of being elected because they possess campaign skills, political experience, and other characteristics that help them raise the campaign funds needed to get their message and persona across to the electorate.

Incumbency is a particularly important aspect of a candidate's profile. An incumbent governor running for reelection stands an excellent chance of victory; about three-quarters of incumbents have retained their seats since 1970. Incumbents enjoy a number of important advantages, including the opportunity while in office to cultivate popularity with the voters and collect campaign donations from interest groups. However, reelection is no sure thing. Budget and tax woes can lead voters to toss chief executives out of office, particularly those who, as candidates, pledged not to raise taxes but then do so after election.[19] Besides these state concerns, midterm gubernatorial elections are also affected by presidential popularity. One recent study of gubernatorial elections from 1994 through 2014 concluded that presidential approval ratings had a modest effect on midterm gubernatorial results.[20]

Incumbents sought reelection in nineteen of the thirty-six gubernatorial elections in 2018; the remaining seventeen governors were either term-limited and could not run for reelection (thirteen states) or decided to retire (four states). Two incumbents lost in the general election (Illinois and Wisconsin), and one lost in the primary election (Kansas). The situation in Kansas was complicated. Governor Sam Brownback was term-limited and could not seek reelection in 2018. He resigned in early 2018 to become a U.S. ambassador. His successor, Jeff Coyler, lost the Republican primary to Kansas secretary of state Kris Kobach, who then lost in the general election to the Democratic candidate, state senator Laura Kelly. Illinois challenger J. B. Pritzker outspent the incumbent governor by a huge margin. In Wisconsin, incumbent Republican Scott Walker lost to Democrat Tony Evers. Walker had become a controversial figure both because of policies he had sponsored in Wisconsin and his failed attempt to win the Republican nomination for the presidency in 2016. Walker's campaign and outside groups spent some $58 million on the race, actually outspending Tony Evers, whose campaign and outside groups spent $35 million. The $93 million spent on the race made it the most expensive in Wisconsin history, topping the 2014 Wisconsin race by some $11 million.[21] Incumbents in the remaining seventeen states won their elections. Eleven states held gubernatorial elections in 2020. Incumbents were reelected in nine. Republican Spencer Cox was elected to succeed retiring Gary Hebert in Utah. Only in Montana did party control of the governorship change from Democratic to Republican.

Being Governor: Duties and Responsibilities

LO 7-2
To discuss the diverse roles of the governor.

In performing the duties of the office, the governor wears the hats of top policy maker, chief legislator, chief administrator, ceremonial leader, intergovernmental coordinator, economic development promoter, and political party leader. Sometimes several of these hats must be balanced atop the governor's head at once. All things considered, these roles make the governorship one of the most difficult and challenging, yet potentially most rewarding, jobs in the world.

Developing and Making Policy

Transforming good ideas from concept to practice is an exciting but extraordinarily difficult challenge for governors. A governor is the leading formulator and initiator of public policy in their state, from their first pronouncements as a gubernatorial candidate until their final days in office. The governor's role as chief policy maker involves many other players, including those in the legislature, bureaucracy, courts, interest groups, and the voting public. Most major policies are initiated by the governor, and success or failure depends largely on how competently the governor designs and frames policy proposals and develops public support for them. The governor must also follow through to see that adopted policies are put into effect as originally intended.

Some issues are by nature transitory, appearing on the agenda of state government and disappearing after appropriate actions are taken. These issues are often created by external events such civil unrest; a federal court decision that mandates a reduction in prison overcrowding; or an act of nature such as a hurricane, tornado, pandemic viral outbreak, or flood.

Most policy issues, however, do not emerge suddenly out of the mists. Perennial concerns face the governor each year: education, corrections, social welfare, health care, the environment, and economic development. Cyclical issues also appear, increase in intensity, and slowly fade away. Examples of the latter are consumer protection, ethics in government, reapportionment, and budget shortfalls. Of course, national policy issues sometimes absorb the governor's time as well, such as preparing for and addressing an influx of illegal immigrants, economic downturns, and proposals to drill or "frack" for oil and gas in the state or near state shorelines.

Several factors have contributed to stronger policy leadership from the chief executives in recent years, including larger and more capable staffs who are knowledgeable in important policy fields; a more integrated executive branch with department heads appointed by the governor; strengthened formal powers of the office, such as longer terms and the veto and budget powers; and the assistance of the NGA along with regional associations, which offer ideas for policy and program development.

LO 7-3
To appraise the dynamics of working with the legislature to enact policy.

Marshaling Legislative Action

The gubernatorial role of marshaling legislative action is closely related to that of policy maker, because legislative action is required for most of the chief executive's policies to be put into effect. In fact, the governor cannot directly introduce bills; party leaders and policy supporters in the statehouse and senate must put the bills in the hopper. Dealing with legislators is a demanding role for a governor, consuming more time than any other role and representing for many the single most difficult aspect of the job.

Relationship with the Legislature Developing a positive and productive relationship with the legislature requires great expenditures of a governor's time, energy, and resources. Several factors hinder smooth relations between the chief executive and the legislature, including partisanship and personality clashes. Even the different natures of the two branches can cause conflict. Governors are elected by a statewide constituency and therefore tend to take a broad, comprehensive, long-range view of issues, whereas legislators, representing relatively small geographical areas and groups of voters, are more likely to take a piecemeal, parochial approach to policy making. Conflicts inevitably erupt during budget time, when critical spending decisions are at hand.[22]

According to one study, the amount of strife between the two branches is influenced by three factors: the size of the majority and the minority parties, the personalities of the governor and legislative leaders, and the nearness of an election year.[23] Following the 2019 elections, there were twenty-four Democratic governors and twenty-six Republicans. Today, the governor has to deal with a one- or two-house majority from the opposing political party. When the opposition party is strong, the governor must seek bipartisan support to get favored legislation passed. Often a governor facing a large legislative majority from the opposing party has only the veto and the possibility of mobilizing public support as weapons against the legislature. Democratic Montana governor Steve Bullock faces a Republican-controlled state legislature and says, "The only way I can get progressive things done is working with Republicans. Even if it were otherwise . . . just because you have the power to do it by one vote doesn't mean that's necessarily the way to exercise it."[24] Likewise, Maryland Republican governor Larry Hogan faces a large majority of Democrats in both houses of the Maryland General Assembly. He tries to avoid losing fights with the legislature and says, "I let a lot of pitches go by. Where there is common ground, we work together."[25] Bullock was reelected as governor in 2016 and Hogan in 2018.

A governor who ignores or alienates members of the opposing political party can quickly find himself in the desert without a drink of water. North Carolina Democratic governor Roy Cooper has faced a combative Republican-controlled General Assembly since he was elected in 2016. For his first two years as governor, Cooper faced a veto-proof Republican majority in both houses of the state legislature. Nevertheless, Cooper vetoed twenty-eight bills the legislature passed on topics such as state elections, abortion, and the state budget. The legislature easily overrode twenty-three of these vetoes. In the 2018 elections, Democrats increased their share of the lower house of the state legislature so that it no longer had a veto-proof majority. None of the nineteen vetoes Cooper issued in 2019 or 2020—including the state budget—was overridden by the legislature. Cooper was reelected as governor in 2020 while Republicans kept control of the state legislature.

The approach of elections can also bring gubernatorial-legislative deadlock because incumbents in both branches of government may become extremely cautious or overtly partisan in their efforts to please (or at least not to offend) the voters while discrediting their opponents. Gridlock may result.

These three conflict-producing factors of partisanship, personalities, and proximity of an election are intensified during debates on the budget, when the principal policy and financial decisions are made. In some instances, including in Maine and New Jersey in 2017, executive-legislative stalemates have produced state government shutdowns, with negative outcomes for many, if not most, state residents.

Even in states in which the governor's own party enjoys a large majority in both houses of the legislature, factions are certain to develop along ideological, rural-urban, geographical, institutional (house versus senate), or other divisions. Ironically, a large legislative majority can create the greatest problems with factionalism, primarily because a sizable opposition doesn't exist to unite the majority party. The stronger the numbers of the majority party, the more likely it is to degenerate into intraparty rivalries beyond the governor's control. As one Democratic governor lamented in the face of a four-to-one majority of his own party in the legislature, "You've got Democrats, you've got moderate Democrats, you've got suburban Democrats, you've got urban Democrats, you've got rural Democrats."[26]

Executive Influence on the Legislative Agenda Despite the difficulties in dealing with the legislature, most governors dominate the policy agenda, usually by working hand in hand with legislative leaders. The governor's influence begins with the State of the State address, which kicks off each new legislative session and continues in most states with the annual budget message. In 2019, governors stressed education, jobs, infrastructure, opioids, the environment, housing, violence prevention, child welfare, and justice.[27] During the legislative session itself, the governor might publicly (or privately) threaten to veto a proposed bill or appeal directly to a particular legislator's constituency. Governors may also take their fight to the people, as Idaho governor Brad Little did in pressuring the state legislature to sustain his veto of a 2019 bill tightening the procedures to get citizen initiatives on the ballot.[28]

Most of the drama, however, takes place behind the scenes. The governor might promise high-level executive branch jobs or judgeships (either for certain legislators or for their friends) to influence legislative votes. Kentucky governor Steve Beshear, a Democrat, appointed two Republican legislators to posts in the executive branch to gain the legislative majority needed to pass a bill expanding betting on horse races.[29] Or a governor might offer some sort of **pork barrel** reward, such as funding a highway project in a legislator's district or approving a special appropriation for the local Strawberry Festival. Private meetings or breakfasts in the governor's mansion flatter and enlist support from individuals or small groups of legislators. Virginia governor Terry McAuliffe (2014–2018) governed by happy hour, stocking the executive mansion with top-shelf spirits and craft beer, and inviting legislators over for nightly receptions. For teetotalers, McAuliffe served daily breakfasts.[30] Successful governors can usually relate to representatives and senators on a personal level. Many are former members of the state legislature, so they can rely on personal connections and experiences to win over key members. One of the

pork barrel Favoritism by a governor or other elected official in distributing government monies or other resources to a particular program, jurisdiction, or individual.

most successful governors recently, for example, was Mike Beebe (2011–2014) of Arkansas, who labored in the state senate for twenty years and as attorney general for four, before winning the state's top office.

In addition, all governors have legislative liaisons who are assigned to lobby for the administration's program. Members of the governor's staff testify at legislative hearings, consult with committees and individuals on proposed bills, and even write floor speeches for friends in the legislature. Some governors designate a floor leader to steer their priorities through the legislature.

Most governors, however, are careful not to be perceived as unduly interfering in the internal affairs of the legislature. Too much meddling in legislative affairs can bring a political backlash that undermines a governor's policy program. The role of chief legislator, then, requires a balancing act that ultimately determines the success or failure of the governor's agenda.

Governors and the Courts

Sometimes the best laid plans of governors are squelched by the courts, either state or federal. Former Florida governor Rick Scott's attempt to require nursing homes immediately to install back-up electrical generators (after twelve people died in an overheated nursing home when its power failed during Hurricane Irma) was struck down by an administrative court judge in 2017 who called the order "impossible for the vast majority of nursing homes."[31] Maine governor Janet Mills, elected in 2018, inherited a number of lawsuits that originated against her predecessor—Paul LePage—over the limits of gubernatorial power. As attorney general, Mills often found herself opposing LePage's actions in court during his tenure in office.[32] Such court actions demonstrate the need for governors and their legal staffs to be attentive to the legality of their actions and decisions.

Administering the Executive Branch

As chief executive of the state, the governor is (in name, at least) in charge of the operations of numerous agencies, departments, boards, and commissions. In the view of many voters, the governor is directly responsible not only for pivotal matters, such as the condition of the state's economy, but also for more mundane concerns, such as clearing the snow off state highways in a timely manner. Most governors are sensitive to their chief administrative responsibilities and spend a great amount of time and energy attending to them. Constitutional and statutory reforms, including the concentration of executive power in the office of the governor and the consolidation of numerous state agencies, have considerably strengthened the governor's capacity to manage the state. If governors are diligent and expeditious in appointing talented and responsive people to policy-making posts, they should feel no compulsion to micromanage the state's day-to-day affairs. Instead, they can focus their energies on leadership activities such as identifying goals, marshaling resources, and achieving results.

In many respects, the governor's job is comparable to that of the CEO of a very large corporation. Governors must manage tens of thousands of workers, staggering sums of money, and complex organizational systems. They must establish priorities, handle crises, and balance contending interests. But there are important differences as well. For one, governors are not paid comparably for their responsibilities. In terms of expenditures and employees, most states are as big or bigger than Fortune 500 companies, whose CEOs typically earn tens of millions of dollars a year in salary, stock options, and other forms of remuneration. Yet the fifty governors average only about $142,826 in annual salary. (The highest paid is the governor of California, at $201,680; the lowest is Maine's, at $70,000.)[33]

In addition to being woefully underpaid, today's governors experience high levels of stress from interest group criticism, legislative sniping, extraordinarily long hours on the job, and constant media attention to every possible misstep.

Restraints on Management Reforms of the executive branch have allowed far more active and influential gubernatorial management, but significant restraints remain. For example, the separation-of-powers principle dictates that the governor shares their authority with the legislature and the courts, either or both of which may be politically or philosophically opposed to any given action. Changes in state agency programs, priorities, or organization typically require legislative approval, and the legality of such changes may be tested in the courts.

The governor's ability to hire, fire, motivate, and punish is severely restricted by the courts, merit-system rules and regulations, collective bargaining contracts, independent boards and commissions with their own personnel systems, and other elected executive branch officials pursuing their own administrative and political agendas. Thus, most employees in the executive branch are outside the governor's formal sphere of authority and may challenge that authority almost at will. Career bureaucrats, who have established their own policy direction and momentum over many years of seeing governors come and go, usually march to their own tune. In sum, governors must lead and manage through third parties and networks in the three branches of government, as well as in the private and nonprofit sectors. They have little unilateral authority.

Governors as Managers Some governors minimize their managerial responsibilities, preferring to delegate them to trusted staff and agency heads. Others provide strong administrative and policy leadership in state government. The honor of "Best Run State" in 2019 went to Utah where Gary Herbert is governor. Low unemployment, strong economic growth, a high level of education, and stable fiscal management all contributed to this high rating.[34] But there are substantial constraints on the governor's managerial activities, along with associated political liabilities. The governors who courageously wade into the bureaucratic fray must invest a great deal of time and scarce political resources, yet they risk embarrassing defeats that can drag their administrations into debilitation and disrepute. After all, "Reorganized the State Bureaucracy" hardly resonates as a campaign slogan.

Meanwhile, in the face of social, political, and economic change, the management of state government has become increasingly complex, yet the need for strong administrative leadership more critical than ever before.

Master of Ceremonies

Some governors thrive on ceremony and others detest it, but all spend a large portion of their time on it because it helps garner reelection votes. Former governors remember ceremonial duties as the second most demanding of the gubernatorial roles, just behind working with the legislature.[35] Cutting the ribbon for a new highway, celebrating the arrival of a new business, welcoming potential foreign investors, receiving the queen of the Collard Green Festival, announcing "Respect Your Parents Week," opening the state fair, and handing out diplomas are the kinds of ceremonial duties that take a governor all over the state and often consume a larger portion of the workweek than does any other role. Even a seemingly pleasant task can have its personal horrors. George A. Aiken, the late governor of Vermont, dreaded having to pin the ribbon on the winner of the Miss Vermont contest because he couldn't figure out how to put the pin in without getting his hand under the bathing suit.

Coordinating Intergovernmental Relations

Governors serve as the major points of contact between their states and the president, Congress, and federal agencies. Everything from emergency response to settling disputes over cross-border water pollution issues are carried out through the governor's office. At the local level, governors are involved in allocating grants-in-aid, promoting cooperation and coordination in economic development activities, and various other matters. Governors also provide leadership in resolving disputes with Native American tribes involving casino gambling and related issues.

The role of intergovernmental coordinator is most visible at the national level, where governors are aided by the NGA and the state's Washington office. The NGA meets twice a year in full session to adopt policy positions and to discuss governors' problems and "best practice" policy solutions. The governors also meet in separate regional organizations. (C-SPAN covers national meetings of the governors.) The NGA's staff analyzes important issues, distributes its analyses to the states, offers practical and technical assistance to the governors, and holds a valuable seminar for new governors. The NGA, however, has come under fire from conservative Republicans, who objected to the organization's perceived "tax-and-spend" agenda, even when it benefitted their own states. In fact, Republican governors of Texas, Florida, Idaho, Maine, South Carolina, and Ohio withdrew from the NGA for a few years over this and related concerns, such as NGA's role in developing the Common Core state education standards, preferring to work with the Republican Governors Association instead.

Most states have established Washington offices to fight for their interests in Congress, the White House, and, perhaps most important, the many federal agencies that interact with states on a daily basis. A governor's official inquiry can help speed up the progress of federal grant-in-aid funds or gain special consideration for a new federal facility. Washington offices are commonly assisted by major law and lobbying firms under contract to individual states.

The governor's role as intergovernmental coordinator is of great importance. It reflects the elevated position of the states in the scheme of American federalism and the increasing state importance in national and international affairs. It is also a reaction to provocations and intrusions from the national government, such as unfunded mandates, poorly framed laws, and unwelcome blundering into state affairs. Acting together and as individuals, the governors have exercised national policy leadership on critical issues such as environmental protection, climate change, taxation of internet sales, public education, and health care reform. Frequently, when the national government confronts a policy problem, it turns to the states for solutions. Yet political polarization in Congress, and increasingly in the states, discourages compromise and lessens state influence in Washington, D.C.[36]

Promoting Economic Development

Unfairly or not, governors may be held responsible by the voters for their state's economic health. As promoter of economic development, a governor works to recruit businesses and tourists from out of state and to encourage economic growth from sources within the state. Governors attend trade fairs, visit the headquarters of firms interested in locating in the state, telephone and e-mail promising business contacts, and welcome business leaders. The role may take the governor and the state economic development team to Mexico, China, Germany, and other countries, as well as to other states. Governors also work hard to promote tourism. But mostly, economic development entails making the state's climate "good for business" by improving infrastructure, arranging generous tax and service incentives, and engaging in other strategies designed to entice out-of-state firms to relocate and encourage in-state businesses to expand or at least stay put.

When a state enjoys success in economic development, the governor usually claims a major portion of the credit. Sometimes the personal touch of a governor can mean the difference between an industrial plum and economic stagnation. Success stories are heralded proudly. Are incumbent governors punished in a reelection effort when promised economic growth falls short? Research findings on this question are mixed.[37]

Leading the Political Party

By claiming the top elected post in the state, the governor becomes the highest-ranking member of their political party. This role is not as significant as it was several decades ago, when the governor controlled the state's party apparatus and legislative leadership and had strong influence over party nominations for seats in the state legislature and executive branch offices. Primaries have replaced party conventions and put nominations largely in the hands of the voters. And legislative leaders are a much more independent breed than they were, for example, in Illinois, when Governor Richard Ogilvie (1969–1973) brought up the need for income tax legislation during a breakfast meeting at the mansion. Senate president Russ Arrington angrily asked, "Who is the crazy son of a bitch who is going to sponsor this thing?" The governor calmly replied, "Russ, you are." And he did.[38] Such an order is unlikely these days. Still, some governors get involved in legislative elections through campaign aid, endorsements, or other actions. If the governor's choice wins, they may feel a special debt to the governor and support them on important legislation.

The political party remains useful to the governor for three principal reasons.[39] Legislators from the governor's own party are more likely to support the chief executive's programs. Communication lines to the president and national cabinet members are more likely to be open when the president and the governor are members of the same party. And finally, the party remains the most convenient means through which to win nomination to the governor's office.

Formal and Informal Powers of the Governor

LO 7-4
To explain the formal powers of the office today and how they are used.

A variety of powers are attached to the governor's office. A governor's **formal powers** include the tenure of the office, power of appointment, power to veto legislation, responsibility for preparing the budget, authority to reorganize the executive branch, and the right to hire professional staff in the governor's office. These institutional powers give governors the *potential* to carry out the duties of office as they see fit. However, the formal powers vary considerably from state to state. Some governors' offices (Illinois, New York) are considered strong and others (Alabama, Georgia) weak. Also, the fact that these powers are available does not mean that they are used effectively. Equally important are the **informal powers** (sometimes called personal powers) that governors have at their disposal. These are potentially empowering features of the job or the person that are not expressly provided for in the law. Many of the informal powers are associated with personal traits on which the chief executive relies to carry out the duties and responsibilities of the office. They are especially helpful in relations with the legislature. Within any state, the governor's formal powers change only slowly because changes require new state laws or constitutional amendments. But as the occupant of the office of governor changes, new governors make better or worse use of their informal powers, either enhancing or diminishing their role in state government.[40] For example, Brad Little was elected governor of Idaho in 2018, replacing Butch Otter. Both are Republicans; both had Republican-controlled state legislatures. The formal powers of the Idaho governor had not changed recently, but Little is using his informal powers much more effectively in working with the state legislature than did Otter.[41]

Both sets of powers have increased over the past several decades. And governors are more influential than ever before, primarily because of their

formal powers
Powers of the governor derived from the state constitution or statute.

informal powers
Powers of the governor not derived from constitutional or statutory law.

enhanced formal powers; charisma, however, remains as important as ever. The most successful governors are those who employ their informal powers to maximize the formal powers. The term for this concept is *synergism*, a condition in which the total effect of two distinct sets of attributes working together is greater than the sum of their effects when acting independently. An influential governor, then, is one who can skillfully combine formal and informal powers to maximum effectiveness. Counted among the most effective governors today are those who do so: Charlie Baker (R-Massachusetts), Larry Hogan (R-Maryland), Andrew Cuomo (D-New York), Doug Burgum (R-North Dakota), Kay Ivey (R-Alabama), Brad Little (R-Idaho), and Gary Herbert (R-Utah): All are experienced state leaders who are not term-limited in their next election and whose states give them high levels of institutional power.[42] Interestingly, while Cuomo, Burgum, Ivey, Little, and Herbert enjoy large majorities of their own party in their respective state legislatures, Baker and Hogan face legislatures with large opposing majorities.

Tenure

The governor's tenure power has two characteristics: the duration (number of years) of a term of office and the number of terms that an individual may serve as governor. From the onerous restriction of a single one-year term of office placed on ten of the first thirteen governors, the duration has evolved to today's standard of two or more four-year terms (only New Hampshire and Vermont restrict their governors to two-year terms). In addition, gubernatorial elections have become distinct from national elections because thirty-nine states hold them in nonpresidential election years. This system encourages the voters to focus their attention on issues important to the state rather than allowing national politics to dominate state election outcomes.

The importance of longer consecutive terms of office is readily apparent. A two-year governorship condemns the incumbent to a perpetual reelection campaign. As soon as the winner takes office, planning and fundraising must begin for the next election. For any new governor, the initial year in office is typically spent settling into the job. In addition, the first term, first-year chief executive must live with the budget priorities adopted by their predecessor. A two-year governorship, therefore, does not encourage success in matters of legislation or policy. Nor does it enable the governor to have much effect on the bureaucracy, whose old hands are likely to treat the governor as a mere bird of passage, making them almost a lame duck when his term begins. As Governor Alfred E. Smith of New York observed after serving four two-year terms during the 1920s, "One hardly has time to locate the knob on the State-house door."[43]

By contrast, Virginia's governor, the only one who is restricted to a single four-year term, is a bit less confined in carrying out his responsibilities. But he really has only two years to put his programs and priorities in place, sandwiched on one side by the initial learning year and on the other by the lame-duck period. The incumbent needs another four-year term to design new programs, acquire the necessary legislative support to put them into place, and get a handle on the bureaucracy by appointing loyal, competent people to top posts. Eight years in office also enhances the governor's intergovernmental role, particularly by giving him sufficient time to develop and nurture key relationships and win leadership positions in organizations such as the NGA. The record of an eight-year chief executive stands on its own, untainted by the successes or failures of the office's previous inhabitant.

The average time actually served by governors has grown with fewer restrictions on tenure. The first gubernatorial graybeard was Illinois governor Jim Thompson, who stepped down after serving his fourth consecutive term in 1990—a twentieth-century record.[44] Recent "comeback governors" have been elected in California (Jerry Brown, 1975–1983, 2011–2019), Iowa (Terry Branstad, 1983–1999, 2011–2019), and Oregon (John Kitzhaber, 1995–2003, 2011–2015). Long periods in office strengthen the governor's position as policy leader, chief legislator, chief administrator, and intergovernmental coordinator, and leave strong policy legacies.

Appointment Power

Surveys of past governors indicate that they consider appointment power to be the most important weapon in their arsenal when it comes to managing the state bureaucracy. The ability to appoint one's supporters to top positions in the executive branch also enhances the policy management role. When individuals who share the governor's basic philosophy and feel loyal to the chief executive and their programs direct the operations of state government, the governor's policies are more likely to be successful. Strong appointment authority can even help the governor's legislative role. The actual or implicit promise of important administrative and especially judicial positions can generate a surprising amount of support from ambitious lawmakers.

Unfortunately for today's governors, the long ballot lives on in the **plural executive**. Most states continue to provide for popular election of numerous officials in the executive branch, including insurance commissioners, public utility commissioners, and secretaries of agriculture. The Council of State Governments lists forty-eight such positions in its annual *Book of the States*. Mississippi and North Dakota elect the largest number—nine in each state—while Alaska, Hawaii, Maine, New Hampshire, New Jersey, and Tennessee choose all these officials in ways other than popular election. Proponents of popular election claim that these officials make political decisions and therefore should be directly responsible to the electorate. Opponents contend that governors and legislators can make appointment decisions more properly, because they are not beholden to special interests that offer up generous campaign contributions.

Perhaps appointment authority should depend on the office under consideration. Table 7.1 shows the number of states that popularly elect various executive branch officials.

The It's Your Turn box gives you a chance to offer your opinion.

plural executive
A system in which more than one member of the executive branch is popularly elected on a statewide ballot.

Professional Jobs in State Government The vast majority of jobs in the states are filled through objective civil service (merit-system) rules and processes. Governors are generally quite content to avoid meddling with civil service positions. Gubernatorial sacrifice of **patronage** power is understandable in view of the time and headaches associated with naming political supporters to jobs in the bureaucracy. There is always the possibility of embarrassment or scandal if the governor accidentally appoints a person with a criminal record, a clear conflict of interest, or a propensity for sexual harassment or other inappropriate behavior, or someone who causes harm through simple incompetence. Moreover, those who are denied coveted appointments may become angry. One governor is quoted as stating, as he was about to name a new member of a state commission, "I now have twenty-three good friends who want [to be] on the Racing Commission. [Soon] I'll have twenty-two enemies and one ingrate."[45] Governors who abuse the merit hiring system can be prosecuted, as were Kentucky governor Ernie Fletcher and fifteen members of his administration, who were indicted in a hiring scandal in 2006. A governor benefits from a stable, competent civil service that hires, pays, and promotes on the basis of knowledge, job-related skills, and abilities rather than party affiliation, friendship with a legislator, or campaign donations.

The Power to Fire The power of the governor to hire is not necessarily accompanied by the power to fire. Except in cases of extreme misbehavior or corruption, it is very difficult to remove an appointed subordinate from office. For instance, if a governor attempts to dismiss the secretary of agriculture, he can anticipate an orchestrated roar of outrage from legislators, bureaucrats, and farm groups. The upshot is that the political costs of dismissing an appointee can be greater than the pain of simply living with the problem.

A good appointment to a top agency post is the best way for a governor to influence the bureaucracy. By carefully choosing a competent and loyal agency head, the governor can more readily bring about significant changes in the programs and operations of that agency. Where appointment powers are circumscribed, the chief executive must muster their informal powers to influence activities of the state bureaucracy or rely on the seasoned judgment of professional civil servants.

Veto Power

The power to veto bills passed by the legislature bolsters the governor as chief policy maker and chief administrator. A bill may be vetoed because its contents are contrary to a governor's principles or preferences, or for many other reasons. A veto accompanied by an explanation makes a powerful symbolic statement or can instruct the legislature about how the bill might be amended for the governor's signature. A veto can also punish an offending legislator or state agency by eliminating a favored program or severely cutting its budget. Often the mere threat of a veto is enough to persuade a recalcitrant legislature to see the governor's point of view and compromise on the language of a bill. Vetoes are not easy to override. Most states require a majority of three-fifths or two-thirds of the legislature.

patronage
The informal power of a governor (or other officeholder) to make appointments on the basis of party membership and to dispense contracts or other favors to political supporters.

? It's Your Turn

Should Executive Branch Officers Be Elected?

As seen in Table 7.1, fourteen officials are popularly elected in at least one state, including mines commissioner and adjutant general of the National Guard. There are arguments to be made both pro and con for offering voters a "long ballot."

What do you think? Are long ballots preferable to short ballots?

PROS	CONS
It makes sense to elect an auditor and an attorney general, because they require some independence in carrying out their responsibilities. (The auditor oversees the management and spending of state monies; the attorney general is concerned with the legality of executive and legislative branch activities.)	Some of these offices tend to cater to special interests, such as agriculture, insurance, and education. These special interests can be expected to contribute generously to their preferred candidates.
The number of elected branch officials has remained virtually the same for decades. Why change it now?	Governors are weakened by their inability to directly appoint the heads of major state agencies, boards, and commissions. These high-ranking officials make policy decisions in the executive branch, but if they owe their jobs in whole or in part to popular election, the governor's authority as chief executive is significantly diminished. Although nominally in charge of these executive branch agencies, the governor is severely constrained in his ability to manage them.
Incumbent education superintendents, agricultural commissioners, and others have strong supporters in the electorate.	It would be unthinkable in a corporation to preclude the CEO from appointing their own top staff members.
Interest groups will fiercely resist proposals to make certain offices appointive.	The fragmented nature of power in the executive branch diminishes accountability and frustrates governors.
Most citizens simply like having an opportunity to vote on a large number of executive branch officials. Surveys show that they want the long ballot.	Most reformers interested in "good government" agree on the need to consolidate power in the governor's office by reducing the number of statewide elected officials and expanding the power of appointment to more policy-related, or "unclassified," posts in the executive branch.

Types of Vetoes The veto can take several forms. The **package veto** is the governor's rejection of a bill in its entirety. All governors hold package veto authority. The **line item veto** allows the governor to strike out one or more objectionable sections of a bill, permitting the remaining provisions to become law. Only Nevada, Maine, and six other states forbid this gubernatorial power. Several states permit a hybrid form of line item veto in which the governor may choose to reduce the dollar amount of a proposed item to hold down state expenditures or cut back support for a particular program. In some states, the line item veto is permitted only in appropriations bills.

package veto
The governor's formal power to veto a bill in its entirety.

line item veto
The governor's formal power to veto separate items in a bill instead of the entire piece of proposed legislation.

The **pocket veto**, which is available in fourteen states, allows the governor to reject a bill by refusing to sign it after the legislature has adjourned. In two states (Hawaii and Utah), the legislature can reconvene to vote to override a pocket veto; otherwise, the bill dies. A governor might use the pocket veto to avoid giving the legislature a chance to override a formal veto or to abstain from going on record against a proposed piece of controversial legislation.

A fourth type of veto is the **executive amendment**, formally provided in fifteen states and informally used in several others. With this amendatory power, a governor may veto a bill, recommend changes that would make the bill acceptable, and then send it back to the legislature for reconsideration. If the legislature concurs with the suggestions, the governor signs the bill into law.

Use of the Veto
The actual use of the veto varies by time, state, and issue. Some states, such as California and New York, often record high numbers of vetoes, whereas others, like Virginia, report few. On average, governors veto around 4 percent of the bills that reach their desks.[46] The variation among states reflects the tensions and conflicts that exist between the governor and the legislature. The largest number of vetoes typically occurs in states with divided party control of the executive and legislative branches. Occasionally, the governor stands as the last line of defense against a flawed bill backed by the legislature because of powerful interest groups or a bill passed just to score political points. It is not unknown for legislators to secretly ask the governor to veto a questionable bill they have just passed because the bill's contents, although problematic, are politically popular.[47]

Differences in party affiliation between the governor and the legislative majority probably provoke more vetoes than any other factor, especially when party ideology and platforms openly clash. In 2015, Maine governor Paul LePage followed through on a threat to veto all bills sponsored by Democrats unless the legislature approved his call for a constitutional amendment to abandon the income tax, vetoing ten bills in a single day. The legislature rebuked LePage two days later by overriding nine of his vetoes.[48] In his eight years as governor (2011–2019), LePage issued more vetoes than all previous governors of Maine combined. New York governor David Patterson vetoed some 6,700 budget items during a single week in 2010.[49] But when mutual respect and cooperation prevail between the two branches, the governor rarely needs to threaten or actually use the veto.[50] In some states there is more of a tradition of governors issuing vetoes—and state legislatures overturning governors' vetoes—even when the governor and state legislature are in the same party's hands. For example, former Republican governors of South Carolina— Mark Sanford (2003–2011) and Nikki Haley (2011–2017) made extensive use of the veto, only to see many overridden by the heavily Republican majority in the South Carolina legislature. Current South Carolina governor Henry McMaster has been more judicious in the use of his veto power, but one of his recent vetoes of a bill lowering electrical rates charged by the South Carolina public utility was so unpopular that it was overridden by a vote of 110 to 1 in the House and 39 to 0 in the Senate.[51] Former Democratic governor Jerry

pocket veto
The governor's power to withhold approval or disapproval of a bill after the legislature has adjourned for the session, in effect vetoing the measure.

executive amendment
A type of veto used by the governor to reject a bill and also to recommend changes that would cause the governor to consider the bill's approval.

Brown of California (2011–2019) vetoed 17 percent of 2,194 bills sent to him in the 2017–2018 legislative session even though the California state legislature had a large Democratic majority. Brown's vetoes in 2017 and 2018 were not unusual behavior for him. Over his eight years in office, he vetoed 11 percent to 17 percent of the bills sent to him, higher than governors in most other states.[52]

Most governors interact with the legislature throughout the bill-adoption process. Before rejecting a bill, the governor will request comments from key legislators, affected state agencies, and concerned interest groups. He may ask the attorney general for a legal opinion. And before actually vetoing proposed legislation, the governor usually provides advance notification to legislative leaders, along with a final opportunity to make amendments.

The veto can be a powerful offensive weapon that may be used to obtain a legislator's support for a different bill dear to the governor's heart, particularly near the end of the legislative session. The governor may, for instance, hold one bill hostage to a veto until the legislature enacts another bill that he favors, as did Maine's governor LePage. Former California governor Arnold Schwarzenegger also did this in 2008, when he began vetoing all bills sent to his desk until the legislature approved a budget bill; all told, he vetoed 35 percent of the bills sent to him that session.[53] Wisconsin's storied history includes the "Vanna White Veto" and the "Frankenstein Veto." The first, abolished in 1990, permitted the governor to delete individual letters and numbers to change a bill's content. The second, killed by a 2008 voter referendum, allowed the governor to strike out some words and piece together others to alter a bill's content. For instance, Governor Jim Doyle (2003–2011) used the Frankenstein Veto to delete 752 words from a bill, which effectively shifted $427 million from transportation to education.

Budgetary Power

The governor's budget effectively sets the legislative agenda at the beginning of each session. By framing the important policy issues and attaching price tags to them, the governor can determine the scope and direction of budgetary debates in the legislature and ensure that they reflect their overall philosophy on taxing and spending. All but a handful of governors have the authority to appoint (and remove) the budget director and to formulate and submit the executive budget to the legislature. In Mississippi and Texas, budget authority is shared with the legislature or with other elected executive branch officials. And in these two states, two budgets are prepared each year, one by the governor and one by a legislative budget board.

Because budgetary authority is normally housed in the office of the chief executive, the governor can not only drive the budgetary process in the legislature but also enjoys a source of important leverage in the bureaucracy. The executive budget can be used to influence programs, spending, and other activities of state agencies. For example, uncooperative administrators may discover that their agency's slice of the budget pie is smaller than expected, whereas those who are attentive to the concerns of the governor may receive strong financial support. Rational, objective criteria usually determine departmental budget allocations, but a subtle threat from the governor's office does wonders to instill a cooperative agency attitude.

The governor's budget requests are rarely, if ever, enacted exactly as put forward. Rather, they are argued and debated thoroughly in both houses of the legislature. A legislature dominated by the opposing political party is nearly certain to scorn and disparage the governor's budget as "dead on arrival." Governors, who are elected statewide, must appeal to a large and diversified electorate. Legislatures must please localized geographic constituencies. Ultimately, "the governor proposes, but the legislature disposes." In fact, no monies may be appropriated without formal action by the legislature. Which branch of government is most powerful in a budgetary sense? Research is inconclusive—it depends.[54]

During state budget crises, governors find themselves in an extremely vulnerable political positions, particularly if they signed a "no new taxes" pledge when running for office. Legislatures struggle with the governor over the question of who will assume primary responsibility for reducing state expenditures or hiking taxes. Usually, governors take the heat, and even light the match, by cutting spending, introducing tax increases, or both.[55] Such bold actions, though fully appropriate, are not taken without due caution by the governor because the electoral consequences can be direct and negative.

Reorganization Power

Reorganization power refers to the governor's ability to create and abolish state agencies, departments, and other offices and to reallocate administrative responsibilities among them. Reorganizations are usually aimed at the upper levels of the bureaucracy in an effort to streamline the executive branch and thereby make it work more efficiently and effectively. The basic premise is that the governor, as chief manager of the bureaucracy, needs the authority to arrange administrative structures and processes to meet changing demands. For instance, serious and recurring problems in coordinating the delivery of social services among several existing state agencies may call for a consolidated human services department with expanded powers. A governor with strong reorganization power can bring about such a department without approval of the legislature.

Traditionally, legislatures have been responsible for the organization of state government, and in the absence of a constitutional amendment to the contrary or a statutory grant of reorganization power to the governor, they still are. But today, thirty-five states specifically authorize their chief executive to reorganize some or all elements of the bureaucracy through **executive order**, through which the governor can make needed administrative changes when they deem it necessary.

executive order
A rule, regulation, or policy issued unilaterally by the governor to change executive branch operations or activities.

Administrative reorganization today takes place under the assumption that streamlined government improves bureaucratic performance and saves money by cutting down on duplication, waste, and inefficiency. Achieving a more efficient and user-friendly government is a top priority of most governors.

Initiatives to reinvent or reinvigorate government aim to make the bureaucracy more flexible and responsive by changing incentive systems for state employees; privatizing certain operations; reducing layers of bureaucracy; implementing e-government; and consolidating information technology, purchasing and payroll, and human resource management activities.

Executive branch reorganization is widely practiced, but its actual benefits are often ephemeral. Reorganization typically achieves modest financial savings, if any at all, and it can produce bureaucratic infighting, delays, unanticipated financial costs, and widespread confusion. Reorganization is not a panacea for state fiscal ills. However, executive branch reorganization may help to provide a clearer focus on a particular problem, such as the needs of children; or help to contain administrative costs, such as by eliminating superfluous or unnecessary boards, commissions, and task forces, and it may serve various political purposes, such as rationalizing the pain of employee layoffs.[56]

The Politics of Reorganization Reorganization is a politically charged process. Mere talk of it sounds alarms in the halls of the legislature, in the honeycombs of state office buildings, and in the offices of interest groups. Reorganization attempts usually spawn bitter controversy and conflict both inside and outside state government as assorted vested interests fight for favorite programs and organizational turf. Accordingly, comprehensive reorganization proposals are frequently defeated or amended by the legislature or abandoned by discouraged chief executives. One study of proposed state reorganizations discovered that almost 70 percent resulted in rejection of the plan either in part or in its entirety.[57] Even when implemented, reorganizations may generate fierce opposition from entrenched interests in the bureaucracy and, in the final analysis, be judged a failure. In the memorable words of former Kansas governor Robert F. Bennett:

> In the abstract, [reorganization] is, without a doubt, one of the finest and one of the most palatable theories ever espoused by a modern-day politician. But in practice . . . it becomes the loss of a job for your brother or your sister, your uncle or your aunt. It becomes the closing of an office on which you have learned to depend. . . . So there in many instances may be more agony than anything else in this reorganization process.[58]

Most governors who have fought the battle for reorganization would concur. Perhaps such predictable opposition helps explain the rarity of far-reaching state agency restructuring and the preference for small, incremental steps to reorganize and streamline state agencies.

Staffing Power

The governor relies on staff to provide policy analysis and advice, serve as liaisons with the legislature, assist in managing the bureaucracy, and provide constituent services. Professional staff members are a significant component of the governor's team, composing a corps of political loyalists who help the governor cope with the multiple roles of the office. From the handful of political cronies and secretaries of several decades ago, the staff of the governor's office has grown in number, quality, and diversity. Today, the average number of professional and clerical staff members is approximately fifty-six. In some larger, more highly populated states, staff members number well over 100: Texas reports 277 staffers and Florida 276.[59] The principal staff positions of the governor's office include those of chief of staff, legislative liaison, budget director, policy director, legal counsel, scheduler, press secretary, and intergovernmental coordinator.

Perhaps the most important to the governor is their chief of staff. Among the wide range of duties discharged by the chief of staff are chief operating officer, office manager, chief strategist, policy advisor, gubernatorial proxy, gatekeeper, headhunter, crisis coordinator, and personal confidant.[60]

A question of serious concern, especially in the states whose governors have large staffs, is whether these nonelected officials have too much power and influence. Clearly, professional staff members have been highly influential in developing and promoting policies for governors in some states, particularly in states where the governor lacks a coherent set of priorities and lets the staff have free rein to advance their own agenda. In other states, the chief executive is very much in charge, relying on staff primarily for drafting bills and providing technical information. Given their physical and intellectual proximity to the governor, staff members are in a highly advantageous position to influence their boss. In their role as the major funnel for policy information and advice, they can affect the governor's decisions by controlling the flow of information and individuals into his office.

The Relevance of Formal Powers

In Table 7.2, the states are scored according to the strength of the governor's formal powers of office. As noted, governors have won stronger powers over time. But how helpful are the formal powers? Despite the major transformation of the governor's office, governors remain relatively weak because of the setting of state government. They must function within a highly complex and politically charged environment with formal authority that is quite circumscribed by the legislature, the courts, and constitutional and statutory law. Owing to the nature of our federal system, the national government effectively strips them of control over many policy and administrative concerns. Moreover, the business of state government is carried out in a fishbowl, open to regular scrutiny by the media, interest groups, talk-show hosts, bloggers, Tweeters, and other interested parties. Notwithstanding the continued constraints on the exercise of their authority, however, today's governors as a group are probably more effective than their predecessors were in carrying out their varied responsibilities.

In at least three states, the partisan turnover of the governorship from Republican to Democratic in 2016 or 2018 has led the state legislature to attempt to reduce the formal powers of the governor. In North Carolina, Democrat Roy Cooper beat incumbent Republican governor Pat McCrory in a close election in 2016. The Republican-controlled General Assembly responded by passing legislation requiring legislative approval for gubernatorial cabinet choices and

Table 7.2 Relative Power of the Governors' Offices (Formal Powers)

2.5	2.75	3.0	3.25	3.5	3.75	4.0
RI	NH	IA	AL	KS	KY	AK
NC	TX	VA	HI	PA	MD	
OR	AR	WV	MO	NM	OH	
	CA	FL	WY	NY	ND	
	MS	NE	ID	TN	MA	
	OK	GA	IL	UT	MI	
	SC	LA	MN	WA	CT	
		CO	AZ	DE	SD	
		WI	ME	NJ		
		VT	MT	IN		
				NV		

U.S. Average: 3.24

Source: Adapted from Margaret Ferguson, "Governors and the Executive Branch," in Virginia Gray and Russell L. Hanson, eds., *Politics in the American States: A Comparative Analysis*, 11th ed. (Washington, D.C.: Congressional Quarterly Press, 2018), Table 8.4.

reducing the number of employees the governor could hire and how many appointees the governor could make to the state elections board. In Michigan and Wisconsin, similar actions were taken by Republican-controlled legislatures after Democratic governors were elected in 2018. Governors have responded by challenging these actions in state courts with varying degrees of success.[61]

In theory, governors with strong formal powers, such as the governors in Alaska, Kentucky, and Maryland, should be more effective than their counterparts in Vermont, North Carolina, and Oregon. In practice, that tends to be true—but not always. The potential for power and influence must not be confused with action. A governor with strong formal powers enjoys the capacity to serve effectively, but he may choose not to do so or, for various reasons, be unable to utilize the formal powers properly. This point is indirectly confirmed by a study that finds that formal gubernatorial power does not translate into greater success for incumbent governors seeking reelection.[62] Alternatively, a governor with weak formal powers can nonetheless be an effective, strong chief executive if they actively and skillfully apply the levers of power available in the constitution and in statutes.

Informal Powers

No doubt a governor with strong formal powers has an advantage over one without them. But at least equally important for a successful governor is the exploitation of the informal powers of the office. These powers carry authority and influence that are not directly attached to the governorship through statute or constitution, but rather are associated with the human being who

LO 7-5
To analyze the informal powers of the office, their importance, and how they can enhance the formal powers.

happens to occupy the governor's mansion. Governors who can master these powers can be highly effective, even in the absence of strong formal powers.

The informal powers help transform the capacity for action into effective action. They react in synergy with the formal powers to create a successful governorship. An incumbent chief executive in the strong-governor state of Massachusetts will be hopelessly weak unless he also uses his personal assets in performing the multiple roles of the office. Alternatively, a chief executive in a weak-governor state such as South Carolina can be remarkably successful if they fully employ their informal powers to excel in persuading the legislature and the people in the state to adopt new ideas. The informal powers are not as easy to specify as the formal powers are. However, they generally include such tools of persuasion and leadership as popular support; prestige of the office; previous elected experience; public relations and media skills; negotiating and bargaining skills; pork barrel and patronage; and personal characteristics such as ambition, experience, and energy.

Tools of Persuasion and Leadership

Popular support refers to public identification with and support for the governor and his priorities. It may be measured in terms of the margin of victory in the primary and general elections or in terms of the results of public opinion polls. Governors with large victory margins and high levels of public support can lay claim to a popular mandate. They can parlay popular support into legislative acceptance of a policy proposal, channeling the pressures of public opinion to their advantage.

Popular support can quickly vanish when a governor's words or actions alienate voters and/or powerful interest groups, as demonstrated by the cases of two recent governors. Pennsylvania governor Tom Corbett was reported to be a member of a club that traded pornographic photos and videos on safe e-mail accounts during the workday.[63] In a televised appearance, Corbett also equated same-sex marriage to incest. Neither helped him with voters. Governor Paul LePage of Maine "told the state chapter of the NAACP to kiss his butt, likened the Internal Revenue Service to the Nazi Gestapo, issued blanket gag orders to the state's largest newspaper chain (whose headquarters he also joked about bombing), and denounced—on camera—a Democratic state legislator for always wanting to 'give it to the people without Vaseline.'"[64] Remarkably, LePage was returned to office by the voters in 2014 for a second term.

The *prestige of the office* helps the governor open doors all over the world that would be closed to an ordinary citizen. National officials, big-city mayors, corporate executives, foreign officials, and even the president of the United States recognize that the governor sits at the pinnacle of political power in the state, and they treat them accordingly. Governors of California, Texas, Florida, and New York—the largest states—almost automatically assume roles of national and even international prominence. Within the state, the governor typically makes use of the prestige of the office by inviting important individuals for an official audience or perhaps to a special meal or celebration at the mansion. Previous electoral experience is a valuable asset. Those who have made their way up the state's political ambition ladder by serving in the state legislature or serving as attorney general or lieutenant governor have learned how to find their way through political briar patches and avoid tar pits.[65] They can also take advantage of political friends and allies they cultivated along the way. Arkansas governor Mike Beebe (2007–2011) leveraged the experience of twenty years in the state senate and four years as AG to get just about everything he asked for from the legislature.[66]

Public relations and media skills help the governor command the "big mike": the captive attention of the press, radio, and television. Any governor can call a press conference at a moment's notice and get a substantial turnout of the state's major media representatives, an advantage enjoyed by precious few legislators. Some chief executives appear regularly on television to explain their policy positions and initiatives to the people. Others write regular newspaper columns. Nearly all use blogs, Tweets, or Facebook messages for the same purpose. Frequent public appearances, staged events, telephone calls, YouTube videos, and even state-funded "public interest" advertisements delivered through the mass media are also tools in the governor's media kit. Governors have used such techniques to attain statewide voter approval ratings of up to 90 percent. The ability to improvise in unpredictable, chaotic situations doesn't hurt. Former New York governor David Paterson illustrated that point effectively. When the wife of Jonathan Lippman, whom Paterson had just nominated as a judge, fainted at a press conference during Lippman's remarks, the governor quipped to the audience, "It's the usual reaction when Jonathan is speaking."[67] Spontaneity may serve the governor well, but one must also weigh his words carefully before speaking.

Effective governors know instinctively that the media can be a strong ally in carrying out their programs and responsibilities, and they cultivate the press like a flower garden. But media relations are a two-way street. The media expect the governor to be honest, forthright, and available. If he instills respect and cooperation, the governor's media relations can be "of incalculable value in his contest for the public eye and ear."[68] After all, most or even all of what the public knows about the governor comes from the media.

Negotiating and bargaining skills are leadership tools that help the governor to convince legislators, administrators, interest groups, and national and local officials to accept his point of view on whatever issue is at hand. These skills are of tremendous assistance in building voting blocs in the legislature, particularly in divided-power settings. They also help persuade new businesses to locate in the state and help the governor effectively represent a state's interests before the national government.

Pork barrel and patronage are aspects of the seamier side of state politics. Although they are utilized much less frequently now than they were before the civil service reforms of the first half of the twentieth century, governors are still known to promise jobs, contracts, new roads, special policy consideration, electoral assistance, and other favors to influential citizens, legislators, donors, and others in return for their support. All governors have discretionary funds with which to help out a special friend who has constituents in need. And although patronage appointments are now severely limited in most jurisdictions, a personal telephone call from the governor can open the door to an employment opportunity in state government.

Characteristics of a Successful Governor

The *personal characteristics* of an effective governor are nearly impossible to measure. However, leadership is generally agreed to be a very important quality. Leadership traits are difficult to define, but former Utah governor Scott Matheson identified the best governors as:

> men and women who have the right combination of values for quality public service—the courage to stick to their convictions, even when in the minority; integrity by instinct, compassion by nature, leadership by perception; and the character to admit wrong and when necessary, to accept defeat.[69]

A successful governor achieves their objectives by blending these qualities with the formal and informal powers of office. For example, following the political campaign to win the election, the governor must conduct a "never-ending campaign" to win the loyalty and support of their cabinet, state employees, the legislature, and the people if she is to be effective.[70] Sixteen-hour days and 100-hour workweeks are not uncommon. Some governors demonstrate amazing determination and commitment to the job. On an African vacation, former Virginia governor Terry McAuliffe (2014–2018) fell from a horse and broke seven ribs. Yet he returned to Virginia and immediately resumed his obligations (though he was later briefly hospitalized after complications developed).

At the outset, successful governors are careful not to allow eloquent and elevated campaign promises to greatly exceed practical political possibilities. Realizing that to try to do everything is to accomplish nothing, they focus on a few critical issues at a time and marshal their formal and informal resources behind them. Eventually, the determined governor can wear down opponents. But more important, the successful governor exercises leadership by convincing the public that he is the person to pursue their vision and their interests. He prevails in the legislature by applying the pressure of public opinion and by building winning blocs of votes, and leads the bureaucracy by personal example. Above all else, the successful governor must be persuasive.

In short, the formal powers of the office are important to any governor, but even strong formal powers do not guarantee success. As noted earlier, they must be combined with the informal powers to be effective. Whatever approach the governor chooses as chief executive, their individual skills are probably more important than formal powers. Evidence of this conclusion is provided by governors who have won and held their state's top job and successfully pursued their policy agendas in the face of significant opposition. Of course, how a governor proceeds to govern is in part situational.

Leaving Office

Upon leaving office, the vast majority of governors simply continue their public service in another venue. Four out of the last seven presidents were ex-governors. Former Indiana governor Mike Pence is the current vice president. President Trump's Secretary of Agriculture Sonny Perdue from Georgia and former Secretary of Energy Rick Perry from Texas were governors, as was his first United Nations Ambassador—Nikki Haley of South Carolina. California governor Jerry Brown was elected mayor of Oakland following his first years as governor, then as state AG, and in 2010 and 2014, as governor again; Colorado's Roy Romer became superintendent of Los Angeles, California's public schools; former Indiana governor Mitch Daniels was named president of Purdue University; and former governor of Hawaii, Linda Lingle, became chief operating officer for Illinois governor Bruce Rauner. Ten former governors were serving in the U.S. Senate in 2020.

A handful of former governors, however, have served time in prison for illegal actions or gross conflicts of interest. All states but one provide in their constitutions for the impeachment of the governor and other elected officials (in Oregon, they are tried as regular criminal offenders). Impeachment proceedings are usually initiated in the state house of representatives, and the impeachment trial is held in the senate. A two-thirds vote is necessary for conviction and removal of the governor in most states. Of the more than 2,100 governors who have held office, only twenty-three have been either impeached and removed from office or resigned under a cloud of legal problems. Besieged governors are much more likely to resign than face a lengthy public scourging through impeachment and legislative trial, or to be prosecuted upon expiration of their term.

The most recent governors to leave office in disgrace were Eric Greitens of Missouri, Robert Bentley of Alabama, John Kitzhaber of Oregon, Robert McDonnell of Virginia, Eliot Spitzer of New York, and Rod Blagojevich of Illinois. Greitens resigned in 2018 after admitting to an extra-marital affair with his hairstylist. Bentley resigned in 2017 after pleading guilty to two misdemeanor campaign finance charges having to do with covering up an extra-marital affair. Kitzhaber resigned in 2015 over ethical questions about his live-in fiancée's dealings as a consultant while also advising the governor. McDonnell and his wife were prosecuted in 2014 for illegally accepting gifts, vacations, and large loans from a Richmond businessman. (McDonnell's conviction was overturned in a unanimous U.S. Supreme Court decision in 2016.) Spitzer resigned after getting snared in a federal prostitution sting operation. The Blagojevich saga involved a host of federal criminal charges, including trying to sell the U.S. Senate seat that was vacated when Barack Obama assumed the presidency. It ended with the former governor being impeached and removed from office and then convicted on seventeen federal corruption accounts and sentenced to fourteen years in prison (after serving eight years, the remainder of his sentence was commuted by President Trump in 2020).

But these fallen unfortunates are the gubernatorial black sheep—the political throwbacks of state government who spawn media feeding frenzies. They deflect proper attention from the vast majority of hard-working, capable, and honest chief executives who typify the American state governorship today.

LO 7-6

To explain the responsibilities of the other elective statewide executive branch offices.

Other Executive Branch Officials

The states elect more than 300 officials to their executive branches, not counting the fifty governors, ranging from attorneys general and treasurers to railroad commissioners. The four most important statewide offices are described here.

Lieutenant Governor

This office was originally created by the states for two major reasons: to provide for orderly succession to a governor who is unable to fulfill a term because of death or other reasons, and to provide for an official to assume the responsibilities of the governor when the incumbent is temporarily incapacitated or out of the state. Five states do not see a need for the office: Arizona, Maine, New Hampshire, Oregon, and Wyoming. Others attach little importance to it, as indicated by an extremely low salary or the absence of official responsibilities.

The historical reputation of the lieutenant governor was that of a corpse at a funeral; you are needed for the ceremony but no one is expecting much from you; or, as one wag suggested, "dismissed as a ribbon-cutting version of the appendix—prominently situated but without any discernible function."[71] The absence of significant responsibilities gets some lieutenant governors into mischief. Three resigned in 2013 amid scandals and the lieutenant governor of Alaska resigned in 2018 after making unspecified inappropriate comments to a woman.

But several recent lieutenant governors have risen to occupy the executive office because of a death, impeachment, or resignation. Even when a governor's unplanned exit is not the cause of a vacancy in the executive mansion, the lieutenant governorship can be a springboard to the state's top elected office.[72] Twelve governors in 2020 had paid their dues as lieutenant governor.

The lieutenant governorship in the majority of states has become a more visible and responsible position. Many lieutenant governors hold important powers in the state senate, including serving as presiding officer, making bill assignments to committees, and casting tie-breaking votes in the senate. They are official members of the cabinet or of the governor's top advisory body in twenty-one states.[73] Indiana's lieutenant governor serves as secretary of agriculture and runs six state agencies; Colorado's directs the department of higher education. And virtually all lieutenant governors accept special assignments from the chief executive, some of which are quite visible and important. For example, Utah's heads up that state's homeland security efforts. Several lieutenant governors act as agency heads. In general, lieutenant governors' salaries, budget allocations, and staff have grown markedly.

A lingering problem is that twenty states continue to elect the governor and lieutenant governor independently. This system can result in conflict when, for example, the chief executive is out of state and the two officeholders are political rivals or members of opposing political parties. On several recent occasions, a lieutenant governor, assuming command, has proceeded to make judicial appointments, veto legislation, convene special sessions of the legislature, and take other actions at odds with the governor's wishes.

To avoid partisan bickering and politicking in the top two executive branch offices, twenty-five states require team election. In addition to avoiding embarrassing factionalism, team election has the advantages of promoting party accountability in the executive branch, making continuity of policy more likely in the event of gubernatorial death or disability, and ensuring a measure of compatibility and trust between the two state leaders.

Attorney General

The AG is the state's chief legal counsel. The AG renders formal written opinions on legal issues, such as the constitutionality of a statute, administrative rule, or regulation, when requested to do so by the governor, agency heads, legislators, or other public officials. The AG can also independently question the constitutionality of actions by the governor and even the federal government. In most states, the AG's opinions have the force of law unless they are successfully challenged in the courtroom. Many high-profile AGs have successfully positioned themselves for the governorship, including seven sitting governors in 2020.

The AG represents the state in litigation in which the state government is a legal party, represents the state in federal and state courts, and can initiate civil and criminal proceedings in most states. More active today than ever before, AGs regularly contest national government statutes and administrative rulings in controversial fields such as consumer rights, environmental protection, education reform, and business regulation. AGs today are bringing litigation against the national government that argues against portions of the national health care law (the ACA), air pollution regulations, and immigration policy. Activist AGs have initiated actions to protect consumers against mail fraud, mortgage fraud, cybercrime, Medicaid fraud, misleading advertisements by pharmaceutical companies, predatory student loan lending, mortgage fraud and illegal foreclosure actions by banks, and other white-collar crimes.

Some of their collective actions have helped to reform corrupt corporate behavior and to push the national government to regulate business more aggressively. Conservative AGs have taken quite a different tack, litigating for looser environmental, financial, and other regulations. Their litigation and arguments often push issues onto the policy agenda of Congress and to the U.S. Supreme Court. Predictably, the AGs' activism has spawned intense interest and participation in AG elections. A 2014 *New York Times* investigation uncovered numerous cozy relationships between certain AGs and corporate lobbyists in the energy, pharmaceutical, food, and financial industries,[74] raising important questions about the AGs' integrity and independence.

What should be done when an AG is told by the governor or legislature to defend a law they are convinced is unconstitutional? Some AGs mount a defense as best they can, but others refuse to do so. For example, in 2017, North Carolina's Roy Cooper refused to defend the state law that reduced protections for gay and transgender people, and, in 2018, Tennessee's Herbert

Slatery refused to file suit against the federal government's refugee resettlement program in that state.

Treasurer

The treasurer is the official trustee and manager of state funds and the state's chief financial officer. He collects revenues and makes disbursements of state monies. (The treasurer's signature is on the paychecks of all state employees and on citizens' state tax refunds.) Another important duty is the investment of more than $3.2 trillion in state funds, including state employee pension monies and college savings plans. The failure to make profitable investments can cost the treasurer his job. West Virginia treasurer A. James Manchin (uncle to current West Virginia senator Joe Manchin) was impeached for losing $279 million in state funds through bad investments. Other treasurers have been criticized for taking lucrative private-sector jobs in the middle of their terms (Connecticut, New Jersey), accepting gifts from financial firms (Massachusetts), or using their post to raise large sums of campaign money from investment companies. Arkansas treasurer Martha Shoffner was convicted in 2014 on federal charges of taking kickbacks and directing state bond transactions to a single, favored broker. She was sentenced to two and a half years in federal prison.[75]

Secretary of State

In the past, the duties of the secretary of state were rather perfunctory, entailing record keeping and election responsibilities. But voting system reforms, e-government, and other changes in how states run elections have substantially elevated the responsibilities of the position. Secretaries of state typically register corporations, securities, and trademarks, and commission people to be notaries public. The typical secretary of state also maintains state archives, files agency rules and regulations, publishes statutes and copies of the state constitution, and registers lobbyists.

In their election-related responsibilities, they determine the ballot eligibility of political parties and candidates, receive and verify initiative and referendum petitions, supply election ballots to local officials, file the expense papers and other campaign reports of candidates, maintain voter registration rolls, and deter voter fraud. This often puts them in the forefront of the voter identification controversy. A function of growing importance in the secretary of state's offices is to protect citizens and businesses against identity theft.[76]

The Capability of U.S. Governors

The governor, as chief executive, enjoys extensive powers, both formal and informal. Today's governors are capable, active, and, in general, impressive political actors. However, severe national political divisions over such issues as same-sex marriage, gun control, health care, and immigration threaten to conscript governors into the bitter, dysfunctional partisanship that characterizes the nation's capital. This is a development that raises concern and bears close attention.

In addition, today's governors are better educated, more experienced in state government, and more competent than their predecessors. Unfortunate exceptions notwithstanding, their strength and policy influence impresses. They are better able to employ the informal powers of their office in meeting multiple and complex responsibilities. In sum, the governorships display both capability and vigor.

Chapter Recap

- The American governorship historically was institutionally weak, with limited formal powers.

- Today's governors are generally well qualified for the office, but some recent governors have disappointed. Winning the office is increasingly expensive.

- Duties of the governors include making policy, marshaling legislative action, administering the executive branch, serving as master of ceremonies, coordinating intergovernmental relations, promoting economic development, and leading their political party.

- Formal powers of the office, which have strengthened over time, are tenure, appointment, veto, budgeting, reorganizing the executive branch, and staffing.

- To be successful, a governor must master the informal powers of the office and integrate them with the formal powers. Among the informal sources of power are tools of leadership and persuasion, such as public relations skills and negotiating and bargaining skills.

- Governors who violate the law may be removed from office through impeachment, while unpopular governors may be recalled.

- Other key executive branch officials are the AG, lieutenant governor, treasurer, and secretary of state. Like the governors, they too have been expanding their importance in state government.

Key Terms

pork barrel *(p. 184)*
formal powers *(p. 189)*
informal powers *(p. 189)*
plural executive *(p. 191)*

patronage *(p. 192)*
package veto *(p. 193)*
line item veto *(p. 193)*
pocket veto *(p. 194)*

executive amendment *(p. 194)*
executive order *(p. 196)*

Internet Resources

Each state's governor has his or her own website, which can be located through the state homepage or from links at **www.nga.org**, the NGA's website. It features, among other items, governors' biographies, the latest State of the State addresses, and a subject index on various state and local issues.

For information about the attorneys general, see **www.naag.org**. State treasurers can be audited at **www.nast.org**, and lieutenant governors at **www.nlga.us.** Even secretaries of state have a national organization: see **www.nass.org/**.

8

Public Administration: Budgeting and Service Delivery

A firefighter rescues a boy after an auto accident.

Learning Objectives

LO 8-1 To identify the size, scope, and characteristics of state and local government employment.

LO 8-2 To summarize the state government budgetary process, including key actors and critical processes.

LO 8-3 To describe the components of merit systems.

LO 8-4 To explain the challenges of representative bureaucracy and affirmative action, sexual harassment, and public employee unionization and collective bargaining.

LO 8-5 To explain the clash of politics and bureaucracy.

LO 8-6 To describe New Public Management, its strategies, and its pros and cons.

Bureaucracy is a paradox. On one hand, bureaucracy is portrayed as "the problem" with U.S. government at all levels. From the ponderous department of social services, to the dilatory department of motor vehicles, to the extractive county tax assessor's office, it is depicted as all-powerful, out of control, inefficient, wasteful, and drowning in red tape. Public employees ("bureaucrats") are often portrayed as insensitive and uncaring, yet they stay in their jobs forever. Nearly everyone, from elected officials—presidents, governors, mayors, and legislators at all levels—to talk-show commentators, television and film script writers, bloggers, and even product advertisers have stridently bashed the bureaucrats, blaming them for all imaginable sins of omission and commission (and all too often for their own personal shortcomings). The answer to the problem is no less than bureaucratic liposuction to "get the fat out" and surgery to "get the government off our backs."

On the other hand, bureaucracy can be beautiful.[1] Bureaucratic organization is indispensable to public administration. Legislative bodies and chief executives enact public policies through vague laws and then must depend on various state and local agencies to deal with the specifics, such as operationally defining key components of the policies and putting the policies into effect. Some bureaucracies make our lives more difficult, but others improve the quality of our existence by enforcing the laws and punishing the criminals, putting out the fires, repairing and maintaining the roads, and helping the poor and disadvantaged among us. Heroic, life-saving actions by police and firefighters are commonplace but seldom recognized publicly.

A theme of this chapter is that state agencies and local departments (the public administration) should not be treated as scapegoats for all the social, economic, and political maladies that befall society, and that they should be respected—not rebuked. The quality and capacity of public administration have improved markedly in the vast majority of the country's states, municipalities, and counties in terms of the characteristics of employees and the efficiency, effectiveness, and professionalism with which they perform their duties. In fact, studies comparing public employees with cohort groups in the private sector find few important differences between them. Government workers are just as motivated, competent, and ethical as private-sector workers. Moreover, public employees tend to be more sensitive to other human beings and more highly educated than their counterparts in business and industry, and most are imbued with a "public service" ethos that motivates them (see Table 8.1).[2]

State and local employees are responding to citizen demands by providing a wider range of services, in greater quantities, to more people than ever before, and publicly provided services are perceived to be just as good as the same services provided by private firms. Public employees are much more accountable and responsive to political actors and to the public than they are popularly perceived to be. And contrary to popular opinion, government work does not consist of pay without labor. Public employees perform some of the most unpleasant (but necessary) tasks imaginable, from saving abused or threatened children from their parents to caring for the mentally ill and guarding prisoners who hurl feces at them. Many jobs are dangerous, as public employees must contend daily with clients who are criminals, deadbeats, emotionally disturbed, drug abusers, and worse,[3] and expend considerable quantities of "emotional labor."[4] They serve as our first—and continuing—response to disasters and terrorist events.

It is only on those rare occasions when someone fouls up that a public outcry is raised and a media investigation is noisily launched; praise for consistency and excellence in public-service delivery is seldom heard. When government fails to perform effectively, blame can occasionally be laid at the feet of public employees. But more often than not, good government workers are the scapegoats for vague and poorly designed statutes and policies, failed political and corporate leadership, insufficient resources, and other factors

bureaucracy
The administrative branch of government, consisting of all executive offices and their workers.

Table 8.1 Comparing Public- and Private-Sector Employees

CHARACTERISTIC	ADVANTAGE
Motivation	Equal (though public workers favor intrinsic rewards and private workers prefer extrinsic rewards)
Work habits	Equal
Competence	Equal
Personal achievement	Private employees
Educational achievement	Public employees
Values of civic duty and public service	Public employees
Ambition	Private employees
Compassion and self-sacrifice	Public employees
Ethics	Public employees
Helping other people	Public employees
Making a difference	Public employees
Concern for compensation	Private employees

Sources: Adapted from Mary K. Feeney, "Sector Perceptions Among State-Level Public Managers," *Journal of Public Administration Research and Theory* 18(3) (2008): 465–94; Richard W. Stackman, Patrick E. Connor, and Boris W. Becker, "Sectoral Ethos: An Investigation of the Personal Values Systems of Female and Male Managers in the Public and Private Sectors," *Journal of Public Administration Research and Theory* 16 (October 2006): 577–97; Alice Munnel, et al., "Comparing Compensation: State-Local Versus Private Sector Workers," *Issue Brief*, Center for State and Local Government Excellence (September 2011); Kathryn Hendren and Sanjay Pandey, "Motivation in Public Management: Seeing the Forest Through the Trees," in Edmund C. Stazyk and H. George Frederickson, eds., *Handbook of American Public Administration* (Northampton, MA: Edward Elgar, 2018), pp. 172–91.

beyond the control of civil servants. It must also be pointed out that occasional lapses in government administrative ethics often pale in comparison to corporate scandals such as recent ones involving defense contractors, pharmaceutical firms, and banking and finance companies.

LO 8-1
To identify the size, scope, and characteristics of state and local government employment.

Public Employees in State and Local Governments: Who They Are, What They Do

Just over twenty million employees work for states and localities. Their numbers have grown fairly steadily since accurate counts were first compiled in 1929, though they have tailed off since the Great Recession. The distribution of government employees is of interest (see Figure 8.1). Government work tends to be labor-intensive. As a result of this fact and because of inflation, personnel expenditures for states and localities have risen even faster than the

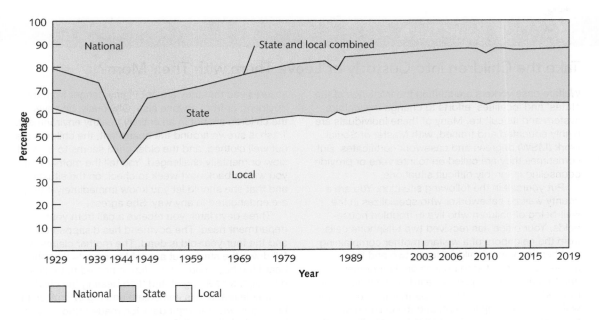

Figure 8.1 Distribution of Full-Time Equivalent Employment, 1929–2019

Since the end of World War II, the percentage of state and local employees, as a proportion of the total government work force, has increased, except when the Great Recession produced a slight downturn.

Source: Bureau of Labor Statistics, 2020.

number of workers. Total payroll costs for state and local governments are about $64 billion per month.[5]

Of course, the number of employees varies greatly among jurisdictions. Generally, states and localities with large populations and high levels of per capita income provide more services and thus employ larger numbers of workers than do smaller, less affluent jurisdictions. California, for instance, has some 1.8 million state and local employees on its payroll, compared with only 45,441 in Vermont. Employment figures are further influenced by the distribution of functions and service responsibilities between states and their local jurisdictions. Such figures do not adequately represent the real people who work for states, cities, counties, towns, townships, and school districts. These workers include the police officer on patrol, the eleventh-grade English teacher, the state trooper, and even your professor of state and local government (if you attend a public institution).[6] Their tasks are as diverse as their titles: sanitation engineer, animal-control officer, heavy-equipment operator, planner, caseworker, and so on. Many of these jobs are quite difficult (see the It's Your Turn feature). The diversity of state and local government work rivals that of the private sector, although important distinctions are made in the nature of the work. As Table 8.2 shows, public- and private-sector management

? **It's Your Turn**

Take the Children into Custody or Leave Them with Their Mom?

Welfare caseworkers are staffing the frontlines of the states' and localities' efforts to change the welfare system and its culture. Many of these individuals are highly educated and trained, with Master of Social Work (MSW) degrees and casework certificates. But sometimes they are called on to intervene or provide counseling in terribly difficult situations.

Put yourself in the following situation. You are a county welfare caseworker who specializes in the well-being of children who live in troubled households. Your office has received two telephone calls from the neighbors of a welfare mother complaining that her two young children (ages two and four) appear to have suffered bruises on their bodies, and that they are frequently heard crying when their mother's boyfriend is in their apartment. You visit the welfare mother's apartment, and the children look fine, except for a couple of minor bruises. The mother

assures you that they are not in any danger from the boyfriend or from anyone else. Obviously, however, the children are not in an entirely healthy environment. Trash is strewn around the apartment, the children are not well clothed, and the older child seems to be a bit slow or mentally challenged. You tell the mother that you will be back next week to check on the situation and that she should let you know immediately if they are endangered in any way. She agrees.

Three days later, you receive a call from your department head. The boyfriend has disappeared, and the four-year-old is dead. The mother claims he fell down the stairs, but a neighbor reports that she heard the boyfriend, who often appeared to be high on drugs, screaming at and then beating the child.

Media reaction is immediate and highly critical. In hindsight, was the right decision made? Should you have acted differently?

PROS	CONS
Department policy did not require you to remove the children from the home based on neighbors' allegations of concern.	Your office had been called twice by neighbors worried about the children.
Caseworkers are encouraged to give the benefit of the doubt to the family so that the children can remain with their relatives.	You saw that the children were poorly clothed and living in a potentially unsafe environment.
You had no clearly convincing evidence that the children were in immediate danger.	You should have erred on the side of caution and recommended that the children be removed immediately and placed in a foster home until their well-being could be assured.

Table 8.2 Public Management and Private Management: What Are the Distinctions?

	PUBLIC MANAGEMENT	PRIVATE MANAGEMENT
CONSTRAINTS	Politics, public opinion, resources	Markets, competitors, resources
CLIENTS	Citizens, legislatures, chief executives, interest groups	Customers who purchase products or services
ACCOUNTABILITY	To citizens and elected and appointed officials	To customers, boards of directors, and shareholders
PURPOSE	To serve the public interest and the common good	To make profits and grow the organization

differ in terms of constraints, clients, accountability, and purpose. From the sewer maintenance worker to the director of human resources, all are public servants—often known as bureaucrats. Almost one of every six working Americans is employed by government at some level. If bureaucrats are the enemy, we have met them and they are us.

Budgeting in State and Local Governments

LO 8-2
To summarize the state government budgetary process, including key actors and critical processes.

The budget is the very lifeblood of public administration. Without a budgetary appropriation, state and local organizations would cease to exist. The monies are allocated (usually on an annual basis) by legislative bodies, but the politics of the budgetary process involves all the familiar political and bureaucratic players: chief executives, interest groups, other government employees, the general public, firms and industries, and, of course, the recipients of legislative appropriations—the state highway department, the municipal police department, the county sanitation office, and so on. In a phrase, budget making is a highly charged political poker game with enormous stakes. To understand public administration, one must have a grasp of budgetary politics.

An often-quoted definition of politics is Harold Lasswell's famous line: "Politics is who gets what, when, where, and how."[7] The budget document provides hard dollars-and-cents data in answer to this question. It is a political manifesto—the most important one you will find in state and local governments. It is a policy statement of what government intends to do (or not do), detailing the amount of the taxpayers' resources that it will dedicate to each program and activity. The outcomes of the budgetary process represent the results of a zero-sum game—for every winner there is a loser—because public resources are limited. An extra million dollars for corrections can mean that much less for higher education; an expensive new fleet of sanitation trucks may require higher trash collection fees from residents. Much of the recognition of the important political function and the controversy surrounding budgeting is exemplified in the recent "Defund the Police" movement which calls for redirecting funding away from policing to other governmental functions.[8]

The Budget Cycle

The process of governmental budgeting is best understood as a cycle with overlapping stages, five of which can be identified: preparation, formulation, adoption, execution, and audit (see Figure 8.2). Several stages are simultaneously taking place at any single time. For example, while the 2020 budget is being executed and revenues and expenditures are being monitored to guard against an operating deficit, the governor and the legislature are developing the 2021 budget. Meanwhile, the 2019 budget is being audited to ensure that monies were properly spent and otherwise accounted for.

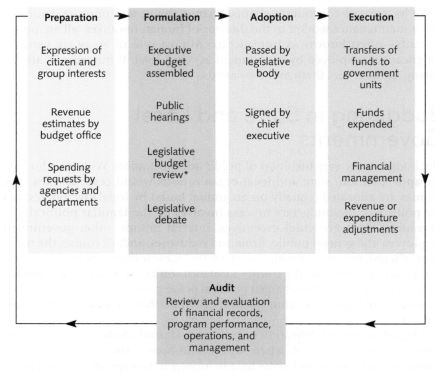

Preparation →	Formulation →	Adoption →	Execution
Expression of citizen and group interests	Executive budget assembled	Passed by legislative body	Transfers of funds to government units
Revenue estimates by budget office	Public hearings	Signed by chief executive	Funds expended
Spending requests by agencies and departments	Legislative budget review*		Financial management
	Legislative debate		Revenue or expenditure adjustments

Audit
Review and evaluation of financial records, program performance, operations, and management

*It is not uncommon for legislatures to develop their own budgets independent of the executive budget.

Figure 8.2 The Budget Process
The budget process has built-in checks and balances because all spending is approved or audited by more than one agency or branch.

Budgets are normally based on a *fiscal* (financial) *year* rather than on the calendar year. Fiscal years for all but four states run from July 1 through June 30 (the exceptions are Alabama, Michigan, New York, and Texas). Nineteen states, including Montana, Nevada, and Texas, have biennial (two-year) budget cycles. Most local governments' fiscal years also extend from July 1 to June 30.

The initial phase of the budget cycle involves demands for slices of the budget pie and estimates of available revenues for the next fiscal year. State and local agency heads join the chorus of interest groups and program beneficiaries seeking additional funding. (With no concern for "profits," agencies have little incentive to ask for less funding instead of more.) Large state agencies are typically represented by their own lobbyists, or "public information specialists." State and local finance administrators and analysts develop estimates of revenues based on past tax receipts and expected economic conditions, and they communicate them to their respective state agencies or municipal departments, which then develop their individual spending requests for the fiscal year. Such spending requests may be constrained by legislative and executive guidance, such as agency or program dollar ceilings, program priorities, or performance-based budgeting considerations.

Formulation, or initial development, of the budget document is the formal responsibility of the chief executive in most states and localities. Exceptions include states in which the balance of power rests with the legislature (such as Arkansas, Mississippi, and South Carolina) and local governments in which budgeting is dominated by a council or commission. Legislatures sometimes develop their own budgets, essentially ignoring those of the governors. Once finalized, the executive budget is then presented to the appropriate legislative body for debate, review, and modification. The lengthy review process that follows allows agencies, departments, interest groups, lobbyists, and citizens to express their points of view. Finally, the legislative body enacts the amended budget. Usually the budget moves forward in accordance with mandated deadlines. Sometimes fiscal crises or political disputes delay budget passage, forcing legislators into all-nighters and casting state and local operations into a sea of uncertainty over what they can and cannot afford to do. For various reasons, New York state is famously tardy in adopting its annual budget, chronically missing its April 1 deadline.

The state legislature or city council ensures that the final document balances revenues with expenditures. Balanced-budget requirements are contained in the constitutions or statutes of forty-eight states and operate through precedent and custom in Vermont and Indiana. These requirements usually apply to local governments as well and are also enforced through municipal ordinances in many localities. Balanced-budget requirements force state and local governments to balance projected expenditures with revenues, but they may be circumvented to some extent (see Figure 8.3). Big-ticket items, for instance, may be funded in a capital budget with payments scheduled over several years.

Before the budget bill becomes law, the chief executive must sign it. Last-minute executive-legislative interactions may be needed to stave off executive vetoes or to override them. Once the chief executive's signature is on the document, the budget goes into effect as law, and the execution phase begins. During budget execution, monies from the state or local general fund are periodically allocated to agencies and departments to meet payrolls, purchase goods and materials, help average citizens solve problems ranging from a rabid raccoon in the neighborhood to a car-swallowing sinkhole in a front yard, and generally achieve program goals.

Accounting procedures and reporting systems continually track revenues and outlays within the agencies. If revenues have been overestimated, the chief executive or legislative body must "rebudget" by making adjustments to keep the budget in the black. They may draw on a rainy-day fund to meet a shortfall or, if the deficit is a large one, order such actions as shown in Figure 8.3. In a crisis, the governor may call the legislature into special session, or the mayor may request a tax increase from the city council. Governments are forced into a dilemma of whether to raise taxes, reduce expenditures, cut services, delay or cancel needed capital expenditures, or use some combination thereof to

Revenue Enhancement Strategies	Spending Reductions
• Hike taxes or fees. • Borrow from employee pension funds. • Borrow from next year's anticipated revenues. • Assume extra new revenues from a prosperous tax year. • Sell excess land, buildings, or other assets. • Aggressively collect delinquent tax payments.	• Postpone infrastructure and equipment maintenance. • Exempt certain costs or projects from the operating budget by creating an "off-budget". • Reduce spending across the board. • Reduce services. • Impose a hiring freeze, unpaid furlough, or travel restrictions. • Refuse to transfer promised funds to local governments (a version of "shift-and-shaft federalism" that imposes new and unforeseen costs of local governments). • Use volunteers to perform appropriate jobs. • Reduce contributions to employee health care or pensions. • Shift state expenditures to local governments. • Privatize a public service.

Figure 8.3 Coping Strategies to Balance an Unbalanced Budget

Sources: Jonathan Walters, "Richard Ravitch: How Budgets Really Work," www.governing.com (accessed April 28, 2014); Kimberly L. Nelson, "Municipal Choice During a Recession: Bounded Rationality and Innovation," *State and Local Government Review* 44 (July 2012): 44–63; John Goodman, "Budget Gimmicks Explained: Five Ways States Hide Deficits," www.stateline.org (accessed June 23, 2011); Mayra Rodriguez Valladares, "Forty U.S. States Cannot Afford to Pay All Their Bills," *Forbes*, https://www.forbes.com/sites/mayrarodriguezvalladares/2018/09/24/fortyusstatescannotaffordtopayalloftheirbills/#10425f67718a (September 24, 2018).

balance the budgets—unpopular choices all. Rainy-day funds are tapped as well. Eventually, real pain is experienced by many different organizations and individuals.

The final portion of the budget cycle involves several types of audits, or financial reviews—each with a different objective. Fiscal audits seek to verify that expenditure records are accurate and that financial transactions have been made in accordance with the law. Performance audits examine agency or department activities in relation to goals, objectives, and outcomes, and ensure that the government is serving its citizens efficiently and effectively. Operational and management audits review how specific programs are carried out and assess administrators' performance.

A performance measurement and management trend has firm traction in state and local governments today, reflecting these jurisdictions' genuine determination to improve service provisions to citizens.[9] Washington state, a leader in outcomes-based budgeting, solicits public and agency input to help prioritize statewide goals and thereby develops a set of priorities to guide and inform agency spending. Those programs that accomplish their goals and objectives are funded; those that fail are not.[10] Many other states have now implemented similar models.

The Actors in Budgeting

Four main institutional actors participate in the budget process: interest groups, agencies, the chief executive, and the legislative body. Interest groups organize testimony at budget hearings and pressure the other three actors to pursue favored policies and programs. The role of the agency or department is to defend the base—the amount of the last fiscal year's appropriation—and to advocate spending for new or expanded programs. Agency and department heads are professionals who believe in the value of their organization and its programs, but they often find themselves playing Byzantine games to get the appropriations they want, as set forth in Table 8.3, which lists tactics used by state and local officials to maximize their share of the budget during negotiations and hearings with governors, local chief executives, and the legislative body.

Table 8.3 The Games Spenders Play

MASSAGE THE CONSTITUENCY	Locate, cultivate, and utilize clientele groups to further the organization's objectives. Encourage them to offer committee testimony and contact legislative members on your behalf.
ALWAYS ASK FOR MORE	If your agency or department doesn't claim its share of new revenues, someone else will. The more you seek, the more you will receive.
WHINING FOR DOLLARS	Keep whining to your boss until his annoyance level is so high that he coughs it up to shut you up.
SPEND ALL APPROPRIATED FUNDS BEFORE THE FISCAL YEAR EXPIRES	An end-of-year surplus indicates that the elected officials were too generous with you this year; they will cut your appropriation next time.
CONCEAL NEW PROGRAMS BEHIND EXISTING ONES	Incrementalism means that existing program commitments are likely to receive cursory review, even if an expansion in the margin is substantial. An announced new program will undergo comprehensive examination. Related to this game is *camel's nose under the tent*, in which low-program start-up costs are followed by ballooning expenses down the road.
"HERE'S A KNIFE; CUT OUT MY HEART WHILE YOU'RE AT IT"	When told that you must cut your budget, place the most popular programs on the chopping block. Rely on your constituency to organize vigorous opposition. Alternatively, state that all your activities are critically important so the elected officials will have to decide what to cut (and answer for it to voters).
A ROSE BY ANY OTHER NAME	Conceal unpopular or controversial programs within other program activities. And give them appealing names (for instance, call a sex education class "Teaching Family Values").
"LET'S STUDY IT FIRST" (AND MAYBE YOU WON'T BE REELECTED)	When told to cut or eliminate a program, argue that the consequences would be devastating and should be carefully studied before action is taken.
SMOKE AND MIRRORS	Support your requests for budget increases with voluminous data and testimony. The data need not be especially persuasive or even factual, just overwhelming. Management writer James H. Boren calls this "bloatating" and "trashifying."
A PIG IN A POKE	Place an unneeded item in your budget request so you can gracefully give it up while protecting more important items.
END RUN	If the chief executive initiates a budget cut, scurry quickly to friends in the legislature.
EVERY VEIN IS AN ARTERY	Claim that any program cut would so completely undermine effectiveness that the entire program would have to be abandoned.

Political scientist Aaron Wildavsky described the basic quandary of agency and departmental representatives as follows:

> Life would be simple if they could just estimate the costs of their ever-expanding needs and submit the total as their request. But if they ask for amounts much larger than the appropriating bodies believe is reasonable, their credibility will suffer a drastic decline. . . . So the first decision rule for agencies is: do not come in too high. Yet the agencies must also not come in too low, for the assumption is that if the agency advocates do not ask for funds they do not need them.[11]

What agency heads usually do is carefully evaluate the fiscal-political environment. They take into consideration the previous year's events, current and estimated agency expenditures, the composition of the legislature, the economic climate, policy statements by the chief executive, the strength of clientele groups, and other factors. Then they put forward a figure somewhat larger than they expect to get.

The chief executive has a much different role in the budget process. In addition to tailoring the budget to their preferred program priorities as closely as possible, they act as an economizer. Individual departmental requests must be reconciled, which means that they must be cut because the sum of the requests will greatly exceed estimated revenues. Of course, an experienced governor or mayor recognizes the games played by administrators; they know that budget requests are likely to be inflated in anticipation of cuts. In fact, various studies on state and local budgeting indicate that the single most influential participant is the chief executive.[12] Not surprisingly, astute public administrators devote time and other resources to cultivating the chief executive's support for their agency's or department's activities.

Unless it develops its own budget independently, the role of the legislative body in the initial stage of the budget cycle is essentially to respond to and modify the initiatives of the chief executive. The governor, mayor, or city manager proposes, and the legislature or council reacts. Later in the budget cycle, the legislative body performs other important functions through its review of agency and department spending and its response to constituents' complaints. Occasionally, a state court will find a budget to violate constitutional or statutory law and invalidate it.[13]

What about the taxpayers whose salaries, homes, and vehicles will be taxed to fund the budget? The traditional approach is essentially to exclude them from the process. But more and more state and local governments offer budget transparency by encouraging citizens to attend and speak in budget hearings, focus groups, coffees, or to participate through web-based applications. Web access to government revenues and expenditures is increasingly being made available by state and local governments. Unfortunately, few taxpayers avail themselves of the opportunity. In the early 2000s, Boston; St. Louis; Hampton, Virginia; and several other cities began experimenting with "participatory budgeting," in which citizens decide how public funds should be spent in their neighborhoods. By 2020 there were some sixty cities and more than 250 neighborhoods, wards, or districts in the United States who used some form of participatory budgeting.[14]

Pervasive Incrementalism

In a perfect world, budgeting would be a purely rational enterprise. Objectives would be identified, stated clearly, and prioritized; alternative means for accomplishing them would be considered; resulting revenue and expenditure decisions would be coordinated within the context of a balanced budget.

That is how budgeting *should* be done. But state and local officials have to allocate huge sums of money in a budgetary environment where objectives are unclear or controversial and often conflict with one another. It is nearly impossible to prioritize the hundreds or thousands of policy items on the agenda. Financial resources, time, and the capacity of the human brain are severely stretched.

To cope with such complexity and minimize political conflict over scarce resources, decision makers "muddle through."[15] They simplify budget decision making by adopting decision rules. For example, instead of searching for the optimal way to address a public policy problem, they search only until they find a feasible solution. As a result, they sacrifice comprehensive analysis and rationality for **incrementalism**, in which small adjustments (usually an increase if times are good) are made to the nature and funding base of existing programs. Thus, the policy commitments and spending levels of ongoing programs are accepted as a given—they become the base for next year's funding. Decisions are made on a very small proportion of the total budget: the increments from one fiscal year to the next. If the budget has to be cut, it is done decrementally—small adjustments are subtracted from the base. In this way, political conflict over values and objectives is held to a minimum.

The hallmarks of incremental budgeting are consistency and continuity: The future becomes an extension of the present, which is itself a continuation of the past. Long-range commitments tend to be made and then honored indefinitely. This is not to say that state and local budgeting is a pedestrian affair. On the contrary, it is as tangled and intricate as the webs of a thousand spiders on methamphetamines. (If in doubt, the reader is urged to access their state or local budget online and see for themself.)

Types of Budgets

A budget document can be laid out in various ways, depending on the purposes one has in mind: control, management, or planning. Historically, *control*, or fiscal accountability, has been the primary purpose of budgeting, incrementalism the dominant process, and the line item budget the standard document.

Control Through Line Item Budgets The **line item budget** facilitates control by specifying the amount of funds each agency or department receives and monitoring how those funds are spent. Each dollar can be accounted for with the line item budget—which lists every object of expenditure, from police uniforms to toilet paper—on individual lines in the budget document. Line item budgets show where the money goes, but they do not tell how effectively the money is spent.

incrementalism
A decision-making approach in the budgetary process in which the previous year's expenditures are used as a base for the current year's budget figures.

line item budget
A budget that lists detailed expenditure items such as personal computers and paper, with no attention to the goals or objectives of spending.

Budgeting for Performance Budget formats that are intended to help budget makers move beyond the narrow constraints of line items and incrementalism toward more rational and flexible decision-making techniques that help attain program results are known as performance budgets. Chief executives and agency officials seek to ensure that priorities set out in the budget are properly carried out. Formal program and policy evaluations are necessary to ensure program performance and public accountability.

In **performance budgeting**, the major emphasis is on services provided and program outcomes. The idea is to focus attention on how effectively goals are attained rather than on what is acquired or spent. Whereas line item budgets are input oriented, performance budgets are output and outcome oriented. Governments and their managers decide what they want to accomplish and then measure these accomplishments versus expenditures. For example, the performance of a fire department can be evaluated by response times to emergency calls and by how quickly a fire is contained once the firefighters arrive on the scene. Police departments can track arrests, clearance rates, crime rates, and citizen satisfaction surveys. Results can be compared to those of similar jurisdictions. By focusing on program objectives and work performance, performance budgets can assist managers, elected officials, and citizens in improving the quality of government operations.[16]

A specific form of performance budgeting is **zero-based budgeting** (ZBB), which is often described as an antidote to incrementalism. ZBB started in the private sector but moved into the public sector with its introduction by Governor Jimmy Carter in Georgia in the 1970s. Carter attempted to use ZBB in the federal budgeting process (with less success) after he was elected president in 1976. In ZBB budget proposals are built from the ground up rather than beginning with the previous year's budget. Agencies are required to start off with a budget of zero and then estimate costs of their highest-priority items, gradually building the budget by adding lower-priority items. This then allows the legislative or executive approving bodies to be able to reduce the agency's budget request by eliminating only the low-priority budget items. ZBB fell out of favor because of the paperwork associated with prioritizing agencies' activities and the controversies over what higher- or lower-priority spending items might actually be. States that experimented with ZBB—such as Georgia and Iowa—used hybrid forms and did so only for short periods of time. However, a form of ZBB is still in use in several large cities; Houston and San Diego are examples.[17]

Capital Budgets The budget formats just described apply to operating budgets, whose funds are depleted within a year. Capital outlays are made over a longer period of time and are composed of big-ticket purchases such as hospitals, university buildings, rapid transit systems, and bridges. They represent one-time, nonrecurring expenditures that call for special funding procedures, or a **capital budget**. Because such items cannot be paid for within a single fiscal year, governments borrow the required funds, just as most individuals borrow when buying a house or an automobile. The debt, with interest, is paid back in accordance with a predetermined schedule.

performance budgeting Budgeting that takes into account the outcomes of government programs.

zero-based budgeting Budgeting that requires agencies to justify all expenditures greater than zero.

capital budget A budget that plans large expenditures for long-term investments, such as buildings and bridges.

Capital projects are funded through the sale of general obligation or revenue bonds. *Bonds* are certificates of debt sold by a government to a purchaser, who eventually recovers the initial price of the bond plus interest. *General obligation bonds* are paid off with a jurisdiction's regular revenues (from taxes and other sources). In this instance, the "full faith and credit" of the government is pledged as security. *Revenue bonds* are usually paid off with user fees collected from use of the new facility (e.g., a parking garage, auditorium, or toll road). Payments for both types of bonds are scheduled over a period of time that usually ranges from five to twenty years. The costs of operating a new facility, such as a school or a sports arena, are met through the regular operating budget and/or user fees.

Human Resource Policy in State and Local Governments: Patronage Versus Merit

LO 8-3
To describe the components of merit systems.

Whether the tasks of state and local governments are popular (fighting crime, educating children), unpopular (imposing and collecting taxes and fees), serious (saving a helpless infant from an abusive parent), or mundane (maintaining the grass on municipal sports fields), they are usually performed by public employees. The 5.3 million state workers and 14.7 million city, county, and town employees are the critical links between public policy decisions and how those policies are implemented. Agencies and departments must be organized to solve problems and deliver services effectively and reliably. Human resource (personnel) rules and procedures determine how public employees are recruited, hired, paid, and fired.

In the nation's first decades, public employees came mainly from the educated and wealthy upper class and, in theory, were hired on the basis of fitness for office. During the presidency of Andrew Jackson (1829–1837), who wanted to open national government jobs to all segments of white, male society, the *patronage* system was adopted to fill many positions. Hiring could depend on party affiliation and other political alliances rather than on job-related qualifications.

Patronage became entrenched in many states and localities, where jobs were awarded almost entirely on grounds of partisan politics, personal friendships, family ties, or financial contributions. This system made appointees accountable to the governor, mayor, or whoever appointed them, but it did nothing to ensure honesty and basic competence. By the beginning of the Civil War, the spoils system permeated government at all levels, and the quality of public service plummeted.

The Merit System

The concept of the **merit system** is usually associated with the national campaign to pass the federal Pendleton Act of 1883. Two key factors led to its realization. First, Anglo-Saxon Protestants were losing political power to urban political machines dominated by new Americans of Catholic faith and Irish, Italian, and Polish descent. Second, scandals rocked the administration of

merit system
The organization of government personnel to provide for hiring and promotion on the basis of knowledge, skills, and abilities rather than patronage or other influences.

President Ulysses S. Grant and spawned a public backlash that peaked with the assassination of President James Garfield by an insane attorney seeking a political appointment. The Pendleton Act set up an independent, bipartisan civil service commission to make objective, merit-based selections for federal job openings.

The *merit principle* was to determine all personnel-related decisions. Those individuals best qualified would receive a job or a promotion based on their knowledge, skill, and abilities. Far from perfect, the federal merit system was thoroughly overhauled by the Civil Service Reform Act of 1978, and strong calls for further changes are being made today. But as a result of the Pendleton Act, the negative effects of patronage politics in national selection practices were mostly eliminated. **Neutral competence** became the primary criterion for obtaining a government job, and public servants are expected to perform their work competently and in a politically neutral manner.

During the period of national merit system reform, the state and local governments were also busy. New York was the first state to enact a merit system, in 1883, and Massachusetts followed its example in 1884. The first municipal merit system was established in Albany, New York, in 1884; Cook County (Chicago), Illinois, became the first county with a merit system, in 1895. (Ironically, both Albany and Cook County, Chicago, were later consumed once again by machine politics and spoils-ridden urban governance, a condition not entirely eradicated even today.)[18]

Most states and numerous local governments enacted merit-based civil service systems on their own. Congressional passage of the 1939 amendments to the Social Security Act of 1935 gave additional impetus to such systems. This legislation obligated the states to set up merit systems for employees in social service and employment security agencies, and departments that were at least partly funded by national grants-in-aid under the Social Security Act. Thus, all states were required to establish a merit system for a sizable segment (around 20 percent) of their workforce; most of them have in fact developed comprehensive systems that encompass almost all state employees. Common elements of these merit-based personnel systems include recruitment, selection, and promotion according to knowledge, skills, and ability; regular performance appraisals; and employee incentive systems.

Some merit systems work better than others. In a handful of states and localities, they are mere formalities around which a shadowy world of patronage, spoils, favoritism, and incompetence flourishes.[19] Such conditions came to public attention when terrorists at Boston's Logan airport boarded, hijacked, and ultimately crashed two commercial aircraft on 9/11. For years, gubernatorial patronage appointees with little or no experience in security or law enforcement had run Logan's security operations.[20]

neutral competence
The concept that public employees should perform their duties competently and without regard for political considerations.

Rigid personnel rules, a lack of training programs, and inadequate salaries continue to plague some jurisdictions. Political control over merit-system employees is limited because most cannot be fired without great difficulty, and many are rigidly protected by union contracts. However, there is a movement in some states to increase political control of public employees by hiring new employees on fixed-term contracts, with no guarantee of tenure in the job, and by expanding the number of positions "exempt" from merit system procedures.

State and Local Advances

State and local governments are experimenting with recruitment and testing innovations, pay-for-performance plans and other incentive systems, participative management innovations, new performance-appraisal methods, and many other concepts. Virtually every state has reformed its civil service in some way.[21] General public dissatisfaction with government at all levels, combined with increasing needs for government to become more sophisticated and responsive to its clients, means that efforts to "reinvent" human resource management are certain to continue.

These reforms are designed to make the executive branch leaner and more responsive to the chief executive; to improve service efficiency and effectiveness; to shift the overarching focus to outputs and outcomes from inputs and processes; and, through decentralization of authority, to enhance flexibility for chief executives, agency heads, city managers, and other officials.[22] Old-style reformers have expressed grave concerns that political blows to the merit system in Georgia, Florida, and other states herald a return of patronage and favoritism in hiring, leading inevitably to a less qualified, politicized public service.[23]

These reformers remain dedicated to the principle of protecting the civil service from unnecessary and gratuitous interference by politicians with patronage considerations in mind. But new-wave reformers want to increase the capacity of government executives and political appointees to manage programs and people in their organizations and to achieve desired results.

Merit System Controversies

As we shall see, state and local governments have been leaders in addressing controversial questions that involve merit-system principles and practices, including **representative bureaucracy** and **affirmative action**, sexual harassment, and public employee collective bargaining.

Representative Bureaucracy The concept of representative bureaucracy—which is related to another key concept, affirmative action—suggests that the structure of government employment should reflect major gender, racial, socioeconomic, religious, geographic, and related components in society. The assumptions behind this idea are that (1) bureaucrats have discretion; (2) a workforce representative of the values, points of view, and interests of the people it governs will be responsive to their special problems and concerns; and (3) a representative bureaucracy provides strong symbolic evidence of a government "of the people, by the people, and for the people." In some situations, representative bureaucracy has "active" dimensions through decisions that may favor a class of people, such as women and minorities.[24]

Women and minority public workers sometimes use their discretion to improve the treatment of and outcomes for minority clients. For instance, female employees tend to be more active in representing female child support recipients than male recipients.[25] Elected officials tend to advance the interests

LO 8-4

To explain the challenges of representative bureaucracy and affirmative action, sexual harassment, and public employee unionization and collective bargaining.

representative bureaucracy
The concept that all major groups in society should participate proportionately in government work.

affirmative action
Special efforts to recruit, hire, and promote members of disadvantaged groups to eliminate the effects of past discrimination.

of those who most resemble them in gender and race.[26] Blacks are more likely to perceive police interactions as legitimate when African American officers are present.[27] Black and white police officers tend to treat victims and suspects differently, according to their race.[28] And African American local government administrators tend to be more supportive of governmental decisions that specifically serve the interests of the black community.[29] The symbolic, or "passive," aspects of representative bureaucracy are also important. A government that demonstrates the possibility of social and occupational mobility for all sorts of people gains legitimacy in the eyes of its citizens and expands the diversity of views taken into account in bureaucratic decisions.

A controversial question is how to *achieve* a representative workforce, particularly at the upper levels of government organizations, without sacrificing the merit principle. *Equal employment opportunity (EEO)*—the policy of prohibiting employment practices that discriminate for reasons of race, sex, color, religion, age, disability, or other factors not related to the job—is mandated by federal law. This policy has been the law for well over a century, yet progress was slow until affirmative action policies were adopted throughout government.

Affirmative action recognizes that equal opportunity has not been sufficient because employment discrimination against women, minorities, and the disabled persists. Governments must take proactive steps to hire and retain those categories of workers legally defined as "protected classes" who have suffered discrimination in the past. These measures may be adopted voluntarily, but they are required under certain conditions (such as a history of deliberate discrimination) specified by the U.S. Equal Employment Opportunity Commission (EEOC), the regulatory body created to enforce EEO and, in some instances, by the courts. Measures include goals, timetables, and other preferential selection and promotion devices intended to make the workforces of public and private organizations more representative of the racial, gender, and other characteristics of the available labor pool.

Under affirmative action, the absence of overt or intentional discrimination in employment may not be sufficient; organizations can implement preferential recruitment, hiring, and promotion schemes to redress existing imbalances. However, the legitimacy of affirmative action policies imposed on employers by the EEOC has been seriously questioned in a series of U.S. Supreme Court decisions and by state legislative actions and referendums.[30]

Obviously, affirmative action is highly controversial. Establishing specific numerical goals and timetables for hiring and promoting minorities does not necessarily correspond with selection or promotion of the best person for the job. In other words, affirmative action appears to conflict with the merit principle. It has also alienated many white males, who feel that they have become victims of "reverse discrimination."

Legal clashes among the federal courts, Congress, and the states and localities continue but have not produced an entirely coherent interpretation of affirmative action's legal standing. Two examples illustrate the complexity of the issues surrounding affirmative action policy. The first concerns the 1996 passage of Proposition 209 in California, which amended the state constitution by prohibiting race and gender consideration in contracting decisions and in hiring for state and local jobs. The initiative was approved by nearly 55 percent of the voters. However, a federal judge blocked enforcement on grounds that Proposition 209 was discriminatory and therefore unconstitutional. Judges for the Ninth Circuit Court of Appeals reinstated Proposition 209, an action that was affirmed by the Supreme Court in a 2014 decision upholding an identical Michigan law adopted through referendum. The Court's reasoning was that voters have the right and capability to decide such issues.[31] Seven other states have banned preferential treatment on the basis of race through similar actions. The second example of confusion and complexity involves a U.S. Supreme Court ruling concerning admissions procedures at the University of Michigan and the University of Texas. In a 2008 decision involving the University of Michigan law school, the Supreme Court held that higher education institutions have a "compelling interest" in enrolling a diverse student body.[32] The court stated that consideration of race to meet diversity goals was permissible only if improper admissions criteria were not employed, such as a numerical quota of African American or Latino students.

After the court disallowed the University of Texas's use of race in the admissions process, Texas adopted a rule such that 10 percent of the top graduating high school seniors would be admitted automatically. This passed the Court's "strict scrutiny" test. But then the university went a step further by implementing a policy in which race was included as one factor in the admissions process for individuals not graduating in the top 10 percent. The Court held that this was a step too far and sent the case back to the lower court for more careful consideration of the strict scrutiny standard. After lower courts weighed in, the Supreme Court reheard the case in 2016, upholding the University of Texas's two-part admissions process.[33]

Despite such confusion, substantial progress toward representative bureaucracy has been made, especially in recruiting and hiring protected-class individuals for entry-level positions. Indeed, African Americans are *overrepresented* relative to their presence in the overall civilian labor force in most state governments. Latinos, however, have had much less success in gaining public jobs at all levels.[34] Granted, some minorities and women continue to bump against a "glass ceiling" as they try to penetrate the upper levels of state and local agencies,[35] as well as "glass walls" that restrict their access to certain agencies, departments, or occupations.[36] And women in public service, as in the private sector, continue to face barriers that most men do not, including work–life conflicts and biased perceptions by men.[37] But progress is being recorded even with respect to these barriers to representative bureaucracy; the number of female, African American, and Latino professionals in state and local governments has grown dramatically in recent years.[38] The Great Recession was a threat to that progress as budget shortfalls forced many state and local governments to lay off workers. Although it is clear that these layoffs adversely affected minority workers, the reasons are unclear. "Last hired, first fired" would predict that workers with the least seniority would be those first laid off, and minority employees typically have less seniority than do white employees. But at least one study has found that "presented with more layoff decisions, managers have more opportunities to discriminate."[39]

The COVID-19 pandemic in 2020 has also posed a major threat to the progress of minority hiring in the public sector. As state and local budgets suffered from reduced revenues from all sources, budgets needed to be adjusted. Many jurisdictions furloughed public employees at facilities such as schools and recreational facilities that were closed by government order. As much as decisionmakers attempted to protect lower paid employees in these furloughs, it was the hourly worker—many of whom are minorities—who suffered the greatest reduction in employment.[40] As the pandemic continued over several months, some of the temporary furloughs turned into permanent layoffs. In some states, furloughed workers cannot collect unemployment benefits while laid off workers can. In April 2020, Congress partially addressed this by enacting legislation appropriating $600 per week for employees who were temporarily furloughed.[41]

Indeed, state and local governments today widely recognize the need to recruit, motivate, and manage a workforce that reflects an increasingly diverse general population. EEO and affirmative action approaches have been recast as "diversity" policies.[42] Of course, when employees working together differ in terms of gender, color, religion, customs, and other key characteristics, misunderstandings and miscommunications are inevitable. The astute public manager helps employees recognize and accept such differences while leveraging the different experiences, perspectives, and knowledge of a diverse workforce to maintain and even raise levels of organizational productivity and effectiveness.[43]

Sexual Harassment Sexual harassment has long been a problem in public and private employment. Sexual harassment can consist of various behaviors: unwanted touching or other physical contact of a sexual nature, implicit or overt sexual propositions, or (in one of its worst forms) extortion of a subordinate by a supervisor who demands sexual favors in return for a promotion or a raise. A "hostile working environment" that pervasively discriminates on the basis of gender also constitutes sexual harassment.[44] Examples in this category include repeated—and unwelcome—leering, sexual joking or teasing, sexually inappropriate remarks, or lewd calendars or electronic communications at the workplace. Isolated incidents of sexual teasing or innuendo do not constitute sexual harassment; a pattern must be present. For instance, three female sheriff's detectives in King County, Washington, settled outside of court for $1 million after showing that they had been subjected to repeated acts of sexual harassment and verbal abuse for years. One sergeant regularly boasted about his sexual prowess and exploits. Others ridiculed the detectives about their buttocks and breasts.[45]

Sexual harassment is illegal according to federal and state laws, and a form of punishable employee misconduct under civil service rules. It is also prosecuted in the courts. Such behavior subverts the merit principle when personnel decisions such as hiring or promotion are influenced by illegal or discriminatory considerations of a sexual nature, or when an employee cannot perform their assigned duties effectively because of sexual harassment.

Sexual harassment can exact a high price on organizational productivity, not to mention the cost of monetary settlements with victims. Unfortunately for the recipient of unwanted sexual attention, there are seldom any witnesses. The matter becomes one person's word against another's. And when one of the parties is the supervisor of the second party, a formal complaint may be decided in favor of the boss.

Much of the official activity aimed at stopping sexual harassment has been concentrated in the states, with local governments following suit. Michigan was the first to adopt a sexual harassment policy, in 1979; since then nearly every state has adopted a statewide policy through legislation or executive order. State and local governments offer employee-training programs that help workers and supervisors identify acts of sexual harassment, establish procedures for effectively addressing it, and enforce prompt, appropriate disciplinary action against offenders.

The consequences of sexual harassment go far beyond the personal discomfort, stress, or injury suffered by victims. The problem also results in significant financial costs to organizations whose employees lose productive work time. Such misconduct is unacceptable today in a national workforce that is almost 50 percent female.

Much research finds that sexual harassment in both private- and public-sector employment is tremendously underreported. Victims often feel that the established procedures for reporting incidents are too cumbersome or burdensome, that the requirements for proof are too strict, and that their reputations within the agency or business will be damaged if they report they were harassed by coworkers or supervisors.[46] The #MeToo movement, which spread widely after accusations of sexual harassment and assault surfaced against movie producer Harvey Weinstein and others in 2017, stimulated other reports of harassment, indicating it was much more prevalent in the workplace than previously thought. A national survey conducted later in 2017 found that more than three in four women and one in three men had experienced some form of harassment in their lifetimes. Nearly 40 percent of women and 13 percent of men reported being harassed in their places of work.[47] An analysis of sexual harassment charges filed by the EEOC between 2005 and 2015 showed that some 6.5 percent of all cases were filed in the broad field of public administration, a lower percentage than in such industries as hotel and food services, retail trade, manufacturing, or health care but a higher percentage than in industries such as education, construction, real estate, or arts entertainment and recreation.[48] Given the degree of underreporting of such incidents, the true figures most likely are much higher. Although public administration has come a long way in facing up to the reality of sexual harassment in the workplace, there is still a long way yet to go.

Unions Nearly always controversial in government, *public-employee unions* present a potentially serious threat to the merit principle. They usually insist on seniority as the primary criterion in personnel decisions, often seek to effect changes in merit-system rules and procedures that benefit their membership, and regularly challenge management authority. Moreover, unions aggressively seek higher pay and benefits, threatening to drive up the costs of government and, in some instances, prompting tax increases.

Until the 1960s, unionization was largely a private-sector phenomenon. Federal legislation protected the rights of workers in industry to organize and engage in **collective bargaining** with their employers over wages, benefits, and working conditions. Workers then organized in record numbers. Unionization in state and local governments developed and flourished in the 1960s and 1970s, some thirty years after the heyday of private-sector unionism. Why the sudden growth? Several reasons are apparent.

First, the rise of unionism in government was spurred by the realization by state and local employees that they were underpaid and otherwise poorly treated in comparison with their counterparts in the private sector, who had progressed so well with unionization and collective bargaining. Second, the bureaucratic and impersonal nature of work in large government organizations encouraged unionization to preserve the dignity of the workers. A third reason for the rise of state and local unionism was the employees' lack of confidence in many civil service systems. Not only pay and benefits were inadequate, but also grievance processes were controlled by management; employees had little or no say in setting personnel policies; and merit selection, promotion, and pay were often fraught with management favoritism.

Perhaps most important, the growth of unions in government was facilitated by a significant change in the legal environment. The rights of public employees to join unions and bargain collectively with management were guaranteed by several U.S. Supreme Court rulings, state legislation, local ordinances, and various informal arrangements that became operative during the 1960s and 1970s. Wisconsin was the first state, in 1959, to permit collective bargaining for state workers. Today, forty-one states specifically allow at least one category of state or local government employees to engage in collective bargaining.

The extent of unionization and collective bargaining is greatest in the states of the Midwest and Northeast—the same areas so fertile for the growth of private-sector unions. Traditionalistic states, including Mississippi, Arizona, Virginia, and the Carolinas, continue to resist the incursion of state and local unions (see Figure 8.4). Public employees in these jurisdictions have the legal and constitutional right to join a union, but their government employers do not have a corresponding duty to bargain with them over wages, benefits, or conditions of work.

Approximately 29 percent of state and 39 percent of local government workers are represented by unions, compared with only 6.2 percent of workers in private industry. The highest proportions of union workers are found in education, highway departments, public welfare, police and fire protection, and sanitation.[49]

The surge in the fortunes of state and local unions was partially arrested by the taxpayer revolt of the late 1970s and by President Ronald Reagan's successful effort to "bust" a federal air traffic controllers' union. Additional resistance to unions developed in the 1990s and has stiffened today as a

collective bargaining
A formal arrangement in which representatives of labor and management negotiate wages, benefits, and working conditions.

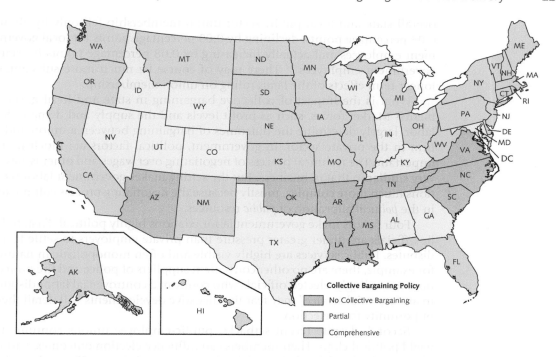

Figure 8.4 Public Employee Collective Bargaining Rights in the States

determined crop of Republican governors and legislatures has taken control of traditionally union-friendly states such as Michigan and Wisconsin. In these and other states, unions have been stripped of collective bargaining rights and suffered cuts in pension, health care, and other benefits. Wisconsin governor Scott Walker declared that "we can no longer live in a society where the public employees are the haves and the taxpayers who foot the bill are the have nots."[50] In many states, budget balancing means extensive public-employee layoffs, which, in conjunction with voter anger, have weakened the unions both economically and politically. Despite these recent attacks, unions remain an important and highly visible component of many state and local governments.

In 2018, the U.S. Supreme Court issued an important decision on public-sector unions. Under provisions of the Taft–Hartley Act of 1947, unions in some twenty states were allowed automatically to collect fees from workers who were not union members if the union represented those workers in labor negotiations. In *Janus v. American Federation of State, County, and Municipal Employees (AFSCME),*[51] the Court ruled that collecting these fees from non-members violated individuals' First Amendment guarantee of freedom of speech. Although many observers agreed with Associate Justice Elena Kagan in her dissenting opinion in the *Janus* decision that there would be large-scale consequences affecting millions of employees who worked for state and local government, those effects have yet to be seen. Between 2018 and 2019, overall state and local public-sector union membership fell only by about 0.03 percentage points, declining by 0.09 percentage points for local government employees and actually increasing by 0.08 percentage points for state government employees.[52] There may of course be much more substantial longer-term effects of the *Janus* ruling on union membership.

What is the impact of collective bargaining in state and local governments? Market forces, such as profit levels and the supply and demand for labor, largely determine the outcomes of bargaining between a union and a firm in the private sector. In government, political factors are much more important. The technical process of negotiating over wages and other issues is very similar to that in business. But the setting makes government labor relations much more complex, mostly because the negotiating process culminates in the *political* allocation of *public* resources.

Four factors make government labor relations highly political. First, public officials are under greater pressure than private employers to settle labor disputes. Public services are highly visible and often monopolistic in nature; for example, there are no other convenient suppliers of police and fire protection. Accordingly, elected officials who confront a controversial labor dispute in an "essential service" may fear that negative developments will derail their opportunity for reelection.

Second, despite recent setbacks, public-employee unions continue to wield political clout. Their members can influence election outcomes, particularly at the local level. A recalcitrant mayor or city council member who opposes a generous union wage or benefit increase may suffer defeat at the polls in the next election if the municipal union members vote as a bloc. Unions actively engage in politics by raising money, writing letters to the editor about candidates, knocking on doors to get out the vote, endorsing candidates, or using any of the other electoral techniques employed by interest groups. Many unions have professional lobbyists to represent them at the state capitol or in city hall.

A third politicizing factor in government labor relations is the symbiotic relationship that can develop between unions and elected officials. In exchange for special consideration at the bargaining table and perhaps elsewhere, the unions can offer public officials two valued commodities: labor peace and electoral support.

Finally, a hard-pressed union can use the strike or a related job action (such as a slowdown or a picket line) as a political weapon. In the private sector, a strike is not likely to have widespread public repercussions unless it involves goods or services that the nation relies on for its economic well-being (such as air transportation, automobile manufacturing, or communications). In government, however, a strike can directly involve the health and safety of all the citizens of a jurisdiction. Striking workers shut down Minnesota state government for twenty days in 2011. A general strike involving police officers, firefighters, and sanitation workers has the potential to turn a city into filthy, life-threatening anarchy. At a minimum, any strike leaves the public inconvenienced. Strikes and other job actions by public employees are illegal in most jurisdictions, although twelve states permit work stoppages by certain "nonessential" workers under strictly regulated conditions. Even where strikes are forbidden, teachers, health care workers, firefighters, and others sometimes walk off the job anyway. It is extremely rare for police or firefighters to strike today, and it is illegal everywhere. But parents angry about a teacher strike or commuters paralyzed by a transportation walkout have convinced many an elected official to seek prompt settlement of an impasse.

In 2018 and 2019, a wave of public-school teacher strikes moved through U.S. states. Teachers walked out in Arizona, Oklahoma, Virginia, and West Virginia, demanding higher pay from state legislatures that had largely resisted pay increases for public-sector employees since the end of the Great Recession in 2011. In 2019, unionized teachers in Los Angeles and Chicago—two of the largest school districts in the United States—walked out, for eleven days in Chicago and six days in Los Angeles. Both cities settled the strikes by offering teachers better pay, smaller class sizes, and partially meeting other demands.[53] The lessons from these work stoppages were not lost on other states; in 2020, teachers in Florida and North Carolina contemplated strikes to gain better pay and working conditions from their respective state legislatures. What are the results of this public teacher political activism? Teachers who walked out or who threatened to strike generally won fairly significant pay increases, either statewide or in their local school districts. On top of this, there seems to be new electoral activism among teachers. One report showed that in 2018, 25 percent of the races for state legislative seats nationwide included at least one candidate who was an educator.[54]

Even when formal strikes are not called (or may be illegal by city ordinance or state law), informal job actions can be organized by public sector unions. Police unions who have been unhappy about local government reactions to the Defund the Police movement have engaged in "blue flu" actions where police officers call in sick in mass, having the effect of a strike without formally calling one. Just such a job action occurred in Atlanta in June 2020 after the Fulton County District Attorney charged two police officers in the death of Rayshard Brooks.[55] A similar type of job action in Chicago did not have a specific incident as its cause but was rather a more generalized reaction to negotiations over a new police contract.[56]

Given these politicizing factors, one might expect unions in government to be extravagantly successful at the bargaining table. Public-employee unions have raised wages and salaries an average of 4 to 8 percent, depending on the service, place, and time period under consideration (e.g., teachers earn around 5 percent more and firefighters around 8 percent more if represented by a union). These figures are much lower than the union-associated wage effects identified in the private sector, and the union advantage dissipated during and after the Great Recession. Greater success has come in the form of better benefits, particularly pensions and health care insurance, though these, too, have experienced significant reductions as a consequence of budget shortfalls and political assaults. It should be noted that union-driven wage and benefit hikes in the private sector are absorbed through profits, layoffs, or higher product prices. In government, by contrast, the choices are to raise taxes or fees, cut services, increase productivity, or contract out.[57]

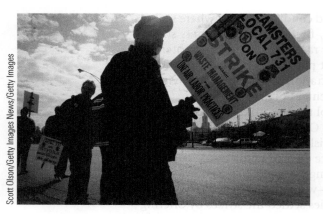

Local sanitation workers on strike in Illinois

Certain personnel impacts have also been associated with collective bargaining in government. Clearly, unions have gained a stronger employee voice in management decision making. All personnel-related issues are potentially negotiable, from employee selection and promotion procedures to retention in the event of a reduction in force. As a result of collective bargaining, many government employers have altered civil service rules, regulations, and procedures. In heavily unionized jurisdictions, two personnel systems coexist uncomfortably—the traditional merit-based civil service system and the collective bargaining system.[58]

Certainly, the rights of public employees have been strengthened by unions, but in the view of critics, it damages the merit principle.

Generally speaking, governments and collective bargaining have reached an uneasy accommodation. The principle of merit in making personnel decisions is still largely in place, and it is usually supported by the unions as long as seniority is fully respected as an employment decision rule. However, political attacks on collective bargaining are likely to continue and even sharpen in the near future.

LO 8-5
To explain the clash of politics and bureaucracy.

The Politics of Bureaucracy

In an ideal representative democracy, political officials popularly elected by the people would make all decisions regarding public policy. They would delegate to public administrators in the executive branch the duty of carrying out these decisions through the agencies of state and local governments. In the real world of bureaucratic politics, however, the line dividing politics (policy) and administration is anything but clear. Politicians frequently interfere in administrative matters, as when a legislator calls an agency head to task for not treating a constituent favorably. Administrators practice politics at the state capitol and in city hall by participating in and influencing policy formulation decisions.

Joining Administration and Politics

Bureaucrats are intimately involved in making public policy, from the design of legislation to its implementation. Government workers often plant and tend the seed bed for policy ideas that grow to become law, in large part because they are more familiar with agency, departmental, and clientele problems and prospective solutions than anyone else in government. It is not unusual, for instance, for law enforcement policy to originate with police administrators or highway policy to be the brainchild of transportation officials.

Passage of a bill usually "signal(s) not the end of the policy story, only the start of a new chapter."[59] State and local employees must interpret the language of the legislation to put it into effect. Because most legislation is written in general terms, civil servants must apply a great deal of **bureaucratic discretion** in planning and delivering services, making rules for service delivery, adjudicating cases and complaints, and otherwise managing the affairs of government. All states have legal systems for hearing and acting on disputes over agency rules and regulations, such as environmental permitting and determination of social service eligibility. These administrative procedures allow individuals, firms, and local governments to challenge agency rules and regulations before an administrative law judge, who issues an order settling the dispute.

In a very real sense, the ultimate success or failure of a public policy depends on the administrators and "street-level bureaucrats" who are responsible for its implementation.[60] Experienced legislators and chief executives understand this, and they bring relevant administrators into the legislative process at an early stage. The knowledge and expertise of these administrators are invaluable in developing an appropriate policy approach to a specific problem, and their cooperation is essential if a policy enacted into law is to be carried out as the lawmakers intend.

Thus, bureaucratic power derives from knowledge, expertise, information, and discretionary authority. It also comes from external sources of support for agency activities—that is, from the chief executive, legislators, and interest groups. Those who receive the benefits of government programs—the clientele, stakeholders, or customers—are also frequently organized into pressure groups. All government programs benefit some interest—agriculture policy for the farm community; tourism policy for the hotel and restaurant community; public assistance policy for the poor; education policy for parents, students, teachers, and administrators—and these **clientele groups** are often capable of exerting considerable influence in support of policies that benefit them. Their support is crucial for securing the resources necessary to develop and operate a successful government program. They serve as significant political assets to state agencies and municipal and county departments that are seeking new programs or additional funding from legislative and executive bodies, and they can become fearsome political in-fighters when their program interests are threatened. Often, clientele and other concerned interest groups form ad hoc coalitions with relevant government agencies and legislative committees to dominate policy making and implementation in a particular policy field.

The problem of politics and administration, then, has two dimensions. First, elected officials have the duty of holding administrators responsible for their decisions and accountable to the public interest, as defined by the constitution and by statute. Second, political oversight and intrusion into administrative activities should be minimized so that administrative decisions and actions are grounded in objective rules and procedures—not in the politics of favoritism. For example, legislators have the duty of ensuring that decisions by a state department of environmental protection guard the public from the

bureaucratic discretion
The ability of public employees to make decisions interpreting law and administrative regulations.

clientele groups
Groups that benefit from a specific government program, such as contractors and construction firms in state highway department spending programs.

harmful effects of pollution while treating polluting companies fairly. Nevertheless, state representatives should not instruct agency employees to go easy on a favored business constituent. Most government agencies discharge their tasks competently and professionally, and therefore require little direct oversight. Occasionally, however, a rogue agency or department head may strike out in the wrong direction.

An example of the proper balance of politics and administration is in the attempt by legislators to influence public administrators. This typically occurs when elected officials or their staff members perform casework for constituents. Although the legislator may occasionally seek favorable treatment that borders on illegality, the bulk of legislative casework comprises responses to citizens' inquiries or complaints, or requests for clarification of administrative regulations or decisions. Such legislative casework is useful because it promotes both feedback on the delivery of services and helpful exchanges of information between elected officials and administrators. If inquiries determine bias or error in the means by which services are delivered, corrective actions can be taken.

In sum, state and local politics are intricately joined with administration. Public policy is made and implemented through the interaction of elected officials, interest groups, and public administrators. Nonetheless, the vast majority of administrative decisions are based on the neutral competence and professionalism of public employees. When the municipal transportation department must decide which streets to repave, for example, a formula is applied that takes into account factors such as the date of the last repaving, intensity of public usage, and the condition of the road.

This is not to say that such decisions are never made on the basis of political favoritism. Sometimes political pressures influence bureaucratic discretion. For example, a telephone inquiry from the mayor or city council member can advance the road-paving schedule in front of the house of a powerful constituent. On the whole, however, state and local services are provided in an unbiased fashion through applying professional norms and standards.

LO 8-6

To describe New Public Management, its strategies, and its pros and cons.

New Public Management

State and local government employment has burgeoned at a rate much faster than that of population growth. In Texas, for instance, the number of state workers jumped from 223,000 in 1990 to 361,356 in 2018. The total monthly state payroll today in the Lone Star State nearly $1.6 billion.[61] Explanations for this huge expansion in the size and costs of state governments are numerous, including federal mandates, expanding levels of services, partisan politics, and the power of incremental budgeting. The Great Recession (2008–2011), however, wreaked havoc on state budgets and resulted in significant reductions in state jobs through attrition and layoffs. Some of the larger jurisdictions experienced reductions of tens of thousands of workers. States are attempting to use employee reductions only as a last resort to cope with the financial effects of the COVID-19 pandemic. Still, hard budget choices will need to be made to address much lower-than-expected revenues combined with increased needs in public health, safety, and welfare. Congressional action on financial assistance to state and local governments is one policy under consideration.[62]

Fueled by economic fires over the states and burning conservative criticism, taxpayer ire and criticism of government are high at all levels. Moreover, state and local employees find little public sympathy for their plight. New strategies are being tried in an effort to solve this perplexing puzzle for public administrators, particularly those intended to make government more productive, responsive, and efficient. But many agencies and departments suffer personnel and resource shortages that have produced service delivery backlogs in everything from restaurant inspections to crime lab testing.

A far-reaching approach to performance enhancement is called **New Public Management (NPM)**. It is a global movement, but, in the United States, it is often associated with the widely read book *Reinventing Government*, by David Osborne and Ted Gaebler.[63] According to NPM proponents, governments today are preoccupied with rules, regulations, and hierarchy; their bureaucracies are bloated, inefficient, and altogether poorly suited for meeting the demands made on them. The solution is for governments to free up managers to tap their powers of entrepreneurship and market competition to design and provide efficient and effective services to state and local "customers." In short, governments should "steer, not row," by stressing a facilitative or cooperative approach to getting services to citizens rather than delivering all services directly. Governments should act as collaborators, catalysts, and partners with the objective of creating public value.[64] Among the alternative service-delivery systems are public-private partnerships, intergovernmental cooperation, volunteerism, and voucher plans. Once transformed, the governments would be enterprising, mission driven, outcome oriented, focused on the needs of their customers, and prepared to "do more with less."

Among the formidable obstacles to such profound change in government activities and behavior are labor-intensive tasks such as teaching and policing that do not readily lend themselves to labor-saving technology; rule-bound civil service systems, which tend to discourage management and entrepreneurial risk taking; the inevitable inertia that plagues public organizations having no bottom line and few market-driven incentives; the difficulties of innovating in organizations created essentially to regulate; the need for politicians to buy into and support the movement, which implies greater autonomy and discretion for administrative agencies but more risks and more mistakes as well; and the certain opposition by powerful vested interests, such as public-employee unions, that feel threatened by change.

New Public Management An administrative reform movement that argues government should manage for results, through entrepreneurial activity, privatization, and improvements in efficiency and effectiveness.

Undeterred by the carping critics and maligning malcontents, many state and local governments have adopted a reinventing attitude in tackling various problems. Principally, they have placed their bets on (1) alternative service delivery mechanisms and (2) e-government.

Alternative Service Delivery Mechanisms

Three popular alternatives to traditional service delivery arrangements are intergovernmental cooperation, **coproduction**, and privatization.

Intergovernmental Cooperation Governments can compete, or they can cooperate. One common means of achieving efficiencies in service provision is coordination of services with neighboring jurisdictions.[65] Though intergovernmental cooperation in such areas as law enforcement, fire protection, and water and sewer service have long histories as shared services, cooperation is today being extended into new service functions.

A recent study found that 24 percent of local governments share some services with another jurisdiction. Common examples include ambulance and emergency management services, libraries, tax assessment, workforce development, and transit systems.[66]

Coproduction Traditionally, states and local governments have produced and delivered public services to citizens. But citizens themselves, as well as other entities, may also become partners in service delivery. In a traditional arrangement, for example, garbage is collected from residential containers by municipal government and taken to the landfill. When residents sort recyclables and cart them to a central municipal location, they are partnering—or coproducing—to reduce waste.[67] Both residents and public employees are involved. But if the recycling center is operated by a business under contract with the city, then a third party is involved in coproduction. As government has become more complicated and costly, coproduction of services has expanded at both the state and local levels. When a partnership entails a government contracting with a business to deliver a public service, such as building and operating a prison or toll bridge, for instance, coproduction has moved into the realm of privatization.

Privatization Privatization is service delivery through such arrangements as vouchers, franchises, public-private partnerships, and contracting out. It is an alternative that garners much support today, especially among conservatives, Republicans, and others who want to see a "businesslike" approach to government. Virtually any government service is a candidate for contracting out (outsourcing), from jails to janitorial work, from teaching to trash collection. Incorporated in 2005, Sandy Springs, Georgia, a wealthy suburb of Atlanta with nearly 107,000 residents, contracted out everything except police, fire protection, and ten staff positions.[68] Recently, that model seems to be under reconsideration as a result of studies showing higher service costs and lower effectiveness than nearby cities like Alpharetta, Johns Creek, and Milton.[69] (In theory, most government facilities can even be sold to private interests and operated as businesses; airports and bridges are examples.) The purported benefits of privatization include cost savings, higher-quality services, the acquisition of highly specialized skills, and more efficient service delivery. It is a popular strategy for reducing service costs.

coproduction
Coproduction involves service delivery through combined efforts of government, citizens, nonprofits, and/or businesses.

To date, privatization has been used most frequently to outsource vehicle towing, solid waste collection, building maintenance and security, street repair, ambulance services, printing, information technology, human resource management tasks, and social welfare services.[70]

In choosing the privatization route to reinventing government, Massachusetts has contracted out mental health care, prison health care, various highway maintenance functions, and operations of interstate highway rest stops, among many other functions. Chicago outsources window washing, sewer cleaning, compost processing, and parking garages. Privately built and operated toll roads and bridges operate in a growing number of states. Indiana leased a toll road to a foreign consortium, raising $3.85 billion; but when tolls were set at much higher levels, a sharp political backlash ensued.[71]

Privatization isn't as easy as it sounds, and it doesn't always generate savings.[72] It usually elicits virulent opposition from public-employee union members, who fear the loss of their jobs or reductions in pay and benefits. Unless governments carefully negotiate and then monitor the quality and effectiveness of privatized services, performance may decline and costs may actually rise. Contracts that are vaguely worded or filled with loopholes, and insufficient contract oversight on the part of some jurisdictions, have resulted in cost overruns, shoddy services, and fraud or corruption by the contractors. For instance, Indiana's $1.3 billion contract with IBM to administer state welfare services met with so many complaints and delays that Governor Mitch Daniel was forced to cancel the contract, but at a cost of $10 million in legal bills and a $52 million court judgment.[73]

Successful outsourcing requires not only careful government planning, design, and analysis of what the jurisdiction and its citizens need and want to have done but also a recognition that government accountability cannot be negotiated. The state, county, or city must remember that ultimately *it* will be held accountable for long-term successful, reliable delivery of a service. If anything goes wrong, government officials—not the private provider—will be blamed and held responsible. Successful contract monitoring requires careful inspections, comprehensive "on-time" performance reports, and assiduous investigations of citizen complaints.

Early efforts to privatize municipal services were "more of a political than an economic act,"[74] and as indicated in the preceding Sandy Springs example, sometimes privatized services are neither less costly nor more effective than publicly provided services. In some communities, this has resulted in shifting away from privately provided services back to those delivered by the public sector. This has been termed "re-municipalization" by some scholars. A recent survey of such actions concluded that re-municipalizing services was based on the practicalities of contract management rather than on politics or ideology.[75]

To keep contractors honest, some governments use multiple, competing firms, government agencies, or nonprofit organizations to deliver the same service to different state or local activities. In Phoenix, Arizona, for example, garbage workers compete head-to-head with private trash collection firms. Such collaboration among governments, nonprofit organizations, and private firms saved Indianapolis some $100 million in four years through negotiated arrangements in waste-water treatment, recycling, sewer billing, street sweeping, and many other services.[76]

Is privatization worthwhile? Local officials believe that outsourcing improves service delivery in most cases, and some research indicates that it saves cities and states up to about 20 percent for some service categories, but little or nothing for others. After all, firms must figure a profit margin into their costs, whereas government providers do not. And there are many notable failures of privatization, particularly those involving sweetheart deals, no-bid contracts, or inept contract administrators. Businesses are known to underestimate costs to win a contract, then submit "change orders" for "unanticipated costs," adding to the total price tag. Privatization is not a cure-all for the problems besetting states and local governments, but it does represent one potentially useful alternative for delivering services.

E-Government and Social Media

E-government involves reengineering the way various government activities are conducted and making the face of government more user-friendly. Some improvements are rather mundane and commonsensical, such as permitting online tax filing and renewal of licenses and registrations. To both improve government-citizen communications and to relieve pressure on overburdened 911 calls, Chicago, Denver, Charlotte, and many other cities have launched 311 apps, web chats, and Twitter for citizens to report service problems and communicate directly with city hall.

Other improvements run the gamut. Arizonians can vote in primary elections on the web and view live proceedings of the state legislature through their state's "digital democracy." Cities mount computer-coordinated attacks on crime that electronically track incidents and suspects, detect emerging crime patterns, and coordinate crime-fighting activities with other state and local jurisdictions. Many jurisdictions send mass alerts to their citizens on their tablets, PCs, and cell phones. Facebook, LinkedIn, and other social media platforms enable citizens to connect and interact with their governments in new, convenient, and timely ways. New York City tracks citizen posts on reported food-borne illnesses acquired from restaurants.

"Virtual offices" operating through the internet are establishing convenient, 24/7 connections among citizens, businesses, nonprofit organizations, and their governments. Beyond e-government, which is mostly a one-way (asynchronous) flow of information, comes social media, which essentially features a two-way (synchronous) conversation between government and citizens. Despite great enthusiasm, various hurdles must be cleared for e-government and social media to function fully as intended: the substantial investments required to pay for the computer hardware, software, and trained personnel; staff expertise may be lacking; sticky, unresolved legal questions of liability, privacy, and security are troublesome; like all users, governments and their sensitive data are vulnerable to cyberattacks; it is difficult to integrate

e-government
The use of information technology to simplify and improve interactions between governments and citizens, firms, public employees, and other entities.

software across multiple agencies and departments; and, there exists a "data paradox"—the explosion of data and information sometimes overwhelms public officials, rendering them unable to decide or act. Other problems have also appeared; the Controversies in States and Localities box presents some of them for your consideration. Nevertheless, the potential of e-government and social media to make government more accessible, understandable, and efficient is enormous.

Although e-government has often been narrowly defined as having to do with communication between government and the public, the reality is much broader. E-government actually involves the use of all kinds of new technologies to make government more efficient and effective. Examples of these technologies are numerous—red light cameras that automatically photograph the license plates of automobiles violating traffic lights,[77] facial recognition software that assists the police in addressing crime issues,[78] smart technology uses in municipal transit systems and traffic flow management,[79] and so on. In 2016, San Diego began using a gunshot detection system (ShotSpotter) that reports the sounds of gunfire directly to the police, addressing the issue of neighborhood residents' potential uneasiness in reporting such incidents.[80] That system is now used in more than 100 cities nationwide. All of these technologies are not without controversy. Because of potential misuse by police departments and inaccuracy in the results the system generates, Amazon recently announced a one-year moratorium on the use of its facial recognition technology (Rekognition) by the police.[81] Nevertheless, this (and many other new technologies) have the potential to make government more responsive to the needs of the public. And modern technologically savvy citizens simply *expect* government to operate in a technologically advanced fashion.

The Quality of Public Administration

Despite the cascade of criticism and virulent vitriol hurled at government agencies, departments, and workers by the media, elected officials, and others, the quality of public administration in state and local governments has improved markedly. Of course, there is considerable variance among jurisdictions; that capacity generally is of a higher quality in affluent, highly educated, and urban jurisdictions.

Administrative quality is a critical factor in support of revitalization and responsiveness of states and localities. State and local governments, particularly through partnership with other governments and private and nonprofit organizations, have the capacity to accomplish more on a grander scale than ever before. The basics of providing services, from disposing of dead animals to delivering healthy human babies, will continue to depend on government employees with high standards of performance and professionalism. But adequate financial and human resources are required to make and keep state and local government what it should be: efficient, effective, responsive, and transparent.

Controversies in States and Localities

Social Media: Problematic or Panacea?

The advantages of social media for citizens and government are numerous and impressive. Problems, from potholes to crime, can be identified and resolved more quickly; the pulse of the people can be gauged through posts, tweets, chats, and other devices. Residents can be informed immediately about anything from traffic pileups to dangerous weather events. Perhaps most importantly, citizens can become directly engaged with their state or local government and feel more a part of it.

But problems with social media are legion. A balance between free speech rights and prohibited content must be maintained. Some postings are obscene, vulgar, inflammatory, or personally insulting. Sometimes government officials and politicians shoot from the hip. When Washington state representative Joe Fitzgibbon tweeted after his Seattle Seahawks lost to the Arizona Cardinals, "Losing a football game sucks. Losing to a desert racist wasteland sucks a lot," he stirred up a "twit storm."[1]

Unintended consequences of social media sometimes appear. After the New York City police department created the hashtag #myNYPD, citizen critics began tweeting photos and videos of cops clubbing, teargassing, and tackling citizens.[2] Within a short period of time, the hashtag was transformed into a "bashtag," resulting in a do-it-yourself protest.[3]

The Wild West world of social media offers plenty of advantages for state and local governments, to be sure, but at a price some officials might not be willing to pay.

Critical Thinking Questions

1. Where should a line be drawn between free speech and messages that should be censored or deleted? Who should decide—a committee? A single individual?

2. What social media policies might states and localities adopt to discourage or prevent unintended consequences, confusing messages, and unwise or potentially embarrassing messages from public officials?

References:

1. Jonathan Walters, "Governments Struggling to Get Social Media Right," www.governing.com (July 2014).
2. Jonathan Walters, "Lost in Translation," Governing (July 2014): 46–49.
3. Tracey Hayes, "#MyNYPD: Transforming Twitter into a Public Place for Protest," Computers and Composition 43 (January 2017): 118–34.

Chapter Recap

- The quality and capacity of public administration have greatly improved in the majority of the states and local governments.

- State and local government employment has grown rapidly but declined during the Great Recession and its aftermath.

- State and local operating budgets must be balanced each year.

- The four principal actors in the budgetary process are interest groups, agencies, the chief executive, and the legislative body.

- Budgets tend to expand (or contract) incrementally.

- The trend in accounting for revenues and expenditures is performance-based budgeting.

- Most state and local jobs are part of a merit system and are filled based on knowledge, skills, and experience, but there are challenges to traditional merit systems.

- Affirmative action led to gains in the advancement of minorities and women in state and local employment, but it is very controversial.

- Unions and collective bargaining present special challenges to many state and local governments.

- Bureaucratic discretion makes public employees important decision makers.

- NPM is aimed at reinventing government through privatization, e-government, coproduction, intergovernmental cooperation, and other steps.

Key Terms

bureaucracy *(p. 209)*
incrementalism *(p. 219)*
line item budget *(p. 219)*
performance budgeting *(p. 220)*
zero-based budgeting *(p. 220)*
capital budget *(p. 220)*
merit system *(p. 221)*

neutral competence *(p. 222)*
representative bureaucracy *(p. 223)*
affirmative action *(p. 223)*
collective bargaining *(p. 228)*
bureaucratic discretion *(p. 233)*
clientele groups *(p. 233)*

New Public Management *(p. 235)*
coproduction *(p. 236)*
e-government *(p. 238)*

Internet Resources

All major municipalities and states have webpages. Many provide links to jobs, NPM initiatives, service-provision information, and other data. Innovative, award-winning websites include Indianapolis's "Electronic City Hall" at **www.indygov.org**, Service Arizona at **www.servicearizona.com**, NC@YourService at www.ncgov.com, and AccessWashington at **www.access.wa.gov**.

An informative public-employee union website is AFSCME's at **www.afscme.org**.

An interesting site on technology, e-government, and social media is **www.govtech.com**.

9

The Judiciary: Independence vs Accountability

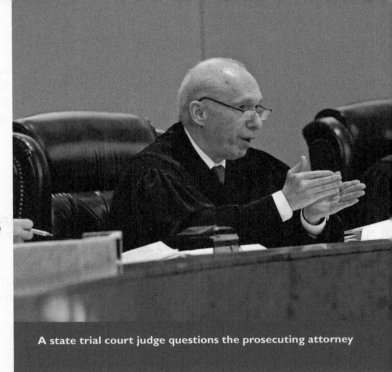

A state trial court judge questions the prosecuting attorney

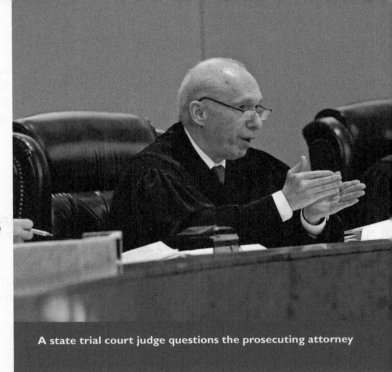AP Images/Mel Evans

Learning Objectives

LO 9-1 To demonstrate an understanding of what state courts do, their position within the federal system, and the types of law they address.

LO 9-2 To demonstrate an understanding of how state courts are organized into two tiers.

LO 9-3 To describe how structural reforms have been implemented to make the courts more effective.

LO 9-4 To compare and contrast the five methods for selecting judges.

LO 9-5 To recognize the trade-offs between judicial independence and accountability.

LO 9-6 To describe some of the factors that influence judicial decision making.

LO 9-7 To demonstrate an understanding of how judicial federalism is related to increased capability and judicial activism in many state courts.

LO 9-8 To describe efforts to reform state courts.

In the 1991 U.S. Supreme Court case *California v. Hodari D,* the court ruled that the Fourth Amendment's guarantees against unreasonable searches and seizures did not apply to a person being chased by a police officer.[1] Hodari D—a young man in Oakland, California—was being chased by an officer who thought that he was selling drugs. During the chase, Hodari D threw away a small rock that the police later recovered and identified as crack cocaine. The Court ruled that the chase was not an unlawful seizure and so the cocaine could be admitted as evidence of guilt. Some seven years later, the Washington state Supreme Court ruled that a police officer shining his patrol car's light on a suspected drug dealer *was* a seizure under state law and so the small amount of drugs the individual allegedly discarded when the light was shone on him was not admissible as evidence in court.[2] In a similar New York Supreme Court case, the court wrote about the Fourth Amendment's protections against unreasonable searches and seizures: "Our State provision, for reasons peculiar to New York, is subject to its own interpretation."[3]

And the New Jersey Supreme Court went so far as to state: "To conform our doctrine now to *Hodari D* would require too radical a change in our search-and-seizure law. We shall continue to define a seizure under New Jersey constitutional law in accordance with our existing precedent."[4] Thirteen other state supreme courts have disagreed with the U.S. Supreme Court definition of a seizure developed in *California v. Hodari D* on the basis of state law or their interpretation of their own state constitution.[5]

State courts have become more open to individuals and groups advocating causes such as civil rights, free speech, and privacy. All sorts of conflicts and problems find their way to state and local courts, from policy issues (abortion rights) to technical ones (what constitutes a seizure). Decisions of "state courts play a decisive role in allocating wealth and power in the United States."[6] Courts at this level are busy; 99 percent of the nation's cases are filed in state courts—approximately 90 million cases a year! New York state's cases alone outnumber those filed in all federal courts by a factor of nine to one. Many of the state courts are innovative in their decision making and administration; in addition, all are far more accessible to the people and responsive to their concerns than are the federal courts. Surveys show that Americans have greater confidence in their state courts than in the legislature or governor.[7]

As the third branch of government, the judiciary is the final authority on the meaning of laws and constitutions and the ultimate arbiter of disputes between the executive and legislative branches. It also makes public policy through rulings on questions of political, social, and economic significance and may serve as the last chance for minority interests to defend themselves from the decisions of the majority. State courts have become more active policy makers in recent years and have increasingly based important decisions on state constitutions rather than on the national constitution. As with the other branches of state government, their structures and processes have been reformed and modernized. In our lifetimes, nearly all of us will personally experience the judicial branch as direct participants (juror, plaintiff, defendant, or witness). At times, the courts are more accessible to us than are the other branches of government. Disputes that cannot be resolved through ordinary legislative, executive, and political processes frequently wind up before a judge, as litigation.

The work of the fifty state court systems is divided into three major areas: civil, criminal, and administrative. In **civil cases**, one individual or corporation sues another over an alleged wrong. Occasionally, a governmental body is party to a civil action. Typical civil actions are divorces, property disputes, and suits for damages arising from automobile or other accidents.

LO 9-1
To demonstrate an understanding of what state courts do, their position within the federal system, and the types of law they address.

civil case
A case that concerns a dispute involving individuals or organizations.

Criminal cases involve the breaking of a law by an individual or a corporation. The state is usually the plaintiff; the accused is the defendant. Murder, assault, embezzlement, disorderly conduct, and tax fraud are common examples. **Administrative cases** concern court actions such as probating wills, revoking driver's licenses, or determining custody of a child. Some administrative cases involve administrative law judges and quasi-judicial (less formal) proceedings. A government entity is usually a party to an administrative case.

State courts adjudicate (resolve disputes and administer justice) by interpreting state statutes, the state and federal constitutions, and **common law**. In developing and deciphering the common law, courts are concerned with the legal rules and expectations that have developed historically through the citizens' custom, culture, and habits and that have been given standing through the courts' decisions rather than from statutes. The most important applications of common law today concern enforcing contracts (contract law), owning and selling property (property law), and establishing liability for death or injuries to people, as well as damage to property (tort law).

The Structure of State Court Systems

State courts have evolved in response to changes in their environments. In colonial days, they developed distinctively, influenced by local customs and beliefs. Because of a shortage of trained lawyers and an abiding distrust of English law, the first judges were laymen who served on a part-time basis. It did not take long for the courts to become overwhelmed with cases: Case overloads were reported as long ago as 1685.[8] More than three centuries later, case backlogs still plague our state judiciaries.

We are a litigious people. As the population and the economy grew, so did the amount of litigation. Courts expanded in number and in degree of specialization. However, their development was not carefully planned. Rather, new courts were added to existing structures. The results were predictably complex and confusing, with overlapping, independent jurisdictions and responsibilities. For instance, Chicago offered an astounding array of jurisdictions, estimated at one time to number 556.[9] State court systems were beset as well by a host of other serious problems, including underfunding, administrative inefficiency, congestion, and excessive delays. In short, the American system of justice left much to be desired.

The organization of the state courts is important because it affects the quality and pace of judicial decisions and the access of individuals and groups to the legal system. It also influences how legal decisions are made. An efficiently organized system, properly staffed and administered, can do a better job of deciding a larger number of cases than a poorly organized system can. Court structure is of great interest to those who make their living in the halls of justice—lawyers, judges, and court staff. It is also an issue of concern to citizens who find themselves in court.

criminal case
A case brought by the state against persons accused of violating a law.

administrative case
Usually, a case in which a government agency applies rules to settle a legal dispute.

common law
Unwritten law based on tradition, custom, or court decisions.

The Two Tiers of Courts

Most states today have a two-tiered court structure: trial courts and appellate courts. There are two types of trial courts: those of limited jurisdiction and major trial courts. Each tier, or level, has a different *jurisdiction*, or range of authority. *Original* jurisdiction gives courts the power to hear certain types of cases first, in contrast to *appellate* jurisdiction, which grants the courts the power to review cases on appeal after they have been tried elsewhere. Trial courts, which comprise the lower tier, include (1) minor courts of limited jurisdiction and (2) major trial courts of general jurisdiction.

Limited jurisdiction trial courts, also known as special trial courts, handle minor, specialized cases, such as those involving juveniles, traffic offenses, and small claims. Most states have several courts of limited jurisdiction, with names that reflect the type of specialized case: traffic court, police court, probate court, municipal court, and so on. Criminal cases here are usually restricted by law to misdemeanor violations of municipal or county ordinances that are punishable by a small fine, a short jail term, or both. Additional courts of limited jurisdiction, sometimes called "boutique" or "problem-solving" courts, have been created to deal with special types of cases or circumstances. For example, all states have created drug courts, with the dual aims of processing drug-related offenses more efficiently and reducing the recidivism rates of drug offenders on probation or parole. Domestic violence and mental health courts are common as well. "Water courts" in Colorado and Montana hear disputes over water rights. Illinois, Texas, Colorado, and other states have created special "veterans courts" to hear minor offenses charged against Iraq and Afghanistan war vets who have had scrapes with the law. In San Francisco, "neighborhood courts" grant individuals charged with minor offenses the option of accepting "restorative justice" in exchange for having their records expunged. For instance, a graffiti artist might be required to clean up their artwork and apologize at a neighborhood meeting.[10]

Present in almost all states are *small claims courts*, which offer a relatively simple and inexpensive way to settle minor civil disputes without either party having to incur the financial and temporal burdens of lawyers and legal procedures. Small claims courts are usually divisions of county, city, or district trial courts. In cases they hear, the plaintiff (the person bringing the suit) asks for monetary recompense from the defendant (the individual or firm being sued) for some harm or damage. Claims are limited to varying amounts, usually around $1,000. The proceedings are informal. Each party presents to a judge the relevant facts and arguments to support their side. The party with the preponderance of evidence on their side wins. Most disputes involve tenant–landlord conflicts, property damage, or the purchase of goods (e.g., shoddy merchandise or the failure of a customer to pay a bill).

The plaintiff usually wins in small claims court. About half the time, defendants do not show up to plead their case and thereby lose by default. In contested cases, plaintiffs win a large percentage of cases. Unfortunately for the plaintiff, winning a case is often easier than collecting from the defendant. It is the plaintiff's responsibility to get written court permission to extract the

LO 9-2
To demonstrate an understanding of how state courts are organized into two tiers.

limited jurisdiction trial courts
Those courts with original jurisdiction over specialized cases such as juvenile offenses or traffic violations.

amount due from the debtor's wages, bank account, or other assets, and to retain the local sheriff or constable to deliver and enforce the court order.

The second type of trial court is the **major trial court**, which exercises general authority over civil and criminal cases. Most cases are filed initially under a major trial court's original jurisdiction. However, trial courts also hear cases on appeal from courts of limited jurisdiction. Major trial courts are often organized along county or district lines. Their names (circuit courts, superior courts, district courts, courts of common pleas) vary by state.

The upper tier of the two-tiered state court system consists of appellate courts: **supreme courts** (sometimes called "courts of last resort") and, in most states, **intermediate appellate courts**. Oklahoma and Texas have two supreme courts: one for criminal cases and the other for civil disputes. Forty states have intermediate appellate courts. Alabama, Oklahoma, Oregon, Texas, Pennsylvania, and Tennessee have two, typically one each for criminal and civil cases. Most intermediate appellate courts are known as courts of appeals. Their work generally involves cases on appeal from lower courts. Thus, these courts exercise appellate jurisdiction by reviewing a trial court's interpretation and application of the law. By contrast, state supreme courts have original jurisdiction in certain types of cases, such as those dealing with constitutional issues, as well as appellate jurisdiction.

Intermediate appellate courts represent an important element in the landscape of state courts. They are intended to increase the capability of supreme courts by reducing their caseload burden, speeding up the appellate process, and improving the quality of judicial decision making. The weight of the evidence points to moderate success in achieving each of these objectives. Appellate case backlogs and delays have been somewhat reduced, and supreme court justices are better able to spend an appropriate amount of time on significant cases. Counteracting this positive trend, however, is the growing number of mandatory appeals, such as for death penalty cases, which can make up more than 60 percent of the caseload.

If a state supreme court so chooses, it can have the final word on any state or local case except one involving a federal constitutional question. Some cases can be filed in either federal or state court. For example, a person who assaults and abducts a victim and then transports them across a state line can be charged in state court with assault and in federal court with kidnapping. Some acts violate nearly identical federal and state laws; possession or sale of certain illegal drugs is a common example. Other cases fall entirely under federal court jurisdiction, such as those involving treason, mail theft, or currency law violation.

Thus, there exists a *dual system* of courts that is sometimes referred to as *judicial federalism*. Generally, state courts adjudicate, or decide, matters of state law, whereas federal courts deal with federal law. The systems are separate and distinct. In some instances, however, there is jurisdictional overlap and even competition for a case. Following the 2013 Boston Marathon bombings, one of the suspects, Tamerlan Tsarnaev, was killed, and his brother Dzhokhar was arrested. The state of Massachusetts first sought jurisdiction over the case, but because this was an act of terrorism, the U.S. Department of Justice brought

major trial court
Court of general jurisdiction that handles major criminal and civil cases.

supreme court
The highest state court, beyond which there is no appeal except in cases involving federal law.

intermediate appellate court
A state appellate court that relieves the case burden on the supreme court by hearing certain types of appeals.

the multiple murder case to trial first (three victims were killed in the bombings). A much more complicated case involved the "Beltway Snipers," who killed people in Virginia, Maryland, and the District of Columbia in 2002. All sought to bring the case to trial first. (Virginia was given the honor of first prosecution.) Robert Gregory Bowers, the accused killer of eleven worshippers at the Tree of Life Jewish synagogue in Pittsburgh in 2018, has been charged with multiple counts of assault and murder—crimes against the state of Pennsylvania—and sixty-three violations of federal hate crime statutes. He will be tried in both state and federal court.[11] Although state courts cannot overturn federal law, they can base certain rulings on the federal constitution. Recently, state courts have decided cases governed by both state and federal laws in hate crimes, freedom of speech, the right to die, and gay rights. It is very unusual for a case decided by a state supreme court to be heard by the U.S. Supreme Court or any other federal court. Even if such a review is done, the U.S. Supreme Court usually upholds the state high court decision. Exceptions do occur. Though Alabama's and other states' supreme courts upheld bans on gay marriage, federal courts later overrode them.

Structural Reforms

Although the two tiers of state courts appear to represent a hierarchy, in fact they do not. Courts in most states operate with a certain degree of autonomy. They have their own budgets, hire their own staff, and use their own procedures. The decisions of major and specialized trial courts usually stand unchallenged. Only a fraction of lower-court cases are appealed, mainly because great expense and years of waiting are certainly involved.

Unified court systems consolidate the various trial courts with overlapping jurisdictions into a single administrative unit and clearly specify each court's purpose and jurisdiction. The aim of this arrangement, which includes centralized management and rulemaking, is to make the work of the courts more efficient, saving time and money and avoiding confusion. Instead of a system whereby each judge runs their own fiefdom, such responsibilities as rulemaking, recordkeeping, budgeting, and personnel management are standardized and centralized, usually under the authority of the state supreme court or the chief justice. As of 2020, twenty-six states operated unified court systems.[12]

Centralization relieves judges from some of the mundane tasks of day-to-day court management so that they can concentrate on adjudication. Additional efficiencies are gained from *offices of court administration*. Court administration involves actively managing, monitoring, and planning the courts' resources and operations. Information technology is enabling tremendous improvements in the way the courts manage criminal cases. Courts are moving to paperless systems in which documents are submitted, disseminated, and stored electronically. Judges and attorneys access case information on their laptops or tablets.

Responsiveness to the public is also growing. An increasing number of state courts are electronically disseminating court documents to reporters and

LO 9-3
To describe how structural reforms have been implemented to make the courts more effective.

SIMPLE SYSTEM	COMPLEX SYSTEM
Alaska	*Georgia*

TRIAL COURTS

General Jurisdiction

Superior Court	Superior Court

Limited (Special) Jurisdiction

District Court	▌ Civil Court ▌ Municipal Court ▌ State Court ▌ County Recorder's Court ▌ Magistrate Court ▌ Probate Court ▌ Municipal Court and the City Court of Atlanta

APPELLATE COURTS

Supreme Court	▌ Supreme Court ▌ Court of Appeals

Figure 9.1 Simplicity and Complexity in State Court Systems

Source: National Center for State Courts (www.ncsc.org).

the public; judicial rulings; speed and efficiency measures; and general information such as instructions for jury duty, maps showing directions to the courthouse, and answers to commonly asked questions about the courts. Some display photographs and biographies of judges, many permit interested citizens to ask questions via e-mail, and others even provide performance evaluations of judges and broadcast cases live over the internet.

Despite consolidation and centralization, court structures and processes continue to vary widely among the states, as shown in Figure 9.1. Generally, the most modern systems are found in the "newer" states, including Alaska and Hawaii, whereas some of the most antiquated are situated in southern states, among them Arkansas and Georgia.

LO 9-4
To compare and contrast the five methods for selecting judges.

How Judges Are Selected

The quality of a state court system depends heavily on the selection of competent, well-trained, impartial judges. According to the American Bar Association (ABA), the leading professional organization for lawyers, judges should be chosen on the basis of solid professional and personal qualifications, regardless of their political views and party identification. Criteria for choosing judges should include experience, integrity, professional competence, judicial temperament, and service to the law and contribution to the effective administration of justice.[13] They should be good listeners. They should be broadly educated and professionally qualified as lawyers, although Arizona, New Mexico, New York, Texas, and Utah have a large number of non–law-degreed judges. An appellate or general trial court judge should also have relevant experience in a lower court or as a courtroom attorney.

Since the founding of the nation itself, controversy has swirled around the selection of state judges. Should they be elected by popular vote? Should they be appointed by the governor? By the legislature? Some critics insist that judicial selection be free from politics and interest group influences, so that judges act independently. Others claim that judges should regularly be held accountable to a majority of the voters or to elected officials for their decisions.[14]

The historic conflict between judicial independence and accountability is manifest in the five types of selection systems used in the states: legislative election, partisan popular election, nonpartisan popular election, the merit plan, and gubernatorial appointment. Figure 9.2 shows the presence of these selection techniques for appellate and major trial courts. Most states use a single selection system for all appellate and major trial court judges. Others take separate approaches to selecting judges, depending on the tier, and four states combine different methods within the trial court tier. Some states have rather elaborate systems that defy simple categorization.

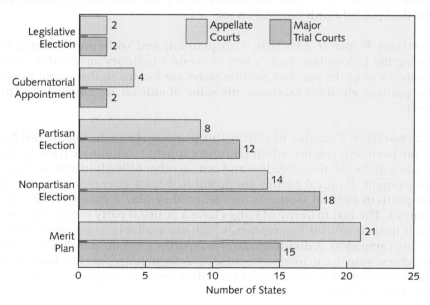

Figure 9.2 State Appellate and Major Trial Court Selection Plans

Note: Kansas and Missouri select some major trial court judges through a merit plan and others through partisan elections; Arizona and Maryland choose some major trial court judges through a merit plan and others through nonpartisan elections. All four states are counted as merit plan states in this chart.

Source: Ballotpedia.org (https://batllotpedia.org/judicial_selection_in_the_states)

Legislative Election

In South Carolina and Virginia, the legislature elects judges by majority vote from among announced candidates. (In South Carolina, the candidates must first clear an election commission.) Not surprisingly, a large majority of judges selected under this plan have been former legislators (at one time in South Carolina, all five state supreme court judges were former state legislators).[15] In these two states, a judgeship is viewed as a highly valued reward for public service and a prestigious cap to a legislative career.

Few people other than legislators approve of legislative election. The public has no role in either choosing judges or reelecting them, so democratic accountability is minimal. The judges may be independent, but because the major criterion for selection is service as a legislator, they often lack other qualifications. Prior legislative service has little connection to the demands of a judgeship.

Popular Election

Judges on one or more courts face elections in thirty-eight states. Some are listed on the ballot by party identification; others are not. In theory, elections maximize the value of judicial accountability to the people. Judges must run for office on the same ticket as candidates for other state offices. Like other candidates, they must raise and spend money for their election campaigns and deal publicly with political issues.

Partisan Popular Election This plan enjoyed widespread popularity during the Jacksonian era as a way to create a judiciary answerable to the voters. Most of the partisan election states are located in the South. In theory, partisan elections maximize the value of judicial accountability to the voters.

Nonpartisan Popular Election This plan won favor during the first half of the twentieth century, when reformers sought to eliminate party identification in the election of judges and certain other officials in state and local government. Political parties are prohibited from openly taking sides in nonpartisan judicial elections. In reality, they play a covert role in such contests. The vast majority of judges have a political party preference. Most list it in their official biographies, which are available to interested voters during campaigns. A disadvantage of nonpartisan elections is that they tend to depress voter participation because incumbent judges are less likely to be challenged; another is that party identification is an important voting cue for many citizens.

The Problems with Popular Elections It is worth observing that electing judges is virtually unknown in the rest of the world, where they are appointed or selected through merit systems. Voter turnout is very low in most judicial elections, whether partisan or nonpartisan. This fact is a major criticism of both methods of electing judges: The winners may not be truly accountable to the people, which is the principal advantage commonly associated with elections. Low rates of voter interest and participation frequently combine with low-key, unexciting, and issueless campaigns to keep many incumbent judges on the bench as long as they run for reelection. From 2016 to 2018, nearly 87 percent of the incumbent judges who ran for reelection were successful,[16] a rate comparable to state legislative races involving an incumbent.

Judicial independence is a problem. Research finds that a state electorate can be mobilized by engaging candidates, distressing events, controversial issues, or cases with emotional content. On controversial issues, judges today seem increasingly vulnerable, particularly in partisan election states in which the voters' views on crime and punishment are harsher than those of the incumbent judge.[17] Public opinion particularly affects judges' decisions when seemingly noncontroversial issues become the subject of campaign attack ads.[18] Taken together, these research findings indicate that judicial races can elevate judicial accountability over independence.

Two problems have become increasingly troublesome: the politicization of judicial races and the creeping realization that campaign donations influence decisions from the bench.[19] The ABA Code of Judicial Conduct forbids judicial campaigning on legal issues, but this prohibition is increasingly ignored in close contests and in elections in which crime-related concerns, such as the death penalty or an accused murderer freed on a legal technicality, claim voters' attention. Moreover, federal courts have ruled that judicial campaigning is protected speech. As in other electoral contests, negative campaigning is on the rise in judicial elections. Judicial candidates energetically sling mud at their opponents for allegedly letting drug abusers free, being corrupt, sympathizing with terrorists, and acting soft on crime. Several states have tried to restrict aggressive judicial politicking through ethics rules and other limitations. When challenged in federal or state courts, such restrictions are usually overturned as intrusions on the candidates' First Amendment rights to free speech. However, in 2015, the U.S. Supreme Court seemed to back away a bit from overturning all state restrictions on judicial candidates when it upheld a Florida law forbidding judges from personally soliciting campaign contributions. In this case Chief Justice Roberts stated, "Judges are not politicians, even when they come to the bench by way of the ballot."[20]

Nevertheless, elected state court judges may view the electorate as their constituency, and that perception can influence their decisions. Former West Virginia Supreme Court Justice Richard Neely wrote about this in his review of product liability laws:

> "As long as I am allowed to redistribute wealth from out-of-state companies to in-state plaintiffs, I shall continue to do so. Not only is my sleep enhanced when I give somebody else's money away, but so is my job security, because in-state plaintiffs, their families and their friends will re-elect me."[21]

Neely served on the West Virginia Supreme Court from 1973 through 1995 and ran unsuccessfully for a Supreme Court seat in the June, 2020 judicial election in that state.[22]

Even more serious is the problem that occurs when judges elected on a partisan ballot are accused of pandering to special interests during election campaigns and paying back campaign support through favorable court decisions. In Texas, for instance, supreme court justices deciding a $10.5 billion judgment against Texaco in favor of Pennzoil were criticized for accepting huge campaign contributions from both companies.

In some recent Ohio Supreme Court decisions, all seven judges accepted money from lawyers for the plaintiffs or defendants.[23] Nonpartisan elected judges have been open to similar charges, especially because political action committees (PACs) have boosted their contributions to candidates for state court judgeships. Research has found systematic empirical evidence that judicial decisions have followed dollars. Similar conclusions have been drawn from case study research on judicial decision making in Alabama, Ohio, West Virginia, and Georgia.[24] Elected judges themselves are troubled by the role of money in judicial elections. As an Ohio Supreme Court justice remarked, "I never felt so much like a hooker down by the bus station . . . as I did in a judicial race."[25]

In addition, popular elections are criticized for the growing amount of money necessary to win a state judgeship. As in other political contests, money talks: The candidate who spends the most is likely to win the election.[26] The implication is that judges have sacrificed their independence and professionalism for crass electoral politics. Following the trend set in executive and legislative contests, special interest groups spent a record $27.8 million in seventy-six 2015–2016 state supreme court campaigns, and political parties invested another $39.4 million. Total spending in that election cycle was an estimated $69.3 million. In the 2017–2018 cycle, total spending actually declined to $39.7 million ($28.7 million by campaigns and parties and $10.8 million by special interest groups) on sixty-six campaigns.[27] Eight of the top ten spenders in 2017–2018 were groups that were not required to disclose the sources of funds. The conservative Judicial Crisis Network spent a reported $3.8 million, the largest amount of any outside group.[28]

The largest campaign contributors are usually trial lawyers, corporations, corporate attorneys, and other groups with an interest in judges' decisions, such as labor unions; business interests desiring to limit the amount of jury awards through tort reform; the U.S. Chamber of Commerce; and various professions, such as insurance or medicine.[29] In some states, attorneys complain that judges "shake them down" for campaign contributions. A supreme court incumbent was brought down in West Virginia largely through the efforts of a corporate CEO who had a lawsuit pending before the court. In "a race noted for money and malice," the CEO provided some $2.3 million to the incumbent's "friendlier" opponent. The CEO in question, Don Blankenship of Massey Energy, had shamelessly vacationed in Monte Carlo with one sitting justice whom he favored in the election while the case was under appeal.[30]

It looks as though judges running for election are forfeiting their independence in certain legal disputes while offering accountability only to the highest bidders instead of to the general public. A very high percentage of the public (87%) believe that campaign dollars influence judicial decisions "a great deal," according to a 2013 survey.[31] If justice is indeed for sale or rent, this is highly disturbing; neither independence nor accountability is achieved, and faith in the legal system is being eroded. According to the president of the Ohio State Bar Association, "The people with money to spend who are affected by court decisions have reached the conclusion that it's a lot cheaper to buy a judge than a governor or an entire legislature, and he can probably do a lot more for you."[32] This sentiment is supported by research showing a positive correlation between campaign contributions and judges' decisions.[33]

If it is unethical for a judge to rule on a case in which they have accepted money from one or more of the interested parties, then it would be difficult to bring together enough judges to hear cases in some election states. Increasingly, the general sentiment is that judges should be both qualified and dignified and that elections do not further either objective. In 2011, Wisconsin joined New Mexico to launch public financing for judges' campaigns to help contain spiraling costs. Other states are imposing restrictions and penalties for false campaign advertising, but all such actions are seriously threatened by the U.S. Supreme Court's *Citizens United* decision on free speech, noted previously.[34] However, the U.S. Supreme Court ruled, in an important 2009 case involving the West Virginia saga mentioned earlier, that justices must recuse or disqualify themselves from ruling on cases in which interested or involved campaign donors have spent large sums of money.[35] All too often, they do not do so.

Merit Plan

Dissatisfaction with other methods for selecting judges has led to the popularity of the so-called *merit plan*. Incorporating elements of gubernatorial appointment and elective systems, the merit plan attempts to provide a mechanism for appointing qualified candidates to the bench while permitting the public to evaluate a judge's performance through the ballot box.

Strongly supported today by almost the entire legal community, the merit plan has been adopted by nearly all of the states that have changed their selection systems. Missouri became the initial adopter in 1940. Another twenty-one states have adopted the merit plan, and others are considering it.

Three Steps Commonly referred to as the Missouri plan, the basic merit plan involves three steps:

1. A judicial nominating commission meets and recommends three or more names of prospective judges to the governor. Members of this bipartisan commission usually include a sitting judge (often the chief justice), representatives chosen by the state bar association, and laypersons appointed by the governor. The nominating commission solicits names of candidates, investigates their records, chooses those it believes to be the best-qualified individuals, and then forwards three or more names and their files to the governor.
2. The governor appoints the preferred candidate to the vacant judgeship.

3. A retention election is held, usually after one or two years, in which the newly appointed judge's name is placed before the voters on a nonpartisan, noncompetitive ticket. The voters decide whether the judge should be retained in office. If she is rejected by a majority vote, the judicial nominating commission begins its work anew. Subsequent retention elections are held every eight or twelve years, depending on the merit plan's provision.

Various hybrids of the basic plan are also in use. For example, California's plan for choosing appellate judges begins when the governor identifies a candidate for a vacancy on the bench and sends that person's name to the Commission on Judicial Appointments. The commission, composed of two judges and the attorney general, hears testimony regarding the nominee and votes to confirm or reject. The new judge is then accepted or rejected in a retention election in the next regularly scheduled gubernatorial contest. Thus, although the governor appoints, the new judge is subject to confirmation by both the Commission on Judicial Appointments and the voters. In New Mexico's multistage merit plan, a judge is nominated by a commission and appointed by the governor. During the next general election, the judge must run in a partisan election. If they win, they then run unopposed in a nonpartisan retention election on the next general election ballot.

The object of the merit plan is to permit the governor some appointive discretion while removing politics from the selection of judges. If it works as intended, election or direct gubernatorial appointment is replaced with a careful appraisal of candidates' professional qualifications by an objective commission. The process is intended to ensure both the basic independence of judges and their accountability to the people.

The Politics of Merit Selection The merit plan looks great on paper, but in practice it has not fulfilled its promise. First, it has not dislodged politics from judicial selection. A judgeship is too important a political office in any state ever to be immune from politics. It is a prized job and an important point of judicial access for numerous individuals, firms, and interest groups, especially the powerful state bar association.

Politics—partisan or nonpartisan—is rampant in the judicial nominating commission's review and selection of candidates. For better or worse, the legal profession often dominates the process. Counting the judge who presides over the nominating commission, lawyers make up a majority of the commission in most of the states. Bar association lobbying is often the prime reason that merit plans are adopted in the first place. However, the legal profession is not monolithic in its politics: It is often divided into two camps—plaintiff's attorneys and defendant's attorneys.

Furthermore, the governor's influence can be exceptionally strong. The laypersons they appoint to the nominating commission are there to represent the governor's point of view and sometimes to promote specific candidates or the agenda of the governor's political party. In six states, the majority of commission members are laypersons. The member who is a judge may also respect the governor's preferences, particularly if the judge owes their appointment to that chief executive.

A second criticism of the merit plan is that the procedure intended to ensure judicial accountability to the people—the retention election—rarely generates voter interest and seldom results in the departure of an incumbent judge from office. Turnout in retention elections is normally very low and, on average, favors the incumbent by more than 70 percent.[36] Few incumbent judges have been voted out in retention elections. In most cases, merit selection means a lifetime appointment.

Voter backlashes, however, do occur against judges whose decisions are distinctly out of step with public opinion. In 1986, California Chief Justice Rose Bird and two associate justices were swept from the state supreme court by large margins in retention elections, as voters reacted negatively to a series of supreme court rulings that significantly expanded the rights of the accused and of convicted felons. Bird had voted to overturn all sixty-one capital punishment cases brought to the court during a period when polls showed 80 percent of the public supported the death penalty in California.[37] Ten years later, Tennessee Supreme Court Justice Penny White was rejected in a retention election for failing to support the death penalty for the perpetrator of a particularly heinous crime.[38] In 2010, Iowa voters tossed out of office three supreme court justices for a ruling that a state gay marriage ban violated the state constitution's equal protection guarantee. Increasingly, campaigns to oust justices are spearheaded by conservative groups who pour money into attack ads against "liberal justices." But national efforts to remove three Tennessee supreme court judges, two judges in Kansas, and three justices in Florida failed.[39]

The final charge leveled against the merit plan is that despite reformers' claims to the contrary, it does not result in the appointment of better-qualified judges or of more women and minorities. When background, education, experience, and decision making are taken into account, judges selected through the merit plan are comparable with those selected through other plans. A large majority are white males. Most leave private practice for the bench and stay there until retirement. And a substantial majority were born, raised, and educated in the state in which they serve. One study on judicial qualifications showed that in nine states, merit-selected judges were disciplined for offenses such as willful misconduct, failure to perform their duties, or a felony conviction at a lower rate than were elected judges.[40]

Gubernatorial Appointment

All but one gubernatorial appointment states are former colonies, reflecting the early popularity of the plan. As a method per se, gubernatorial appointment rates fairly high on independence because the judge is directly appointed without an election, but it is weak on accountability because the judge is beholden to only one person for his job.

Although only a handful of states formally recognize it, gubernatorial appointment is in fact the most common method for selecting a majority of appellate and major trial court judges in the United States. Judges in states with popular elections or merit plans often resign or retire from office just before the end of their terms.[41] Under most state legal systems, the governor has the power to make interim appointments to vacant seats until the next scheduled election or the commencement of merit-plan selection processes. The governor's temporary appointee then enjoys the tremendous advantage of running as an incumbent for the next full term. Gubernatorial appointment is also used to replace a judge who dies before the expiration of the term.

What criteria do a governor apply in making appointments to the bench? Political considerations usually come first. The governor can use the appointment to reward a faithful legislator, shore up support in certain regions of the state, satisfy the demands of party leaders and the state legal establishment, or appeal to women's groups or to minority groups.[42]

LO 9-5
To recognize the trade-offs between judicial independence and accountability.

Which Selection Plan Is Best?

Endless debate endures over which selection plan among the five formal selection systems best achieves a healthy balance of (1) judicial independence from interest groups, attorney organizations, the next election, and other influences and (2) accountability to the people. It is unlikely ever to be settled. Legislative election and gubernatorial appointment probably maximize the value of independence but may be the least desirable because judges selected under these systems tend to come from a rather specific political occupation (the legislature), and the general public has little opportunity to hold them accountable. Judicial accountability is maximized when judges and judicial candidates must face voters, but few incumbents are defeated in elections. (Perhaps the vast majority of sitting judges are capable and competent.) As noted earlier, however, significant policy issues involving the courts and aggressive campaign spending can rouse the voters to the polls in certain instances, meaning that elected judges who want to stay on the bench must pay attention to public opinion.[43]

None of the prevalent selection systems produces "better" judges, however gubernatorial appointment is more likely to benefit women and minorities than the other selection systems are, although minorities are underrepresented under any selection plan.[44] Gubernatorial appointments and nonpartisan elections apparently increase the selection opportunities for minority judges, but larger gains probably await development of a larger pool of minority attorneys.

Politics, of course, is what raises all judges to the bench, regardless of the selection method. According to research by political scientists, what matters is the path a judge takes to the bench. Those chosen through elective systems tend to view the judiciary in more political—as opposed to juridical— terms than those who reach the bench through gubernatorial or merit appointment systems. Elected judges also tend to be more activist in their decision making and more attentive to voter concerns close to election time, and they are more likely to dissent from other judges in their opinions than are appointed judges.[45] Judges who vote to overturn a popular state law are also vulnerable. Voter preferences carry extra weight in a judge's decision making when facing competitive elections, particularly with respect to issues of criminal justice and abortion rights.[46] Those in merit-plan states have less to fear from an angry electorate; they can be guided more by personal ideological preferences and their interpretation of the law.

? It's Your Turn

Judges: Elected, Appointed, or Merit-Selected?

Select a state—any state except the one in which you currently reside. Determine how judges are selected for the appellate and trial courts. Based on what you have read in this chapter and other materials you can access, answer the following questions:

1. What are the pros and cons of the judicial selection process in the state you have chosen?
2. Is this the "best" or most appropriate system for this particular state? Why or why not?

In other words, judges who attain their jobs through electoral politics tend to behave similarly as other elected state officials by emphasizing political, rather than legal, factors in their decision making. The irony is that voters prefer to elect their judges, but they believe that campaign spending influences what judges decide in court. The It's Your Turn feature box offers you an opportunity to weigh in on the issue of selecting judges.

Removal of Judges

Like anyone else, judges can and do break the law or become physically or emotionally incapable of carrying out their responsibilities. If a judge displays serious deficiencies, they must be removed from the bench. Forty-five states provide for impeachment, wherein charges are filed in the state house of representatives and a trial is conducted in the senate. Other traditional means for removing justices include the legislative address and popular recall. In the legislative address, both houses of the legislature, by two-thirds vote, must ask the governor to dismiss a judge. Popular recall requires a specified number of registered voters to petition for a special election to recall the judge before their term has expired. But these traditional mechanisms are cumbersome and uncertain, and hence, seldom successful.

Today, states generally use more practical methods to remove judges. Problems related to senility and old age are ameliorated in at least thirty-seven states by a mandatory retirement age (generally seventy years) or by the forfeiture of pensions for judges serving beyond the retirement age. Such measures have the added benefit of opening the courtrooms to new and younger judges, even in situations where advancing age does not impair performance.

Most states have established special entities to address behavioral problems. *Courts of the judiciary*, whose members are all judges, and *judicial discipline and removal commissions*, composed of judges, lawyers, and laypersons, are authorized to investigate complaints about judges' qualifications, conduct, or fitness. These entities may reject allegations if they are unfounded, privately warn a judge if the charges are not serious, or hold formal hearings. Hearings may result in dismissal of the charges; recommendation for early retirement; or, in some states, outright suspension or removal. Finally, in some states, chief justices or a majority vote of the supreme court can suspend a lower-court judge indefinitely for misbehavior. For example, in 2019, the Indiana Supreme Court suspended three lower-court judges after they were involved in a failed attempt to enter a strip club that resulted in a brawl "with two strangers outside of a White Castle in a drunken melee that ended with two of the judges shot and in critical condition in a hospital."[47] And the Florida Supreme Court suspended a lower-court judge for three months for making "scandalous and inaccurate" claims about his opponent's driving record in a judicial election debate.[48]

The discipline, suspension, or removal of state court judges is uncommon, but it becomes necessary in all states at one time or another. Judges have been found guilty of drunkenness and drug abuse, sexual misconduct with witnesses and defendants, soliciting and accepting bribes, using state-paid staff members to work on their campaigns, buying and selling verdicts, and just about every other kind of misconduct imaginable, including choking a law clerk.[49]

Sometimes judicial ethics seem to be in short supply. In Rhode Island, a state seldom celebrated as a paragon of political virtue, two consecutive supreme court chief justices vacated the bench when faced with impeachment. One resigned following allegations and testimony that he associated with criminals and had adulterous relations with two women in a Mafia-linked motel, among other things. Later, another pleaded guilty to using court money to pay for personal expenses, fixing friends' and relatives' speeding tickets, and ordering his secretary to destroy financial records.[50] Alabama chief justice Roy Moore was removed by the Court of Judiciary for defying federal and state court orders to haul away a two-and-a-half-ton Ten Commandments monument he had installed in the state judicial building. Reelected as chief justice in 2012, Moore was suspended a second time in 2016 when he refused to honor a federal court decision allowing gay marriage in Alabama to proceed.[51] Moore could not run for a third term on the Alabama Supreme Court because he had reached the age of 70, the mandatory retirement age for Alabama judges. Instead, he ran unsuccessfully for the U.S. Senate in the 2017 special election in Alabama.

Judicial Decision Making

LO 9-6
To describe some of the factors that influence judicial decision making.

What factors influence the rulings of state court judges? Why are some courts widely recognized as liberal (California, Hawaii) and others as tough on crime (Arizona, Mississippi)? Why does a prosecutor "judge shop," preferring to file a case before one judge rather than another? Isn't justice supposed to be blind, like its symbol of the woman holding the scales?

Judges, alas, are mortal beings like the rest of us. The formalities and legal jargon of the courtroom tend to mask the fact that judges' decisions are no less discretionary and subjective than the decisions of a governor, legislator, or agency head. Before we examine the factors that affect judicial decision making, however, we must distinguish between the legal settings of appellate courts and trial courts.

In And Out of the Trial Court

Approximately 90 percent of all civil and criminal cases are resolved outside the courtroom or through guilty pleas. In many civil cases, the defendant never appears in court to defend themselves, thereby implicitly admitting their guilt and therefore losing the case by default. Other civil cases are settled in a pretrial conference between the defendant and the plaintiff (where, for instance, payments on an overdue debt might be rescheduled) or through voluntary dispute resolution procedures such as mediation or arbitration.

The process of settling criminal cases out of court at the discretion of the prosecutor and the judge is called **plea bargaining**. Although some defendants plead guilty as originally charged, acknowledging guilt for a lesser charge is more typical in criminal proceedings. With the possible exceptions of the victim and the general citizenry, everyone benefits from plea bargaining, a fact that helps account for its extensive use. The accused gets off with lighter punishment than they would face if the case went to trial and they lost. The defense attorney frees up time to take on additional legal work. The prosecuting attorney increases their conviction rate, which looks good if they have political ambitions. The judge helps cut back the number of cases awaiting trial. Even police officers benefit by not having to spend time testifying (and waiting to testify) and by raising the department's clearance rate (the number of cases solved and disposed).

Out-of-court settlements through plea bargaining are negotiated in an informal atmosphere in the judge's chamber, between attorneys in the halls of the court building, or over drinks in a neighboring pub. This is a disturbingly casual way to dispense justice. The process is secretive and far removed from any notion of due process. The prosecuting (district) attorney enjoys enormous discretion in making deals. Often the propensity to settle depends on the length of the prosecuting attorney's court docket or their professional relationship with the accused's attorney, not on the merits of the case. All too often an innocent person pleads guilty to a lesser offense for fear of being wrongly convicted of a more serious offense, or because they cannot post bail and don't want to spend any unnecessary time behind bars. Equally disturbing, particularly to a victim, is the fact that plea bargaining can soon put a guilty person back on the streets, perhaps to search for another victim.

Nonetheless, plea bargaining is widely practiced. It is almost inevitable when the prosecutor's case hinges on weak evidence, police errors, a questionable witness, or the possibility of catching a bigger fish. Negotiation of a guilty plea for a lesser offense can occur at any stage of the criminal justice process. Plea bargaining replaces the common law idea of innocence until proven guilty with the presumption of some degree of guilt to which the defendant is willing to admit.

If the accused is unable to make a deal with the prosecuting attorney, they face either a **bench trial** by a single judge or a **trial by jury**. Both involve a courtroom hearing with all the legal formalities. In some jurisdictions and for certain types of cases, the defendant has a choice. In other situations, state legal procedures specify which trial format will be utilized. A jury trial is always mandatory for murder cases.

In a bench trial, the judge alone hears all arguments, determines the facts, and makes rulings on questions of law. Jury trials depend on a panel of citizens who decide the facts of the case; the judge instructs the jury on the applicable law. Although judges and juries would usually reach the same decision, the uncertainty introduced by twelve laypersons is usually great enough

plea bargaining
Negotiation between a prosecutor and a criminal defendant's counsel that results in the defendant pleading guilty to a lesser charge or pleading guilty in exchange for a reduced sentence.

bench trial
Trial by a single judge, without a jury.

trial by jury
A trial in which a jury decides the facts and makes a finding of guilty or not guilty.

Controversies in States and Localities

What if the Jury Pool Becomes a Puddle?

Many courts experience problems in getting people to perform their civic duty of jury service. Jury service is required for a large cross section of the population so that trials can be scheduled in reasonable amounts of time and defendants can receive fair and considered treatment from a jury of one's peers. Moreover, research shows that serving on a jury tends to heighten levels of civic participation in other ways, including voting and other forms of engagement.[1]

Juror shortages can seriously impede the value of a speedy trial. Many individuals ignore jury summons. Some individuals shirk from jury duty to avoid the accompanying loss of income from their regular job. Some may not be able to arrange day care or elder care. Others show up but try to avoid jury duty by exaggerating or lying about the hardships jury duty would impose on them. With increasing frequency, some people simply shrug off their responsibility to serve. Judges may respond to those who ignore their summons by sending the sheriff or bailiff to round them up and haul them before the judge. In North Dakota, New Jersey, and elsewhere, their names are published in the local newspaper. Turning to positive incentives, some states are improving the jury duty experience by installing computer workstations, snack rooms, libraries, and other amenities in the jury lounge.

What can be done to increase jury compliance rates? Among the options being tried are:

- Increase juror pay from a paltry $10 to $20 a day to a more attractive amount, such as $50 to $100.
- Provide day care for children of prospective jurors who have child-care responsibilities.
- Make the juror experience more attractive by providing wireless internet, snack rooms, coffee or tea, libraries, or other amenities for use when not actively hearing a case.
- Send a court officer to the home or place of employment of jury scofflaws and take them to court.
- Fine shirkers for noncompliance with a jury summons.

Critical Thinking Questions

1. What actions do you think are feasible to accelerate jury participation rates? What actions would you consider to be unacceptable? Can you think of any not listed here?

2. Do you feel a personal responsibility to comply with a jury duty summons? Why or why not? Have you been summoned to jury duty? If so, what was your experience?

[1] Andrew J. Bloeser, Carl McCurley, and Jeffery J. Mondak, "Jury Service as Civic Engagement: Determinants of Jury Summons Compliance," *American Politics Research* 40 (2, 2012): 179–204.

to convince a defendant to choose a bench trial or, if offered, alternative means of resolving the dispute such as mediation. Less than 2 percent of all criminal cases and less than 1 percent of civil cases are resolved by jury trial.[52]

When jury trials do occur, attorneys seek to limit the unpredictable nature of juries by extensively questioning individuals in the jury pool. Each side in the dispute has the right to strike the names of a certain number of potential jurors without giving a specific reason. Others are eliminated for cause, such as personal knowledge of the case or its principals. In high-stakes cases, the jury-selection process involves public opinion surveys, individual background investigations of potential jurors, and other costly techniques. Many courts experience problems in getting people to perform their civic duty of jury service, as the Controversies in States and Localities feature box illustrates.

As with many other governmental institutions, trial courts have had to adapt to the changed environment of the COVID-19 pandemic. Social distancing is nearly impossible in a courtroom, especially for jury trials and so courts began experimenting with virtual trials. By the spring of 2020, some sixteen states were allowing videoconference pretrial hearings. Florida courts held several bench trials over Zoom; one concerned a child abduction and a second was about the voting rights of convicted felons but the move to videoconference jury trials is much more problematic. Constitutional issues arise in such an arrangement. What does it mean to confront witnesses if the witnesses are testifying online? How can jury privacy and security be guaranteed if the jurors are sitting at home rather than in the courtroom? Do all trial participants have internet access with speed high enough to allow videoconferencing without annoying delays? Would a defendant need to go to the local library or some other public place in order to access the internet? What about defendants who are in jail or prison?[53] While no state has used videoconference jury trials for criminal offenses, Texas has experimented with one in a civil case with some success. As the trial court judge in that case stated, "No one is saying tomorrow we're going to start trying serious felonies over Zoom.... But I think there are many civil trials where parties might agree that this is a good way to resolve it given the uncertainty of when you're ever going to get an in-person civil trial."[54]

Inside the Appellate Court

Appellate courts are substantially different from trial courts: No plaintiffs, defendants, or witnesses are present; no bargaining or pre-decision settlement is allowed. The appeal consists of a review of court records and arguments advanced by the attorneys, who frequently are not the same lawyers who originally represented the parties. Appellate court rulings are issued by a panel of at least three judges who are tasked with deciding if legal errors have occurred. Unlike decisions in most trial courts, appellate court decisions are written and published. The majority vote prevails. Judges voting in the minority have the right to make a formal, written dissent that justifies their opinion.

State supreme courts vary dramatically in ideology. Those in Hawaii, Rhode Island, and Maryland are much more liberal than those in Arizona, Mississippi, and New Hampshire. There is marked variation in the dissent rates of state appellate courts. Some courts maintain a public aura of consensus on even the most controversial matters by almost always publishing unanimous opinions. Justices may disagree, but they do not necessarily dissent formally.

Other courts are rocked by public disputes over legal questions. Personal, professional, partisan, political, and other disagreements can spill over into open hostility over casework. As an Illinois chief justice observed, "Dissents are born not of doubt but of firm convictions."[55] Supreme courts in states such as California, New York, Michigan, and Mississippi have a history of contentiousness, whereas others, like those in Rhode Island and Maryland, are havens of harmony. Dissent rates appear to be positively related to a state's socioeconomic and political complexity, such as urbanization and partisan competition. Judges with long tenure and who do not have to face the voters in elections are more likely to dissent. More dissent also occurs in courts with a large number of justices and with intermediate appellate courts. The more time justices have at their disposal, the more likely they are to find reasons to disagree.[56]

Influences of the Legal System

In addition to the facts of the case itself, judicial decision making is influenced by factors associated with the legal system, including institutional arrangements, accepted legal procedures, caseload pressures, and the ease with which certain interested parties gain access to the legal process.

1. Institutional Arrangements The level, or tier, of court is a structural characteristic that influences decision making. Trial court judges enforce legal norms and routinely *apply* the law as it has been written and interpreted over the years. The trial court permits direct interpersonal contacts among the judge, the jury, and the parties (usually individuals and small businesses). Divorce, personal injury, traffic violations, and minor criminal violations are the types of cases that predominate in trial courts.

Appellate courts are more apt to *interpret* the law and create public policy. State constitutional issues, state–local conflicts, and challenges to government regulation of business are the kinds of issues likely to be found in appellate courts. Cases typically involve government and large corporations. A particular case in a high court sometimes has an enormous impact on public policy, particularly when judges depart from established precedent or offer new interpretations of the law. The Wisconsin Supreme Court essentially overturned a constitutional amendment guaranteeing the right to carry a concealed weapon. Nevada's highest court nullified a state constitutional provision that two-thirds of the legislature must approve tax increases. Florida's supreme court struck down an education voucher system that permitted children to attend private and religious schools at the public's expense. Washington's supreme court found unconstitutional a popular initiative that required either a public vote or a two-thirds legislative majority to enact a tax increase, and also voted to hold the state legislature in contempt for failing to obey a court order to appropriately fund public schools.

Another important institutional arrangement is the selection procedure for judges. For instance, judicial decisions may be influenced by partisan electoral competition. Especially when a judge facing reelection must vote on an issue highly salient to voters, public opinion can affect the judge's ruling.[57] Death penalty cases provide a good example of this point. A study of judicial decision making in Texas, North Carolina, Louisiana, and Kentucky found that judges seeking reelection tend to uphold death sentences. In these traditionally conservative states, a decision in support of the death penalty helps to avoid unwanted preelection criticism from political opponents. As one former state supreme court justice put it, "Judges who are running for reelection do keep in mind what the next 30-second ad is going to look like."[58]

precedent
The legal principle that previous similar court decisions should be applied to future decisions.

stare decisis
The legal doctrine that precedent set in earlier cases should guide judges' rulings.

2. Legal Procedures and Precedent On the basis of **precedent** and under the legal doctrine of **stare decisis**, the principles and procedures of law applied in one situation are applied in any similar situation. In addition, lower courts are supposed to follow the precedents established by higher courts. An individual decision may seem unimportant, but when it is made in the context of other similar cases, it helps judicial precedent evolve. Through this practice, the doctrine of equal treatment before the law is pursued. When lower-court judges refuse to follow precedent or are ignorant of it, their decisions can be overturned on appeal. Of course, several conflicting precedents may relate to a case; in such instances, a judge will choose among them in justifying his ruling. A previous decision may become obsolete, may be manifestly absurd, or may simply clash with a judge's values or point of view.

Where do judges find precedent? In previous judicial rulings, state supreme court decisions set the norms. Supreme courts themselves, however, scan the legal landscape beyond state boundaries. Decisions of the U.S. Supreme Court may influence those of the state supreme courts. Increasingly, however, state supreme courts are practicing doctrinal diversity and looking to one another for precedent. State appellate judges borrow from and cite the decisions of other states. They especially tend to rely on the more professional, prestigious supreme courts, such as those of California, Colorado, and Washington. State courts also tend to network with courts in the same region of the country, where cultural and other environmental factors are similar.[59]

3. Caseload Pressures Caseloads affect judges' decisions. The number of cases varies in accordance with crime rates, socioeconomic characteristics of the jurisdictions, state laws, the number of judges, and many other variables. It stands to reason that the quality of judicial decision making is inversely related to caseload. Judges burdened by too much litigation are hard-pressed to devote an adequate amount of time and attention to each case before them.

4. Access to the System The final legal-system characteristic affecting judicial decisions is the access of individuals, organizations, and groups to the court system. Wealthy people and corporations are better able to pay for resources (attorneys, legal research, etc.) and therefore enter the legal system with a great advantage over poorer litigants (perhaps helping account for why African Americans and Latinos tend to receive harsher sentences than white defendants). Special-interest groups also enjoy certain advantages in influencing judicial decisions. They often have specialized knowledge in areas of litigation, such as environmental or business regulation. Lobbying by interest groups is much less prominent in the judicial branch than it is in the legislative and executive branches, but groups can affect outcomes by providing financial aid to litigants in important cases and by filing *amicus curiae* (friend of the court) briefs supporting one side or the other in a dispute. Most importantly, making monetary contributions to a judge's reelection campaign can influence a judge's decision.

The states have implemented several reforms to increase access to the judicial system for those who are disadvantaged. For example, court interpreters are available in states with large Latino and Asian populations. Physical and communication barriers have been removed so that persons with disabilities can participate fully in all aspects of the legal system. Racial, ethnic, and gender biases against attorneys, plaintiffs, defendants, witnesses, and other court participants are being addressed (although women still tend to receive less severe sentences than men who commit similar crimes).[60] Night courts remain open late for people who have difficulty getting off their day jobs to appear in court. And day care is being provided for children of plaintiffs, defendants, witnesses, and jurors. Gradually, state courts are responding to changes in the nature of society.

Personal Values, Attitudes, and Characteristics of Judges

Simply put, judges do not think and act alike. Each is a product of individual background and experiences, which in turn influence decisions made in the courtroom. Studies of state court justices have found that decisions are related to the judges' party identification, political ideology, prior careers, religion, age, and gender. In other words, personal characteristics predispose a judge to decide cases in certain ways.

For example, Democratic judges tend to favor the claimant in civil rights cases, the injured party in liability (tort) cases, the government in tax disputes, the employee in worker's compensation cases, the government in business regulation cases, the defendant in criminal contests, the union in disagreements with management, and the tenant in landlord–tenant cases. Republican judges tend to support the opposite side on all these issues. Female judges, who now occupy one out of three seats on supreme courts, are more supportive of women on sex discrimination and other feminist issues; more likely to favor the accused in obscenity and death penalty cases; and, in general, are more liberal than their male colleagues.[61] And, finally, the judge's race appears to have little effect on the sentences handed down to black and white defendants, although African American judges tend to be tougher than Latino judges when sentencing all defendants.[62] Obviously, these distinctions do not hold in all situations, but the point is that *justice* is an opaque concept. No wonder attorneys try to shop around for the most sympathetic judge before filing a legal action.

LO 9-7
To demonstrate an understanding of how judicial federalism is related to increased capability and judicial activism in many state courts.

Judicial Federalism

During the 1950s and 1960s, the U.S. Supreme Court was the leading judicial actor in the land. Under Chief Justice Earl Warren (1953–1969) and his liberal majority, the Court handed down a long series of rulings that overturned racial segregation, mandated legislative reapportionment, extended voting rights, and expanded the rights of accused criminals. Significant reversals of state court decisions were commonplace. "Impeach Earl Warren" billboards sprouted up across the South like kudzu.

As a growing proportion of conservative justices filled the Supreme Court, however, it changed direction. Since 1988, a conservative majority has been in control. The Court has been somewhat less intrusive in state and local affairs and has flashed a green light to state courts inclined to activism. The result is **judicial federalism**, in which state courts look first to state constitutional and statutory laws in rendering legal judgments on important state and local issues rather than to the federal courts.

judicial federalism State constitutional and statutory laws are consulted and applied before federal law.

judicial activism The making of judicial public policy through decisions that overturn existing law or effectively make new laws.

Judicial Activism in the States

Judicial activism is a value-laden term with ideological dimensions.[63] When associated with politically liberal court decisions, it is decried by conservatives. However, conservative judges (such as those in the majority of the U.S. Supreme Court) are also activists. Whether liberal or conservative, all tend to show strong ideological tendencies.

An objective definition of judicial activism, then, points to court-generated change in public policy that is perceived as illegitimate by opponents who favor the status quo. Judicial activism is in the eye of the beholder. All too often, an "activist" judge is one who doesn't decide a case the way one *thinks* they should.[64]

Regardless of one's feelings on the matter, state supreme courts have clearly become *more* activist by expanding into new policy areas. They are more likely to be involved in the policy-making process by making decisions that affect policy in the executive branch, and many preempt the lawmaking responsibility of the legislature when, in exercising the power of judicial review, the courts invalidate a statute based on constitutional grounds.

How can state courts override the decisions of the highest court in the United States? The answer is that they are grounding their rulings in their own constitutions instead of basing them on the national constitution. In several decisions, the U.S. Supreme Court has upheld the right of the states to expand on the minimum rights and liberties guaranteed under the national document. Of course, when there is an irreconcilable conflict between state and federal laws, the latter prevails.

Current Trends in State Courts

The wave of state court activism is not carrying all the states with it. Some state supreme courts remain caught in the doldrums, consistently endorsing —rather than repudiating—U.S. Supreme Court decisions. Some of them are so quiet, as one wag suggested, "that you can hear their arteries harden." But even traditionally inactive courts in states such as Wisconsin and North Carolina have been stirred into independent actions recently. State court activism seems to be contagious, as courts utilize their own information and case networks instead of those of the U.S. Supreme Court.

Of course, with rare exceptions, judges cannot seize issues as governors and legislators can; they must wait for litigants to bring them to the courthouse. And although judges can issue rulings, they must depend on the executive and legislative branches to comply with and enforce those rulings. Nonetheless, many state supreme courts are becoming more active in the policy-making process. The reluctance of the federal courts to address important and controversial issues comprehensively has resulted in more cases for state supreme courts to decide.

State court activism does have some negative points. First, courts may appear to overstep their authority and try to go too far in policy making, intruding into the proper domain of executive and legislative actors—not to mention that of the voters. For example, courts in California, New Jersey, and elsewhere issued decisions that certain state legislative budget actions violated constitutional obligations.[65] Second, judges have little knowledge or expertise in the substance of public policy or in the policy-making process. They have no specialized staff to perform in-depth policy research on particular policy issues, and they cannot realistically depend on lawyers to do policy research for them. After all, lawyers are trained and practiced in legal reasoning and process, not social or political science. Third, state courts are increasingly issuing policy decisions that have significant budgetary implications. Court rulings on school finance, prison overcrowding, and treatment of the mentally ill have severely affected state budgets. Such court actions rarely take into account their related financial effects. A fourth problem is that in the context of state constitutional rights, geography is limiting. A state-by-state approach may not be appropriate for policies in areas such as civil rights, clean air and water, and safe food, which should be provided equally to all citizens.[66] In fact, at least one study has shown that federal courts are expanding into areas in which state courts traditionally exercised power, partially as a result of national business interests looking for decisions carrying precedence in all states and partially the result of state court budget problems.[67]

LO 9-8
To describe efforts to reform state courts.

Administrative and Organizational Improvements in State Courts

We have already discussed several important judicial reforms: intermediate appellate courts, court consolidation, merit-selection plans for judges, more practical means for disciplining and removing judges, and administrative and organizational improvements, including those of a financial nature. This last category deserves further consideration.

Financial Improvements and Financial Pressures

The exorbitant costs of some trials can bankrupt local jurisdictions if state financial assistance is not forthcoming. For example, one child molestation case in Los Angeles County lasted two and a half years and carried a tab of $15 million. (Neither of the two defendants was convicted.) The price tag for a murder trial and subsequent appeals can also be counted in the millions. A high-profile multiple murder case in Georgia effectively drained the public defender system of funds and halted proceedings in seventy-two other capital cases.[68]

The national economic recession of 2008–2011 resulted in substantial cuts to state court budgets, with serious consequences for indigent defendants and all parties interested in justice and speedy trials. The budget situation for state courts had gotten so bad by 2011 that Massachusetts chief justice was moved to observe that state courts had reached "the tipping point of dysfunction."[69] Until recently, state court budgets improved somewhat—a 2018 survey of court administrators showed that some 60 percent of courts were in better financial shape than they had been in 2009, but a quarter said their financial shape had deteriorated in the last year.[70] To make matters even worse, some legislatures have been known to threaten and even implement court budget cuts because of displeasure with unpopular rulings. At the same time, the federal court system has been recruiting prominent state court judges to serve on the federal bench, further depleting state court resources.[71] It is too soon to determine what the effects of the COVID-19 pandemic are on state court systems but coping with the pandemic will most likely require additional funding for such things as remote access licenses, personal protection for court officers, and so on.

In response to such budget crises in the past and to even out resources throughout the court system, more than half of the states assume full financial responsibility for the operation of state and local courts. Through centralized budgeting (also referred to as *unified court budgeting*), a consolidated budget for all state and local courts is prepared by the chief administrative officer of the state court system, detailing all personnel, supplies, equipment, and other expenditures. This is intended to enhance financial management and maintain judicial independence from the executive and legislative branches.

Dealing with Growing Caseloads

Case backlogs are a commonly recognized problem, and they are getting worse with budget shortfalls. State trial court cases peaked at over 100 million per year in 2008 but have shown a slow but steady decline to around 90 million in 2017, still a remarkable number.[72] Some judges hand down more than 300 opinions annually. Delays of two years or more are not uncommon for appellate court hearings, and the unprecedented pressure is growing. Calls for **tort** reform to reduce the number of personal injury cases and the escalating size of jury awards have become increasingly insistent. (Torts account for about two-thirds of all civil trials; the average award in a tort trial, however, is only $30,000.)

Excessive caseloads are caused by numerous factors, including the greater propensity of losing parties to appeal lower-court decisions, the tremendous growth in litigation, heightened interest group activity, huge increases in drug-related and drunk-driving cases, and poor caseload-management procedures. Exacerbating the problem is the high demand for litigation aggravated by the prodigious quantity of lawyers in the United States, which accounts for nearly two-thirds of all the lawyers in the world. The American Bar Association counted nearly 1,352,000 lawyers in 2019. The demographics are interesting: 64 percent are male, 85 percent white. But more than half of the 2019 law school first-year enrollment was female and 31 percent was minority.[73] These lawyers are distributed unevenly: There are more than 182,000 in New York state, but only some 1,700 in North Dakota.[74]

The larger concern is that long delays thwart the progress of justice. The quality of evidence deteriorates as witnesses disappear or forget what they saw, and victims suffer from delays that prevent them from collecting damages for injuries incurred during a crime or an accident. Innocent defendants can be harmed by the experience of being held in jail for long periods while awaiting trial. Increasingly, criminal cases are thwarted because of witness intimidation by the accused, his friends, or others who desire to end the prosecution and free the accused.

Reducing excessive caseloads is not a simple matter. Common sense dictates establishing intermediate appellate courts and adding new judgeships. But much like a new highway draws more traffic, intermediate appellate courts, by their very existence, tend to attract more appeals. Although additional judges can speed up the trial process in lower courts, they may also add to appellate backlogs. Expanding the number of judges in an appellate court is also problematic: Hearings may take longer because of more input or factional divisions among judges. And, for better or worse, the law schools continue to spew out new lawyers, looking for something to do.

The stubborn persistence of case backlogs has led to some interesting and promising new approaches.

1. *Alternative dispute resolution.* Mediation, arbitration, or other techniques help settle litigation prior to or during formal courtroom proceedings. Mediation involves a neutral third party who tries to help the opponents reach a voluntary agreement. Arbitration consists of a binding ruling by a neutral party in

tort
A civil wrong that causes harm to another person, such as an auto accident, product liability, or defamation.

favor of one party or the other. In a growing number of states, civil litigants in search of timely settlement hire private judges to arbitrate their disputes.

2. *Fines against lawyers and litigants.* Laws or court rules allow judges to levy monetary fines against lawyers and litigants guilty of delaying tactics, frivolous litigation.

3. *Case management systems.* Judges can take charge of their dockets and impose a no-nonsense case management system. Although individual systems vary widely, a typical approach is multitracking, or *differentiated case management.* It distinguishes between simple and complex cases, as well as between frivolous and potentially significant cases, and treats them differently. Complex and significant cases are waved down the traditional appellate track. Simple and frivolous cases take a shorter track, usually under the direction of staff attorneys. In Vermont, this case management system is referred to as the "rocket docket." Experiments with multitracking have been successful in reducing case delays in Arizona, Maine, New Hampshire, and other states. As previously noted, another case management innovation designed to speed the wheels of justice is problem-solving, or *boutique,* courts, in which environmental law disputes, drug cases, domestic violence cases, or others with special characteristics are heard by judges in specialized courts.

4. *New technology.* Technological innovations are also improving the quality and quantity of court operations. Electronic databases (e.g., LEXIS and WESTLAW) store case information and legal research and transmit information from law offices to courts. Electronic filing of court documents and online access to court information for attorneys and citizens help track child support payments, store case data for legal research, transmit data from law offices to courts, and, in general, save the courts money and staff time. Arraignment procedures, during which suspects are formally charged, are videotaped to save time or to prevent potential problems from a disruptive defendant. Video courtrooms, in which trials are filmed, create a more accurate trial record and cost much less than a written transcript by a court stenographer. Lawyers in high-tech courtrooms speed up proceedings by using PowerPoint, video clips, and internet sources, displayed for jurors on individual monitors. Audiovisual technology permits hearings, motions, pleas, sentencing, and other proceedings to be conducted long distance between the jail and the courthouse, thereby saving money and enhancing security. And as noted above, states are experimenting with virtual court proceedings.

5. *Performance standards.* The National Center for State Courts has developed performance standards for state trial courts to aid self-assessment and improvement.[75] A growing number of states are not only adopting quantitative indicators of the speed with which cases are processed but are also trying to measure broader concerns such as access to justice, fairness and integrity, public trust and confidence, and the quality of judges' decision making.

Compensating the Judges

At first glance, judicial salaries seem high enough. In 2019, state supreme court judges earned an average of approximately $176,000. For a general jurisdiction trial court, it was $157,763. The variation is great: California chief justices make $256,000, whereas their counterparts in New Mexico are paid only $133,174. Trial court judges are paid 10 to 20 percent less.[76]

However, these amounts are substantially below what an experienced, respected attorney can expect to make. A successful lawyer who gives up private practice and perhaps a lucrative partnership for the bench must be willing to take a considerable cut in income. Unlike legislators, state judges are permitted little outside income. Therefore, it is reasonable to ask whether the best legal minds will be attracted to judgeships, given that judicial compensation is relatively low. This dilemma exists at all levels and in all branches of public service, from the municipal finance officer to the highway department director, because most state and local government compensation lags behind that for comparable professional jobs in the private sector. If we expect our judges, law enforcement officers, and other public employees to be honest, productive, and highly qualified, perhaps they should be compensated fairly.

Judicial Performance Evaluation

Who judges the judges? In popular election and merit system states, the voters hold judges accountable. But voters have no voice in gubernatorial and legislative selection states. And even when judicial elections are held, how much do the voters really know about the candidates?

Judicial performance evaluation (JPE) offers an objective process to assess the performance of judges. Voters are educated, and judges are encouraged to use evaluation results for self-improvement. First adopted by Alaska in 1975, JPE programs are now mandated in sixteen additional states and under active consideration in several others. JPE involves confidential surveys of attorneys, court professionals, witnesses, jurors, and other court participants. Respondents are questioned about how the judge interprets the law, manages their workload, and interacts with people in the courtroom, among other factors.[77]

Research indicates that JPE can contribute to judicial self-improvement and provide valuable, job-related information on judges' performance to the voters. Used appropriately, JPE helps preserve the hallmark characteristics of independence and accountability of the judiciary.[78]

State Courts Today

Like the other two branches of government, the state judiciary has been reformed significantly. Court systems have been modernized and simplified, intermediate appellate courts have been added, processes have been streamlined, and case delays are being addressed as resources permit. Disciplinary and removal commissions now make it easier to deal with problem judges, and JPE furnishes useful data on judicial performance. But courts are still striving for adequate funding and greater independence from political pressures and favoritism. Justice may appear at times to be an ephemeral ideal, and an expensive one at that, but it is more likely to be approximated in state judicial decisions today than ever before. The courts, like the rest of society, are participants in the technological age. New innovations and approaches will follow the recommendations of commissions in states now studying the needs of state judicial systems in the future.

Court modernization and reform have been accompanied by increased judicial activism. The newly assertive state courts have far surpassed the federal courts in public policy activism. They sometimes blatantly disagree with federal precedents and insist on decisions grounded in state constitutional law rather than in the national constitution. In short, the state courts are proactively responding to public concerns with the administration of justice, and, by inference, to the perennial issues of crime and criminal justice.

 # Chapter Recap

- State courts are organized into two tiers: appellate courts and trial courts.

- The five methods for selecting judges are legislative election, partisan election, nonpartisan election, merit plan, and gubernatorial appointment. Each selection plan has certain advantages and disadvantages —there is no "one best way."

- Many factors influence judicial decision making, including institutional arrangements; legal procedures; case precedent; caseload pressures; access to the legal system; and the personal values, attitudes, and characteristics of judges.

- Judicial federalism is related to increased capability and judicial activism in many state courts.

- Efforts to reform state courts include financial improvements, better caseload management, and improved compensation for judges.

Key Terms

civil case *(p. 243)*
criminal case *(p. 244)*
administrative case *(p. 244)*
common law *(p. 244)*
limited jurisdiction trial courts *(p. 245)*

major trial courts *(p. 246)*
supreme court *(p. 246)*
intermediate appellate court *(p. 246)*
plea bargaining *(p. 259)*
bench trial *(p. 259)*

trial by jury *(p. 259)*
precedent *(p. 262)*
stare decisis *(p. 262)*
judicial federalism *(p. 264)*
judicial activism *(p. 264)*
tort *(p. 267)*

Internet Resources

The National Center for State Courts (NCSC) maintains a list of courts and their websites. NCSC's website at **www.ncsc.org** is a rich source of information on the courts, including state court decisions, caseload statistics, and court organization. There are also links to all state court websites at **www.ncsc.org/Information -and-Resources/Browse-by-State/State-Court -Websites.aspx**.

Interesting state sites include the following: California at **www.courts.ca.gov/**, Florida at **www .flcourts.org**, and Alaska at **courts.alaska.gov**.

The American Bar Association's website at **www .abanet.org/** provides an analysis of current controversial cases and other legal information.

To watch live performances of Indiana's court proceedings, see **www.in.gov/judiciary/webcast**.

10

Local Government: Types and Functions

City Hall in Santa Monica, California

Learning Objectives

LO 10-1   To classify local government into five types: counties, municipalities, towns and townships, special districts, and school districts.

LO 10-2   To examine the functions, organization, and performance of county government.

LO 10-3   To identify the forms and functions of city government and the issues confronting municipalities around the country.

LO 10-4   To evaluate the roles and future of town and township government.

LO 10-5   To analyze the need for special districts and the concerns about them.

LO 10-6   To examine the politics and issues affecting school district government.

LO 10-7   To evaluate the issue of "good" governance at the local level.

In 2015, Illinois governor Bruce Rauner created a task force with the avowed goal of streamlining local governments and making them function more efficiently. Supporters of the task force hoped that it would come up with recommendations to reduce the number of local governments and potentially save millions of dollars and improve public services.[1] With nearly 7,000 units of local government of various types and sizes—far more than any other state—Illinois is ripe for a rethinking of its local government landscape. In December 2015, the task force delivered its final report, making twelve recommendations for consolidation and reduction in local governments. As of 2020, five of these recommendations had been enacted into law by the Illinois state legislature, five were rejected, and the remaining two were still under consideration.[2]

What do citizens want from their local governments? The answer is, to be governed well. They want governmental structures that work and leaders who are effective. They want jurisdictions with adequate capacity to resolve the tough public problems of our times. But as this chapter demonstrates, "governed well" is hard to achieve. Even with improved capacity, local governments continue to confront a series of challenges, some perennial, some episodic.[3]

Orientations to Communities

Communities and their governments can be discussed in many different ways. Theoretically, at least three different orientations have some appeal. When you move from the theoretical realm to legal realities, five types of local governments can be differentiated.

Theoretical Orientations

In the early days of the United States, communities were idealized as *civic republics*.[4] In a civic republic, community government is based on the principle of mutual consent. Citizens share fundamental beliefs and participate in public affairs. Their motivation for civic involvement is less materialistic self-interest than altruistic concern for community welfare. Although this idea continued to have theoretical appeal, its reality was threatened by the growing and diverse nineteenth-century populace, which preferred to maximize individual liberty and accumulation of wealth. An economically inspired conception of community, that of the *corporate enterprise*, gradually emerged. Economic growth and the ensuing competition for wealth sparked extensive conflict.[5] With the guidance of state government, local governments adopted policies and juggled the clashing interests.

These two theoretical orientations, the community as a civic republic and the community as a corporate enterprise, remain viable. An alternative orientation has emerged, however—one that portrays the community as a *consumer market*.[6] In a consumer market, citizens are consumers of public services, and governments are providers. This idea places increased emphasis on quality of life and cost-effectiveness. Individuals make choices about where they will live—in the heart of the city, a suburban jurisdiction, or a rural portion of the county. In each of these locales, the individual will encounter government or, more accurately, *governments*. The range of government services and the cost of these services vary from one place to another. Informed consumers, so the theory goes, seek communities that are in line with their preferences. You say that you want to live in the Los Angeles area? You have many jurisdictional choices: Twenty-one cities share a border with the city of Los Angeles. Each one provides a different package of services, in terms of type, quality, and cost—a consumer market, indeed.

Five Types of Local Governments

Local government is the level of government that fights crime, extinguishes fires, paves streets, collects trash, maintains parks, provides water, and educates children. Some local governments provide all of these services; others, only some. A useful way of thinking about local governments is to distinguish between general-purpose and single-purpose local governments. **General-purpose local governments** are those that perform a wide range of governmental functions. These include three types of local governments: counties, municipalities, and towns and townships. Single-purpose local governments, as the label implies, have a specific purpose and perform one function. School districts and special districts are single-purpose governments.

The boundaries of single-purpose districts may or may not coincide with the general-purpose local governments in the area. For example, the boundaries

LO 10-1
To classify local government into five types: counties, municipalities, towns and townships, special districts, and school districts.

general-purpose local government
A local government that performs a wide range of functions.

Figure 10.1 Cities, Townships, and School Districts in St. Joseph County, Indiana

Note: The St. Joseph County border is indicated by the thick line. The New Prairie United School Corporation, the John Glenn School Corporation, and the Union-North Union United School Corporation extend beyond the county's borders. City names are italicized; township names are in boldface type. City land areas are shaded light blue.

Source: Adapted from STATS Indiana, 2000, "Northwest Indiana Townships by County," https://www.stats.indiana.edu/maptools/maps/boundary/townships_2000/index.asp (accessed March 23, 20120; STATS Indiana, 2006, "Northwest Indiana Unified School Districts," http://www.stats.indiana.edu/maptools/maps/boundary/school_districts/region1_unified.gif (accessed March 23, 2020).

of a school district may be coterminous with the county, they may cover smaller portions of the county, or they may even extend over sections of two or more counties. Figure 10.1 maps the boundaries of several cities (South Bend, for example), townships (Olive is one), and school districts (such as the John Glenn School Corporation) in, and extending beyond, St. Joseph County, Indiana. Not shown are four library districts and two other special districts within the county, overlapping some of the other jurisdictions. The web of boundaries shown in Figure 10.1 is not unique to northern Indiana— it characterizes most places in the United States. These noncongruent, overlapping boundaries can produce significant coordination problems for local governments in an area.[7]

In the United States, the number of local governments exceeds 90,000. Figure 10.2 shows the number of local governments at two points in time: 1952 and 2017. Among general-purpose local governments, the number of counties and towns and townships decreased slightly over the sixty-year

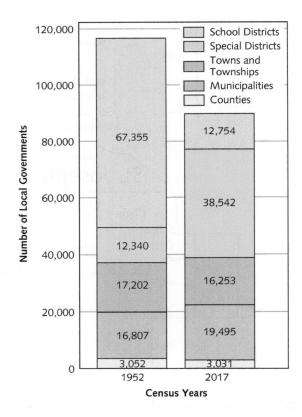

Figure 10.2 Numbers of Local Governments, by Type of Government: 1952 versus 2017

Source: U.S. Census Bureau, "2017 Census of Governments, Table 2: Local Governments by Type and State" (accessed March 3, 2020).

period as the number of municipalities increased. In terms of **single-purpose local governments**, the trends are more dramatic. From 1952 to 2017, nearly 81 percent of America's school districts were abolished or consolidated with surrounding districts; in the same period, special districts have tripled in number.

Native American reservations are not considered a formal type of local government, even though they perform many local government functions. **Metropolitan areas**, which are composed of a central city and its surrounding county (or counties), are not local governments either. The label *metropolitan statistical area (MSA)* is used by the federal government to designate urban areas that have reached a minimum 50,000-population threshold. As of 2020, the United States contained 392 MSAs. Another federal designation, **micropolitan statistical area**, refers to places with populations between 10,000 and 49,999. There were 542 micropolitan statistical areas in the United States in 2020. The MSA and micropolitan labels are used for statistical data collection and, in some instances, in federal grant programs.

Regardless of the purpose of a local government, we must remember that it has a lifeline to state government. In short, state government gives local government its legal existence. Local citizens may instill a community with its flavor and its character, but state government makes local government official. Over time, most states have gradually relaxed their control over localities through grants of **home rule**, which give local governments more decision-making power.

American local governments were not planned according to some grand design. Rather, they grew in response to a combination of citizen demand, interest group pressure, and state government acquiescence. As a consequence, no rational system of local governments exists. What does exist is a collection of autonomous, frequently overlapping jurisdictional units. The prevalence of **jurisdictional overlap** creates layers of local governments and raises questions about their number and function. As indicated in the introduction to this chapter, the number of local governments varies from state to state. Consider the case of Pennsylvania, second only to Illinois in the number of local governments. Pennsylvania's 4,830 local jurisdictions include 66 counties, 1,013 cities, 1,546 townships, 1,691 special districts, and 514 school districts.[8] Nevada, on the other hand, has a grand total of 189 local governments.

Being so close to the people offers special challenges to local governments. Citizens are well aware when trash has not been collected or when libraries do not carry current bestsellers. They can contact local officials and attend public hearings. A recent survey asked a national sample of Americans about their interactions with government. Some 20 percent said that they had contacted an elected official, and nearly 30 percent attended a community meeting in the last year.[9] The interactive nature of local government makes the questions of capacity and responsiveness all the more critical.

single-purpose local government
A local government, such as a school district, that performs a specific function.

metropolitan area
A central city of at least 50,000 people and its surrounding county (or counties); often called an *urban area*.

micropolitan statistical area
An urban cluster with a population between 10,000 to 49,999.

home rule
A broad grant of power from the state to a local government.

jurisdictional overlap
The existence of multiple local governments in the same territory.

LO 10-2

To examine the functions, organization, and performance of county government.

County Government

State governments have carved up their territories into 3,031 discrete, general-purpose subunits called counties (except in Louisiana, where counties are called *parishes*, and in Alaska, where they are called *boroughs*). Counties exist everywhere, with only a few exceptions: Connecticut and Rhode Island, where there are no functional county governments; Washington, D.C., which is a special case in itself; some municipalities in Virginia that are independent jurisdictions and are not part of the counties that surround them; and cities like Baltimore and St. Louis, which are not part of a county because of past political decisions. Also, some jurisdictions—Philadelphia and San Francisco, for example—are considered cities but they are actually consolidated city-county government structures.

Not All Counties Are Alike

Counties can be differentiated according to their urban/rural nature. Urban, or metropolitan, counties contain one or more large cities and surrounding suburbs and serve as the employment hubs for the area. Los Angeles County, California, with more than ten million residents—and larger than most states—is the largest population county in the United States. Even though most Americans live in metropolitan areas, most counties are actually non-metropolitan—that is, they contain one or more small cities, with the rest of the area sparsely settled. More than three-fourths of American counties have fewer than 100,000 inhabitants. Counties that contain no incorporated places with more than 2,500 residents are the most rural of all. Loving County, Texas, with 134 people spread over its 677-square-mile territory, is an example of an extremely rural jurisdiction.

The Role of County Government

Counties were created by states to function as their administrative appendages. In other words, counties were expected to manage activities of statewide concern at the local level. Their basic set of functions traditionally included property tax assessment and collection, law enforcement, elections, record keeping (land transactions, births, and deaths), and road maintenance. The county courthouse was the center of government.

The twin pressures of modernization and population growth placed additional demands on county governments. As a result, their service offerings have expanded and now include health care and hospitals, pollution control, mass transit, industrial development, social services, and consumer protection. Examples of the traditional and new functions of counties appear in Table 10.1. The more new services that a county provides, the more it is delivering city-type services to its residents and businesses.[10] As a result, counties are increasingly regarded less as simple functionaries of state government and more as important policy-making units of local government. Thirty-eight states have adopted home rule provisions for at least some of their counties.[11] This has made it easier for counties to change their organizational structures and reform their practices.

Table 10.1 County Government Functions

FUNCTION	TRADITIONAL FUNCTION	NEW FUNCTION
Building and housing code enforcement		X
Disaster preparedness		X
Water supply/sewage disposal		X
Parks and recreation		X
Judicial administration	X	
County jail maintenance	X	
Planning and land-use control		X
Record keeping: land transactions, births, deaths, marriages	X	
Airports		X
Public hospitals		X
Law enforcement	X	
Local roads and bridges, construction and maintenance	X	
Consumer protection		X
Mass transit		X
Property tax assessment and collection	X	
Election administration	X	
Natural resource preservation		X
Welfare and social-service programs	X	
Libraries		X
Stadiums, convention and cultural centers		X
Pollution control		X
Public health, including clinics		X
Community development and housing		X

Sources: David R. Berman, *County Governments in an Era of Change* (Westport, CT: Greenwood Press, 1993); Tanis J. Salant, "Overview of County Governments," in Roger L. Kemp, ed., *Forms of Local Government* (Jefferson, NC: McFarland, 1999); J. Edwin Benton, et al., "Service Challenges and Governance Issues Confronting American Counties in the 21st Century: An Overview," *State and Local Government Review* 40 (2008): 54–68.

Even with their gradual empowerment, counties, like other local governments, continue to chafe at the traditionally tight reins of state government control. Counties resent state requirements that the counties themselves have to pay for. In addition, they dislike the limits that states place on their authority. The issue of empowerment is unlikely to fade anytime soon.

How Counties Are Organized

The traditional structure of county government is based on an elected governing body, usually called a board of commissioners or supervisors, which is the central policy-making apparatus in the county. The board enacts county ordinances, approves the county budget, and appoints other officials (such as the directors of the county public works department and the county parks department). One of the board members acts as presiding officer. Historically, this form of government has been the most popular; more than half of U.S. counties use it, although its predominance is decreasing. A typical county commission has five members and meets in regular session twice a month.

The board is not omnipotent, however, because several other county officials are also elected, forming a plural executive structure. In most places, these officials include the sheriff, the county prosecutor (or district attorney), the county clerk (or clerk of the court), the county treasurer (or auditor), the county tax assessor, and, in some states, even the coroner. These officials can become powerful political figures in their own right by controlling their own bureaucratic units. Figure 10.3 sketches the typical organizational pattern of county government.

There are two primary criticisms of this type of organizational structure. First, it has no elected central executive official, like the mayor of a city or the governor of a state. County government is run by a board. Second, it does not

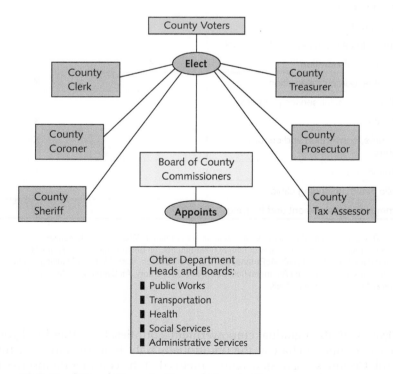

Figure 10.3 Traditional Organization of County Government
The most common form of county government lacks a central executive.

have a single-professional administrator to manage county government in the way a city manager does in a municipality. Elected officials are responsible for administering many major county functions.

These criticisms have led to calls for reform of the structure of county government. Two alternative county structures have grown in popularity over the past three decades. In one, called the *county council-elected executive plan*, the voters elect an executive officer in addition to the governing board. The result is a clearer separation between legislative and executive powers—in effect, a two-branch system of government. The board still has the power to set policy, adopt the budget, and audit the financial performance of the county. The executive's role is to prepare the budget, administer county operations (in other words, implement the policies of the board), and appoint department heads. More than 400 counties have adopted this arrangement; among the most recent is Cuyahoga County, Ohio, where Cleveland is located. Utah County (Provo area) rejected changing to this plan in the November 2020 election. In the other alternative structure, the *council-administrator plan*, the county board hires a professional administrator (sometimes called a "county manager") to run the government. The advantage of this form of government is that it brings to the county a highly skilled manager with a professional commitment to efficient, effective government. Approximately 1,000 counties have variations of the council-administrator structure. One of the most recent large counties to adopt such a plan is Bexar County, Texas, population 1.8 million, where San Antonio is located.

Determining the most effective structural arrangements for county government is an ongoing issue. Defections from the long-standing commission form of county government and experimentation with alternatives continue, especially in the most populous counties. Los Angeles County, which employs 100,000 people and has a budget of $20 billion, recently empowered its county administrator by giving her the authority to hire and fire most department heads.[12] Does structure matter? Research has shown that policy consequences are attributable, at least in part, to structure. For example, among fast-growing counties in Florida, the adoption of a reformed structure led to an expansion of the counties' services to its residents.[13] A national study has found a link between reformed structures and county spending on redistributive programs such as child welfare, homeless shelters, and mental health services.[14] However, other studies have raised questions about the impact of reformed structures on policy outcomes, suggesting that this question has not been answered definitively.[15] The It's Your Turn box raises a related question that several counties have confronted recently: whether to impose residency requirements on their employees.

The Performance of County Government

Counties are now more prominent than they were in the old days when they were considered the shadowy backwaters of local governments. As urban populations spill beyond the suburbs into the unincorporated territory of counties, the pressure on all local governments grows. A county and the cities located within it may find themselves at odds on myriad issues. The county–state relationship can be rocky, primarily because of the spiraling costs of state-imposed

? It's Your Turn

Should Public Employees Have to Live Where They Work?

Some counties and cities require their employees to live within their territorial boundaries. Other counties and cities that had these requirements in the past have repealed them. What do you think?

PROS	CONS
Living in the county or city gives employees a greater stake in the community.	People should be able to live where they want to, regardless of their employer.
Residents feel safer when police officers, sheriff's deputies, and firefighters, in particular, live in nearby neighborhoods.	Public employees may not be able to afford to buy or rent housing within the city or county.
Public employees are more likely to shop at local stores if they live there, thus strengthening the local economy.	Having residency requirements may discourage otherwise qualified applicants from seeking city or county employment.

mandates for programs such as indigent services and long-term health care. In addition, counties are expected to tackle tough dilemmas of affordable housing and environmental compliance at the same time that they are expanding their services to include disaster preparedness and consumer protection.

The pressures on county government are many. One novel idea for relieving the burdens on counties was suggested in California a while back, when the legislature considered a proposal to divide the state into seven regions that would be governed by thirteen-member elected boards.[16] These regional "super governments" would assume many of the development and infrastructure functions currently assigned to county governments. Although the bill did not pass, the performance of county government remains an issue in other parts of the nation. In Massachusetts, where cities and towns provide most local services, the state legislature abolished several counties, contending that they were superfluous in the Bay State. Clearly, county governments must continue to modernize and focus on the big picture or run the risk of being bypassed. With that in mind, voters in Allegheny County, Pennsylvania (the Pittsburgh area), approved a restructuring plan in 2005 that merged several elected county positions and made some elective offices appointed.[17]

LO 10-3
To identify the forms and functions of city government and the issues confronting municipalities around the country.

Municipal Government

Municipalities are cities; the words are synonymous and refer to a specific, populated territory, typically operating under a charter from state government. Cities differ from counties in terms of how they were created and what they do. Historically, they have been the primary units of local government in most societies—the grand enclaves of human civilization.

Creating Cities

A city is a legal recognition of settlement patterns in an area. In the most common procedure, residents of an area in a county petition the state for a charter of incorporation. The area slated for **incorporation** must meet certain criteria, such as population or density minimums. In Alabama, for instance, the population threshold required for incorporation is 300 people; in Arizona, the number is 1,500. In most cases, a referendum is required. The referendum enables citizens to vote on whether they wish to become an incorporated municipality. If the incorporation measure is successful, then the state grants a **charter**, and the newly created city has the legal authority to elect officials, levy taxes, and provide services to its residents. Not all cities have charters, however. Most California cities, for example, operate under general state law rather than a charter.

New cities are created every year. For instance, during a single six-year period, 145 places incorporated (and thirty-three cities disincorporated, or ceased to exist as official locales).[18] Although most new cities tend to be small, some begin with sizable populations. For example, more than 94,000 people were living in Jurupa Valley, California, when the city incorporated in 2011.

Like counties, cities are general-purpose units of local government. But unlike counties, they typically have greater decision-making authority and discretion. Almost all states have enacted home rule provisions for cities, although in some states, only those cities that have attained a certain population size can exercise this option. (One of the few states without home rule for cities, New Hampshire, sought to provide it through a constitutional amendment in 2000, but voters defeated the measure.) In addition, cities generally offer a wider array of services to their citizenry than most counties do. Police and fire services, public works, and parks and recreation are standard features, supplemented in some cities by publicly maintained cemeteries, city-owned and operated housing, city-run docks, city-sponsored festivals, and city-constructed convention centers. Municipal government picks up garbage and trash, sweeps streets, maintains traffic signals, and plants trees.

City Governmental Structure

Nearly all city governments operate with one of three structures: a mayor–council form, a council–manager form, or a city commission form. In each structure, an elected governing body, typically called a *city council*, has policy-making authority. What differentiates the three structures is the manner in which the executive branch is organized.

Mayor–Council Form In the mayor–council form of government, executive functions such as the appointment of department heads are performed by elected officials. This form of government can be subdivided into two types, depending on the formal powers held by the mayor. In a **strong-mayor-council structure**, the mayor is the source of executive leadership. Strong mayors run city hall the way governors run the statehouse. They are responsible for daily administrative activities, the hiring and firing of top-level city officials, and budget preparation. They have a potential veto over council actions.

incorporation
The creation of a municipality through the granting of a charter from the state.

charter
A document that sets out a city's structure, authority, and functions.

strong-mayor-council structure
The mayor is empowered to perform the executive functions of government and has a veto over city council actions.

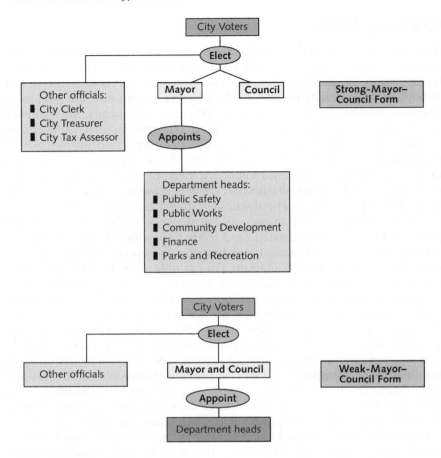

Figure 10.4 Mayor–Council Form of Government

The primary difference between these two structures concerns the power and authority possessed by the mayor. Strong mayors are more ideally situated to exert influence and control.

weak-mayor–council structure
The mayor lacks formal executive power; the city council (of which the mayor is a member) is the source of executive and legislative power.

The strong-mayor–council structure grew out of dissatisfaction in the late nineteenth century with the **weak-mayor–council structure**. The weak-mayor–council structure, which has its roots in the colonial period of American history, limits the mayor's role to that of executive figurehead. The council (of which the mayor is a member) is the source of executive power and legislative power. The council appoints city officials and develops the budget, and the mayor has no veto power. They perform ceremonial tasks such as speaking for the city, chairing council meetings, and attending ribbon-cutting festivities. A structurally weak mayor can emerge as a powerful political figure in the city, but only if they posses informal sources of power. For example, Chicago has a weak-mayor–council form of government, but the mayor of Chicago has historically been a powerful figure in the city.[19] Figure 10.4 highlights the structural differences between the strong- and weak-mayor–council forms of city government.

Figure 10.5 Council–Manager Form of Government

The council–manager form of government places administrative responsibility in the hands of a skilled professional. The intent is to make the operation of city government less political.

Mayor–council structures are popular both in large cities (in which populations are greater than 250,000) and in small cities (with populations under 10,000). In large cities, the clash of conflicting interests requires the leadership of an empowered politician, a strong mayor. In small communities, however, the mayor–council structure is a low-cost, part-time operation. Many large cities in which the administrative burdens of the mayor's job are especially heavy have established the position of general manager or chief administrative officer to assist the mayor.

Council–Manager Form The second city government structure, the council–manager form, emphasizes the separation of politics (the policy-making activities of the governing body) from administration (the execution of the policies enacted by the governing body). Theoretically, the city council makes policy, and administrators execute policy. Under this structure, the council hires a professional administrator to manage city government. Figure 10.5 illustrates this structure. (An important variation within the council–manager form is whether the mayor is directly elected by the voters [in 63 percent of council–manager cities] or selected by the council from its membership [37 percent].[20])

The administrator (usually called a **city manager**) appoints and removes department heads, oversees service delivery, develops personnel policies, and prepares budget proposals for the council. These responsibilities alone make the manager an important figure in city government. But add to them the power to make policy recommendations to the city council, and the position becomes even more powerful. In council–manager cities, the council and the manager typically have a working understanding about how far the manager

city manager
A professional administrator hired by a city council to handle the day-to-day operation of the city.

can venture into the policy-making realm of city government. Because a manager's job carries great responsibilities and requires advanced education and training, it typically pays well. The International City/County Management Association (ICMA) annual salary study showed median salaries of about $80,000 for managers serving in communities under 2,500 in population to more than $300,000 for managers in cities of 250,000 or more.[21]

More than half of U.S. cities use the council–manager form of city government. Among cities of 25,000 to 75,000 people, the council–manager structure predominates; it is also popular in more homogeneous suburban communities and in the newer cities of the Sunbelt region. Examples of large cities with a council–manager structure include Phoenix, San Antonio, and Dallas.

City Commission Form Under the city commission form of government, illustrated in Figure 10.6, legislative and executive functions are merged. Commissioners not only make policy as members of the city's governing body but they also head the major departments of city government. In other words, they are both policy makers and policy executors. One of the commissioners is designated as mayor simply to preside over commission meetings.

The commission form of government was created as a reaction to the mayor–council structure. Its origins can be traced back to the inability of a mayor–council government in Galveston, Texas, to respond to the chaos caused by a hurricane in 1900 that demolished the city and killed 6,000 people. Bowing to gubernatorial pressure, the Texas legislature authorized the creation of a totally new form of city government—a commission form—and by 1904, the new city government had entirely rebuilt Galveston. The success of the commission led to its adoption first by other Texas cities (Houston, Dallas, Fort Worth) and then, within a decade, by 160 other municipalities (such as Des Moines, Iowa; Pittsburgh, Pennsylvania; Buffalo, New York; Nashville, Tennessee; and Charlotte, North Carolina). Its appeal was its ostensible reduction of politics in city government.

But almost as fast as the city commission form of government appeared, disillusionment set in. One problem stemmed from the predictable tendency of commissioners to act as advocates for their own departments. Each commissioner wanted a larger share of the city's budget allocated to their department. Another problem had to do with politicians acting as administrators: Elected officials do

Figure 10.6 City Commission Form of Government

Executive leadership is fragmented under a commission form of government. Each commissioner heads a department; together, they run city hall.

not always turn out to be good managers. The result was that public enthusiasm for the city commission form declined. By 1990, when Tulsa, Oklahoma, installed a mayor–council form in place of its commission system, only a few cities continued to use a commission structure. Notable among them was Portland, Oregon, with its modified commission form of government. And Portland likes its commission form. A measure to change to a council–manager structure was handily defeated by voters in 2007. The issue re-emerged in 2019 when the City Club of Portland commissioned a major study evaluating Portland's government. Residents of Portland may get to vote again soon to scrap the commission.[22]   (Some council–manager cities such as Ft. Lauderdale, Florida, and Grand Rapids, Michigan, call their city council a "commission," but they do not have a formal commission structure as described here.)

Which Form of City Government Is Best?

Experts disagree about which city government structure is best. Most would probably agree that structures lacking a strong executive officer are generally less preferable than others. By that standard, the weak-mayor–council and the commission forms are less favorable. The strong-mayor–council form of government is extolled for fixing accountability firmly in the mayor's office, and the council–manager system is credited with professionalizing city government by bringing in skilled administrators to run things. Yet strong-mayor structures are criticized for concentrating power in the mayor's office; council–manager forms are taken to task for placing too much power in the hands of an unelected city manager. One study adds some clarity with its finding that cities that lack a professional administrator tend to have more conflict and less cooperation in formulating public policy.[23] Ultimately, it is up to community residents to decide which form of government they want, and several have made structural changes over the years.

In 2004, Richmond, Virginia, switched from a weak-mayor structure to a strong-mayor form; in 2006, San Diego replaced its city manager with a strong mayor. In Sacramento, it was the mayor who personally took up the strong-mayor cause; the city council put the question on the 2014 ballot, where it was rejected by voters. El Paso, Texas, however moved in a different direction and abandoned its strong-mayor structure and joined the ranks of council–manager cities. For some cities, a hybrid form that combines features of several structures may be the answer. For instance, both Oakland, California, and Cincinnati, Ohio, amended their council–manager form of government by adding a strong-mayor position and retaining the position of city manager. In fact, the distinction between the mayor–council form and the council–manager form may be blurring as more cities tinker with their structures, designing entities that contain elements of both.[24] A 2009 study of Michigan cities found just such a pattern.[25]

Pressing Issues for Cities

The pressing issues in city governments these days include planning and land use, annexation, finances, representation, and technology. Although the issues are discussed separately in the following subsections, they are frequently intertwined.

For instance, decisions about land use can affect the city's finances; the annexation of new territory may alter representation patterns; and technology affects everything.

Planning and Land Use Land is important to city governments for their economic and political well-being. City governments control land uses within their boundaries and frequently use a comprehensive plan (often called a *general* or *master plan*) to guide them. The plan divides the city into sections for commercial, industrial, and residential uses. In addition, a city might set aside areas for recreation and open space. For example, the general plan for Santa Barbara, California, designates portions of the city for parks, bikeways, and a bird refuge.

New York City enacted the first modern zoning **ordinance** in 1916; since then, cities have used *zoning* to effect land-use planning and control. Through zoning, the designations established in a city's plan are made specific. For example, land set aside for residential use may be zoned for single-family dwellings, multifamily units, or mobile homes. Commercial areas may be zoned for offices, shopping centers, or hotels. Industrial sections of the city are often separated into "light" and "heavy" zones. In addition, cities can overlay special zones onto existing ones. For instance, cities intending to restore older sections of the commercially zoned downtown area may establish historic preservation zones. Once these zones are so designated, property owners are prohibited from tearing down old structures there and, instead, are encouraged to renovate them. A city eager to transform the appearance of a particular area may also create special zones so it can regulate architectural style or the height of buildings and thus achieve the right "look." Cincinnati has a special zoning overlay that created a gas streetlamp district where street lighting is provided solely by old-fashioned gas lamps.[26]

Once set, zoning can be altered through applications for variances and rezoning, usually heard by a city's planning commission, and subsequently approved or denied by the city council. A variance is a waiver of a zoning requirement such as a minimum lot size or a building height limit. Rezoning involves a change in zoning designation, either to allow more intense use of the land (an upzoning) or to restrict use (downzoning). Applications for variances and rezoning are often controversial. A study of fourteen years' worth of applications to upzone parcels in Wilmington, Delaware, demonstrated that community sentiment played an important role in the outcome.[27]

Zoning is ultimately a political exercise with economic consequences. Cities use zoning to promote "good" growth such as upscale residential areas and to limit "bad" growth such as low-income housing.[28] Some cities have engaged in a practice that became known as *exclusionary zoning*. For example, a city might restrict its residential zones to 4,500-square-foot single-family dwellings on five-acre lots. The resulting high cost of housing would effectively limit the pool of potential residents to the wealthy. Recent research has documented greater segregation by income in metropolitan areas in which suburbs restrict the density of residential construction compared with places with more permissive density zoning rules.[29] Court decisions have not only found exclusionary

ordinance
Enacted by the governing body, it is the local government equivalent of a statute.

zoning illegal, but they have also instructed local governments to provide housing opportunities for low- and moderate-income people.

Annexation **Annexation** has been a popular means by which cities can add territory, population, and tax base. In the past fifty years, many cities have found themselves squeezed by the rapid growth and incorporation of territory just outside city limits and hence beyond their control. What is worse (from a central city's perspective), some of these suburban cities have begun to threaten the central city's traditional dominance of the metropolitan area. People and jobs are finding suburban locales to their liking, and many have left the central city. To counteract this trend and to ensure adequate space for future expansion, some cities have engaged in annexation efforts. During one six-year period, U.S. cities added nearly 3.5 million acres of land via 45,000 annexations.[30]

Not all cities can annex, however. They run up against two realities: the strictures of state laws and the existence of incorporated suburbs on their borders (which means the territory cannot be annexed). State governments determine the legal procedures for the annexation process, and they can make it easy or hard.[31] Texas is a state that made it easy for cities to annex (e.g., by not requiring consent of those who live in the area to be annexed) and, not surprisingly, big Texas cities (in terms of population) have vast territories: Houston covers 600 square miles; San Antonio, 465 square miles; and Dallas, 386 square miles. In 2019, the Texas annexation law changed to require voter approval in areas to be annexed by cities. Will this end municipal annexation in Texas? Not if lessons from another state are applicable. In 2011, North Carolina ended involuntary annexation and now requires voter approval in areas cities are seeking to annex. While this slowed down city annexations in North Carolina, it hasn't ended them. Most post-2011 annexation now comes from voluntary annexation petitions from landowners and developers.[32] Both Texas and North Carolina cities can still use their power of **extraterritorial jurisdiction (ETJ)** to supplement annexation. Under ETJ, they can control subdivision practices in unincorporated bordering territory. (The amount of territory varies from a half-mile for small cities to five miles for cities with more than 250,000 people.)

Some states make it difficult for their cities to annex. Cities may have to wait for landowners in an adjoining area to petition to be annexed. In some instances, a city bent on annexation will put pressure on landowners outside the city who use city services such as water or sewer. Agree to be annexed, they say, or the price of the service may skyrocket or, even worse, the service might be curtailed.[33] In some states, even when a majority of the landowners request annexation, referendum elections must be held if the proportion is less than 75 percent. State law may require that the annexation be approved by referendum by both the existing city and the area to be annexed. This stipulation is known as a *dual majority*, and it complicates the annexation process.

Some of the most prominent U.S. cities have rather confined city limits. The most extreme cases are Newark, New Jersey (covering 24.2 square miles); Miami, Florida (35.9); Buffalo, New York (40.4); San Francisco, California

annexation
The addition of unincorporated adjacent territory to a municipality.

extraterritorial jurisdiction (ETJ)
The ability of a city government to control certain practices in an adjacent, unincorporated area.

(46.9); and Boston, Massachusetts (48.3).[34] On the other hand are cities with large areas such as Jacksonville, (747.0 square miles), Oklahoma City (606.4), Houston (599.6), and Phoenix (516.7). But the largest big city by far is Anchorage, Alaska, with a whopping land area of 1,705 square miles—larger than the state of Rhode Island. In the older, established metropolitan areas, a central city has little room to expand because it is hemmed in by incorporated suburbs. Suburban areas incorporate—that is, become legal municipal entities—for many reasons. The threat of being annexed by a neighboring city frequently stimulates the creation of new cities. Sometimes this has odd results. For example, the city of Hamtramck, Michigan, is surrounded by Detroit. Hamtramck incorporated in the early twentieth century in order to prevent annexation by Detroit.

Finances City governments, like other local governments, must balance their fiscal resources against their fiscal needs. Unlike the national government, however, these governments have to operate within the constraints of a balanced budget. As a result, they have become fairly creative at finding new sources of revenue in hard times.

One standard approach to budget-balancing is to reduce the rate of growth in operational spending (expenditures related to service provision, such as city employee salaries). Another popular mechanism is to increase the level of fees and charges. For instance, a city might increase the cost of a building permit or charge more for health inspections at restaurants. It can also hike the cost of parking in a metered space or in a city-owned parking garage. (Commuting students at urban colleges with inadequate parking have probably marveled at how adept city officials are at the "make students pay" strategy.) Indeed, cities can boost revenues in several seemingly small ways. A city service that used to be free, such as a city park, may now have an admission fee. Cities can postpone or reduce their capital spending (expenditures for big-ticket items such as installation of sewer systems or the purchase of fire engines) and contract out services to private providers, for example, allowing a waste-disposal firm to collect residential garbage or a local charity to take over the operation of homeless shelters. The Controversies in States and Localities feature takes up one remedy that many cities are pursuing: the outsourcing of city services.

Cities and other local governments found the financial going tough during the recessionary period late in the first decade of the twenty-first century.[35] Figure 10.7 shows how rapidly the fiscal situation deteriorated in city governments. In 2007, 70 percent of city finance officers reported that they were better able to meet their city's financial needs than in the year before. By 2009, only 12 percent reported this to be the case, the lowest figure in decades. From 2011 to 2016, the fiscal situation improved; then it dropped in 2017 but improved until the COVID-19 pandemic in 2020. As of 2019, views of the economy began to decline. Growth in revenue slowed (especially in large Midwestern cities), and two in three finance officers saw a recession coming as soon as 2020.[36] Very few, however, foresaw the extent of the COVID-19 recession that hit the nation in spring 2020. The National Bureau of Economic

Controversies in States and Localities

Outsourcing City Services

When cities face budget deficits, they seek to reduce costs. For some cities and towns, outsourcing city services—contracting with nonprofit organizations, private firms, and other governments to provide the services—can be part of the solution. In San Jose, California, in 2010, as the reality of a $118 million-dollar deficit became clear, city officials cast about for any cost-savings they could find. One solution was to hire private janitorial firms to clean both city hall and the airport, saving the city $4 million. Sandy Springs, Georgia, a newly incorporated city outside Atlanta, has gone even further by contracting out a range of services to a private firm.

For some localities, outsourcing is a way of life. Consider the city of Weston, Florida, an affluent planned community that was incorporated in 1996. The city has a population of 65,000, an annual budget of $135 million, and only ten city employees. City services, ranging from park maintenance to public safety, are provided through thirty-five contracts with private firms and with county government. A visitor to City Hall might see individuals working in various offices, but they are employees of private companies that are paid by the city. What makes Weston even more different from other outsourcing cities is that the city's charter expressly discourages hiring city employees. The only way for the city to bring a service under the purview of city government is for four of the five city council members to approve an exception.

Outsourcing offers several potential advantages to cities. The most obvious is that outsourcing usually saves cities money. If several private firms bid on a contract, the resulting cost competition works to a city's benefit. Another advantage that cities enjoy

through outsourcing is flexibility: Employees can be hired and laid off as demand necessitates, avoiding labor disputes with unionized city employees.

However, outsourcing is not a perfect solution. Many critics assert that outsourcing makes employees less accountable to the city and its residents. And there is always the risk that the private firm may not deliver the service as specified by the terms of the contract. Finally, negotiating contracts and monitoring compliance can be a complicated and arduous process. City governments need to exercise due diligence to make outsourcing work.

Weston, Florida, and Sandy Springs, Georgia, have moved much farther along the outsourcing path than most cities have. But it is clear that even among the most traditional city governments that have relied on city employees to provide services, the attraction of outsourcing some city services is strong.

Critical Thinking Questions

1. Does your city government outsource the delivery of certain public services? If so, what are they?

2. From the city government's perspective, what are the differences between contracting with a private firm, a nonprofit organization, or another local government?

3. What can a city government do if a contractor fails to deliver an agreed-upon public service? What are the possible consequences of the city's actions?

Sources: Jonas Prager, "Contract City Redux: Weston, Florida as the Ultimate New Public Management City," *Public Administration Review* 68 (January/February 2008); John Ruch, "Is the 'Sandy Springs Model' of Government Changing?" *Reporter Newspapers*, www.reporternewspapers.net (July 8, 2016).

Research's Business Cycle Dating Committee officially declared the United States to be in a recession as of February 2020 when extreme volatility hit stock exchange transactions. For example, the Dow Jones Industrial Average declined from a high of over 29,000 in early February to a low of just over 18,000 a month later.[37] While many think this recession will be short lived—perhaps only as long as COVID-19 remains at pandemic levels—the Federal Reserve has projected a much longer road to full economic recovery, as long as two years.[38]

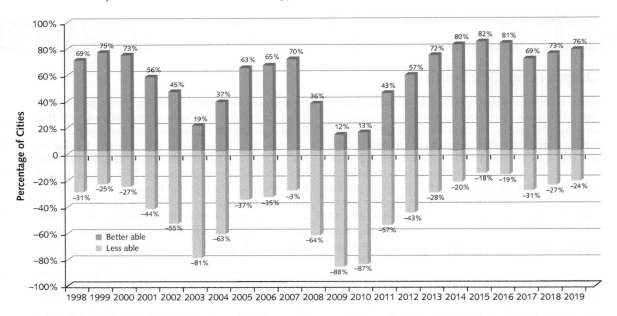

Figure 10.7 Percentage of Cities "Better Able/Less Able" to Meet Financial Needs, 1998–2019

Source: National League of Cities, "City Fiscal Conditions 2019," https://www.nlc.org/sites/default/files/2019-10/CS_Fiscal%20Conditions%20 2019Web%20final.pdf (accessed February 22, 2020).

at-large elections
Citywide (or county-wide) contests to determine the members of a city council (or county commission).

district (ward) elections
Elections in which the voters in one district or ward of a jurisdiction (city, county, school district) vote for a candidate to represent that district.

reform movement
An early twentieth-century effort to depoliticize local governments through nonpartisan elections, at-large representation, shorter ballots, and professional management.

Representation Representation in city government is another fundamental concern. How can citizens' preferences be represented effectively in city hall? In the colonial days of town meetings and civic republics, it was simple: A citizen showed up at the meeting hall, voiced their opinion, and the majority ruled. When this procedure proved to be unwieldy, a system of representative democracy seemed the perfect solution.

In city governments, city council members are elected in one of two ways: either at large or by districts (also called wards). In **at-large elections**, a city voter can vote in each council race. (One modification of the at-large approach requires candidates to compete for a specific seat or "place" on the council; however, the vote is citywide.) In **district (ward) elections**, a city voter can vote only in the council race in their district. From the perspective of candidates, the at-large system means that a citywide campaign must be mounted. With districts, a candidate's campaign is limited to a specific area of the city. The structural **reform movement** during the Progressive Era advocated at-large elections as a means of weakening the geographic base of political machines. Candidates running in citywide races must appeal to a broad cross section of the population to be successful.

The use of at-large electoral systems has significant consequences. An in-depth study of almost 1,000 city council members across the country revealed that at-large members tended to be wealthier and more highly educated than council members elected from districts.[39] At-large council members also differ from district members in terms of their relationships with constituents. Council members elected at large devote less time to answering individual complaints and direct their attention to a citywide and business constituency.

Almost half of U.S. cities with populations of 2,500 or more use an at-large method for electing their council members, but the popularity of the method decreases as the size of a city's population increases. For example, less than 15 percent of cities with populations above a half-million use at-large elections. This approach to city council representation is increasingly under attack for diminishing the likelihood that a member of a minority group can be elected. Research on more than 1,000 southern communities indicated that the abolition of at-large elections resulted in dramatic gains in black representation.[40] And the impact is not confined to the South. When New York City redrew city council district lines and increased the number of seats after the 2010 census, the resulting council was composed of more African Americans and Latinos than ever before.

Although research on the topic continues, studies have shown that changing the electoral system from at-large to districts has other effects, too, such as an overall increase in citizen participation in terms of greater attendance at council meetings, higher voter turnout, and a larger number of candidates. These findings are not universal, however. For example, one study of fifty-seven cities compared voter turnout in the two different electoral systems and found that turnout in district elections actually outpaced turnout in at-large elections by nearly six percentage points.[41] Furthermore, it is not altogether clear that changing to districts will translate into policy benefits for the previously underrepresented sectors of the city. Earlier research suggested that in terms of attitudes toward public policy, there was really no significant difference between council members elected at large and those elected from districts.[42] However, this tendency may not hold up when it comes to minority employment. Research in Texas showed that, even after accounting for other factors, school systems in which school board members were elected from wards hired more minority school administrators than at-large systems did.[43]

Several alternatives have been tried in jurisdictions where minority candidates have met with persistent electoral defeat. Two of these are **cumulative voting** and **ranked-choice voting**. In cumulative voting, candidates run at large, and voters cast as many votes as there are seats to be filled. The voter may allocate these votes as they wish, either as a bloc for one candidate or spread out among the candidates. In a community with a history of racially or ethnically polarized voting, the chance of minority-candidate success increases under a cumulative-voting arrangement. For example, when Alamogordo, New Mexico, adopted cumulative voting, a Latino candidate who would have finished fourth in a standard at-large election placed third in total votes cast.[44] Because three seats were being contested, the difference between a third- and fourth-place finish meant the difference between winning and losing. In ranked-choice voting (sometimes called instant runoff), voters rank the candidates on the ballot by their preference—first choice, second choice, and so on. First choices are tallied and if one candidate gets more than a majority, that candidate is declared the winner. If no candidate gets a majority,

cumulative voting
Candidates compete at large and voters can cast as many votes as there are seats to be filled, either as a bloc for one candidate or spread out among several candidates.

ranked-choice voting
Voters rank candidates as first choice, second choice, and so on. If a candidate receives a majority of first-choice preferences, the candidate wins. If no candidate gets a majority, second-choice preferences are consulted. Sometimes called instant runoff.

Entryway to Oakland Park, a city in Broward County, Florida.

the candidate with the fewest first choice votes is eliminated and that person's votes are redistributed based on second choices. This goes on until one candidate attains a majority. There has been a flurry of recent interest in both of these alternative voting systems recently. Ranked-choice voting has been used in Cambridge, Massachusetts, for many years but has recently been adopted in Berkeley, Oakland, and San Francisco, California, and Santa Fe and Las Cruces, New Mexico, and other cities. New York City will begin using ranked-choice voting in its mayoral and city council elections in 2021. Cumulative voting is being used in some elections in sixty-three jurisdictions in the United States, including Amarillo, Texas; Peoria, Illinois; Port Chester, New York; and Mission Viejo, California.[45]

Technology Smart Cities is a phrase that is often used to refer to the use of technology—in particular the internet of things (IoT)—by cities to collect data, analyze it, and develop city services and programs to address the needs expressed in the data. The initiative involves the use of sensors to feed real-time data to city offices on activities so that services can be customized accordingly. Examples are numerous. Sensors in public trash cans can provide data on the level of trash in the can, allowing city sanitation trucks to skip some cans and service others more frequently, cutting costs while increasing responsiveness. Sensors embedded in curbs can tell drivers looking for parking spaces where the open spaces are, reducing the amount of time spent searching for parking. This can result in less air pollution, traffic congestion, and lower levels of driver frustration. Sensors in traffic lights can increase the time that green lights are on when traffic is heavy on one street at certain times of the day, speeding commuters to work or home after work.

U.S. cities have been experimenting with Smart City technology for the last decade. New York City, for example, is replacing pay telephones with

Smart City
The use of the internet of things (IoT) to enable cities to customize services by collecting data from a variety of sensors.

smart kiosks. The city's LinkNYC initiative offers free Wi-Fi and nationwide calling as well as a charging station for cell phones, weather forecasts, maps, transit updates, and a connection to the city's 311 service. The technology is free because advertising supports its cost.[46] In 2015, the federal Department of Transportation (DOT) hosted the Smart City Challenge where large cities proposed ambitious Smart City plans whose implementation would be assisted by federal funding. Seventy-eight cities submitted proposals; the winner was Columbus, Ohio. With $40 million in federal funds and $10 million in private funding, Columbus is implementing its plan, which calls for such things as electric autonomous shuttles that will ferry commuters from parking lots outside of the downtown area to their places of business and then back to their cars in the evening; truck platooning that will allow connected long-haul trucks to be able to convoy by adapting speeds, braking, and navigation; and the installation of some 3,000 communication units in cars and 175 at intersections to help prevent car collisions and ease traffic congestion.[47]

Smart City technology promises to make cities more efficient and effective in delivering services to residents, commuters, and visitors. But is it worth the investment? Upgrading technology by large cities around the world was recently estimated to cost $41 trillion over the next twenty years.[48] Chattanooga, Tennessee, was an early leader in the Smart City movement. It used a $110 million grant from the 2009 American Reinvestment and Recovery Act to build a fiber optic network along its public utility routes. The result was a citywide internet system with speeds some 200 times faster than the average of other cities in the United States. Within five years, Chattanooga turned the initial $110 million investment into attracting 671 companies with 14,000 employees and creating more than $1.8 billion in value.[49] But to follow Chattanooga's or Columbus's lead, other cities need to develop the initial investment, which may no longer be available from the federal government.

Related to Smart Cities is the recent development of 311 technology in U.S. cities. Beginning in 1996, Baltimore developed a system to allow residents to report graffiti or potholes or other urban annoyances to a centralized city office, avoiding the use of emergency 911 services that people had been using for these reports. The idea caught on and is being used throughout the country as a method of reporting conditions that might be important to the complainer but don't require immediate or emergency response by city government.[50] The system—now available not only by phone but also by the internet, social media, or mobile phone app—has become incredibly popular in large cities throughout the United States. New York City reported more than 44 million 311 contacts in 2018 alone.[51] Questions, of course, have arisen about the use of 311 services—what do people complain about on 311? Does 311 benefit everyone or do some groups and neighborhoods benefit more than others? An analysis of 2018 311 calls in New York City shows that 28 percent were about buildings (no heat, no hot water, etc.), 17 percent were about public spaces (illegal parking, blocked driveways, unsanitary conditions), 16 percent were about noise, 11 percent about street conditions, 2 percent about social disorder, with 26 percent about all other conditions. Less than 0.2 percent of the calls concerned drug activity, disorderly youths, or public drinking.[52] A second recent study of fifteen cities addresses the equity of 311, showing no systematic differences in city responses to service requests between predominantly minority and nonminority neighborhoods or between wealthier and poorer neighborhoods.[53]

LO 10-4
To evaluate the roles and future of town and township government.

Towns and Townships

The word *town* evokes an image of a small community where everyone knows everyone else, where government is informal, and where local leaders gather at the coffee shop to make important decisions. This image is both accurate and inaccurate. Towns generally are smaller, in terms of population and land area, than cities or counties. And the extent of their governmental powers depends on state government. But even where they are relatively weak, town government is increasingly becoming more formalized.

How Do We Know a Town when We See One?

Towns and townships are general-purpose units of local government, distinct from county and city governments. Only twenty states, primarily in the Northeast and Midwest, have official towns or townships. In some states, these small jurisdictions have relatively broad powers; in others, they have a more circumscribed role. In some states, the word *town* simply means a municipality smaller than a city but larger than a village, a definition used by geographers.[54]

In New England, towns offer the kinds of services commonly associated with cities and counties in other states. Many New England towns continue their tradition of direct democracy through a **town meeting** form of government. At a yearly town assembly, residents make decisions on policy matters confronting the community. They elect town officials, pass local ordinances, levy taxes, and adopt a budget. In other words, the people who attend the town meeting function as a legislative body. Although the mechanism of the town meeting exemplifies democracy in action, it often falls short of the ideal, primarily due to the relatively low rate of citizen participation in meetings. Often, fewer than 10 percent of a town's voters actually attend the meeting. Those who do show up tend to be older and, not surprisingly, more engaged in politics in general. Research has found that "some citizens are in fact turned off by the lack of civility of the face-to-face interactions at town meetings."[55] Larger towns in Connecticut and Massachusetts rely on representatives elected by residents to vote at the meetings.

town meeting
An annual event at which a town's residents enact ordinances, elect officials, levy taxes, and adopt a budget.

Towns in New England, along with those in New Jersey, New York, and Pennsylvania, enjoy fairly broad powers. In large measure, they act like other general-purpose units of government. Townships in Michigan and in Wisconsin (townships are called towns in the Badger State) are similarly empowered. In the remainder of the township states (Illinois, Indiana, Kansas, Minnesota, Missouri, Nebraska, North Dakota, Ohio, and South Dakota), the nature of township government is more rural. Rural townships tend to stretch across 36 square miles of land (conforming to the surveys done by the national government before the areas were settled), and their service offerings are often limited to roads and law enforcement. In one state, Indiana, townships actually cover the entire territory and population with other jurisdictional units superimposed on them. (Revisit Figure 10.1 near the beginning of this chapter.) A part-time elected board of supervisors or trustees commonly rules the roost in townships. In addition, some of the jobs in government may be staffed by volunteers rather than salaried workers. However, the closer these rural townships are to large urban areas, the more likely they are to offer an expanded set of services to residents.

The Future of Towns and Townships

The demise of the township type of government has long been expected. As rural areas become more populated, they will eventually meet the population minimums necessary to become municipalities. In 2000, for instance, residents of a Minnesota township decided to incorporate as a municipality to ward off annexation by a neighboring city.[56] Even in New England, questions of town viability have arisen. For example, many Connecticut towns with populations exceeding 15,000 have found it increasingly difficult to operate effectively through town meetings.[57] Accordingly, some are adding professional managers, whereas others are considering a shift to a strong-mayor form of government.

Some other towns face a different problem. Many are experiencing substantial population exodus and, in the process, losing their reason for existence. These towns may die a natural death, with other types of government (perhaps counties or special districts) providing services to the remaining residents. The question is: Do towns and townships make sense in contemporary America? Despite dire predictions of their pending demise, towns and townships have proved to be remarkably resilient. The U.S. Census Bureau counted 16,253 towns and townships in 2017, down only 111 from the 2012 figure. Most of the decline came in Midwestern states.

Towns and townships have not sat idly by while commentators speculated on their dim future. They formed an interest group, the National Association of Towns and Townships (NATaT), to lobby on their behalf in Washington, D.C. Seven states have statewide town or township associations that offer services to member governments and promote town-related issues in the legislature. Also, many small towns have embarked on ambitious economic development strategies—industrial recruitment, tourism promotion, and amenity enhancement—in an attempt to stimulate new growth. Even as they grow in population, many towns want to maintain the image of a small community where everyone knows everyone else. The town of Cary, North Carolina, has a population of 162,000, larger than the cities of Wilmington (122,607) or Asheville (92,452). Cary has refused to retitle itself as a city partially because of evidence from a recent study of the Phoenix, Arizona, area that found "people viewed towns as more affordable than cities, cleaner, more charming, safer and better to retire to."[58] Many respondents in that study said they preferred living in towns but shopping in nearby cities.

LO 10-5
To analyze the need
for special districts
and the concerns
about them.

Special Districts

Special districts are established to meet certain service needs in a particular area. In other words, they do what other local governments cannot or will not do. Special districts can be formed in three different ways:

- States can create them through special enabling legislation.
- General-purpose local governments may adopt a resolution establishing a special district.
- Citizens may initiate districts by petition, which is often followed by a referendum on their creation.

Some districts have the power to levy taxes; others rely on user fees, grants, and private revenue bonds for funding. Taxing districts typically have elected governing boards; nontaxing districts—called **public authorities**—ordinarily operate with appointed boards.[59] The United States has approximately 38,500 special districts, and that number is increasing. In the fifteen-year period from 2002 to 2017, the number of special districts grew by nearly 3,500.[60] As one might expect, the pattern of special-district creation (and abolition) varies from one state to another. Colorado (1,214), Texas (553), and Florida (513) accounted for a large portion of the increase from 2002 to 2017. Indiana and Pennsylvania, however, reduced their special districts count by more than 400 and nearly 200, respectively, during that period.

Not all special districts are organized alike. Ninety-two percent of them provide a single function, but the functions vary. Natural resource management, fire protection, housing and community development, and water and sewer service are the most common. Among the 2,798 special districts in Texas are drainage districts, utility districts, river authorities, emergency services districts, sports facility authorities, community college districts, and hospital districts. Most states have other, state-specific districts, such as Colorado's mine drainage districts and tunnel districts or Florida's beach and shore preservation districts and mobile home park recreation districts. The budget and staff size of special districts range from minuscule to mammoth. Some of the more prominent include the Port Authority of New York and New Jersey, the Chicago Transit Authority, the Washington Public Power Supply System, and the Los Angeles County Sanitation District. The states of Illinois and California have the highest number of special districts (3,204 and 2,894, respectively). Alaska and Hawaii have the fewest by far, with fourteen and fifteen, respectively.

Why Special Districts Are Needed

Special districts overlay existing general-purpose local governments and address deficiencies in them.[61] Three general categories of "deficiencies" are worth examining: technical conditions, financial constraints, and political explanations.

First are the technical conditions of a general-purpose local government. In some states, cities cannot extend their service districts beyond their boundaries. Moreover, the problem to be addressed may not fit neatly within a single jurisdiction. A river that runs through several counties may periodically overflow its banks in heavy spring rains—a problem affecting small portions

public authority
A type of special district funded by nontax revenue and governed by an appointed board.

of many jurisdictions. A flood control district covering only the affected areas may be a logical solution. Problems of scale must also be considered. A general-purpose local government simply may not be able to provide electric service to its residents as efficiently as a special utility district that covers a multitude of counties. Finally, some states prohibit the jurisdictional co-venturing that would allow localities to offer services jointly with other jurisdictions. In that case, operation of a two-county library would require the establishment of a special two-county library district.

A second set of deficiencies has to do with financial constraints. Local general-purpose governments commonly operate under debt and tax limitations. Demands for additional services that exceed a jurisdiction's revenue-raising ceiling or lead to the assumption of excessive debt cannot be accommodated. By using special districts, existing jurisdictions can circumvent the debt and tax ceilings. (A study of Indiana's special districts found that they accounted for 8 percent of local government expenditures but carried approximately 38 percent of total local government debt in the state.[62]) Furthermore, special districts are better suited than general-purpose governments for service-charge or user-fee financing, whereby the cost of the service can be directly apportioned to the consumer (as with water or sewer charges). Research has confirmed that the more stringent the financial limitations that a state imposes on its county governments, the greater the number of special districts that are created in those counties.[63]

Technical and financial deficiencies of general-purpose local governments help to explain the creation of special districts, but political explanations shed even more light. Restrictive annexation laws and county governments with limited authority are political facts of life that encourage the use of special districts. For residents of an urban fringe area, a public-service district (which may provide more than one service) may be the only option. Some special districts owe their existence to a federal mandate. For example, national government policy has spurred the establishment of soil conservation and flood control districts throughout the country.

Once created, a special district may become a political power in its own right. In places where general-purpose governmental units are fully equipped legally, financially, and technically to provide a service, they may encounter resistance from special-district interests fighting to preserve an existing district.

Concerns About Special Districts

The arguments in favor of special districts revolve around their potential for efficient service provision and the likelihood that they will be responsive to constituents whose demands are not otherwise being met.[64] For the most part, however, scholarly observers look at special districts with a jaundiced eye. The most frequently heard complaint is that special districts lack accountability. The public is often unaware of their existence, so they function free of much scrutiny. A study of 100 airport and seaport districts found that those with an elected governing board were no more likely to be responsive to public preferences than those with appointed boards.[65] And as research by Nancy Burns reminds us, the establishment of special districts is a costly political act.[66]

Well-placed groups such as businesses, developers, and homeowners' associations are among the beneficiaries of special-district creation.

One thing is certain: The proliferation of special districts complicates the development of comprehensive solutions to public problems. It is not uncommon for cities and counties to be locked in governmental combat with the special districts in their area. All of these governmental units tend to be turf-protecting, service-providing, revenue-seeking rivals.[67] Despite the claims of district advocates, special districts may actually drive up the costs of service delivery. An analysis of 300 metropolitan areas compared services provided by special districts with those provided by general-purpose governments and found that districts actually had a higher per capita cost.[68]

Cognizant of these concerns, state governments are looking more closely at special districts and the role they play in service delivery. Several states have taken actions that give their general-purpose local governments more input into the decision to create special districts.

LO 10-6
To examine the politics and issues affecting school district government.

School Districts

School districts are a type of single-purpose local government. They are a distinct kind of special district and, as such, are considered one of the five types of local government. The trend in school districts follows the theory that fewer is better. Before World War II, more than 100,000 school districts covered the countryside. Many of these were rural, one-school operations. In many small towns, community identity was linked to the local schoolhouse. Despite serving as a source of pride, small districts were so expensive to maintain that consolidations have occurred throughout the nation, and by 2017 the number of districts was just under 13,000. Nebraska exemplifies the trend. In 1952, there were 6,392 school districts in the state; by 2017, the Cornhusker State had only 269. Now the states with the highest number of school districts by far are Texas (1,073) and California (1,011). The entire state of Hawaii is one school district.

School districts in the United States vary tremendously in the number of students they serve. All of New York City is one school district with a student population of more than one million students. The smallest is Washington Island, Wisconsin, with a student population of seventy-two. In southern states it is common for each county to be one school district. North Carolina, for example, has 100 counties and 115 school districts. Wake County Schools has a student population of more than 160,000, whereas Hyde County Schools only has 619 students. Many northern suburban areas have counties split up into multiple school districts. Nassau County, a Long Island suburb of New York City with a population of nearly 1.4 million, has fifty-six school districts, with student enrollment ranging from under 1,000 to just over 8,000 students.

School Politics

The school board is the formal source of power and authority in the district. The board is typically composed of five to seven members, usually elected in nonpartisan, at-large elections. Their job is to make policy for the school district. One of the most important policy decisions involves the district budget—how the money will be spent. Similar to what happens in special districts, some school districts have independent taxing authority, allowing them to collect taxes separately from the public. Other districts rely on the unit of general government in which they are located to collect taxes to fund schools. In some states, such as New York, Minnesota, and Wisconsin, independent school districts' budget proposals go to the public as referendums and must pass before money can be spent.

School districts are governed by these boards and managed by trained, full-time educational administrators. Like city governments, school districts invested heavily in the reform model of governance, and the average district has become more professional in operation in the past 40 years.[69] An appointed chief administrator (a superintendent) typically heads the school district staff, the size of which depends on the size of the district. (Superintendents of public schools are elected in only about 2 percent of school districts in the country.) Like city managers, the superintendent's job pays well. Median salaries in 2019 ranged from $92,000 for districts with fewer than 300 students to $232,000 for districts with 25,000 students or more.[70] The staff plays an important role in making sure that new laws adopted by the state are implemented by schools in the district.

Revamping public education has been a hot topic for the past two decades. Concern over mismanagement of funds and low student achievement has led some states to shift control of schools away from the school district itself and place it in the hands of city government, typically in the mayor's office, for a period of time. New York City, Chicago, Baltimore, Cleveland, and Detroit are among the most prominent examples. At the same time, other school districts have sought to decentralize, shifting power to the individual school level. This school-based management approach has meant greater involvement of the private sector in some schools; in others it has enhanced the role of teachers and parents. Regardless, these efforts all share the same basic objective: improving the performance of public schools.

School District Issues

Among the myriad challenges faced by school districts is one persistent conundrum: how to secure sufficient funding for public education. Although the relationship is a bit more complex than the old saying "you get what you pay for," there is widespread agreement that children in well-funded school districts are better off educationally than those in poorly funded ones.

Serious disparities in school funding, caused by wide differences in the available property taxes that provide much of the revenue for public education, have led to the increasing financial involvement of state government in local school districts. State governments use an **equalization formula** to distribute funds to school districts in an effort to reduce financial disparities. Under this formula, poorer school districts receive a proportionately larger share of state funds than wealthier districts do. Although these programs have increased the amount of funding for education, they have not eliminated the interdistrict variation. Wealthier districts simply use the state guarantee as a foundation on which to heap their own resources; poorer school districts continue to operate with less revenue. This situation prompted many state supreme courts around the country to declare their public-school finance

equalization formula A means of distributing funds (primarily to school districts) to reduce financial disparities among districts.

systems unconstitutional. Legislatures struggled to design new, more equitable financial arrangements. Michigan lowered property taxes for schools and substituted sales taxes and other revenues. Other states have established lotteries and earmarked the proceeds for education. The issue of money for schools stays at the top of legislative agendas, year in and year out.

LO 10-7
To evaluate the issue of "good" governance at the local level.

Communities and Governance

Let us return to the governance issue that was raised early in this chapter and has been alluded to throughout: How do we know when a community is well governed? This chapter is full of examples of communities restructuring their governments in hopes of improving governance. Voters oust incumbents and elect new council members in a similar effort. Conflict over local government spending priorities ensues. Local jurisdictions embark on innovative efforts to respond to their citizens' concerns. And on and on. The good news is research has found evidence that the policies enacted by city governments do tend to reflect the preferences of their citizens.[71] Cities with more liberal populations adopt more liberal policies; cities with conservative electorates enact more conservative policies.

On the whole, the American public seems to be reasonably satisfied with their local governments. Table 10.2 reports the results of Gallup polls conducted periodically that ask respondents about their trust and confidence in local government. Public opinion tends to be positive and stable over time with between 68 and 72 percent of respondents answering either "a great deal" or "a fair amount" of trust and confidence in localities.

Table 10.2 Public Opinion: Trust in Local Government

Poll Question: How much trust and confidence do you have in the local governments in the area where you live when it comes to handling local problems—a great deal, a fair amount, not very much, or none at all?

	GREAT DEAL (%)	FAIR AMOUNT (%)	NOT VERY MUCH (%)	NONE AT ALL (%)	NO OPINION (%)
2020	24	47	20	9	0
2019	24	47	21	8	1
2018	24	48	20	8	0
2017	23	47	20	9	1
2016	23	48	21	8	1
2015	19	51	20	9	1
2014	24	48	18	8	1
2013	21	50	19	9	1
2012	23	51	16	8	1
2011	19	49	21	11	1
2010	19	51	20	10	1
2009	19	50	22	8	1
2008	23	49	17	9	2

Source: Adapted from Gallup poll, "Trust in Government." https://news.gallup.com/poll/5392/trust-government .aspx (accessed November 7, 2020).

Although there is no universally accepted set of criteria for evaluating the quality of governance, several researchers and organizations have come up with proxy measures.[72] For example, the National Civic League bestows its "All-America City" designation on ten jurisdictions (cities, counties, and metro areas) that successfully tackle serious community problems in a collaborative way. These jurisdictions won the accolade in 2020:

- Algoma, Wisconsin
- Danville Virginia
- El Paso, Texas
- Franklin, Tennessee
- Miami Gardens, Florida
- Muncie, Indiana
- Pitt County, North Carolina
- Portsmouth, Ohio
- Rancho Cucamonga, California
- Rochester, New York[73]

The award-winning projects dealt with civic engagement in issues ranging from improving the health of young people to neighborhood revitalization, disaster recovery, and neighborhood garden development.

The governance question goes back to Plato and Aristotle, and we are unlikely to resolve it here. But the approach used in identifying All-America cities—tackling serious community problems in a collaborative way—offers some guidance for continued discussion about government structure and function.

 # Chapter Recap

- Theoretically, communities can be considered civic republics, corporate enterprises, or consumer markets. Legally, there are five types of local governments: counties, municipalities, towns and townships, special districts, and school districts. The United States has more than 90,000 local governments.

- Counties were created by states to serve as their local administrative extensions. Over time, they have taken on more functions and, especially in urban areas, they provide municipal-type services.

- The United States has more than 19,000 municipalities, or cities. The strong-mayor–council form of city government invests power in an elected mayor; the council–manager structure relies heavily on a professional administrator to run the city. The issue

about which structure is better instigates much debate.

- Towns and townships are general-purpose local governments, like counties and cities. Twenty states, primarily in the Northeast and Midwest, have official towns or townships. Some have fairly broad powers; others, especially rural Midwestern townships, offer more limited services. Many experts have predicted that towns and townships will gradually disappear as the nation urbanizes.

- Special districts are the most prevalent and at the same time the least understood of the five types of local government. They provide a service to an area that other local governments do not provide because of technical, financial, or political considerations. Natural resource management, fire protection, housing and community development, and water and sewer service are the most common special districts. Their financing varies: some have the power to tax; others rely on user fees, grants, or bonds.

- The number of school districts has declined because of mergers and consolidations to a current level of fewer than 13,000. School districts are typically governed by elected boards and managed by trained, full-time educational administrators. School politics can create rivalries as issues such as parental choice, neighborhood schools, and effective financing are debated.

- The public wants well-governed communities. Local governments redesign their structures in the hope of improving governance. Polls show that the public's trust and confidence in local government is fairly positive and stable. Analysts continue to develop criteria such as managing for results in an effort to identify the best performing localities.

Key Terms

general-purpose local government (*p. 273*)
single-purpose local government (*p. 275*)
metropolitan area (*p. 275*)
micropolitan statistical area (*p. 275*)
home rule (*p. 275*)
jurisdictional overlap (*p. 275*)
incorporation (*p. 281*)

charter (*p. 281*)
strong-mayor–council structure (*p. 281*)
weak-mayor–council structure (*p. 282*)
city manager (*p. 283*)
ordinance (*p. 286*)
annexation (*p. 287*)
extraterritorial jurisdiction (*ETJ*) (*p. 287*)

at-large elections (*p. 290*)
district (*ward*) elections (*p. 290*)
reform movement (*p. 290*)
cumulative voting (*p. 291*)
ranked-choice voting (*p. 291*)
Smart City (*p. 292*)
town meeting (*p. 294*)
public authority (*p. 296*)
equalization formula (*p. 299*)

Internet Resources

Most of the five types of government are represented by national associations: **www.naco.org** (National Association of Counties); **www.nlc.org** (National League of Cities); **www.natat.org** (National Association of Towns and Townships); **www.nsba.org** (for school districts, the relevant website is that of the National School Boards Association).

To explore a specific school district, see **www.kcpublicschools.org** (the website of the Kansas City, Missouri, school district).

Special districts, by virtue of their specialized nature, tend to have function-specific national organizations. For example, the National Association of Conservation Districts can be found at **www.nacdnet.org**. A fifteen-county district, the Colorado River Water Conservation District, whose website can be found at **www.crwcd.org**, is an example of an individual special district. The website of one of the most famous special districts, the Port Authority of New York and New Jersey, is **www.panynj.gov**.

Cities and counties have learned that maintaining websites is a good way to connect with the public. The website for the city of Los Angeles can be found at **www.lacity.org**; the website for the county can be found at **www.lacounty.gov**. The website for the largest county in Michigan is **www.waynecounty.com**; the largest county in Nevada is at **www.clarkcountynv.gov**.

You can find information about the Big Apple at **www.nyc.gov**; for the city of New Orleans, **www.nola.gov**. The websites for the cities of Atlanta and Minneapolis are **www.atlantaga.gov** and **www.ci.minneapolis.mn.us**, respectively.

A scholarly journal that contains the latest research on local governments is *Urban Affairs Review*. Its URL is **uar.sagepub.com**.

11

Local Leadership and Governance: Continuity and Change

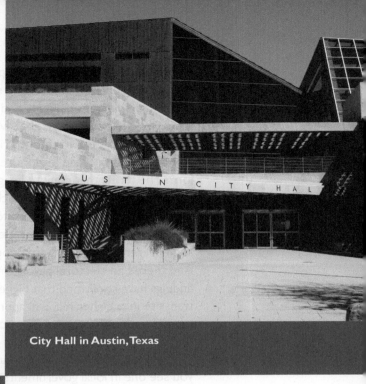

City Hall in Austin, Texas

Brandon Seidel/Shutterstock.com

Learning Objectives

LO 11-1 To appraise various theories of community power.

LO 11-2 To recognize disputes over property rights as manifestations of power.

LO 11-3 To compare different types of local executives and the challenges they face.

LO 11-4 To recognize the conflict inherent in local legislative bodies.

LO 11-5 To articulate why localities need leadership.

Since 1973, there have been six proposals to replace the at-large election of city council members in Austin, Texas with a district election system. All of the proposals failed until 2012. That year, two options were put before the voters: the 8-2-1 plan, which featured eight district seats, two at-large seats, and a mayor elected citywide, and the 10-1 plan, which did away with all at-large council seats in favor of electing ten council members from districts and a mayor voted on citywide. Austinites for Geographic Representation pushed adoption of the 10-1 plan; the Austin Community for Change supported the 8-2-1 system.[1] Voters approved the 10-1 plan, and, in 2014, Austin elected its first council members from districts. What was the city trying to accomplish with this structural change? The intent was to produce a more diverse city council that would be responsive to the interests of the different neighborhoods in Austin. In other words, the goal was to ensure that the leadership of the city reflected the city itself. Once the 10-1 plan was in place, some in

Austin began to ponder another possible change with leadership consequences: adoption of a strong-mayor structure.[2]

Leadership goes hand in hand with governance. It can make the difference between an effectively functioning government and one that lurches from one crisis to another. Local government requires talented leaders, regardless of their structural form. The terms that conjure images of leadership in local government circles these days include *initiative*, *inventiveness*, *risk taking*, *high energy level*, *persistence*, *innovation*, and *vision*. These words share a common element: They denote activity and engagement. Leaders are people who make a difference. And there's an electoral payoff for doing a good job. Research findings have confirmed that higher job performance ratings translate into higher mayoral approval levels.[3] Not surprisingly, mayors with high approval are more likely to be reelected.

One of the popular labels for contemporary leaders is *entrepreneur*. How do you know an entrepreneurial leader when you see one in local government? You can identify such leaders by their advocacy of innovative ideas. They are the people "who actively seek opportunities for dynamic changes in policy or politics."[4] Some may occupy positions of power in local government; others may emerge from the ranks of ordinary citizens. Regardless of their background, they share a commitment to new ideas and a willingness to take risks. For example, a study of Colorado communities found that entrepreneurs—experts and citizens alike—were essential in changing policy toward recreational use of various river basins in the state.[5]

The spirit of entrepreneurialism is not limited to individuals: Communities exhibit leadership too. At some point, on some issue, a jurisdiction may try something new; it may "think outside the box." For instance, in 2013, Indianapolis became the first major city to pledge to convert its entire fleet of city vehicles to alternative fuels by 2025. Replacing city-owned sedans with plug-in or hybrid vehicles was the first step, followed by transitioning heavy vehicles such as garbage trucks, fire engines, and snowplows to compressed natural gas. The final piece will be converting the city's 1,900 police car fleet to alternative fuel vehicles.[6] Other cities with similar perspectives on energy security and the environment are likely to follow in Indianapolis's direction. Leading cities become models for other jurisdictions.

Community Power

LO 11-1
To appraise various theories of community power.

Real questions arise about who is running the show in local government. At the risk of sounding naive, we might suggest that "the people" run government; however, much of the evidence can persuade us otherwise. But we should not become too cynical, either. Citizen preferences do have an impact on public policy decisions.[7] Can we assume, therefore, that those who occupy important elected positions in government, such as the mayor and the city council, are in fact in charge? Are they the leaders of the community? These questions have interested scholars for a long time.

Two theories have been influential in sorting through the issue of who's running the show. One, **elite theory**, argues that a small group of leaders called an *elite* possesses power and rules society. Conversely, **pluralist theory** posits that power is dispersed among competing groups whose clashes produce societal rule.

Elite Theory

One of the earliest expositions of elite theory argued that any society, from underdeveloped to advanced, has two classes of people: a small set who rule and a large mass who are ruled.[8] The rulers allocate values for society and determine the rules of the game; the ruled tend to be passive and ill-informed and cannot exercise any direct influence over the rulers. This division is reflected elsewhere in society. In organizations, for example, power is inevitably concentrated in the hands of a few people. Given the pervasiveness of elite systems, should we expect decision making in communities to be any different?

A famous study of power in the community given the name of Middletown (actually Muncie, Indiana) in the 1920s and 1930s discovered an identifiable set of rulers.[9] The researchers, sociologists Robert and Helen Lynd, determined that Family X (the Ball family) was at the core of this ruling elite. Through their economic power, Family X and a small group of business leaders called the shots in Middletown. Government officials simply did the bidding of Family X and its cohorts.

Another widely read study of community power confirmed the basic tenets of elitism. Sociologist Floyd Hunter's study of Regional City (Atlanta, Georgia) in the 1950s and his follow-up research in the 1970s identified the top leadership—a forty-person economic elite—who dominated the local political system.[10] Hunter argued that an individual's power in Regional City was determined by his role in the local economy. Local elected officials merely carried out the policy decisions of the elite. To illustrate this point, Hunter compared the relatively limited power enjoyed by the mayor of Atlanta to the extensive power possessed by the president of a firm headquartered in Regional City: Coca-Cola.

Assume for a moment that elitist interpretations of community power are accurate; where do these interpretations take us? Do not be confused about the intent of an economic elite: They are not running the community out of a sense of benevolence. The following statement captures the larger meaning of elitism:

Virtually all U.S. cities are dominated by a small, parochial elite whose members have business or professional interests that are linked to local

elite theory
A theory of government that asserts that a small group possesses power and rules society.

pluralist theory
A theory of government that asserts that multiple, open, competing groups possess power and rule society.

development and growth. These elites use public authority and private power as a means to stimulate economic development and thus enhance their own local business interests.[11]

To most people, this conclusion is disturbing.

Pluralist Theory

The findings of the studies just discussed did not square with the prevailing orthodoxy of American political science: pluralism. Not everyone saw community power through the elitist lens, and many questioned whether the findings from Middletown and Regional City applied to other communities.

Pluralist theory views the decision-making process as one of bargaining, accommodation, and compromise. According to this view, no monolithic entity calls the shots; instead, authority is fragmented. Many leadership groups can become involved in decision making, depending on the nature and importance of the issue at hand. Granted, the size, cohesion, and wealth of these groups vary, but no group has a monopoly on resources. Pluralism sets forth a much more accessible system of community decision making than the grimly deterministic tenets of elitism do.

A study conducted by Robert Dahl in New Haven, Connecticut, challenged the sociologists' findings, particularly those of Hunter.[12] According to Dahl, decisions in New Haven in the 1950s were the product of the interactions of a system of groups with more than one center of power. Except for the mayor, no single leader was influential across a series of issue areas, and influential actors were not drawn from a single segment of the community.

Further explication of the pluralist model revealed that, although community decision making is limited to relatively few actors, the legitimacy of such a system hinges on the easily revoked consent of a much larger segment of the local population. In other words, the masses may acquiesce to the leaders, but they can also speak up when they are displeased. Success in a pluralistic environment is determined by a group's ability to form coalitions with other groups. Pluralism, then, offers a more hopeful interpretation of community power.

New Haven: Is It All in the Approach?

reputational approach
A method for studying community power in which researchers ask informants to name and rank influential individuals.

decisional method
A method for studying community power in which researchers identify key issues and the individuals who are active in the decision-making process.

New Haven, the setting for Dahl's affirmation of pluralist theory, has been examined and reexamined by skeptical researchers. Some of the debate between elitists and pluralists is a function of methodology—that is, the particular approach used in studying community power. Sociologists have tended to rely on what is called a **reputational approach**, whereby they go into a community and ask informants to name and rank the local leaders. Those whose names appear repeatedly are considered to be the movers and shakers. This approach is criticized on the grounds that it measures not leadership per se but the reputation for leadership. Political scientists approach the power question differently, through a **decisional method**. They focus on specific community issues and, using various sources, try to determine who is influential in the decision-making process. It is easy to see that the two different approaches can produce divergent findings.

Users of the decisional method claim that it allows them to identify overt power rather than just power potential. In addition, it offers a realistic picture of power relationships as dynamic rather than fixed. Critics of the decisional method argue that when researchers select key issues to examine, they are being arbitrary. Also, a study of decision making may ignore the most powerful actors in a community—those who can keep issues *off* the agenda, who are influential enough to keep certain issues submerged. Table 11.1 reports the perceptions of mayors and council members in eight communities in the Kansas City metropolitan area regarding the involvement of various types of

Table 11.1 Various Groups Ranked by Their Level of Activity and Influence in Local Politics

TYPE OF GROUP	LEVEL OF ACTIVITY	AMOUNT OF INFLUENCE
Chamber of Commerce	4.51	4.01
Neighborhood groups	3.96	3.82
Developers	3.76	3.46
Task forces	3.64	3.39
Democrats	3.37	2.89
Nonprofit organizations	3.30	2.98
Historical preservationists	3.09	2.55
Churches	3.03	2.65
Republicans	2.99	2.59
Public employees	2.83	2.57
Bankers	2.73	2.58
Labor in private sector	2.51	2.26
Women's groups	2.21	1.94
Professional groups	2.14	1.93
National businesses	2.07	2.14
Clientele groups	2.04	1.96
Morality groups	1.86	1.53
Minority groups	1.82	1.66
Global businesses	1.70	1.77
Environmental groups	1.70	1.61
GLBT groups	1.42	1.23
Ethnic groups	1.27	1.18
Community action groups	0.97	0.96
Other parties	0.23	0.18
Overall average	2.47	2.24

Source: Adapted from Paul Schumaker, "Group Involvements in City Politics and Pluralist Theory," *Urban Affairs Review* 49 (March 2013): p. 26.

groups in local politics.[13] Officials used a five-point scale ranging from 1 (very low) to 5 (very high) to assess group activity and influence in their communities. Not surprisingly, the Chamber of Commerce and neighborhood groups were at the top of the list.

Dahl found New Haven to be a pluralist's delight. Convinced that the finding was affected by Dahl's methods, another researcher, G. William Domhoff, examined New Haven and emerged with a contrary view of the power structure.[14] He claimed that Dahl missed the big picture by focusing on issues that were of minor concern to the New Haven elite and that Dahl's finding of an accessible decision-making process in which many groups were involved was not an adequate test of the presence of an elite. Domhoff investigated the urban redevelopment issue and discovered that the long-time mayor, whom Dahl had seen as leading an executive-centered coalition, was in fact being actively manipulated by a cadre of local business leaders. Domhoff contended that New Haven was not quite the pluralistic paradise it was made out to be.

The Dynamics of Power

The work of Hunter and that of Dahl remains significant, but neither elitism nor pluralism adequately explains who's running the show. Not all communities are organized alike; even within a single community, power arrangements shift as time passes and conditions change. Two examples—Miami and Boston—offer insight into the dynamics of power. In Miami, a diverse city in which economic divisions are exacerbated by racial and ethnic tensions, an elite-dominated power structure continues to hold sway in important local decisions. According to Judith Gainsborough, who has studied the power structure in Miami, "The power to actually influence decision making is not widely dispersed."[15] Even so, the composition of the elite has changed over time, becoming more diverse itself. In Boston, power is much more diverse. The city's political leaders joined forces with local economic leaders in the effort to bring the Olympics to the city. The U.S. Olympic Committee chose Boston as its nominee for the 2024 games. In January 2015, Boston mayor Marty Walsh called the nomination "an exception honor." Within a few weeks, opposition began to grow, originally among young professionals who formed a group called No Boston Olympics. They conducted a series of polls with the public radio station WBUR that showed that near majorities of the public opposed the Olympic bid.[16] Eventually Mayor Walsh refused to sign the Olympic host city contract, stating, "I cannot commit to putting the taxpayers at risk." The USOC withdrew Boston's bid and eventually the International Olympic Committee awarded the 2024 games to Paris.

regime
The informal arrangements that surround and complement the formal workings of governmental authority.

Regime Theory Is pluralism an accurate description of the power dynamics in communities across the land? Probably not. The penetration of the government's domain by private economic interests in American communities is deep. Consequently, to understand the dynamics of power in a community, one must look to the **regime**. Political scientist Clarence Stone defines regime as "the informal arrangements that surround and complement the formal workings of governmental authority."[17] Stone uses the concepts of *systemic power* and *strategic advantage* to explain why community decisions so frequently favor upper-strata interests.[18]

The starting point of his argument is that public officials operate in a highly stratified socioeconomic system with a small upper class; a large, varied middle class; and a relatively small lower class. According to Stone, "Public officeholders are predisposed to interact with and to favor those who can reciprocate benefits."[19] Two considerations define the environment in which public officials operate: electoral accountability (keeping the majority of the public satisfied) and systemic power (the unequal distribution of economic, organizational, and social resources). Decision makers are likely to side with majority preferences on highly visible issues; but on less visible ones, the possessors of systemic power—the upper strata—will win most of the time. With their superior resources, they can set the agenda in the community and instigate (or block) change. In other words, they enjoy a strategic advantage.

An urban regime brings a certain degree of stability to a community because key leaders share a vision for the future—that is, they have an agenda that they want to implement—and they interact with one another. An analysis of New Orleans found that the city's lack of a regime contributed mightily to the problems the city faced preparing for and responding to Hurricane Katrina in 2005.[20] In nonregime cities such as New Orleans, temporary coalitions spring up around various issues, but there is little shared understanding of the city's problems. Leaders do not communicate regularly, and cooperation is in short supply. The result is haphazard governance, an outcome that was on display in New Orleans in the aftermath of Katrina.

Nonprofit Organizations as Power Players **Nonprofit organizations** have become fully integrated into the government and politics of many communities. Four types of governmentally active nonprofit organizations can be identified:

- Civic nonprofits
- Policy advocates
- Policy implementers
- Governing nonprofits[21]

The first type, civic nonprofit organizations, plays a watchdog role, monitoring government and educating the public. A local citizens' league acts in this way, attending city council meetings and publicizing council decisions. Policy advocates, the second type, move beyond the provision of information to become active supporters of particular policies or programs. For instance, if an education advocacy group endorses year-round schools, it would lobby the school board vigorously in support of such a policy change. The third type of nonprofit organization, policy implementers, actually delivers services, often through a contract with a local government. For example, homeless shelters in many communities are operated by nonprofit groups supported by city funds, federal grants, and charitable contributions. Governing nonprofits, the fourth type, are different because they may work through or with local government, but they also act independently. These nonprofits are the most powerful of the four types because they offer an alternative venue for decision making.

nonprofit organizations Private sector groups that carry out charitable, educational, religious, literary, service, or scientific functions.

Have nonprofit organizations upset community power structures? Policy advocates and governing nonprofits have the potential to reset agendas and effect real change. Research on the city of Detroit offers some insight into the long-term impact of nonprofit organizations. Richard Hula and Cynthia Jackson-Elmoore studied the influence of two nonprofits created in the aftermath of Detroit's civil disturbances of the late 1960s: New Detroit and Detroit Renaissance.[22] For many years, these organizations have been important players in the city's politics. Although they had a similar genesis, "both were born as an elite response to and fear of civil unrest,"[23] their styles and foci have varied. New Detroit has more of a social agenda, focusing on race relations and education reform. Detroit Renaissance, a smaller organization made up of the corporate elite from the Detroit area, concentrated its energies on economic renewal. Both organizations have been active on the Detroit scene, advocating ambitious reforms and new policies over four decades. And although both organizations have enjoyed some successes, neither has been able to transform the local political agenda. Yet Hula and Jackson-Elmoore contend that the presence of New Detroit and Detroit Renaissance has had an important catalytic effect. When nonprofits join with local elected leaders, their impact increases. In other words, to become power players, nonprofit organizations must become part of the regime.

Hyperpluralism Our understanding of community power structures continues to evolve. What is certain is that some interests, especially those of the economically powerful, seem to prevail more often than others. Still, different communities have developed different arrangements for governance. In some places, weak political leadership and a dispersed business elite have resulted in a condition called **hyperpluralism**. In hyperpluralistic communities, where many interests clash, competing groups cannot form coalitions and the distribution of power tends to be unstable. Research on medium-size cities revealed at least seventeen different types of interest groups that were both active and influential on the local scene.[24] The range of interests represented by these groups is extensive, from taxes and traffic to economic development and public safety. The question of who's in charge remains an interesting one.

Property Rights: A Matter of Power

The issue of property rights raises interesting questions about the exercise of power. You may have heard someone say, "I own this land; therefore, I can do anything I want with it," but that would be far from accurate. Through zoning and other regulations, government can limit what you can do with your property. Moreover, government can actually take that property away from you for a public purpose. All it has to do is follow proper procedures and compensate you—that is, pay fair market value—for the **taking**. Suppose you own a half-acre vacant lot near the central business district of your city. The city may be eyeing your lot as the site for the new library it plans to construct. If you are not willing to sell the land, the city can use its power of eminent domain—that is, it can take your property. You can haggle over the value of the lot, perhaps demand an administrative hearing, and maybe even file a lawsuit to try to stop the city; but in the end, if the taking is for a public purpose, the city has the power to do so. Where the issue gets a little dicey is over the notion of "public purpose." Obviously, a library is a public purpose, but can the city use its eminent domain power to take that same lot and sell it to a developer so that they can construct an office building? The answer may surprise you.

The city council of New London, Connecticut, had voted in 2000 to take 90 acres of land for a redevelopment project. The city's development corporation would redevelop the area with a hotel, marina, and upscale residences that would generate much-needed jobs and tax revenue for the financially stressed city. Most of the property owners sold their land to the city, but a small group refused and, instead, filed suit claiming that the action represented an illegal taking. The plaintiffs argued that the city's plans for the land would destroy an established neighborhood to benefit private developers. In essence, they contended that the city had violated the public purpose requirement of a taking. The case, *Kelo v. City of New London*, went all the way to the U.S. Supreme Court, which, in a 5-to-4 decision in 2005, ruled in favor of the city. The reasoning went like this: New London wanted to use the land to promote economic development, which is a traditional function of government; ergo, the city's plan fulfilled a public purpose.[25]

Property rights advocates deplored the Court's decision, arguing that working-class residents and small business owners were being displaced so that the city could pursue a more productive use of the land. They had an advocate in Justice Sandra Day O'Connor, who dissented, saying, "The beneficiaries [of the Court's ruling] are likely to be those citizens with disproportionate influence and power in the political process, including large corporations and development firms."[26] Localities, not surprisingly, welcomed the decision, claiming that eminent domain was an essential tool in their efforts to regain and maintain economic vitality. They pointed to other examples of the use of eminent domain to benefit private firms, particularly a Nissan automobile facility in Canton, Mississippi, and a speedway in Kansas City, Kansas.

The court did invite states to place restrictions on localities' use of eminent domain if they so desired; and, forty-three states did so, either by legislative action or by citizen initiative. Clearly, the exercise of eminent domain is costly, not only in terms of dollars but in terms of goodwill. Polls conducted in Connecticut, and Florida after *Kelo*, found that majorities opposed *any* use of eminent domain by government, and 91 percent of Minnesotans opposed local government taking of private property for another private development project.[27] This sentiment is one of the reasons why Washington, DC, as it acquired land for the construction of a new stadium for the Washington Nationals baseball team, explicitly refused to take property. But by the same token, New York City was not reluctant to condemn property and take it as the site for a new basketball arena for the Brooklyn Nets. The definition of *public purpose* is likely to continue to unleash a power struggle in many communities.

Local Executives

The mantle of leadership in local government falls most often on chief executives: mayors and managers. Although it is possible for chief executives to eschew a leadership role, they rarely do.

LO 11-3
To compare different types of local executives and the challenges they face.

Mayors

Mayors tend to be the most prominent figures in city government, primarily because their position automatically makes them the center of attention. Occasionally, a city council member emerges as a leader on a specific issue or stirs up some interest with verbal attacks on the mayor (which many observers interpret as jockeying for position to run against the mayor at the next election). But for the most part, attention is drawn to the mayor.

A lot is expected of the mayor. The city comptroller of New York once described the former mayor, Michael Bloomberg, positively: "He's hired a very talented group. He's run city services well. He's approached things in a balanced fashion." However, the comptroller continued, "But the mayor is not just a CEO. The mayor is an emotional leader, an inspirational leader, and in that regard, I don't think he's done nearly as good a job."[28] A similar theme was echoed by Los Angeles city councilman Bernard Parks as he mulled a bid for the mayor's job. "This is a big city, a thriving city. The mayor's office doesn't make you a leader. You have to have a leader in the mayor's office."[29]

Differences Between Strong and Weak Mayors It is important to note that the labels strong and weak mayor refer to the *position*, not to the person who occupies it. A structure simply creates opportunities for leadership, not the certainty of it. True leaders are those who can take what is structurally a weak-mayor position and transform it into a strong mayoralty.

A *strong-mayor* structure establishes the mayor as the sole chief executive who exercises substantive policy responsibilities. In this kind of structure, the position of city manager, someone who can expand an administrative role and become a policy rival to the mayor, does not exist. As an ideal type, a strong mayor has the following features:

- Is elected directly by the voters, not selected by the council
- Serves a four-year, not two-year, term of office
- Has no limitations on reelection
- Plays a central role in budget formulation
- Has extensive appointment and removal powers
- Has veto power over council-enacted ordinances

The actual powers of a specific strong mayor may not include all these items; but the more of these powers a mayor can exercise, the stronger their position is and the easier it is for them to become a leader.

A *weak-mayor* structure does not provide these elements. Its design is such that the mayor shares policy responsibilities with the council and perhaps a manager and serves a limited amount of time in office. (In an especially weak-mayor system, the job is passed around among the council members annually, each of whom takes a turn at being mayor.) A weak-mayor structure often implies strong council involvement in budgetary and personnel matters. The

? It's Your Turn

Should All Cities Have a Strong Mayor?

PROS	CONS
Having a strong mayor increases accountability. There's no confusion about who is in charge in city government. It's like former President Harry Truman said: "The buck stops here."	Too much power in one office introduces the possibility of abuse of power. As British Baron Acton said in the nineteenth century: "Power tends to corrupt, and absolute power corrupts absolutely."
Highly qualified candidates will seek the office of mayor if it is imbued with sufficient authority to make things happen.	Someone might be a good campaigner and win the office, but that doesn't mean that he or she will be an effective government leader. A professional city manager is trained to make city government function effectively.
The issues of the twenty-first century require smart, decisive actions. An empowered mayor will be better equipped to take those actions on behalf of the city.	Most of the issues in most city governments these days are not so complicated or contentious that they require a full-time mayor.

variation in mayoral power is reflected in mayoral remuneration: Weak mayors receive token salaries. If a mayor in a weak-mayor structure is to become a leader, he has to exceed the job description.

Mayoral leadership has been the subject of discussion in the popular press.[30] An article, "The Lure of the Strong Mayor," argued that large, diverse communities grappling with complex problems are better served by a structure that fixes leadership and accountability in the mayor's office. In response, "Beware the Lure of the 'Strong' Mayor" contended that a too powerful mayor could run amok, building political machines based on the exchange of benefits. Structural differences can indeed have consequences. It is important to remember, however, that individuals who work within structures are the essential factor. Leaders can make structures work for them sometimes by performing minor surgery on the structure. As David Morgan and Sheilah Watson note, "Even in council-manager communities—where mayors have the fewest formal powers—by negotiating, networking, and facilitating the efforts of others, mayors clearly rise above the nominal figurehead role."[31] The It's Your Turn box invites you to consider the advantages and disadvantages of a strong mayor.

Black Mayors By 2018, African American mayors headed more than 40 percent of cities with populations of 40,000 or more across the country. Not only can you find black mayors leading cities where the population is predominantly black, but you also can find them in majority-white cities, too, as Table 11.2 shows. Today's African American mayors tend to be problem solvers, not crusaders; political pragmatists, not ideologues.[32]

Table 11.2 Black Mayors in Large Cities, 2019

CITY	STATE	MAYOR	POPULATION (2019 CENSUS ESTIMATE)	% AFRICAN AMERICAN
Chicago	IL	Lori Lightfoot	2,670,406	30.1
Houston	TX	Sylvester Turner	2,378,146	22.5
Dallas	TX	Eric Johnson	1,400.337	24.3
San Francisco	CA	London Breed	906,419	5.2
Charlotte	NC	Vi Alexander Lyles	904.675	35.1
Denver	CO	Michael Hancock	745,172	9.4
Washington	DC	Muriel Bowser	601,723	46.4
Baltimore	MD	Jack Young	587,712	52.5
Atlanta	GA	Keisha Lance Bottoms	510,730	51.8
Kansas City	MO	Quinton Lucas	507,652	29.0
New Orleans	LA	LaToya Cantrell	398,523	59.7
Cleveland	OH	Frank Jackson	377,797	49.6
Stockton	CA	Michael Tubbs	317,088	11.8
Saint Paul	MN	Melvin Carter	313,878	16.0
Plano	TX	Harry LaRosiliere	297,285	8.4
Newark	NJ	Ras Baraka	284,420	49.7
Buffalo	NY	Byron Brown	251,106	38.7
Norfolk	VA	Kenneth Alexander	241,055	41.6
Richmond	VA	Levar Stoney	237,338	47.8
Baton Rouge	LA	Sharon Weston-Broome	229,295	55.0
Tacoma	WA	Victoria Woodards	225,745	10.0
Birmingham	AL	Randall Woodfin	210,613	70.5
Fayetteville	NC	Mitch Colvin	209,419	42.3
Rochester	NY	Lovely Warren	205,464	40.3

Sources: Ballotpedia, "List of the Current Mayors of the Top 100 Cities in the United States," https://ballotpedia.org/List_of_current_mayors_of_the_top_100_cities_in_the_United_States (accessed March 5, 2020); U.S. Census, "Quick Facts," https://www.census.gov/quickfacts/fact/table/US/PST045219 (accessed March 7, 2020).

For example, the two-term mayor of Plano, Texas—Harry LaRosiliere—ran for reelection, stating "Our City will protect you. Our schools will educate you, and our community will nurture you."[33]

Increased success by blacks in mayoral elections has led some observers to talk of **deracialization**, or the de-emphasis of race as a campaign issue in an effort to attract white voter support.[34] Instead of making racial appeals, candidates offer a race-neutral platform that stresses their personal qualifications and political experience.[35] In cities where the white electorate outnumbers the black electorate, such as Dallas and Denver, neither Eric Johnson nor Michael Hancock could have been elected without the support of white voters. Even in cities where white voters constitute a minority, they often control

deracialization
The de-emphasis of race in politics, especially in campaigns, so that there is less racial bloc voting.

the electoral balance when two African American candidates square off in the mayoral race.

Deracialization works both ways. Detroit, a majority African American city, elected a white mayor—Mike Duggan—in 2013 (he was reelected in 2017) after having had black mayors since 1975. Duggan's successful campaigns focused on economic recovery and redevelopment of downtown, issues that both black and white residents of Detroit support.[36] Deracialization of local campaigns, and the manner in which a mayor elected by a multiracial coalition governs once in office, is a compelling subject for research. For example, a study of Houston found that when minority mayors run for reelection, evaluations of job performance are more important to voters than racial group affiliation is.[37]

Some have argued that deracialization is simply the latest step in an attempt not to address racial issues. By focusing on race-neutral issues, they say, deracialization may be ignoring the existence of racial injustice. The rise of the Black Lives Matter movement is a serious critique to deracialization. One can see this in the interplay between the Black Lives Matter slogan and the response of All Lives Matter. All Lives Matter carries with it the connotation that creating a level playing field in which all can compete equally is enough to eliminate bias. Black Lives Matter focuses on the idea that some classes of people come onto the playing field at a distinct disadvantage that cannot be addressed by simply leveling the field. The complexity of this interplay is displayed well by Berkeley Law professor John Powell who argues:

The idea that all lives matter is certainly true. All lives should matter . . . the problem with 'all lives matter' is that it's based on the myth that all racial groups are situated similarly, that we all have equal opportunity. . . . All lives matter also ignores history and resists efforts to improve the lives of Black people specifically, who have been struggling for 400 years under the weight of anti-Black racism to belong in this country and to have our humanity seen. . . . When you say 'all lives matter,' you are making a statement based on a false perception of a post-racial society, which means we're free from racism. We know that's not true.[38]

Women Mayors More women are running for and winning local elective offices. The data from cities with populations of 30,000 or more are instructive. In 1973, fewer than 2 percent of the cities in that population range had female mayors. A quarter-century later, the number of women mayors had increased

Washington, D.C., mayor Muriel Bowser at a press conference.

to 21 percent, a level around which it has fluctuated. (In 2019, 22 percent of cities of 30,000 or more were governed by women.) Thirty-five women were at the helm of large U.S. cities in 2019, nearly 30 percent of the 120 cities with populations of 200,000 or more. Table 11.3 demonstrates this marked increase over the numbers from just a few years earlier.

Table 11.3 Women Mayors in Large Cities, 2019

CITY	STATE	NAME	POPULATION (2019 CENSUS ESTIMATE)
Chicago	IL	Lori Lightfoot	2,670,406
Phoenix	AZ	Kate Gallego	1,743,469
Fort Worth	TX	Betsy Price	933,881
San Francisco	CA	London Breed	906,419
Charlotte	NC	Vi Alexander Lyles	904,675
Seattle	WA	Jenny Durkan	787,740
Las Vegas	NV	Carolyn Goodman	674,768
Washington	DC	Muriel Bowser	601,723
Tucson	AZ	Regina Romero	539,756
Atlanta	GA	Keisha Lance Bottoms	510,730
Raleigh	NC	Mary Ann Baldwin	454,612
Omaha	NE	Jean Stothert	453,758
Oakland	CA	Libby Schaaf	428,545
Tampa	FL	Jane Castor	411,849
New Orleans	LA	LaToya Cantrell	398,523
Bakersfield	CA	Karen Goh	391,996
Lexington	KY	Linda Gorton	333,177
Henderson	NV	Debra March	325,341
Irvine	CA	Christina Shea	307,318
Saint Louis	MO	Lyda Krewson	297,520
Lincoln	NE	Leirion Gaylor Barid	295,376
Greensboro	NC	Nancy Vaughan	294,011
Chula Vista	CA	Mary Casillas Salas	275,696
Madison	WI	Satya Rhodes-Conway	268,303
Reno	NV	Hillary Schieve	263,607
Gilbert	AZ	Jenn Daniels	255,069
Fremont	CA	Lily Mei	239,996
Boise	ID	Lauren McLean	234,646
Tacoma	WA	Victoria Woodards	225,745

(continued)

Table 11.3 Women Mayors in Large Cities, 2019 (*continued*)

CITY	STATE	NAME	POPULATION (2019 CENSUS ESTIMATE)
Baton Rouge	LA	Sharon Weston-Broome	225,295
Fontana	CA	Acquanetta Warren	220,753
Grand Rapids	MI	Rosalynn Bliss	210,849
Rochester	NY	Lovely Warren	205,464
Amarillo	TX	Ginger Nelson	204,526
Salt Lake City	UT	Erin Mendenhall	202,968

Sources: Ballotpedia, "List of the Current Mayors of the Top 100 Cities in the United States," https://ballotpedia .org/List_of_current_mayors_of_the_top_100_cities_in_the_United_States (accessed March 5, 2020); U.S. Census, "Quick Facts," https://www.census.gov/quickfacts/fact/table/US/PST045219 (accessed March 7, 2020).

The 2017 race for mayor of Seattle took on an interesting dimension when two female candidates squared off in a runoff election. Former U.S attorney Jenny Durkan and community activist Cary Moon finished one-two in the twenty-one-candidate primary, but neither had won a majority of the vote. The cost of housing and the increasing homeless population were two of the major issues that the two women disagreed on. When the votes were tallied, Durkan beat Moon 56 percent to 44 percent to become the first openly lesbian mayor of a large U.S. city. Seattle wasn't the only large U.S. city to witness a woman versus woman contest in 2017. Two African American women ran against each other for mayor of New Orleans. LaToya Cantrell, a city council member beat Desirée Charbonnet, a local judge with 60 percent of the vote in a runoff after neither won a majority of the votes in the eighteen-candidate nonpartisan primary.[39] And then, in 2019, former federal prosecutor Lori Lightfoot beat Cook County Board president Toni Preckwinkle 71 percent to 29 percent in the Chicago mayoral race. Lightfoot became the first African American female mayor of the third largest city in the United States.

Studies of female mayoral candidates have dispelled several electoral myths.[40] For example, women do not appear to experience greater difficulty in raising money or gaining newspaper endorsements than men do. Women mayors, however, do tend to be political novices. Few female mayors in Florida, for instance, had held elective office before their mayoral election; if they had, it was usually a city council seat. Female mayors also have a policy impact: Research conducted by political scientist Mirya Holman found that cities led by women mayors allocate more funds for social welfare programs than cities with male mayors do.[41] Female mayors are, however, treated much worse by some constituents than are male mayors. A recent study found female mayors of cities of 30,000 or greater to be twice as likely as male mayors to experience psychological abuse and almost three times as likely to experience physical violence. As the title of this study suggests, the job is "not for the faint of heart."[42]

Increasing Mayoral Diversity Beyond race and gender, U.S. mayors are becoming more diverse in terms of ethnicity and sexual orientation. As of 2019, four big city mayors were Asian American and nine were Latino (see Table 11.4). The LGBTQ Victory Fund lists forty-five mayors in the United States who are openly gay or lesbian. Five large cities are headed by mayors who are openly gay or lesbian—Chicago (Lori Lightfoot), Seattle (Jenny Durkan), Tampa (Jane Castor), Madison, Wisconsin (Satya Rhodes-Conway), and Long Beach, California (Robert Garcia). Former mayors of Houston (Annise Parker, 2004–2010); Lexington, Kentucky (Jim Gray, 2011–2019); Portland, Oregon (Sam Adams, 2009–2012); Salt Lake City (Jackie Biskupski, 2016–2020); and Seattle (Ed Murray, 2014–2017) were openly gay or lesbian. And then, of course, there is Pete Buttigieg, the openly gay former mayor of South Bend, Indiana (2012–2020), who ran unsuccessfully for the 2020 Democratic nomination for president.

By comparing Tables 11.2, 11.3, and 11.4, you can see that the same names appear in pairs of tables. Lori Lightfoot of Chicago is both African American and female, as are eight of the other twenty-five African American mayors of large cities. Two of the eight Latino mayors and two of the four Asian American mayors are also female. Harry LaRosiliere (Plano, Texas) was born in Haiti, and Harry Sidhu (Anaheim, California) and Karen Goh (Bakersfield, California) were born in India. All are naturalized American citizens. Some mayors are

Table 11.4 Latino and Asian American Mayors of U.S. Cities, 2019

LATINO MAYORS				
CITY	STATE	NAME	POPULATION	% LATINO
Los Angeles	CA	Eric Garcetti	4,085,014	48.6
Tucson	AZ	Regina Romero	539,786	43.2
Miami	FL	Francis Suarez	504,439	72.5
Santa Ana	CA	Miguel Pulido	335,009	76.8
Chula Vista	CA	Mary Salas	275,896	58.8
Laredo	TX	Pete Saenz	233,775	95.4
San Bernardino	CA	John Valdivia	218,995	64.8
Moreno Valley	CA	Yxstian Gutierrez	213,743	58.0
ASIAN AMERICAN MAYORS				
CITY	STATE	NAME	POPULATION	% ASIAN AMERICAN
San Antonio	TX	Ron Nirenberg	1,590,402	2.8
Bakersfield	CA	Karen Goh	391,996	7.3
Anaheim	CA	Harry Sidhu	358,063	16.7
Fremont	CA	Lily Mei	239,996	58.4

Sources: Ballotpedia, "List of the Current Mayors of the Top 100 Cities in the United States," https://ballotpedia.org/List_of_current_mayors_of_the_top_100_cities_in_the_United_States (accessed March 5, 2020); U.S. Census, "Quick Facts," https://www.census.gov/quickfacts/fact/table/US/PST045219 (accessed March 7, 2020).

virtually a showcase of the multiethnic cities they serve. Eric Garcetti (Los Angeles) is Mexican American on his father's side and Russian Jewish on his mother's side.[43] Frank Jackson (Cleveland) is African American on his father's side and Italian American on his mother's side.[44] Ron Nirenberg (San Antonio) was born in Malaysia where his father met his Malaysian mother while serving in the Peace Corps. His father's family is Polish and Russian Jewish while his mother's family is a mixture of Filipino, Malay, Indian, and British.[45]

Visionary Mayors   For mayors to become leaders, they need to have vision—that is, they need the ability to identify goals for their city and achieve them, which is easier said than done. As a former Dallas mayor commented, "Mayors work in real time. You have to limit your agenda to the big stuff."[46] Three erstwhile mayors widely hailed as visionary when they were in office put their heads together to come up with a how-to list.[47] Their rules for creating and implementing successful city visions included several obvious items such as "borrow from everyone" and "build on existing strengths." But the list also instructed mayors to market their vision on a human scale so that local residents and business interests can understand its relevance to them. Getting cooperation from the community goes a long way in bolstering mayoral leadership. But the immediate tasks of keeping the city running smoothly can cause some mayors to lose sight of the vision or, at the least, put it aside as they worry about potholes, garbage collection, and budget deficits. In that vein, Los Angeles mayor Eric Garcetti, who was elected in 2013 and reelected in 2017, has said that his goal is to make L.A. the "best run city in America."[48]

City Managers

City managers (as well as county administrators and appointed school superintendents) exemplify the movement toward reformed local government. Local government reform was a **Progressive era** movement that sought to depose the corrupt and inefficient partisan political machines that controlled many American cities. To the reformers, local government had become too political; what was needed, they believed, was a government designed along the lines of a business corporation. To achieve their goals, reformers advocated fundamental structural changes in local government such as the abolition of partisan local elections, the use of at-large electoral systems, and the installation of a professionally trained city manager. Altering the structure of local government has had profound consequences for local government leadership. City managers—the professional, neutral experts whose job is to run the day-to-day affairs of the city—have become key leaders.

In the original conception, managers were to implement but not formulate policy. Administration and politics were to be kept separate. The managers' responsibility would be to administer the policies enacted by the elected officials—the city councils—by whom they were hired (and fired). In other words, they were to act as the agents of their political principals. But it is impossible to keep administration and politics completely separate.

Progressive era
A period in the early twentieth century that focused on reforming or cleaning up government.

City managers are influenced not only by their training and by the councils that employ them but also by their own political ideologies.[49] When it comes to making choices, they balance professional norms, the politics of the issue, and their own predispositions. Hence, city managers typically end up being far more influential on the local government scene than their neutral personas might suggest.

Managers as Policy Leaders According to the International City/County Management Association, the city managers' professional association, the role of the manager is to help the governing body function more effectively. "Managers—and their staffs—need to build political capacity so they can assist the elected body in framing community issues."[50] Ways in which the manager can assume a larger role in policy making include proposing community goals and service levels; structuring the budget preparation, review, and adoption process so that it is linked to goals and service levels; and orienting new council members to organizational processes and norms. This approach has had the intended effect. James Svara, who surveyed officials in large cities, concluded that managers have become "more assertive in attempting to focus the council on long-range concerns and in shaping the tone of the policymaking process."[51]

One indisputable role for the city manager is as an information source for the busy, part-time city council. For instance, suppose that some enterprising college students are requesting a change in a city ordinance that prohibits street vendors. The council asks the manager to study the pros and cons of street vending. At a subsequent meeting, they report on other cities' experiences: Has it created a litter problem? Does it draw clientele away from established businesses? How much revenue can be expected from vendor licensing fees? The manager then offers alternative courses of action (allow street vending only at lunchtime, restrict pushcarts to Main Street) and evaluates their probable consequences. In some councils, the manager is asked to make a formal recommendation; in others, their recommendation is more along the lines of "Well, what do you think?" At some point, a vote is called and the council makes an official decision.

Working with Councils and Mayors City managers are not cut from one mold; they vary in terms of experience, outlook, and style. Ideally, a manager should be a near-perfect match for the community they serve. A manager who is focused on making the city function smoothly might be poorly suited for a community in need of an innovative, big-picture kind of leader. And the converse is true: a manager who wants to take on an expansive leadership role would find themself stymied in a city seeking a technical problem solver. Obviously, it is important that the city council and the city manager share similar views on the role the manager is expected to play.[52] However, a good council–manager fit can be difficult to maintain. The composition of the city council can change, new issues will emerge, and managers may shift their orientation toward the job. It is no wonder that the average tenure of a manager in a city is between six and seven years. Some are fired, of course, but some are "ladder climbers" who move on to larger cities, whereas others are "lateral movers," relocating to similar-size communities.[53] Consequently, the search for the "right" manager is nearly constant in many places.

A veteran city administrator in Missouri offered new managers this advice about dealing with elected officials:

- Don't substitute your political judgment for the judgments of the elected officials.
- Don't cut red ribbons, cut red tape . . . in other words, keep a low profile.
- Listen, count to three, and choose your words wisely.
- The council–manager relationship is not a game won on points.
- There's no great honor in being fired, but there's no shame in being fired for the right reason.[54]

As noted earlier, one new trend is the hiring of professional managers in cities that do not use the council–manager form of government. Cities are adapting their structures to employ officials with titles such as managing director or chief administrative officer (CAO).[55] These individuals have the educational credentials and professional experiences of city managers, and their role in a strong-mayor city is typically limited to administrative matters.

Local Legislatures

LO 11-4
To recognize the conflict inherent in local legislative bodies.

Local legislatures include city councils, county commissions, town boards of aldermen or selectmen, special district boards, and school boards. They are representative, deliberative policy-making bodies. In this section, we focus on city councils because that is where most of the research has taken place, but many of the points are also applicable to the other local legislative bodies such as county commissions and school boards. Although the ensuing discussion focuses on patterns across councils, it is important to remember that significant variations may exist from one city to another. For example, in some communities, council members receive high salaries, are assisted by clerical and research staff, and have no limits on the number of terms they can serve. In Chicago, for instance, city council members (called **aldermen**) earn more than $122,000 per year, have office staffs, and can serve an unlimited number of four-year terms. (To put it in perspective, the mayor of Chicago has an annual salary of $216,000.) But in Oklahoma City, a council–manager city, council members receive a yearly salary of $12,000; the mayor earns $24,000. In many smaller places, council service is considered a volunteer activity, with members receiving virtually no compensation whatsoever.

The issue of elected officials' pay can be a sensitive one. An example comes from Miami-Dade County, Florida, where voters rejected a proposal in 2012 to raise county commissioners' base pay from $6,000 annually to $92,000 a year. (The pay raise would have been accompanied by term limits and a ban on outside employment while serving on the commission.) This was the thirteenth time in fifty years that a proposed salary hike for commissioners had gone down to defeat. Since that time, Miami-Dade commissioners have discussed the issue several times but have rejected putting it before the voters again for fear that it would again be rejected.[56]

aldermen
A label used in some communities for members of a local legislative body, such as a city council.

City Council Members: Old and New

A former member of the city council of Concord, California, harkening back to an earlier time, commented, "When I first came on the city council, it was like a good-old-boys' club."[57] The standard description was that the city council was a part-time, low-paying haven for public-spirited white men who did not consider themselves politicians. Most councils used at-large electoral mechanisms, so individual council members had no specific, territorially based constituency. Council members considered themselves volunteers. Research on city councils in the San Francisco Bay area in the 1960s found that these volunteer members were fairly unresponsive to public pressures and tended to vote according to their own preferences.[58] In other words, there was not much representation going on.

Today, the circumstances have changed. City councils are less white, less male, and less passive than they were in the past. Now, city councilors are more engaged and active. Some of this change is due to modifications in the electoral mechanism, such as the switch from at-large or citywide elections to district (or ward) elections.[59] Table 11.5 shows the wide variation in both

Table 11.5 City Councils of the Twenty Largest U.S. Cities

CITY	STATE	POPULATION (2019 CENSUS ESTIMATES)	COUNCIL SIZE	NUMBER ELECTED AT LARGE	NUMBER ELECTED FROM DISTRICTS
New York	NY	8,622,357	51	0	51
Los Angeles	CA	4,085,014	15	0	15
Chicago	IL	2,670,406	50	0	50
Houston	TX	2,378,146	16	5	11
Phoenix	AZ	1,743,469	8	0	8
San Antonio	TX	1,590,402	10	0	10
Philadelphia	PA	1,579,504	17	7	10
San Diego	CA	1,469,490	9	0	9
Dallas	TX	1,400,337	14	0	14
San Jose	CA	1,036,242	10	0	10
Austin	TX	1,018,842	10	0	10
Jacksonville	FL	934,439	19	5	14
Fort Worth	TX	933,881	9	1	8
San Francisco	CA	906,419	11	0	11
Charlotte	NC	904,675	11	4	7
Columbus	OH	900,274	7	7	0
Indianapolis	IN	866,640	29	4	25
Seattle	WA	787,740	9	2	7
Denver	CO	745,172	13	2	11

Sources: U.S. Census, "Quick Facts," https://www.census.gov/quickfacts/fact/table/US/PST045219 (accessed March 7, 2020); Ballotpedia.org, "List of Current City Council Officials of the Top 100 Cities in the United States," https://ballotpedia.org/List_of_current_city_council_officials_of_the_top_100_cities_in_the_United_States, (accessed March 8, 2020).

council size and number of members elected at large and from districts in the twenty largest American cities. Columbus, Ohio, is the only one of these large cities that continues to elect all of its council members at large; Detroit did so until voters approved a change in the city's charter in 2009. The rest of these cities use a combination of at-large and district seats or they elect all of their council members from districts. Figure 11.1 displays the district map for Detroit, a city with a strong-mayor–council structure and seven of its nine council members elected from districts.

Council Diversity

Racial and ethnic minorities are making inroads into local politics in increasing numbers. There are some 1,070 city council seats in the 100 largest cities in the United States. As of 2019, nearly 40 percent of these seats were held by women, more than 25 percent by African Americans, and 15 percent by Latinos.[60] A study conducted in 2009 found nearly 4,000 African Americans serving in elected city and county offices across the country (the number is undoubtedly higher now).[61] In 2018, there were nearly 2,400 Latinos serving in elected city and county offices.[62] And although Asian Americans accounted for just under 1 percent of locally elected officials, their numbers are also growing, especially in California.

City Council Districts

At-Large: Brenda Jones (*President*)
District 1: James Tate
District 2: Roy McCalister, Jr.
District 3: Scott Benson
District 4: Andre Spivey
District 5: Mary Sheffield
　　　　　　(*President Pro Tem*)
District 6: Raquel Castañeda-López
District 7: Gabe Leland
At-Large: Janeé Ayers

Figure 11.1 Detroit City Council District Map

Source: City of Detroit, Council District Map, https://detroitmi.gov/sites/detroitmi.localhost/files/2019-07/headernewsletter.jpg.

Despite the rise in minority representation, the percentages remain relatively low. Much research has been done on the impact of structural considerations—for example, the at-large election format, the size of the council, and the use of nonpartisan elections—on minority representation on the council.[63] Other factors such as the size of a minority group, its geographical concentration, and its political cohesiveness affect electoral success. In general, a higher proportion of African American council members can be found in central cities that use a mayor–council structure, on larger councils, and in southern cities with large black populations. Councils with higher-than-average Latino representation tend to be found in the Southwest and Far West and in larger central cities that use council–manager structures. Thus far, Asian representation has been clustered primarily in the Pacific Coast area in larger council–manager central cities. Native American representation is highest in small communities using commission structures in the southwestern and Pacific Coast areas of the country. The increase in nonwhites on councils has policy consequences. Data from 351 city council members indicates that nonwhites tend to pursue a more liberal agenda than whites do.[64]

Given the finite number of council seats in any community and the fact that more groups are now clamoring for representation, two outcomes are possible: Minority groups may try to build coalitions, or they may opt for a more independent, competitive approach. Although temporary electoral coalitions have emerged in a few cities, it appears that interminority group competition is on the rise.[65] Research in ninety-six cities demonstrates, for example, that an increase in the Latino population has a negative effect on black representation on city councils.[66] Another interesting question is the extent to which the concept of deracialization can be extended to Latinos and Asian Americans in their bids for local offices. Research on the Little Saigon area of Orange County, California, showed evidence of racial bloc voting in every election for city council or school board between 1998 and 2002 in which a Vietnamese American competed against a white candidate.[67]

An early 1990s national survey of city council members showed that, compared with males, female council members were much more likely to view the representation of women, environmentalists, abortion rights activists, racial minorities, and good-government organizations as extremely important.[68] Other research of that period found that men and women on the council saw each other through different lenses. As Susan Adams Beck pointed out, "Men often express frustration that women ask too many questions, while women see themselves as well-prepared and think their male colleagues are often 'winging it.'"[69] These days, with respect to the public's perceptions of leadership, few notable gender differences exist. Polls show few differences between perceptions of men and women on traits such as honesty, respectfulness, decisiveness, or working well under pressure. Although majorities see no difference between the sexes, those who do see differences think women are better at serving as role models for children, working out compromises, and being compassionate. Men are seen as better at being willing to take risks.[70]

Local governing boards in cities and counties are becoming more diverse in another way: The number of local elected officials (the tally includes more than city council members) who are openly gay or lesbian has risen to more

Members of the Mobile, Alabama, city council listen to a city staffer as she discusses the city's budget

than 500.[71] The Gay and Lesbian Victory Fund is a political action committee that provides technical and financial support for openly gay and lesbian candidates, many of whom are seeking local offices. Major changes in LGBTQ representation began to surface in 2017 with several candidates winning seats on city councils. For example, Phillipe Cunningham and Andrea Jenkins—both transgender—won seats on the Minneapolis city council (Jenkins became the first African American transgender person elected to public office in the country). Gay candidates also won seats in Toledo, Lansing, and Cincinnati. While much attention was on congressional races in 2018, the "rainbow wave" grew in city council races. Then, in 2019, nearly 100 LGBTQ candidates won local council elections. Not only did LGBTQ candidates win in traditionally liberal states such as Massachusetts, New York, and California, but they also won in more conservative states like Kansas, Virginia, and Utah.[72] An earlier study found that gay and lesbian electoral success was more likely in larger cities; in jurisdictions with higher numbers of nonfamily households (such as university communities); and in places with partisan, district election of council members.[73] The recent success of LGBTQ candidates, however, indicates that these candidates are competing in and winning races throughout the United States.

Councils in Action: Increasing Conflict

In earlier times, when members of the council came from the same socioeconomic stratum (in some communities, *all* members of the at-large council came from the same neighborhood) and when they shared a common political philosophy, governing was easier. Members of the council could come together before the meeting (usually at breakfast in a restaurant near City

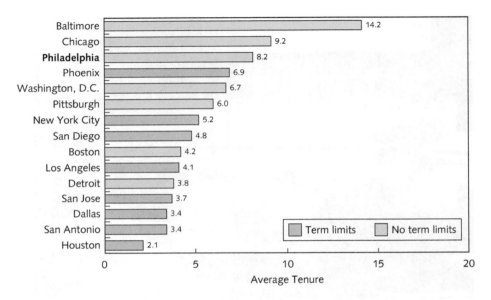

Figure 11.2 Average Tenure (in Years) of City Council Members in Fifteen Cities, as of 2016

Note: Cities in bold type impose term limits on their city council members.

Source: Thomas Ginsberg and Katie Martin, "Salaries Up, Tenure and Share of Women Down on Philadelphia City Council: Changes Reflect Trends Across 15 Major Cities," Pew Charitable Trusts Philadelphia Research and Policy (January 25, 2016).

Hall) and discuss the items on the agenda. Thus, they could arrive at an informal resolution of any particularly troubling items and thereby transform the actual council meeting into a rubber-stamp exercise. No wonder that the majority of council votes were often unanimous; members were merely ratifying what they had already settled on. Nowadays, councils appear to be less collegial. In many cities, average council tenure is relatively brief, as Figure 11.2 suggests. However, when incumbent city council members seek reelection, they have a strong advantage over their challengers.[74]

Intracouncil Conflict Council members elected by districts report more factionalism and less unanimity than do their counterparts elected at large. Research confirms the link between district elections and lower levels of cooperation on city councils.[75] As more cities adopt district-based electoral mechanisms, council conflict may rise in the future. However, concerns that council members elected from districts will ignore citywide interests in favor of the narrower interests of their particular district appear to be overstated, if a study of Los Angeles can be extended to other cities.[76]

Battles with the Mayor Although mayors and city councils get along most of the time, relationships can become conflictive, to say the least.

In fact, they can be downright hostile at times. A former mayor of Philadelphia did not pull any punches when he referred to the city council as "the worst legislative body in the free world."[77] Budget allocations and spending decisions can spark conflict. In Boston, when Mayor Martin Walsh took office in 2014, he referred to the city council as his partner in city government. That partnership frayed within months when the mayor vetoed a $20,000 salary increase (from $87,500 to $107,500) that the council had approved for itself.[78] The Controversies in States and Localities feature describes a significant tension involving the mayor and council in a Missouri city.

Council–mayor conflict is not necessarily unproductive. Conflict is expected in a political system that operates on the foundation of separation of powers. Clashes between the legislative branch and the executive branch can produce better government. But when the disagreements between the council and the mayor escalate to the point of gridlock, effective governance is stymied.

Leadership and Capacity

LO 11-5
To articulate why localities need leadership.

In the final analysis, the concept of leadership remains somewhat ephemeral. Regardless of the difficulty we might have in defining it precisely, it is a central, critical concern in local government. Much is being made of a new pragmatism among America's big-city mayors, an orientation that is independent of race or ethnicity. It is a back-to-basics approach to governing, one that emphasizes service delivery, balanced budgets, and working with the private sector to cure the city's ills. This new breed of mayor also seeks to build alliances with adjacent suburbs. Witness the pragmatism of Atlanta's former mayor, Bill Campbell, who wanted to greet visitors coming to his city for the 1996 Olympics with a sign reading "Welcome to Atlanta—a real city with real problems and real people working real hard every day to solve them."[79] Leave it to former New York City mayor Michael Bloomberg to put it in perspective. When asked whether he would run for higher office, he responded, "I think I have a better job than the governor and the president."[80] Nevertheless, Bloomberg made an unsuccessful run for the Democratic nomination for president in 2020.

At the same time, local governments are becoming more entrepreneurial. Local governments are confronting their problems and challenges by trying new ideas, exploring alternatives, and reaching out for solutions. New approaches do not necessarily work and therein lies the risk. But when they do, other places are quick to embrace them. As a result, local governments change and, one hopes, improve. Consider the case of Baltimore. In 2016, Catherine Pugh was elected for a four-year term as mayor, but she resigned in May 2019 after a scandal concerning self-published children's books. Pugh was the second mayor of Baltimore in ten years to resign as a result of a corruption scandal. She was succeeded by council member Jack Young who failed to be renominated as mayor in 2020. Baltimore has been plagued by high

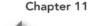

Controversies in States and Localities

The Mayor, the City Council, and Walmart . . . and the Community

The development of a Walmart store can be a divisive issue in a community. Opponents often cite the threat to local mom-and-pop stores, whereas supporters appreciate the employment opportunities and lower prices that a Walmart brings. Ellisville, Missouri, a city of almost 10,000 near St. Louis, offers an interesting example of mayor–council conflict. A developer looking to build a Walmart Supercenter in Ellisville sought a $15 million subsidy from the city to develop the property. The subsidy quickly became a hot-button issue and sparked the formation of pro-subsidy and no-subsidy groups.

Tensions escalated when the city council voted to provide a subsidy to the developer, an action that the newly elected mayor, Adam Paul, strongly opposed. (He had campaigned on a "No Walmart" platform.) There was talk in some neighborhoods of recalling the pro-subsidy members of the council. The mayor's relationship with the council soured as he railed against their decision and it wasn't long before the council levied several charges against the mayor (giving illegal orders to employees, holding illegal meetings, among other charges) and voted to impeach him. A circuit judge reinstated Mayor Paul three months later. In the meantime, city elections had changed the composition of the council to one more favorable to the mayor's position. As numerous lawsuits were being filed by groups on both sides of the issue, the council fired the city manager who was seen by many as being supportive of the Walmart project, and it denied the developer an extension of his development permit. In the fall of 2013, Walmart

announced that it was dropping its plans to build in Ellisville.

So, in the end, the mayor prevailed: No subsidy was provided. Walmart does have stores in the area, but not one in Ellisville. In the aftermath, the mayor and the council sought to move forward, restoring harmonious relations in City Hall and with the citizenry . . . and to attract new, nonsubsidized retail businesses to the community.

Critical Thinking Questions

1. If you had been on the Ellisville city council, would you have voted for or against the subsidy to develop a Walmart Supercenter?

2. As a member of the council, what types of information would you need to help you make the best decision for the community?

3. How should a council member who is elected from a specific district balance the interests of his or her constituents with the interests of the city as a whole?

4. Is the position of mayor of Ellisville strong or weak? Why?

Sources: Stephen Deere, "Ellisville Walmart Deal Dead—Again," *St. Louis Post-Dispatch*, https://www.stltoday.com/news/local/metro/ellisville-walmart-deal-dead-again/article_30ddad97-8b66-5300-9fc5-7c2d6d38eb89.html (October 15, 2013); Paul Hampel, "Judge Permanently Reinstates Adam Paul as Ellisville Mayor," *St. Louis Post-Dispatch*, https://www.stltoday.com/news/local/govt-and-politics/judge-permanently-reinstates-adam-paul-as-ellisville-mayor/article_37aafdc7-719f-569b-a52e-b1e430333690.html (July 1, 2013).

rates of violent crime, pervasive poverty, and persistent unemployment; in addition, its school system is being sued for failing to provide an adequate education, as Maryland state law requires. The new mayor was optimistic, stating, "I need every citizen to be part of what I'm trying to do in terms of reducing crime and cleaning the city. Together we all can do it."[81] Despite his optimistic attitude, Young lost the Democratic nomination to Brandon Scott who was later elected mayor. Scott, the youngest mayor in Baltimore history, ran on a platform of reducing gun violence, restoring trust in government, and ending illegal dumping in the city, and other conditions that drew derogatory comments from President Donald Trump in July 2019.[82]

Chapter Recap

- Elite theory (a small group of leaders possesses power and rules society) and pluralist theory (power is dispersed among competing groups) have dominated the study of community power. Attention has been focused more recently on regime theory and the related concepts of systemic power and strategic advantage.

- Nonprofit organizations have become increasingly important in communities.

- Mayors tend to be the central figures in city politics and government, even if they operate in formally weak-mayor structures.

- City managers have become policy leaders. Even in cities without a formal city manager structure, chief administrative officers are being hired to take on some of the management responsibilities.

- City councils have changed from the good-old-boy clubs of the past. They are more active, they are more diverse, and more conflict occurs among city council members. One of the reasons for these changes is the switch from at-large, or citywide, elections to district (or ward) election of council members.

- Leadership is the ability to realize goals. It varies from one place to another, as a function of the situation. Leadership also comes from the grassroots.

Key Terms

elite theory (p. 305)
pluralist theory (p. 305)
reputational approach (p. 306)
decisional method (p. 306)

regime (p. 308)
nonprofit organizations (p. 309)
hyperpluralism (p. 310)
taking (p. 310)

deracialization (p. 314)
Progressive era (p. 319)
aldermen (p. 321)

Internet Resources

The association of mayors of cities with populations of 30,000 or more, the U.S. Conference of Mayors, has a website at **www.usmayors.org**.

Mayors in a state frequently belong to a statewide organization such as **www.njcm.org** in New Jersey. In the Tar Heel State, the North Carolina Metropolitan Mayors Coalition actively represents cities' interests in state government. Its website is **http://ncmetromayors.com/**.

Specialized constituency groups often have their own organizations and websites, as does the African American Mayors Association at **ourmayors.org**.

The website for the Center for American Women and Politics at Rutgers University, **www.cawp.rutgers.edu**, contains a wealth of data on women and politics.

Information about the city and county management profession can be found at the International City/County Management Association's website, **www.icma.org**.

12

State-Local Relations: Fifty Different Systems

Protesters rally outside the North Carolina State Capitol in 2016.

AP Images/Chuck Liddy

Learning Objectives

LO 12-1   To identify the fundamentals of the state–local relationship, its variations, and its changes.

LO 12-2   To analyze the issues of urban sprawl and smart growth.

LO 12-3   To evaluate the various forms of regionalism.

LO 12-4   To assess the urban impacts of state policies on housing and infrastructure.

LO 12-5   To compare differing futures of rural America.

In February 2016, the Charlotte City Council passed an ordinance that added gay and transgender people to the list of those protected against discrimination. One of the provisions in the ordinance would allow people to use public restrooms according to the gender they identify with. Before this vote was taken, North Carolina governor Pat McCrory warned Charlotte that taking such action would trigger "immediate state legislative intervention."[1] Some thirty-one days after the Charlotte ordinance passed, and before it could go into effect, a special session of the North Carolina General Assembly passed House Bill 2, which overrode the Charlotte ordinance and all other such ordinances passed by local governments in the state. The bill also forbade local governments in North Carolina from raising minimum wages above the state's rate of $7.25 per hour. Although modeled on legislation that had passed in Arkansas and other states, the North

Carolina law was much more sweeping in scope. "Nobody has passed a law like this," said a University of North Carolina law professor.[2] After a year of negative reaction to "the bathroom bill"—including several major project cancellations in Charlotte—the General Assembly repealed it but said it would revisit the issue of local antidiscrimination ordinances in three years.

Can state governments supplant local preferences? Can they limit what their localities can do? The answer is an emphatic "yes." A state can impose its will on local governments within its boundaries. The relationship between states and their communities is often strained. On the one hand, state government gives local governments life. States create the rules for their localities. On the other hand, state governments historically have not treated their local governments well. Over time, some states have realized that mistreating their governmental offspring is counterproductive and have launched a sometimes uncoordinated process of assistance and empowerment of local government. Other states, however, have not been so inclined.

Capturing this evolution is the statement of the National Conference of State Legislatures (NCSL) Task Force on State-Local Relations: "Legislators should place a higher priority on state-local issues than has been done in the past. The time has come to change their attitude toward local governments—to stop considering them as just another special interest group and to start treating them as partners in our federal system."[3] Stronger, more competent local governments are an asset to state government.

This chapter examines broad issues for state and local governments and related trends. Let us first consider the most fundamental issue: the distribution of authority between the state and its constituent units.

The Distribution of Authority

In essence, local governments are creatures of their states. The relationship is that of a unitary system: The state holds all legal power. Federal and state courts have consistently upheld the dependency of localities on the state since

LO 12-1
To identify the fundamentals of the state–local relationship, its variations, and its changes.

Iowa's judge John F. Dillon first laid down **Dillon's rule** in 1868. Dillon's rule established that local governments may exercise only those powers explicitly granted to them by the state, those clearly implied by the explicit powers, and those absolutely essential to the declared objectives and purposes of the local government. Any doubt regarding the legality of any specific local government power is resolved in favor of the state.[4] This perspective runs counter to the more Jeffersonian conception that local governments are imbued with inherent rights, an argument that was elaborated in a Michigan Supreme Court ruling in 1871.[5]

In the words of the U.S. Advisory Commission on Intergovernmental Relations (ACIR), "State legislatures are the trustees of the basic rules of local governance in America. The laws and constitutions of each state are the basic legal instruments of local governance."[6] The ACIR statement denotes the essence of the distribution of authority between a state and its localities. In short, it is up to the state to determine the amount and type of authority a local government may possess. As specified by Dillon's rule, localities depend on the state to give them sufficient power to operate effectively.

The Amount and Type of Authority

In general, states' regulatory reach is great. For example, states may regulate local governments':

- Finances (by establishing debt limits and requiring balanced budgets)
- Personnel (by setting qualifications for certain positions and prescribing employee pension plans)
- Structure (by establishing forms of government and outlawing particular electoral systems)
- Processes (by requiring public hearings and open meetings and mandating financial disclosure)
- Functions (by ordering the provision of public safety functions and proscribing the pursuit of enterprise activities)
- Service standards (by adopting solid waste guidelines and setting acceptable water-quality levels)

The preceding list makes the point: The state capitol casts a long shadow.

In actuality, the amount and type of authority that states give their local governments vary widely. Some states grant their localities wide-ranging powers to restructure themselves, impose new taxes, and take on additional functions. Others, much more conservative with their power, force local governments to turn to the legislature for approval to act. Empowerment also depends on the type of local government. General-purpose governments such as counties, cities, and towns have wider latitude than special-purpose entities like school districts. Even general-purpose governments possess different degrees of authority; counties tend to be more circumscribed than cities in their ability to modify their form of government and expand their service offerings.

A look at building codes offers an illustration of the variability of state-local authority. Twenty-five years ago, researcher Peter May examined all fifty

Dillon's rule
A rule that limits the powers of local government to those expressly granted by the state or those powers closely linked to the express powers.

states to determine the amount of discretion given local governments to adopt and enforce building codes.[7] He found several different patterns. Twelve states (Kentucky and Michigan among them) played an aggressive role by imposing mandatory building codes on their local governments and overseeing local compliance. Thirteen states (including Indiana and Wyoming) had mandatory local codes but stopped short of state review or oversight. The rest of the states gave their local governments more leeway. In eight states (Iowa and Nebraska among them), local governments themselves decided whether to enforce the state building code. And seventeen states (including Delaware and Oklahoma) had no comprehensive building codes; thus, local governments were free to design and enact their own ordinances. In the years since the study was done, states have modified their building codes in numerous ways. But the fundamental point remains valid: States vary in their treatment of local government.

Many state constitutions set forth a provision for home rule. Although home rule falls short of actual local self-government, it is an important step in the direction of greater local decision making.[8] And local jurisdictions tend to be extremely protective of whatever power they have wrested from state government. For example, the beleaguered Baltimore school system rejected a state plan to take over the schools because, in the words of the one local official, "the solution to the problems in Baltimore city starts with Baltimore city."[9]

Devolution (the shift in power from the national government to the states) has also occurred between some states and their local governments. In the state-local case, it is called **second-order devolution**. For example, in 2011, the Alabama legislature authorized its cities and counties to create public organizations to promote tourism; in Oklahoma, municipalities were given more leeway to tear down abandoned buildings. In both cases, the state did not require local governments to act but rather gave them the authority to act if they so desired. What kinds of states tend to give their localities comparatively more power? On average, states that operate with traditional citizen-style, part-time legislative bodies are more likely to empower their local governments, as are states with slower rates of population growth and less robust economies.[10]

A State–Local Tug of War

Local governments want their states to provide them with adequate funding and ample discretion. Local officials are supremely confident of their abilities to govern, given sufficient state support. These same local officials express concern that neither their policy-making power nor their financial authority has kept pace with the increased administrative responsibilities placed on them by state government. The recognition and correction of such conditions are the state's responsibility. The state of Michigan, for example, has used its statutory authority to appoint emergency financial managers for several of its financially troubled local governments. The most famous case is the city of Detroit, which had amassed a budget deficit of more than $320 million by 2013 when a state-appointed emergency manager took control of the city's finances away from local elected officials. (Detroit eventually declared

second-order devolution
A shift in power from state government to local government.

? It's Your Turn

Should a State Bail Out Its Financially Stressed Local Governments?

PROS	CONS
Restoring the financial health of local governments is in the best interest of the state.	The local government got itself into the financial mess, it should figure out a solution.
A state has more resources to draw on to help a troubled locality.	There is little incentive for local officials to make hard choices about expenditures and revenues if the state is going to step in and override them.
Sometimes local officials are just too close to the situation to be able to see it clearly and resolve the problems; a state official can offer fresh thinking.	It is undemocratic for appointed state officials to usurp the policy-making power of local elected officials.

bankruptcy in 2014, allowing the city to restructure its debt, slash expenditures, and develop a plan for seeking new revenue; the state's emergency manager then returned control to local officials.) The issue of state takeovers of localities is considered in the It's Your Turn box.

States are not at all reluctant to exercise power vis-à-vis their local jurisdictions. Consider these laws passed in legislative sessions in 2019[11]

- Pennsylvania banned local governments from enacting bans on plastic grocery bags.
- North Dakota prevented cities from raising minimum wages above the $7.25 per hour level set by the state and federal governments.
- Arkansas prohibited municipalities from passing sanctuary policies that put limits on cooperation with federal immigration officials.

A persistent theme runs through the preceding list: State government can impose its will on local governments. These examples do not mean that states and localities are invariably at each other's throats. Plenty of examples of state–local partnerships exist, such as Florida's and Palm Beach County's joint effort to attract biotechnology industries. The county purchased the land to build a research facility ($200 million); the state is paying the facility's operating costs for seven years ($300 million).[12] Still, the relationship between a state and its local governments often involves conflict as each level tries to exert its will. As tensions escalate, state courts may become involved in determining whether the actions of a state or its local jurisdictions violate the provisions of the state's constitution.

The diagram presented in Figure 12.1 reflects the two fundamental ways that states can influence the authority of local governments. One way is through the vertical state–local government relationship: States can choose to retain power (centralize) or disperse power (decentralize). The other way is horizontal—the power relationships that local governments have with each

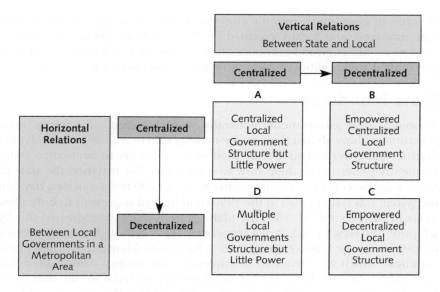

Figure 12.1 Typology of Governance Structure of Metropolitan Regions

Source: David K. Hamilton, David Y. Miller, and Jerry Paytas, "Exploring Horizontal and Vertical Dimensions of the Governing of Metropolitan Regions," *Urban Affairs Review* 40 (November 2004): 152.

other. Combining the two dimensions, vertical and horizontal, produces the four square-shaped boxes on the right half of the diagram.[13] Box A reflects a state that centralizes vertically and horizontally; box C is a state that decentralizes on both dimensions. In a metropolitan area in A states, there are few local governments, and they lack power. In states characterized by the pattern described in box C, many local governments exist and they enjoy substantial power. The states depicted by boxes B and D have one centralizing feature and one decentralizing feature. A state's political history, its constitution, and actions of the legislature combine to determine where a state fits in this diagram. Too, some shifts can occur over time, especially as metropolitan areas develop.

The ability of states and localities to work together effectively has been tested by the issue of homeland security. Concerned that state and local governments were ill prepared to respond to a disaster in a comprehensive and cooperative way, the federal government funded two antiterrorism exercises. One simulation, a bomb and chemical weapons attack, took place in Connecticut; the other, a bioterrorism incident, was set in New Jersey.[14] The exercises exposed weaknesses in response capability, especially communications among responders. The results of the mock disasters sent state and local officials throughout the nation back to the drawing boards to try to determine how to improve their response systems. One outcome has been the creation of the federal National Response Framework (NRF), an "all-hazards" emergency operations plan that identifies and assigns responsibilities to state and local agencies—and to nonprofit organizations—in the event of a disaster. The NRF states, "most incidents begin and end locally" but "when all levels of government become engaged, a response is federally supported, state managed, and locally executed."[15] Plans such as this are designed to improve coordination and communication not only vertically (between the state government and localities) but also horizontally (among local jurisdictions).

State Mandates

Although local governments generally want increased autonomy, state governments have shared their policy-making sphere with reluctance. Rather than let subgovernments devise their own solutions to problems, states frequently prefer to tell them how to solve them. For instance, the state of Idaho's online court records are estimated to get 200,000 requests a day, but the system was last updated in the 1990s and limited requestors to only a few items in each record. In 2016, the Idaho State Legislature addressed this by adopting Odyssey, a product of a Texas company.[16] Although this was a major innovation in the Idaho court system, it had its problems. Individual Idaho counties—which were required to implement the system—complained that the system didn't work the way the developers promised it would, that it was time-consuming and cumbersome. The state said that the system would not cost counties any additional funds to implement and would also save on personnel costs, but a survey of Idaho county officials found that 29 percent said they had to increase revenues to pay for the new system, whereas 42 percent said they had to hire additional employees. Adapting to the new system was rated the most difficult state mandate for counties to implement, with 78 percent of the county officials citing it as the most troublesome.[17] Requirements or orders like these are examples of *mandates*. Unfunded mandates, especially those with a large price tag, are a persistent source of friction between state and local levels of government.

From the perspective of state government, mandates are necessary to ensure that vital activities are performed and desirable goals are achieved. State mandates promote uniformity of policy from one jurisdiction to another (for instance, regarding the length of the public school year or the operating hours of precinct polling places). In addition, they promote coordination, especially among adjacent jurisdictions that provide services jointly (as with a regional hospital or a metropolitan transportation system).

Officials at the local level tend to see state mandates as unnecessary, and often costly, intrusions into local matters. A nationwide survey of city managers and state legislators captured the differing perspectives of the two groups. When asked about the impact of state mandates in twelve policy areas, city managers judged them as negative across the board, while state legislators viewed nine of twelve as positive or neutral.[18]

Local officials offer several suggestions for fixing the mandate problem. Three solutions supported by more than 80 percent of officials surveyed in a Minnesota study of state mandates are as follows:

- The state should provide a clear statement of the rationale behind the mandate; in other words, the state should justify its action.

- Localities should be given greater flexibility in implementing the provisions of the mandate.
- Financial aid to local governments should be increased so that they can deal with mandates effectively.[19]

As might be expected, these solutions are substantially less popular with state officials. But certainly, more communication between state policy makers and local officials, especially at the outset, would reduce some of the friction generated by mandates. Allowing local governments more leeway in implementation, either through extension of time or variation in rules, would lessen the punch that mandates pack. Even more central to any type of mandate reform is adequate state funding of mandates. This action would go a long way toward improving state–local relationships. Recognizing that funding is one of the key considerations, many states have adopted **mandate-reimbursement requirements**. These measures require states either to reimburse local governments for the costs of state mandates or to give local governments adequate revenue-raising capacity to pay for them.

New Jersey goes one step further in addressing unfunded state mandates on local government. The Council on Local Mandates was established as an independent body in 1996. Its members are appointed by the governor, majority and minority leaders of the state senate and house of representatives, and the chief justice of the state supreme court. The council is empowered to overturn state-imposed mandates on local governments if a county municipality or school district files a complaint. In its twenty-four-year history, the council has only overturned twenty-two mandates, the most recent of these being the state law that required counties to automatically send 2018 mail-in ballots to any voter who had voted by mail in 2016. The New Jersey Association of Counties argued that counties were required to send out more than 437,000 mail-in ballots for the 2018 elections—costing an extra $2.8 million—and that the costs would be much greater in 2020.[20]

State–Local Organizations

Legal, administrative, and financial ties link state and local governments. Additional interaction occurs when state governments establish organizations such as local government study commissions and advisory panels of local officials. Among the most prevalent structures are task forces, advisory commissions on intergovernmental relations, and departments of community affairs.

Task forces tend to be focused organizations set up by the governor or the state legislature in response to a perceived local-level problem. If a state wants to investigate the ramifications of changing its annexation statutes, the legislature might create a task force on annexation and boundary changes (or something similar). The task force would probably be composed of state and local officials, community leaders, and experts on the subject of annexation.

mandate-reimbursement requirements Measures that take the financial sting out of state mandates.

First, the task force would collect information on how other states handle the annexation question; second, it would conduct a series of public hearings to get input from individuals and groups interested in the issue; finally, it would compile a report that included recommendations suitable for legislative action. Its work completed, the task force would then disband, although individual members might turn up as advocates when the task-force recommendations receive legislative attention. Task forces are quick organizational responses to local problems that have become too prominent for state government to ignore. A task force is a low-cost, concentrated reaction that undertakes specific tasks and, in some instances, actually influences legislative deliberations.

In a more comprehensive effort at state-local cooperation, twenty-five states established state-level *advisory commissions on intergovernmental relations* (*ACIRs*), modeled after the commission, now defunct, created by the U.S. Congress in 1959. State-level ACIRs are designed to promote more harmonious, workable relations between the state and its governmental subdivisions. They are intended to offer a neutral forum for discussion of long-range state–local issues—a venue in which officials can engage in focused dialogue; conduct research on local developments and new state policies; promote experimentation in intergovernmental processes, both state–local and interlocal; and propose solutions to state–local problems.

Despite their promise, many state ACIRs met their demise in the 1990s and early 2000s, among them the ACIRs in Oklahoma and Virginia, victims of state budget cuts and insufficient legislative support. (Kansas bucked the trend by creating an ACIR in 2002.) The most recent count shows that only ten state ACIRs remain viable.[21] Those that have managed to survive have been able to demonstrate their utility and steer a nonpartisan path in a partisan environment. The Connecticut ACIR, for instance, has as one of its statutory responsibilities the tracking and reporting of the mandates adopted by the state's General Assembly during the legislative session.

Another way in which states can generate closer formal ties with their local governments is through specialized administrative agencies. All fifty states have created *departments of community affairs* (*DCAs*) that are involved in local activities. They have different names (Kentucky calls its DCA the Department for Local Government; Washington's is the Department of Community, Trade, and Economic Development), but their function is similar: to offer a range of programs and services to local governments. DCAs are involved in housing, urban revitalization, anti-poverty programs, and economic development; they also offer local governments services such as planning, management, and financial assistance. DCAs vary on several dimensions: their niche in state government, the sizes of their budget and staff, and whether they include an advisory board of local officials. Compared with state-level ACIRs, DCAs function much more as service deliverers and much less as policy initiators. Therefore, these two types of organizations tend to complement rather than compete with one another. Both function as advocates for local government, however, at the state level.

Metropolitics: A New Challenge for State Government

State governments often find their dealings with local governments to be confounded by the side effects of urbanization. Regardless of which state we examine its urban areas show the effects of three waves of suburbanization. An early wave occurred during the 1920s, when automobiles facilitated the development of outlying residential areas. Although the dispersion slowed during the Great Depression and World War II, its resurgence in the 1950s triggered a second wave during which retail stores followed the population exodus, the so-called malling of America. Now a third wave of suburbanization is upon us, one fueled by what has been called America's "exit ramp economy." Office, commercial, and retail facilities are increasingly located along suburban freeways.[22] This phenomenon is occurring nearly everywhere, from New York City to San Diego, from Milwaukee to Miami. This third wave of suburbanization has caught the attention of state governments.

As a result of the transformation of American metropolitan areas, central cities have lost some of their prominence as the social, economic, and political focal points of their areas. People have moved to surrounding suburbs and beyond; businesses and firms have sprung up in the hinterlands; communities have formed their own service and taxing districts. The outward flow of people and activities has fundamentally altered metropolitan areas. As noted earlier, these new boom towns are not simply residential but also include business, retail, and entertainment activities.

Continued outward growth beyond the central city suggests the need for changes in outmoded state government policy toward metropolitan jurisdictions. A serious concern is that rapid, unplanned growth is producing sprawl and fostering what are called shadow governments. A logical question is: What is state government doing while all of this is occurring? More than it used to, as we shall see.

Urban Sprawl Versus Smart Growth

Population growth is, of course, something that states and localities desire. But the consequences of rapid and unplanned population growth test the capability of governments to provide services efficiently and effectively. As growth spills beyond city limits into unincorporated areas, as **edge cities** spring up along interstate highways, the result is often traffic congestion and overcrowded schools. Far from the central city, subdivisions and strip malls sprout on land that was recently forests and farms. It costs a lot of money for government to provide infrastructure—streets, water and sewer lines, schools—to these new developments. Meanwhile, many inner cities, where the infrastructure is already in place, are plagued by empty storefronts, vacant lots, and abandoned factories. Many states and localities have struggled to balance the benefits of new growth against the attendant costs.

LO 12-2
To analyze the issues of urban sprawl and smart growth.

edge cities
New boom towns featuring retail shops and malls, restaurants, office buildings, and housing developments, far from the central city.

Sprawling Growth In many parts of the country, one of the hottest issues of the early twenty-first century is **urban sprawl**, a term that carries negative connotations. It refers to development beyond the central city that is characterized by low densities, rapid land consumption, and dependence on the automobile. It is often called *leapfrog development* because it jumps over established settlements. Exit-ramp communities and edge cities are a manifestation of sprawl. Urban sprawl is resource intensive and costly, and it is also the subject of political debate.

Until the mortgage crisis in 2008 and the subsequent recession, Las Vegas, Nevada, offered perhaps the best contemporary example of a fast-growing, sprawling city. According to the city's statistics, 200 new residents arrived in Las Vegas every day; a house was constructed every fifteen minutes.[23] Traffic congestion intensified, as did concern over maintaining an adequate water supply in this desert city. As human settlement pushed ever outward to lower-cost land, local government was pressed to provide schools, parks, and roads. Growth quickly outstripped the infrastructure needed to support it. The mayor of Las Vegas proposed a $2,000-per-house **impact fee** to mitigate the effects of growth, but the city lacked the authority to levy the fee. The Nevada legislature had to approve the proposal before it could take effect.

Although the pace of growth has slowed in Las Vegas and the surrounding area, the issues related to planning and paying for new development remain. Even though revenues for local governments will increase as a result of development, costs of providing services will also rise and not necessarily commensurately. One study of Georgia counties found that for every $1.00 of revenue brought in by new housing developments, the cost of services was between $1.23 and $2.07.[24] Public education was the big-ticket item pushing up service costs. This is the primary explanation for the popularity of impact fees. Research on Florida counties found that rapid population growth stimulates the adoption of impact fees, especially if nearby counties have adopted them already.[25] Only when commercial and industrial development complements subdivision growth do local governments typically enjoy a net revenue gain.

Urban sprawl also raises environmental and public safety issues. In California, the high costs of housing in major cities has led to the development of more moderately priced suburban housing developments on lands that have experienced wildfires over the years. When recurring wildfires affect these areas, homes are burned. One recent study compared the effects of the wind-driven 1964 Hanly and the 2017 Tubbs wildfires, both occurring in similar areas in Napa, Sonoma, and Lake counties near Santa Barbara. Only a small part of the area had housing units in 1964 but by 2017, a very large percentage of the area had been developed with low- or high-density housing. The result was the destruction of more than 2,000 homes and the loss of some twenty-two lives in the Tubbs Fire.[26] Four of the five largest fires in California history have occurred since 2012, each burning more than 250,000 acres of land (larger than the land area of New York City).

The relentless creep of urban sprawl has prompted reactions in many states and communities. In 2018, nineteen land conservation measures appeared on ballots throughout the country; eighteen of them passed. These measures

urban sprawl Development characterized by low population density, rapid land consumption, and dependence on the automobile.

impact fee A charge levied on new development to offset some of the costs of providing services.

committed more than $1.2 billion in new funding for land conservation. Voters in Connecticut approved a constitutional amendment requiring the state legislature to hold public hearings and attain a two-thirds majority before state-owned public land can be sold or given away.[27] One major defeat occurred in California where Fresno voters rejected a $1.1 billion citizen initiative to update and improve city parks and trails.

Smart Growth The majority of land-use decisions occur at the local level, and many states offer guidance and provide localities with tools to manage growth. Hawaii was a pioneer in this effort with its State Land Use Law, adopted in 1961; Vermont and Oregon got on board in 1970 and 1973, respectively, with growth management acts designed to control the pace of development and protect environmentally sensitive areas. The **smart growth** movement represents the new generation in state growth management. It is an effort to reduce the amount of sprawl and minimize its impact. Communities tend to define "smart growth" in ways that fit their own particular circumstances, but the basic principles of the movement are listed in Table 12.1.

Maryland was one of the first states to take action to limit sprawl. Calling sprawl "a disease eating away at the heart of America," Governor Parris Glendening signed the Smart Growth Areas Act into law in 1997.[28] In effect, the state rewards local governments that target new growth in areas that already have infrastructure, and it denies state funding for infrastructure projects that encourage sprawl. Several other states moved quickly to follow Maryland's lead. The following year, Arizona adopted a Growing Smarter Act; by 2003, another twenty states had taken anti-sprawl actions of one sort or another.[29]

A word of caution is necessary. Not everyone thinks that sprawl is so bad. In fact, to some, sprawl is simply the consequence of the unfettered workings of a free-market system.[30] Given a choice, they contend, Americans prefer a spread out, car-centered lifestyle. Obviously, there is some truth to that

smart growth
Government efforts to limit urban sprawl by managing growth.

Table 12.1 Ten Principles of Smart Growth

- Mix land uses.
- Take advantage of compact building design.
- Create a range of housing opportunities and choices.
- Create walkable neighborhoods.
- Foster distinctive, attractive communities with a strong sense of place.
- Preserve open space, farmland, natural beauty, and critical environmental areas.
- Strengthen and direct development toward existing communities.
- Provide a variety of transportation choices.
- Make development decisions predictable, fair, and cost-effective.
- Encourage community and stakeholder collaboration in development decisions.

Source: Smart Growth Online, "Smart Growth Principles," http://smartgrowth.org/smart-growth-principles/ (accessed March 14, 2020).

argument. Smart growth inevitably means higher density, that is, smaller lot sizes and taller buildings to accommodate more people. High-rise condominium complexes and soaring office towers appeal to some folks, but to most suburbanites, increased density is not something they want.[31] And then there are private property advocates who argue that any kind of growth management legislation interferes with what people can and cannot do with their own property.[32]

Shadow Governments

As new development pushes into the hinterlands, new forms of governance are emerging. They have become known as **shadow governments**, and although they may not be official government units, in many important ways they behave as if they were. They levy fees, regulate behavior, and provide services. Three types of shadow government exist:

- Private enterprise shadow governments, such as homeowners' associations
- Public–private partnership shadow governments, common examples of which are development corporations and business improvement districts
- Subsidiaries of conventional governments with unusual powers, such as area-wide planning commissions

Shadow governments exist within the confines of state law, but most states have not taken an active role in overseeing them.

Estimates place the number of private enterprise shadow governments at more than 350,000, the majority located in suburban areas. A condominium community provides an illustration. The property owners' association makes rules for residents (from the speed limit on community streets to the color of the condo), provides services (security, maintenance, landscaping, operating the community swimming pool), and assesses fees (based on the size of the unit). Residents typically vote for the board of directors of the association (in some instances, developers of the project retain seats on the board), and votes tend to be weighted according to the value of the housing unit. Owners with a greater financial investment have a greater say in the governing of the community, which is a far cry from the one-person, one-vote principle.

Shadow governments, especially the first two types, raise questions about matters of power and equity (but not about their efficiency because, by most accounts, they tend to operate fairly efficiently). The power issue centers on information, influence, and accountability. Shadow governments control information, restrict influence to those who belong or can pay, and have little public accountability. They are not subject to the same legal standards as are typical governments.[33] The equity issue addresses the class discrimination inherent in these governments. A poor family out for a Sunday drive may be able to traverse public streets in their ramshackle automobile, but if they turn their car onto a private street patrolled by private police, they are likely to be

shadow governments
Entities, especially unofficial ones, that function like governments.

followed and perhaps even stopped, questioned, and escorted out of the neighborhood. One extension of this is the gated community in which the homes are literally separated from the surrounding area by a wall or a gate. Entry is controlled by a guard or an electronic device that opens the gate. Guests of residents can typically only access the community by approval of the individual resident. As of 2017, some 9.2 million of the 121.5 million housing units in the United States (just over 7.5 percent) were located in gated communities.[34]

Whatever our uneasiness over power and equity issues related to shadow governments, their number is increasing. Shadow governments are especially popular in metropolitan areas, because local government boundaries do not necessarily jibe with economic realities and development patterns. Their vaunted efficiency makes them a force to be reckoned with. Research on private enterprise shadow governments in California, Florida, and New Jersey showed each state taking vastly different approaches to their regulation.[35]

The social and economic changes in U.S. metropolitan areas have had a tremendous impact on urban governance. Urban expansion and shadow governments make up extended webs of interdependent jurisdictions. How can these places be governed best? Some observers have advocated a broad regionally focused approach.

Regional Governance

A typical metropolitan area in the United States is fragmented—that is, it is comprised of many local governments. One alternative to the fragmentation is the creation of a **regional government**, a larger entity to replace some of the smaller jurisdictions. State legislatures are important players in this process because, aside from the state constitution, they create the rules of the game. Their actions either facilitate or hinder local government reorganization into regional units.

City–County Consolidation In the United States, the closest thing to regional government is **city–county consolidation**, whereby area jurisdictions are absorbed into a single countywide government. In a pure form of consolidation, one police department, one fire department, and one water and sewer system exist for the area. The functions of local government— public safety, public works, health and human services, community and economic development, and recreation and arts programs—are provided by a single jurisdiction. Thirty-four consolidated city–county governments exist in the United States. Some of these consolidated jurisdictions reflect political decisions of the nineteenth century, such as the combined city– county governments of Philadelphia, San Francisco, and New Orleans. Among the most prominent mergers of the past forty years are those in Indianapolis–Marion County, Indiana; Jacksonville–Duval County, Florida; Nashville–Davidson County, Tennessee; and, Louisville–Jefferson County, Kentucky. The state of Georgia leads the nation in the number of consolidated

LO 12-3
To evaluate the various forms of regionalism.

regional government
An area-wide structure for local governance, designed to replace multiple jurisdictions.

city–county consolidation
The merger of city and county governments into a single jurisdiction.

city–county governments with seven, the most recent occurring in Macon–
Bibb County in 2014.

Regional government seems so rational, yet it has proven to be quite dif-
ficult to achieve. Voters usually defeat proposals to consolidate city and
county government, such as the 2012 effort in Evansville and Vanderburgh
County, Indiana. At various times, voters have rejected the mergers of Des
Moines and Polk County, Iowa; Spokane and Spokane County, Washington;
Wilmington and New Hanover County, North Carolina; and Knoxville and
Knox County, Tennessee—just to name a few. Opponents of jurisdictional
consolidation often include city and county governing boards, city and county
employees, and taxpayer organizations. Support for merging governments
typically comes from the local chamber of commerce, real estate developers,
local newspapers, and civic organizations.[36]

To reformers, this lack of success is perplexing. The logic is straightforward: If small local governments in a metropolitan area merge to form a larger
local government, two positive outcomes will occur. First, stubborn public
policy problems can be tackled from an area-wide perspective. For example,
the pollution generated by City A that affects City B can be handled as a
regional problem rather than as a conflict between the two cities. Second,
combining forces produces *economies of scale* in service delivery. Instead of
each jurisdiction constructing and operating separate jails, for example, one
large regional facility can be maintained. Jail service can be provided at a
lower cost to each participating jurisdiction. These anticipated outcomes are
persuasive arguments in favor of consolidation.

Regional government does not always perform as expected, however.
Research has shown that city–county consolidation does not necessarily
reduce the costs of government and may even increase them.[37] Another criticism of regional government is that it can be inaccessible and destructive of
the hard-won political gains of minorities. Compared with a city or town
government, regional government is farther away, both literally and figura-
tively. Residents of small towns fear the loss of identity as their community
gets swept into bigger government. The effect on minority political strength
is no less troublesome. Because the proportionate number of minorities may
be lessened when jurisdictions are combined, their voting strength can be
diluted. For instance, African Americans made up 34 percent of pre-merger
Louisville but only 19.5 percent of consolidated Louisville–Jefferson Metro
Government.[38]

A competing perspective on regional government comes from **public
choice theory**. According to this theory, the existence of many jurisdictions
in a metropolitan area gives people options, that is, they can choose to live
in the central city, in nearby suburbs, or in the county. Each of these jurisdictions offers a particular mix of tax rates, policies, and public services. In
deciding where to reside or open a business, individuals seek places that are
in line with their own tax, policy, and service preferences.[39] To public choice
theorists, consolidating cities and counties or creating regional governments
robs people of important choices and creates inefficiencies. The consolidation of the city of Louisville and Jefferson County borrowed a page from

public choice theory
The theory that
individuals shop
around to find a local
government whose
taxes and services are
in line with their own
preferences.

Jefferson County   Independent Cities   Louisville

Figure 12.2 Map of Louisville, Jefferson County, and Small Cities

Source: H.V. Savitch and Ronald K. Vogel, "Suburbs without a City: Power and City-County Consolidation," *Urban Affairs Review* (July 2004): 769. Copyright 2004 by Sage Publications Inc. Journals. Reproduced with permission of Sage Publications Inc. Journals in the format Textbook via Copyright Clearance Center.

public choice theory when, in a political compromise, it left eighty smaller jurisdictions in the county out of the merger. Figure 12.2 shows the boundaries of pre-consolidated Louisville and Jefferson County, as well as the other jurisdictions.

A City and Its Suburbs The former mayor of Albuquerque, New Mexico, David Rusk, after thinking long and hard about the relationship between a central city and its suburbs, jumped into the regionalism debate with this statement: "The real city is the total metropolitan area—city and suburb."[40] He uses the concept of elasticity (and inelasticity) to signify the ability of a city to expand its city boundaries (or not). In a sense, a city's elasticity is its destiny. Elastic cities have been able to capture suburban growth; by adjusting their boundaries through annexation, they can keep pace with urban sprawl. Conversely, many inelastic cities trapped in existing boundaries have suffered population loss and tax-base erosion, resulting in higher levels of racial and class segregation.

The solution offered is a familiar one: regional government. But to be effective, the regional government must include the central city and at least 60 percent of the area's population, according to Rusk. How to do this? It depends on the characteristics of the metropolitan area. In single-county metropolitan areas, empowerment of the urban county would effectively create regional government, as would city–county consolidation. And in multi-county metropolitan areas, a single regional government could be created out of existing cities and counties. Obviously, the restructuring of local governments in these ways would engender substantial opposition; as Rusk acknowledges, however, few alternatives are available to areas with low elasticity.

The argument for a metropolitan-wide government is simple: Because economies are essentially regional in nature, governance can (and should) be, too. As discussed earlier, however, regional government has never been a popular alternative in this country. Overcoming traditional anti-regionalism sentiment will not be easy, but regional approaches may be necessary for effective competition in an increasingly global economy. And there is some evidence that thinking regionally is gaining favor. Maybe the mayor of Missoula, Montana (a college town), said it best when he commented: "It is not possible for Missoula to understand itself, or its future, except in a regional context. The city draws its strength from the region."[41]

It's up to the States Both Portland, Oregon, and the Twin Cities area of Minnesota have embraced regionalism. In Oregon, Portland joined with its suburbs and outlying jurisdictions to develop a region-wide vision for the future. The 2040 Plan, as it is called, aims at accommodating orderly growth while maintaining a desirable quality of life in the region. The planning process involved extensive public participation, including citizen surveys and public forums. In addition, the plan's backers launched media campaigns and loaned videos to acquaint residents with the proposal. The 2040 Plan is enforced by an elected, region-wide council that works to secure the compliance of local governments.[42]

In the Minneapolis–St. Paul area of Minnesota, jurisdictions contribute 40 percent of their new commercial and industrial tax base to a regional pool. The money in this pool is redistributed to communities throughout the region on the basis of financial need, thereby reducing fiscal disparities across jurisdictions. Thus, for instance, a new industry locating in one city becomes a benefit to neighboring cities as well. With regional tax-base sharing as a start, Minnesota went even further in 1994 when the state legislature placed all regional sewer, transit, and land-use planning in the hands of a regional organization—the Metropolitan Council of the Twin Cities.[43] This significantly empowered council makes crucial decisions about growth and development in the Twin Cities area from a regional perspective.

In the final analysis, it is up to state government to provide a sufficiently supportive environment in which regionalism can take root. It was Oregon and Minnesota that created the legal environment for Portland and the Twin Cities, respectively. As political scientists Margaret Weir, Harold Wolman, and Todd Swanstrom declared in their research on city–suburban coalitions, "States are critical players; they set the terms and conditions under which regionalism occurs."[44] They have to because the natural tendency for officials in cities and their suburbs is to see each other as rivals rather than allies or partners. An extreme example of regionalism comes from California, where there were efforts to get initiatives on the 2016 ballot that would have created six regional Californias and on the 2018 ballot to create three regional Californias. Read about this in the Controversies in States and Localities feature.

Regional Coordination **Councils of government (COGs)** or regional planning commissions are examples of regional coordination. They do not involve a formal merger or combination of governments; instead, COGs are loose collections of local governments designed to increase communication and coordination in an area. They provide a neutral forum in which local leaders can come together to identify and discuss issues of common concern.[45] Several COGs and regional planning organizations have recently conducted planning exercises organized to address "what-if" scenarios. Some of these different scenarios are:

- What would be the effect on Denver-area water usage if future households move from less dense to more dense residential patterns of land use? (Colorado Water and Growth Dialogue, 2018)[46]
- What if the Biloxi, Mississippi, area invests more in transit, or in pedestrian and bicycle facility improvements? (Gulf Regional Planning Commission, 2016)[47]
- What if a major tornado strikes Dallas-Fort Worth? (North Texas COG, 2019)[48]

The point of the scenario planning process is to get local leaders thinking about how large-scale events could affect the area's jurisdictions in the future.

State governments, in fact, were not active in the creation of COGs; national government programs spurred their development. For example, the federal government requires states to create metropolitan planning organizations (MPOs) to coordinate transportation programs in urban areas.[49] Nearly half of the MPOs are part of their area COG. Currently, there are more than 500 COGs active in the United States, serving some 35,000 of the 39,000 local general-purpose governments.

Although area-wide planning is the most common activity of COGs, they also perform other tasks. Member governments can turn to them for technical assistance (such as help in writing federal grant applications), professional services (planning, budgeting, engineering, legal advice), and information (economic data for the region).

The impact of these councils has been less significant than their creators hoped, but they have had two positive effects. First, COGs have elevated the concept of area-wide policy planning from a pipe dream to a reality. They have been heavily involved in criminal justice, water quality, housing, and especially transportation planning. Second, councils have substantially improved the operational capacity of rural local governments by providing expertise to small local jurisdictions that cannot afford to hire specialized staff.

Some localities have taken a more informal route to regional coordination through service sharing. In service sharing, jurisdictions agree to consolidate specific services, cooperate in their provision, or exchange them. For instance, recreational facilities may be provided jointly by several jurisdictions, one government may rent jail space from another, or county residents may use the city library in return for city residents' use of the county's solid waste landfill. Service-sharing arrangements are popular because they hold the promise of greater efficiency in service delivery, *and* they do not threaten

councils of government
Formal organizations of general-purpose governments in an area, intended to improve regional coordination.

Controversies in States and Localities

One Big California or Several Regional Californias?

California is a big state, both in terms of population and land area. Since joining the United States in 1850, many proposals to split the state in two—usually into northern and southern states—have emerged. The groups promoting a split are usually unhappy with state policy on certain issues or believe that their area is not getting its fair share of resources from the legislature.

Since 2000, there have been five proposals to split the state into smaller states. In 2014, California venture capitalist Tim Draper's proposed ballot initiative on the question of dividing the state into six separate states was rejected for inclusion on the 2016 ballot by the California secretary of state, who found the initiative didn't have a sufficient number of valid signatures. Not to be deterred, in 2018 Draper started a new plan called CAL 3 to divide the state into three new states: Northern California, California, and Southern California (see the accompanying map). This time the proposal did get sufficient signatures to get it on the ballot. Why propose such a dramatic change? In the view of Draper and

his supporters, the Golden State had become ungovernable and it needed to be refreshed. The solution was to create smaller states that would be more responsive to their residents, more accountable for their actions, and more innovative in their policies.

The CAL 3 proposal attracted a lot of attention and plenty of pushback. The California Planning and Conservation League brought suit against CAL 3, arguing that the proposed changes were so fundamental that they should have been approved by a two-thirds vote of the state legislature before they could appear on a ballot. In July 2018, the California Supreme Court removed the CAL 3 initiative from the 2018 ballot but said it would be willing to hear further arguments about it appearing on a later ballot.

Critical Thinking Questions

1. What advantages does California enjoy as the largest state in the nation? What disadvantages does it face?

2. Why are smaller states thought to be more responsive and accountable than larger states?

3. Would a layer of multi-county regional governments be a better alternative to breaking up the state?

Sources: Casey Tolan, "This Is Really Happening: Measure to Split California into Three States Qualifies for November Ballot," *The Mercury News*, https://www.mercurynews.com/2018/06/12/ballot-measure-split-california-three-states/ (June 12, 2018); Glynn Custred, "To Fix California, Break It Up," *National Review*, https://www.nationalreview.com/2018/08/fix-california-by-breaking-it-up-cal-3-initiative/ (August 15, 2018); Bob Egelko, "Splitting Up California: State Supreme Court Takes Initiative Off Ballot," *San Francisco Chronicle*, https://www.sfchronicle.com/politics/article/Splitting-up-Calif-State-Supreme-Court-takes-13085880.php (July 18, 2018).

The Three Californias

the power and autonomy of existing jurisdictions the way consolidation does. Research suggests that local officials may be more receptive to this type of interjurisdictional cooperation than is commonly thought.[50] Still, the ability to hammer out agreements that benefit all participating governments is contingent upon numerous factors related to the problem itself and the jurisdictional context.[51] COGs and service-sharing agreements provide for a modicum of regional governance . . . without a regional government.

States and Urban Policy

LO 12-4
To assess the urban impacts of state policies on housing and infrastructure.

If you had attended an urban policy conference recently, you would have heard the phrase *state government* used repeatedly. Many states have replaced some of their policies that had a negative impact on urban areas with urban-friendly programs. Michigan was one of the leaders when, in 1998, its Urban Caucus began a process of identifying state programs that hindered investment in central cities. Since then, other states have followed suit. Three significant contemporary issues—housing, infrastructure, and new urbanism—are of particular interest in an urban environment. Let us consider each of these contemporary issues in terms of state-local interaction.

Housing Policy

For middle- and upper-income city residents, the housing market can be counted on to produce affordable units, but what is affordable to these residents is out of reach for low-income households. The mechanics of market economics effectively shut them out of the system. Low-cost housing does not generate the return that higher-cost housing does. As a result, governments have intervened to create incentives for developers to produce low-income housing units and, where incentives do not work, to become providers of housing themselves. One of the aims of the federal Housing Act of 1949 was "a decent home in a suitable living environment" for all Americans.

Over time, the national government has backed away from this goal and altered its approach to housing. In 1968, it was willing to become the nation's housing provider of last resort, but by the 1980s the push was to deregulate and let market forces prevail. Modifications of national tax laws have had a negative effect on rental housing stock. Deliberate actions and inaction resulted in a decline in home ownership, an increase in the proportion of household income that is spent on housing, a decrease in the number of affordable rental units, an increase in the number of physically inadequate and abandoned structures, and an increase in the number of homeless people.[52]

In response, state governments have set up housing finance agencies, non-profit corporations have entered the low-income housing market, and local governments have adopted regulations to preserve their affordable housing stock. New Jersey, for example, mandated that all of its 567 communities provide their fair share of affordable housing for low- and moderate-income people. In some places, housing vouchers—a form of consumer subsidy that would open currently unaffordable housing to low-income residents—have been instituted. Another approach is for local governments to require developers to include a fixed proportion of affordable units in their market-rate projects as a condition for approval of a building permit. This approach works, however, only where developers are clamoring for access.

Connecticut has been particularly innovative in addressing its affordable-housing problem. As part of its statewide plan, the state conducted a housing needs assessment. In a pilot program, Connecticut entered into mediated negotiations with local jurisdictions in a specified area to develop a fair-housing compact for the area. To encourage communities to pursue the goals of the compact, it established a housing infrastructure fund to provide state financial assistance. As a result, thousands of new affordable housing units were constructed.[53] Connecticut's effort to address the scarcity of affordable housing has been emulated by other states.

Some local jurisdictions are also playing active roles. Seattle has pioneered the resurgence of backyard cottages—small, affordable units that are constructed behind existing single-family homes. Although some homeowners use these "accessory dwelling units" to house their extended family, most rent them to tenants. Initially, the city's policy met with criticism that it would change the feel of a neighborhood, but a recent study showed this not to be the case.[54] Other cities such as Los Angeles, Denver, and Austin have followed Seattle's lead in adopting this affordable housing option, with many more expected to soon allow such development.[55] In some regions of the country, cities are dealing with the phenomenon of **gentrification**, in which new development occurs in underinvested and predominately poor neighborhoods. That might seem to be a positive development, but it typically leads to steep rises in housing prices that eventually displace a community's longtime residents.[56]

In states hit particularly hard by the downturn in the housing market in 2008 and 2009, problems of a different sort arose. In California, Arizona, Nevada, and Florida, plunging home values and mortgage foreclosures meant lower property tax revenues for local jurisdictions. In addition, the number of homeless people rose in many cities, straining the capacity of shelters and leading to the creation of tent cities and encampments. By 2012, the housing market had rebounded somewhat in many areas of the country; by 2015, most areas in the United States were experiencing increased demand for housing. But as the cost of housing in large cities such as Miami, St. Louis, Denver, and Boston increased rapidly, homelessness also increased. A 2018 study showed that when housing costs increase to more than a third of income, homelessness can be expected to rise rapidly.[57] Housing costs can exceed one-third of income under two different sets of circumstances: income declines as a result of unemployment or underemployment while housing costs are stable or housing costs increase dramatically while income doesn't keep pace.

As with many other policy areas, the COVID-19 pandemic affected housing. As a large number of hourly workers—many of whom were renters rather than homeowners—were furloughed or laid-off, rent payments became problematic. More than 30 percent of renters made either partial or no rent payments in May 2020, up from 25 percent in April.[58] Many state governors or state legislatures placed moratoriums on evictions for non-payment of rent as a result of COVID-19 (some also prohibited late fees and shutting off utilities) but many of these moratoriums had relatively short life spans and were due to expire after 30 to 60 days.[59] The federal CARES Act imposed moratoriums on federally subsidized apartments for 120 days.[60]

gentrification
The replacement of lower-value housing and businesses with higher-value residential and commercial development. Property values increase and longtime residents are often displaced.

Infrastructure Policy

Infrastructure is the physical network of a community, that is, its roads and bridges, airports, water and sewer systems, and public buildings. Its importance lies in its connection to development; the simplest equation is no infrastructure = no development. Infrastructure has become an issue in many communities because of its crumbling condition and the high cost of repair or replacement. Bridges that are structurally deficient, airport runways in poor condition, drinking water facilities that are substandard, sewer pipes that overflow—all of these infrastructure problems present major challenges. Every four years, the American Society of Civil Engineers (ASCE) assigns grades to U.S. infrastructure. In 2017, the average across the sixteen areas surveyed was a D+. The only grade above C went to rail lines, which had an average grade of B.[61] Cost estimates to improve U.S. infrastructure are staggering: $300 billion to $450 billion in essential upgrades to water and sewer systems;[62] $836 billion for necessary transportation infrastructure improvements;[63] and so on. Repairing drinking water infrastructure in one city— Flint, Michigan—where drinking water was heavily contaminated by lead leaching from water pipes, may cost upward of $216 million. And there are dozens of other U.S. cities that have similar lead pipes used for drinking water.[64] The federal stimulus program (formally, the American Recovery and Reinvestment Act of 2009) provided some relief, with approximately $110 billion in funding for shovel-ready infrastructure projects. Clearly, substantially more money will be needed to maintain and modernize the nation's infrastructure, and all levels of government will be involved. President Trump's 2018 infrastructure improvement plan proposed $200 billion in federal funding coupled with $1.5 trillion in private funding.[65] As the economic effects of the COVID-19 pandemic dramatically affected the country in 2020, the Trump administration reformulated this plan as a $1 trillion economic stimulus package [66]

The stock of aging, sometimes unsafe infrastructure has prompted states and localities to cast about for solutions. In the area of transportation infrastructure, one approach receiving greater scrutiny is privatization.[67] Some states have allowed the construction of private toll roads; a few states have leased existing highways to private companies. For example, in 2006, Indiana signed a seventy-five-year lease with a foreign firm to operate a 157-mile toll road that traverses the state. For an upfront lease payment of $3.8 billion, the investors get to keep toll road revenues during the seventy-five-year lease period and are responsible for maintaining the roadway. Privatized highway projects are criticized on two counts. Some argue that private roadways will produce a have/have-not distinction, with the affluent traveling on pay roads and the poor being dispatched to congested freeways. Others claim that privatization offers a Band-Aid solution to the enormous transportation problems facing the nation. Despite these concerns, privatization remains an attractive option to governors and legislatures intent on holding down highway taxes.

At the local level, interest in innovative infrastructure plans has grown. Two large Midwestern cities offer illustrative examples.[68] In Indianapolis, the merger of separate utilities into a single quasi-governmental organization has resulted in cost savings, freeing up $425 million for a series of infrastructure improvements. The program, dubbed "RebuildIndy," relies heavily on

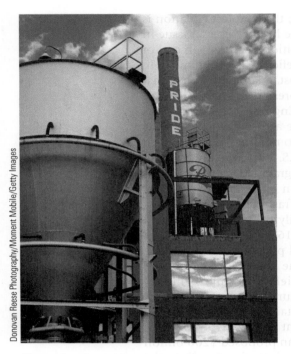

Donovan Reese Photography/Moment Mobile/Getty Images

The redeveloped Pearl Brewery, a twenty-two-acre mixed-use complex in San Antonio.

the input of the public, local businesses, and experts in deciding which projects to prioritize. The plan has stimulated increases in sidewalk, greenway, and bike lane construction, turning the car-dependent city into a much more walkable community.[69] In Minneapolis, a "Development Infrastructure Fund" was created for investment in public infrastructure that will generate private development. Small amounts of bond funds were utilized to leverage private capital for projects that would eventually expand the city's tax base. In 2019, the Minneapolis City Council adopted Minneapolis 2040, a twenty-year comprehensive plan based partially on funding from the development fund.[70] In both Indianapolis and Minneapolis, the goal is to cement the link between infrastructure improvement and economic development.

New Urbanism

One of the most intriguing efforts at transforming the urban experience has its roots in architecture and urban planning. Called **new urbanism**, the approach rejects the suburban model of development in favor of a traditional small-town style. Proponents of new urbanism, especially Miami-based architects Andres Duany and Elizabeth Plater-Zyberk, have advocated what is essentially a high-density, pedestrian-friendly, environmentally sensitive design for communities.[71] In theory, residents of these new urban places will acquire a sense of community and become engaged in civic life. One of the first experiments with new urbanism was the development of Seaside, Florida. (Movie buffs will remember it as the town where *The Truman Show* was filmed.) Another, called Celebration, has been created by the Walt Disney Company on 5,000 acres on the fringe of Orlando, Florida. It is a corporate-planned town with a private government.

The real test for new urbanism will be in an existing city, not in a geographically separate enclave. Can new urbanism work in a place plagued by social disorder and disinvestment? The answer to that question will not be known for years, and many observers are skeptical. But the Congress for the New Urbanism (CNU), a nonprofit organization committed to promoting the concept, is forging ahead. Annually, CNU selects exemplary projects, both in the United States and abroad, that embrace new urbanism principles. Table 12.2 lists four of the projects that won the 2019 award.

new urbanism
An anti-suburban, pro–small-town version of city planning.

So far, states have not taken new urbanism to heart, but interest is growing. As states seek ways to revitalize declining central cities, new urbanism may be a promising approach.

Table 12.2 Award-Winning Projects, Congress of New Urbanism, 2019

REGIONAL/CITYWIDE SCALE:	
Las Cruces and Dona Ana County, New Mexico	Plan 2040 contains a unified development code that attempts to recreate pre-automobile development patterns in the area.
NEIGHBORHOOD SCALE:	
New York City, New York	Essex Crossing is a more than 1,000-unit development with more than 50 percent designated for affordable housing, located on Manhattan's Lower East Side. Most shopping and many recreational needs can be met on site.
Carmel, Indiana	Monon Boulevard Corridor is a walkable downtown mixed-use development being built on a former industrial site.
Charleston, South Carolina	Upper King Street Gateway Development is a mixed-use development that will provide a gateway to downtown Charleston from the north.

Source: Congress for the New Urbanism, "Charter Awards 2019," https://www.cnu.org/sites/default/files /CharterAwardsBook_2019_r_0.pdf (accessed March 15, 2020). Reprinted by permission.

States and Their Rural Communities

LO 12-5
To compare differing futures of rural America.

When the local Dairy Queen closes its doors, a small town in rural America knows that it is in trouble. The Dairy Queen, like the coffee shop on Main Street, serves as a gathering place for community residents. Its demise symbolizes the tough times that a lot of rural communities face. Throughout the late twentieth century and into the twenty-first, this was the pattern in rural communities. Recently, things have begun to change. Between 2011 and 2018, rural counties in the United States experienced a small increase in population, narrowing the gap in the urban–rural county population growth rate. Likewise, while rural poverty rates remain higher than urban poverty rates, the difference has narrowed.[72] Rural areas also tend to have an older, less-educated population that is more likely to be disabled, resulting in lower rates of employment and lower incomes than urban areas.[73] By 2018, some 14 percent of the U.S. population lived in rural counties, down from 19 percent in 2012 (some of this decline is the result of counties being reclassified from rural to urban). There are great regional differences in these numbers—rural counties in Florida, the Upper Great Lakes (Huron, Michigan, and Superior), and the Pacific Northwest seem to be growing in population and doing better economically, whereas rural counties in northern Appalachia and the southern Coastal Plain seem to be doing worse.[74]

One major threat to agriculturally dependent rural areas is the trade war with China, Canada, the European Union, Mexico, and Turkey set off by President Trump's imposition of tariffs on imports from those areas. As prices for U.S. agricultural exports increased internationally, demand fell. The U.S. Department of Agriculture (USDA) estimated that agricultural exports such as

A rural area that has been bypassed by the interstate highway system

cotton, soybeans, sorghum, and wheat from this country declined on average by some 4 percent in 2019. To compensate partially for this, USDA distributed $28 billion in assistance in 2018 and 2019 to U.S. farmers.[75]

What can state governments do to encourage the right kind of growth in rural areas? Short of pumping enormous amounts of money into the local economy, they can encourage the expansion of local intergovernmental cooperation, whereby small rural governments join together to increase their administrative capacity to deliver services and achieve economies of scale. Two state actions facilitate such cooperation. One is the reforming of state tax codes so that jurisdictions can share locally generated tax revenues, similar to the Twin Cities model discussed earlier. Rather than competing with one another for a new manufacturing plant or a shopping mall, local governments can cooperate to bring the new facility to the area; regardless of where this facility is located, all jurisdictions can receive a portion of the tax revenue. A second useful state action is the promotion of statewide land-use planning. As one observer has noted, "Currently too many rural local governments engage in wasteful inter-community competition, mutually antagonistic zoning, and contradictory development plans."[76]

Several small towns in Kansas have embraced a new strategy to reverse population loss: offering free land to relocating families. By 2009, Marquette, a central Kansas town of 500 people a few years earlier, had given away forty free residential lots and had seen its population reach 682.[77] Others of these proverbial one-stoplight towns offer additional inducements to new residents or business developers: free water and sewer hookups, no-cost building permits, and memberships at nearby golf courses.

In an effort to find new ways to compete, rural places are getting entrepreneurial. For instance, an action that may bear fruit is the attempt to foster business by installing high-speed internet connections to isolated rural areas. Indiana created its I-Light program to bring broadband to its farming communities; Alabama and Alaska give tax credits to broadband firms committed to investing in rural areas.[78]

As states are shifting from traditional sources of electrical power (coal, natural gas, or nuclear power plants) to renewable sources, rural areas become attractive for wind or solar farms. Since 2002, each household in Sherman County, Oregon (population 1,765), has received $590 each year for allowing the county to be the host of a major wind farm (landowners on whose property the wind turbines are located receive much more—up to $8,000 for each megawatt generated).[79] Solar farm development can have equally positive economic effects, obviously in states such as Arizona, New Mexico, or Texas but also in rural areas in Ohio or upstate New York. One analysis of the costs and benefits of a proposed 149-megawatt solar farm in Jefferson County, Wisconsin (population approximately 85,000), showed the project would create nearly $500,000 per year in increased income in the county, resulting in nearly $900,000 in increased economic activity.[80]

Controversy exists about both wind and solar farm development. Arguments run from the aesthetic—wind or solar farms are not as attractive as farmland—to economic—converting fertile farmland to energy production can reduce the nation's food supply and drive up the price of food—to environmental—reduction in bird and bat populations as a result of collisions with wind vanes.[81]

Still, the future of rural America continues to be debated, as large cities get larger and many rural areas experience population decline. The median age of rural residents is some seven years older than urban residents. Productivity of rural workers is lower than urban workers; rural families have lower incomes than urban families. The economy of rural America has been declining for twenty-five or more years. Crime and opioid addiction are increasing rapidly in rural areas, and the list of woes goes on.[82] But one characteristic of rural Americans is resiliency, so the search for innovative economic development strategies continues.

The Interaction of State and Local Governments

Constitutionally, state governments are supreme in their dealings with local governments. New York City, Los Angeles, and Chicago are large, world-class cities, but even they have to follow the dictates of their respective state governments. For example, when the mayors of these cities sought to increase their control over local public schools, it took action by their respective state legislatures to make it happen. Even so, power does not flow in only one direction. The political realities are such that these cities and their smaller counterparts influence what happens in their state capitols. Suffice it to say, the state–local relationship is subject to constant adjustment. A Governor's Task Force to Renew Montana Government, for instance, adopted several provisions aimed at diminishing the influence of the state in what are considered purely local issues. But in a different vein, when Philadelphia's mayor proposed closing some fire stations to cut costs, state legislators intervened, passing a bill to prevent the city from doing so.[83] (The governor of Pennsylvania at the time, himself a former mayor of Philadelphia, vetoed the bill, saying it infringed on the city's home rule power.)

Some issues or problems require a statewide, uniform response, whereas others are the particular concern of a single local jurisdiction. New York governor Andrew Cuomo and New York City mayor Bill de Blasio have been at such personal and policy odds with each other that one observer noted, "it should be on HBO boxing."[84] Nevertheless, when COVID-19 cases began showing up in New York in February 2020, the two officials presented a unified state and local response in a rare public appearance together.[85] Consider the problem of opioid addiction. Many areas—particularly rural ones—show high rates of the legal or illegal use of opioid pain killers. Former Ohio governor John Kasich convened a state-level task force to address this problem in his state in 2011. The task force immediately saw that it would require cooperation between state and local law enforcement, public health officials, addiction experts, and educators. The result of this intergovernmental cooperation has been a decline in the number of opioid-related deaths in Ohio each year since 2015.[86] Thus, even with the constitutional superiority of the state, the state–local relationship is much more nuanced.

When he was elected governor of New York, George Pataki said that, "as a former mayor, I know firsthand the importance of freeing our cities, towns, and counties from the heavy hand of state government."[87] But as Governor Pataki quickly learned, a governor has to engage in big-picture, statewide thinking, and it is awfully tempting to impose the state's will on those same localities. To make sure their voice is heard, many local governments do what those in California do: hire lobbyists to represent their interests in the state legislature. Localities in the Golden State spent nearly $55 million lobbying lawmakers in 2018.[88] Even so, cities and counties found themselves on the losing side of several key measures, including one that capped impact fees that cities can charge on new housing developments. The state–local relationship can be rocky indeed.

 ## Chapter Recap

- States vary in the amount and type of authority they give their local governments. The general trend has been toward increased state assistance and empowerment of localities, but some states continue to keep their local governments on a short leash.

- The issue of mandates is a particularly contentious state–local matter.

- Three types of state–local organizations are common: task forces, advisory commissions on intergovernmental relations, and departments of community affairs.

- Urban sprawl has become a major issue in state–local relations. States have begun to adopt smart growth laws that are designed to help localities manage growth.

- Regionalism continues to be advocated as a solution to many local problems. More jurisdictions are creating regional organizations to link their local governments.

- States are looking for innovative solutions to challenging housing and infrastructure problems.

- New urbanism promotes a back-to-the-future community that appeals to a particular segment of the market.

- With many rural communities in decline, states are seeking ways of revitalizing them.

- Even as the interaction of states and localities becomes more positive, the tug of war between the two levels continues.

Key Terms

Dillon's rule *(p. 332)*
second-order devolution *(p. 333)*
mandate-reimbursement requirements *(p. 337)*
edge cities *(p. 339)*

urban sprawl *(p. 340)*
impact fee *(p. 340)*
smart growth *(p. 341)*
shadow governments *(p. 342)*
regional government *(p. 343)*

city–county consolidation *(p. 343)*
public choice theory *(p. 344)*
councils of government *(p. 347)*
gentrification *(p. 350)*
new urbanism *(p. 352)*

Internet Resources

The National Association of Regional Councils maintains a website at **www.narc.org/**. It shows the differences and similarities of regional councils across the country.

The Association of Bay Area Governments' award-winning site can be found at **www.abag .ca.gov**.

The website for the regional planning agency that deals with 189 cities and six counties in Southern California is **www.scag.ca.gov**.

For information on the activities of a state-level ACIR, see the Tennessee ACIR at **www.tn.gov /tacir**. Utah replaced its ACIR with the Utah Intergovernmental Roundtable at **https://gardner .utah.edu/utah-intergovernmental-roundtable/**

The Urban Institute's site for research on economic and social policy can be found at **www .urban.org**. It is a useful source of information on states and localities.

To learn more about new urbanism, see **www .cnu.org**, the website for the Congress for the New Urbanism.

The Kansas Free Land program is described at **www.kansasfreeland.com/**.

Georgia's rural development council maintains an informative website at **www.ruralgeorgia .org**. Other states with rural development councils have similar websites.

13

Taxing and Spending: Where the Money Comes from and Where It Goes

The old Detroit Central Station, abandoned since 1988, was recently purchased by Ford Motor Company who plans to redo the building by 2022.

Learning Objectives

LO 13-1 To recognize the principles of government finance.

LO 13-2 To identify criteria for evaluating taxes.

LO 13-3 To describe where state and local governments get revenue, and how they spend it.

LO 13-4 To evaluate the political economy of taxation.

LO 13-5 To discuss how state and local governments manage money.

LO 13-6 To be able to discuss current issues in state and local political economy.

Detroit, Michigan, became the largest U.S. city ever to file for Chapter 9 bankruptcy on July 18, 2013. Once, Detroit was an industrial dynamo of 1.8 million people. Virtually all American automobiles were manufactured there. But Motor City melted down to only 675,000 residents, surrounded by tens of thousands of abandoned buildings and houses. Public services were cut to the bone and debts rose to an estimated $18.5 billion—about $27,000 per person.

What brought Detroit to this sorry state? Auto manufacturing moved overseas and to the southern states in pursuit of cheaper labor; jobs fled with the auto industry. Employee pension and health care liabilities mounted to unsustainable levels. Taxes were raised to fund growing operating deficits. And as employment opportunities and quality of life declined, people moved to suburban municipalities, leaving Detroit with a shrunken tax base to maintain a huge 139-square-mile municipal jurisdiction.[1]

The state assumed financial control of the city. Former Michigan governor Rick Snyder appointed an emergency manager to guide the city back to solvency, granting him the powers to diminish labor contracts, reduce pensions and health care payouts, eliminate city departments, and even sell city assets. Sixteen months later, a federal judge approved a plan for Detroit to exit bankruptcy. Perhaps realizing the enormity of the challenges before them, interested parties, including the largest creditors, worked together to forge a recovery plan that lopped off $7 billion in liabilities and debts. The court permitted the city to invest $1.7 billion to purchase new fire trucks, ambulances, and other outdated equipment, remove blighted buildings and houses, and to take other actions to help move Motown to a measure of financial stability.[2] Elected officials were restored to power in city hall. Detroit's financial situation began to improve. Within thirteen months, the city emerged from bankruptcy and the city's debt was restructured by a public-private partnership. By 2020, Detroit seems to be on an upswing. For example, the new Little Caesars Arena (where both the NHL's Red Wings and the NBA's Pistons play) opened downtown in 2017. And Ford Motor Company bought the 1.2 million-square-foot Michigan Central Station and plans to redo the building as its headquarters for autonomous and electric vehicles, bringing some 2,500 jobs back to the central city.[3]

This chapter deals with state and local finance: the politics and policies of taxing and spending. Finance is a topic of continuing, visceral interest in state and local jurisdictions, and it is an activity characterized by much change and experimentation. From taxpayer revolts to spending mandates, the fiscal landscape has changed profoundly. More change is certain as state and local governments strive to meet taxpayer service demands economically and creatively.

The Principles of Finance

LO 13-1
To recognize the principles of government finance.

A major purpose of government is to provide services to citizens. But this costs money: Equipment must be purchased, and employees must be paid. Governments raise needed funds through taxes, fees, and borrowing. In a democracy, the voters decide what range and quality of services they desire, and they register their decisions through elected representatives. Sometimes, when elected officials don't listen voters revolt and take matters directly into their own hands.

Two basic principles describe state and local financial systems: *interdependence* and *diversity*. State and local fiscal systems are closely interlinked and heavily influenced by national financial activities. Intergovernmental sharing of revenues is a pronounced feature of our interdependent federal fiscal system. Yet our state financial structures and processes are also highly diverse. Though affected by national activities, their own economic health, and competitive pressures from one another, the states enjoy substantial autonomy in designing individual revenue systems in response to citizens' policy preferences.

Interdependence

U.S. governments raise huge amounts of money. The states and localities collected about $1.65 trillion in taxes in 2017. Total **own-source revenue** was $2.4 trillion when charges and fees applied to people, services, and products within the jurisdiction of each level of government were counted. State and local governments also benefit from **intergovernmental transfers**. The national government contributes about one-quarter of all state and local revenues; however, more than 60 percent of this federal money is "passed through" to *individual* recipients such as those receiving Medicaid. For their part, states pass on some $533 billion to their cities, counties, and special-purpose governments, whereas local governments receive some $69 billion directly from the federal government.[4] Some states are economic powerhouses. California's economy exceeds $3 trillion, making it the fifth largest in the world.

Local governments rely heavily on the states and, to a lesser degree, on the national government for financial authority and assistance. *Only the states* can authorize localities to levy taxes and fees, incur debt, and spend money. State constitutions and laws place many conditions on local government taxing and spending. In return, states provide monetary support of local governments through state grants-in-aid and revenue sharing; they also assume financial responsibility for activities carried out by localities—in particular, education and social welfare costs. Most local governments are fine with this arrangement. But the role of the states as senior financial partners in state–local finance is criticized in some quarters as being both inadequate and unduly restrictive of local financial flexibility.

State–local finances are linked closely to activities of the national government. For instance, when the federal government changes the tax code, it can wreak havoc on those thirty-five states that base their own income taxes on the federal tax code. The Tax Cuts and Jobs Act (TCJA) of 2017 made major revisions to the federal income tax code and these changes affected state and local tax revenue, depending on how individual states link state income taxes to federal income taxes. One analysis of four different states showed that TCJA would have large negative effects on tax revenue in Missouri, small positive impacts in Colorado and Utah, and virtually no impact on New York.[5]

Of course, the outbreak of COVID-19 was a major shock to the national, state, and local economies in 2020. As governors closed restaurants and bars and as music festivals and other types of events where people gather in large

own-source revenue Monies derived by a government from its own taxable resources.

intergovernmental transfers The movement of money or other resources from one level of government to another.

numbers were canceled, many businesses laid off workers or were forced to close. Many large employers were able to carry workers on payroll, even though they were forced to limit employee hours. Most smaller retailers simply didn't have the cash flow needed to pay furloughed workers and so unemployment claims spiked in March 2020. By early June, some 42.6 million Americans had filed for unemployment benefits.[6] And even this large number may understate the actual severity of the problem as state systems for processing claims crashed under the weight of unprecedented demand.[7] The federal government and many states extended the deadline for taxpayers to file income tax forms, but the longer-range implications of reductions in sales tax revenue and possible property tax losses as businesses close are unclear.

When the national economy takes such a hit, state and local governments suffer most. They cannot, after all, print money or run an operating budget deficit into the future. This fact is sometimes recognized by Congress, which is providing substantial amounts of **countercyclical aid** to the states and localities to help them recover from the ravages of the COVID-19 crisis and past major shocks such as the Great Recession. In late March 2020, for example, Congress passed a $2.2 trillion aid package—the largest in U.S. history—that provided checks of up to $1,200 per person to stimulate the U.S. economy.

Diversity

The second basic principle of state and local finance systems is diversity of revenue sources. Each level of government depends on one type of revenue device more than others. For the national government, it is the income tax; for the states, the sales tax; and for local governments, the property tax. But diversity triumphs among the states. Differences in **tax capacity** (wealth), **tax effort** (burden), and tax choices are obvious even to the casual traveler. Most states tax personal income and merchandise sales, but a handful do not. Several states garner substantial revenues from severance taxes on oil, gas, and minerals.

Some states, such as New Jersey and New York, tax with a heavy hand. Others, including Nevada and Alaska, are relative tax havens. Most fall somewhere in the middle. If the basic objective of taxing is to pluck the maximum number of feathers from the goose with the minimum amount of hissing, the wealthy states hold a great advantage. They can reap high-tax revenues with much less effort than can poor states, which must tax at high rates just to pull in enough money to pay for the basics. Per capita state and local tax revenues vary from $7,869 in Connecticut to $2,742 in Mississippi. The U.S. average is $4,420.[8]

There is a close relationship between state wealth (as measured by personal income) and tax burden. Table 13.1 shows how the states compare in state and local tax burdens (taxes, controlling for personal income). Tax levels also reflect factors such as citizen preferences, population characteristics and trends, business climate, limitations on tax increases and/or expenditures, and the quality, as well as quantity, of government services. And taxing is only

countercyclical aid
A transfer of federal dollars to states and localities to counteract a downturn in the economic cycle.

tax capacity
The taxable resources of a government jurisdiction.

tax effort
The extent to which a jurisdiction exploits its taxable resources.

one means of plucking the public goose. State and local governments increasingly rely on fees and charges for services rendered. Examples include entrance fees for parks and recreation facilities, sewer and garbage fees, and motor vehicle fees.

Table 13.1 State/Local and Total Taxes by State, as a Percentage of Personal Income and Per Capita

STATE	STATE/LOCAL TAXES AS A % OF INCOME	STATE/LOCAL TAX COLLECTION PER CAPITA ($)
U.S. Average	9.9	4,420
New York	12.7	6,993
Connecticut	12.6	7,869
New Jersey	12.2	6,926
California	11.0	5,237
Illinois	11.0	5,235
Wisconsin	11.0	4,734
Maryland	10.9	5,920
Minnesota	10.8	5,185
Rhode Island	10.8	4,998
Massachusetts	10.3	5,872
Oregon	10.3	4,095
Vermont	10.3	4,557
Delaware	10.2	4,412
Hawaii	10.2	4,576
Maine	10.2	3,997
Pennsylvania	10.2	4,589
Arkansas	10.1	3,519
North Carolina	9.8	3,659
Ohio	9.8	3,924
West Virginia	9.8	3,331
Utah	9.6	3,556
Indiana	9.5	3,585
Kansas	9.5	4,131
Kentucky	9.5	3,298
Michigan	9.4	3,631
Idaho	9.3	3,318
Missouri	9.3	3,591
Virginia	9.3	4,623
Washington	9.3	4,541

(continued)

Table 13.1 State/Local and Total Taxes by State, as a Percentage of Personal Income and Per Capita (*continued*)

STATE	STATE/LOCAL TAXES AS A % OF INCOME	STATE/LOCAL TAX COLLECTION PER CAPITA ($)
Iowa	9.2	4,037
Nebraska	9.2	4,197
Georgia	9.1	3,426
North Dakota	9.0	4,867
Colorado	8.9	4,304
Florida	8.9	3,738
Arizona	8.8	3,276
Alabama	8.7	3,067
Montana	8.7	3,389
New Mexico	8.7	3,141
Mississippi	8.6	2,742
Oklahoma	8.6	3,515
South Carolina	8.4	2,936
Nevada	8.1	3,349
New Hampshire	7.9	3,961
Louisiana	7.9	2,950
Texas	7.6	3,340
Tennessee	7.3	2,805
South Dakota	7.1	3,318
Wyoming	7.1	4,407
Alaska	6.5	3,229

Source: https://taxfoundation.org/facts-and-figures-2020/. Data are current as of 2012.

Revenues

Although the state and local finance systems have their own strengths, weaknesses, and peculiarities, certain trends can be found in all of them. The property tax is always unpopular. It is no longer a significant source of state revenue; its contribution to total own-source local coffers, though, remains strong. States collect only 3 percent of all the property taxes in the United States; the other 97 percent is collected by local governments. States continue to depend heavily on the sales tax, but alternatives are being used more widely. Intergovernmental revenues from the federal government make up more than one-quarter of the total. In fact, tax diversification is an important trend in all state and local tax systems (see Figure 13.1). The largest portion of state and local revenue, however, comes from charges and fees—such things as tuition at state and city universities and community colleges, charges at public hospitals, tolls on highways, parking revenue, user fees for parks and recreation facilities, and so on.

LO 13-2
To understand criteria
for evaluating taxes.

Criteria for Evaluating Taxes

Numerous criteria can be used to evaluate taxes. What one person or interest group likes about a tax may be what another dislikes. Nevertheless, political scientists and economists generally agree that among the most important criteria are equity, efficiency, yield, political accountability, and acceptability.

Equity If citizens or firms are expected to pay a tax, they should view it as fair. In the context of taxation, *equity* usually refers to distributing the burden of the tax in accordance with ability to pay: High income means greater ability to pay and therefore a larger tax burden. Equity includes other dimensions as well, such as the relative tax burden on individuals versus firms and the impact of various types of taxes on income, age, and social class. It is interesting to observe that despite the constant complaints about taxes, the typical American pays much less in total taxes today (as a percentage of income) than he or she did thirty years ago.[9]

Taxes may be regressive, progressive, or proportional. A **regressive tax** places a greater burden on low-income citizens than on high-income citizens. Thus, the ability-to-pay principle is violated, with the result that upper-income groups contribute a smaller portion of their incomes than do lower-income groups. Most state and local levies, including property and sales taxes, are considered regressive. For example, both low-income and high-income people would pay, say, a 7 percent sales tax. The latter will likely make more purchases and contribute more total dollars in sales tax, but at a lower percentage of their total income, than the low-income individuals.

A **progressive tax** increases as a percentage of a person's income as that income rises. The more you make, the greater proportion of your income is extracted by the progressive tax. Thus, those better able to pay carry a heavier tax burden than do the poor. California's personal income tax is the most progressive, varying from 1.4 to 13.3 percent of taxable income. The more you earn, the higher your *income tax bracket.*

regressive tax
A tax in which the rate falls as the base or taxable income rises, advantaging those with higher income.

progressive tax
A tax in which the rate rises as the base or taxable income rises, advantaging those with lower income.

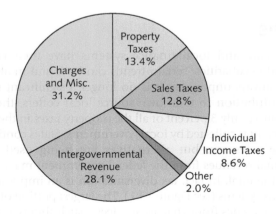

FIGURE 13.1 State and Local General Revenues, by Source

Source: Tax Policy Center, The Urban Institute (February 10, 2020).

A **proportional tax**, sometimes called a **flat tax**, burdens everyone equally, at least in theory. For instance, a tax on income of, say, 10 percent that is applied across the board is a proportional tax. Whether you earn $100,000 or $10,000, you pay a flat 10 percent of the total in taxes. Of course, a low-income person is more burdened by a proportional income tax than is a high-income person (as in the case of the sales tax).

In place of ability to pay, some people advocate the **benefit principle**. Under this principle, those who reap more benefits from government services should shoulder more of the tax burden than people who do not avail themselves of service opportunities to the same degree. As a hypothetical example, it might be argued that parents whose children attend public schools should pay higher taxes for education than should senior citizens, childless couples, or single people without children. The benefit principle is the theoretical underpinning for user fees, which charge a taxpayer directly for services received. The unfortunate downside is that it disadvantages those who have the least ability to pay.

Efficiency This refers to the amount of money a tax contributes to government coffers compared to the effort and expense it takes to administer and collect it. Taxes that return substantial sums of money at minimal collection costs to the government are preferred to taxes that require large outlays for moderate revenues. Income and sales taxes have high yields because they raise large sums of money at low expense. They are simple to understand and fairly easy to collect. Property taxes, however, have lower yields because they are more expensive to assess and collect. Property values must be regularly appraised, which involves a certain degree of subjectivity.

Yield Yield depends on base and rate: The broader the tax base and the higher the rate, the higher the yield. As a simple example, a sales tax applied to all purchases yields much more than a sales tax on cigarette purchases, and a $1-per-pack tax produces more money than a 25-cent tax.

Political Accountability Tax increases should not be hidden. Instead, state and local legislative bodies should have to approve them deliberately—and publicly. Citizens should know how much they owe and when it must be paid. For example, some state income taxes are silently hiked as wages rise in response to cost-of-living increases. After inflation is accounted for, taxpayers make the same real income as they did before, but they are driven into a higher-income bracket for tax purposes. This phenomenon, known as *bracket creep*, can be eliminated by **indexing** income tax brackets to changes in the cost of living.

Tax expenditures, also known as tax breaks, or more cynically as corporate welfare, depress political accountability. These are tax preferences that benefit certain taxpayers through credits, exemptions, deductions, and other favorable treatment. For example, specified manufacturing companies may pay a lower sales tax on new equipment than other companies, or receive payments for each new job created. Tax expenditures have little or no visibility to the voting public.

proportional (flat) tax
A tax in which people pay an identical rate regardless of income or economic transaction.

benefit principle
The principle that taxes should be levied on those who benefit directly from a government service.

indexing
A system in which tax brackets are automatically adjusted to account for inflation.

Acceptability The type and mix of taxes imposed should be congruent with citizen preferences. No tax commands wild enthusiasm, and a portion of the citizenry will *always* be opposed to *any* tax, but some are less disagreeable than others. Tax acceptability varies, depending on numerous factors, including equity implications and the perceived pain of paying. Large, one-time payments, such as the annual property tax, inflict greater pain than small, frequently paid sales taxes. And a tax on someone else is always preferable. As former senator Russell Long of Louisiana put it many years ago, "Don't tax me, don't tax thee; tax that man behind the tree."

LO 13-3
To describe where state and local governments get revenue, and how they spend it.

Major State and Local Taxes

The principal types of taxes are those on property, sales, and income. Various miscellaneous taxes and fees also provide revenue for state and local governments.

Property Tax Taxes on personal and corporate property account for about one-third of state and local tax revenue. States hardly utilize the property tax at all today (it represents less than 1 percent of their total revenues), but local governments continue to depend on this fiscal workhorse for more than one-third of all their own-source revenues. Other revenue sources have augmented the property tax, so its proportionate contribution has diminished. As always, there is considerable state-by-state variation. Less than 10 percent of state and local revenue in Alabama, Delaware, Kentucky, New Mexico, and North Dakota comes from the property tax, whereas nearly 40 percent does in New Hampshire.[10]

Property taxes are widely reviled. Assessments of value may seem to change suddenly or appear to stack up unfavorably against similar properties, and to appeal assessments involves a frustrating process. Acceptability, efficiency, and accountability rank low in relation to other taxes. The best feature of the property tax is that it is certain: Owners of property must pay it or the government may seize and sell their land, buildings, or other taxable possessions. But it tends to be regressive and sometimes must be paid in a large lump sum.

On first thought, it seems that property taxes cannot be truly regressive because only those people who own property pay taxes on it directly; however, renters pay property taxes indirectly through their monthly rent checks to the landlord. When property tax assessments climb, so do rental charges. Property taxes can also violate the ability-to-pay principle when housing values spiral upward. Retirees and other homeowners on fixed incomes may discover with alarm that their annual property tax bills are doubling or tripling as housing prices escalate. Alternatively, as property values plummet, as they did during the Great Recession of 2008–2011, tax values remain the same until the next scheduled reassessment.

Just this sort of situation helped precipitate California's Proposition 13, which was credited with kicking off a taxpayer revolt across the United States. In the Los Angeles and San Francisco Bay areas during the 1970s, property taxes doubled and then tripled in only a few years. Some senior citizens were forced to sell their homes to pay their property taxes. Proposition 13 reduced property tax bills by approximately $7 billion in the first year, and it imposed strict limitations on the ability of local governments to raise property and other taxes in the future. California dropped from the eighth-highest property tax state to the twenty-eighth. This example illustrates the importance of political accountability.

Property taxes are difficult to administer and somewhat arbitrary. The process of levying an annual fee on "real property" (land and buildings) begins with an assessor making a formal appraisal of the market value of the land and the buildings on it. Then property values are "equalized" so that similarly valued real estate is taxed at the same level. Time is set aside to make corrections and to review appeals on appraisals that the owner believes are too high. Next, an assessment ratio is applied to the property. For instance, houses might be assessed for tax purposes at 80 percent of market value. A rate is placed on the assessed value to calculate the annual tax amount. (Assessed at a market price of $100,000, taxed at a ratio of 0.80 and a rate of $3 per $100 [30 mils], a house would produce a tax due of $2,400.) Determining market value may seem fairly straightforward, but ultimately the appraised market value depends on the findings of the assessor, who may or may not be unbiased, properly trained for the job, or fully aware of conditions in the local housing market (statistical models remove some of the guesswork). Property can thus be underappraised or overappraised. For the sake of equity, property should be appraised regularly (e.g., every two or three years). Otherwise, property that does not change ownership becomes increasingly undervalued or overvalued, depending on the local real estate market. Property tax systems are further criticized for exempting certain types of real estate and buildings. Government buildings such as hospitals and state and federal offices are not taxed, even though they utilize police and fire protection, trash collection, and other local government services. Churches, synagogues, mosques, and related property used for religious purposes are also partly or wholly exempted in the vast majority of jurisdictions, as is property owned by charitable and nonprofit organizations.

The amount of tax-exempt property in most populous cities has been growing as more land and buildings are acquired by nonprofit organizations, particularly those in education and health care. Nearly 30 percent of Baltimore's entire tax base escapes property taxation.[11] A relatively small portion of this "lost" revenue is captured through payments in lieu of taxes (PILOTs), which are agreements negotiated by state and local governments and the nonprofit owner. In addition, some state and local governments are sharpening the definition of which organizations qualify for tax exempt status.

In an effort to make property taxation more equitable and more in keeping with ability to pay, most states have enacted some form of **circuit breaker**. For instance, the property of low-income individuals is excluded from taxation in some states; others assign lower-assessment ratios to the homes of senior citizens or set a top limit on the tax according to the owner's income (e.g., 4 percent of net income). Many states have "truth-in-taxation" laws that

circuit breaker
A limit on taxes applied to certain categories of people, such as the poor or elderly.

roll back property tax rates as appraised values rise rapidly. Most also offer homestead exemptions, in which owner-occupied homes are taxed at lower rates or assessed at lower values than are rental homes or business property. Massachusetts municipalities permit seniors to earn credits against their tax bills through public service activities.

Despite such attempts to make the property tax fairer, differences in property values among cities, counties, and school districts still have important implications for the quality and distribution of services. Jurisdictions with many wealthy families, capital-intensive industries, or rapid construction growth can provide high levels of services with low tax rates, whereas areas with weak property tax bases must tax at high rates merely to yield enough revenue to maintain minimal services. Residential property tax rates vary widely from city to city. Altering the unequal distribution of property values is essentially beyond the control of local governments. As a result, "wealthy suburbs remain wealthy, poor communities remain poor, and services remain unequal."[12]

Sales Tax States currently collect more of their revenues from the general sales and gross receipts tax than from any other source. It accounts for almost one-quarter of total state general revenues. Only five states do not levy a general statewide sales tax: Alaska, Delaware, Montana, New Hampshire, and Oregon (Alaska allows municipalities to levy individual sales taxes). State sales tax rates vary from 7.5 percent in California to 2.9 percent in Colorado. Some states, particularly those that do not have personal income taxes, are exceptionally dependent on the sales tax: Washington, Tennessee, Louisiana, South Dakota, and Nevada derive approximately 40 percent of their own-source revenues from the sales tax.

The sales tax has remained in favor for two major reasons. First, citizen surveys have consistently shown that when a tax must be raised, voters reluctantly prefer the sales tax. Although the reasons are not entirely clear, this tax is perceived to be fairer than other forms of taxation. Second, there is an abiding belief that high state income taxes depress economic development, and the property tax is widely detested.

Thirty-eight states authorize at least some of their municipalities and counties to levy local sales taxes. When state and local sales taxes are combined, the total tax bite can be painful. In Chicago, you will pay 10.25 cents on every $1 item you purchase, as you will in Glendale and Long Beach, California. Sales taxes are usually optional for the local jurisdiction but may require state legislative approval in some cases. Typically, states impose ceilings on how many pennies the localities can attach to the state sales tax; states also specify which sizes and types of local governments are permitted to exercise this option.

When applied to all merchandise, the sales tax is clearly regressive. Poor folks must spend a larger portion of their incomes than rich people spend on basics, such as food and clothing. Therefore, the sales tax places a much heavier burden on low-income people. Most of the forty-five states with a sales tax alleviate its regressive nature by excluding certain "necessities."

Thirty-two states that have sales taxes do not tax food purchased from the grocery store; only a handful tax prescription drugs; most exempt consumer electric and gas utilities; and five exclude clothing.[13] New Jersey excludes paper products. When the sales tax was extended to paper products in 1990, enraged Jerseyites mailed wads of toilet paper—some of it used—to horrified legislators, who quickly rescinded the tax. Seventeen states hold "sales tax holidays" in which specified merchandise, such as hurricane supplies and clothing, are exempt from the sales tax for a weekend or longer.[14]

States can improve the yield of the sales tax by broadening the base to include services. In this way, more of the burden is passed on to upper-income individuals, who are heavier users of services. Approximately half of the states tax services such as household, automobile, and appliance repairs; barber and beauty shop treatments; printing; rentals; dry cleaning; cable television service; and interior decorating. Hawaii, Texas, and South Dakota tax almost all professional and personal services. New Jersey taxes hair transplants and tummy tucks, and Arkansas taps into tattoos and nose rings. Colorado, Washington, Hawaii, and Alaska tax recreational marijuana sales. Maryland residents must pay an annual "flush tax" of $60 on their sewer bills to help clean up polluted Chesapeake Bay. However, states can move too far and too fast with taxes on services. Florida, Massachusetts, and Michigan broadened the base of their sales tax to services, only to have it repealed shortly afterward through lobbying efforts by the business community. Sweeping proposals to tax services are typically defeated by vested interests. These setbacks may be temporary. Services are the largest and fastest growing segment of the U.S. economy. Eighty-five percent of new jobs are in services. As one political commentator asked, "How can one rationalize taxing autos, videocassettes, and toothpaste, but not piped-in music, cable TV, parking lot services, or $100 beauty salon treatments?"[15] Pet grooming services, legal and financial services, and many others from landscaping to vehicle repairs have lost their tax-favored status as states extend sales taxes to services incrementally, fighting industry and lobbyists one at a time.

Whatever form the sales tax takes, elasticity is not a strong point, although its productivity falls when consumer purchases slow and rises as consumers boost their spending. Broadening the base helps. States sometimes attempt to make the sales tax more responsive to short-term economic conditions by increasing it on a temporary basis, to make up for lower-than-anticipated revenues, and then reducing it when needed monies are collected. A problem with these tactics, however, is that consumers tend to postpone major purchases until the tax rate falls.

The sales tax is relatively simple for governments to administer. Sellers of merchandise and services are required to collect it and remit it to the state on a regular basis. Political accountability is also an advantage because legislative bodies must enact laws or ordinances to increase the sales tax rate. And, as we have observed, the sales tax is the least unpopular of the major taxes.

Tax evasion is a major problem in collecting sales taxes. Since the tax is collected by merchants and then remitted to the state, a merchant may be tempted to report lower sales than actually occur. In the old days, this might have meant two sets of books or even two cash registers. Nowadays, the schemes have gotten more electronically sophisticated. Sales suppression software—known as tax zappers—can be attached to electronic cash registers to report a lower level of cash sales than what really occurs. Each sale that is underreported or deleted means the merchant gets to keep the sales tax that should have been remitted for that sale or to charge the buyer a lower total price than a nearby store that is collecting the tax. Sales tax evasion in the restaurant industry alone has been estimated to cost state governments some $21 billion a year in lost revenue.[16]

There has been a continuing fight over state and local governments' right to collect sales taxes on electronic commerce on the internet. In the past, twenty-one states levied taxes or fees on internet access, data downloads, or goods purchased on the internet. Then pressures from internet interests, including servers, media companies, and retail businesses, led Congress to pass the Internet Tax Freedom Act, in 1998, which imposed a moratorium on taxing internet access and online sales. State and local officials strongly opposed such limitations, citing estimates that it costs them more than $23 billion in annual revenues because more and more goods are purchased on the internet or otherwise from out of state. Already states estimate that they forfeit another $5 billion a year in uncollected taxes from interstate catalog sales. Only internet and catalog sales to citizens living in the same state in which the vendor company has a physical presence in the state are taxed. And many states require citizens to declare and pay such sales taxes in their annual state income tax returns, but usually to little avail because of the difficulty of enforcement.

Taxation of internet sales is both complicated and controversial, and it has become a compelling issue for the states. A 1992 U.S. Supreme Court ruling blocked taxation of catalog sales on the grounds of violating the Interstate Commerce Clause, a ruling that has obvious applicability to taxing internet commerce today.[17] The Court reversed course in a 2017 case, ruling that a South Dakota law taxing internet companies that don't have a physical store in the state was not a violation of the Interstate Commerce Clause. However, the ruling in *South Dakota v. Wayfair* was narrow, mainly addressing online retailers who had distribution centers in several states. The Court said it would be more critical of broadly based internet state sales taxes.[18] In anticipation of being required to collect sales taxes, Amazon began collecting state sales tax (but not local taxes) in 2017 on internet purchases originating in the forty-five states that have such a tax. Amazon has 183 fulfillment centers in thirty-six states. On the other hand, L. L. Bean, the large online and catalog retailer, continues to collect sales taxes only in the states in which it has a physical presence.[19] L. L. Bean has fifty-five stores in nineteen states.

Income Tax Most states tax personal and corporate income. Wisconsin was the first, in 1911, two years before the national government enacted its own personal income tax. Forty-one states have broad-based taxes on personal income; two states (Tennessee and New Hampshire) limit theirs to capital gains, interest, and dividends. Only Alaska, Texas, South Dakota, Florida, Nevada, Washington, and

Wyoming leave all personal income untaxed. Nevada, Texas, Washington, and Wyoming also abstain from taxing corporate income. Personal income taxes garner 38 percent of all state own-source taxes, and the corporate tax brings in about 4.7 percent.[20] Seventeen states permit designated cities, counties, or school districts to levy taxes on personal income.[21]

State and local income taxes are equitable when they are progressive. Progressivity normally entails a sliding scale, so that high-income filers pay a greater percentage of their income in taxes than do low-income filers. California has the steepest scale, ranging from 1.0 to 13.3 percent of taxable income. Most states do not levy a personal income tax on people whose earnings fall below a certain floor—say, $10,000. Overall, state personal income taxes are moderately progressive. Nine states, however, tax income at a flat rate varying from 3.07 percent in Pennsylvania to 5.25 percent in North Carolina.

Personal and corporate income taxes are superior to other taxes on the criteria of yield and elasticity. By tapping almost all sources of income, they draw in large sums of money and respond fairly well to short-term economic conditions (though the income tax has become more volatile, particularly during periods of boom and bust).[22]

Through payroll withholding, income taxes are fairly simple to collect. Also, many states periodically adjust income tax rates in response to annual revenue needs. As mentioned earlier, political accountability can be problematic with respect to income taxes during periods of rising prices. Unless income tax rates are indexed to inflation, as they are in seventeen states, cost-of-living increases push salaries and corporate earnings into higher tax brackets.

Miscellaneous Taxes A wide variety of miscellaneous taxes are assessed by state and local governments. "Sin taxes" raise a small—but growing—percentage of all state revenues. All states tax cigarettes and many have boosted this tax during the past few years. The $4.35 tax in Connecticut and New York boosts the average price per pack to $9.20. Some cities levy additional taxes on smokes; the price per pack in New York City is now $13. Yet Missouri charges only 17 cents per pack. This startling disparity in prices has led to a flourishing trade in cigarette smuggling from low- to high-tax states. A 2015 study by the Tax Foundation found that more than half of the cigarettes smoked in New York came from smuggled sources. New York wasn't alone—nearly half the cigarettes smoked in Arizona, Washington, and New Mexico also had out-of-state origins.[23] The estimated annual revenue loss for New York alone was $1.5 billion in 2016.[24]

In 1998, the states experienced the equivalent of winning the lottery. A court settlement with tobacco companies sent as much as $206 billion into state coffers over a period of twenty-five years. Ideally, the funds would be used for public health and smoking prevention programs. But few strings are attached, and states have spent the windfall on economic development initiatives, balancing the budget, new government office buildings, and even golf courses.[25] Nine states took the fiscally unsound step of selling bonds to be paid off with future projected tobacco settlement money, thus mortgaging the future for dollars today. Ironically, the amount of tobacco settlement dollars pledged to the states is based on the number of packs of cigarettes sold. But all states are experiencing shrinking sales as smokers beat the habit or take advantage of Indian reservations, internet sales, and black-market cigarettes.

States are also suing opioid producers and distributors in suits similar to those waged against the tobacco industry. In 2019, Oklahoma settled its lawsuit against opioid manufacturers Purdue and Teva Pharmaceuticals for $355 million. Its suit against the pharmaceutical giant Johnson and Johnson is under appeal. Oklahoma then turned around and sued three distributors for "supplying massive and patently unreasonable quantities of opioids to communities around the United States, including Oklahoma."[26] A recent offer of $18 billion by three distributors of legal opioids was rejected by twenty-one states that have brought suit. The states are seeking a settlement of between $22 and $32 billion.[27]

So far, taxes on recreational marijuana sales in the states permitting them have come in slightly above or below expectations. Taxes on medical marijuana in twenty-three states produce relatively insignificant revenues. The It's Your Turn feature raises questions on when and how marijuana should be taxed.

Alcoholic beverages are taxed in all fifty states, although rates vary according to classification: beer, wine, or spirits. Beer guzzlers should steer clear of Tennessee, where the tax per gallon of beer is $1.29; frequent imbibers are invited to visit Wyoming, where the tax is only 2 cents per gallon. Excise taxes on a gallon of wine range from $3.26 in bourbon-swilling Kentucky to 20 cents in California. Likewise, liquor taxes vary greatly, from $2 per gallon in Missouri to $32.52 in Washington. Though not a "sin," gasoline falls under taxation's shadow as well. The highest state tax on gasoline in 2020 was in California (62.5 cents per gallon). The lowest was in Alaska (13.8 cents). Alas, the gas tax is running toward empty as motorists reduce the number of miles they drive and as vehicles are becoming more fuel efficient. The surprising decline in the price of gasoline at the pump from 2012 on further reduced gas tax revenues in some states. And the shelter at home orders many states imposed during the COVID-19 pandemic reduced gasoline consumption even further. The result is depletion of road construction and maintenance funds for which gasoline taxes are earmarked.

Most states tax death in one form or another. Estate taxes must be paid on the financial assets and property of a deceased person in fourteen states before the remainder is disbursed to the survivors. Inheritance taxes are imposed in six states on non-spouses who inherit substantial assets (typically valued at more than $1 million). Rates are generally staggered according to the value of the estate and the survivors' relationship to the deceased. A reduction of the federal estate tax has resulted in a decline for such state taxes as well, unless the states amend their estate tax laws.

Other miscellaneous sources of revenue include hunting and fishing licenses, business licenses, auto license fees, parking tickets, traffic violation fines, and telecommunications fees. Utah imposes a 10 percent "pole tax" on strip clubs and on escort services. Another interesting instrument is the "jock tax."

? It's Your Turn

Should Medical Marijuana Be Taxed?

Put simply, a sales tax is exacted on the buyer of a good; it is applied to a retail transaction on purchases, such as clothing or groceries. An excise tax is imposed on a particular product, such as gasoline or tobacco. Both increase the buyer's cost. Colorado exacts a 15 percent sales tax and a 15 percent excise tax on recreational marijuana. Washington state's excise and sales taxes total 37 percent on weed-for-fun.

But what about medical marijuana? Should states apply both excise and sales taxes, one of them, or neither? How about infused medical marijuana products such as cookies or candies?

PROS	CONS
State and local governments should apply both sales and excise taxes to all medical marijuana products at relatively high levels because they raise needed revenues.	Medical marijuana should not be taxed at all; it should be treated like prescription medications, which most states do not tax.
High marijuana taxes will discourage abuse or overuse of the drug.	Medical marijuana should not be taxed, or only taxed minimally, because it is for an approved medical condition (that currently is not covered by health insurance).
Buyers should be willing to pay taxes because they no longer have to worry about arrest for possession and use of illegal marijuana.	If medical marijuana is taxed too heavily, users will purchase the herb on the black market instead of from approved dispensaries.

Twenty states and several cities require professional athletes to pay a prorated income tax for games played in their jurisdiction. For example, Golden State Warrior Stephen Curry, whose gross salary is $37.5 million, pays a jock tax of $24,895 for each game he plays against the Pistons in Detroit (he also gets a tax credit on his California state income tax for the tax he pays to Detroit).[28] For highly paid baseball, basketball, and football players, the jock tax is a minor itch. But for the lower-paid athletes, the jock tax burns. Some professional athletes must file tax returns in as many as twenty different states, depending on which states tax their team's visit.

User Fees

Setting specific prices on goods and services provided by state and local governments is one method that clearly pursues the *benefit principle*: Only those who use the goods and services should pay. User fees have been in existence for many years. Examples include college tuition, water and sewer charges, and trash collection assessments. Toll roads and bridges are coming back in fashion as well. Building and inspection fees, food truck licenses, and even fire service charges are assessed in some local jurisdictions. Today, user fees are being applied broadly as state and especially local officials attempt to tie services to their true costs. Such fees are increasingly being levied on "nonessential" local government services, such as parks and recreation, libraries, and airports. User fees make up approximately 12 percent of local governments' own-source revenues.

User fees offer several advantages. If priced accurately, they are perfectly fair under the benefit principle, and they enjoy a relatively high level of political acceptability. But those people who do not have enough money to purchase the goods and services may have to do without—a circumstance that violates the ability-to-pay principle. A good case in point is higher education, which is shifting increasingly from state funding to tuition and fee-based funding. (Rebates, scholarships, fee waivers, and reduced-fee schedules help mitigate ability-to-pay difficulties among low-income residents.)

User fees are structured to yield whatever is needed to finance a particular service. An added benefit is that service users who do not live in the taxing jurisdiction must also pay the price, say, for a day at the state zoo. Yield may be achieved if the amount of the charge is varied so that it always covers service costs. In many instances, user fees can be levied without specific permission from the state.

Because service users must be identified and charged, some user fees can be difficult to administer. Political accountability is low because the charges can be increased without legislative action. However, a special advantage of user fees is that they can be employed to ration certain goods or services. For instance, entrance charges can be increased to reduce attendance at an overcrowded public facility or varied according to the day of the week to encourage more efficient utilization. If the city museum has few visitors on Mondays, it can cut the entrance fee on that day of the week by half.

An increasingly popular and specialized form of user charge is the local impact fee, or exaction, requiring private land developers to contribute roads, sewers, and other infrastructure as the price for local regulatory approval for development projects such as subdivisions or retail facilities. The cost of infrastructure is thus shifted to firms and, ultimately, to those who purchase or use their buildings or facilities. A related concept is applied through a special sales tax on travel and tourism-related services. Here, taxes on lodging, rental cars, and other services paid largely by out-of-towners are imposed at rates averaging 12 percent.

Table 13.2 summarizes the discussion of various taxes and fees based on the five criteria described at the beginning of this section.

Severance Tax

States blessed with petroleum, coal, natural gas, and minerals tax these natural resources as they are taken from the land and sold. A fortunate few (Alaska, North Dakota, and Wyoming among the most fortunate) are able to "export" a substantial portion of their tax bite to people living in other states. In-staters, however, must pay the same tax rate as out-of-staters.

A large majority of states (thirty-eight) place a severance tax on some form of natural resources, but just ten states collect 90 percent of all severance

Table 13.2 Summarizing State and Local Taxes According to Five Criteria

TAX	EQUITY	YIELD	POLITICAL ACCOUNTABILITY	ACCEPTABILITY	EFFICIENCY
Property	Fair	Fair	Poor	Poor	Poor
Sales	Poor	Good	Excellent	Good	Excellent
Personal and corporate income	Good	Excellent	Fair	Fair	Good
User fees	Fair	Good	Fair	Good	Excellent

tax revenues. Taxes on oil and natural gas account for billions of dollars in state revenues in Alaska, North Dakota, and Wyoming. These three states bring in about half of their revenues from severance taxes on coal, oil, and gas (which may explain why these states are able to forgo personal income taxes). Several states are rather creative in applying the severance tax. Washington levies the tax on oysters, salmon, and other food fish; and Louisiana, on freshwater mussels.[29]

Severance taxes are popular in states rich in natural resources because they help keep income, property, and sales taxes relatively low. Severance tax revenues also help to pay for environmental damage resulting from resource extraction operations, such as strip mining and fracking. The major disadvantage is that a state economy too dependent on severance taxes can be damaged badly when the price or supply of its natural resources declines, as severance-tax-dependent states have experienced because oil and natural gas have remained low since 2012. Even so, natural resources have been individually enriching for Alaskans. For more than twenty years, every man, woman, and child resident of Alaska has received a rebate from the state's Permanent Fund. Checks went as high as $3,269 in 2008 (including a one-time $1,200 rebate approved by the state legislature). That amount fell to only $900 in 2013 but then gradually rose to $1,606 in 2019. Established primarily with severance taxes on petroleum, the Permanent Fund's $62 billion in principal and reserves are diversified through investments in office buildings, industrial complexes, stocks, and bonds.[30]

Gambling: Lotteries and Casinos

The lottery is an old American tradition; initially established in the 1600s, it was popular from the colonial days until the late 1800s. Lotteries flourished throughout the country as a means of raising money for good causes such as new schools, highways, canals, and bridges. But scandals and mismanagement led every state and the national government to ban "looteries." From 1895 to 1963, no legal lotteries operated. Then New Hampshire established a new one, followed in 1967 by New York. Forty-three more states operate lotteries today.

Several factors account for the rebirth of "bettor government." First, lotteries can bring in meaningful sums of money—some $23.6 billion in "profits" in 2018.[31] Second, they are popular and entertaining. And they are voluntary—you do not have to participate. In addition, lotteries help relieve pressure on major taxes. In some states, net lottery earnings take the place of a 1 cent increase in the sales tax.

But lotteries also have disadvantages. They are costly to administer and have low yields; average state profits only amount to just over 30 percent of gross receipts. Prize awards must be great enough to encourage future ticket sales—the higher the payout, the more people play. New games must be created to retain enthusiasm. Ticket vendors must be paid commissions. And tight (as well as expensive) security precautions are required to guarantee the game's integrity. As a result, lotteries generate only a small percentage of most states' total revenues. The average yield for players is low: About 65 percent of the total revenue is returned to players in prize money, far below the returns of other games of chance, such as slot machines, roulette, or craps. And lottery winners must pay income taxes on their winnings. Although many states earmark lottery proceeds for popular programs, especially education, the result is often a shell game. For instance, Florida's lottery officially benefits schools and colleges; but in reality, lottery money simply replaces general-fund revenues rather than actually enhancing education funding.

Lotteries can also be attacked on the grounds of equity. Although the purchase of a ticket is voluntary and thus seemingly fair, studies indicate that low-income individuals are more likely to play. Participation is also higher among African Americans, Latinos, males, seniors, and those with low levels of education. The lottery, then, is a regressive way to raise money.[32] Furthermore, lotteries also tend to encourage compulsive gambling (one could further assert that states themselves become addicted to gambling revenues). In recognition of this problem, some states earmark a portion of lottery proceeds for treatment programs.

As interstate lottery competition has saturated markets and depressed profits, states have adopted other forms of legalized gambling, including pari-mutuel betting on horse and dog races; "racinos," with slot machines at the tracks; as well as gaming on river boats, Indian reservations, and at Old West historical sites. Once restricted to Atlantic City and Las Vegas, casino gambling and slot parlors are now offered in forty states, including operations on about 440 Native American reservations. Gambling establishments virtually blanket Minnesota and Mississippi. Touted as producers of jobs, tourist attractions, and generators of higher revenues, casinos and slot parlors share many of the same disadvantages as lotteries, including diminishing returns as new casinos open monthly across the country. Yet they do rake in a significant sum of revenues.

Previously forbidden by the federal government under the 1961 Federal Wire Act, internet gambling (other than sports wagering) was approved in a U.S. Justice Department ruling in 2011. Nevada was the first to proceed with "ultimate poker," soon followed by Delaware and New Jersey. Although Congress will probably need to regulate internet gambling, the potential take for the states is substantial, estimated to be $2 to $4 billion in tax revenues.[33] And then in 2018, the U.S. Supreme Court decided that the congressional ban on internet sports betting was unconstitutional and allowed states to authorize (and tax) this form of gambling. By 2019, eleven states had legalized internet sports betting, generating approximately $155.7 million in tax revenue in a year.[34] As of 2020, another thirty-one states were in the process of legalizing this lucrative new source of state revenue.[35]

The Political Economy of Taxation

LO 13-4
To evaluate the political economy of taxation.

Decisions to raise or lower taxes and fees are inherently political. There are winners and losers, payers and receivers, both in the taxing and in the spending that follows.

Spending

Taxes fuel government spending. The principle of diversity in state and local finance is evident, given what state and local governments choose to do with their revenues. First, these governments spend a great deal of money. State and local spending has ascended much faster than the gross national product and the level of inflation. The functional distribution of spending varies from state to state. As indicated in Figure 13.2, education (K–12 and higher education) consumes the largest total portion of state and local spending, followed by Medicaid.

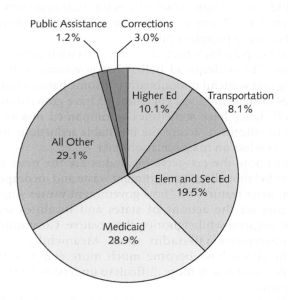

Figure 13.2 Total State Government Spending by Service Delivered

Source: National Association of State Budget Officers, "2019 State Expenditure Report," www.nasbo.org (accessed March 20, 2020).

Within each of these functional categories lies a wide range of financial commitments. For instance, higher-education expenditures in 2019 ran from 26.7 percent of total state spending in Iowa to only 1.7 percent in Vermont. Hawaii dedicated 14.0 percent to transportation, whereas Wyoming set aside just 2.8 percent for the same purpose.[36] Such differences represent historical trends, local economic circumstances, and citizens' willingness to incur debt to pay for services. Demographic factors also play a role. For instance, states with high populations of children invest more money in schools than do states with large proportions of senior citizens. State population growth drives up expenditures for such services as water and sewer systems, street maintenance, and law enforcement. The largest expenditure gains in recent years have been registered in Medicaid, as populations of the medically indigent have swelled.

One of the most difficult decisions for an elected official is to go on record in favor of raising taxes (lowering taxes is always popular). The political heat can scorch even the coolest incumbent. But when revenues do not equal service costs and citizens do not want to cut services, raising taxes may be the only answer. However, most people do not want higher taxes. This dilemma is the familiar **tax–service paradox**: People demand new, improved, or at least the same level of government services but do not want to pay for them through taxes. For instance, the people of Washington state, in their collective wisdom, voted in a 1999 constitutional initiative to slice taxes. But the very next year, they passed another initiative to reduce class sizes and boost teacher pay—without, of course, providing any new money. Voters in a dozen other states have taken similar action. As a former legislator put it, "I wouldn't say voters are stupid. But the same voter who wants unlimited services also does not want to pay for it. There is a disconnect."[37] Is it any wonder that user charges have become a popular option?

The tax–service paradox reflects a certain alienation between government and its citizens. The widespread belief that government at all levels has become too big and wasteful undoubtedly has some basis in fact. The size and responsibilities of state and local governments have grown dramatically, and waste and inefficiency have sometimes accompanied this growth. But the unwillingness of citizens to accept the inevitable reductions in services that follow tax cuts borders on mass schizophrenia.

Helping promote the tax–service paradox are the news media, which enthusiastically belabor alleged government waste and incompetence. Prime-time television news features on "how government wastes your money" and typical reporting on the actions of states and localities search for and emphasize the negative while ignoring the positive. Government bashing is a popular conservative talk-radio sport. Meanwhile, state and local government functions have become much more complex and technical, tending to make government more difficult to understand, interact with, and communicate with.

State and local governments are responding with outreach efforts designed to educate citizens about what their governments are doing for them and where their tax dollars are going. Local governments send notices showing

tax–service paradox Situation in which people demand more government services but do not want to pay for them through higher taxes.

taxpayers what their money goes to pay for. In several recent cases, most notably in California, state voters have repealed or loosened up restrictions on taxing and spending, indicating, perhaps, the ability of state leaders to get their "dollars and sense" messages across to voters. Thus, the **political economy**—the set of political choices that frames economic policy—has become enormously perplexing for state and local officials. Several features of contemporary state and local economies merit additional discussion: the tax revolt, fiscal stress, limited discretion in raising new revenues, and underfunded retiree pensions and health care benefits.

Tax Revolt

Taxpayer resentment of property taxes and changes in assessment practices and the general perception that government is too big, too costly, and too wasteful first took on a tangible form in 1978 with the passage of Proposition 13 in California. Its most Draconian embodiment was adopted by Colorado voters in 1992 as the Taxpayer's Bill of Rights, known as TABOR.[38] (Some of TABOR's severity was lessened in a subsequent referendum adopted in 2005, but in 2019 voters rejected a ballot proposition that would have further loosened TABOR's effect on transportation and education funding.) Today, nearly every state has enacted statutory or constitutional limitations on taxing and spending by restricting personal or corporate income tax increases, indexing their income taxes to the cost of living, limiting expenditures to increases in cost of living, and other measures. In most instances, citizens have taken tax matters into their own hands through the initiative process. In other cases, state legislators jumped in front of the parade and cut taxes and spending themselves.

Taxpayer revolts come and go today. Their legacy, however, remains enormously important. Watchdog organizations such as the Americans for Tax Reform, led by famous taxophobe Grover Norquist, insist that candidates for elective office sign a "no-tax" pledge. Public officials must work hard to justify tax increases; otherwise, they risk a voter uprising and perhaps political death. Indeed, the stirrings of new tax revolts are constantly in evidence. In 2019, Texans approved a ballot measure that would require a two-thirds vote of the state legislature if they wanted to impose an income tax in the state, and in the 2017 through 2019 election seasons many states passed a variety of property tax exemptions for veterans, surviving spouses of first responders killed in the line of duty, senior citizens, those with property in disaster areas, and many others without measures to compensate for the revenue lost.

Taxation and expenditure limitations (TELs), then, are restrictions on government taxing and spending. Forty-six states have some sort of property tax restrictions in effect, and many place limitations on other forms of taxation as well. Raising taxes now requires a constitutional amendment, voter approval, or an extraordinary legislative majority in quite a few states. States and localities usually resist reducing service levels, opting instead to shift tax burdens or find new sources of revenues, such as user charges.[39]

political economy Political choices that have economic outcomes.

taxation and expenditure limitations (TELs) Restrictions on state and/or local government taxing and spending.

Political and economic consequences of the tax revolt have been much studied. In many cases, TELs have made state and local finance an extraordinarily difficult undertaking: Voters insist on passing spending mandates for education, law enforcement, or other popular programs while at the same time tying the hands of legislatures with restrictions on new revenue raising, spawning political and bureaucratic legerdemain and new fees to gather sufficient funds to pay for essential services. So far, TELs have not significantly reduced the size and cost of government, or exerted positive effects on employment or per capita income, as had been advertised. However, TELs have led local governments to depend more on the states and to greater recognition by public officials of the continuing need to measure the taxpaying public's pulse on tax issues.[40]

Fiscal Stress

During national and regional economic downturns, many state and local jurisdictions experience severe **fiscal stress**: They struggle to pay for programs and provide services that citizens want and need without taxing the citizens at unacceptably high levels. Many factors contribute to fiscal stress. Typically, adverse social and economic conditions, mostly beyond state and local government control, establish an environment conducive to financial problems. Between 2008 and 2020, two major events created financial problems for state and local government. First, the unwinding of the national economy during the Great Recession in 2008–2011 was due largely to the deregulation of the financial industry, personal and corporate greed, the housing and mortgage loan meltdowns, and other macroeconomic factors (though some jurisdictions incurred unrealistic long-term spending obligations even as taxes were lessened). Second, the COVID-19 pandemic in 2020 greatly increased health expenditures by state and local governments. In addition, claims for unemployment compensation rose dramatically as businesses closed in response to government attempts to enforce social distancing. All forms of tax revenue and user fees declined steeply. The long-term economic effects of this health crisis remain to be seen, but the immediate effects have been devastating on areas like Seattle, Los Angeles, San Francisco, and New York City. Early COVID hotspots such as Washington state, Illinois, New Jersey, and New York began to see declines in new cases by summer of 2020, but other states saw dramatic increases in cases. By July 2020, there were thirty-four states classified as COVID hotspots in the United States.[41] State governors in Texas, Florida, and Georgia who had reopened bars, beaches, and restaurants in May had to close some of them again in June in response to growing caseloads. These second set of closings had dramatic financial effects on individual workers and state economies.[42]

fiscal stress
Financial pressure on a government from factors such as revenue shortfalls and taxing and spending limitations.

Older industrial cities are particularly vulnerable during traditional recessions. Many jobs and manufacturing industries have been lost because of the gradual but inexorable shift to a service- and information-based economy and company relocation to the Sunbelt and foreign sites. In cities such as Detroit and Philadelphia, the exodus of jobs and firms has eroded the value of taxable resources (mostly property), yet citizens left behind have growing service demands. In New Orleans and other Gulf Coast communities, the local tax base was essentially wiped out by Hurricane Katrina in 2005, and, after modest recovery, was badly damaged again as a result of the 2010 BP oil spill.

The COVID-19 pandemic resulted in a different kind of economic impact. Although industrial workers were certainly affected, many of them were at least somewhat protected because they worked for companies large enough to be able to keep workers on the payroll or they had union contracts that covered these conditions. Many hourly employees were not so fortunate. Service-based workers in the retail, hospitality, travel, food service, and entertainment sectors of the economy were hard hit as Americans stopped going out to eat or for a drink, attending concerts, flying on commercial airlines, and traveling on cruise ships. Especially hard hit were individuals who worked for small businesses—the "ma and pa" restaurant that employed fewer than a dozen people, for example. When these types of workplaces are forced to stop operations, owners typically cannot afford to continue to pay workers. Early estimates of the pandemic were that the unemployment rate could go as high as 20 percent, twice what it was in October 2009 and rivaling unemployment rates in the Great Depression of the 1930s.[43]

Concentration of the poor and minorities in deteriorating housing, the shortage of jobs, high levels of crime, the illegal drug trade, homelessness, large expanses of blighted property, and related factors have produced crisis-level situations. Declining infrastructure also plagues older cities: Water and

Miami Herald/Tribune News Service/Getty Images

Collapsed pedestrian bridge at Florida International University in Miami visually illustrates the problems of aging infrastructure.

sewer lines, treatment plants, streets, sidewalks, and other components of the urban physical landscape are in dire need of restoration or replacement. The American Society for Civil Engineers estimates that $4.5 trillion in infrastructure spending is needed by 2025.[44] The estimated amount needed to replace New York City's crumbling and leaking natural gas lines alone is a shocking $10 million *a mile* and there are some 6,000 miles of gas lines in the city![45] Most of these problems, it should be noted, will require tax or fee increases and national government attention if they are to be addressed effectively.

Political contributions to fiscal stress typically compound the economic problems of cities. Mismanagement of resources and inefficient procedures and activities are common complaints. Pressures from city workers and their unions have also driven up service-provision costs in some localities. Thus, service demands and the costs of providing services grow while taxes and intergovernmental revenues decline. This is a well-tested recipe for fiscal stress that evokes fears of bond defaults and even bankruptcy. Recessions and public health crises come and go, but many states and localities face chronic fiscal shortfalls because of structural problems deeply embedded in their revenue systems. Structural imbalances result from out-of-date tax systems developed for radically different state economies of fifty years past, as well as from unwise financial management practices.

Limited Discretion

TELs have placed ceilings on the rates and amounts of taxation and spending, thus limiting the discretion of the nonnational governments. Other constraining factors, too, keep state and local governments from falling prey to the temptation of taxing and spending orgies. One important factor is interstate competition for jobs and economic development. High-tax states run a risk of having jobs, firms, and investments "stolen" by low-tax states.

Earmarking taxes for popular programs also limits state and local taxing and spending discretion. Earmarking is well established: Fuel taxes have been set aside for road and highway programs since automobiles first left ruts in muddy cow pastures. Approximately 25 percent of state tax revenues are earmarked. What differs today is the levels of specificity and creativity in earmarking. Surpluses may accumulate in some dedicated funds, such as highways, whereas other important needs such as education or law enforcement are not sufficiently met. The hands of government officials are tied, however, because they cannot move the funds around. Typical state earmarks fund local drainage, water, or sewer projects; enhance fisheries or environmental cleanups; or pay for municipal or county building improvements. Cigarette buyers in Washington cough up millions of dollars each year to help clean up Puget Sound. Several states earmark a penny of the sales tax for public education.

Financial discretion is partly determined by one's position on the fiscal food chain. The national government can essentially tax and spend as it wishes, subject only to its highly underdeveloped capacity for self-discipline.

States must meet federal spending mandates for Medicaid, education, and other services while somehow balancing their budgets each year. Local governments, in addition to suffering reductions in state aid during tough times in this seemingly eternal game of "shift and shaft federalism," must comply with an increasing number of state spending mandates, even as their legal authority to raise revenues remains severely circumscribed in most states. In some ways, local governments are not masters of their own fiscal fate.[46]

Pensions and Health Care When the U.S. General Accounting Standards Board (GASB) issued standards requiring state and local governments to publicly report the funding status of employee pension and health care benefits, most jurisdictions were caught with their financial pants down. As noted earlier, for many years most states and many localities have been underfunding the future liabilities of employee retirement benefits. The estimated gap between what states have promised their retirees for pension benefits and what they have available to pay for them was estimated to be $1.28 trillion in 2017. Chicago's unfunded pension liability alone is estimated to be $30 billion.[47]

Equally serious are the unfunded billions in future liabilities of health care for retirees and their families. California is in the red for $87.7 billion, New York for $88.4 billion, and Texas for $88.7 billion. The larger the state employment numbers, the higher the future debt in most cases. But on a per capita basis, states such as Delaware and New Jersey are particularly hard hit. Delaware is underfunded by more than $8,500 per state resident, and New Jersey for nearly $7,700 per resident.[48] Cities are overstretched as well, falling some $259 billion short of full health care funding. Counties are some $141 billion short and school districts $138 billion short of full funding.

There are several reasons for these huge pension and retiree health care debts. The baby boom bulge in the government workforce has now reached retirement age. Unwise state borrowing from pension funds during difficult economic times is a major cause in some jurisdictions. Overly optimistic assumptions about health care inflation have been common. And, of course, legislators have a tendency to spend today and worry about the future tomorrow (or let the next generation of lawmakers worry about it).

One attempt to defuse the ticking pension and health care bomb is for state and local governments not to pay for retiree benefits. Several states have recently taken such steps. In 2014, South Dakota removed state subsidies from retiree health care coverage. Kansas followed suit in 2016. Both states had relatively small health plan liabilities. In 2017, North Carolina eliminated the health insurance benefit for newly hired employees in an attempt to reduce its $34.4 billion liability in this fund. Such action would seem to be politically difficult in states that either had a small liability or powerful public employee associations. On the other hand, in states like Alabama, Georgia, South Carolina, and Texas, where health care liabilities are large and public sector unions are weak, action like North Carolina's would seem to be more likely.[49]

LO 13-5
To discuss how state
and local governments
manage money.

Managing Money

Every state except Vermont is constitutionally or statutorily required to balance its *operating budgets* each fiscal year. In turn, the states require that local governments balance *their* budgets. However, these requirements apply only to operating budgets, which are used for daily financial receipts and disbursements. *Capital budgets,* used for big purchases that must be paid for over time (for instance, a new bridge or school building), typically run substantial deficits. Operating budgets may also run in the red during the fiscal year, so long as expenditures equal revenues at the end of the year. Consequently, the reliability of revenue estimates is a vital consideration.

Estimating Revenues

Not so long ago, state and local governments estimated their annual revenues simply by extrapolating from past trends. This approach was simple, inexpensive, and worked well during periods of steady economic growth, but it failed miserably during years of boom or bust. The finance officers of states and most larger cities and counties are much more sophisticated today. Using computer software, they employ econometric modeling to derive mathematical estimates of future revenues. Economic forecasting firms and/or academics assist or provide independent projections.

Econometric modeling places key variables in equations to predict the fiscal-year yield of each major tax. A wide variety of variables are used, including employment levels, food prices, housing costs, oil and gas prices, consumer savings levels, interest rates, intergovernmental aid projections, and state and local debt obligations. Because state and local economies are increasingly linked to national and international factors, estimates often include measures for the value of the dollar, international trade and investment, and national fiscal policy. Despite sophisticated econometric models and financial software, predictions can be wildly off the mark. State revenue estimates fell short by an average of more than 10 percent in 2009 as the Great Recession wreaked havoc.[50] Although most states have improved their revenue forecasting abilities, tax revenues from all sources—income, sales, and even property—have become more volatile, as have projections of revenue from sin taxes. This makes even more sophisticated revenue projection techniques open to error.[51]

Two critical factors determine the accuracy of revenue estimates: the quality of the data and the validity of the economic assumptions. Indeed, econometric modeling of state and local economies can be a voyage into the unknown. Data problems include difficulty in measuring key variables; periodic revisions of historical economic data, which require new calculations; and modifications in tax laws or fee schedules. But the major sources of error are the economic assumptions built into the models. Examples are legion: The national economy may not perform as expected; federal financial policy can change to either benefit or harm state and local revenues; federal government shutdowns and sequesters, as occurred in 2013–2014, ripple through the state and local economies; energy prices may plummet or soar; natural or human disasters may disrupt state or local economic growth. Recessions are particularly damaging to fiscal stability because state and local sales and income taxes are highly sensitive to economic downturns.

Rainy Day Funds

Because a balanced budget is mandatory, but estimation errors are inevitable, forty-eight states and many localities have established contingency, "budget stabilization," or reserve funds. Popularly known as *rainy day funds,* these savings accounts help insulate budgets from fiscal distortions caused by inaccurate data or faulty economic assumptions; they are also available to alleviate revenue shortfalls. In years of economic health, the funds accumulate principal and interest. When the economy falters, governments can tap into their savings accounts to balance the budget and avoid imposing tax and fee increases.

During sunny days, the states typically fill up their contingency funds to as much as 10 percent of total spending. Amidst the recessionary storms of 2008–2011, states were forced to dig deeply, simply to retain essential services. Many states completely drained their rainy day funds.[52] The task of balancing the budget is especially daunting to local governments, given their lack of economic diversity, dependency on state taxes and financial aid, and sensitivity to economic dislocations. The departure of a single large employer can disrupt a local economy for years. So can weather: Snowstorms, hurricanes, tornadoes, and other weather events close businesses and disrupt tax revenues as well as damage homes, infrastructure, and people's lives. So, the potential advantages of rainy day funds are numerous in the fragile fiscal context of cities and counties.

Other Financial Management Practices

State and local governments, of necessity, are becoming more knowledgeable about how to manage cash and investments. Cash reserves that once sat idly in non-interest-bearing accounts or a desk drawer are now invested in short-term notes, money market accounts, U.S. Treasury bills, certificates of deposit, and other financial instruments so that governments can maximize interest earnings. Most states have local government investment pools that manage billions of dollars in short-term assets. The process of spending and collecting monies is also manipulated to advantage. For example, large checks are deposited in interest-bearing accounts on the day they are received; conversely, payable checks are drawn on the latest date possible. In general, state and local financial management today resembles that of a large corporation instead of the mom-and-pop approach of years ago. After all, the nonnational governments spend and invest more than $3 trillion annually.

The most important state or local investment is usually the public-employee pension fund. In the past, these funds were conservatively managed and politically untouchable. Today, however, they tend to be invested in more aggressive instruments such as corporate stock. They also represent a tempting honey pot for financially strapped states, whose governors have dipped their hands in the funds and pulled out billions to balance the budget. As described previously, many state retirement plans have very large unfunded liabilities. State and local investments must not be managed too aggressively nor too recklessly, as the case of Orange County, California, illustrates. One of the nation's biggest and wealthiest counties, Orange County became the largest at the time to file for federal bankruptcy in 1994. (Read about how much responsibility a state should take when a local government declares bankruptcy in the Controversies in State and Local Government box below.) The county's financial nightmare commenced when its investment pool manager, Robert L. Citron, placed millions of dollars in financial instruments called derivatives. These instruments "derive" their value from underlying assets such as stocks, bonds, or mortgages. The derivatives' value changes when the price of the underlying assets changes. Orange County lost $1.5 billion when its derivatives, which were tied to interest rates, declined precipitously in value. In effect, Citron was borrowing money from stocks, bonds, and other assets to bet on the direction of interest rates. He lost, and so did Orange County's taxpayers.[53]

Long-Term Borrowing Like corporations, state and local governments issue long-term debt obligations, typically for five to twenty-five years. Bonds are the most common form of long-term borrowing. Because of federal and state tax breaks for investors, the state and local governments are able to finance bonded indebtedness at significantly lower rates than corporations. There are three conventional types of bonds: general obligation bonds, revenue bonds, and industrial development bonds.

The principal and interest payments on **general obligation bonds** are secured by the "full faith, credit, and taxing power" of the state or local jurisdiction issuing them. General-obligation bonds are used to finance public projects such as highways, schools, and hospitals. Lenders are guaranteed repayment as long as the bond-issuing government is solvent; defaults are nearly nonexistent, but downgrades of cities' credit worthiness occur from time to time.

Revenue bonds are backed by expected income from a specific project or service; examples include a toll bridge, a municipal sewer system, or sports complex. Revenue bonds are payable only from the revenues derived from the specified source, not from general tax revenues. Because they typically represent a riskier investment than general-obligation bonds, they command a higher rate of interest.

The **industrial development bond (IDB)** is a type of revenue bond issued by a local government on behalf of a private company to further economic development, such as a new manufacturing facility. The payment of principal and interest on IDBs depends solely on the ability of the industry using the facilities financed by the bond to meet its financial obligation. If the user fails to make payments, creditors can seize and sell any real or personal property associated with the facility. Private interests, such as developers and

general obligation bond
A debt instrument supported by the full financial resources of the issuing jurisdiction.

revenue bond
A bond paid off from income derived from the facility built with the bond proceeds.

industrial development bond (IDB)
A type of revenue bond issued to fund the construction of a facility to be used by a private firm.

Controversies in States and Localities

The State's Responsibility in Local Bankruptcy Events

Harrisburg, Pennsylvania, won the dubious award for first state capital to file for bankruptcy on October 12, 2011, attributing the action to a failed plan to finance and construct an incinerator and to "cash flow problems." On November 9, 2011, Jefferson County, Alabama, surpassed Orange County as the largest county government bankruptcy declaration in history, seeking relief from a debt of more than $4 billion. Jefferson County, home of Birmingham, ran up its huge debt thanks to political corruption, a bad investment in a sewer system, and dumb spending decisions. And as stated in the introduction to this chapter, Detroit became the largest municipality to file for bankruptcy.

For these and a handful of other local governments that declared bankruptcy during and after the Great Recession, the decisions were not made without deliberation (and desperation). The consequences of bankruptcy are dire. Businesses may flee, as well as residents concerned about property values. Services, even police and fire, are drastically reduced or eliminated altogether. And the reputation of the city or county is seriously damaged.

The process of filing for bankruptcy is challenging. Only local governments—not states—may do so under federal law, and they must have state approval. To be eligible, the local government must demonstrate insolvency and that it has made a good-faith effort to settle with creditors. Once declared, the bankruptcy proceedings move into the state courts to help chart a path toward financial relief. Though painful, bankruptcy does have the advantages of providing legal protection from creditors and additional time for the local government to get its financial

house in order.[1] It may take years to emerge from bankruptcy with a balanced budget and stable finances. But the city or county may prefer the bankruptcy option, which does permit a good deal of local decision-making space, to a state takeover of the locality, its finances, and even its government. Nineteen states have adopted laws enabling them to intervene in local government financial crises, and other states can do so with special legislation.[2]

Critical Thinking Questions

1. When a city or county goes under water financially, what should the state do? Let the local jurisdiction find its own way back financially? Help it out with loans, grants, or other financial assistance? Take over the jurisdiction and turn over its budget and operations to an external emergency manager?

2. What conditions (e.g., mismanagement, corruption, a declining tax base, etc.) should guide state action?

[1] Campbell Robertson, Mary Williams Walsh, and Michael Cooper, "Bankruptcy Rarely Offers Easy Answer for Counties," https://www.nytimes.com/2011/11/11/us/bankruptcy-rarely-offers-easy-answer-for-counties.html(November 10, 2011); John Gramlich, "Municipal Bankruptcy Explained: What It Means to File for Chapter 9," https://www.pewtrusts.org/en/research-and-analysis/blogs/stateline/2011/11/22/municipal-bankruptcy-explained-what-it-means-to-file-for-chapter-9 (November 22, 2011); Ryan Holeywell, "How Bad Is It?" *Governing* (May 2011): 26–30.

[2] Elaine S. Povich, "States Intervene in City Fiscal Crises," https://www.pewtrusts.org/en/research-and-analysis/blogs/stateline/2014/07/01/states-intervene-in-city-fiscal-crises (July 1, 2014); Liz Farmer, "The 'B' Word: Is the Stigma of Municipal Bankruptcy Going Away?" *Governing* (March 2013): 36–41; Liz Farmer, "Exiting the Penalty Box," *Governing* (December 2014): 54–6.

retailers, are the primary beneficiaries of IDBs. Conventionally, these private-purpose bonds are issued by local governments to attract economic activity and investments; in fact, they are frequently used to furnish loans at highly favorable interest rates to small- or medium-size firms.

The **qualified private activity bond** is a municipal security that enables a firm to finance certain projects with bonds exempt from federal taxes. These financial instruments have been criticized for favoring select businesses with

qualified private activity bond
A tax-exempt state or municipal security issued to a private firm to finance a project or facility.

government subsidies. Among the questionable uses have been for a Pakistani company's fertilizer plant in Indiana whose chemicals appeared in improvised explosive devices in Afghanistan, and financial offices for large and wealthy firms such as Goldman Sachs Group and Bank of America.[54] Any "public purpose" for such private activity bonds is hard to discern.

Short-term borrowing is available to state and local governments that need temporary funds just to help tide them over or to meet unexpected circumstances. To borrow money on a short-term loan (e.g., one to six months), governments may access capital markets or even secure a loan from a bank or credit union.

Limits on Borrowing Almost all states place constitutional or statutory restrictions on their own and local government borrowing. Some have set maximum levels of indebtedness; others require popular referenda to create debt or to exceed specified debt limits. They tightly restrict local government debt, especially general-obligation bonds. (State-imposed constraints normally do not apply to revenue bonds.)

The bond market places its own informal limitations on debt by assessing the quality of bonds, notes, and other debt instruments. Investors in government bonds rely on Moody's Investors Service, Standard and Poor's Corporation, Fitch Ratings, and other investment services for ratings of a jurisdiction's capacity to repay its obligations. Criteria taken into consideration in bond ratings include existing debt levels, rainy day funds, market value of real estate, population growth, per capita income, employment levels, and other measures of overall financial health and solvency. Highly rated bond issues receive ratings of *aaa*, *aa*, and *a*. Variations of *b* indicate medium to high risk. A rating of *c* is reserved for bonds in immediate danger of default. The average interest rate on low-rated bonds usually exceeds that of top-rated ones by 1½ to 2 percentage points, which translates into a considerable difference in interest payments.

Bond ratings tend to rise during periods of economic growth but can fall rapidly during recessions, driving up borrowing costs. Downgrades in general obligation bond ratings cost states or localities millions of dollars. States recently suffering rating declines include Illinois and New Jersey.

LO 13-6
To be able to discuss current issues in state and local political economy.

Current Issues in State and Local Finance

Dollars define state and local relations. Local governments today recognize that their financial futures depend more on the states than on Washington, D.C.

The Unpleasant Reality

State and local governments are experiencing significant long-term problems in political economy. Tax systems designed for a primitive industrial age are badly out of step with today's service- and information-based global economy. Beset with its own chronic, self-inflicted financial travails and a record high budget deficit from wars and overspending, the budget-impaired federal government is not a consistently reliable fiscal partner. Indeed, the federal government threatened to revoke the tax-exempt status of municipal bonds during the 2013 sequestration.

The spiraling costs of health care, Medicaid, corrections, and public education cannot be shouldered by a single level of government. Mandates without money are certainly no help. When mandates and program responsibilities are pushed to a different rung of the government ladder, funds should follow. Local governments in particular require more revenue-raising authority and broader tax bases to pay for the services they deliver. Most states have been receptive to these principles, but during the Great Recession many states cut funding to local governments, pulled back local governments share of sales and other tax revenues, while foisting even more service delivery responsibilities on them.

The need to increase state and local capability and responsiveness by reinventing and reinvigorating government has perhaps never been greater. The financial structures and processes of state and local governments must be made more appropriate to the social and economic environment in which they operate, which includes a service-based economy; global markets; aging baby boomers; and the changing gender, racial, and ethnic composition of the labor force. These challenges to state and local governments are not being met sufficiently by present revenue systems. The longer they remain unmet, the more severe the problems and the actions that will have to be taken to rectify them.[55]

Education is also needed for taxpayers, who do not always grasp the relationship between taxes paid and services rendered. Resistance to new or existing taxes is to be expected, but campaigns can educate citizens that the result of reducing or eliminating taxes will be fewer or lower-quality services.

 # Chapter Recap

- The two basic principles of state and local financial systems are the interdependence of the three levels of government and the diversity of revenue sources.

- Among the criteria for evaluating taxes are equity, yield, political accountability, acceptability, and efficiency.

- The major state and local taxes are those assessed on property, sales, and income. Other taxes and fees are also imposed.

- Legalized gambling and gaming also raise money.

- Taxpayer resistance has produced tax and expenditure limitations in many states, increased sensitivity of state and local officials to taxpayer preferences, and in some cases fiscal stress for governments.

- State and local governments estimate annual revenues and set aside money in rainy day funds for emergencies and contingencies.

- State and local financial relationships are characterized by sharing and cooperation but also by conflict over mandates and limited local discretion.

Key Terms

own-source revenue *(p. 360)*
intergovernmental transfers *(p. 360)*
countercyclical aid *(p. 361)*
tax capacity *(p. 361)*
tax effort *(p. 361)*
regressive tax *(p. 364)*
progressive tax *(p. 364)*

proportional *(flat) tax (p. 365)*
benefit principle *(p. 365)*
indexing *(p. 365)*
circuit breaker *(p. 367)*
tax–service paradox *(p. 378)*
political economy *(p. 379)*
taxation and expenditure limitations *(TELs) (p. 379)*

fiscal stress *(p. 380)*
general obligation bond *(p. 386)*
revenue bond *(p. 386)*
industrial development bond *(IDB) (p. 386)*
qualified private activity bond *(p. 387)*

Internet Resources

The National Conference of State Legislatures' Principles of a High-Quality Tax System are available for viewing at **www.ncsl.org**.

One of the best individual sites on state tax and budget information is "where the money goes" at the Texas State Comptroller at **www.window .state.tx.us**.

Comparative state and local revenue, tax, and expenditure data may be found at the U.S. Census Bureau's website (**www.census.gov**) and at the Tax Foundation's website (**www .tax-foundation.org**).

See **www.usa.gov/state-taxes** for general tax resources and official state tax sites.

14

Economic Development: Competing for Growth

VA governor Ralph Northam announcing the Amazon deal

Learning Objectives

LO 14-1 To recognize regional differences in economic prosperity.

LO 14-2 To distinguish the four waves of economic development policy.

LO 14-3 To assess the politics inherent in economic development.

LO 14-4 To explain strategic planning and four economic development approaches popular with states and localities.

LO 14-5 To defend both sides of the three persistent questions about government's role in the economy.

In 2017, the internet sales giant Amazon announced that it was interested in developing a second headquarters unit to complement its facility in Seattle. Competition was fierce for the $5 billion facility and the 50,000 high-paying jobs it would create, with 238 areas in the United States, Canada, and Mexico submitting proposals. Amazon's preferences for awarding the facility were very specific: metropolitan area of more than one million in population, a stable business-friendly environment, an area with the potential to attract technological talent, and a community that thinks "big and creatively when considering locations and real estate options."[1] States and municipalities developed proposals that touted their education, recreation, and entertainment offerings and promised infrastructure improvements and tax abatements. Creative proposals came from cities like Columbus, Ohio, who offered to waive property taxes for fifteen years; Chicago, who said it would lower income taxes paid by Amazon employees by at least 50 percent; and

Kevin Dietsch/UPI/Alamy Stock Photo

Fresno, California, who offered to make Amazon an equal partner in deciding how the benefits of the new facility would be used in the city.[2] Eventually, Amazon announced it would create two facilities, one near Arlington, Virginia, and the other in the Long Island City area of New York City, each employing 25,000 workers (with an additional smaller facility in Nashville, Tennessee, employing 5,000). New York promised $1.85 billion, whereas Virginia's incentives were valued at *only* $819 million (Nashville promised $102 million).[3] Although the project was welcomed by northern Virginia, opposition arose from some Queens politicians in New York who objected to the size of the incentive package, the effects the facility would have on existing neighborhoods, and Amazon's opposition to unionization. In February 2019, Amazon announced it was canceling its plans in New York and would increase its investment in the planned Virginia facility and elsewhere.[4] One thing is clear from this: Amazon did not choose Virginia because it offered the best financial incentives. Proposals like New Jersey's $7 billion for a facility located in Newark and Maryland's $8.5 billion for one north of Washington, D.C., were rejected. The Amazon official who led the search said proposals were rejected because of an absence of a regional transportation system or a lack of a tech-savvy workforce rather than the amount of economic incentives offered.[5] Less than a year after canceling the HQ2 project in New York City, Amazon announced it would expand its presence in the city, adding 1,500 jobs—without any public economic incentives.[6]

Attracting new investment like Amazon is what **economic development** is all about these days. Capital investment, employment rates, income levels, tax base, and public services—all are linked to economic development. And it is a competitive process, often pitting one state against another. Reflect on the salvo fired in 2010 by former Texas governor Rick Perry. He sent letters to ninety top businesses in Washington, saying, "As the State of Washington considers a multibillion dollar tax increase for citizens and businesses, I invite you to consider your future in America's new land of opportunity: the State of Texas."[7] Not surprisingly, then Washington governor Chris Gregoire unleashed a counterstrike claiming that the Evergreen State had for several years ranked ahead of Texas in its business friendliness.

economic development
A process by which a community, state, or nation increases its level of per capita income, high-quality jobs, and capital investment.

(Washingtonians voted down the proposed tax increase, perhaps coincidentally.) And when the city of Irwindale, California, complained that the fumes from the production of sriracha sauce were bothering local residents, Huy Fong, the producer of the sauce, informed the city that more than two dozen other cities were happy to have the $50 million facility relocate. Irwindale backed down.[8] As these dust ups suggest, resurgent state and local governments are pursuing economic development with a vengeance.

Regional Differences in Economic Prosperity

LO 14-1
To recognize regional differences in economic prosperity.

The United States continues to be a nation of diverse regional economies. When the headline in *USA Today* trumpets "Nation's economy improves," be assured that not all places are experiencing the same level of improvement. As economist Mark Crain notes, during the last three decades of the twentieth century, living standards (measured by real income per capita) in the United States increased by 50 percent.[9] However, this average figure masks a considerable range in the data: from a low of 28 percent in Alaska to a high of 64 percent in North Carolina. Even within regions, economies can vary. Detroit and Columbus are both located in the Midwest, but the largest city in Michigan and the largest city in Ohio are worlds apart economically.[10] Different economic mixes of manufacturing, services, and retail employment mean different economic conditions. The effects of global economic restructuring coupled with a prolonged national recession hit states and communities hard in the early twenty-first century. Some places have done better than others in adjusting to the new economic realities.

The business network CNBC evaluates the states annually on fifty-six different measures related to business competitiveness.[11] The individual measures—tax burden, job training programs, wage rates, regulatory environment, venture capital, and quality of life, among others—are weighted and aggregated to produce scores and rankings. Figure 14.1 organizes the states into quintiles based on these rankings. Virginia and Texas were the top two scoring states in CNBC's 2019 analysis; Rhode Island edged out Hawaii for the lowest score.

Remember that economies are dynamic—that is, economic momentum can slow down and speed up. The personal income growth in a state, the change in unemployment rates, and the level of population change are three indicators that can be combined into a useful index of economic momentum, or change. The figures for December 2019 showed Utah, Idaho, and Arizona at the top of the list, with Connecticut and West Virginia at the bottom. The rankings throughout 2019 showed great stability; eight of the same states stayed in the top ten all year, while five of the lowest ten stayed in the bottom ten.[12] By June 2020, state scores began to show the effects of the

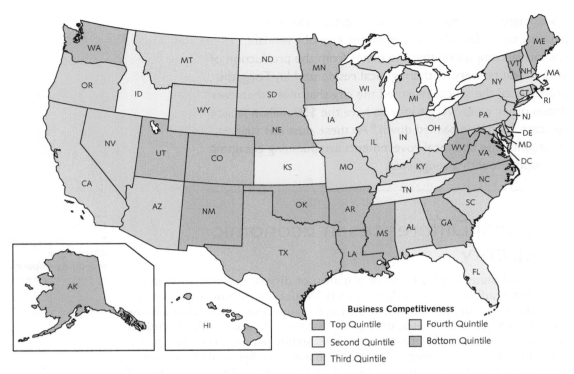

Figure 14.1 State Business Competitiveness

Source: "America's Top States For Business in 2019," CNBC, https://www.cnbc.com/2019/07/10/americas-top-states-for-business-2019.html
(January 27, 2020).

COVID-19 pandemic.[13] While the same states (Idaho, Utah, Arizona) remained at the top of the list, states at the bottom of the list changed partially because of the negative economic effects of the coronavirus pandemic. Michigan, New York, and Hawaii were the lowest ranked states in June. In December 2019, Utah had the highest score (1.50 percentage points higher than the national average set at 0.0) while West Virginia had the lowest score (−1.69) for a difference of just over three percentage points. By June 2020, Idaho had the highest score (3.23) while Hawaii had the lowest (−3.45) for a difference greater than 6.5 percentage points. This larger range in scores reflects the differential effects the coronavirus was having on states. Some states that had low infection rates through spring (such as Nebraska and South Dakota) did well on the June rankings while other states that had high infection rates in the spring such as (New York and Michigan) continued to be negatively affected by the virus.

Local economies are also dynamic. Some cities that were once the economic engines of the country—Cleveland, Detroit, St. Louis—have been replaced by others—Austin, Raleigh, San Jose. As some cities decline, others surge. The Controversies in States and Localities feature discusses cities that have become magnets for what has been called the "creative class."

Controversies in States and Localities

The Creative Class and Cool Cities

What's the hottest thing for cities these days? Well, to be cool. Metropolitan areas across the country are in a race for the informal title of the coolest city in America. They want to be considered hip, trendy, and sophisticated. This is because the cool cities attract well-educated, talented young professionals to their environs. They are magnets for the creative class, people whose work involves producing new ideas, new technology, or new creative content. It is this demographic of innovators that is, some contend, the driving force for economic development. And with a recent study showing that two-thirds of college graduates will choose where to live before looking for employment, this gives states and localities considerable leverage in attracting the urban crowd.

Cool cities possess what Richard Florida calls in his book *The Rise of the Creative Class* the three T's: technology, tolerance, and talent. Their economies are knowledge based, their policies promote social tolerance, and their communities nurture the arts and culture. Jobs are plentiful, gays and lesbians are welcomed, and the nightlife is lively. Cities that embrace such a culture experience an influx of entrepreneurial, ambitious, and creative young people. And this trend has a snowball effect, attracting a continual stream of well-educated, mobile fun-seekers to cool cities. Consequently, cities lacking in some or all of the three T's fall more and more behind, out of step with the cool places.

This three T's framework has proven so insightful that many state and local governments are implementing its precepts. Florida's consulting agency has helped begin thirty-three initiatives across seven cities, all with the end goal of developing a local "cool" culture. There are initiatives that promote the work of local artists, such as the creation of a sculpture garden in El Paso, Texas, which features exclusive work from the area's most talented sculptors. Promoting local events and workshops is another popular initiative, such as Tacoma's "Love Tacoma" social networking program, which sponsors cultural activities like glass blowing, boutique tours, and farmers' markets. Environmental awareness and initiatives that cater to the eco-friendly crowd are gaining a lot of momentum. Pedestrian-friendly downtowns, public transit systems, trails, bike paths, and local parks are all selling points to the creative class.

So, based on the preceding criteria of what defines cool, which cities top the list? *Forbes* magazine publishes a list every four years. In 2017, the top ten were San Francisco, Seattle, San Diego, New Orleans, Portland (Oregon), San Jose, Los Angeles, New York, Boston, and Denver. According to one study, the top five cities for young Generation Y singles are Dallas, Houston, Austin, Phoenix, and Orlando. Their strong employment opportunity and good salaries, coupled with colorful social events and local flair, give them a unique cultural personality tailored just for the creative class. Meanwhile, many other cities are implementing their own "cool" initiatives that could rival the current leaders.

Critical Thinking Questions

1. Has your city tried to cultivate a "cool" image? If so, what indicators can be used to determine how successful it has been?

2. All cities have a unique culture. What culture could your area leverage to develop a more hip or unique image?

3. Should cities expend resources trying to create a cool image, or is this a distraction from other ways to develop the economy?

Sources: Ann Markusen, "Creative Cities: A 10-Year Research Agenda," *Journal of Urban Affairs* 36 (August 2014): 587–89; Samantha Sharf, "San Francisco Tops Our List of America's Coolest Cities," *Forbes*, https://www.forbes.com/sites/samanthasharf/2017/10/26/san-francisco-tops-our-list-of-americas-coolest-cities/#3f83e07540f1 (October 26, 2017); Casey Leins, "The 10 Most Desirable U.S. Cities for Millennials," *U.S. News and World Report*, https://www.usnews.com/news/cities/slideshows/the-10-most-desirable-us-cities-for-millennials (December 18, 2019); Richard Florida, *The Rise of the Creative Class* (New York: Basic Books, 2019).

LO 14-2
To distinguish the four
waves of economic
development policy.

Approaches to Economic Development

Governments devise elaborate strategies *and spend a lot of money* to promote economic development within their boundaries. The approaches they use have evolved over time, but even some of the oldest tools remain viable today.

Early Approaches: First and Second Waves

Community efforts to spur economic development have a long history, but the first statewide program of industrial recruitment was created during the Great Depression. Mississippi, with its Balance Agriculture with Industry plan, made it possible for local governments to issue bonds to finance the construction or purchase of facilities for relocating industry. Other southern states followed suit, luring businesses from elsewhere with tax breaks, public **subsidies**, and low wages. Called *smokestack chasing*, aggressive industrial recruitment had spread beyond the South by the 1970s. By the end of that decade, as states raided other states for industry, statistics showed that between 80 and 90 percent of new jobs came from existing firm expansions and start-up businesses, not from relocating businesses. About the same time, pressure from foreign competition intensified. Policy makers feverishly cast about for strategies that would spawn new businesses and keep state economies strong. These efforts began a new era, or second wave, in economic development. States established **venture capital pools**, created **small-business incubators**, and initiated workforce training programs in an attempt to support homegrown enterprise. Even with these new initiatives in place, many states continued to chase out-of-state industry.

Newer Approaches: Third and Fourth Waves

The 1990s saw a third wave gather strength. This wave represented a rethinking of the role of government in promoting economic growth. Second-wave programs, well-intentioned perhaps, simply did not have sufficient scale or focus to transform state economies. An **enterprise zone**, for example, may revitalize a neighborhood, but unless an extensive network of such zones exists throughout the state, the overall impact is marginal. Third-wave efforts sought to correct some of the deficiencies of second-wave programs. One of the keys to the third wave was moving economic development programs out of state agencies and into private organizations. Rather than directly supplying the program or the service, as it had done in the first and second waves, government would provide direction and seed capital.

The latest ripple flowing from the third wave is called **clusters**. It reconfigures the economy as clusters of firms that compete and trade with one another and have common needs. By focusing on interconnections and working relationships among businesses, nonprofit organizations, and government, a state gets a better sense of its economic foundations.[14] Arizona pioneered the concept in its Strategic Plan for Economic Development. The state identified ten clusters ranging from food, fiber, and natural products to environmental technologies, to mining and minerals.[15] Each cluster has spawned an

subsidy
Financial assistance given by a government to a firm or enterprise.

venture capital pools
Special funds earmarked for new, innovative businesses that cannot get conventional financing.

small-business incubators
Facilities that provide services aimed at nurturing start-up businesses.

enterprise zone
Areas of a community that offer special government incentives aimed at stimulating investment. Also called an *empowerment zone*.

clusters
Geographically concentrated firms that compete and trade with each other and have similar needs.

organization in which ideas can be shared, common strategies developed, and joint ventures negotiated. In Connecticut, the clusters are tourism, aerospace, and bioscience. To nurture and support its clusters, the Connecticut legislature redesigned the state's research and development tax credits. High technology remains an important cluster in many places around the country despite the slowdown the industry experienced in the early 2000s.[16]

Third-wave thinking continues to influence states and localities, but a fourth wave has already developed. Political scientist Susan Clarke and geographer Gary Gaile contend that a distinctively different set of strategies is needed.[17] This new set, or fourth wave, is more attuned to global markets, especially localities' use of trade and telecommunications to their economic advantage. The fourth wave is also more focused on human capital—that is, on educating and training its workforce. Even as states and localities turn to these third- and fourth-wave approaches, however, they continue to use strategies from the first and second waves. How to pursue economic development remains a hotly debated subject.

A leading figure who has headed economic revitalization efforts in three states points to five key trends that states must understand as they design their economic development policies:

- The economic playing field is the world, not the neighboring county or state.
- The new infrastructure is technology and telecommunications.
- Regionalism provides an opportunity for states and others to work together. Boundaries are falling.
- Sustainable development strategies that recognize the interdependence of the economy and the environment are necessary.
- Successful economic development efforts are built on a high-quality workforce.[18]

The Fourth Wave and the "New Economy"

The fourth wave in economic development approaches is linked to what some are calling the "**new economy**." The list of trends at the end of the preceding section identifies fundamental changes in the U.S. economy. According to adherents of the new economy, states that fail to adapt their development strategies to these new circumstances will be left behind. A public policy think tank, the Information Technology and Innovation Foundation (ITIF), lays it out: "The New Economy is a global, entrepreneurial, and knowledge-based economy in which the keys to success lie in the extent to which knowledge, technology, and innovation are embedded in products and services."[19] ITIF recently evaluated the states according to how close each one is to achieving a new economy. A total of twenty-five indicators was used; among them were items such as state export capacity, in-migration of knowledge workers, number of fast-growing companies, residential use of broadband technology, and industry investment in research and development. Weighting each of the twenty-five indicators according to its importance, ITIF calculated scores for each state. The map in Figure 14.2 groups the states into quintiles based on

new economy
An economy based in global technology and knowledge, as opposed to the old economy based in national manufacturing.

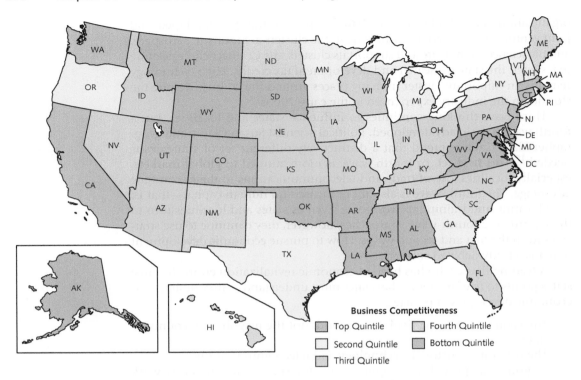

Figure 14.2 State Scores on the "New Economy"

Source: Robert D. Atkinson and John Wu, "The 2017 New State Economy Index," https://itif.org/publications/2017/11/06/2017-state-new
-economy-index (November 6, 2017).

the aggregate scores. Leading new economy states are Massachusetts, California; and Washington; at the other end of the score sheet are West Virginia, Arkansas, and Mississippi.

LO 14-3

To assess the politics inherent in economic development.

The Politics of Economic Growth

Economic development occupies a central role in campaigns for state and local elective office. Like reducing crime and improving education, it is a consensus issue: Everybody is in favor of it. Thus, each candidate tries to convince the voters that their approach to economic development will be the most effective. At both the state and local levels, candidates' campaign rhetoric typically emphasizes jobs and employment, and candidates talk in terms of "sustaining and expanding economic growth."

Most states have created several mechanisms to implement economic development strategies.[20] Ideally, a state government should be internally united for its economic development effort, but several natural cleavages—partisan politics, legislative–executive disputes, and agency turf battles—make cohesion difficult. Because economic development is a central issue, it inspires a lot of political posturing. In the end, a state government with a unified, cohesive approach to economic development is likely to be more successful than a state without one.

As a state's top elected official and chief executive, the governor commonly takes the lead in economic development. For example, when he took office in 2009, Utah governor Jon Huntsman reorganized state agencies to create a new Governor's Office of Economic Development (GOED), declaring, "Economic development is the cornerstone of my administration."[21] Organizations like GOED try to come up with fresh ideas and new tactics, maximizing the state's strengths and minimizing its weaknesses. And states are more than willing to borrow ideas that have been successful in other states.

Once an economic development strategy is in place, the next challenge is implementation. During what we earlier referred to as the first wave of economic development strategies, the responsibility for implementation belonged to state agencies. Adherents to the third wave argue, however, that state agencies have not responded creatively and effectively to the challenges confronting them. Third-wave advocates want government agencies out of the economic development business, with more flexible, public–private hybrids or private-sector organizations as their replacements. Florida was the first state to replace its Department of Commerce with a public–private organization, which it named Enterprise Florida (or eFlorida). Arizona was one of the most recent converts to the public–private approach when it abolished its Department of Commerce to create the Arizona Commerce Authority.

Greater involvement by nongovernment organizations in providing economic development programs and services is risky. The key issue is how much control the state can maintain and how much it cedes to the private sector. This further issue then is whether the priorities of the nongovernment organizations are in their own interest or in the public interest. The executive director of Good Jobs First, a frequent critic of state privatizing economic development has said, "We think it's a recipe for mischief, if not corruption," referencing several studies they have done that highlight problems with the privatization approach.[22]

State governments have always had a complex relationship with the private sector. They must contend with demands from various interests, of which business is only one (albeit a powerful one). Nevertheless, state policy makers have generally tried to accommodate the demands of the business community. In fact, one persistent criticism of state legislatures is that they have been *too* receptive to the entreaties of business. Business leaders believe that because their success is central to a state's economy, they ought to be treated as a public-interest rather than as a special-interest group. A state may thus feel that it is less a partner than a prisoner. In response to the question "Who runs Massachusetts?" one state legislator responded, "The businesses that threaten to move out of the state. They have a chokehold on us."[23] Much of private industry's decisions about location is out of control of state or local governments. For example, when the large packaged food company Conagra decided to relocate its headquarters from Omaha, Nebraska, to Chicago in 2016, it reportedly passed up $28.5 million in incentives from the state of Nebraska and accepted less than half that much in tax credits from Illinois.[24] Conagra officials said no incentives offered by Nebraska would have kept them in Omaha since the move was designed to keep the company competitive in a changing market.

A successful partnership that has emerged in some states is the one between industries and universities. The Committee for Economic Development, a national group of prominent business executives and educators, identifies five ways in which states can facilitate these partnerships: through state-established centers, state grants to university research centers, research incubators, small-business development centers, and research parks.[25]

A potentially fertile area for industry–university collaboration is bioscience, especially stem cell research. Minnesota was one of the first states to take action when it established a Stem Cell Institute at the University of Minnesota and set up tax-free zones for bioscience companies; Wisconsin, another pioneer, has its nonprofit WiCell Research Institute. New Jersey passed legislation in 2004 that legalized stem-cell research in the Garden State and promptly budgeted $6.5 million a year through 2010 in support of it. California, where many biotech companies are located, approved a massive spending initiative on its 2004 ballot. The California Stem Cell Research and Cures Initiative allocated a whopping $300 million a year for ten years. The California Institute for Regenerative Medicine was created; it in turn has funded twelve stem cell research facilities and distributed millions of dollars in grants. Stem cell research could lead to significant advances in health, but for states, the economic development benefits are just as—and maybe more—appealing. Accordingly, when President Barack Obama lifted the federal ban on funding stem cell research in 2009, the promise of new federal grants had many states paying attention. In the words of former Missouri governor Bob Holden, "Whether it's pharmaceuticals, biotechnology, or medical research—life sciences technologies will create the jobs of tomorrow."[26] When the Trump administration reversed the Obama policy and put restrictions on federal funding for embryonic stem cell research, efforts like California's were solidified enough that they appear to be able to withstand the change in federal policy.[27]

Current Approaches

LO 14-4
To explain strategic planning and four economic development approaches popular with states and localities.

State governments, aware that their economic development activities have appeared incoherent and even counterproductive to the outside world, have attempted to clarify their role. In doing so, many states have engaged in strategic planning. Economic sectors commonly targeted by states include travel and tourism, the arts, sports, and international trade.

Strategic Planning

strategic planning
An approach to economic development that emphasizes adaptation to changing conditions and anticipation of future events.

Strategic planning can be useful for several reasons. First, it produces an understanding of the state's economic bedrock. Second, it provides a venue in which public- and private-sector leaders can exchange perspectives and develop a consensus about the state's economic future. In addition, strategic planning moves the economic development issue from goal setting to implementation. Finally, it provides a mechanism for adjusting and correcting the state's actions to match emerging economic trends.

Wisconsin was one of the first states to engage in strategic planning for economic development. A twenty-three–member strategic development commission was established by the governor during a time of economic turmoil growing out of the loss of industrial jobs. The commission's assignment was to analyze the Wisconsin economy and identify avenues for government action. Eighteen months and half a million dollars later, it produced its strategic plan. The focus was on preserving the existing job base, fostering new jobs, and adopting the ethos that "Wisconsin is first in quality."[28] More than 100 specific recommendations were included in the plan.

Since then, most states have undertaken strategic planning exercises. Missouri's 2011 "Strategic Initiative for Economic Growth" is typical. With the goal of transforming the Show Me State's economy within five years, the plan identified eight strategies:

- Attract, retain, and develop a workforce with the education and skills to succeed in the twenty-first–century economy.
- Support local developers in the retention and expansion of existing businesses and employers.
- Optimize state tax, incentive, and regulatory policies to best support the growth of high-value target sectors.
- Invest in technology and innovation to attract, launch, and sustain the growth companies of the future.
- Aggressively market the state to select domestic and international audiences.
- Develop a best-in-class foreign trade initiative.
- Develop a culture that encourages small and minority business development and entrepreneurism.
- Provide the infrastructure necessary for companies and communities to be successful.[29]

Five years after Missouri adopted the plan, its implementation was seen as successful. By 2016, Missouri led all states in new business creation.[30]

Strategic planning is an important first step. The actual programs and tools that state and local governments employ to accomplish their economic development objectives are many and varied. Four that have maintained their popularity are travel and tourism, the arts, sports, and international trade.

Michigan has launched a major promotional effort to attract tourists to the state.

Dennis MacDonald/Alamy Stock Photo

Travel and Tourism

Travel and tourism are big business. According to the U.S. Travel Association, direct spending by travelers reached $1.1 trillion in 2019, generating 15.6 million jobs and contributing $179.7 billion in tax revenue.[31] States are actively marketing the virtues of their coasts, mountains, national parks, regional cuisine, and casinos—whatever might attract a tourist dollar. States develop advertising campaigns around a catchy slogan: The South with a Twist (Georgia), Come See for Yourself (New Jersey), Restart Your Engines (Indiana), Possibilities . . . Endless (Nebraska). The most famous of these is, of course, "Virginia Is for Lovers," adopted in 1969. As Iowa's tourism director noted, "We're looking for a type of kick-butt theme that gets on people's minds."[32] Major cities do the same thing. "That's So LA" and "Second to None" are the marketing slogans of Los Angeles and Chicago, respectively.

Appealing images abound on state travel and tourism websites. For example, read how Oregon's coast is described on the state's official tourism website:

> Thoughts fade away along this wind-swept shoreline, home to soaring sand dunes, pristine state parks and bustling harbors. It doesn't get much more coastal than this region. And thanks to a pioneering beach bill, all 363 miles of Oregon's coastline remain free and public. That means endless opportunities to comb for agates or glass floats, catch your own Dungeness crab or razor clam, watch for whales, seals and puffins, make footprints in the sand or simply be captivated by a winter storm from inside a cozy beachfront lodge. No matter the season, the Oregon Coast is a rejuvenating getaway.[33]

On its tourism website, Idaho focuses on its rivers, promising "Endless miles of smiles;" Kansas, in a tribute to *The Wizard of Oz*, has identified a series of "yellow brick road trips" throughout the state.

Travel and tourism are especially appealing because of the tax yield. Most states levy an **accommodations tax** (commonly referred to as a bed tax), and the money spent by travelers and tourists is also subject to state as well as local sales taxes. All in all, nonresidents contribute a significant sum to the tax base of tourism-rich locales. However, recent fiscal stress led many states to cut their advertising and tourism-promotion budgets, some rather substantially. Michigan's "Pure Michigan" campaign, funded with $25 million a year in state funds, fell prey to a line-item veto by Governor Gretchen Whitmer in 2019, although the governor added $15 million for the campaign to her 2021 budget proposal.[34] In 2011, Washington went so far as to shut down its tourism promotion office, prompting several tourism-related businesses to create an alliance to advertise the state.[35] In the meantime, the state of Montana rented several billboards in the Seattle area advertising the beauty of Big Sky Country. No doubt about it: Tourism is a competitive activity for states and localities. The COVID-19 pandemic in 2020 threatens this lucrative industry in states around the country. Especially hard hit are the states of Washington, Florida, and New York. While New York City alone attracted a record 67 million tourists in 2019, the number of tourists visiting the Big Apple was much smaller in 2020. Some 300,000 jobs in the city are tourism-related and the loss of even some of these has had a dramatic effect on the city's economy.[36] Some 41 percent of Orlando's workforce is involved in tourism. The closures in March 2020 of Disney World,

accommodations tax
A tax on hotel- or motel-room occupancy, with the revenues usually earmarked for tourism-related uses.

Universal Orlando Resort, and Sea World Orlando resulted in a loss in tourism revenue of more than $200 million a day and spike in unemployment to 16.5 percent in that city. The Florida theme parks reopened in late summer 2020 but with reduced attendance and thus lower revenue generation.[37]

The Arts

Throughout the country, in medium size to large cities, performing arts lovers (patrons of dance, opera, theater, and orchestra) are joining with business leaders to forge a coalition. Their intent is to use the arts as a development strategy. Promoting the arts as a development tool may not be as far-fetched as one might initially think.[38] Cities hope that, by sponsoring world-class concerts in acoustically perfect arenas, they can bring audiences of white-collar workers back to the city's center. Such events would also generate secondary spending by the audience (and participants) at restaurants, retail shops, parking garages, and hotels. And just as important, a new sense of liveliness and vitality would infuse the nightlife. In fact, the accessibility of community **amenities** such as the arts is a factor that frequently contributes to business-relocation decisions. Members of arts coalitions argue that company officials might look more favorably on their city if it regularly attracts Broadway shows and the Bolshoi Ballet. They point out that a successful performing arts center could stimulate additional physical development in the downtown area. Indeed, a community might invest in an arts strategy for many reasons.

Aware that the arts can provide a valuable boost, several cities have cast an envious eye at Chicago's Millennium Park, a sculpture garden that opened to rave reviews (and a lot of visitors) in 2004. St. Louis took a page from the same book and created Citygarden in 2009, a three-acre sculpture park on downtown land that was previously vacant. Both San Francisco and Minneapolis invested in massive overhauls of their art museums, and Louisville built a brand-new performing arts and educational center. Denver sports a new opera house, and Atlanta advertises the Georgia Aquarium, billed as the largest indoor fish tank in the world.[39]

But the arts need not be highbrow to affect development. Popular culture—be it multiplex theaters, theme restaurants, sports arenas, or entertainment-oriented stores—is turning around many central cities. Street art, especially sculptural displays, is another popular art form that many places have embraced. Chicago kicked it off with that city's colorful and clever Cows on Parade: 320 life-size fiberglass bovines. Cultural leaders in other cities took the idea and ran with it. There were pigs in Cincinnati, Ohio; horses in Lexington, Kentucky; geckos in Orlando, Florida; and cornstalks in Bloomington, Illinois. Clearly, the arts have become an important economic development tool.

Sports

Professional sports and big-league cities go hand in hand. Hosting a profes-sional sports franchise is evidence that a city has arrived—that it is not simply a large city but a major-league city. Only sixty cities in the country host a top-level professional baseball, basketball, football, or hockey team. Smaller cities eagerly court minor-league teams to enhance the quality of life in the community.

amenities
Comfort and conve-niences that contrib-ute to quality of life.

The Las Vegas Raiders opened the 2020 NFL season in Allegiant Stadium built partially with public money.

Acquiring or retaining professional sports teams has become an important element in local economic development plans. Cities want professional sports franchises, but they don't come easily. In fact, ownership groups have to bid for franchises, typically with some sort of public subsidy. This subsidy usually comes in the form of below-market-rate leases and tax breaks for the stadium (depending on whether the facility is publicly or privately owned). City leaders defend these subsidies, arguing that the return, both economically and symbolically, is worth it. Las Vegas and the state of Nevada ponied up almost $750 million of the total $2 billion to build a domed stadium to house the Oakland Raiders even before the Raiders decided to move to Las Vegas (eventually the NFL granted the Raiders permission to move). But the public is increasingly skeptical. Even in football-friendly Texas, some residents of Arlington, the home of the Dallas Cowboys' $1.12 billion mega-stadium, balked at the use of local tax revenue ($325 million) and the city's **eminent domain** power in support of the stadium.[40]

When public financial support is not forthcoming, team owners frequently threaten to relocate. The threat can be a potent one, as Seattle found out when the Supersonics basketball team left town to become the Oklahoma City Thunder. Few politicians want a treasured professional team to relocate. Thus, the governor of Minnesota, an opponent of stadium bills when he was a state legislator, proposed the construction of new stadiums for the Twins (baseball) and the Vikings (football). Governor Tim Pawlenty explained his flip-flop this way: "Bottom line: I don't want to lose the Twins or the Vikings on my watch."[41] (The Twins got their new stadium in downtown Minneapolis in 2010; the Vikings moved into their new stadium in 2016). When the NFL Colts decided to move from Baltimore to Indianapolis in 1984, the city of Baltimore tried to use eminent domain to keep the team in Maryland. While such an effort seems outlandish, it had some legal precedent—Oakland, California, used similar

eminent domain The right of a government to seize private property for public use, in exchange for payment of fair market value.

tactics to try to keep the Raiders from moving to Los Angeles in 1980 (the Raiders played in Los Angeles from 1982 to 1994, then returned to Oakland but moved to Las Vegas in 2020). So frightening was Baltimore's threat of eminent domain that the mayor of Indianapolis sent fifteen trucks free of charge to Baltimore to move the team's equipment in the middle of the night. When the trucks entered Indiana, they were escorted by the state police.[42] (In 1996, Baltimore got some revenge when the NFL Cleveland Browns franchise relocated and became the Baltimore Ravens. Not to be left out, Cleveland received a reactivated Browns franchise in 1999). Table 14.1 shows the wide range in the percentage of public money in recent stadium and arena construction.

Table 14.1 Public Financial Support of Sports Stadiums and Arenas since 2000

MLB			NFL		
TEAM	YEAR	PUBLIC FUNDS (%)	TEAM	YEAR	PUBLIC FUNDS (%)
Atlanta Braves	2017	58	Arizona Cardinals	2006	76
Cincinnati Reds	2003	82	Atlanta Falcons	2016	100
Detroit Tigers	2000	38	Cincinnati Bengals	2000	89
Houston Astros	2000	68	Dallas Cowboys	2009	30
Miami Marlins	2012	80.3	Denver Broncos	2001	73
Milwaukee Brewers	2001	77.5	Detroit Lions	2002	36
Minnesota Twins	2010	64	Houston Texans	2002	73
New York Mets	2009	20.5	Indianapolis Colts	2008	50
New York Yankees	2009	32	Las Vegas Raiders	2020	39
Philadelphia Phillies	2004	50	Los Angeles Chargers/Rams	2020	0
Pittsburgh Pirates	2001	70	Minnesota Vikings	2016	51
San Diego Padres	2004	66	New England Patriots	2002	0
San Francisco Giants	2000	0	New York Giants/Jets	2010	0
St. Louis Cardinals	2006	12	Philadelphia Eagles	2003	39
Washington Nationals	2008	100	Pittsburgh Stealers	2001	69
			San Francisco 49ers	2014	12
			Seattle Seahawks	2002	83
NBA			MLS		
TEAM	YEAR	PUBLIC FUNDS (%)	TEAM	YEAR	PUBLIC FUNDS (%)
Brooklyn Nets	2012	40	Atlanta United FC	2017	58.3
Charlotte Hornets	2005	100	Chicago Fire	2006	100
Dallas Mavericks	2001	30	Colorado Rapids	2007	50
Detroit Pistons	2017	37.5	DC United	2018	37.5

(continued)

Table 14.1 Public Financial Support of Sports Stadiums and Arenas since 2000 (*continued*)

NBA			MLS		
TEAM	**YEAR**	**PUBLIC FUNDS (%)**	**TEAM**	**YEAR**	**PUBLIC FUNDS (%)**
Golden State Warriors	2019	0	FC Dallas	2005	85
Houston Rockets	2003	100	Houston Dynamo	2012	32
Memphis Grizzlies	2004	100	Los Angles FC	2018	0
Oklahoma City Thunder	2002	100	Los Angeles Galaxy	2003	0
Orlando Magic	2010	87.5	Minnesota United	2019	0
Sacramento Kings	2016	46	Montreal Impact	2008	0
San Antonio Spurs	2002	84	New England Revolution	2002	22.1
			New York City FC	2009	0
			New York Red Bulls	2010	0
			Orlando City SC	2017	0
			Philadelphia Union	2010	61
			Real Salt Lake	2008	41
			San Jose Earthquakes	2015	0
			Seattle Sounders FC	2002	66
			Sporting Kansas City	2011	0
			Toronto FC	2007	55

NHL		
TEAM	**YEAR**	**PUBLIC FUNDS (%)**
Arizona Coyotes	2003	82
Columbus Blue Jackets	2000	0
Dallas Stars	2001	30
Detroit Red Wings	2017	100
Edmonton Oilers	2016	50
Las Vegas Golden Knights	2016	0
Minnesota Wild	2000	74
New Jersey Devils	2007	66
New York Islanders	2012	40
Pittsburgh Penguins	2010	0
Winnipeg Jets	2004	30

Source: *Sports Facility Reports*, 2019, National Sports Law Institute, Marquette University, https://law.marquette.edu/national-sports-law
-institute/sports-facility-reports-volume-20-2019 Appendix 1 (MLB); Appendix 2 (NBA); Appendix 3 (NFL); Appendix 4 (NHL); Appendix 5
(MLS) (accessed March 24, 2020).

A study on the impact of sports stadiums on local economies found that the stadiums had negligible effects on jobs and development; instead, they diverted economic development from manufacturing to the service sector.[43] And a cost-benefit analysis of minor-league stadiums turned up negative.[44] But economic analyses of hosting the Olympics are more positive. The 1996 Summer Olympics in Atlanta produced an estimated $5.1 billion for Georgia's economy. And the tax revenues were put at $165 million. The 2002 Winter Olympics in Utah generated a surplus (profit) of $163.4 million; $59 million went to partially pay back state and local governments for their investments while $76 million was earmarked for maintenance and operation of the Olympic venues constructed for the games.[45] Called by some the "world's largest economic development opportunity," the Olympic Games are the ultimate sports prize.

International Trade

States are no longer content to concentrate on domestic markets for the goods and services produced in their jurisdictions—they are venturing abroad. States pursue international trade for two reasons. First, foreign markets can be important consumers of state goods. Second, foreign investors may have capital to commit to projects in a state. Thus, the promotion of international trade is a two-way street: State products are exported, and investment capital is imported.

One highly visible means by which state governments pursue international markets and investments is through trade missions in which the governor, top business leaders, and economic development agency officials make formal visits, most often to Europe and Asia. The state delegation exchanges information with representatives of the country's public and private sectors and establishes ties that delegation members hope will lead to exports and investments.

State governments perform three important roles in export promotion:

- Brokering information
- Offering technical support
- Providing export financing[46]

As information brokers, states conduct seminars and conferences, sponsor trade shows, provide market research, publish export handbooks, and offer individual counseling to American businesses. Oklahoma, for instance, has set up an international division in its commerce department to encourage export activity. One of its key functions is to identify export opportunities for Oklahoma's business firms. Once an opportunity has been identified, the division provides technical support to help the relevant firm become more knowledgeable about the exporting process.

Technical support is critical because U.S. firms may not be aware of the details involved in exporting: working with international banks, complying with another country's laws and regulations, securing the necessary licensing agreements, designing appropriate packaging for products, and the like. Thus, states conduct seminars to inform businesses of the details. Export finance is also important because without it, a state's information brokerage and technical support functions are weakened. The first state to tackle the export finance issue was Minnesota; it provides a firm with operating capital for the period between the signing of a sales agreement and the delivery of a product. In addition to working capital, some states offer insurance and export credit. The availability of financing converts the fantasy of exporting into reality. Texas and California, not surprisingly, led the other states in terms of the value of exports, with 20.1 and 10.5 percent of the U.S. total, respectively.[47]

State government is also involved in promoting the state as a place for foreign investment. According to the U.S. Bureau of the Census, more than 7.3 million jobs were a direct result of foreign investment in 2017. (More than 10 percent of them are in California.)[48] New Jersey and South Carolina led all states in 2019 with 8.2 percent of their workforce in foreign-owned businesses, followed by New Hampshire (7.5 percent) and Connecticut and Indiana (7.2 percent).[49]

The enactment of foreign trade agreements such as the North American Free Trade Agreement (NAFTA) and its replacement, the U.S.-Mexico-Canada Agreement (USMCA), add another dimension to the globalization of trade for states and localities. NAFTA gradually eliminated trade barriers and investment restrictions among the United States, Canada, and Mexico. NAFTA opened new markets to a state's industries, but it also put pressure on those industries to remain competitive. In addition, the agreement imposed new limitations and duties on state governments. Under NAFTA, for example, states could no longer discriminate in favor of homegrown service-providing firms, nor could they restrict foreign ownership of land, unless these policies were specifically grandfathered into the agreement. In 2018, President Donald Trump announced he would formally terminate NAFTA, claiming, "It's been a disaster for the United States."[50] To replace NAFTA Trump proposed USMCA, which Congress passed in early 2020. The new law is very much like NAFTA in many respects but stipulates tougher regulations on labor and automobile components.[51]

Foreign direct investment (FDI) in the United States peaked in 2016 and then began a multiyear decline. Some $251.8 billion was invested in the United States in 2018, down about 9 percent from 2017. Major investors in the United States are the United Kingdom, Japan, Luxembourg, Canada, the Netherlands, and Switzerland.[52] The downturn in FDI in the United States is both the result of recent U.S. policy changes such as USMCA; the Tax Cut and Jobs Act of 2017; and recent tariffs increases, as well as uncertainties in the international market from events like Britain's exit from the European Union (Brexit), low oil prices, and the threat of an international recession. Like its effect on much of everything else, the COVID-19 pandemic has had a dramatic negative on FDI, with worldwide reduction projected to be some 40 percent in 2020.[53]

LO 14-5
To defend both sides of the three persistent questions about government's role in the economy.

Persistent Questions

A robust economy provides jobs for residents and revenues for governments. Therefore, economic health is a central public policy concern. Government actions intended to spark economic development are typically considered to be in the public interest. Still, three questions in particular are associated with government involvement in the economy, and they pertain to the impact, the extent, and the fairness of government action.

Do State and Local Government Efforts Make Much Difference?

Views about the impact of government actions on the economy diverge widely. Some studies suggest that many of the important factors that affect an economy are beyond the control of state and local governments, whereas others contend that government action can greatly influence the fate of a local economy.[54] Both views contain a kernel of truth. One widely cited study of the location decisions of large firms found that a favorable labor climate and proximity to suppliers and consumers were important criteria to most firms.[55] Governments can affect the first factor but not the second. Also, states vary in the degree to which their economies are influenced by external forces.

Questions about impact and return on investment continue to haunt state and local development officials. Can the actions of states and localities affect employment levels, income, and investment? Statistical tests suggest that the outcomes are both mixed and marginal. Research has shown that, in some places, at some times, some economic development tools produce the intended outcomes.[56] A study of forty government-assisted development projects in ten medium-size cities reached similar conclusions.[57] Regardless of the modest results, however, governments continue to intervene in their economies. This behavior may rest in the political benefits of successful development projects to elected officials. Or it may be an outgrowth of business influence in public policy making. Whatever the explanation, the behavior continues.

An example illustrates the dilemma that states face. After the South Carolina General Assembly voted down a proposal in 2011 to give sales tax incentives to an Amazon distribution center, the company immediately ceased construction of the facility. On the heels of Amazon's decision, two other manufacturing firms dropped their plans to build major plants nearby, citing an uncertain political climate. Moreover, one of the Palmetto State's largest homebuilders shelved plans to construct hundreds of new houses in the area.[58] A political firestorm ensued and supporters of the tax breaks—or more likely, the 2,000 jobs that Amazon had projected—prevailed upon the legislature to reconsider its decision. It did so, approving the tax break late in the legislative session, and Amazon's distribution center began operations in 2012. Would the company have built the facility eventually without the tax breaks? South Carolina and plenty of other states do not appear willing to take the risk.

If the fourth wave in economic development is upon us, then perhaps states should heed the words of a former Maryland governor:

> We are all having to learn new rules for the new economy. Under the old rules, states attracted businesses based on tax structures or incentive packages. But the high-tech companies that are the driving engines in this new economy can locate anywhere. They are motivated by the quality of the work force and the quality of life that is offered.[59]

Initial research findings suggest that grants and loans in support of technology development can increase an area's share of high-technology employment.[60] Other fourth-wave approaches such as increased local–global links and investment in human capital have been shown to contribute to state economic growth.[61]

Does Government Spend Too Much?

Some observers claim that government gives away too much in its pursuit of economic health. This concern develops out of the fundamental relationship between a federal system of government and a capitalistic economic system. Governmental jurisdictions cover specific territories, but capital is mobile, so business firms can move from one location to another. Because these firms are so important to a local economy, governments offer incentives to influence their location decisions. As noted, the impact of these incentives on firms' decisions is not clear, but most jurisdictions believe that they cannot afford *not* to offer them. Concern is increasing, however, that competition among jurisdictions to attract business may be counterproductive and too costly to government. As a consequence, citizens are beginning to look more closely at the **incentive packages**—tax breaks, low interest loans, and infrastructure development—that their governments offer to business.

Examples of government concessions to the automobile industry abound—the Kia plant in Georgia, the Hyundai facility in Alabama, the Volvo plant in South Carolina. The fundamental question is: How extensive should incentives be? The answer typically involves calculation of the return on the state's investment. In the late 1980s, Kentucky put together one of the first big automotive deals when it attracted a new Toyota assembly plant to the community of Georgetown. Twenty-five years later, the investment seems to have paid off—the facility employs 6,300 full-time workers and is credited with spurring the creation of an additional 25,000 jobs in the Bluegrass State.[62] South Carolina offered more than $200 million to land the Volvo production facility in 2015. The result was the initial creation of 1,500 jobs with another 2,500 planned for 2021. Volvo's investment in South Carolina will top $1 billion when the facility is complete.[63] To complement its auto-producing plants, Volvo will build a $600 million battery-producing facility for the all-electric vehicles it will build in South Carolina.[64] Other component manufacturers are expected to build facilities near the Volvo plant and a nearby $500 million Mercedes van plant, creating many jobs.

Jurisdictions compete for major investments such as automobile manufacturing facilities, and that competition has the effect of ratcheting up the value of incentive packages. When German automaker Mercedes-Benz announced that it was seeking a location for its first U.S. facility, more than thirty-five states expressed interest. Five states—Alabama, Iowa, Nebraska, North Carolina, and South Carolina—survived the winnowing process. Each state tried to outdo the others by offering generous packages of tax breaks and

incentive packages
The enticements that state and local governments offer to retain or attract business and industry.

low-cost land. In the end, Mercedes selected Vance, Alabama, as the site of the $300 million facility. But the price that Alabama paid was a dear one. The state provided $92.2 million in land and facility construction costs, $77.5 million in infrastructure development, $60 million in training, and a twenty-five–year tax abatement. Estimates put the state costs at approximately $179,000 per job. The extravagant bidding for the Mercedes-Benz plant raised some eyebrows; but in the words of one Alabama economist, "The symbolism [of winning the Mercedes facility] may be as important as the direct economic impact."[65] The Amazon incentive packages offered by New Jersey and Maryland described at the beginning of this chapter would have cost Maryland $340,000 and New Jersey $280,000 per job created.

Figuring out how much in economic benefits a new facility will yield the local economy is difficult. Some of the benefits are in the form of site preparation and construction jobs for the facility itself and these jobs are of course temporary. Other jobs are more permanent, but will they benefit the local labor force? Many times, a company that locates in a community brings in trained workers from its other facilities. Relocating these jobs will most likely improve the local economy and its tax revenues but local workers who are not educationally and technologically trained to meet a new company's hiring requirements may have to settle for lower-wage positions.

Likewise figuring out how much in incentives is being offered to lure a company is also difficult. Such things as property tax abatements or income tax breaks for specific companies are fairly simple to compute, but other items are more difficult. Should infrastructure improvements be considered as an incentive? Although these are designed to attract a company, they also benefit the larger community by making commuting time to other locations quicker and easier. Job training programs designed to make local workers more attractive for employment in a new facility also make those workers more attractive for other kinds of employment. The best economic impact analyses take these and other factors into account when they project the benefits and costs of locating a new facility.

Concern about government overspending lingers, and it extends beyond the automobile industry. For instance, Wisconsin found that its efforts to attract the film industry bore fruit, but at a high price. An analysis of one big-budget film showed that two-thirds of the money filmmakers spent went out of state; moreover, Wisconsin's incentives package meant that the state refunded 90 percent of what filmmakers spent in the state.[66] The It's Your Turn box takes up the issue of incentives for the film industry.

To gauge whether economic development subsidies are working as anticipated, states are encouraged to:

- Build evaluation of incentives into policy and budget debates,
- Develop a schedule to review incentives,
- Use solid data and analysis to measure the economic impact of incentives, and
- Clarify the goals of incentives, then evaluate incentives against those goals.[67]

It's Your Turn

Should a State Government Provide Tax Incentives to the Film Industry to Make Movies There?

In 2000, four states offered tax incentives to the film industry; by 2010, that number had risen to forty-four states. Since that time thirteen states have ended their incentive programs. States are rethinking their generosity and wondering whether it is worthwhile. What do you think: Should states offer tax incentives to moviemakers?

PROS	CONS
Movies can be made anywhere; a state has to offer incentives to attract the industry, especially if other states are doing so.	Offering tax breaks to one industry has the effect of increasing the tax burden on other industries.
Subsidies to moviemakers may be costly, but there are substantial indirect economic benefits to the state from being the site for a film.	It's a competition in which states try to emulate and outdo one another. It becomes an escalating "arms race" of incentives that is ultimately inefficient.
Serving as the setting for a major film can generate a positive buzz about a state in the media. In other words, it is another way to advertise the state to a wide audience.	Film production does not create permanent jobs and many of the temporary jobs go to out-of-state workers.

Figure 14.3 displays the states that are leading the way in these evaluations, those that are lagging, and those that are making progress. One example of a leading state is Oregon, where a law sets expiration dates for most tax credits for economic development. This means that the legislature will reexamine each subsidy to determine if it is performing as expected, and if not, abolish or redesign it.

Clearly, as state governments continue to offer these packages, many are becoming more savvy about the potential risks. Concern that a government-supported development project might turn sour has led to the imposition of **clawbacks**. Clawbacks require a subsidized firm that fails to deliver on its promises (regarding number of jobs, say, or amount of investment) to repay some or all of its subsidy. In this way, generous states and localities are not left holding the bag. Consider the case of United Airlines and its maintenance facility in Indianapolis. To attract United to Indiana, the state offered the company a deal that contained $300 million in assorted tax breaks but with several clawback provisions. When it failed to create the number of jobs the agreement called for, United Airlines had to return more than $30 million to the Hoosier State.[68]

Does Government Spend Fairly?

clawbacks
Requirements that subsidized firms repay some or all of the subsidy if they fail to deliver on their promises.

Traditionally, government involvement in economic development has taken the form of efforts to reduce costs to business. According to economic development professionals, the central business district, local developers, the local labor force, and existing business firms derive the greatest benefit from city-sponsored economic development activity.[69] As citizens began to ask *who* benefits, however, some state governments refocused their efforts toward direct investments in human resources. Based on research on minority entrepreneurs, this approach should pay dividends: investment in human capital and access to financial resources can lead to the creation of new firms.[70]

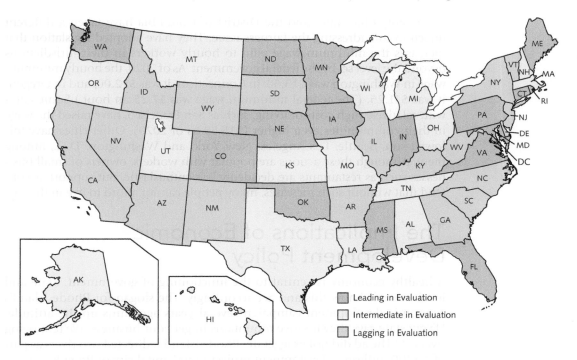

Figure 14.3 State Evaluations of Economic Development Incentive Programs

Source: State Tax Incentive Evaluation Ratings, Pew Trusts, https://www.pewtrusts.org/en/research-and-analysis/articles/2017/05/03/state-tax-incentive-evaluation-ratings (August 19, 2019).

Local governments have been especially active in expanding the concept of economic development beyond a narrow concern with business investment. Led by the pioneering efforts of San Francisco and Boston, some U.S. cities are tying economic development initiatives to the achievement of social objectives, an approach called **linkaging**. For instance, local governments have linked large-scale commercial development (office and retail buildings and hotels) to concerns such as housing and employment. This movement grew out of frustration over the disappearance of older low-income neighborhoods from revitalized, commercially oriented downtown areas.[71] The upscaling of formerly low-income neighborhoods—a process known as gentrification—displaces existing residents. With linkaging, developers are required to provide low- or moderate-income housing or employment to targeted groups or to contribute funding to programs that support these objectives. In return for the opportunity to enter a lucrative local market, a developer pays a price. This process has been called "the cities' attempt to share the profits of their prospering sectors with their poor."[72]

Linkaging works best in cities with booming economies. But even in cities with more stable economies, local government can negotiate with developers for social concessions. In Richmond, Virginia, for example, city officials convinced developers to provide substantial minority participation in a major retail project in the downtown area. In return for city approval of a massive redevelopment project in Jersey City, New Jersey, developers agreed to reserve a certain percentage of dwelling units for low- and moderate-income individuals.

linkaging
A method by which local governments use large-scale commercial development projects to accomplish social objectives.

Twenty-nine states and the District of Columbia have taken a different direction in addressing the fairness issue: They have adopted legislation that increases the minimum wage paid to hourly workers in their jurisdictions beyond the level set by the federal government. As of 2020, the hourly minimum wage in Washington was $13.50; in Connecticut, it was $12.00; and in Oregon, it was $11.25. (The federal minimum wage was $7.25 an hour.) Some cities with relatively high costs of living, such as San Francisco, have raised the wage in their communities even higher ($15.59 as of 2020). Other cities have followed suit, Seattle, Los Angeles, New York, and Washington, D.C., among them. Although these actions are popular with workers, owners of small businesses such as restaurants are decidedly less enthusiastic. But supporters contend that without such increases, many people cannot afford to live in the city.

The Implications of Economic Development Policy

A healthy economy is central to the functioning of government. State and local officials know this and act accordingly. The slogan for Rhode Island's economic development campaign several years ago sums up the attitude: "Every state says they'll move mountains to get your business. We're moving rivers."[73] The ad did not exaggerate: Rhode Island redirected two rivers as part of a $200 million redevelopment project in its capital city of Providence.

Yet when an observer steps back and ponders such strategies and deals, a degree of skepticism is inevitable. Could New York City have better spent the millions it committed to Chase Manhattan Bank to keep the financial institution from moving 4,600 office workers to New Jersey? The deal involved $235 million worth of tax abatements, discounted utilities, site improvements, and job-training tax credits over the next twenty years.[74] And which state really won when a division of Eastman Kodak turned down Maryland's $4.5 million package of subsidized land, tax breaks, and employee training in favor of Pennsylvania's $14 million deal? Some might conclude that corporations are staging raids on public treasuries. But many state and local government officials would argue that concessions for business serve an important function by creating jobs and generating economic activity, thus improving the local tax base, which in turn funds public services. Maybe the third and fourth waves of economic development will be characterized by more creative and productive efforts at achieving this outcome.

Local economies are evaluated, compared, and ranked on the basis of numerous indicators. Most common among the indicators are quality of life, the number of start-up businesses, the growth in population, and the level of employment. Table 14.2 compares the ten large metropolitan areas that in 2019 were considered by many to be the most favorable places for small businesses.[75] Of interest is the variation in both the average unemployment rate and the change in housing prices across the ten areas.

As one might expect, states and localities scoring high on these rankings place far more value on them than their low-scoring counterparts do—at least publicly. But allowing for the inherent biases in the rankings, they certainly suggest that some communities are faring quite well in the economic development wars.

Table 14.2 Top Ten U.S. Metropolitan Areas for Small Businesses, 2019

CITY	AVERAGE 2019 UNEMPLOYMENT	FIVE-YEAR CHANGE IN HOUSING PRICES 2014–2019
Seattle, WA	3.6	57.7%
Denver, CO	2.8	55.0%
Tampa, FL	3.2	58.2%
Miami, FL	3.1	43.7%
Portland, OR	3.7	46.9%
Atlanta, GA	3.3	45.5%
Orlando, FL	3.1	52.6%
Los Angeles, CA	4.1	38.3%
New York, NY	3.7	24.5%
Minneapolis, MN	3.0	35.2%

Sources: Melissa Wylie, "Best Places for New Small Businesses," https://www.lendingtree.com/business/small/best-places-for-new-small-businesses/ (February 20, 2020); U.S. Bureau of Labor Statistics, "Metropolitan Area Employment and Unemployment Archived News Releases (Monthly), https://www.bls.gov/bls/news-release/metro.htm#2019; Federal Housing Finance Agency, "Housing Price Index (HPI), Quarterly Report," https://www.fhfa.gov/AboutUs/Reports/ReportDocuments/2019Q4_HPI.pdf (December 2019).

Critics claim that competition for economic development is nothing more than the relocation of a given amount of economic activity from one community to another, with no overall increase in national productivity. Mercedes-Benz was going to open a U.S. manufacturing facility anyway; the question was simply, where? By playing states against one another, Mercedes-Benz was able to exact a subsidy of unheard-of proportions from Alabama.[76] Many critics call for increased cooperation among jurisdictions in their quest for economic development. However, this objective has been elusive at both the state and local levels, and jurisdictions continue to use financial carrots to gain an edge in the competition.

Thus far, the courts have not been receptive to legal challenges seeking to outlaw the use of corporate tax incentives. The U.S. Supreme Court rejected the arguments of a group of Ohio taxpayers who sought to undo a $281 million package of tax breaks given to Daimler Chrysler for a Jeep plant in Toledo.[77] Even when jurisdictions agree not to raid companies from each other, the agreements can unravel. Within months after signing a cooperative no-poaching pact, Miami-Dade, Broward, and Palm Beach counties in south Florida reverted to their old competitive behaviors.[78] Economic development continues to be a singular proposition, with each jurisdiction pursuing its own destiny.

Chapter Recap

- The economic performance of the states varies. Even in an individual state, its economic health changes over time. The same is true for localities: Their economies are dynamic.

- Economic development has had four waves of different approaches or strategies. The first wave was characterized by smokestack chasing. The latest, or fourth, wave emphasizes globalization and human capital. Even now, states continue to use approaches from the earlier waves.

- The relationship between state government and the private sector can be complicated. Some states have begun to use public–private hybrid organizations in economic development functions.

- States have offered huge incentives to attract automobile manufacturers. But with trends showing a decline in manufacturing as a proportion of the job base, the emphasis is shifting toward research and technology. Many states have begun to invest in bioscience research.

- States have taken on many different economic development initiatives, including strategic planning, travel and tourism, the arts, sports, and international trade.

- Three major questions continue to surface with regard to government involvement in the economy: Do state and local government efforts make much difference? Does government spend too much to attract and grow new business and to retain old business? Does government spend fairly; that is, does reducing costs for business come at a cost to other groups?

- Many organizations rank states and localities on aspects of economic development. In evaluating these rankings, it is important to consider the criteria used in their compilation.

- Economic development is a competitive activity, pitting one jurisdiction against others. Efforts are underway to foster more cooperative behavior among jurisdictions.

Key Terms

economic development (p. 392)
subsidy (p. 396)
venture capital pools (p. 396)
small-business incubators (p. 396)

enterprise zone (p. 396)
clusters (p. 396)
new economy (p. 397)
strategic planning (p. 400)
accommodations tax (p. 402)
amenities (p. 403)

eminent domain (p. 404)
incentive packages (p. 410)
clawbacks (p. 412)
linkaging (p. 413)

Internet Resources

Two economic development organizations, one with a national focus, the other with an international emphasis, maintain useful websites. These are the Prosperity Now (formerly the Corporation for Enterprise Development) at **https://prosperitynow.org** and the International Economic Development Council at **www.iedconline.org**.

All states have a web presence in economic development, typically through a state agency. The comprehensive website of the Arizona Commerce Authority can be found at **www.azcommerce.com**.

Explore a more targeted approach to economic development at **commerce.idaho.gov**, which is a part of Idaho's Department of Commerce website.

Other examples of states with less traditional economic development websites are the state of Kentucky's new economy website at **www.kyin-novation.com** and Enterprise Florida at **www.enterpriseflorida**.

A statewide organization devoted to local economic development is the California Association for Local Economic Development, **www.caled.org**.

The website for the New York City Economic Development Corporation is **https://edc.nyc**.

For economic development from a private sector perspective, check out the website of *Site Selection* magazine at **www.siteselection.com**. It tracks new business activity around the nation.

15

Education Policy: Reading, Writing, and Reform

Enthusiastic students in a public school.

Fuses/Corbis/Getty Images

Learning Objectives

Can you interpret a bus schedule? Follow a map? Balance a checkbook? Fill out a job application? Were you able to follow the last chapter? If not, you are functionally illiterate, like one in four of your fellow adult Americans. Convincing evidence reports that too many students cannot read, write, and do math at grade level. And a substantial proportion of U.S. teenagers are shockingly ignorant of history and government. This is not breaking news. In a much cited 1983 report *A Nation at Risk*, the National Commission on Excellence in Education lamented the erosion of the educational foundations of society "by a rising tide of mediocrity that threatens our very future."[1]

Disturbing studies document the persistent underperformance of U.S. students in comparison with students in other developed countries. Despite much higher per-pupil spending on schools, scores in mathematics, science, and reading earned by U.S. 15-year-olds—even those from well-to-do and educated families—consistently rank poorly, behind such countries as China, Poland, and South Korea.[2] U.S. firms corroborate these concerns with stories about their frustration in finding new employees who can read, write, and perform basic math functions. But the other side of the coin is that many public-school systems are doing an outstanding job of preparing youngsters for college and the work world, especially those in middle-class and upper-middle-class communities where funding is adequate, and education is considered important. An important portion of the perceived crisis in public education is a product of demographics—poverty, homelessness, culture, dysfunctional or unsupportive families, and poor health and nutrition. A large percentage our public-school students come from low-income families, and most of them begin first grade already behind their more privileged peers.[3] These societal problems are factors that cannot be corrected by teachers or principals.

In the opinion of many Americans, education is the most important function performed by state and local governments. The facts support this point of view. Education consumes more of state and local budgets than any other service. More than $694 billion is spent on public elementary and secondary schooling by the states and localities. That translates to around $12,201 per pupil.[4] The importance of education is also demonstrated by the sheer number of people involved in it as students, parents, teachers, administrators, and staff. Some 7.6 million people are employed in K–12 public education in the United States, more than half of all state and local government employees. Citizens have high expectations for their schools, assuming that they will teach everything from the basics to good citizenship. To a great extent, the future of this country and its economy is linked to the quality of public education.

But which level of government is—or should be—responsible for ensuring that American children receive a public education commensurate with this nation's economic and military power? Governmental role confusion prevails. Once overwhelmingly a local government responsibility, public education has evolved into a shared responsibility of the national, state, and local governments. Business and nonprofit organizations are increasingly engaged as well. This chapter maps the education landscape along with its dead ends, pitfalls, and promising paths.

Is There a Crisis in Education?

LO 15-1
To discuss the
perceived crisis in
education.

Education policy is controversial and frequently proclaimed to be in crisis.
Policy makers, parents, teachers, and others have long debated how schools
should be organized and financed, and what should be taught. If there is an
education crisis, it is a perennial and permanent condition. There are, however, significant shortcomings of our current education efforts and outcomes,
and the public is intensely aware of them. Despite billions of dollars in
federal, state, and local government spending, along with a spate of institutional and classroom reforms, these shortcomings are not easily resolved.

One seemingly straightforward sign of problems in the quality of schooling makes headlines in newspapers throughout the country each year: student
performance on standardized college entrance exams. Scholastic Aptitude Test
(SAT) and American College Test (ACT) scores on verbal and math sections
dropped almost annually from 1963 to 1982, to levels below those existing
at the time of the last declared crisis in education (see Figure 15.1). Following
a brief rally during the mid-1980s, scores again began eroding slowly, but
then stabilized. The recent scores for both SAT and ACT tests have been slowly
dropping again.

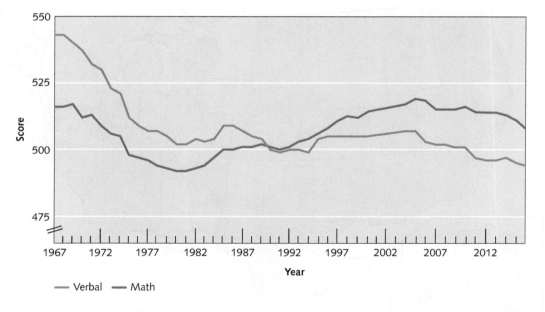

Figure 15.1 Average SAT Verbal and Mathematics Scores, 1963–2016

Average SAT verbal and math scores began a prolonged period of decline in the early 1960s but
turned upward in 1982. The current trend is moderately to the downside.

Note: Minimum 200, maximum 800 for each score. All scores have been recentered to match the 1996 College Board Scale. The SAT was
changed in 2017, so post-2016 scores are not comparable to earlier scores. Post-2016 scores are excluded from this chart.

Source: College Board, "Class of 2017 SAT Results," https://reports.collegeboard.org/archive/sat-suite-program-results/2017
/class-2017-results (accessed June 27, 2020).

Striking differences in SAT scores among the states reflect population characteristics such as race and ethnicity, immigration, poverty levels, and urban–suburban–rural population. But the greatest variation is accounted for by the percentage of high school students taking the SAT. Generally, the higher the percentage of high schoolers who take the test is, the lower the state scores will be. A more comprehensive assessment of the quality of education in the states is found in Figure 15.2, which grades them using composite scores calculated from three different measures not related to the SAT.

Is the U.S. education system failing? Or is perception more pessimistic than reality? Public opinion surveys reveal that Americans are mostly satisfied with their own public schools but generally critical of everyone else's. The media bombardment about failing public schools notwithstanding, many school systems are academically strong, and most others have shown recent improvements. State scores on the National Assessment of Educational Progress (NAEP), given to fourth, eighth, and twelfth graders, have also shown gains since 1992 in reading and math, but no improvement, or even some decline, in the scores of twelfth-grade students.[5] Dropout rates dropped to a

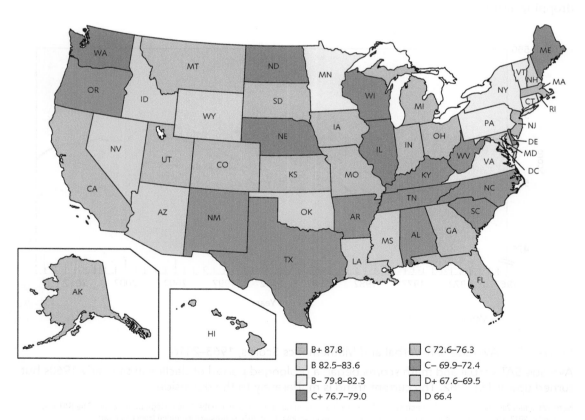

B+ 87.8		C 72.6–76.3	
B 82.5–83.6		C– 69.9–72.4	
B– 79.8–82.3		D+ 67.6–69.5	
C+ 76.7–79.0		D 66.4	

Figure 15.2 Quality Counts 2019: State Report Cards

Source: "Quality Counts 2019: Grading the States," *Education Week* (September 4, 2019). Reprinted by permission of Editorial Projects in Education. (No state received a score of "A.")

record low in 2017 (the latest year for which figures are available), as students are staying in school longer. But few would dispute that the U.S. education system suffers serious problems and needs improvement. The most widely recognized policy problems can be reduced to four major variables: standards, students, teachers, and the education bureaucracy.

Standards

Schools have suffered from a malady that might be called *curriculum drift*. Courses designed to teach basic reading comprehension, writing, and mathematics are sometimes de-emphasized, as nonessential topics become popular. State legislatures and school boards have mandated courses and topics on slavery, the Holocaust, genocide, "green literacy," gay and lesbian contributions (California), climate change denial (Texas, Louisiana), and the Irish potato famine—worthy topics, perhaps, but no substitute for the basics. To many critics, education sometimes seems to neglect instruction in basic skills and the ability to think analytically. Business, military, and university leaders complain about having to invest millions of dollars in remedial education before ill-prepared high school graduates are ready to work, serve in the armed forces, or succeed in college. They further lament the prevalence of social promotions and a basic ignorance of history, culture, and government. Many students graduate from high school prepared for neither college nor the job market. The argument that the native intelligence of U.S. youth has declined has no basis, so considerable blame has been placed on weak and vacillating educational standards for curricula and courses.

Students

Students themselves have not escaped criticism. Some choose to soften their curriculum with easy nonacademic courses rather than English, math, science, social studies, and foreign languages. Today's students are said to be poorly motivated and lazy in comparison with their predecessors. They are faulted for seeking instant gratification through television, video games, the internet, drugs, alcohol, and sex instead of seriously applying themselves to coursework. In a typical year and depending on the school, anywhere from 1 to 40 percent of students give up high school altogether by dropping out. The overall national high school dropout rate was 5.4 percent in 2017. Dropout rates for all groups have been declining, but the 2017 rates were still high for Native Americans (10.1 percent), Hispanic (8.2 percent), and African Americans (6.5 percent). Rates for whites (4.3 percent) and Asians (2.1 percent) are lower and have also declined.[6]

Clearly, however, the legal and moral responsibility for providing direction to a young person's life rests with their parents; school readiness starts at home. This responsibility includes encouraging the child to complete homework assignments and regulating extracurricular activities, television, video game, cell phone, and internet access. Researchers have found that U.S. children start the first grade with fewer academic skills than their Asian counterparts, whose parents give them a head start by regularly working with them at home before they enter school. Coaching after school helps children in several Asian countries maintain their early advantage. But U.S. parents tend to abdicate to the schools the responsibility for educating their children. Often parents have little choice; as a result of the high percentage of single-parent and two-worker households, many parents have little time, and less energy, to spend helping their children. The shortage and expense of professional day care and after-school learning opportunities compound the problem.

Teachers

Teachers are the linchpins between students and the learning process and the single most important factor in student success. Effective teaching can bestow lifelong learning skills, whereas poor teaching can result in academic indifference among good students and dropping out for marginal students. One problem with teaching is that, for many years, the quality of individuals who choose to enter the teaching profession has declined. The gradual decline in the quality of teachers is partly due to changes in the nature of the workforce and the elevated expectations and demands placed on teachers. (However, behavioral expectations have certainly changed for the better, as shown by the socially repressive teacher contract from 1922 reproduced in Figure 15.3.)

THOU SHALT NOT

1922 Contract, Salisbury, N.C.

Miss _____ agrees:

1. Not to get married. This contract becomes null and void immediately if the teacher marries.
2. Not to have company with men.
3. To be at home between the hours of 8:00 pm and 6:00 am unless in attendance at a school function.
4. Not to loiter downtown in ice cream stores.
5. Not to leave town at any time without the permission of the Chairman of the Trustees.
6. Not to smoke cigarettes. This contract becomes null and void immediately if the teacher is found smoking.
7. Not to drink beer, wine, or whiskey. This contract becomes null and void immediately if the teacher is found drinking beer, wine, or whiskey.
8. Not to ride in a carriage or automobile with any man except her brother or father.
9. Not to dress in bright colors.
10. Not to dye her hair.
11. To wear at least two petticoats.
12. Not to wear dresses more than two inches above the ankles.
13. To keep the classroom clean:
    (a) to sweep the classroom floor at least once daily.
    (b) to scrub the classroom floor at least once weekly with soap and hot water.
    (c) to clean the blackboard at least once daily.
    (d) to start the fire at 7:00 am so that the room will be warm at 8:00 am when the children arrive.
14. Not to wear face powder, mascara, or to paint the lips.

From "North Carolina Women: Making History" by Margaret Supplee Smith and Emily Herring Wilson.

Figure 15.3 Thou Shalt Not

Many top-notch young men and women enter the noble profession of teaching. But academically gifted women who once would have chosen the teaching profession are now more likely to seek out higher paying, more prestigious positions in government; the legal, medical, and other professions; and the private sector. In their place, less able college graduates elect to become teachers, resulting in a severe shortage of qualified teachers in some states. In 2019, verbal (retitled Evidenced-Based Reading and Writing) and math SAT scores for education majors averaged 1,022, somewhat lower than 1,059 for other subject majors, and much lower than high-scoring intended majors such as math (1,243), physical science (1,203), or social science (1,164).[7] Also reflecting the drop in quality of the teaching labor pool is that many of those hired to teach each year lack the proper qualifications and preparation for the courses they teach. For example, passing rates for the 2019 General Knowledge Test—a required statewide exam for applicants for a teaching license in Florida—only ranged from 60 to 70 percent in the areas of math, writing, reading, vocabulary grammar, and spelling.[8]

Part of the blame must also be placed on universities, whose teacher programs continue to emphasize educational methodology courses, which teach prospective instructors how to teach rather than giving them substantive knowledge of their subject matter. Another reason it has been difficult to find good teachers is that, in some states, teaching remains a low-wage occupation, with the starting salary comparing unfavorably with starting salaries in other professional fields.

In an effort to help improve pay and working conditions, most teachers join unions such as the American Federation of Teachers (AFT) and the National Education Association (NEA). According to some critics, these unions have become part of the problem with public education because they further teachers' narrow self-interest and protect incompetents from being fired. (See the Controversies in States and Localities feature.)

Meanwhile, many of those who do become teachers quickly exit the profession. About 15 percent of all teachers call it quits each year. Teacher dropout rates are particularly high at high-poverty schools, making the teacher dropout rate exceed that of students![9] Many discouraged teachers feel that they are not valued or respected by students, the public, and state legislators, and even scorned by some of them. Excessive testing inhibits their ability to teach—other than to tests. Seemingly endless busy-work, including detailed lesson plans and reports, suck up teaching time. The frustrations of teaching also come from lack of parental interest and support, and students' absence of discipline and use of drugs. Noisy, disruptive behavior by a handful of students spoils the learning environment for all. Teachers are assaulted in the classroom, and violent crimes occur on or near school grounds. Empty gestures by elected officials such as mandating posting of the Ten Commandments (Jackson County, Kentucky) on classroom walls, requiring uniforms (Memphis, New York City), or requiring students to address teachers as *ma'am* and *sir* (Louisiana) do not help. Teacher stress is augmented, especially in poor schools, by crumbling buildings, chronic supply and equipment shortages, overcrowded classrooms, crushing paperwork burdens, and the threat of being fired or laid off. Further, problems with the supply of teachers are being worsened by the retirement of baby boomers. Because of this demographic fact and the dissatisfactions just noted, severe shortages of qualified teachers have developed, especially in the fields of mathematics, science, foreign languages, and special education. Shortages are most severe in the Sunbelt, where student populations are growing. Acute teacher shortfalls force too many school districts to hire unqualified, ill-prepared people simply to put a warm adult body in the classroom.

The Education Bureaucracy

Bureaucracy is publicly vilified everywhere, and the schools are no exception. A strong case can be made that the United States has too many school administrators, rules, reports, and restrictions and too few teachers. The ratio is as high as one nonteaching employee for every eight teachers in some districts. Critics say that school districts and their bureaucracies act like classic monopolies. They are guaranteed customers (students) and income (tax revenues), yet they face little or no competition because parents have limited choice about where to send their children to school. The results of these monopolistic school bureaucracies allegedly include a lack of accountability to parents and the community (and ultimately to students and teachers), unnecessary rules and red tape, inefficient use of human resources, and time constraints and odious mounds of paperwork for teachers. Like most bureaucracies, those in the education establishment are reactive and resistant to innovation and change and therefore viewed as recalcitrant enemies of reform.

Research is inconclusive on the bureaucracy issue. Some research finds that large, centralized bureaucracies with restrictive rules and red tape tend to reduce school effectiveness.[10] Findings of other scholars show no significant effects of bureaucracy and that school bureaucracies tend to grow larger when schools perform poorly because administrators take actions to improve performance. In other words, bureaucracy does not harm school performance; rather, it is a rational response intended to arrest decline and boost performance by developing and putting into place new policies, programs, and oversight.[11]

Before reviewing the responses of the national, state, and local governments to these critical problems in public education, we will look at how the complex intergovernmental relationships in education have evolved.

LO 15-2

To be able to explain intergovernmental roles in education.

Intergovernmental Roles in Education

The responsibility for establishing, supporting, and overseeing public schools is reserved to the states under the Tenth Amendment and expressly provided for in the state constitutions. Day-to-day operating authority is delegated to local governments by all states except Hawaii, which has a unitary, state-run system, and Oregon, which centralizes control over the public-school system in the governor's office. A large majority of U.S. primary and secondary school systems are operated by independent school districts, but cities, counties, towns, or townships run the schools in some states. Although local control is the tradition, the states are the dominant policy makers, deciding important issues such as the duration of the school year, curriculum requirements, textbook selection, teacher certification and compensation, minimum graduation requirements, and pupil–teacher ratios. But the national government's role in education has become more prominent in recent years, heavily influencing what states and local school districts decide to do or not to do. The selection and dismissal of teachers, certain budget decisions, and management and operating details are typically carried out locally.

State involvement has also intensified, largely because of recognized inequalities among schools and school districts, the accountability demands of federal education policy, and forceful actions by governors and legislatures to address the perceived education crisis. Centralization of state authority in education policy is greatest in the South, where poverty and race relations have called for high levels of state intervention. Conversely, the tradition of local education autonomy is strongest in New England. But in the final analysis, it is difficult to identify a single important school policy issue today that is not subject to state or federal, rather than local, determination.

Another reason more state and federal involvement in the public schools has occurred is because of financial difficulties and the fact that some citizens and policy makers have lost confidence in the schools' ability to provide a quality education. In several instances, local school systems have essentially lost their independence as the states and some municipalities have assumed full operational responsibilities—an especially likely outcome when the local school districts are unable to respond adequately to political and financial pressures. States and some cities have imposed the ultimate sanction on failing schools by shutting them down entirely.

Generally, states take over local school districts either because of poor financial conditions in a district or because of poor academic performance as demonstrated by annual test scores. Often these two are related—poorly funded and administered schools often have underperforming students. Michigan, California, Nevada, New Jersey, Pennsylvania, and Rhode Island have been the most active states in taking over local school districts for financial reasons, composing some 70 percent of all state financially related takeovers by 2019.[12] Tennessee and Louisiana have been active in taking over local schools for poor student-performance–related issues. Former Georgia governor Nathan Deal proposed such action, but the constitutional amendment granting the state power to implement this plan failed in a 2016 referendum. Tennessee organized the special Achievement School District and transferred thirty underperforming schools in Memphis and Nashville from local control to state control under this district. Louisiana's state-administered Opportunity School District originally took over some schools in Baton Rouge and New Orleans beginning in 2003 but the number increased dramatically after Hurricane Katrina devasted New Orleans in 2005.[13]

The National Government Presence in Education

The federal government traditionally played a minimal role in primary and secondary education, especially when compared with the governments of most other countries, where public education is treated as a national responsibility. The first grant of money for education came only in 1917, when the Smith-Hughes Act financed vocational education in secondary schools. Much later, the National Defense Education Act of 1958 provided funds to improve math, science, and foreign-language education.

The national role was substantially enlarged during the 1960s and 1970s, primarily through the Elementary and Secondary Education Act (ESEA) of 1965. The ESEA established a direct national subsidy for education, providing funds to almost every school district in the United States. Amounts were allocated for library acquisitions, audiovisual materials, teachers' aides, and compensatory programs for children of poor families and for the mentally and physically disabled. Parochial (religious) schools also benefit from ESEA funding, although no funds are provided for religious materials, courses, or teacher salaries. Until recently, Congress used the opportunity of each reauthorization of ESEA to pile on all manner of mandates about how the money must be spent.

During the 1960s and 1970s, the federal government exercised targeted policy leadership in education. The Head Start program helped prepare poor children for school and provided many of them with their first medical, dental, and nutritional care. Matching grants encouraged states and localities to experiment with other programs, and research findings, statistics, and new policy information were disseminated by the National Institute of Education and the National Center for Education Statistics. The national commitment to public schools received an important symbolic boost in 1979 with the creation of the U.S. Department of Education.

These new commitments brought the national share of total school expenditures from 4.4 percent in 1960 to 9 percent in 1980 and has stayed around that level since. Federal aid varies widely from state to state. New Jersey is lowest with 4.1 percent of all K–12 education funding coming from the feds, whereas New Mexico is highest with 14.4 percent. Head Start—demonstrated to be successful in several evaluations—was reauthorized and expanded to Early Head Start: all-day, all-year programs for low-income, at-risk infants and toddlers. The National and Community Service Act established scholarships and tuition reimbursements for community service. New federal monies were also provided for school modernization and construction, to improve technological literacy of teachers and students, and to promote charter schools.

The 2002 reauthorization of ESEA—No Child Left Behind (NCLB)— insinuated the federal government in the schools debate as the "national schoolmarm, hovering over state school reform efforts and whacking those states that fail to record satisfactory and timely progress toward federal education goals with financial penalties and mandatory corrective actions."[14] NCLB was viewed as particularly onerous in its testing and performance mandates. The law significantly increased federal financial support for the schools, but it also required substantial new state and local education spending.

The $12 billion No Child Left Behind law promised to transform public education but saddled the states and their schools with significant new (and mostly unfunded) mandates, including mandatory and frequent testing and a stipulation that failing schools not making sufficient progress in any one of numerous student demographic categories would have to restructure, offer students a transfer or private tuition, or even close down entirely.

The broad goals of NCLB were admirable and widely accepted: No child would be neglected and left behind in school, and all would have an equal chance to succeed. But the devil was in the details of implementation. Teachers, principals, chief state school officers (CSSOs), governors, and state legislators soon howled like scalded hounds as they became aware of their predicament. The costs of annual testing amounted to millions of dollars more than what Congress provided. Established, and demonstrably effective, state standards and testing programs were threatened with replacement by cumbersome federal mandates. Local control of public education appeared to be the victim of a "regime change" replete with federal mandates and regulations.

Implementation of NCLB did not go smoothly as intergovernmental conflict immediately erupted. Michigan, Texas, Vermont, and the NEA filed suit against the federal government on the grounds that NCLB illegally imposed unfunded mandates on the states. Other states also litigated or threatened to refuse to comply with NCLB. Gradually, accommodations to state and local concerns were made by the U.S. Department of Education through waivers of certain requirements.

The state and school district issues with NCLB were many. To take one example, when schools and districts failed to meet their goals for a certain period of time, the U.S. Department of Education could declare them "failed," leading to closure or a state takeover. In 2012, an estimated 49 percent of the nation's schools had been officially declared to be "failing, though very few were shut down and most escaped the 'failing' category the next year through federal waivers of accountability requirements."[15] To relieve pressure on the states while Congress was deadlocked for several years over NCLB's reauthorization, the Obama administration approved waiver requests from forty-four states to relieve them of some of the most vexing requirements. A 2009 federal initiative designed to help states cope with the ravages of the Great Recession, labeled Race to the Top, required states to compete for competitive, discretionary grants, with priority given to those that adopted federal standards-based priorities. The stakes were high: More than $4 billion was divvied out to winning (and compliant) states. Eventually, in 2015, Congress reauthorized ESEA as the Every Student Succeeds Act (ESSA). ESSA maintained the concept of standardized testing but reduced the emphasis on these tests that NCLB mandated. Even more important, ESSA shifted the adoption of educational standards from the federal government to the states. ESSA represented the first reduction in the role of the federal government in K–12 education since the passage of ESEA in 1965 first expanded that role.[16]

The Political and Financial Pressures on Public Schools

Political pressures constantly roil the waters of public education as teacher organizations, nonprofit foundations, minority groups, businesses, conservative and religious organizations, and parents make new demands on their schools. Teachers and their unions want more control over what goes on in the classroom. Minority groups are concerned with inequities and poor performance of heavily minority schools. Bilingual education is an issue in states with large Hispanic or other non-English–language populations. And religious groups fight to keep prayer, abstinence education, antidrug programs such as DARE, and "intelligent design" in the classroom and Charles Darwin, "safe sex," and secular values out. If local school boards wilt under the crescendo of demands, then parties interested in education policy take their demands to higher political levels—the governor, the state legislature, the courts, and the state board of education, none of which may be in agreement on what to do about any given issue. In this way, school politics, once the province of local school boards and professional educators, has evolved into highly contentious interest group politics.

Financial Pressures Increased financial pressure on the schools is a second factor producing education policy centralization. Historically, schools have been funded mostly through revenues derived from the property tax. A school district can assess taxes only on property within its local boundaries, so wealthy districts with much highly valued residential and/or commercial property can afford to finance public schools at generous levels, whereas poor districts (even though they often tax their property at much higher rates than wealthy districts) tend to raise fewer dollars because of their lower property values. The consequence of such financial inequities is that some children receive a more expensive, and probably higher-quality, education than other children do, even though the parents of the advantaged group of children may contribute fewer tax dollars. Predictably, it is the children of the poor and minorities who fare the worst.

The states' assumption of primary financial responsibility for public schools has important constitutional components. In the landmark case of *Serrano v. Priest* (1971), the California Supreme Court declared that inequalities in school-district spending resulting from variations in taxable wealth were unconstitutional. The court observed that local control is a "cruel illusion;" poor districts simply cannot achieve excellence in education because of a low tax base, no matter at how high a rate property is taxed.[17] Therefore, education must be considered a fundamental interest of the state; in other words, the state must ensure that expenditures on education are not determined primarily by the taxable wealth of the school district.

Following *Serrano*, lawsuits were filed in other states by plaintiffs who sought to have their own property tax-based systems declared unconstitutional. One of these cases, *San Antonio Independent School District v. Rodriguez* (1973), made its way to the U.S. Supreme Court. A federal district court had found the Texas school finance system to be unconstitutional under the equal protection clause of the Fourteenth Amendment. However, the Supreme Court reversed the lower court, holding that education is not a fundamental right under the U.S. Constitution (in which it is not even mentioned).[18] The issue was thus placed exclusively in the constitutional domain of the states, in which plaintiffs would have to rely on their own constitutions—and courts—to prevent arbitrary circumstances from predetermining the quality of a child's education.

All but a handful of state supreme courts have heard cases on educational financing; litigation is ongoing in approximately half of the states. Some thirty states have determined that existing funding schemes were unconstitutional because they did not provide an adequate education for all children or give them reasonable opportunity to attain state education goals, and have ordered equal funding for poor districts.

All states have made efforts to equalize funding among school districts, usually by applying distribution formulas for state aid that take into account property values and property-tax effort in individual districts. Most increased state support has been targeted to districts with low property values through **foundation programs**, which ensure that all school districts receive a minimum level of funding per pupil. State education allocations also take into account the characteristics of students. For instance, a New Jersey formula distributes state aid based on the difference between what the state calculates a district needs to provide a "thorough and efficient education" and what the district can afford to budget for that education. The state then funds the difference.[19] The tendency over time is for states to "level up" so that aid to poor districts does not come at the expense of more affluent districts.[20]

Figure 15.4 displays the intergovernmental revenue contributions for public schools over time. Note that the federal portion, averaging only about

foundation program
A means of state education funding that allocates a basic level of funding to all districts.

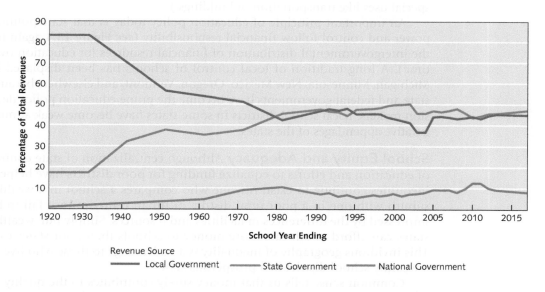

Figure 15.4 Trends in Revenue Sources for Public Elementary and Secondary Education
Elementary and secondary education receives the greatest portion of revenues from state and local government. The national contribution rose to 12.4 percent in 2011 but has since declined.

Source: U.S. Bureau of the Census, Public Education Finances: 2012 (Washington, D.C.: U.S. Government Printing Office, May, 2014).

9.0 percent since 1970, grew to more than 12 percent in 2012, then returned to its pre-2012 average of 9.0 percent.

A disturbing legacy of the Great Recession is that many school districts have been rapidly escalating the amount of fees imposed on students for particular courses, extracurricular activities such as sports, and even for riding the bus. The principle of a free public education is becoming an historical artifact of the twentieth century.

The Impact of Property-Tax Cuts Additional impetus to the state assumption of school costs may be attributed to state legacies of the taxpayer revolt. Statutory and constitutional limitations on taxing were typically aimed at the unpopular property tax. If public schools were to avoid such draconian measures as closing their doors, the states had to increase their education contributions.

One state, Michigan, completely tossed away its local property tax-based school-financing system. Prompted by numerous voter defeats of proposed property-tax increases to fund public schools, the Michigan legislature repealed all local property taxes supporting the public schools. The legislature then gave voters a choice: increase the state sales tax from 4 to 6 percent; impose a statewide property tax of 6 mils and triple the cigarette tax; or raise the state income tax. In a statewide constitutional referendum in 1994, voters picked the first option. Indiana followed suit in 2009 shifting funding for public schools from the local property tax to a one percentage point increase in the state sales tax (local school districts can still impose property taxes for special uses like transportation or buildings.)

An important principle of education policy today is that state political power and control follow financial responsibility (see Figure 15.4 again for the intergovernmental distribution of financial resources for education over time). A long tradition of local control of schools has been displaced in Michigan, Minnesota, New Mexico, Oregon, Vermont, and elsewhere because state and federal governments have become the prime education policy decision makers. Local school districts in some states have become weak administrative appendages of the states.

School Equity and Adequacy Although centralization of state control of education and efforts to equalize funding for poor districts have helped, inequities continue to exist. Anyone who compares a school in a wealthy suburb with one in a poor rural district or urban center cannot fail to be impressed by the differences in facilities and resources. Simply put, wealthy states can afford to allocate more money to schools than poor states can. This invidious geography of inequality is an advantage to those who live in a wealthy school district in a prosperous state.[21]

Common sense tells us that money surely contributes to the quality of schooling. Modern, well-designed buildings, up-to-date technology, the latest learning materials, low pupil-teacher ratios, and well-paid teachers should enhance student achievement, as should a rich offering of honors and advanced placement (AP) courses. But research has revealed an astonishing paradox: There is no consistent, significant statistical relationship between school spending and student performance.[22] Table 15.1 ranks the states on

Table 15.1 Average Teacher Salaries and Expenditures per Pupil, Graduation Rates, and Quality Counts Ranks 2014

STATE	EXPENDITURE RANK	TEACHER SALARY RANK	GRADUATION RATE RANK	QUALITY COUNTS RANK
Alabama	40	36	15	43
Alaska	3	6	47	31
Arizona	48	44	38	45
Arkansas	39	37	15	41
California	17	2	31	27
Colorado	32	30	44	23
Connecticut	5	4	15	3
Delaware	15	13	21	19
Florida	42	45	27	25
Georgia	34	21	44	29
Hawaii	14	17	31	24
Idaho	50	43	38	44
Illinois	11	10	21	15
Indiana	46	35	15	22
Iowa	29	20	1	20
Kansas	30	40	21	26
Kentucky	33	27	4	35
Louisiana	28	38	44	47
Maine	16	25	15	13
Maryland	12	7	9	4
Massachusetts	4	3	9	2
Michigan	37	12	38	32
Minnesota	18	19	35	10
Mississippi	45	50	35	46
Missouri	31	42	4	33
Montana	26	29	21	28
Nebraska	23	24	4	18
Nevada	43	23	49	49
New Hampshire	8	18	9	5
New Jersey	2	5	2	1
New Mexico	35	47	50	50
New York	1	1	38	8
North Carolina	41	33	21	36
North Dakota	13	28	9	14

(continued)

Table 15.1 Average Teacher Salaries and Expenditures per Pupil, Graduation Rates, and Quality Counts Ranks 2014 (*continued*)

STATE	EXPENDITURE RANK	TEACHER SALARY RANK	GRADUATION RATE RANK	QUALITY COUNTS RANK
Ohio	24	16	29	21
Oklahoma	47	48	35	48
Oregon	21	11	48	37
Pennsylvania	7	8	21	9
Rhode Island	10	9	31	12
South Carolina	27	49	31	42
South Dakota	36	46	29	34
Tennessee	44	34	4	39
Texas	38	26	4	40
Utah	49	41	27	30
Vermont	6	14	9	7
Virginia	22	31	15	11
Washington	19	22	38	17
West Virginia	20	49	2	38
Wisconsin	25	32	9	16
Wyoming	9	15	38	6

Sources: National Center for Education Statistics, *Digest of Education Statistics: 2017* (January 2019); Education Week, "Grading the States" (September 3, 2019).

average expenditures per pupil, teacher salaries, high school graduation rates, and composite Quality Counts scores to illustrate the differential state monetary investments in public education as compared to two outcomes.

The first research to reach this conclusion was the so-called Coleman Report in 1966.[23] Sociologist James S. Coleman examined thousands of school situations and discovered that curricula, facilities, class size, expenditures, and other resource factors were not associated with achievement. He *did* find that the family and socioeconomic backgrounds of students influenced performance, with children of well-off, well-educated parents outperforming those brought up in less-advantageous surroundings, a finding supported in more recent research.[24] Also, black students performed better in predominantly white schools than in predominantly black schools—a finding that later served as the grounds for implementing busing to put an end to school segregation. Coleman's staggering conclusions were reexamined in an extensive review of 120 studies; only eighteen found a statistically significant positive relationship between school expenditures and student performance. The overall conclusion is that no strong or systematic relationship exists between them.[25] However, the research consistently finds that minority students perform at lower levels than white students,[26] and the black–white, Hispanic–white performance gaps worsen with grade level.[27]

The Minority Achievement Gap The performance distance between minorities and whites is a stubborn and troubling issue. According to research in psychology, there is no quantifiable difference between black and white infants.[28] The gap, then, is caused by what happens later. The problem is complicated by the fact that the achievement gap for African Americans who are early high achievers grows faster across the grades than it does for initially low-performing children.[29] And overall, the minority achievement gap expands as all African American and Latino students move through the grade levels. These disparities are as resistant to a cure as is the common cold. Desegregation of the schools has not been the answer, and a 2007 U.S. Supreme Court decision, along with persistent segregated housing patterns, dilutes school diversity efforts.[30] Money has not helped, either.[31] But some important research findings have been reported that could help narrow the achievement gap. For example, it appears that the achievement gap might widen because white children have more extensive summer learning opportunities than children of color.[32] Other intriguing findings are that some high-achieving African American students experience negative peer pressure for "acting white,"[33] and that white students have greater access to high-performing teachers.[34]

The Education Policy Actors

The proliferation of independent school districts in the latter part of the nineteenth century was accompanied by intensive politicization. School districts in big cities and rural areas alike were as inclined to hire teachers and principals on the basis of patronage as on the basis of professional competence. Reformers (mostly professional educators) struggled to remove partisan politics from the public schools by electing school boards on a nonpartisan, at-large basis and by giving the professionals the primary responsibility for running school systems. These efforts were successful, but a new type of politics arose as teachers, school administrators, and state-level education actors began to dominate policy decisions as the "education establishment."

LO 15-3
To analyze the education establishment policy actors and their roles.

The Education Establishment

In the past, the members of the education establishment, popularly referred to as the "education bureaucracy," tried to dominate school policy making by resolving issues among themselves and then presenting a united front before legislative bodies and the governor. They constituted a powerful political coalition that managed to win substantial financial commitments to the schools. Because of the political and financial pressures already mentioned, however, the education establishment is fractured today.

Teachers As noted, teachers had little power or influence outside the classroom until they began to organize into professional associations and unions. Once, teacher organizations, particularly the NEA, focused their primary attention on school improvement rather than on the economic well-being of teachers themselves, and teachers and administrators maintained a common front before the state legislature. Gradually, however, a newer teacher organization challenged the dominance and docility of the NEA, especially in large cities. This rival organization, the AFT, openly referred to itself as a labor union and struggled to win collective bargaining rights for teachers. With the election of the AFT as the bargaining agent for teachers, the teachers began carving a home for themselves outside the cozy family of the education establishment. Both the AFT and then later the NEA lobbied for state legislation permitting collective bargaining and concentrated their efforts on winning better pay and working conditions for teachers. Today, approximately three-fourths of the nation's schoolteachers belong to one of these groups. However, many NEA locals, primarily in the southern and western states, do not engage in collective bargaining, either because they choose not to or because their state does not permit it.

Teacher militancy accompanied unionization. Strikes and other job actions disrupted many local school districts as teachers battled for higher pay, fewer nonteaching duties, and other demands. The rise of teachers' unions forever fragmented the education lobby in most states as teachers sought to look out primarily for their own interests rather than the interests of school administrators. Teachers remain perhaps the most powerful of education interest groups at the state level, although lately they have drawn heavy fire from conservative politicians, dissatisfied citizens, and other education stakeholders. (Former U.S. Secretary of Education Rod Paige famously referred to the NEA as a "terrorist organization.") Each year, the opening day of school is delayed in some districts because teachers go out on strike over concerns such as pay and benefits, working conditions, and education quality issues. In 2018 and 2019, statewide teacher walkouts occurred in Arizona, Colorado, Kentucky, North Carolina, Oklahoma, and West Virginia. Chicago public schoolteachers walked out for two weeks in October 2019—the longest such strike in that city's history. In many states where teachers didn't or couldn't go out on strike, such as Florida, Indiana, Oregon, and South Carolina, they held rallies instead, demanding pay increases, reductions in class sizes, increased levels of education funding, and more input into education policy.

Local School Boards Another member of the education establishment, the local school board, is a legislative body responsible for governing and administering public education at the local level. About 14,000 of these local bodies exist. Local school boards are made up of laypeople, not representatives of the professional education community. Board members are elected by voters in independent school districts in most states.

The original American ideal of local control of public schools lodged its faith in local school boards, which were popularly elected and therefore responsive to citizens' opinions and points of view. In fact, their true authority has never equaled the myth of local control. The status and influence of local boards have diminished, except perhaps for those boards that have the authority to adjust property tax rates. Some school boards have contracted with private entities to run their schools. Others, rife with politics, patronage practices, and scandals, have been pushed aside and effectively replaced by city governments (e.g., Boston, Chicago, Detroit, New York City, and Philadelphia). One critic called local school boards "the worst kind of anachronism . . . ripe for corruption, as a springboard for aspiring politicians, and a venue for disgruntled former school employees to air their dirty laundry."[35]

School boards still commonly do financial planning and oversight, and as noted earlier, some set school taxes on property in the district. They also hire district superintendents of education and school administrators, approve teacher appointments and school assignment policies, determine building and facility needs, and debate program needs. In fact, some local boards are criticized for trying to micromanage the daily minutiae of school operations instead of properly focusing on broad policy issues. Policy issues, however, are increasingly settled by state and federal standards and regulations, collective bargaining contracts, and court decisions.

Many local school boards suffer from yawning public apathy, extremely low turnouts for board elections, and widespread ignorance of what such boards are supposed to be doing. Others teem with partisan politics. About the only events that focus citizen attention on local boards are the occasional bond or tax referendum that proposes to raise property taxes in the school district, or vitriolic debates over conflicting goals and values such as school redistricting, funding equity, sex education, and the respective places of Darwin and Jesus in the classroom.

Other Policy Actors Also known as the state education agency, the *state board of education* (SBE) exercises general supervision over all primary and secondary schools. The SBE members are appointed by the governor or legislature, elected, or selected through some combination of processes. Like local boards, state boards sometimes become consumed by politics. The Texas and Kansas state boards of education have been arguing for years about the proper roles of science, creationism, and global climate change in the classroom and in school texts. Most SBEs make policy and budget recommendations to the governor and legislature. With few exceptions, however, they are not significant policy actors. They tend to lack political clout, policy expertise, and public visibility.

Like local school boards, state boards of education defer to the authority and expertise of another policy actor—in this case, the *chief state school officer* (CSSO). This CSSO, also known as the state superintendent of schools or the commissioner of education, establishes and enforces standards and accountability for local school curricula, teacher certification, standardized student testing, and certain other matters and provides technical and other assistance to the schools. They may be appointed by the SBE, popularly elected on a statewide ballot, or appointed by the governor. Although the formal relationship between the CSSO and the SBE varies, nearly all CSSOs serve as executive officers and professional advisers to their state boards of education. As governors and state legislatures have increasingly provided policy leadership for the schools, the influence of CSSOs has declined.

Yet another administrative creature, *the state department of education* (SDE), is responsible for rulemaking and for furnishing administrative and technical support to the CSSO and the SBE. It also administers national and state-aid programs for public schools. The state department of education is almost exclusively the habitat of education professionals. State departments have grown in size, competency, and power. They have taken on the difficult job of monitoring state education reforms, and they have significantly increased their capacities for research, program evaluation, performance measurement, and testing.

LO 15-4

LO 15-4

To analyze the new education policy actors and their roles.

The State Education Policy Leaders

As the coalition of actors described earlier has fragmented and lost influence, state-level education actors and community and business organizations have increased their interest in school issues and their capacity to respond to them, and governors and legislatures have added staff and augmented their ability to collect data and conduct research. Education policy making today orbits around state and federal governments rather than local education professionals, although the demand for, and tradition of, local control remains important.

Governors State chief executives are deeply involved in all major aspects of education policy making. Education issues often receive passionate attention during campaigns and in state of the state addresses. Occasionally, education clearly dominates governors' policy agendas. Education policy is the most important perennial issue in most states, and a significant concern of voters.

In formulating, lobbying for, and implementing education policy, the governors rely heavily on their staffs. Many governors have special divisions of education. Staff members facilitate the flow of information to and from the governor's office and the desks of other key education policy makers. They analyze information from all levels of government, in and out of state, and from national organizations such as the National Governors' Association and the Education Commission of the States. They also draft bills, lobby legislators and education and business groups, and attempt to influence public opinion on education issues. Recently, Republican governors in Michigan, North Carolina, Wisconsin, New Jersey, and other states orchestrated policies that deprivileged teachers and their unions while enhancing charter schools and voucher programs. The most successful governors have managed to weave delicate advocacy coalitions among all significant education policy actors to increase their chances of winning significant reform programs.

State Legislatures Legislatures have always had the final responsibility for enacting broad education policy and for determining state funding of public schools. They were the leading state policy actors until governors upstaged them, but the critical policy battles are still fought on legislative turf.

Lobbyists for the education establishment are quite busy in the state-house, but their influence has diminished because issue conflicts have precluded a united front. Numerous other interests, including business, minority groups, the disabled, community organizations, the economically disadvantaged, and those promoting school choice also receive a hearing from legislators.

Like governors, legislatures have expanded their capabilities. They have added their own education staff specialists, enhanced their research capabilities, and extended efforts to oversee and even overturn the actions of governors and education agencies.

Courts Federal and state courts, especially the U.S. Supreme Court, are important factors in public education. They have issued rulings on several issues affecting students, such as censorship of school newspapers, personal dress and grooming standards, female participation in sports programs, student discipline, student drug testing, privacy of student lockers, and school prayer. Federal courts imposed desegregation policies on public schools through a series of decisions beginning with *Brown v. Board of Education of Topeka* (1954), which declared that racial segregation violated the Fourteenth Amendment's equal protection clause.[36] Court-ordered busing to achieve school desegregation was mandated in *Swann v. Charlotte-Mecklenburg County Schools* (in North Carolina) in 1971 and in other decisions involving districts that had practiced government-approved racial segregation.[37] These decisions, and the subsequent busing, were highly controversial and contributed to white flight to the suburbs in many places. In some cities, such as Boston, Massachusetts, court-ordered busing led to violent protests.

Racial segregation of the schools remains a serious and intractable problem. Clearly, aggressive busing has not worked: Research shows that although racial segregation within school districts might be declining, segregation between school districts has persisted.[38] Racial and social disparities from housing segregation have created "islands of immunity" to school integration.[39] It appears that a tipping point is reached when nonwhite enrollment surpasses 25 percent, triggering white flight to different school districts or private schools. Remaining behind are the children of poverty and color.[40] African Americans in particular continue to live in segregated housing and attend segregated schools. Yet with the endorsement of a conservative majority of the U.S. Supreme Court, many school districts, including Charlotte–Mecklenburg and Boston, have dismantled desegregation plans in favor of combining neighborhood schools with various "choice" options such as charter, magnet, and private schools.

State courts, too, have ordered changes in education policy. As we have noted, many state supreme courts have mandated school-finance reform to attain greater equity in the funding of public education. State courts are also asked to resolve various legal disagreements spawned by education reforms. Individuals and groups representing minority positions can often capture the attention of top policy makers only through the legal system.

The Corporate Community Because many high school graduates lack the basic skills and knowledge to succeed in the workplace, of necessity, businesses are involved in the public schools. Consequently, some firms have developed their own training and education programs, often incorporating fundamental reading and writing skills.

To members of the education establishment, business leaders are partly to blame for the sad state of the schools. Some industries based primarily on low-wage labor and unsophisticated skills historically opposed education reform as an unnecessary expense. Firms are also criticized for negotiating local property-tax breaks that deprive school districts of much-needed revenues, then complaining about the poor quality of education in those very districts they are starving financially. Today, however, due to the changing nature of work, most corporate leaders are vocal proponents of education improvement at all levels, from preschool to college. They differ significantly, however, on how to attain it.

Corporate involvement encompasses a broad range of activities, including purchasing technology and supplies for local school, sponsoring opportunities in which students may concentrate on a specially designed curriculum in areas such as finance, IT, or biotechnology, and offering work in paid summer internships. Overall, the role of business varies from state to state, but in most locations its contribution is largely rhetorical and episodic. Commercialization of the classroom is a growing problem. Product advertisements, exclusive lunchroom franchises for soft-drink bottler and fast-food chains, and even advertising on school buses raise questions about the true interests of business in the schools.

Recently, large private foundations such as the Gates, Kellogg, and Annie E. Casey foundations, have taken on a more active role in public education by advocating for school and teacher improvement policies, common core standards, and other issues.[41] Moreover, they are strategically ponying up millions of dollars in support of their ideas.

Private Schools The widespread presence of private schools, most of them church sponsored, makes them influential policy actors. They enroll approximately 10 percent of K–12 students nationwide. To their supporters, the superiority of private schools in providing quality education is taken on faith. Private schools do provide a superior education in some instances, but in others, private schools are academically inferior, or they are little more than devices used by parents to keep their children in a religious environment or predominantly white classrooms.

Educational Innovation in the States

In the time since *A Nation at Risk* called national attention to the acute need for educational reforms, the states have responded on a large scale. Hundreds of task forces have thoroughly studied school problems and issued recommendations for resolving them. Many of these recommendations have been enacted into law as innovative programs to improve the quality of public education. The federal ESSA incorporated many principles and innovations first adopted by the states.

A broad and powerful coalition of state and local elected officials, professional educators, community organizations, parents, and business interests has been instrumental in the drive to improve public education. Democrats, Republicans, and independents alike generally agree that the economic future of the United States depends on the quality of schooling. What they do not agree on is how to best obtain improved outcomes.

The states have been busily innovating in the four critical areas of standards, students, teachers, and the education bureaucracy. Every state has recorded remarkable program achievements in at least one of these categories, and, in some instances, prodded by NCLB and ESSA, a majority have implemented reforms in all four. But incremental reforms have not been sufficient to reverse the strong tide of school mediocrity and even failure in many troubled settings, opening up a growing demand for more far-reaching restructuring of public education.

Standards

Standards and levels of assessment have been raised in almost every state. Curriculum and graduation requirements have been strengthened, instructional time has been increased, steps have been taken to minimize overcrowding, and technology has been ushered into the classroom. Special programs have been developed to encourage gifted students and to assist developmentally challenged students.

Competency testing for basic skills and subject matter has been another widely adopted reform. All states now test students at several grade levels to monitor progress in the basics, and most require students to pass a competency test (or exit exam) before graduating from high school. All states require school "report cards" to hold schools accountable for student performance. Successful schools and their teachers may receive financial rewards. Low-performing schools may be overhauled, receive special assistance, or, if hopeless, even be taken over or closed.

Yet many teachers, parents, and students openly wonder if, prodded by the federal government and the states, schools have gone overboard with frequent—and often intrusive—testing. A 2015 study found that students in sixty-six urban school districts were required to take some 112 standardized tests between pre-kindergarten and twelfth grade, an average of eight tests per academic year.[42] The stress associated with over-testing affects not only teachers but also students and parents. In some states, required testing (and test preparation) consumes up to one-third of the school year.[43] Research indicates that many states actually lowered their testing standards to comply with NCLB requirements that all schools be proficient in math and reading.[44] "Teaching to the Test" has become endemic in many schools. And disturbing evidence of teachers and administrators tampering with tests has appeared in Texas, Georgia, Massachusetts, Virginia, and elsewhere.[45] In April 2015, eleven Atlanta teachers and administrators were convicted of racketeering for altering test answer sheets. Other Atlanta educators received lesser punishments.[46]

The National Governors Association and the Council of Chief State School Officers launched the Common Core Standards Initiative in 2009. All but five states adopted the standards for English and math, and the first exams were administered in 2014–2015.[47] The common or national exams were intended to replace previous state tests in English language and math. The common core standards became a political football in 2015 as conservative and other concerned groups attacked it as unwanted federal intrusion into the schools (even though the governors and state school administrators developed the program). Since 2015, four states that initially adopted common core standards—Arizona, Indiana, Oklahoma, and South Carolina—have repealed or replaced them with state-developed standards. ESSA went farther and made the federal government officially neutral in the testing controversy. ESSA states "The Secretary [of Education] shall not attempt to influence, incentivize, or coerce State adoption of the Common Core Standards . . . or any other academic standards common to a significant number of states, or assessments tied to such standard."[48] The It's Your Turn box solicits your views on common core.

Another effort to raise standards is year-round schooling, now required for millions of students in public schools. Three-month summer breaks—the legacy of an agrarian economy in which children were needed to plant and bring in the crops—are being replaced with multi-tracking arrangements in which students and teachers are divided into several groups, or tracks. They attend classes for forty-five, sixty, or ninety days, and then go on break for a two- or three-week intersession.

Although the research remains inconclusive, year-round schooling may improve learning by ensuring that children keep their mental sharpness and do not forget much of what they have learned over the summer. It also saves money by maximizing the use of school buildings and resources. Certain problems arise, however. For example, it is difficult to schedule maintenance on buildings and equipment, and extended schooling can interfere with sports and other extracurricular activities and disrupt family vacations and day-care arrangements. A more effective approach may be to increase the length of the school day or academic year to pack in more time for teaching and learning.

Students

Of course, students are the intended beneficiaries of the improvements and strengthening of standards. In general, expectations for student academic performance and classroom behavior have been raised. However, based on SAT and ACT scores and results of the National Assessment of Educational Programs tests, there are, at best, only modest indications of improvement. Great disparities remain among states, suburban and urban districts, minority groups, and family-income categories.

One commonsense approach is to better prepare students to begin school in the first place. The federal Head Start program is one such program, and states are also helping to build first-graders' learning foundations through

? It's Your Turn

Should States Implement Common Core Standards?

Originally conceived and enthusiastically adopted by the states, common core standards have become a political football, with supporters asserting that the idea is sound and badly needed, while opponents decry national government intrusion into a traditional state and local education policy arena.

Where does your state stand on CCS? Has opposition arisen? If so, from what quarters? What are your thoughts on the desirability of national CCS implemented by the states? Is CCS a good idea?

PROS	CONS
Common core standards were not in fact mandated by the federal government. Rather, they were conceived, developed, and coordinated by the governors and chief state school officers.	Critics assert that the CCS reflects national (Obama administration) priorities and amounts to federal overreach, not state and local priorities.
CCS offer an accurate means of measuring and comparing student achievement across the states.	Public education is a state and local—not national—responsibility and must be treated as such.
The standards identify and test for the knowledge and skills U.S. children need to compete globally.	States should be free to set their own standards and develop their own testing systems.
The federal government offers grant funds to states willing to implement CCS.	Some CCS are actually set below those standards previously existing in some states.
The federal government has granted waivers to nearly all the states to provide flexibility in establishing their own accountability systems.	CCS impose more testing requirements on already over-tested students, who should spend more time learning and less in preparing for tests.
	Opposition to CCS is broad, incorporating Tea Party zealots, liberal-minded teachers and their organizations, and parents.

highly structured and innovative preschool programs. Kindergarten is one step removed from first grade and can be very helpful in preparing kids for school. But the trend is pre-kindergarten initiatives that can involve children as young as three years. Early childhood programs boost reading and math skills for entering kindergarteners by four to six months ahead of those who remain at home[49] and help to identify medical and social service needs. Importantly, they also involve parents in the learning process. Approximately 33 percent of four-year-olds are enrolled in state-funded preschool programs. Head Start enrollment brings the national total to 44 percent.[50]

Virtually all states have raised course requirements for students to graduate from high school. Students are required to take more upper-level math and science courses and more foreign-language classes, and a larger proportion of students are enrolling in honors and AP courses than ever before.

The national education paradigm today is known as **outcomes-based or performance-based education**. National standards, such as a common core curriculum and achievement tests on the basics, are said to enhance school accountability by helping to determine and test for levels of student knowledge, skills, and abilities, as well as for curriculum and teacher development needs. Although almost everyone agrees that standards must be raised and many think that national testing is a good idea, moving beyond broad goals and relatively painless incremental changes is proving to be difficult. Many Americans support national standards, but they distrust the national government and fear federal intrusion into the schools and what they teach. However, outcomes-based education appears to be here to stay.

Student classroom behavior has been a target of reformers in many states. Strict discipline codes are being enforced, as are stronger attendance policies. In especially difficult school settings, police officers, closed-circuit television monitors, metal detectors, airport-style screeners, and other devices help maintain order. Most states have adopted anti-bullying laws. More stringent discipline policies have made it easier for teachers to remove troublemakers from the classroom. Many school districts are using zero-tolerance policies to expel violent students. Other violence prevention programs teach conflict-resolution and anger-management skills to reduce fighting and discourage gang membership. Ironically, corporal punishment (paddling, usually) remains legal in nineteen states and is still used (mostly in the Bible Belt states) to discipline unruly students.[51]

Student drug testing is an active issue in some districts. The U.S. Supreme Court has ruled that schools may perform drug tests on students participating in sports and other extracurricular activities. (Before that ruling, public-school students were presumed to be excluded from drug testing by the Fourteenth Amendment's protection against illegal search and seizure.) Presumably, drug (urine) testing would identify trouble-prone students and send a discouraging message to those contemplating smoking weed, consuming alcohol, or getting involved with more serious substances. Professional educators and health groups oppose drug testing, arguing that students engaging in extracurricular activities are less likely to use drugs, and that requiring screening as a condition of participation in sports, band, clubs, and other activities would deter students from participating. At a more fundamental level remains the matter of overcoming *state* constitutional provisions regarding privacy and illegal search and seizure.

Hungry children cannot learn. Free school lunch and breakfast programs help ensure low-income students have full bellies on school days. To help avoid unnecessary distractions during class time, more than 1,000 public schools segregate classrooms by gender. Students who graduate from high school with a B or better average in New York and several other states are guaranteed state payment of full tuition at a state college or university, as long as they maintain a B average or better. Such scholarship programs have the added benefit of helping stem the brain drain of top students who attend college out of state and never move back. Houston, New York City, Atlanta, Memphis, Baltimore, and other cities are also paying kids for performance.

outcomes-based or performance-based education A reform that strives to hold schools, teachers, and administrators accountable for student performance, primarily based on standardized test scores.

Incentives for regular, punctual attendance are being offered in some locales, including guarantees of admission to college to all graduating seniors with a minimum grade point average and having regular attendance. Some states permit tenth graders who pass certain exams to receive their diplomas two years early and enroll directly in community college.[52] Other states allow high-performing high school students to take community college courses for dual high school and college credit.

Some offer cash for high attendance or for passing AP exams.[53] Taking a punitive tack, North Carolina and other states revoke the driver's license of any high school student who drops out or fails to pass 70 percent of their courses. Naugatuck, Connecticut, fines truant students or their parents $20 a day, and also prohibits withdrawal from school before the age of 17. The goal, of course, is to keep in school some of the hundreds of thousands of students who drop out each year, at a huge cost in lost tax revenues and increased expenditures associated with welfare, unemployment, and crime.

Teachers

Of the many factors influencing student learning, the quality of the teacher in the classroom usually makes the greatest difference. Good teachers not only help raise their students' test scores, but they also contribute to lower rates of teen pregnancy, higher college attendance, and higher lifetime earnings, according to one study.[54] Teachers have been the beneficiaries (or victims, depending on one's standpoint) of the most extensive and far-reaching educational reforms. They welcome higher pay, improved fringe benefits, and more opportunities for professional improvement. Smaller class sizes are particularly desirable, giving teachers more time to interact with each student. Teachers have been much less pleased with paperwork and accountability requirements, performance appraisals, testing of teachers, and teacher merit-pay schemes.

A recent National Education Association analysis shows that although average teacher salaries increased by 11.5 percent between 2010 and 2019, when adjusted for inflation, salaries *declined* by 4.5 percent.[55] Variations among the states continue to be rather pronounced, in response to differences in local cost of living, labor market conditions, and other factors. In 2019, estimated average teachers' salaries in New York were $85,889, while average salaries in Mississippi were estimated to be only $45,574.[56] At least fifteen states raised teachers' salaries in 2019, partially as a result of job actions taken by teachers in 2018. Teachers were pleased with significant salary increases in Arizona, New Mexico, South Carolina, Texas, Virginia, and West Virginia, although some of the raises were accompanied by less popular initiatives such as increased monitoring of teacher performance and increasing the number of public charter schools.[57]

Teacher Shortages Because of retirements, attrition, and a spurt in public-school enrollment, critical shortages of qualified teachers, particularly for math and science courses, continue to exist in many states. Baby boomer retirements are depleting America's classrooms of experienced teachers. Projections of new classroom teacher needs indicate even worse problems to come. Teacher shortages in the highly valued STEM (Science, Technology, Engineering and Math) courses are particularly severe; shortages in these disciplines may have long-range consequences for U.S. technology development.[58]

The states are experimenting with several strategies to relieve teacher shortfalls. Most are taking steps to entice former teachers and education majors who are working in other fields back into the classroom, and nearly all have relaxed or set up streamlined teacher certification requirements. One particularly rich pool for new teachers consists of people who have departed from military service, business, or government. Such nontraditional recruiting not only helps alleviate the teacher-supply problem but also has the added benefit of elevating the quality and diversity of the teaching pool. Approximately one-third of new teachers are such mid-career entrants.[59] Another valuable pipeline is the Teach for America program, which recruits high-performing college graduates to teach in high-need schools in low-income communities. Many states offer special scholarships, signing bonuses, or loans to attract college students into the teaching profession.

Research finds that many education problems stem from the failure to recruit, train, and retain good teachers. Some schools serve as retirement homes for the inept. Some teachers' colleges do an inadequate job of preparing teachers for the classroom. Some schools require teachers to teach out of their field of expertise and training. And once in the classroom, many teachers, especially in urban and low-income schools, soon lose their enthusiasm and confidence in their own abilities when faced with at-risk children.

States are taking steps to solve these and related problems. A majority of states have recently bulked up teacher preparation policies, setting higher academic proficiency requirements for teacher education programs and testing for content-specific knowledge. Teacher-licensing and classroom certification requirements are being tightened up to include longer classroom internships, mastery of subject matter material, and comprehensive classroom readiness assessment including lesson plans, homework assignments, and videotaped teaching sessions. Schools are adopting programs to mentor new teachers with experienced teachers. State education statutes and collective bargaining contracts are being modified to make it easier to end teacher tenure and dismiss teachers who should no longer be in the classroom.

Merit-pay plans that seek to reward high-performing teachers with special pay increases are popular. (See the Controversies in States and Localities feature.) Career ladders, which promote outstanding teachers up several levels to higher job classifications, have also been tried.

For various reasons—including budget cuts, teacher dissatisfaction with the plans, and fierce union opposition—these initiatives generally have not been successful. Teacher shortages in the STEM disciplines, special education, and bilingual education continue to plague many districts. And enrollment in teacher education programs has dropped substantially. Teacher satisfaction with jobs and the profession is also low; a 2019 poll found that over a five-year period, half of public schoolteachers seriously thought about leaving the teaching profession. More than half said they would vote to go on strike for higher wages, better funding of schools, and better working conditions. And large majorities of parents and the public said they would support the teachers if they did go on strike.[60]

Bureaucracy and School Choice

A single, boilerplate plan does not exist for improving the schools, but most strategies hold one factor in common: **school choice**. Its most essential elements include a market-based, decentralized approach that permits individual selection of the school that the child will attend, while providing tax dollars to accompany the student to the chosen school. The expectation is that, in the scramble to attract tuition dollars, heretofore fossilized schools will try new ideas, offer new or specialized curricula, and take other steps to reinvigorate public education, and new schools will be established. Schools unable or unwilling to adapt to and compete within the education marketplace will be forced to consolidate with more successful schools or close their doors altogether.

Magnet Schools A common school-choice program, found in nearly all large urban school districts, is the **magnet school**. A form of public school and under school district control, the magnet school offers specialized curricula to attract students from various backgrounds who share a common interest in areas such as the performing arts, science and technology, engineering, or international studies. Originally conceived as an alternative to busing, successful magnet schools help attract affluent children to the inner city and poor children to the suburbs. More than three million students currently attend magnet schools.

Related to magnet schools are **open enrollment programs** that permit students either to select schools only inside the existing school district or to choose any public school in the state. Within-district choice keeps resources and tax dollars in the same local jurisdiction. Between-district enrollment allows children to attend a school in a different district, perhaps many miles away. Open enrollment plans are intended to increase educational opportunities for students regardless of minority or socioeconomic status. Among the fifty states, only Alabama, Maryland, and North Carolina do not have open enrollment plans.

Open enrollment is not without its problems, however. An important shortcoming is that white and middle-class children tend to "choose" to flee low-performing schools for those that are better performing. Such an outcome has obvious implications for minority and social-class balance in the schools. School-choice proponents claim that children of poor parents can also transfer to more desirable schools, but without special assistance, many poor children cannot afford transportation to outlying districts. This problem has been at least partially addressed in states that furnish or help pay transportation costs for low-income children. However, students still face the additional hurdle of gaining admission to their school of choice, which might be fully enrolled.

school choice
A market-based approach to education improvement that permits parents and students to choose which school the child will attend. Examples include charter schools and voucher programs.

magnet school
A public school whose curriculum emphasizes a specialized area, such as science or performing arts, and that is intended to attract a diverse set of students.

open enrollment program
An option that permits students to attend a public school of their choice within a designated jurisdictional area. The intent is to increase educational options for all children.

Controversies in States and Localities

Should Teachers Have Tenure?

All of us have experienced good teachers and bad teachers. Shouldn't the good ones be encouraged to stay, and the bad ones sacked? Union contracts build in strong protections for teachers in collective bargaining states. Even in non-union settings, it is difficult to dismiss an underperforming or badly behaving teacher. Typically, the inadequate teacher remains in the classroom, to the disadvantage of the students, or is simply transferred to a different school. The difficulty in firing incompetent teachers is a common complaint of school administrators, parents, and education reformers alike.

Teacher tenure, a long-standing job protection right, is the politically charged focal point. Teachers are awarded tenure after three to five years of acceptable performance. Tenure helps keep experienced teachers in the profession. But what happens if a tenured teacher stops trying, becomes emotionally unstable, or commits a felony? To revoke tenure and dismiss a teacher usually requires proof of felonious acts or serious misconduct. Tenure rights are so strong that seldom is simple incompetence or consistently poor performance sufficient to push a teacher out of the classroom without years of charges and appeals. The poster child for the problem is New York City's "rubber rooms," in which hundreds of teachers accused of wrongdoing or incompetence were banned to trailers or unused classrooms to while away their time doing nothing while enjoying full pay for years until the cases were resolved. At one point, $30 million a year was being paid in salaries to teachers in legal limbo. Another egregious example is the case of an eighth-grade science teacher in Ohio, whose dismissal for branding crosses on the arms of public school students took two years and cost $900,000.

Three potential solutions are being tested in the states. The first is simply to terminate tenure and replace it with annual contracts. A poorly performing teacher would not have their contract renewed. South Dakota, Idaho, Florida, and North Carolina have ended tenure altogether. The second is to make it easier to fire teachers who have tenure but receive poor performance reviews. Arizona, Rhode Island, Colorado, and Nevada diluted tenure protections by making the process of dismissing bad teachers easier and faster.

The third solution involves identifying struggling teachers and either helping them improve sufficiently, convincing them to find a different profession, or firing them. The best example of this strategy is found in Toledo, Ohio. Toledo's Peer Assistance Review (PAR) assigns skilled veteran teachers to troubled teachers. The "consulting teachers" must be pulled from their classrooms to perform their mentoring duties, which is certainly a disadvantage of PAR, but recent research finds that significant cost savings are realized when novice teachers are transformed into accomplished performers and the hopeless are weeded out. For example, to fire a tenured teacher averages a cost of $128,941 in legal and other expenses, compared with only about $8,000 to counsel someone out of the profession.

Despite the widely recognized need to usher poor teachers out the door, there is much controversy over how it should be done: the "big stick" approach of the tenure bashers, the "tough love" tactic of Toledo, or something in between. And decisions must be guided by teacher assessments.

Critical Thinking Questions

1. Should teachers have tenure? Why or why not?
2. On what basis should teachers be evaluated? Student test scores? Student progress? Or other factors?

Sources: Adrienne Lu, "Teacher Tenure and Dismissal on Trial," https://www.pewtrusts.org/en/research-and-analysis/blogs/stateline/2014/04/01/teacher-tenure-and-dismissal-on-trial (accessed April 1, 2014); Sharon Otterman, "New York Teachers Still in Idle Limbo," https://www.nytimes.com/2010/12/08/nyregion/08schools.html (December 7, 2010); Trip Gabriel, "Plan Offered to Overhaul Discipline of Teachers," https://www.nytimes.com/2011/01/20/education/20teachers.html (January 19, 2011); Jonathan Walters, "Tough Love for Teachers," *Governing* (March 2011): 40–43.

Charter Schools Unlike open enrollment programs, which provide greater choice among existing schools, charter schools expand the total number of school possibilities for parents to choose from. **Charter schools** are independent entities operating within the public-school system under charters, or contracts that specify operating procedures and performance indicators. The charters are negotiated between their organizers and a sponsoring organization. The sponsor may be a local school board, teachers, parents, private business, or another entity.

Charter schools promise to deliver results in exchange for being unleashed from the bureaucratic chains of the education establishment. Flexibility and innovation are their strong suits. Most design their own curricula, hire and fire teachers, and generally run their own show. Some feature a back-to-basics curriculum; others emphasize math and science. In actuality, however, their degree of autonomy varies widely depending on state authorizing legislation. Using public (mostly state) tax dollars to compete with private and traditional public schools, charter schools are intended to improve responsiveness to parents and enhance the quality of education throughout the jurisdiction. Some public schools have adopted charter school features such as longer school days and one-on-one tutoring.[61]

Charter school laws have been adopted in forty-five states. They are particularly popular in Texas, California, Louisiana, and Florida. There are about three million students enrolled in some 7,000 charter schools nationwide. Charter schools are resisted by teacher unions, and some school boards are also skeptical of charter-reform efforts. Across the United States, charter schools have been closed for various reasons, typically poor student performance and financial problems. Reliable evaluative research is only now appearing on how well they measure up, and the results are mixed for charter schools. Some boost student achievement, but others do no better—or worse—than standard public schools.[62]

Voucher Plans In a system using a **voucher plan**, parents receive a certificate from the state or from their local school district that may be used to subsidize the tuition for a public, private, or religious school of their choice. The concept is quite similar to that of the G.I. bill and Pell grants for federal reimbursements to colleges and universities. Voucher programs are operating in sixteen states, nearly all governed by Republican majorities. Despite displays of public enthusiasm for voucher programs, they have gone down to defeat in several state initiative and referendum votes. Several state courts have also proven to be less than friendly to voucher plans, having blocked them from operating in Colorado, among other states.

The *federal* constitutional legitimacy of spending public money on religious schools was established by the U.S. Supreme Court in 2002 in *Zelman v. Simmons-Harris et al.*, a decision heralded as an important ruling on religion and the schools.[63] The Court's 5–4 majority concluded that Cleveland, Ohio's, plan offered "a genuine choice between religious and nonreligious schools," despite the enrollment of 96 percent of voucher recipients in religious schools.[64] Left undetermined was the constitutionality of such vouchers according to the *state* courts.

charter school
An alternative public school established by contract with a sponsoring agency, school district, business, or other organization.

voucher plan
An arrangement in which the state or school district subsidizes tuition for students to enroll in a school of student/parent choice.

The Florida program, enacted by the legislature in 1999, offered "opportunity scholarships" to students in chronically low-performing schools, permitting them to transfer to a better-performing public school or to any private school. The Florida voucher program was struck down as unconstitutional by the state supreme court in 2006, on the grounds that public money cannot be used to finance private schools.[65] Taking a different tack, Florida then adopted a tax credit for private school tuition, effectively achieving the ends sought by the legislature. Such a tax-credit approach has been adopted by several other states to avoid constitutional issues.

The largest and most-examined voucher experiment began in 1999 in Milwaukee. The Milwaukee school-choice program provides low-income parents with vouchers to send their children to private schools. It is used by nearly 29,000 low- and middle-income students, who receive about $8,300 (grades kindergarten through eight) or $8,946 (grades nine through twelve) each. The majority are enrolled in religious (mostly Catholic and Lutheran) schools.[66] Unlike in Florida, the Wisconsin state supreme court permitted vouchers to be applied to parochial schools. The court's reasoning was that the voucher money was going to parents, not to schools.

Nevada recently became the bellwether for voucher-related programs by providing an Education Savings Account to all public-school students. The ESA offers 100 percent of what the state pays for public school students, currently $5,700 a year, to disabled students and those from poor families, and 90 percent to all others. Dollars may be spent for public, private, or religious schooling, textbooks, and even dual-enrollment college credits.[67] Funding for the plan has been a controversial topic in the Nevada state legislature; in 2017, Republicans in the legislature said they would vote against any budget bills unless Democrats supported funding the ESAs. Democrats resisted this but eventually a compromise was reached. However, the amount of funding authorized only allows full tuition in private schools to be covered for a relatively small number of students.[68]

Overall, it does appear that voucher programs have encouraged parents to participate more in their children's education and that parental satisfaction with schools has increased. There is no shortage of voucher champions, chiefly among political conservatives and religious supporters.[69] But there is only very modest evidence for vouchers improving student achievement. In Milwaukee and Cleveland, the most thorough analyses to date indicate that school-choice students have not performed any better than similar non-choice students.[70] Also undetermined is the effect of shifting public tax dollars from public schools to private ones on the quality of public schools. Will public schools improve so that they can compete with private schools, or will they become education hovels for the remaining poor children? Will vouchers truly benefit children of low-income families who, even with a voucher, still must come up with thousands of dollars annually to pay private-school tuition? Or will vouchers disproportionately help upper- and middle-income families? What will be the impact on minority and social-class segregation?

School vouchers received a major boost when President Donald Trump selected Betsy DeVos, a longtime advocate of vouchers, as his secretary of education in 2017. President Trump's 2020 budget proposal included some

$5 billion to support voucher programs.[71] Trump's proposal could get a big boost from the U.S. Supreme Court's decision in the 2020 case *Espinoza v. Montana Department of Revenue* where the court overturned a provision in the Montana state constitution forbidding public funds from going to religious schools. The 5-4 decision found that the provision discriminated against religious schools and the families who send their children to them on the basis of religion.[72]

Privatization

Perhaps the most radical restructuring plan of all involves turning over management and operation of the public schools to a private firm. K-12 Inc., Connections Education, and other companies operate for-profit standard and charter schools in twenty-three states. One of the most interesting privatization experiments is in Philadelphia. Following a state takeover of Philadelphia's troubled school system in 2002, thirty-eight failing public schools were transferred to seven outside administrators, including Edison, Temple University, and the University of Pennsylvania.[73] Results from the City of Brotherly Love have been mixed. Six of the schools were retaken by the Philadelphia School District in 2008 because of poor performance and financial issues, and several others were placed on notice that they faced the same fate unless improvements were made.[74] Meanwhile, scores of standard Philadelphia schools have been closed because of city budget shortfalls.

Noteworthy failures of schools-for-profit have also occurred in Hartford, Connecticut; Dallas, Texas; and other cities because of high financial costs and disappointing student performance. In an early analysis by the Rand Corporation, comparing student test scores in public schools with privately run schools in six cities, results again were mixed. Students in traditional schools did better on standardized reading and science tests in Cleveland and St. Paul but did worse than test takers in privately managed schools in Denver and San Francisco.[75] Early schools-for-profit providers, Edison and EAI, have left the marketplace or declared bankruptcy, but other firms have stepped in with privately run charter schools. Recently, states have been taking a much more assertive role in regulating for-profit providers. In 2018, California banned for-profit K–12 schools from operating in the state. Increased state regulation of such schools became an issue in the 2018 Ohio gubernatorial race in response to an $80 million financial scandal involving the now bankrupt Electronic Classroom of Tomorrow (ECOT). Richard Cordray, the Democratic candidate, proposed a complete ban on for-profit schools, while Republican Mike DeWine, the eventual winner, called for increased state accountability.[76]

Homeschooling

In addition to the large number of children enrolled in private schools (approximately 10 percent of the student population), it is estimated that up to 2.4 million school-age children are taught at home by their parents.[77] Many homeschoolers are from religious families uncomfortable with the public school's environment, performance, or secular values. The homeschool curriculum, testing, and other factors are regulated by most—but not all—states. Some states accommodate homeschooling by permitting selected public-school activities. For instance, Idaho public schools must allow homeschooled children in their districts to participate in any school activity, including sports. Studies of homeschooled children generally show positive results, with stay-at-home kids outperforming their public-school counterparts on standardized achievement tests.[78] Conclusions concerning the performance of homeschooled students need to be interpreted carefully for at least two reasons. First, homeschooled students are not a random selection from public schools; they are students whose parents have selected them for homeschooling. Second, there is no way of knowing what the performance of homeschooled students would have been if they had remained in the public-school system.

Virtual Schools

Widely available technology makes it possible for students to learn at home from long-distance teachers. The Florida Virtual School serves more than 207,000 students across the state in internet-based instruction. Almost all states offer online courses to at least some students, and most permit certain students to attend virtual schools full time. Idaho requires all high school students to take some online classes.

The virtual school can be particularly appropriate for rural states with great distances between schools, such as Alaska and Wyoming. The COVID-19 pandemic in 2020 tested states' abilities to offer instruction online. As states closed their in-person schools (some for the remainder of the 2019–2020 academic year), classes were shifted online. States like Florida or Idaho that have a history of offering such classes may have had an easier time making the shift than did states that do not have such a history. But even in states with experience, the transition was made difficult because *all* classes needed to be offered online. Teachers experienced in online instruction offer these warnings to states making the transition:

- Not every home has computers or high-speed internet.
- Younger children require lots of adult supervision.
- Even great teachers lack expertise in creating online lessons.
- Students with special needs can be the hardest to teach virtually.
- Schools provide more than academic skills.[79]

Beyond these is the state of the U.S. broadband network and its limited abilities in some areas of the country to serve large numbers of users at the same time. In the second week of March 2020, the broadband speed testing service Ookla reported that internet download speeds had declined by nearly 5 percent from the week before, as larger numbers of users were attempting to work, attend school, read the news, or engage in social networking with friends and relatives.[80] Whereas a slowing internet may be an inconvenience to some users, it is a much larger problem for classroom study, especially where the teachers may want to use synchronous methods of instruction such as online live video lectures, chat rooms, and other technologies requiring large amounts of bandwidth to operate optimally. A major question is how the 2020-2021 school year will proceed—in person or online. While states are planning for the school year to begin with students in classrooms, surges in

COVID-19 cases in summer 2020 threatened this optimistic scenario.[81] Especially troubling is the possible confluence of increased COVID-19 cases and the beginning of flu season later in the fall.[82]

The Report Card on School Choice

Will the school-choice movement save the public schools or destroy them? Is the most salient objective improvement of the quality of public education, or is it something different? The fight over school reform is currently being won by those groups favoring the market-oriented approaches of school choice through vouchers, charter schools, and private schools.[83] The education establishment that dominated school policy for decades has lost ground to a new alignment of interests populated by conservative advocacy groups, foundations, and those seeking reform through standards and accountability approaches. But the education establishment is fighting back by challenging market-based reforms, asserting that the real problems with under-performing schools are poverty, racial segregation, poor parenting, and a lack of resources.[84] During the Obama administration, the federal government seemed to back the education establishment in this battle, but the election of Donald Trump put the federal government on the side of market-based reformers. Although the federal government only provides some 9 percent of school funding resources, its policies and regulations carry heavy weight in how schools operate.

Are parents truly capable and do they have sufficient information to make the best educational choices for their children? Arguments are proffered from various perspectives. So far, relatively small numbers of students participate in school-choice programs, though their numbers are rapidly rising. Still, evaluative data are limited, precluding comprehensive assessment of student performance or possible unintended consequences of school-choice programs.

One thing is certain: School choice is highly controversial and, except for the magnet-school option, is perceived as a threat by almost the entire education establishment, particularly teachers and school board members, who fear losing funding from reduced enrollment and being saddled with the most difficult, at-risk children. When school-choice proposals involve public tax dollars for parochial schools, they are especially controversial.

The Continuing Challenges of Public Education

LO 15-6
To discuss the continuing challenges of public education.

The states, as well as the national government, are serious about excellence in education and providing direction and leadership to attain it. The vitality, innovation, and capability of the states are prominent in education policy, but the federal government is an increasingly influential partner.

A troubling gap separates policy goals and enactment from policy implementation. More time must pass before we can accurately gauge the consequences of many state and federal initiatives. It will take a tremendous act of political will and much hard work to bring to fruition the state and national educational improvement goals and to reinstate the United States as a world leader in K–12 performance.

The continuing problems in public education are manifold and daunting, and reform is extremely controversial, complex, and elusive. As education reform seemingly plods along, many frustrated parents opt for alternative arrangements. The number of private schools and the number of children instructed at home have grown significantly. Meanwhile, during this prolonged period of debate about the future of the public schools, many thorny dilemmas persist. Students and teachers must learn how to utilize information technology productively, billions must be invested in much-needed building repairs and new construction, and the special problems of at-risk and immigrant children must be addressed more effectively.

Putting effective state education reforms into practice requires the cooperation of many fragmented interests, including teachers, school administrators, superintendents, students, parents, conservative groups, foundations, and levels of government, each group with their own interests and turf to defend. Triumph over this fractured and increasingly ideologically driven policy subsystem will come only through civic action that mobilizes a vast array of public, private, and nonprofit actors and interests into a united front committed to reform over the long term—decades or more.

The unfinished portrait for educational excellence has been sketched by governors, legislatures, the state education community, and the national government. States must encourage innovation and creative thinking at the local level while maintaining needed standards and accountability. Constitutionally, and in practice, education remains primarily a state and local responsibility. This truth was recognized in the Obama administration through liberal granting of NCLB waivers to states dissatisfied with provisions of the federal law and through its sponsorship of ESSA.

The national government has an important and legitimate role, but it has been perceived as unduly intrusive and costly. Federal action alone provides no final answer to the persistent problems of public education. State and local reform efforts are hobbled by childhood poverty, broken families, and other social problems that the national government could help address. And by funding and disseminating the results of research and experimental projects, the national government can elevate capacity and stimulate state and local innovation by state and local school districts. If the current education reforms fail to move us toward providing quality education for our children, radical rethinking and restructuring of American public education may well be needed.

Often in American history a crisis has been necessary to change policy dramatically. The Great Depression of the early 1930s, as badly as it hurt the U.S. economy for several years, resulted in the creation of the Social Security system, the Federal Deposit Insurance Corporation (FDIC) that guarantees bank deposits, and other New Deal programs. The COVID-19 crisis may be such a turning point in U.S. education. As states experiment with online delivery systems for public education during this pandemic, promising new ideas will arise. When the pandemic has run its course, will K–12 education return to its earlier state? Or will changing education policies become "the new normal" because they were necessary during the pandemic?

Chapter Recap

- Education is the single most important—and most costly—function in state and local governments.

- There is a perceived crisis in the public schools; criticism involves standards, student performance, teachers, excessive testing, and the education bureaucracy.

- The activities of state, local, national, and private actors and the education establishment largely determine policy development and outcomes.

- The role of the national government in education policy became more important with No Child Left Behind but has lessened somewhat with Every Student Succeeds.

- The education establishment has fragmented; the new key policy actors are governors, legislatures, courts, private schools, the corporate community, conservative groups, and the national government.

- A wave of education innovations in the states has raised standards, attempted to improve student retention and performance, and attempted to address a critical shortage of classroom teachers.

- The most controversial innovations have involved various school-choice programs, including magnet and charter schools, vouchers, and private schools.

- The COVID-19 pandemic of 2020 had dramatic effects on education in the United States. Whether these effects are temporary or permanent remains to be seen.

- The problems of reforming public education are multifaceted and complex, requiring the continual attention of government at all levels.

Key Terms

foundation program *(p. 429)*

outcomes-based or performance-based education *(p. 442)*

school choice *(p. 445)*

magnet school *(p. 445)*

open enrollment program *(p. 445)*

charter school *(p. 447)*

voucher plan *(p.447)*

Internet Resources

For the National Report Card on state school systems, see **www.edweek.org**. This site, which may require payment for access, can also be used to find informative articles on school reform.

School finance data are available from the National Center for Education Statistics at **www.nces.ed.gov** and on the U.S. Department of Education's website at **www.ed.gov**.

State education agencies may be explored at **www.ccsso.org**, home for the Council of Chief State School Officers.

One of the best places to go for education policy information and trends is the website of the Education Commission of the States at **www.ecs.org**.

Teacher salary data and education policy analysis may be found on the American Federation of Teachers' website at **www.aft.org** and at **www.nea.org**, the website of the National Education Association.

16

Criminal Justice: Cops and Corrections

Locks in a single prison door represent the anguish of incarceration.

Learning Objectives

LO 16-1 To explain how much crime there actually is and how it is measured.

LO 16-2 To recognize the ongoing challenge of crime fighting.

LO 16-3 To explain intergovernmental roles in criminal justice.

LO 16-4 To identify the actors in criminal justice policy and their respective roles.

LO 16-5 To explain how policy participants interact.

LO 16-6 To assess the benefits and problems of capital punishment.

LO 16-7 To evaluate state correctional policy.

LO 16-8 To discuss correctional policy alternatives for states and localities.

The headlines could not be starker: "Phoenix Police Shoot and Kill Man Wielding Gun in Parked Car,"[1] "Traffic Stop Escalates into Police Shooting."[2] And then, "Veteran Oklahoma Police Officer Killed, Rookie in Critical Condition, After Suspect Shoots Both in Head,"[3] "Phoenix Police Commander Killed, 2 Others Wounded in Shooting."[4] It seems like a day doesn't pass where there isn't an article in the news about police officers killing civilians or civilians killing police officers.

Police across the country are being accused of regularly abusing suspects with beatings, tasers, and other actions. Alternatively, police officers feel they are under siege; they feel they take their lives in their hands when they conduct routine traffic checks, investigate shop-lifting complaints, or respond to domestic violence calls. Police officers think that many, if not most, of the shootings of civilians by police officers are justified, and civilians feel that police officers threaten their lives with their aggressive policing.[5] In this time of mutual suspicion, police departments have armed themselves with

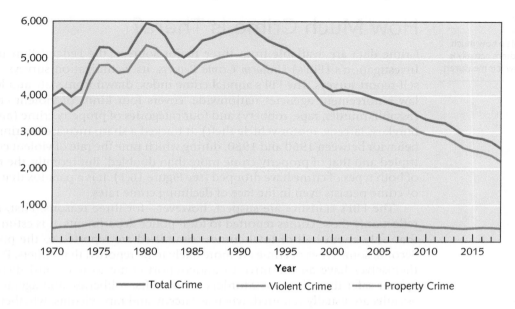

Figure 16.1 States' Rate of Crime per 100,000 People, 1970–2018

Source: DisasterCenter.com; FBI UCS Annual Crime Reports, Table 1.

machine guns, night vision equipment, and armored vehicles, much of it surplus from the U.S. military. To document police interactions with civilians, many police departments around the United States began requiring officers to wear body cameras while on duty; more than half the law enforcement agencies now do so. But these cameras are not a panacea; they come with concerns about cost, necessity, and civil liberties.[6]

Has crime become serious and dangerous enough to warrant aggressive police response to enforcing the law on the one hand, and intrusive public monitoring of police behavior on the other hand? Do we live in such a crime-infested environment that the police and civilians are virtually at war with each other?

According to crime statistics, the answer would appear to be no. Both violent and property crime rates have dropped dramatically over the past twenty-five years, as shown in Figure 16.1. Why? The answers are complex and multifaceted —and sometimes contradictory. More police officers on the beat, aggressive community policing programs, and high-tech policing are some of the reasons for the decline in criminal activity. But there are other factors that may be pushing the crime rate down as well, such as an aging population.

How Much Crime Is There?

Crime data are available from three major sources: the Federal Bureau of Investigation's (FBI's) *Uniform Crime Reports,* its victimization surveys, and self-report surveys. The FBI's annual crime index, drawn from state and local law enforcement agencies nationwide, covers four kinds of violent crime (assault, murder, rape, robbery) and four categories of property crime (arson, burglary, larceny, motor vehicle theft). It tracked a sharp increase in criminal behavior between 1960 and 1980, during which time the rate of violent crime tripled and that of property crime more than doubled. But recently, the rates of both types of crime have dropped (see Figure 16.1). It is a paradox that fear of crime persists even in the face of declining crime rates.

The FBI's statistics are suspect, however—for three reasons. First, they reflect only those crimes reported to local police departments. It is estimated that only about half of total crimes committed are reported to the police. Second, some types of crime are more likely to be reported than others. Police themselves have an incentive to underreport crime to make jurisdictions appear safer than they are. Murders, auto thefts, robberies, and aggravated assaults are usually reported, whereas larceny and rape victims, whether out of embarrassment, fear, or other reasons, may remain silent. Third, the FBI's crime data include only eight types of criminal behavior. Most white-collar crimes and drug crimes are excluded, despite their high numbers. Thus, the index provides only a partial picture of actual criminal activity.

Because of these disadvantages, a second, more accurate approach to measuring crime is used. *Victimization surveys* scientifically survey approximately 160,000 people in jurisdictions in some 90,000 households across the country twice a year, asking them whether they or members of their households have been victims of personal or property crime during the past six months. Also utilized by large metropolitan areas and some states, victimization surveys have been conducted on a nationwide basis by the U.S. Bureau of the Census since 1973. The Uniform Crime Reports (UCR) and the National Crime Victimization Survey (NCVS) are difficult to compare because they include somewhat different crimes, calculate crime rates by person (UCR) or household (NCVS), and define the same crime (like burglary) differently. Even with all these differences, the NCVS shows a much higher rate of crimes than does the UCR. The NCVS also shows some identifiable patterns: African Americans, Latinos, males, and urban dwellers are more likely than others to be crime victims. Like the UCR, the NCVS shows a dropping level of both violent and property crime, but, unlike the UCR, the NCVS shows violent crimes ticking up since 2015 by about one percentage point per year while the incidence of property crime continues to decline.[7]

A third, unofficial source of criminal activity is *self-report surveys,* in which criminologists survey people—and especially juveniles—on their own lawbreaking behavior during the prior year. In the early 2000s, as much as 85 to 90 percent of respondents reported having committed criminal acts.[8] A 2017 survey also reported a high incidence of self-admitted criminal activity but offenses respondents admitted to were not violent. Crimes people admitted committing include illegally downloading music (76 percent), littering (75 percent), being drunk in public (60 percent), possessing or using illegal drugs (52 percent), and driving while intoxicated (40 percent).[9] Self-admitted violations of traffic laws were so widespread (86 percent) that one researcher commented, "We are all criminals."[10]

Prediction is problematic because we do not really know what *causes* crime. We can state, however, that it is associated with certain factors. From a broad perspective, criminal activity is normally associated with economic recessions, joblessness, and opportunity, though the significant decline in crime during the most recent recessions would appear to contradict these associations. Crime is most likely to be committed by young males, many of them from impoverished and/or broken families. Crime rates are higher in densely populated cities and states than in rural areas. Urban areas present more targets of opportunity, various sociocultural problems that promote criminal behavior, a better chance of escape for criminals, and a haven for gangs. Crime also appears to be related to poverty, unemployment, low levels of education, marital instability, drug abuse, and race.[11] A recipe for crime and incarceration is to take a male, unemployed, African American high school dropout from a low-income, unstable family background and place him in an urban setting. Approximately one-third of such individuals have served time by their mid-thirties.[12] Put differently, while African Americans make up some 12 percent of the U.S. population, they compose 40 percent of prison inmates in the United States.[13] But does this mean that African Americans commit a disproportionate percentage of crimes or that police differentially target African Americans for potential criminal offenses?

Crime is complex. Offenses committed by some groups of people are more readily defined as crimes than similar offenses committed by other groups of people. Businesspeople engage in insider trading and fraud, solicit and pay kickbacks, launch Ponzi schemes, and commit other white-collar crimes that cost their victims millions of dollars. Large percentages of the public admit to using or possessing illegal drugs or violating traffic laws. Some contractors rig bids on government construction projects and Pentagon defense contracts; some bankers embezzle money; some judges accept bribes; the occasional priest or minister molests a child. The underlying causes of these and other sad cases cannot be attributed to economic deprivation, age, neighborhood, race, or the entertainment industry. Greed certainly contributes to many crimes, as does opportunity, drug addiction, and psychological disorders; the origins of others remain unknown.

Although reasonable people disagree about the causes of crime, most agree that law enforcement is not as effective as it should be in apprehending and deterring criminals. Fewer than 20 percent of all property crimes reported to the police are "cleared" by an arrest. For violent crimes, the record is better: approximately 45 percent.[14] Probably two-thirds of the arrests, however, do not result in a conviction or in any sort of punishment for the offender. Extrapolation from these somewhat rough estimates indicates that a criminal has only a slight chance —maybe one in a hundred—of being both arrested *and* convicted of a crime.

Fighting Crime

Throwing money at the problem does not seem to be the final answer; research has been unable to find a strong link between higher police expenditures on personnel and materials and a subsequent reduction in crime. Obviously, *how* the money is spent makes a difference. Most criminal activities cannot be prevented by law enforcement officials, and unreported crimes are very difficult to investigate. More prisons and longer sentences have some effect on crime rates. Other factors that appear to be associated with higher arrest rates, and lower crime rates as well, are related to the behavior, tactical deployment, and tools of police officers. Aggressive and active police work in responding to calls from citizens and technology-enhanced prediction and investigation of criminal events seem to help, as does the use of more officers on the streets.

Community policing is the popular terminology for a hands-on law enforcement approach. Typically, officers are assigned specific territorial areas of responsibility and are encouraged to use their imaginations, experience, and personal touch in fighting crime. Police work directly with citizens and with relevant government and nonprofit organizations to identify problems and solve them creatively. If drug houses, junkies, and prostitutes infest a community, the citizens and community police officers find a way to run them out. They converse with children and adults, aiming to foster trust. Minor troublemakers are identified and counseled before they become big-time offenders. To be effective, officers must add community engagement and social work to their law enforcement duties to make their assigned neighborhoods ones they would themselves be willing to live in.[15]

Political scientist James Q. Wilson developed the "Broken Window" approach to fighting crime in a 1982 article he wrote with George L. Kelling. In the authors' words, "If a window in a building is broken and is left unrepaired, all the rest of the windows will soon be broken."[16] The message of a broken window is that no one cares. Of course, the metaphor doesn't apply only to broken windows but extends to all manifestations of neighborhood decay, including dilapidated buildings, public consumption of alcohol and drugs, drug dealing, hookers on street corners, aggressive panhandlers, graffiti, and gang activity. Visual deterioration of a neighborhood leads to social degeneration and makes the area more vulnerable to crime. By preventing or correcting visible manifestations of neighborhood decline, or by "repairing the broken windows," neighborhoods will host fewer criminal activities, and positive forces can take root and flourish. Community policing and attention to "broken windows" are said to be at least partly responsible for the dramatic decline in violent crime in large cities since the 1990s, though research findings are mixed.[17]

More controversial, but also believed to be effective, is "stop and frisk," a straightforward approach to reducing violent crime by removing guns from the street. In New York City, Cleveland, Philadelphia, and other cities, officers were trained to profile individuals on the street for the likelihood of packing a weapon or toting illegal drugs. Constantly hitching one's trousers, tightening one's belt, patting an inside pocket, and wearing a heavy coat in warm weather are all indicators of a weapon. Hundreds of handguns and pounds of drugs were seized in high-crime neighborhoods using stop and frisk tactics. The tactic won approval by the U.S. Supreme Court,[18] but it was very controversial in minority neighborhoods and opposed by civil rights groups. In New York City, for example, there were more than 685,000 police stops in 2011 (the height of the stop and frisk policy); 89 percent of the stops resulted in no further action taken. As community groups organized against seemingly random and heavy-handed street stops and a state judge ruled such practices

?   **It's Your Turn**

Should Potentially Invasive Data-Driven Policing Technology Be Restricted or Prohibited?

The National Security Agency (NSA) is well known for using invasive techniques to track telephone and internet-based communications under the guise of fighting terrorism. But a growing number of state and local governments are learning fast and accessing new technology that raises important questions about the long arm of the law. At least twenty-six states permit federal, state, or local law enforcement agencies to search photo databases, including drivers' licenses, to identify people. Accessing facial recognition technology, Ohio and other states are using facial features from drivers' license photos to help identify criminals from video and other sources. Pinellas County, Florida, can search more than 120 million individuals in photo databases in Florida and elsewhere. Three states—California, New Hampshire, and Oregon—completely ban the use of facial recognition technology in police body cameras.

Facial recognition systems are biometric tools that can be deployed remotely from police laptops, just as license plates scans have for years. Still-emerging biometrics permit individuals to be identified through their irises, vein prints, palm prints, skin tone, and gait.[1] Data can come not only from drivers' licenses but also from video cameras and other means of surveillance. Facebook and other social media networks? They, too, are fair game for data gathering and facial recognition technology.[2] The use of drones as an eye in the sky to keep watch on protests, suspected gang activity, and the whereabouts of suspects has become routine in the United States. Real-time drone use as first responders is becoming possible and was recently tested in Chula Vista, California.[3]

Should state and local governments start restricting such invasive actions to protect our liberties and freedom?

PROS	CONS
What one does, so long as it does not involve breaking the law, is one's own business—not the government's.	These law enforcement technologies protect citizens and governments from criminals and terrorists and help police identify suspects and make arrests.
These are tools for routine, suspicion-less surveillance of vehicles and individuals; as such, they intrude on our freedom and right to privacy.	These are tools to advance law enforcement; they are used cautiously so that privacy rights are not violated.
Facial searches and other biometric techniques ignore the boundaries between criminal and non-criminal databases by placing innocent people's images in what amounts to perpetual digital lineups.	Advanced technology is a weapon in the war on terrorism.
These technologies are first steps toward developing a national ID system through drivers' licenses.	If you are not doing anything wrong, you have nothing to worry about.
	Any restrictions should be the responsibility of the national government—not the states or localities.

illegal, the number of stop and frisk occurrences dropped from its height in 2011 to 13,459 in 2019.[19]

All kinds of police surveillance systems are also increasingly in use, and they too are raising concerns. Video surveillance systems are being widely adopted by cities to keep an eye on crime-ridden areas. Gunshot tracking systems help police respond almost immediately to shootings, assist victims, and nab suspects.

Sound sensors placed in troubled areas transmit a gunshot's distance and direction from the sensor directly to police headquarters. When combined with video surveillance, gunshot tracking can be a powerful law enforcement tool.

Other forms of high-tech, data-driven policing include integrating criminal activity data with day, location, season, and previous crime patterns. GIS technology can map crime and cross reference related variables in a massive database on criminals and criminal activity, helping predict when and where the next incident is likely to occur. This "evidence-based policing" involves targeting, testing, and tracking people and places to better utilize police resources.[20] A growing number of departments are sharing some of the data online so residents can be informed about criminal activity in their neighborhoods. Los Angeles' COMPSTAT system is a good example.[21]

Through such creative adaptation of emerging technology, law enforcement attempts to stay one step ahead of criminals and better protect people and property. A certain balance, however, must be sought between surveillance technology and citizens' right to privacy. It's Your Turn presents more on some disturbing developments.

The Ongoing Challenge of Crime Fighting

LO 16-2
To recognize the ongoing challenge of crime fighting.

The vast proportion of dollars spent on law enforcement comes from states and localities. Congress and the president provide plenty of rhetoric but relatively little material assistance. In the majority of jurisdictions, crime is under control and citizens feel relatively safe. But many jurisdictions, particularly in urban poverty areas, are victims of demographics. High poverty rates, dysfunctional families, free-flowing illegal drug markets, and violent gangs are all factors invariably associated with high crime rates. The hard-pressed police often find themselves simply trying to contend with the worst crimes. As for politicians, it is easy for them to talk "tough on crime" but then offer little extra financial assistance for fighting crime. For the cop on the street, tough and immediate judgment calls must often be made: Arrest or mediate in a domestic dispute? Call for backup now or deal with the situation first? Does this berserk halfwit have a gun? Should I draw and fire now?

Community policing, the broken windows approach, stop-and-frisk, and high-tech policing all are being tried across jurisdictions in the United States. Nonetheless, much of the effectiveness of law enforcement depends on the officers themselves, who work in a most dangerous and stressful occupation.

Intergovernmental Roles in Criminal Justice

LO 16-3
To explain intergovernmental roles in criminal justice.

Problems with the U.S. system of criminal justice cannot be attributed to a lack of human and material resources. About 1.1 million employees work full-time in state and local police agencies. Total state and local payroll for police protection exceeds $5.7 billion.[22] And as of 2020, the U.S. Department of Defense's Law Enforcement Support Office (known as the 1033 program) has transferred some $7.4 billion in surplus equipment—everything from aircraft to armored vehicles to Kevlar vests—to local, state, and federal police agencies at little or no cost.[23]

The states and localities exercise jurisdiction over more than 95 percent of all crime that occurs in the United States. Municipal and county police and sheriff's departments bear much of the burden of law enforcement, employing nearly 90 percent of all sworn police employees; the state law enforcement organizations (highway patrol and special agencies) employ only around 10 percent.[24] These state and local entities enforce state laws and local ordinances. Federal crimes such as treason, kidnapping, and counterfeiting are dealt with by the FBI and processed through the federal courts and correctional system. The two systems are separate, but some cooperation occurs. For instance, the FBI and state law enforcement agencies exchange information such as fingerprints, mug shots, data, and details on the movements of fugitives, suspected terrorists, and drug smugglers; they sometimes work together in criminal investigations, as they have in numerous drug busts and anti-terrorist activities.

Nine out of every ten dollars spent on police protection and corrections come from the coffers of state and local governments—an illustration of the decentralized nature of criminal justice spending in the United States. The national government's resources are concentrated on homeland security and federal corrections agencies. However, Washington provides certain forms of direct financial assistance to the states and localities, totaling more than $1 billion, to hire more police and adopt crime-fighting strategies.

Greater national involvement in state and local law enforcement is being called for, given the rise in sophisticated cybercrime; the growing economic, political, and global dimensions of organized crime; human trafficking; drug trafficking; the ever-present threat of terrorist acts; and the fact that criminal activities do not respect jurisdictional boundaries. States and localities can do only so much to combat the poverty, poor housing, inadequate education, and other social and economic conditions that are conducive to crime.

One innovation that emerged from the nation's reactions to the September 11, 2001, terrorist attacks on the United States was the creation of **fusion centers**. These were originally funded by the federal Department of Homeland Security and Department of Justice to share information and intelligence among federal, state, and local authorities and break down barriers that might exist between different law enforcement agencies. There are currently seventy-eight fusion centers, at least one in each state, the District of Columbia, Guam, Puerto Rico, and the U.S. Virgin Islands. Fusion centers are now owned and operated by state and local government with cooperation and some funding from federal authorities. Although originally designed to combat terrorism, fusion centers have more recently been used to combat all forms of criminal activity.[25]

fusion centers
A joint effort by federal, state, and local law enforcement authorities to share information and resources in order to address terrorist and criminal activity.

Actors in Criminal Justice Policy

LO 16-4
To identify the actors in criminal justice policy and their respective roles.

There is a large cast of characters in state and local criminal justice systems. State policy leadership is exercised by the governor, who sets the tone for the pursuit of law and order through State of the State addresses, proposed legislation, and public presentations. It is the rare governor who does not announce a new law enforcement program of some type.

Legislative bodies decide what a crime is and prohibit it through laws, establish the structure of the legal system, and determine sentencing parameters, including the option of capital punishment. Legislatures tend to be responsive to citizen pressures on law enforcement issues, as demonstrated by lawmakers' activity in areas such as gun control, the death penalty, and sentencing reform.

Law Enforcement Officials

The state attorney general formally heads the law enforcement function in most states; county and city attorneys and district attorneys typically follow the attorney general's lead. These positions call for a great deal of discretion in deciding whom to prosecute for which alleged crimes or civil violations. The prosecution of offenses is a politically charged endeavor, particularly when it is within the authority of people who aspire to higher political office. On the other side of the courtroom are public defenders and private defense attorneys, who try to negotiate dropped charges, a favorable plea bargain, or get their clients declared innocent.

The highway patrol (state troopers), special state law enforcement divisions modeled on the FBI, county sheriffs, police chiefs, local line and staff officers, and civilian employees are also important. They are responsible for implementing the policies decided on by elected officials and for carrying out the basic day-to-day activities connected with enforcing the law. But it is the highway patrol, the county sheriff, and the cops on the street who are the frontline law enforcers. Dangerous and stressful, policing is a profession in high demand.

The Courts

State and local courts decide the innocence or guilt of defendants brought before them, based on the evidence submitted. In the great majority of cases, however, plea bargaining prevails, and the case never goes to trial. Courts can also influence criminal justice through rulings that specify correct police procedures in criminal cases. U.S. Supreme Court decisions, in particular, have shaped the criminal justice process. The federal courts have the final word on cases in which the defendants claim that their federal rights have been violated by state or local law enforcement personnel. (State courts handle alleged violations of state constitutional rights.)

Critics have asserted that the Supreme Court has made it more difficult to convict criminals through decisions that have expanded the rights of the accused. The most controversial and oft-criticized case is *Miranda v. Arizona* (1966).[26] This decision expanded the rights of the accused by requiring police officers to inform anyone suspected of a crime of the right to remain silent; the fact that anything said can and will be used against them in a court of law; and the right to be represented by counsel, paid for by the state if necessary. Evidence obtained when the accused has not clearly indicated their understanding of these *Miranda* warnings or explicitly waived their rights is not legally admissible in the courtroom because it is considered a violation of the Fifth Amendment right not to incriminate oneself.

The U.S. Supreme Court also influenced state and local criminal procedures in the case of *Mapp v. Ohio* (1961). Basing its decision on the due process clause of the Fourteenth Amendment, the Court ruled that evidence obtained illegally by the police cannot be introduced in court.[27] This "exclusionary rule" extended the Fourth Amendment's protection from illegal search and seizure. The police must have a search warrant specifying which person or place will be searched and what will be seized. Over time, these and other early decisions favoring the accused have been relaxed by a conservative Supreme Court.

The Public's Involvement

The voting public also participates in justice policy. Citizens make demands on officials (the governor, legislators, judges, police, etc.) to conform to public opinion on crimes and criminals. Generally, the pressure is on for more law and order, and it results in strict criminal codes and correctional policies. Citizens also participate directly in the criminal justice system by serving on juries. Most citizens consider it their public duty to serve on a jury from time to time, and such service does tend to be an interesting (if not always edifying) experience. Trials usually last fewer than four days, and many prospective jurors are never called into the courtroom. But occasionally, a jury trial will drag out over a lengthy period; one of the longest was concluded in Belleville, Illinois, after a forty-four-month marathon concerning liability for a toxic chemical spill. Attorneys for the losing party then announced that they would appeal.[28]

Citizens also participate in criminal justice by sitting on grand juries. A **grand jury** (which is typically composed of twelve members) serves as a check on the power of the state or local prosecutor by considering evidence in a case and then deciding whether to indict the accused. Twenty states require a grand jury **indictment** for serious crimes. In other states, it is optional, or a preliminary hearing of charges and evidence before a judge is used instead. In practice, grand juries are inclined to rubber-stamp whatever course of action is recommended by the prosecutor. Former district attorney and chief judge of the New York Court of Appeals, Sol Wachtler (later himself convicted of extortion, racketeering, and blackmail), famously quipped that district attorneys had so much prosecutorial discretion that they could get a grand jury to "indict a ham sandwich."[29] Rarely does one question the professional legal opinion of the district attorney or attorney general.

An additional function of the grand jury is to act as an investigatory body for certain types of crimes, particularly vice, political and corporate corruption, and organized crime. In this capacity, the grand jury is empowered to issue subpoenas for evidence and suspects whom it wishes to examine. A statewide grand jury is most appropriate for criminal investigations because it can deal with activities that cross county or district boundaries. Among the states that provide for statewide grand juries are Arizona, Colorado, Florida, New Jersey, South Carolina, and Virginia.

The public may also become involved in the criminal justice process by tackling crime on its own. Telephone-and web-based crime report lines;

grand jury
A group of citizens appointed to determine if there is enough evidence to bring a person to trial.

indictment
A formal, written accusation submitted to a court by a grand jury, alleging a specified crime.

neighborhood crime watches and patrols; neighborhood complaints of prostitution, drug dealing, or gang activity; and similar actions to report "broken windows" help take a bite out of crime.

Finally, the public at times becomes involved in criminal justice through public demonstrations in support or opposed to police actions. The death of George Floyd at the hands of Minneapolis police officers in May 2020 set off a series of public protests. Most were peaceful but some turned violent as protestors clashed with police officers and shops and public buildings were looted. The protestors' rage turned on public displays of what many viewed as symbols of racism—in particular, statues of Confederate soldiers. These demands of the protestors were varied but most focused on several changes to criminal justice policy. First was what was summed up as "defund the police." While this slogan conjures simplistic images of police departments not being able to pay officers or buy supplies for police cruisers, the substance is much more complex. Community-oriented policing expanded the mission of the police, adding new tasks that had social work, mental health, and family relations connotations. For community-oriented policing to work as it was designed, the police need to be trained to take on duties in addition to those cops typically perform. In its broadest interpretation, the defund the police movement means shifting resources currently designated for police functions to other civilian functions more closely aligned with addressing social ills—mental health counselors, intervention specialists, domestic relations experts, and so on.

A second demand of many of the recent protests has been the removal of public symbols of perceived racism. While protests on this issue have occurred for several years, the death of George Floyd and others brought the situation to a head. Nowhere has this been more visible than in the capital of the old Confederacy—Richmond, Virginia. Monument Avenue in downtown Richmond is lined with statues of Confederate military officers and Jefferson Davis, president of the Confederacy. Added to this display in the 1990s was a statue of Arthur Ashe, the international tennis star and civil rights activist, who was born in Richmond. In Summer 2020, protestors tore down the statue of Jefferson Davis. Richmond Mayor Levar Stoney then ordered the removal of statues of Confederate Naval Commander Matthew Fontaine Maury and Generals Stonewall Jackson and JEB Stuart (all three statues were owned by the City of Richmond). Virginia Governor Ralph Northam's order to remove the statue of Robert E. Lee (which is on state-owned land on Monument Avenue) has been blocked by several lawsuits.[30] In response to protestor actions, Confederate statues have been removed in more than twenty large U.S. cities. In some of these cities, the actions were taken to prevent injuries to protestors attempting to remove the statues themselves.[31] Coupled with local action removing such statues and memorials is the possibility of national action changing the names of U.S. military bases named after Confederate officers. President Trump has said that he opposes any renaming of these bases.[32]

And finally, protestors demanded the end to aggressive police tactics in dealing with suspects. The symbol of these tactics is the chokehold, where pressure is applied either to the sides or back of a person's neck restricting blood flow to the brain or to the person's windpipe restricting breathing.

Both holds can cause unconsciousness. Most large police departments in the United States ban the use of such holds but grant exceptions when the police officer's life or safety is threatened. Minneapolis is *not* one of the cities that banned the use of chokeholds and in the time period from 2015 to 2020, police officers in that city had utilized such restraints at least 237 times resulting in some 44 people losing consciousness.[33] (The Minneapolis City Council banned the use of chokeholds by the police a week after George Floyd's death.) A national ban on chokeholds is being considered in congress but the details of such legislation are unclear. Most likely such a ban, if it were to pass congress, would be coupled with continuing federal financial assistance to local law enforcement agencies.

All these policy actions show how spontaneous public outcry outside of the normal course of action can cause governments to respond quickly.

The Victim

An often-ignored influence on criminal justice policy is the victim. Many victims are left psychologically, physically, and/or financially damaged after a crime. States have responded to this sad fact by developing victim compensation programs. These programs are typically administered by a board, which assesses the validity of victims' claims and decides on a monetary award to help compensate for hospital and doctor bills, loss of property, and other financial needs resulting from the crime. Maximum state benefits, supplemented by the federal Victims of Violent Crime Act (VOCA), usually vary from $10,000 to $25,000, depending on the state (60 percent of the money comes from the federal government). Rarely is a victim made whole by these limited payments, but at least some assistance is provided to help the person deal with the various traumas of the crime.[34]

States permit use of victim-impact statements in court before sentencing a convicted criminal. The statements may include victims' and family members' views on how the crime has affected them and their feelings about the crime and the accused. Most states and many counties now provide victim notification systems so that crime victims are made aware of their assailants' subsequent prison release. The federal Megan's Law requires notification of a community when a convicted sex offender moves into the neighborhood. (Megan was a seven-year-old girl who was sexually assaulted and murdered by a neighbor who had recently been released from prison after serving time as a sex offender.)[35] States post their sex offender registry on the web, listing the names and whereabouts of offenders.

How Policy Participants Interact: Two Policy Areas

LO 16-5
To explain how policy participants interact.

All states do not define or treat crimes in the same manner. The states' handling of criminal justice in two policy areas—victimless crimes and capital punishment—illuminates this point.

Victimless Crime

Prostitution, pornography, illegal drug use, music and movie pirating, and flouting mandatory seatbelt and motorcycle helmet laws are all examples of victimless crimes. Statutes enacted by legislative bodies define what constitutes criminal behavior, and public opinion usually influences what activities the legislatures treat as criminal. **Victimless crimes** are voluntary acts that violate the law but no one's individual rights. Some such acts are perceived to present little or no threat to individuals or society. Yet up to 50 percent of all arrests in urban areas is estimated to be on charges of victimless crimes.

One may argue that such crimes should be wiped off the books because those who engage in these activities suffer willingly (if at all). A strong case can be made for legalizing, regulating, and taxing prostitution and recreational drugs. People will pursue these activities anyway, the argument goes, so why criminalize and incarcerate a large portion of the population unnecessarily? Instead, why not get a little piece of the action for the public purse? State regulation of gambling helps diminish the role of organized crime, and regulation of prostitution can help prevent the spread of sexually transmitted diseases by requiring regular medical checkups for prostitutes. Though "massage parlors" and "escort services" exist in all major cities, only Nevada has legalized and regulated prostitution.

Finally, legalizing "recreational" drugs promises to take the profits out of the drug trade and to reduce drug-related crime and corruption. An estimated one-third of all new state prisoners have been convicted of drug-related crimes. The tens of billions of dollars spent annually by the United States on the "war on drugs" have resulted in a pathetic failure, leaving us today with just as many addicts; swelling prison populations containing some half a million (mostly nonviolent) drug offenders; an enormously profitable, gang-driven importation and distribution system that lures young people and even grade-school children into the trade; and a great deal of drug-related violence.[36] By shifting drug enforcement money and efforts to medical and psychiatric treatment of addicts and users, perhaps legalization would even lead to less addiction, while padding the public purse.

In states where legislative bodies define the scope of criminal behavior broadly to include victimless crimes, an extra burden is placed on other actors in the criminal justice system. Prosecutors and law enforcement authorities find much of their time consumed by these relatively minor and nonthreatening activities when they could be concentrating on more serious crimes, such as murder, rape, and robbery. The courts must also spend a great deal of time processing these cases. The legalization of certain victimless crimes would immediately shorten the dockets of prosecutors, police, and judges; render the process more manageable; and reduce the burgeoning prison and jail population. A less radical strategy is *decriminalization*—the prescribing of a minor penalty (usually a small fine) for specified crimes. For example, many states and localities have decriminalized possession of small amounts of marijuana.

Opponents claim that *victimless* is the wrong word to describe these actions. For example, with the selling of sex, prostitutes and their clients can

victimless crimes
Illegal acts that, in theory, do no one any harm.

become infected with the HIV virus and other communicable diseases. It is not uncommon for prostitutes to endure serious emotional and physical costs. Legalization of drugs such as methamphetamines, heroin, or crack cocaine might lead to a significant rise in addiction rates and require higher spending for treatment and health care. And if legalization were selective (say, only marijuana, cocaine, and ecstasy were made available legally), then new, more powerful designer drugs would likely continue to debut on the market.

In practice, hard-pressed prosecutors often drop charges against perpetrators of victimless crimes, judges dismiss the least offensive cases or administer a small fine or a suspended sentence, and law enforcement personnel tend to look the other way when passing near a prostitute or a smoker of weed. De facto decriminalization is the norm for many victimless crimes in much of the United States, especially in the case of legally prohibited sexual behavior between consenting adults, including sodomy, adultery, and the ever-popular fornication.

Capital Punishment

LO 16-6
To assess the benefits and problems of capital punishment.

Capital punishment offers a second example of how states vary in their approach to criminal justice. In this area, the interactions among individuals and institutions are critically important. Public opinion helps determine a legislature's propensity to enact and courts to carry out a death penalty statute. Prosecutors must decide under which circumstances to seek the death penalty. Only juries can find a defendant guilty or innocent in a capital case. Judges apply the penalty of death, subject to lengthy appellate review. Governors have the power to commute a sentence of execution. And the federal courts have played an important role in determining the conditions under which a state can legally put a person to death for a crime.

Criminal executions were once commonplace in the United States. In colonial days, public hangings were considered appropriate for adulterers, religious heretics, blasphemers, and thieves. A total of 717 people was legally executed during the 1950s. But public opinion slowly began to turn against capital punishment and so did the U.S. Supreme Court. In the 1972 case of *Furman v. Georgia*, a 5-to-4 majority held that the death penalty had been applied in a cruel, arbitrary, and racist manner by the states.[37] The Supreme Court expressly declared unconstitutional the capital punishment statutes in Louisiana and North Carolina and implicitly invalidated similar laws in many other states. It held that death penalty laws could be valid only if used in accordance with correct procedures and standards and could be invoked solely for lethal crimes.

The Supreme Court later ruled that the use of the death penalty for those who committed crimes while juveniles is unconstitutional.[38] But in one seemingly bizarre 2003 case, the Court let stand lower court rulings that Arkansas could forcibly administer drugs to an insane murderer to render him sane enough to be executed.[39] However, the Court did prevent the execution of a murderer with mental retardation in 2002 and of a man who raped, but did not kill, his eight-year-old stepdaughter in a 2008 decision.[40]

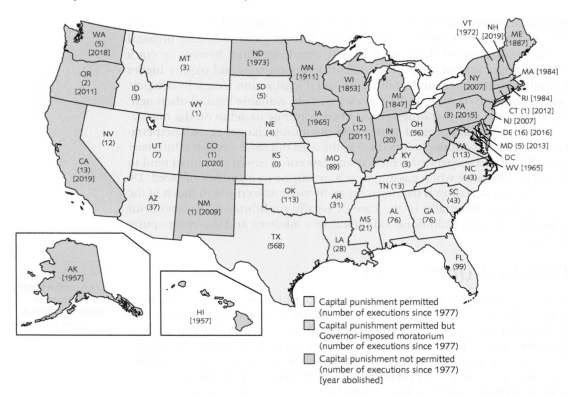

Figure 16.2 States with and Without the Death Penalty, and Post-1976 Executions, March 2020

Most states permit capital punishment, although some have not actually carried out the death penalty for many years.

The map shows the number executed since 1976 or the year the death penalty was abolished.

Source: Death Penalty Information Center (www.deathpenaltyinfo.org).

Several states voluntarily abolished capital punishment in the 1960s and 1970s. The majority, however, rewrote their statutes to conform to the Supreme Court's guidelines (see Figure 16.2). In 2008, the U.S. Supreme Court held in *Baze v. Rees* that the three-drug cocktail used to lethally inject the accused in Kentucky (and by implication in many other states) was constitutionally valid; executions then recommenced in several states following an unofficial six-month moratorium while the case was under review.[41]

A total of twenty-eight states permit executions today, although governors in California, Oregon, and Pennsylvania, where the death penalty is legal, have issued moratoriums on executions. The most commonly used technique is lethal injection. Several states permit the condemned to choose the method of execution, adding to lethal injection the possibilities of lethal gas (six states), electrocution (nine states), hanging (three states), or firing squad (three states). The alternatives listed are also approved in some states, such as Arkansas, Mississippi, and Oklahoma, if lethal injection is invalidated by court order or is "otherwise unavailable." Those states supportive of the death penalty tend to have both a politically conservative population and a high murder rate. Some 2,620 inmates were languishing on death row in state penitentiaries in January 2020. While statutes were being rewritten and clarified between 1968 and 1976, no executions were carried out. Since January 1977, however, 1,512 people have made the long walk from death row to the death chamber, more than 80 percent of them in the South. Texas is the leading executioner; the state used lethal injection to execute 568 felons between 1976 and 2020.[42]

Recent public opinion polls indicate that 56 percent of the American people favor capital punishment, a figure that has been declining. However, when presented with the alternative of life without parole, the "in favor" group drops to 36 percent.[43] Execution remains a rather tedious and enormously expensive endeavor. The prisoners executed today have spent, on average, around eleven years on death row. The appeals process presents numerous opportunities for delay, and it is not unusual for an inmate, after languishing for a decade or more on death row, to escape the death penalty through the legal process. The price tag on death is shocking, averaging millions of dollars per execution when court and other related costs are considered; the price in Maryland recently was estimated at $186 million for five executions from 1978 to 1999. Not surprisingly, arguments have been made that abolishing the death penalty would be positive for state budgets.

An especially troublesome aspect of the death penalty demographic differences in who gets executed. African Americans receive this form of punishment well out of proportion to their numbers. Although African Americans make up about 13 percent of the U.S. population, 34 percent of those executed since 1977 have been black, and 42 percent of death-row inmates are black. Black people who kill white people are significantly more likely to be sentenced to death. Latinos have been executed in rough proportion to their presence in the overall population—8 percent—and they make up 13 percent of death-row inmates. Less than 2 percent of those condemned to death since 1977 have been women, and very few women have been executed.[44]

Under various U.S. Supreme Court rulings, application of the death sentence must not be idiosyncratic or capricious. Critics of the death penalty claim, however, that it is applied capriciously, from the decision of a prosecutor to ask the jury to determine that a given crime is a capital offense to the requisite review of a jury's death sentence by the state supreme court. The offender's race is definitely a consideration, as noted earlier. And those who murder police officers, women, the elderly, children under age 12, or multiple victims are more likely to be sentenced to death, as are those who kill after a sexual assault or robbery.[45]

Obviously, a great deal of controversy surrounds the issue of executing criminals. Researchers generally agree that if punishment is to discourage future criminal behavior, it must be swift and certain. Neither of these conditions is met by the death penalty in the United States. And few reasonable and informed people today argue that capital punishment acts as a deterrent, except in the specific case of the guilty individual who is executed.

Studies comparing homicide rates in states with and without death penalties either find no significant differences in homicide rates or find that states with capital punishment actually have higher rates of homicide.

Also disturbing is the fact that the personal characteristics of judges influence their decisions. Republican judges are much more likely to vote for the death penalty, as are older judges and those with previous experience as a prosecutor.[46] In this sense, the death penalty resembles a judicial lottery. Application of the death penalty can also be cruel and unusual punishment in more ways than one. In one case, Florida's "Old Sparky" overheated, causing flames and smoke to erupt from a leather mask worn by the unfortunate murderer, Pedro Medina. (This gruesome scene helped to convince Florida officials to replace the electric chair with lethal injection.) As noted earlier, even lethal injection has come under fire as a cruel and unusual cause of death. Efforts to locate a suitable vein in a former junkie can take hours. Recently, an Arizona prisoner took two hours to die, struggling for breath. Execution of an Oklahoma inmate was stopped after he grimaced and struggled after his three-drug cocktail, only to die of a heart attack shortly thereafter. Prison officials had searched for a usable vein for nearly an hour before finally inserting the needle into his groin.

Typically, three chemicals are injected into the prisoner: a barbiturate, a paralytic, and then a heart-stopping substance. If the first chemical is improperly administered and therefore ineffective, the other two can cause extreme agony. A U.S. shortage of one of the three drugs began in 2011 and, along with resistance of other countries to exporting it to these shores, resulted in the introduction of a new death drug, pentobarbital. (It is commonly used to euthanize pets.) New drug combinations are being tried in what one critic called "human science experiments." Pharmaceutical companies have weighed in, some refusing to sell their drugs to states where they are to be used in executions. In one execution in Nebraska in 2018, the state used an untested four-drug combination; one of the drugs was the synthetic opioid fentanyl.[47] On top of this, the American Medical Association has said that active physician involvement in administering the lethal injections is a violation of medical ethics.[48] Some seventeen states require lethal injections to be administered by physicians. In North Carolina, physicians began refusing to administer the lethal cocktail in 2006, essentially halting executions in the state.

The public has become increasingly ambivalent about the death penalty because of growing evidence of serious problems in the justice system and a growing citizen concern for possible innocence.[49] Studies have found that two of every three death sentences are eventually overturned, usually due to errors by incompetent defense attorneys or evidence withheld by prosecutors and police officers.

Calls for an end to executions have grown louder, and some states have heeded them. Delaware repealed the death penalty in 2016, New Hampshire in 2019, and Colorado in 2020, and high courts in New York and Washington ruled executions to be unconstitutional. A number of states in which the death penalty is legally condoned have not put anyone to death for years.

Concern is growing that innocent people are being put to death. The arbitrary nature of the death penalty and other public concerns are registered in statistics. From a post-1977 peak of ninety-eight executions in 1999, the number plummeted to only twenty-two in 2019. Similarly, the number of death sentences had declined from 315 in 1996 to just thirty-four in 2019.[50] DNA testing makes identification of a killer a statistical certainty when such evidence is available, and more states are demanding that DNA evidence be submitted before extinguishing a person's life and that inmates proven to be innocent are freed. It is estimated that more than 160 men and women have been exonerated since 1973, many of them as a result of negative DNA tests, and others because of incompetent defense attorneys or prosecutorial or police misconduct.[51] Two mentally deficient North Carolina brothers sentenced to death in 1984 were freed thirty years later when evidence was uncovered that crime scene DNA implicated a different man, since deceased.

On the side of those favoring the death penalty is the argument for the legitimacy of *lex talionis*, the principle that the punishment should fit the crime. According to this view, some crimes are so heinous that only the death of the perpetrator can balance the scales of justice and relieve the moral outrage of society. This argument for justice as retribution cannot be validated on empirical grounds; it is an ethical question that each state must legislatively resolve.

Correctional Policy

LO 16-7
To evaluate state correctional policy.

A person convicted of a crime in a court of law becomes the object of correctional policy, which, as its name implies, aims to correct behavior that society finds unacceptable. In theory, an offender should first be punished, both for retribution and to serve as a lesson for other potential criminals. Second, convicted lawbreakers should be rehabilitated so they can become productive law-abiding citizens after fulfilling the terms of their punishment. Third, criminals who represent a danger to society should be physically separated from the general public.

If correcting criminal behavior is the overarching goal of correctional policy in the states, we have a terrible policy failure on our hands. As already noted, most crimes do not result in an arrest. Even when an offender is detained by the police, she stands a good chance of avoiding conviction or incarceration. Thus, deterrence is a dubious proposition at best. Remember that the best way to prevent undesirable behavior is through swift and certain punishment. Those of us who quizzically stuck a foreign object into an electrical outlet in childhood received the shock of swift punishment. If we were foolish enough to try it a second time, we discovered that the punishment was certain. Only the imbecilic or masochistic among us would subject themselves to such abuse a third time. That is how our correctional policy would have to work if deterrence is to be achieved. But for various reasons, swift and certain punishment is unlikely.

The U.S. Department of Justice estimates that more than 40 percent of former inmates released from state prisons commit another serious offense or violate the terms of parole or probation within three years and return to prison because of it. It appears that prisons actually increase the likelihood that an individual will commit additional crimes when he is freed. Our state prisons have been called breeding pens for criminals. Instead of being rehabilitated, the first-time offender is likely to receive expert schooling in various criminal professions. Overcrowding, understaffing, physical and sexual brutality, gangs, and rampant drug abuse do not help an offender become a law-abiding citizen. Many approaches have been tried—counseling, vocational training, basic education, and others—but none has consistently been able to overcome the criminalizing environment of state prison systems.

Without doubt, most incarcerated offenders see deprivation of their freedom as punishment, and so retribution does occur. For the average felon, "going to jail sucks."[52] Just as surely, prison effectively removes some undesirable characters from our midst. These two objectives of correctional policy are achieved to some degree, although cynics point out that sentencing tends to be rather inconsistent and a significant proportion of criminals are released before serving out their sentences. Most important, and contrary to the conventional wisdom, research consistently shows that state imprisonment rates are not significantly related to crime rates. In fact, supporting the notion that prisons are colleges for criminals, incarceration might actually boost crime.[53]

Sentencing

Sentencing reform has recently received a great deal of attention in the states. The inconsistency of criminal sentencing is obvious if we examine incarceration rates. The United States locks up about 660 people per 100,000 population, but that number varies widely from 990 per 100,000 in Oklahoma to 280 in Vermont and Massachusetts[54] (see Figure 16.3). Southern states tend to be toughest on crime: They are more than twice as likely as other states to convict people arrested on felony charges, and their sentences are more severe than those in other regions. As observed earlier, however, crime rates and incarceration rates are not closely related. Some states with relatively high rates of crime lock up fewer people than do other states with lower crime rates.

One striking inconsistency is the extremely high lockup rate of African Americans in state and federal prisons. Black men are six times as likely as white men to be locked up; they comprise about 40 percent of the male prison population, according to federal statistics. This imbalance has been attributed to poverty, poor education, and other demographics of criminal activity, which drive up the black crime rate, as well as law enforcement's focus on crack cocaine, which is found predominantly in the inner-city black communities.[55] Possession of crack is punished more severely in the courts than offenses involving other illegal drugs. The political climate also matters: States dominated by conservative Republicans tend to imprison disproportionate rates of blacks.[56] Similarly, Latino defendants tend to receive harsher sentences than whites.[57] It should not come as a surprise that blacks

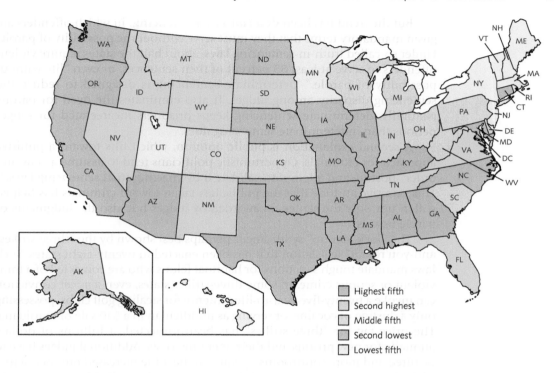

Figure 16.3 Prisoners (per 100,000 Residents) Incarcerated in State and Federal Correctional Institutions, by State, as of 2016

Source: Bureau of Justice Statistics, Annual Surveys of Probation and Parole, Deaths in Custody Reporting Program: Annual Summary on Inmates under Jail Jurisdiction, and National Prisoner Statistics Program, 2013. The adult resident population estimates are based on unpublished U.S. adult state resident populations on January 1, 2014.

and Latinos are much more suspicious of police and distrustful of criminal justice systems than are whites. With some 2.1 million prisoners (226,000 federal, 1.291 million state, and 631,000 local),[58] and an incarceration rate of 660 inmates per 100,000 population,[59] the United States has the highest incarceration rate in the world. With only 5 percent of the earth's people, the United States has about one-quarter of the world's prisoners.

Why is our incarceration rate so high? First, prison sentences are harsh compared with those in other countries. Historically, state courts applied **indeterminate sentencing,** whereby judges have great discretion in deciding the number of years for which an offender should be sentenced to prison. The offender then becomes eligible for parole after a minimum period is served, based on good behavior and meeting prison goals. For instance, a ten- to twenty-year sentence for armed robbery might require the inmate to serve at least five years. After that time, he becomes eligible for parole, subject to the judgment of a parole board, which reviews the case and the prisoner's behavior in prison.

indeterminate sentencing Sentencing in which a judge exercises discretion when deciding on the number of years for the sentence.

But the trend has been **determinate sentencing**, in which offenders are given mandatory terms that they must serve without the possibility of parole. Under so-called truth-in-sentencing laws, about half the states require violent offenders to serve at least 85 percent of their sentences, or even "life without possibility of parole." Determinate sentencing is designed to reduce the sentencing disparity among judges. It also eliminates the need for parole. Naturally, determinate sentencing keeps prisoners incarcerated for longer periods than indeterminate sentencing does.

A second explanation is public opinion, which tilts toward a punitive approach for criminals. Opportunistic politicians tend to assume a "law and order" posture and attempt to validate it by enacting strict sentencing laws.[60] This punitive attitude that the public has taken toward criminals has helped stiffen not only the sentences awarded by judges but also the judgments of parole boards.

The "lock-'em-up" syndrome is perhaps best shown by the "three-strikes-and-you're-out" legislation that has been enacted in twenty-eight states. Such laws mandate tough sanctions for habitual felons who are convicted of a third violent or serious crime. In some three-strikes states, even a *minor* conviction can invoke a twenty-five-year-to-life sentence for stealing golf clubs, possessing only a dusting of cocaine, or serving as middleman in a $10 sale of marijuana. The price tag for "three strikes" has been projected at billions of dollars annually for new prisons and their operating costs. Additional judges have to be hired and more courtrooms operated to hear the increased number of jury trials. As a consequence, three-strikes laws are rarely applied in most states. In California, where the three-strikes law had imprisoned nearly 4,000 offenders for life for committing nonviolent (mostly drug-related) crimes, courts interpreted a 2016 constitutional amendment increasing parole opportunities for nonviolent offenders as applying to "strikers."

A third contributing factor to high imprisonment rates is drug enforcement penalties. Most drug-related offenses do not involve violence and are "victimless," yet they have been severely punished as part of the failed war on drugs. As mentioned earlier, we "lost" the war on drugs many years ago. Drug supplies are ample and cheap, yet large proportions of our jails and prisons are populated with nonviolent drug offenders.

States are rethinking mandatory minimum sentences for drug offenders. Arkansas, Louisiana, New York, Texas, and other states have rolled them back, favoring community-based drug treatment programs instead. California voters passed an initiative that mandates treatment rather than prison for first and second drug offenses. By diverting and treating drug offenders, such policy changes have significantly reduced prison populations in some states.[61]

But most criminals *are* doing more time, and prisons are increasingly serving as expensive geriatric hospitals for relatively harmless criminals who are senior citizens. Prisoners aged fifty-five or older account for about 12 percent of state prisoners, a figure that is expected to rise sharply. Already, states are grouping aging inmates within assisted living correctional facilities and nursing homes for their special health care needs, as well as to protect them from younger, more violent inmates.[62] The average yearly cost of

determinate sentencing Mandatory sentencing that is determined by law, not a judge's discretion.

housing a sickly, geriatric prisoner, who may have ailments ranging from HIV/AIDS, liver or kidney disease, to mental illness or dementia, can run three times the amount for a younger, healthy inmate. Yet "criminal menopause" apparently afflicts felons in their twilight years, making them unlikely to commit a new crime if released.

Prison Conditions

As noted earlier, 1.9 million people are confined to state prisons and local jails in the United States. The number of prisoners was growing by about 4 percent annually until 2010, when lower crime rates and state sentencing reforms helped reverse the trend. Prisons continue to operate beyond official capacity in many states, despite the construction of numerous new facilities to reduce the problems of prison overcrowding and its accompanying conditions of poor sanitation, inadequate health care, and high levels of violence. Traditionally, courts assumed a hands-off policy toward offenders once they were behind prison walls. The administration of state correctional systems was the sole responsibility of corrections officials. But in a series of decisions, the federal courts applied the Eighth Amendment prohibition on cruel and unusual punishment and the Fourteenth Amendment provision for due process and equal protection of the laws to prison inmates. In addition, the Supreme Court permitted inmates of state and local facilities to bypass less sympathetic state courts and file suits alleging violations of their civil rights in federal courts. Such federal court rulings have altered the nature of correctional policy and changed it greatly.

Much of the litigation has concerned overcrowding. As more and more people were sentenced to prison, corrections officials responded by doubling, tripling, and even quadrupling cell arrangements. It was not unusual for inmates to be crowded together at the rate of one per ten square feet of floor space. Drastic improvements were long overdue in Arkansas and other states. At Arkansas's dreaded maximum-security institution, Cumming Farms, inmates were worked in the fields like slaves, ten hours a day, six days a week, in all types of weather. At night they slept in 100-man barracks. Rapes and other forms of physical violence occurred regularly. A federal lawsuit led to the finding that Arkansas's entire penal system was in violation of the Eighth Amendment.

The adult prison systems of several states are presently being run under federal court orders. In 2009, a panel of federal judges ordered California officials to reduce the state prison population by 40,591 inmates, to a total of 110,000, within two years. By operating prisons at 190 percent of capacity, California was found to be in violation of the Eighth Amendment's prohibition of cruel and unusual punishment, particularly for sick and mentally ill inmates.[63] An average of one death per week was being registered as inmates suffered from medical malpractice and inattention.[64] State officials facing decisions on how to comply with the court order transferred certain categories of prisoners to county jails and provided funds to assist the counties in constructing new jails and other expenses. Early release was ordered for thousands of inmates to further reduce crowding.

The intrusion of the federal courts into state correctional policy is quite controversial, particularly when they have taken over full operating responsibility or ordered increased state and local expenditures for prisons or mass inmate releases. Important questions concerning the proper division of power between the national government and the states have been raised, as have questions about the competence of federal court officials to run state prison systems. However these important issues in federalism are ultimately resolved, the immediate problem for many states is providing adequate space for their prison populations and finding the money to pay for it.

Prisons have become financial albatrosses. On average, corrections spending trails only education and Medicaid in state budget allocations. State and local spending on prisons and jails, currently estimated at over $53 billion a year, rose at a startling rate of 166 percent from 1992 to 2018.[65] Room, board, and care for one state prison inmate averages about $30,000 per year but can reach up to $60,000 for maximum security prisons. Prison and jail guards must be paid; prisoners fed and tended to. And each new prison bed space for growing ranks of confined criminals can cost up to $100,000. Prison costs are also escalating as a result of health care inflation. Prisoners are a particularly unhealthy subset of the population: Most smoke, many are drug abusers, some have acute mental problems, a troubling proportion is HIV positive, and a growing number are seniors. One of the unintended consequences of "three strikes and you're out" and similar laws has been the increase in inmates who are serving long sentences or life without parole. In 1984, some 34,000 prisoners in state prisons were serving life without parole sentences; in 2016, that number had increased to almost 162,000. Adding in prisoners with sentences of fifty years or more (virtual life sentences), the number swells to more than 206,000, or one in every seven people currently in prison.[66]

Another large percentage of the current jail and prison population in the United States are those in pretrial detention. Many people detained in local jails are there because they were arrested and are awaiting trial. They typically did not have the financial resources to post bail and await trial without being incarcerated. One recent estimate is that nearly three-quarters of the 631,000 prisoners in local jails have not been convicted of a crime. The same study concludes that the increase in pretrial detainees in local jails from 1997 to 2017 accounted for virtually all of the local jail growth over that twenty-year time period.[67] In 2015, the median income for people who could post bail and wait for trial outside of jail was nearly $40,000 for men and $23,000 for women; for those who were unable to meet bail, the median income was less than $16,000 for men and just over $11,000 for women.[68] Because of this three states—Alaska, New Jersey, and New York—recently abolished cash bail for most criminal cases. Voters in California rejected this in a 2020 statewide referendum.

There seems to be no easy end in sight for prison spending, because of "Murphy's Law of Incarceration": The number of inmates expands to fill all available space, or "if you build them, you'll fill them." However, the prison-building boom is tapering off for three reasons: Many new prisons have already come online, states are adopting alternatives to incarceration, and state budget problems have resulted in significant cuts to corrections budgets.

The COVID-19 pandemic put a huge strain on prisons and jails throughout the United States. Rates of infection in correctional facilities soared as it became difficult or impossible to isolate those infected with the virus from those who were virus free. Early in the pandemic, before prisons and jails limited and then ended visitation, visitors infected prisoners and guards. Infections were then passed from prisoner to guard and from guard to prisoner. In spring 2020, eight of the ten COVID-19 hotspots in the United States were prisons and jails.[69] Cook County Jail in Chicago, Rikers Island in New York, and Harris County Jail in Texas showed widespread outbreaks of the virus. Inmates in Kansas, New York, and Washington state engaged in protests—some violent—over issues of housing healthy prisoners and infected ones together.[70] Public health officials had previously warned that the overcrowded and unsanitary conditions in jails and prisons represented a breeding ground for the virus.[71] As one researcher said, "there's basically no way in the crowded conditions that exist in current jails and prisons to implement social distancing."[72] "Our jails are petri dishes," said the president of the Cook County (Chicago) Board of Commissioners.[73] In response to the pandemic, some states began limiting transfers from local jails to state prisons (North Carolina); others put moratoriums on accepting new inmates (Alabama, Colorado); while a third group began releasing nonviolent inmates who were at risk of developing the disease (California, New York).

Policy Alternatives for States and Localities

LO 16-8
To discuss correctional policy alternatives for states and localities.

In addition to the immediate responses made necessary by federal court actions and budget shortfalls, states and localities are attempting to devise a more comprehensive approach to coping with the problem of prison over-crowding. Whatever their past failings, and primarily for reasons of budget rather than conscience, they are demonstrating today an increasing propensity for experimentation and innovation. Three basic strategies are being employed to bring and keep inmate populations in line with institutional capacity: back-door strategies, front-door strategies, and capacity enhancement.

Back-Door Strategies

Back-door strategies include several methods for releasing offenders from prisons on probation or parole before they have served their full sentences. This strategy is the most conventional of the three, but some interesting innovations are being tested.

One of the less imaginative but nonetheless quite effective ways to deal with prison overcrowding is to grant early release. Most states have early-release programs in place, but the method of implementation varies. In some states, the governor or parole board simply pares off the last few months or weeks of sentences that are nearly completed, until the necessary number of inmates have left the prison. Other states apply a risk analysis approach that predicts the likelihood that certain inmates, if released, will not commit another serious offense. For example, nonviolent offenders are freed before violent offenders, larcenists before burglars, marijuana users before heroin dealers, and so on. An inmate's personal characteristics, prison behavior, and work history may also be taken into consideration. Early release reduces inmate populations quickly, but public outcries are certain to follow when an offender released before expiration of their sentence commits a highly publicized violent crime. Ex-cons discharged without oversight and assistance are not likely to become model citizens overnight. Old habits and felonious friends tend to return, and most employers hesitate to hire a convicted felon. Today, felons incarcerated during the lock-'em-up mentality of the 1990s and early 2000s are returning home in record numbers. Past patterns indicate that many will become repeat offenders within three years, a "revolving door" problem that states and localities ignore at their own peril.

Reinventing Parole Many states are taking a close look at new civilian reentry approaches for convicts to boost their chances for successful transition from behind prison walls to the streets. Job-related skills training, placement services, and alcohol and drug counseling (80 percent of ex-cons are released with substance abuse problems) are typical. New, more comprehensive programs are also receiving experimentation. Maryland's Reentry Partnership develops collaborative transition plans for inmates. The state corrections and parole division, local police and health departments, and community organizations work together to determine (with the prisoner's input) individual needs, including counseling, transportation, and housing. Caseworkers and a prisoner's advocate coordinate the services. Hawaii's Opportunity Probation with Enforcement (HOPE) program has reduced recidivism by half through imposing correctional "time outs" for backsliding offenders. Anyone violating the terms of parole or probation is sent immediately back to jail for a few days, then given another opportunity.[74]

parole
Program in which offenders are released from prison to serve the remainder of their sentence under community supervision.

probation
Instead of incarceration, this program permits minor offenders to remain in the community under supervision, or to serve brief sentences followed by probation.

Programs such as these are much cheaper than what it takes to keep an inmate locked up—a daily cost of less than $10 for probationers and parolees, versus up to $100 to keep an offender behind bars.[75]

Conventional **parole** or **probation** has not been particularly effective, although these programs account for three out of four individuals in the corrections population. In most states that utilize this technique, the parole and probation officers (whose duty it is to keep up with the progress of the released offender) are terribly overworked. An estimated 4.5 million adults are under parole supervision.[76] It is not unknown for one parole officer to be responsible for 200 offenders—a nearly impossible task. (The average is about 60 parolees per case officer and about 100 probationers.)[77] Most probationers and parolees are supposed to receive substance abuse counseling, pay restitution to their victims, or comply with other terms of their release, but many do not. About 19 percent soon end up back behind bars for parole violations.[78]

Innovations in probation and parole can save serious money. Texas expanded drug treatment programs, reformed parole practices, and established drug courts. As a result, it has saved nearly $1 billion in new prison costs.[79]

Electronic House Detention Electronic house detention is a popular way to cope with prison overcrowding. Ankle bracelets monitor a released inmate's movements and if the person strays too far police are notified. Electronic monitoring is much cheaper than jail or prison (the cost is about $5,500 a year in Florida), and it enables a working prisoner to pay their own share of the program and, in some cases, to repay the victim of the crime as well. But it has not been found to significantly reduce new offenses, escapes, or recidivism, though the evidence is mixed.[80] But it is not appropriate for an escape-minded individual, who can cut off the anklet and walk away, perhaps to commit more crimes.

Vocational Programs Another back-door strategy reduces the sentences of prisoners who participate in educational and vocational programs. These programs are intended to teach convicts skills that can help them obtain jobs once they are out of prison, and they have the added benefits of keeping inmates involved in productive, rather than destructive, activities while behind prison walls and saving the state money. Education and vocational training both reduce recidivism and improve job prospects when prisoners are released.[81] This would seem to be a good investment, since 95 percent of prisoners are eventually released back into the community.

The idea of profiting from prison work has considerable appeal. In addition to using their time productively and learning marketable skills, inmates earn wages that can help defray the cost of their room and board, provide monetary restitution to victims, fund savings accounts for the inmates to use after their release, and even earn early release. Several programs have had encouraging results, including making stained-glass windows and restoring classic cars in Nevada prisons, training and socializing rescued dogs for adoption in Oklahoma and Kansas, fighting forest fires in Oregon and Georgia, saddle making and tilapia raising and packaging in Colorado, and sewing everything from bed covers to Victoria's Secret lingerie in South Carolina. Prison industries may include more conventional activities like printing, metalworking, textiles, signs and license plates, and basic manufacturing.

Front-Door Strategies

The second basic strategy used to balance the number of prisoners with the supply of beds is the front-door approach, which aims to keep minor offenders out of prison in the first place by directing them into alternative programs.

Creative Sentencing One front-door strategy is to grant judges more flexibility in determining sentences. **Creative sentencing**, also known as evidence-based sentencing, permits judges or community boards to match

creative sentencing Sentencing in which the punishment matches the crime and the characteristics of the convicted person.

the punishment with the crime while keeping the nonviolent offender in society. A common option is community service—sentencing the offender to put in a specified number of hours cleaning up parks or streets; working in a public hospital; painting public buildings; or performing specialized tasks related to the person's professional expertise, such as dentistry or accounting.

Another option is to link the sentence to available prison space. This about-face from determinate sentencing is applied in an elaborate grid in North Carolina that helps judges balance the seriousness of a crime and the perpetrator's past criminal record with the number of beds available in the prison system. In determining the length of the sentence, the judge refers to the grid for minimum and maximum terms. Offenders must serve at least the minimum term without the possibility of parole. Nonviolent offenders such as petty thieves, embezzlers, and minor drug offenders are assigned to halfway houses, drug treatment, or other programs.

Yet another strategy is for judges to assess fines in lieu of prison for relatively serious nonviolent crimes. A substantial fine, some argue, is just as strong a deterrent as a short stay in jail. So is the loss of a valued personal belonging. A Texas judge ordered a father who physically abused his son to spend the next thirty nights sleeping in the family doghouse (no explanation is offered of where the dog slept).

Regional Restitution Centers Another front-door strategy used in Florida, Texas, Georgia, and other states is the *regional restitution center* (also known as *diversion centers*), a variation on the standard work-release center. Nonviolent offenders are housed in restitution centers near their homes and work in the community during the day; they receive regular supervision. Their paychecks are turned over to center staff members, who subtract expenses for food and housing and distribute the remainder to the offenders' victims as restitution, to the court for payment of fines, and to the offenders' spouses and children for support. Anything left over belongs to the inmates.

Diversion of the Mentally Ill from Jail or Emergency Room A surprisingly large amount of police time is given to dealing with the mentally ill who may present a threat to others or to themselves. Usually, police apprehend such a person and take them directly to jail or an emergency room. Neither place is equipped to handle mental illnesses adequately. But San Antonio, Texas, and other cities are trying something different called "smart justice." In San Antonio, police officers take a required forty-hour course learning how to handle mental health crises. Instead of jail or the hospital, the Restoration Center, with a psych unit and medical assistance, is available for the troubled individual.[82]

Intensive Probation Supervision A third front-door strategy is *intensive probation supervision (IPS)*. IPS is somewhat like house arrest because it is designed to keep first-time offenders guilty of a serious but usually nonviolent crime (e.g., drunk driving, drug possession or distribution) out of state institutions. Those who qualify for the program face intense, highly intrusive supervision and surveillance for a prescribed period. Among other things, IPS requires face-to-face contacts between offenders and the IPS staff each week in the office, on the job, or in the home; random alcohol and drug testing and mandatory counseling for abusers; weekly employment verification; and an early nightly curfew (usually 8:00 p.m.). The program is basically self-supporting because probationers pay money into the program, in addition to any restitution they provide to their victims. Prisons get much-needed breathing space and save a substantial sum of money for each offender diverted from prison.

A front-door approach to easing prison overcrowding now losing favor is boot camps, or *shock incarceration*. Young (17- to 25-year-old) first-time felony offenders are given the option of serving their prison term or spending several months in a **shock incarceration** center, which resembles boot camp in the U.S. Marine Corps. In fact, former marine drill instructors are often in charge. Those inmates who successfully complete the three- to six-month program earn early release. Those who fall short are assigned to the regular prison population.

Shock incarceration is aimed at more than just relief of prison overcrowding. It is also intended to teach self-control and self-discipline to young people who come from dysfunctional homes or from selfish, undisciplined personal backgrounds. If shock incarceration had the long-term impact its advocates claim, it should keep thousands of young offenders from becoming recidivists; however, boot-camp dropout rates are high, and in most states the recidivism rate for graduates is similar to that for the regular prison population. Of course, dropouts and recidivists end up in prison, canceling any savings generated from boot camp. Savings are also lost when judges assign youths to boot camp instead of probation. Disappointing results have led several states, including Arizona, New York, and California, to close their camps.

Capacity Enhancement

Capacity enhancement is the third major strategy for matching available prison beds with the number of inmates. Usually it entails construction of new prison facilities, which is very costly; operating them is even more so. Some states, most recently Virginia, completed new facilities but were not been able to afford to staff and run them. Many taxpayers resent spending so much money on the care and feeding of criminals—although, ironically, they want criminals to be locked up. Others oppose having a new prison located in their community. But poor, rural areas often perceive prisons to be a desirable form of economic development. A new prison typically brings 300 institutional jobs with 1,000 inmates. Prisons are supply-driven, and the flow of criminals is dependable. Prisons also purchase local goods and services. They pay sales taxes, water and sewer fees, and landfill charges. Also, because

shock incarceration
Prison boot camps provide this option for young offenders, who receive paramilitary and physical training intended to "shock" the offender into staying out of trouble and learning self-discipline.

inmates are considered residents of local jurisdictions, their presence means more federal and state funding.

The prison construction boom seems to have hit pause for now, primarily for financial reasons, a falling crime rate, early release policies, and alternatives to incarceration. Some states, however, have saved on the cost of building new prisons by sending prisoners to other states that might have excess prison capacity. Called "the prisoner trade" by one researcher, a state may pay up to $76 a day to another state to house prisoners. While such interstate transfer of prisoners was rare in the early twentieth century, it became much more popular after the 1983 U.S. Supreme Court decision in *Olim v Wakinekona.*[83]

Private Prisons A popular capacity enhancement innovation is private prisons, or prisons for profit, an idea spawned from the near hopelessness of many overcrowded state correctional systems. The private sector has long provided certain services and programs to prisons, including health care, food services, and alcohol and drug treatment. Privately operated prisons existed more than 100 years ago in Louisiana, New York, and a handful of other states, but they were closed down amid revelations of prisoner abuse.

About 8.5 percent of incarcerated adults and juveniles are held in privately run correction institutions today. These institutions include medium-security prisons in Virginia, Texas, Oklahoma, and Tennessee. The two largest prison management firms, Corrections Corporation of America and Geo Group,[84] control 75 percent of the private corrections market (see the Controversies in States and Localities feature).

Does Prison Pay? The construction and operation of prisons has been the fastest-growing budget item in many states. Yet every dollar sunk into correctional facilities is one less to pay for highways, social services, education, and the needs of children. Our priorities seem skewed indeed when we invest only $4,000 to $8,000 per year for a child's education, whereas a prisoner costs up to ten times that amount to keep incarcerated.

Does prison pay by keeping repeat offenders out of action? cost-benefit analyses comparing the costs of incarceration with estimated savings to society from foregone burglaries, larcenies, murders, and rapes do indicate some net benefit to society. One study found that "prison pays for most state prisoners," especially those who are either repeat or violent offenders who pose an immediate danger if released.[85]

Prison does not pay, however, for drug offenders, most of whom could be placed under supervision or substance abuse counseling and treatment or released altogether. And it doesn't pay for older offenders who are no longer high-risk individuals. And as noted earlier, incarceration appears to have no measurable effect on the crime rate. States with the highest incarceration rates also have among the highest crime rates.

Controversies in States and Localities

Are Private Prisons a Good Idea?

Despite its rapid growth to 8.5 percent of the total prison population, prison privatization is controversial. Those who support it claim that prisons built and operated by the private sector save the taxpayers money. Because of less red tape, facilities can be constructed and operated more economically. Most important, advocates point out, private prisons reduce overcrowding.

Opponents of privatization, however, question whether firms can in fact build and operate correctional facilities significantly less expensively than state or local governments can. They believe that the profit motive is misplaced in a prison setting, where firms may skimp on nutritious food, health care, or skilled personnel to cut operating costs. A "prison-industrial complex," whose businesses profit from constructing and filling up cell space, lobbies and contributes campaign dollars to legislators in the interest of stricter sentencing requirements and additional private prisons. CCA and other private prison firms actually require occupancy of 80 to 100 percent to be guaranteed in their contracts.

Lately, evidence on the economics of prison privatization urges caution. Most of the private facilities house juveniles, illegal aliens, and minimum- and medium-security offenders. The majority of studies and several states' experiences indicate that operating cost savings have been marginal or much less than promised. An Arizona study found that operating private prisons actually cost $1,600 more per year than state prisons, even though the firms "cherry pick" healthy, low-maintenance inmates. Several states have taken over privately run prisons because of understaffing, safety issues, contract noncompliance, and other concerns.

Who should be responsible for prisons? Economic considerations are obviously important, but constitutional and legal issues challenge prisons for profit. A basic question is whether the delegation of the corrections function to a private firm is constitutionally permissible. So far, no major court has ruled to the contrary. However, the Supreme Court spoke on one related issue by declaring that private prison guards who violate inmates' rights are not entitled to qualified immunity—unlike public-sector guards.

Another set of considerations concerns practical accountability for the day-to-day operation of jails and prisons. Who is responsible for developing operational rules, procedures, and standards and for ensuring that they are carried out? What happens if prison employees strike? (Strikes by state correctional employees are illegal, but those by their private-sector counterparts are not.) What if the corporation hikes its fees substantially? Or shuts its doors because of an unprofitable shortage of inmates, as happened Texas in 2011? Or declares bankruptcy because of financial mismanagement or a liability suit? Who is liable if prisoners are abused and have their civil rights violated by a firm's guards, as happened with Missouri felons doing time in a Texas prison run by a Mississippi company? Consider this case: In Texas, two men escaped from a private prison near Houston. They nearly made it to Dallas before they were caught. But Texas authorities couldn't prosecute because by breaking out of a private facility, the men had not committed an offense under Texas law. The men, who had been sent to the private facility from Oregon, could not be prosecuted for escape in Oregon because the event happened in Texas.

Economic and legal issues aside, perhaps the most important question is, who *should* operate our jails and prisons? Legal scholar Ira Robbins suggests that we should remember the words of the novelist Fyodor Dostoevsky: "The degree of civilization in a society can be judged by entering its prisons." The state, after all, administers justice in the courtroom. Shouldn't it also be responsible for carrying out justice in the correctional facilities? Should profits be derived from depriving human beings of their freedom? Or does saving taxpayer dollars deserve consideration, too?

Critical Thinking Questions

1. Are private prisons a good idea? Explain your answer.
2. What are the proper roles of private sector entities in corrections? Are there any lines that should not be crossed?

Source: B. E. Price, *Merchandizing Prisoners: Who Really Pays for Prison Privatization* (Westport, CT: Praeger, 2006); Wharton Public Policy Initiative, "Private Prisons: An Evaluation of Economic and Ethical Implications" (January 25, 2018); Richard A. Oppel, Jr., "Private Prisons Found to Offer Little in Savings," https://www.nytimes.com/2011/05/19/us/19prisons.html (May 18, 2011); *Richardson v. McKnight* 138 L. Ed. 2d 540 (1997).

The Current Challenge in Crime and Corrections

The idea of placing people in prisons to punish them with deprivation of their freedom was devised only 200 years ago. Until fairly recently, brutality was the operating norm. Deliberately painful executions, maiming, flogging, branding, and other harsh punishments were applied to both serious and minor offenders. Misbehavior in prison was likely to be met with beatings or with more elaborate tortures such as stretching from ropes attached to a pulley in the ceiling or long confinement in an unventilated sweat box. By contrast, prison conditions in the states today seem almost luxurious. Inmates typically enjoy recreational activities, training and educational opportunities, televisions and other entertainment devices in their cells, and other amenities. Rules enforcement is also much more civilized and respectful of inmates' human rights. But a backlash is evident in some states. Surveys show that most citizens don't want criminals coddled. They agree with former Massachusetts governor William Weld that prisons should offer "a tour through the circles of hell"—not the easy life. Maricopa County, Arizona, sheriff Joe Arpaio became the icon for this idea when he opened a tent city prison made of Korean War–era tents in 1993. The prison remained in operation until 2017 when it was closed by his successor.

But state budget problems have forced a reality check. To cut corrections costs, states continue to shift money into community programs and treatment programs—both saving money compared to prison or jail. Several states, including Kansas and Michigan, have recently closed correctional facilities, generating savings from payroll and operating expenses. Both conservatives, such as Charles and the late David Koch, and liberals, such as the Center for American Progress, are questioning the cost-effectiveness of our current criminal justice system, especially as to how it addresses low-level drug offenses.[86] On the other hand, recidivism continues to haunt state corrections systems, and early release could produce more criminal activities. The result could be renewed citizen pressures to "lock 'em up."

Crime and corrections present major challenges to state and local governments. Certainly, any long-term success will have to come from the recognition that all major components of the criminal justice system are interrelated to some extent. Thus, a broad approach to courts, crime, and corrections is called for. That means beginning with the identification of at-risk children, creating an educational and social welfare support system for them, providing alcohol and drug abuse rehabilitation for prisoners and minor offenders, and helping to repair families and communities that are lacking in resources. It means addressing homelessness, poverty, and gangs. Some policies do seem to be driving down the crime rate. The aging of the U.S. population is an important factor, but so are technology enhancements and community-based activities such as community policing, drug treatment, and citywide crackdowns on gang leaders and serial offenders. Before the states can fully cope with the challenges described in this chapter, we must understand such complex relationships more fully and attack the causes of crime, as well as its effects.

Chapter Recap

- Crime data are collected through the FBI's *Uniform Crime Reports*, victimization surveys, and self-reports. All three sources show a reduction in crime.

- Criminal justice is overwhelmingly a state and local government responsibility, with modest federal involvement.

- Key actors in criminal justice policy are law enforcement officials, the courts, the public, victims, and the accused.

- Victimless crimes and capital punishment are two policy issues that illustrate the variation in state approaches to criminal justice policy.

- Corrections policy deprives some criminals of their freedom, but little rehabilitation occurs.

- Policy alternatives for addressing prison capacity problems include back-door and front-door strategies and making additional prison cells available. Prison privatization is one controversial approach.

- Crime and corrections have become perennial challenges for state and local governments.

Key Terms

fusion center (*p. 461*)
grand jury (*p. 463*)
indictment (*p. 463*)
victimless crimes (*p. 466*)

indeterminate sentencing (*p. 473*)
determinate sentencing (*p. 474*)

parole (*p. 478*)
probation (*p. 478*)
creative sentencing (*p. 479*)
shock incarceration (*p. 481*)

Internet Resources

Law enforcement and corrections-related sites proliferate on the web. A few of the more interesting include the Federal Bureau of Investigation (FBI) homepage at **www.fbi.gov** and the Police Guide at **www.policeguide.com**.

For community policing, see the Office of Community Oriented Policing (COPS) at **www.cops.usdoj.gov**.

Chilling yet fascinating collections of "last words" from Texas's busy death chamber may be read at **www.goodbyewarden.com** or **www.tdcj.state.tx.us**.

Links to most major criminal justice policy issues are available at **www.corrections.com**.

www.sentencingproject.org is a nonprofit organization that promotes alternatives to prison.

For corrections and sentencing data, and other valuable information, see **www.ojp.usdoj.gov/bjs/** and **www.ncjrs.org**. Another general source is the web address of the National Archive of Criminal Justice Data at **www.icpsr.umich.edu/NACJD**.

The Death Penalty Information Center (**www.deathpenaltyinfo.org**) provides a wealth of statistics and reports on capital punishment.

17

Social Welfare and Health Care Policy: Addressing Poverty and Sickness

A family with two children begs for money at a gas station.

Learning Objectives

LO 17-1 To explain the meaning of poverty and how it is measured.

LO 17-2 To analyze social welfare and ideology.

LO 17-3 To describe current social welfare policy.

LO 17-4 To define the types of social welfare programs.

LO 17-5 To discuss state innovations in social welfare.

LO 17-6 To explain how welfare checks can be turned into paychecks.

LO 17-7 To analyze federal and state health care policy.

Brandi Harris, a 30-year-old mother of two young children, is in desperate straits. Her live-in boyfriend left her eighteen months ago with nothing but a rented trailer and a 15-year-old Dodge. Unable to arrange day care, find work, and with the car barely running, Brandi sells everything of value she has. Following numerous eviction notices for unpaid rent, she now lives in the car and on the streets with her kids. The youngest child, a girl six years old, is ready to join her eight-year-old sister in school—but to which school district do they belong? And because of COVID-19, the local schools are telling parents to go online or to home school. The only internet service Brandi can find is at the public library and that has a long waiting list for users. The local homeless shelter looks to be unsafe for the children, and they cannot stay there for more than a few weeks anyway. Where should they go? What should they do? What resources are offered by the city, community organizations, state, or federal offices to help them in this time of need?

State and local governments must interact with people and situations such as these every day. There will always be people who, for various reasons, need help coping with poverty, unemployment, physical disabilities, drug or alcohol addiction, mental illness, or other burdens that afflict them either temporarily or permanently. Most of those who need assistance actively seek it out through federal, state, local, and nonprofit social welfare and health care programs. Some do not receive welfare benefits but choose to fight their battles themselves or perhaps with family assistance; some need temporary help until they get back on their feet again; and some will be dependent on government assistance for the rest of their lives. Many of the poor work full-time jobs at low wages; others have never drawn a paycheck.

Welfare and health care policy is an abiding concern in the states. With Congress bogged down in a swamp of rhetoric and partisan mudslinging, the states have embarked on a path of unprecedented health and welfare innovations. The growth in the states' capacity to design, develop, and administer such programs is remarkable. It is confirmation of their responsiveness to the problems besetting their citizens and to their capability to address some of the most difficult and persistent problems of our time both creatively and effectively.

Thinking About—and Measuring —Poverty

LO 17-I
To explain the meaning of poverty and how it is measured.

There are few cases of absolute deprivation in this country. The necessities of life—food, clothing, housing—are available to almost everyone through government programs and nonprofit organizations (the homeless represent a perplexing and painful exception). For many years, we took some comfort in the idea that the extreme, life-threatening poverty found in Sudan or Haiti simply does not occur here. (The World Bank defines absolute poverty as $1.90 a day or less to live on.) Then in 2015, the World Bank decided to measure extreme poverty not only in poor countries but also in wealthy ones. And the analysis showed some 3.7 million people (1.2 percent of the population) in the United States lived in extreme poverty.[1] This incredible finding prompted a two-week visit in 2017 by United Nations Special Rapporteur on Extreme Poverty and Human Rights. The rapporteur toured California, Alabama, Georgia, Puerto Rico, West Virginia, and Washington, D.C., and basically confirmed the World Bank findings,[2] a conclusion that created immediate controversy.[3] Most Americans tend to think of poverty in the United States not in this extreme form but as relative deprivation: People are poor when they have substantially less wealth and income than most others; and despite their best efforts, they have grave difficulty making ends meet. Within this wealthy nation, relative differences in wealth and income equality are profound and worsening. The United States has the highest degree of economic inequality among all advanced nations and one of the highest in the entire world.

The federal government uses a statistic called the *poverty threshold* to define poverty in quantitative terms. The amount has been set at three times the amount of income necessary to purchase essential food. The official poverty threshold changes each year as the cost of food rises (or, very rarely, falls). In 2020, it was pegged at $26,200 for a family of four and at $12,760 for an individual under age 65.[4] The poverty figure is important because it helps determine who qualifies for various forms of public assistance. More than thirty-eight million "officially" poor people lived in the United States in 2018, or around 11.8 percent of the population. In Louisiana and Mississippi, 19.8 percent of the state's population is officially poor; in New Hampshire, only 6.4 percent of the population is. In race and ethnicity comparisons, poverty rates ranged from 20.8 percent for African Americans and 17.6 percent for Latinos to 8.1 percent for whites and 10.1 percent for Asian Americans.[5]

Measuring poverty is far from an exact science. Government statistics fail to account for regional cost-of-living differences; variations in states' ability and willingness to fund welfare programs; a decline in the inflation-adjusted value of the minimum wage; changes in consumption patterns; the cost of housing, energy, child care, and health care; in-kind assistance such as food stamps; the earned income tax credit; and the value of off-the-books income and barter income earned by individuals. And the poverty threshold is based on outdated assumptions about relative food costs and preferences taken from the year 1963! It is widely acknowledged that the official poverty numbers are inexact. Some economists say the figures significantly understate the actual degree of poverty, but others believe the opposite is true.[6]

Poverty in the United States was once associated largely with old age, but this view is no longer true. As the population has grown older, senior citizens have organized as a formidable interest group. Social Security benefits, federal programs such as Medicare, and age-based preferences in local property and state income taxes have eased elderly people's financial burdens. Today, only 9.7 percent of those aged 65 and older are considered poor. The most alarming poverty victims are children: Some 16 percent live in poverty, including almost 30 percent of African American children from birth to age 18.[7] In the context of limited government resources, a generational reckoning is inevitable; society will have to decide how to allocate its resources between the old and the young. Social Security and Medicare outlays to seniors are growing rapidly as a proportion of federal spending, while children's poverty statistics and youth unemployment remain disturbingly high.

Household composition also affects poverty. While some 9 percent of all households were below the poverty line in 2018, single parent–headed households had much higher poverty rates than families with two parents. Nearly 25 percent of female-headed households with no husband present were below the poverty line while just under 13 percent of male-headed households with no wife present were. In comparison, less than 5 percent of married couple families were below the poverty line.[8]

Social Welfare and Ideology

LO 17-2
To analyze social welfare and ideology.

Intense debates over political ideology and values have always stormed across the social welfare policy landscape, resulting in confused policy goals and a faulty, confusing patchwork of programs. Conservatives and liberals have propounded starkly opposing points of view on the causes of poverty and the appropriate government response.

Conservatives (usually Republications, Libertarians, or Tea Partiers), who generally believe in a restricted role for government, have tended to accept a modern version of the nineteenth-century view that "the giving of relief is a violation of natural law."[9] According to this viewpoint, the poor are victims of their own deficiencies. If they are to rise above poverty, they must hoist themselves up by their own bootstraps. In other words, they must work hard and live prudently. From this perspective, the poor get what they deserve. Conservatives attack the social welfare system for interfering with "the free market," discouraging more productive allocations of public funds, undermining the work ethic, encouraging immoral behavior, and creating a permanent "underclass" of dependent welfare recipients. Conservatives favor policies that encourage marriage; discourage illegitimacy, unmarried sex, and teen pregnancy; promote individual responsibility; and cut welfare spending and dependency on public support.[10]

For liberals (usually Democrats, or progressives), who generally believe in a broad and active role for government, poverty is a structural problem. People fall into poverty largely because of factors essentially beyond their control, such as inadequate schooling, poor and/or dysfunctional parents, divorce, lack of jobs, various forms of discrimination, and the up-and-down cycles of a capitalistic economy. According to this view, most people cannot help being poor; and so it becomes the responsibility of government not only to relieve their poverty through public assistance programs but also to provide the poor with the appropriate skills and physical environment to enable them to become self-sufficient.

What does the typical American think about welfare? Contrary to conventional wisdom, most Americans favor government efforts to help the poor and are willing to pay taxes to assist them. But people do tend to make a distinction between the "deserving" poor and those who are not willing to work and be personally responsible for their behavior. Media reports, conservative talk shows, and racial stereotyping contribute to the widespread—but erroneous—belief that most welfare recipients are African Americans who lack a work ethic and behave irresponsibly.[11]

The Origins of Social Welfare Policy

Social welfare programs developed later in the United States than in Western European nations. The U.S. programs in place today are also much less uniform and generous than those in Western Europe. These differences have been attributed to the federal system and especially to the competition among states for economic development. States attempt to create an attractive business climate characterized by low taxes and limited social program expenditures. This means less money for social services.

Our fragmented social welfare policy is a reflection of shifting conservative and liberal control of Congress and the presidency, and the inherently controversial nature of redistributive policies—those that result in taking from one group of people to give to another.

Although its roots may be traced back to pensions for Revolutionary War veterans and their widows, the basic foundations of the welfare system were laid by the liberal Democratic administration of Franklin D. Roosevelt in response to the Great Depression of the 1930s. Private charity and state and local relief programs were completely inadequate for combating a 25 percent unemployment rate and a collapsed national economy. The federal government responded with massive programs designed to provide temporary relief through public assistance payments, job creation, and Social Security. Since the 1930s, competing political parties and ideologies have sewn together a patchwork of programs to help the poor and unfortunate. The most far-reaching effort was President Lyndon B. Johnson's "War on Poverty" in the 1960s, which included VISTA, the Job Corps, food stamps, and the Elementary and Secondary Education Act, among many other programs. It is estimated that today there are more than 170 separate federal anti-poverty programs, and many more at the state and local levels.

A Social Welfare Consensus

A social welfare consensus emerged among conservatives and liberals and led to a coalition for reform in the late 1980s. Conservatives admitted government's responsibility to help the truly needy and economically vulnerable, and liberals saw the need to attach certain obligations to welfare and to address the behavioral dependency of the underclass. Behavioral dependency means that poor people become dependent on government for their economic well-being by reason of their own choices, and it is a serious problem for this country's underclass, which is disproportionately young, male, minority, and urban. Many of these people are school and societal dropouts—borderline illiterates with no job skills. A disproportionate number become involved in drugs and crime. Agreement existed that welfare dependency must be reduced so that people can get off the dole and on the job. For those involved in crime and illegal drug activity, aggressive law enforcement, incarceration, substance abuse counseling and treatment, or social work were called for.

The social welfare consensus was broad enough to enable congressional passage of the Family Support Act of 1988. This law incorporated conservative principles of personal responsibility with liberal principles of poverty relief. Then, in 1996, President Clinton made good on his promise to end welfare as we know it by signing a law that eliminated the nation's largest welfare program, Aid to Families with Dependent Children (AFDC). Eligibility for federal welfare benefits was limited to no more than five years. With this law, an enormous challenge was thrown down to state and local governments to assume the lead in helping the poor exchange welfare checks for paychecks.

This consensus reflected a somewhat common, mainstream view of poverty, but disagreement about how to solve the problem persists. The consensus worked well in the good economic times of the late 1990s but began unraveling in the early 2000s. Most agree that different types of poverty should be treated distinctively. For example, children, seniors, the disabled, single parents, working adults, and nonworking adults all have different needs. Many also agree that government should help those who can climb out of poverty through job training and other programs and that able-bodied welfare recipients have an obligation to seek and secure a job or perform public work. Beyond these basic elements, the consensus tends to unravel. Conservatives seek better behavior from the poor, admonishing them to complete high school, find jobs (even at low wages), and either get married and stay married or not have babies at all and get off welfare. Liberals are more willing to utilize social programs to transfer government resources to the poor, with fewer conditions.

It's simple to say that public assistance recipients should just "get a job." But with unemployment soaring to nearly 15 percent during the trough of the COVID-19 pandemic (the highest rate since the Great Depression of the 1930s), jobs were very hard to find, especially for workers paid on an hourly basis. A significant proportion of the population dwells in "deep poverty," without work *or* welfare, struggling to get by from one day to the next.[12] The plight of the poor remains complex and multifaceted. There may be very little absolute poverty in the United States, but relative poverty—referred to today as inequality—has risen at a shocking rate. The top 1 percent of households receives nearly 23 percent of all income today, while the income share of the bottom 10 percent has fallen deeply.[13]

Current Social Welfare Policy

During and after the Great Depression, social welfare policy became primarily the responsibility of the federal government, with limited roles reserved to the states and localities. The states brought the various federal programs into action, administered them, and drew up rules to determine who was eligible for benefits. But with the 1996 welfare reform bill, entitled the Personal Responsibility and Work Opportunity Reconciliation Act (PRWORA), the federal government ceded a large portion of the policy field to the states and localities. Replacing AFDC was a new program, **Temporary Assistance for Needy Families (TANF)**, which emphasized maximum state discretion. As a consequence, state and local governments are in the vanguard of innovation and program experimentation, perhaps even more so than in other public policy fields.

temporary assistance for needy families (TANF) A provision of the Personal Responsibility and Work Opportunity Reconciliation Act (PRWORA) of 1996, which replaced AFDC with a flexible program that allows states to set their own conditions and benefit levels for welfare recipients to help them secure and maintain employment.

LO 17-3
To describe current social welfare policy.

Dramatic variations among the states exist in levels of social welfare spending. Massachusetts, New York, and Alaska generally spend more per person on public assistance than Mississippi, Alabama, and South Carolina. Some states pay relatively high benefits for one program, such as Medicaid, but relatively low benefits for another, such as TANF—the result of battles among various constituencies over a limited social welfare pie. States controlled by the Democratic Party tend to be more generous than Republican-dominated states, and strong party competition within a state drives up benefit levels. Race is important: Eligibility policies are stricter, and benefits are lower in states with high African American caseloads.[14] Political beliefs have an impact as well. The relationship between a dominant liberal or conservative ideology and state welfare spending levels should be obvious.

LO 17-4
To define the types of social welfare programs.

Types of Social Welfare Programs

Together, social welfare programs provide a safety net for those less fortunate and those who have fallen on hard times. They may be sorted into two basic categories: public assistance and social insurance. Public assistance programs, such as Medicaid and TANF, involve government payments of money or in-kind benefits to disadvantaged people who meet various qualifying criteria. Social insurance programs, such as Social Security, include recipient contributions (e.g., the Social Security payroll tax) as well as government payments. Our concern in this chapter is primarily with public assistance programs.

To convey a basic understanding of the complex intergovernmental web of social welfare policies, we examine the most significant ones individually. For purposes of discussion, we divide public assistance policies into two types: direct cash transfers and in-kind benefits. Social insurance programs also receive attention (see Table 17.1). Most social welfare programs are so-called entitlement programs, meaning that these are government spending programs with eligibility criteria. If a recipient meets the criteria (age, income, etc.), they are entitled to the benefit.

Direct Cash Transfers

Direct cash transfers are welfare programs that directly convey money, in the form of government checks, to qualified recipients. Administrative arrangements vary by type of program. *Aid to Families with Dependent Children* was included in the Social Security Act of 1935 to furnish financial aid to poor children whose fathers had died. By 1996, however, AFDC payments went almost entirely (90 percent) to single-parent families in which the living father was absent.

direct cash transfers
The transfer of cash, such as in the form of a disability check, from one level of government to an individual citizen beneficiary.

AFDC was the most costly and most controversial social welfare program in the United States. Critics claimed that it caused marriages to break up or to be consciously avoided; encouraged young, nonworking, unwed women to have babies; promoted migration of the poor to states paying higher AFDC benefits; and perpetuated dependency into future generations. No one professed fondness for AFDC, not even the recipients.

Table 17.1 Major Social Welfare and Social Insurance Programs

PROGRAM CATEGORY AND NAME	NUMBER OF RECIPIENTS (IN MILLIONS)	WHO FUNDS	WHO ADMINISTERS	TOTAL EXPENDITURES (IN BILLIONS OF DOLLARS)
DIRECT CASH TRANSFER				
TANF[a]	3.1	National, state	State	26.8
SSI[b]	8.1	National	National, state	56.4
Earned Income Tax Credit[c]	25	National	National	63
IN-KIND PROGRAM				
Supplemental Nutrition Assistance Program (formerly Food Stamps)[d]	35.7	National	State, local	60.4
Medicaid[e]	70.6	National, state	State, local	406 (national $)
Child Nutrition[f]	35.6	National	State, local	23.5
Children's Health Insurance Program (CHIP)[g]	9.4	National, state	State	17.2
SOCIAL INSURANCE				
Social Security (OASDI)[h]	62.9	National	National	1,044
Medicare[i]	58.7	National, state	National, state	750
Unemployment compensation[j]	3.2	State, private	State	6.4
Worker's compensation[k]	9.3	State, private	State	62

Source: All data are the most recent available. [a]Congressional Research Service, "The Temporary Assistance for Needy Families (TANF) Block Grant: Responses to Frequently Asked Questions, https://fas.org/sgp/crs/misc/RL32760.pdf (December 30, 2019); [b]Social Security Administration, "SSA Budget Information," https://www.ssa.gov/budget/FY21Files/FY21-JEAC.pdf (accessed April 14, 2020); [c]"Earned Income Tax Credit and Other Refundable Credits," https://www.eitc.irs.gov/eitc-central/eitc-information-for-press/eitc-information-for -the-press (accessed April 15, 2020); [d]U.S. Department of Agriculture, "SNAP Data Tables: Participation and Costs," https://www.fns.usda .gov/pd/supplemental-nutrition-assistance-program-snap (accessed April 10, 2020); [e]"State Medicaid and CHIP Applications, Eligibility Determinations and Enrollment Data," https://data.medicaid.gov/Enrollment/State-Medicaid-and-CHIP-Applications-Eligibility-D/n5ce -jxme (accessed April 14, 2020); [f]USDA, "Program Data Overview," https://www.fns.usda.gov/pd/overview (April 10, 2020); [g]Medicaid and CHIP Payment and Access Commission, "Most Current MACStats Compiled," https://www.macpac.gov/publication/macstats-compiled / (December 2019); [h]Social Security Administration, "Fast Facts and Figures About Social Security, 2019," https://www.ssa.gov/policy/docs /chartbooks/fast_facts/2019/fast_facts19.html (accessed April 14, 2020); [i]Centers for Medicare and Medicaid Services, "2018 Medicare Enrollment Section," https://www.cms.gov/files/document/2018-mdcr-enroll-ab-2.pdf (February 13, 2020) and "NHE Fact Sheet" https://www.cms.gov/Research-Statistics-Data-and-Systems/Statistics-Trends-and-Reports/NationalHealthExpendData/NHE-Fact-Sheet (March 24, 2020); [j]U.S. Department of Labor, "Unemployment Insurance Data: 4th Quarter 2019 Summary Tables," https://oui.doleta.gov /unemploy/data_summary/DataSum.asp (March 6, 2020); [k]Elaine Weiss, Griffin Murphy, and Leslie Boden, Workers' Compensation Benefits, Costs, and Coverage (2017 Data), (Washington, D.C.: National Academy of Social Insurance 2019). **NOTE: All data are pre-COVID-19 pandemic.**

As noted earlier, AFDC was abandoned in 1996 with passage of the new welfare reform act, PRWORA, which replaced AFDC grants to individuals with block grants to the states. The states in turn designed programs for promoting work and individual responsibility. The states received vast new authority and flexibility for reinventing welfare, subject to certain federal requirements. States submit TANF plans outlining how the state will assist needy families with children and help prepare parents to become self-sufficient. The law stipulates that adults have up to two years to find a job without losing benefits and a lifetime limit of five years to receive benefits. Up to 20 percent of the state's welfare population may receive hardship exemptions for circumstances such as mental or physical disabilities. This "tough love" approach to getting people off public support also has a financial stick to move any recalcitrant states ahead. States must demonstrate that at least 50 percent of TANF recipients are engaged in work or work-related activities for 20 to 30 hours per week, depending on the age of children; two-parent families must record a total of 35 to 55 hours per week.

The states combined TANF requirements with previously existing state welfare-to-work programs and dropped welfare caseloads dramatically (by 50 to 90 percent in the states and by three-quarters nationwide). Following the initial years of success, the states found themselves hard-pressed to locate jobs for the least able of the welfare population, who experience serious, and often multiple, barriers to employment, even while the federal government tightened up its demands that they do so. Many—if not most—of the available jobs pay minimum wage, which, by itself, is not nearly sufficient to raise a person out of poverty or even provide for basic needs. Moreover, high unemployment levels during and since the Great Recession are indicative of serious labor market problems. The states believe that they are much better suited than the national government to handle welfare-to-work programs. Yet substantial cuts to TANF benefits occurred from 2008 to 2012 as states struggled through their financial difficulties. As states tightened up restrictions to qualify for TANF during the Great Recession, welfare rolls declined even as the number of poor escalated.[15]

Supplemental Security Income (SSI) is financed and operated by the national government, except that state officials determine who is eligible for the program and have the option of enhancing SSI payments. Created in 1974, SSI combines three programs: Old Age Assistance, Aid to the Blind, and Aid to the Disabled. Its recipients are people who are unable to work because of old age or physical or mental disabilities and, increasingly, children with behavioral or learning disabilities. Average monthly payments are about $783.

The *Earned Income Tax Credit* provides cash assistance to low-income working individuals and families through a refundable federal income tax credit. It was created in 1975 to offset the burden of Social Security taxes and to encourage work. Many states offer a state EITC match for state taxes, averaging 3.5 percent in Louisiana up to 32 percent in Vermont.

General Assistance is a state and local program intended to help poor people who do not qualify for other direct cash or in-kind transfer programs, such as the nonworking but physically able poor. State benefit levels vary greatly. Twenty-five states do not offer the program at all, and many of the others reduced benefits during the recent economic difficulties.[16]

in-kind programs
The payment of a noncash social welfare benefit, such as food stamps or clothing, to an individual recipient.

In-Kind Programs

In-kind programs provide benefits in goods or services rather than in cash, as a way to address specific problems of poverty, hunger, illness, and joblessness.

The Supplemental Nutrition Assistance Program (SNAP), formerly known as the Food Stamp Program, provides low-income individuals and families with financial aid for purchasing food. The program was established in 1964, and benefit levels are uniform throughout the United States. Both the working and nonworking poor are eligible if their income falls sufficiently close to the poverty level. More than twenty million new SNAP recipients were added to the rolls during the Great Recession.

Medicaid is a health care assistance program for the poor (SSI recipients automatically qualify). It is jointly funded by the national and state governments (the federal/state share varies from 75–25 in Mississippi to 50–50 in states with higher per-capita income), and it is enormously expensive (more than $406 billion in 2018 federal funding, constituting more than 26 percent of state budgets. The Medicaid program provides free health care services to uninsured poor people and is the principal source of assistance for long-term institutional care for the physically and mentally disabled and the elderly. It must be distinguished from Medicare, which is an entitlement program that grants health care assistance to those aged 65 or older.

Since the inception of Medicaid in 1965, it has been wracked with scandals: Doctors, pharmacists, dentists, and other professionals have been charged with everything from performing unnecessary surgery and inflating fees to filing reimbursements for imaginary patients. Fueled by expansions of the program and rising health care costs, Medicaid has also placed an increasingly onerous burden on state budgets. In a desperate search for Medicaid savings, states cut payments to service providers, cracked down on fraud and waste, reduced benefits, improved care management for the chronically ill, and reformed health care delivery systems to enhance the quality and efficiency of patient treatment and care.

The Patient Protection and Affordable Care Act (ACA, or "Obamacare") of 2010 added an estimated 14.7 million new recipients to Medicaid rolls by 2019. States have the option to accept additional federal Medicaid funds or not; about half of them have decided to accept. Those that choose not to take the federal money generally have Republican-dominated legislatures and governors' offices,[17] whose officeholders were averse to almost any policy associated with former President Obama, and who say they are concerned about the federal government honoring its promise to pay 90 percent of future Medicaid costs.

The *Children's Health Insurance Program (CHIP)* is jointly funded by the federal and state governments to provide health insurance to children in families who cannot afford private insurance but who earn too much income to qualify for Medicaid. Under CHIP, the states enjoy great flexibility in designing and implementing their own plans. The Bipartisan Budget Act of 2018 maintained CHIP and set the federal matching rate from a minimum of 65 percent to a maximum of 80 percent, depending on state per capita income. The Families First Coronavirus Response Act of 2020 temporarily increased the federal match by 6.2 percent because of the COVID-19 pandemic.

Housing programs exist in several forms today. The federal housing program helps pay for public housing or provides rent subsidies directly to the poor, who apply them to private rental units (widely known as the Section 8 program). States administer a portion of approximately 1.2 million subsidized apartment units; the U.S. Department of Housing and Urban Development administers the rest. As homelessness rates soared across the country between 2008 and 2011, emergency shelters were overwhelmed. Tent cities arose in Phoenix, Reno, Sacramento, and many other cities. A majority of the homeless were families with children. States have responded with expanded shelters, new subsidized housing, and other attempts to relieve the problem. As the nation recovered from the Great Recession, homeless percentages gradually declined in most states. By 2018, only eight states (Alaska, Idaho, Montana, Massachusetts, New York, South Dakota, Vermont, and Wyoming) showed higher percentages of homeless population than they had in 2007. Homelessness more than doubled in South Dakota over this period of time, but the number of people—around 1,000—was relatively small in comparison to many other states. The Controversies in State and Local Government feature elaborates on the homeless problem and on state-local efforts to combat it.

Other in-kind programs include numerous types of public assistance, such as the *Child Nutrition* or school lunch program, Head Start, energy assistance for low-income families, legal services, family planning, foster care, and services for the physically and mentally disabled. National, state, and local participation depends on the specific program in question. Under TANF, states have flexibility in offering in-kind aid to help move welfare recipients into jobs and keep them working. Examples include child-care services, job

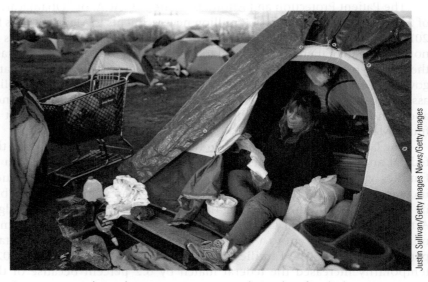

A woman at a homeless encampment packs up her few belongings.

Controversies in States and Localities

Combatting Homelessness

Data indicate that the current size of America's adult homeless population is around 553,000. The Great Recession took the number of homeless to an all-time high of around 750,000. If one loses their job, cannot find another one, goes belly up on the mortgage and has the house foreclosed, can't make car payments and sees that car repossessed, despair may set in. When no friends or relatives are available to help, that leaves the local homeless shelter or the streets. Homeless encampments dot the landscapes of our cities. Many of the victims are children: An estimated 2.5 million are homeless (though not accounted for in official figures), crashing on friends' couches, in all-night cafes, or motels. Some are with one or both parents, others are on the streets or otherwise on their own. These children are highly vulnerable to sex trafficking and other forms of abuse.

Homelessness is a complex problem that often involves more than the loss of income and housing. Minimum wage earners cannot afford apartments at market rates. Mental health problems, substance abuse issues, and post-traumatic stress disorder (PTSD) can also drive individuals to the streets, under bridges, or to wooded areas in a city. And truly, we don't really have a solid grip on the extent of the homeless problem, as the population is notoriously difficult to count. Homelessness puts the police in a bind: Do you arrest and risk packing the jails with the homeless (some of whom prefer a bunk in the county jail—with a meal or two—to a park bench) or let them be, despite citizen complaints? Ship them out of town on a bus? Should more shelters be constructed? If so, where should they be located? Who should pay for treatment, shelter and food expenses, or hospitalization?

Those who study and attempt to resolve homelessness understand that each case is different. The war veteran with PTSD has different issues (and treatment opportunities) than the mother with children

or the elderly alcoholic. Multiple interventions are called for in some cases, including substance abuse treatment, medication for emotional disorders, housing, and food. A network approach is often recommended, with state and local agencies, faith-based organizations, nonprofit service providers, and others offering a range of services.

The Obama administration stepped up the battle against homelessness in 2010 and pledged to end veterans' homelessness by 2015. Federal agencies provided rental-assistance housing vouchers, along with health care services and counseling for veterans. There has been some success in this area—the rate of homelessness for veterans declined by 38 percent from 2007 to 2018. The federal government learned lessons from local governments such as Lee County, Florida; Trenton, New Jersey; and Salt Lake City, Utah. These local governments are combatting homelessness with "rapid rehousing," a strategy that provides housing and stability while the recipient accesses counseling, job planning, and other services until they can get work that pays enough for them to eventually pull their own weight.

Critical Thinking Questions

1. What should the respective responsibilities of federal, state, and local governments be with respect to homelessness? What should be the role, if any, of the nonprofit and private sectors?

2. What is the homelessness situation in your state's largest city? How is it being addressed?

Sources: National Alliance to End Homelessness, "State of Homelessness," https://endhomelessness.org/homelessness-in-america/homelessness-statistics/state-of-homelessness-report/ (accessed April 15, 2020); Jaclyn Gallucci, "Human Trafficking Is an Epidemic in the U.S. It's Also Big Business," *Fortune*, https://fortune.com/2019/04/14/human-sex-trafficking-us-slavery/ (April 14, 2019); U.S. Interagency Council on Homelessness, "Rapid Re-Housing," https://www.usich.gov/solutions/housing/rapid-re-housing/ (August 15, 2018).

training, transportation, technical and college education, workshops on how to find and keep a job, and even state-subsidized salaries until the worker earns full-time employment. The diversity of in-kind programs is compelling evidence of the complexity of the poverty problem.

Social Insurance

Social insurance is distinguished from public assistance programs by the fact that recipients (or their relatives or employers) contribute financially through the Social Insurance and Medicare trust funds, established by federal law. In effect, participants pay in advance for their future well-being through payroll deductions. Although not considered to be a public assistance program, social insurance helps greatly in the broad effort to relieve poverty. Contributions to social insurance come from Social Security payments by individual workers and by their employers.

Social Security (officially known as Old Age, Survivors, Disability, and Health Insurance) is run entirely by the national government and is paid for through a payroll tax on employers and employees. Monthly checks are sent electronically to retired people; to the disabled; and to the spouses and dependent children of workers who retire, die, or become disabled.

Medicare provides federal health care, hospital, and prescription drug benefits for people over the age of 65 in exchange for a monthly premium and co-payments. It was created in 1965 through an amendment to the Social Security Act. Medicare costs have escalated rapidly as a result of the growing number of senior citizens and ballooning health care bills and prescription drug prices.

Unemployment compensation was mandated by the Social Security Act of 1935. It requires employers and employees to contribute to a trust fund administered by the states. Those who lose their jobs through layoffs or dismissals can draw combined state and federal unemployment benefits. States vary in their unemployment compensation time limits. The federal CARES Act, passed in March 2020, allowed states to extend unemployment compensation for an additional 13 weeks because of high unemployment during the COVID-19 pandemic.

Worker's compensation is also part of the Social Security Act. Financed by employers and administered by the states, it establishes insurance for workers and their dependents to cover job-related accidents or illnesses that result in death or disability. Its cost, which is closely associated with the price of health care, has escalated.

Social welfare policy clearly demonstrates the interdependent nature of the federal system. The national government pays for and operates some programs on its own; Social Security is one example. State and local governments take care of others. The states and localities perform key administrative roles in most social welfare efforts and serve as incubators for new ideas and programs, many of which have later been incorporated into national policy. The private and nonprofit sectors contribute through charities such as United Way agencies and through institutions such as hospitals, clinics, nursing homes, and myriad community-based organizations. Contracting by all levels of government with nonprofit service providers has made hidden partners of these organizations, which attend to Americans' problems from cradle to grave.

Social insurance programs assume a traditional view of the U.S. economy where companies employ people for fairly long periods of time over the

social insurance
A jointly funded benefit program made available by a government to its citizens as a right of its citizens.

course of their lifetimes. Workers employed by large industrial firms have portions of their social security, unemployment, and workers' compensation paid by their employers. But this economy has been changing rather rapidly. Nowadays, more than one-third of all U.S. workers (some fifty-seven million people) work in the **gig economy**—working several part-time jobs on a free-lance or contract basis.[18] People working for Uber or Lyft, who sell items on eBay or Etsy, or who eke out a living by completing surveys for Amazon Mechanical Turk don't fit the image of the U.S. economy of those who designed the Social Security system in the 1930s. What does it mean for gig economy workers to become unemployed or to retire? What does the mini-mum wage mean to somebody who operates as an independent contractor for Uber? Much employment and social welfare legislation at both the federal and state levels is based on a notion of the U.S. economy that seems out-moded for many in 2020 America.

Before the advent of the COVID-19 pandemic in spring 2020, the U.S. economy was performing very well. Unemployment in 2019 averaged less than 4 percent and some 176,000 jobs were added each month across the country. People who had been unemployed for some time were beginning to find jobs in the booming economy.[19] The economic boom of 2019 could not survive the coronavirus pandemic of 2020. As retail shops, restaurants, theaters, and theme parks shut down and people self-quarantined or sheltered in place, large sectors of the economy experienced tremendous unemployment. Beyond these retail establishments, especially hard hit were airlines, cruise ship companies, casinos, hotel chains, and all kinds of professional sports organizations. The official unemployment rate of 3.5 percent in December 2019 (some 7.1 million unemployed people) ballooned, by some estimates, to 17.9 percent the first week in April 2020 (more than twenty-nine million). If accurate, this would be the highest unemployment rate in the United States since 1938.[20] Initial claims for unemployment compensation, which had averaged fewer than 220,000 per week through 2019 and into early 2020, increased to 6.6 million by the end of March 2020, and that number increased to almost 12 million in the first week in April.[21] While unemployment eased some in May and June, the rate could increase again as states close businesses in response to increased coronavirus infections. If these numbers persist for a significant period of time (or grow worse) the effects on both state and federal financial resources and their ability to assist unemployed workers will be staggering.

State Innovations in Social Welfare

Public assistance policy today has two critical goals. One pertains to the well-being of children and the family. The other goal is to end welfare depend-ency where possible. The respective roles and contributions of national, state, and local governments in these two policy goals are continually being sorted out. A perplexing array of welfare traps snares even the most carefully devised policy proposals (see Figure 17.1). Undeniably, however, the states and local-ities are important innovators in social welfare policy and the governments closest to the needs of the poor and disadvantaged.

LO 17-5
To discuss state innovations in social welfare.

gig economy
Work characterized by short-term contracts or freelance work as opposed to permanent jobs.

The policy objective seems simple: Make welfare a reciprocal arrangement in which the poor must look for and accept a job in exchange for government assistance in preparing for work. If recipients refuse, they should lose their benefits. Welfare should offer a helping hand, not a lifetime handout. But many traps make achieving this seemingly simple objective both complex and elusive, and they present significant roadblocks to state policy innovation.

Trap 1: Some people *cannot* work. A large number of welfare recipients are simply incapable of holding down a job. Whether because of substance abuse, emotional problems, physical or learning disabilities, or other conditions, these people need long-term support for themselves and their children. It is not always easy to distinguish members of this group from the able-bodied.

Trap 2: Providing financial and other support may actually reduce the potential rewards of working. Taking even a low-wage job forces people to forgo the safety net of Medicaid, food stamps, and other programs.

Trap 3: The creation of community service or make-work jobs for the poor is opposed by labor unions and other groups that fear welfare recipients will displace workers in low-wage, low-skilled jobs, sending *them* onto the welfare rolls.

Trap 4: Unless the government separates children from their parents and places them in foster homes, or other care facilities, help for poor children also means help for their parents. If welfare recipients are denied benefits for not working, their children may suffer hardships. The denial of additional assistance for the single welfare mother's second or third child unfairly punishes the innocent child.

Trap 5: "Deadbeat Dads" who do not pay court-ordered child support present a conundrum. If jailed, they cannot work to pay the support. If laboring in a low-wage job, they cannot afford to shelter and feed themselves plus turn over hundreds of dollars a month to the mother.

Trap 6: To get people off welfare and thus save money in the long term means spending money today. Most welfare reform proposals require spending for education, job training, child care, and related services. Failure to invest sufficiently can result in public assistance programs that are underfunded and doomed to fail. It is cheaper in the short run to send the poor their welfare checks. The long-run solution requires a large financial investment.

Trap 7: Bureaucracy can get in the way of compassion and good sense. The average length of a federal food-stamps form—which is designed by individual states—is twelve pages. Some run more than thirty pages. Confusing legalese and intrusive questions inhibit applications. Some states ask applicants to list the value of a burial plot or what a child earns from cutting grass. Maryland requires applicants to list "deemor expenses" (a phrase not in the working vocabulary of most Americans).

Trap 8: Welfare policy sets a double standard: It pushes the poor mother to exercise "parental responsibility" by leaving her children for a job to support them, yet the middle-class woman is praised for staying home to raise her children.

Trap 9: The typical job-training program requires that participants be job-ready, have a high school diploma, read at the eighth-grade level or higher, and provide their own day care and transportation. But the typical unemployed person has little or no work experience, has a tenth-grade education, reads at the sixth-grade level, has limited access to day care, and has no personal transportation. As a result, job training may not help.

Trap 10: If most new jobs are found in the suburbs, but the majority of the poor live in central cities, access to reliable transportation to their place of work is unlikely. The same is true if the poor live in declining suburbs but the jobs are mostly in the central city.

Figure 17.1 Ten Welfare Traps

Source: The authors; also Kent Weaver, "Old Traps, New Twists," *Brookings Review* (Summer 1994): 14–21.

In addressing the problems and causes of poverty, the states are a beehive of experimentation and creative activity, but they have learned that a great chasm exists between establishing a new program and making it work effectively. Policy implementation is hindered by the complexities of our federal system; the waxing and waning of elected officials' attention; partisan, ideological, and interest group politics; and the enormity of our social welfare problems.[22] Government programs, no matter how well intended, sometimes cannot cause desired behavioral changes in target populations. The ravages of drugs, crime, and poverty, the lack of parenting skills, and other issues place many Americans at risk of long-term welfare dependency.

Saving the Children

Several important reasons explain the plight of children. Many children live with a single parent because of high divorce rates (almost half of all children experience life with a divorced parent during childhood), births to unwed mothers (some 40 percent of all infants, or some four million a year), and irresponsible fathers who refuse to support or even recognize their offspring. And as we saw earlier, single parent–headed households have much higher poverty rates than two parent households. There are some 13.6 million single parents in the United States, raising 22.4 million children. More than 80 percent of the single parents are mothers and nearly 30 percent of those families live in poverty.[23]

Even if single mothers have the necessary education or skills to secure employment, their children often must be placed in the care of older siblings or left on their own if family or friends cannot care for them. Some are at risk of abuse. Opportunities for affordable, subsidized, or free day care are generally limited to Head Start and oversubscribed state-run and charitable programs. Finally, too many children are born not only into poverty but also into sickness. Because of inadequate diets, lack of health insurance, ignorance about prenatal care, drug abuse, and the spread of sexually transmitted diseases, many mothers give birth to premature, underweight, and sickly children. Some infants do not survive.

Children's issues have risen near to the top of national and state policy agendas. Historically, the national government has addressed these problems, and it continues to do so today through programs such as Head Start, which provides preschool education and medical, dental, and social services for approximately 887,125 children up to five years of age. Head Start is a popular program that also promotes parental self-sufficiency. In addition, the states and some local governments have their own approaches. Successful programs that assist children now will eventually help reduce welfare expenditures for future adults and the elderly.

To deal with the growing problem of absentee fathers (97 percent of non-paying parents are male), the states withhold court-ordered child support payments from the wages of absent parents, even if the parent has not fallen behind in payments. States are also required to establish paternity, through blood tests and DNA techniques, for children born out of wedlock. The result is that more fathers are being held financially responsible for their offspring. The states have additional authority to speed up judicial and administrative procedures for obtaining paternal support, to establish guidelines for judges to determine the appropriate size of child support awards, and to monitor support payments. Many states use a "deadbeat dad" approach to publicize and prosecute delinquent fathers. A national database has been established, consisting of each person newly hired by every U.S. employer. States can plug into the database to track down deadbeat parents across state lines and hold them accountable.

Despite these efforts, about one-quarter of women owed child support never receive a dollar, and others receive only a portion of that which is owed. If the father is incarcerated for failure to make his payments or for unrelated reasons, payments halt.

Day Care

The issue of day care for children of working and single parents has received a great deal of attention from the state and local governments, whereas the national government has struggled in vain to produce child-care legislation. Hundreds of thousands of youngsters are home alone each day from the time they return from school until a parent or relative arrives. State and local governments are subsidizing day-care programs through tax breaks and are offering various child-care arrangements under TANF. Nearly all states partly or fully fund child-care expenses for TANF recipients. States are also taking the lead in improving prenatal care, gradually reducing the nation's shameful infant mortality rate, which ranks 33 of 36 industrialized nations. Only Mexico, Turkey, and Chile have higher infant mortality rates.[24] It is certainly less costly to invest at the front end of a person's life than to try correcting medical and other ailments later.

Teenage Mothers

Teenagers are highly likely to produce at-risk children (children more likely to experience school failure than other children). The rate of births to teen mothers accelerated during the 1970s and 1980s, then leveled off, but has since dropped to an historic low of 17.4 births per 1,000 teens, less than half of what it was in 2008.[25] Nearly 90 percent of births to teens occur to unmarried women, and most of these children and their mothers live in poverty. The annual taxpayer bill for aiding these almost certainly dysfunctional families is staggering.

Reductions in the high teen birthrate are attributed not only to greater use of effective birth control methods for those who are sexually active but also to lower rates of sexual activity for all teens.[26] Federal law prohibits using federal Medicaid funds for abortions for poor girls and women unless their pregnancies are the result of incest or rape. Abortion is an extremely controversial "hot stove" issue in the states. State-paid abortions for poor women would undoubtedly reduce the number of unplanned births further and provide a family-planning option that is widely available to middle- and upper-income women. It would also save taxpayers the expense of supporting a substantial number of children born into poverty, perhaps with serious and costly health problems. But abortion is highly distasteful to many and sinful to pro-life advocates. To its most rabid opponents, it is grounds for assassinating physicians who perform abortions. To conservative legislators, abortion is an act to be severely restricted or banned altogether.

State programs to reduce teen pregnancy take several directions. Minnesota integrates teen pregnancy prevention with human immunodeficiency virus (HIV) and sexually transmitted disease (STD) awareness and prevention. North Carolina targets middle-school adolescents and teens who are at risk of sexual activity. Catawba County's Teen Up program, for example, provides classes in sexual abuse, sexuality, drug abuse, handling peer pressure for sex, managing emotions and conflict, and other topics for students identified by school counselors.

California, Delaware, Florida, and many other states attack teen pregnancy by strengthening enforcement of long-neglected statutory rape laws. The goal is to discourage "sexual predators"—older males who prey on girls under the legal age of consent (18 in California and a dozen others, and 16 in most states).

Despite the reduction in teen births, the problem remains serious and perplexing. Teen pregnancy is an unmarried mother's recipe for a lifetime of poverty. It encourages dependency and greatly reduces career and life choices for the mother. Teen pregnancies cost taxpayers billions of dollars for social welfare and health care support for the child and the mother, most of whom receive no assistance from the father. A large majority of teen mothers never complete high school.

Turning Welfare Checks into Paychecks

LO 17-6
To explain how welfare checks can be turned into paychecks.

Before the 1996 Welfare Reform Act and TANF, checks were handed over to AFDC recipients, and little was required of them in return. The driving idea now is to help people find jobs and become independent. Jobs should produce more household income, along with improved self-image and self-reliance for recipients, and financial savings for taxpayers.

The states have taken two different approaches to moving clients from welfare to work. With an eye to meeting required federal work-participation rates, many states have "work-first" strategies that stress immediate job searches. Others, more concerned about the long-term reduction of poverty, focus on helping recipients develop necessary job skills through education, training, and other preemployment preparation. TANF has evolved into additional efforts to help recipients retain jobs and earn promotions and pay increases. Examples of work-first approaches are the widely praised Greater Avenues for Independence (GAIN) program in Riverside County, California, and Wisconsin Works.

In a different direction, several states have privatized all or most major components of public assistance programs. Private firms or nonprofit organizations were given contracts to process forms and applications in Arizona and elsewhere. Some county job centers in Wisconsin are run by private companies and nonprofits. Indiana contracted out management of its entire

TANF program, as well as the food-stamps program, but terminated the $1.16 billion privatization contract because of excruciatingly long client waiting periods for food-stamps processing.[27] Privatization has not proven to be a panacea. Texas' ambitious effort to privatize public assistance program client intake and screening "turned into a dark comedy of bungled work and unanswered and dropped phone calls; applications lost, ignored, and misdirected."[28]

Many additional state and local efforts are underway. A growing number of states and cities have set minimum wages substantially above the $7.25 per hour the federal government imposed in 2009. As of 2020, twenty-nine states had adopted such laws, averaging $10.35 per hour. California hiked its minimum wage to $13 an hour in 2020 and Washington raised it to $13.50. Seventeen states have recently passed legislation raising their minimum as the state cost of living increases.[29]

As indicated by the welfare traps discussed in Figure 17.1, however, divine intervention to settle the welfare conundrum would not be unwelcome. State and local efforts to significantly reform welfare—courageous and well intentioned as they may be—encounter enormous difficulties. Complicating factors abound. For example, what should be done about welfare recipients who truly want but cannot find a job? And what about the high proportion of TANF recipients who have physical or mental impairments? Make-work or community service sounds promising, until one examines the costs of arranging, monitoring, and paying for it. What if a recipient is addicted to drugs or alcohol and cannot hold a job? Detoxification and counseling are not cheap, but kicking the recipient off assistance could well result in a new enlistee in the ranks of criminals, the incarcerated, or the homeless. Most states deny TANF benefits to convicted drug felons, and several jurisdictions have required their general assistance recipients to undergo mandatory drug tests. Those testing positive must submit to treatment or forgo their assistance. The It's Your Turn feature considers the pros and cons of recipient drug testing.

After six decades of public assistance as an entitlement under AFDC, a regime grounded in work and self-sufficiency is firmly in place. Rapidly declining welfare caseloads in nearly every state elated supporters of TANF and state and local innovators. But the early job placements essentially removed the better-educated and job-ready people from the welfare rolls. Those who simply do not want to work also dropped off public assistance. Those still seeking a declining number of low-skill jobs in a national economy characterized by growing inequality and stagnant economic and social mobility are increasingly hard-pressed to make do, let alone achieve "the American Dream." Welfare rolls have been cut, but many—particularly single moms and their kids—live in precarious circumstances.

Fears of a race to the bottom, in which states seek to drive out the poor by cutting welfare benefits to the bare bone, and a "magnet hypothesis," which predicted that poor people would move to states with relatively generous welfare benefits, have not been realized, though research indicates that interstate competition tends to reduce the generosity of state welfare programs.[30] Much is at stake, and state and local governments are engaging the issues as best they can.

? It's Your Turn

Should Welfare Recipients Be Drug Tested?

At least eight states have required that TANF applicants be tested for illegal drug use before they can acquire public assistance. The most onerous requirements were adopted by Florida, which not only mandates the urine test but also makes the person being tested pay for it (refundable if the test is passed). Those in favor of drug testing tend to be, predictably, political conservatives who subscribe to the belief that welfare clients are lazy, drug-abusing individuals whose sorry plight is their own fault. Opponents of client testing are generally those who believe that the downtrodden and unemployed are largely victims of circumstances beyond their control and that mandatory drug testing is unnecessarily punitive, perpetuates negative stereotypes, and "blames the victim."

The American Civil Liberties Union filed a legal action and won a temporary injunction in federal court alleging that testing was an "unreasonable search." In 2014 the 11th U.S. Circuit Court of Appeals issued a permanent injunction confirming that the law was an unconstitutional violation of the Fourth Amendment. Research has revealed that drug testing saved Florida no money, and indeed was cost negative. Few users were identified; only 2.6 percent of tests had positive results, and another 2 percent refused to be tested. Florida's experience with testing was not unique. Nine months of testing 5,550 public assistance recipients in Mississippi produced only eight failed tests. At an average price of $30, the tests cost the states quite a lot of money to identify so few users, the vast majority of whom test positive for marijuana. It appears, then, that welfare applicants are no more likely to use drugs than the general population. Humorist Carl Hiaasen concluded that Florida state legislators themselves should submit to a "patriotic whiz-fest" to determine how many of "them" are drug users.

PROS	CONS
By screening out drug users, the taxpayers will save money on welfare costs and ensure that TANF funds go toward helping recipients secure jobs and get off the dole, rather than to support a drug habit. The Florida and Mississippi research is flawed and unpersuasive.	Opponents cite federal appellate court decisions finding that mandatory testing violates the Fourth Amendment to the U.S. Constitution, which prohibits illegal search and seizure.
Welfare drug testing has been upheld by courts in Texas, Indiana, and New Jersey.	Warrantless, suspicionless testing is coercive and unfairly stigmatizes welfare recipients.
Testing may deter drug use.	Few drug users are identified; the primary beneficiaries of drug testing are the companies that do the testing and reap profits.
Illegal drug use is harmful to a child in the family of the abuser. Drug testing protects these children, who deserve drug-free homes.	
Recipients are unlikely to become self-sufficient if they are using illegal drugs.	

LO 17-7
To analyze federal and
state health care
policy.

Health Care

A national debate has raged over health care reform for many years, with politicians and interest groups' hysteria and hand wringing over each new proposal. Americans have learned a lot about the problems and politics of health care, along with a new vocabulary of health care terms (see Table 17.2). Then finally, in 2010, Congress enacted President Obama's Patient Protection and **Affordable Care Act (ACA)**. Under the ACA, the states have developed innovative policies of their own.

The Problem

**affordable care act
(ACA)**
Also known as
Obamacare, this
2010 congressional
act requires states
to establish Health
Benefits Exchanges, or
to rely on the federal
exchange, and gives
them the option of
accepting a generous
federal subsidy to
expand state Medicaid
rolls, among other
provisions.

Nearly everyone agrees that, although the quality of health care technology in the United States is unsurpassed, the U.S. health care system is far too expensive and dysfunctional. Costs have been soaring for three decades. The nation's total annual health care bill is about $3.6 trillion, or 18 percent of the economy—by far the highest in the world.[31] Medicare alone pays medical bills for nearly sixty million aging citizens. Medicaid costs have soared and now gobble up the single largest proportion of state budgets. These costs include millions of elderly people in nursing homes, children in low-income families, physically disabled individuals who require daily living assistance, and the mentally disabled. The Great Recession of 2008–2011 pushed large numbers of new enrollees into Medicaid as people lost their houses, cars, and jobs. And economic impact projections of the COVID-19 pandemic in 2020 show that the seventy-one million people covered under Medicaid in 2019 could increase to between eighty-two and ninety-four million depending on how high the unemployment rate goes.[32]

Table 17.2 An Essential Dictionary of Health Care Terms

MANAGED CARE ORGANIZATIONS: Involves several types of health plans that seek to contain costs by restricting the physicians and services that patients can access, promoting preventive health care, and capping hospital and physician payments. Managed care is available through private insurance firms and nonprofits, consisting of gatekeeper physicians who direct patients to approved hospitals and other providers, and *preferred provider organizations* (PPOs), which are networks of approved doctors and hospitals. Managed care organizations typically receive a fixed sum per patient from the state to manage the patient's care.

ACCOUNTABLE CARE ORGANIZATIONS: Groups of doctors, hospitals, and other health care providers who voluntarily cooperate to provide coordinated care to Medicaid patients. The goals are to avoid duplication of services while delivering high-quality care, all within a set budget.

MANAGED COMPETITION: Market-driven insurance plans that create incentives for competing insurance companies to provide health care services at low prices through negotiated fees.

PORTABILITY: The ability of individuals to take health care coverage with them wherever they work or live.

SINGLE PAYER: A government agency administrating a health care system financed through taxes. Called "socialized medicine" by its critics, this system is prevalent in Great Britain, Canada, and several European countries. An example in the United States is the federal Medicare program.

FEE-FOR-SERVICE: The traditional means of paying for health care in which providers charge for specific patient services. This approach is known for being unnecessarily expensive and incentivizing unnecessary tests and procedures.

Inflating health care costs are the aging U.S. population, which means a larger number of people with illnesses directly associated with old age; the obesity epidemic; and increased use of expensive medical technology such as MRI. Expansions of eligibility for health care entitlement programs drive up costs. So do fraud and abuse. For example, some physicians sell prescriptions for narcotics. Some nursing homes charge for services not provided, and some home health care companies bill for nursing visits never made. (In some Florida nursing homes, patients in comas were billed for speech therapy.)[33] In pill mills, a conspiracy of doctors, clinic owners, and pharmacists prescribe drugs and obtain government reimbursements, yet no drugs actually change hands. All told, Medicare overpayments ran as high as $28.9 billion in 2019 due to errors, waste, and fraud.

Prior to passage of the ACA, even though per capita U.S. health care spending far exceeded that of other countries, a large portion of the population (estimated to be one in four people under age 65) did not have health insurance. Consequently, the U.S. health care system was inferior to those of most other advanced nations in terms of access, mortality rates, patient safety, efficiency, equity, and many other measures.[34] Uninsured Americans have had to spend their personal resources to the point of bankruptcy before they could qualify for government aid through Medicaid. A layoff or job change could result in the loss of insurance coverage, meaning entire families courted financial disaster. When uninsured, sick, or injured people take advantage of free government health care programs, usually in hospital emergency rooms or free clinics, individuals with health care insurance are the ones who pay. Doctors, hospitals, and others simply garner revenue lost from the uninsured through higher fees charged to those who can pay. The result was a fragmented, profit-driven, two-tiered system in which the insured received state-of-the-art health care and the uninsured experienced health care services that were surpassed by those of some Third World countries.

Medical malpractice suits complicate the financial issues of health care policy. Physicians and other health care providers bemoan astoundingly high jury awards for pain and suffering and soaring insurance premiums. Some doctors in New Jersey, Florida, and West Virginia literally walked off the job in protest. Trial lawyers fight caps on jury awards and defend victims' rights to seek fair and just compensation for preventable medical mistakes. With no action forthcoming from Congress, states are left to grapple with the issue, and a large majority have set limits on jury awards for "pain and suffering" and other noneconomic claims.[35]

The Affordable Care Act of 2010

It would be a challenge to explain the confusion and political furor over the ACA. The Act required citizens and residents of the United States to have health insurance or pay a fine. States were to create Health Benefits Exchanges through which coverage may be purchased. If they chose not to create their own state-run exchange, state residents would be covered by a federal health exchange. Employers were required to either provide health insurance to their workers or pay a penalty for not doing so. Federal subsidies are available to assist uninsured low-income individuals. States were originally mandated to extend

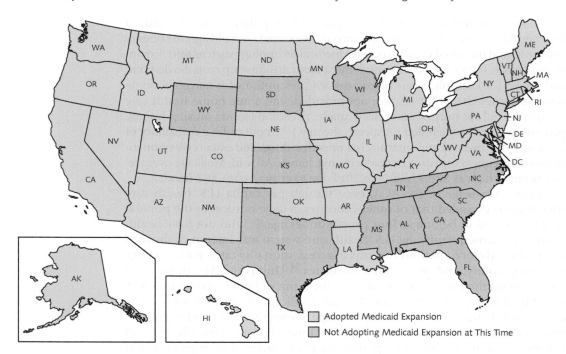

Figure 17.2 Status of State Action on the Medicaid Expansion Decision, November 2020

Source: Kaiser Family Foundation.

Medicaid coverage to residents with incomes of less than 133 percent of the federal poverty level, but this mandate was declared invalid by the U.S. Supreme Court in a 2012 decision, *National Federation of Independent Business v. Sebelius*.[36] States could voluntarily expand Medicaid, accepting generous federal funding to do so. By 2020, thirty-eight states had expanded their Medicaid programs.

While noncooperating states sued in federal courts and their legislatures proposed—and some passed—a raft of anti-ACA bills, other states took advantage of the ACA by creating and operating their own health care exchanges and expanding Medicaid coverage.

Donald Trump's 2016 campaign for the presidency included a promise to repeal the ACA and replace it with a plan that would "expand choice, freedom, affordability." Finding the necessary votes to pass such a plan became a difficult legislative endeavor throughout 2017, 2018, and 2019. The ACA includes some very popular provisions—allowing children to stay on their parents' health insurance until age 26; forbidding health insurance companies from refusing coverage based on preexisting conditions—with some unpopular provisions—the individual mandate. Eventually, what did pass Congress as part of the Tax Cut and Jobs Act (TCJA) of 2017 was reducing the annual penalty for not purchasing health care to $0 effective in 2018. While TCJA did not repeal the individual mandate, it essentially made compliance with this ACA provision voluntary. In 2018, the attorneys general of twenty states brought suit against the federal government, claiming the ACA was unconstitutional since TCJA had actually repealed the individual mandate which they claimed was the keystone of the U.S Supreme Court's decision in *National Federation of Independent Business v. Sibelius*. A federal district court judge agreed with them, as did a panel of appeals court judges, setting the stage for another hearing on the ACA before the U.S. Supreme Court late in 2020.

Of course, health care problems endure and—for better or for worse —will be revisited by Congress. Meanwhile, managed care and managed competition are resulting in mergers and consolidation in the health care industry and monetary efficiencies as doctor, hospital, and pharmaceutical fees and prices are squeezed. But most of the juice is out of the orange, and future state Medicaid costs were expected to grow at an average annual rate of about 6 percent before COVID-19 introduced tremendous volatility in health care costs.[37] More than half of the states reported that their spending on Medicaid in 2020 would exceed what they had projected it to be with only six states reporting lower than expected Medicaid spending.[38]

State and Local Health Care Innovation

Prior to Congress acting on national health care, the states were busily engaged in reforming health care themselves. Innovations tested by states served as models for major provisions of the ACA. Indeed, Massachusetts' "Commonwealth Care" program served as a model for the ACA. Each state has its own perspective on what is wrong with health care and its own approach to fixing it. State actions are also guided by economics and special circumstances.

The ACA provided generous financial support to cooperating states seeking to improve the quality and cost of health care. Several states took early advantage and successfully launched early state health care exchanges. Relatively flawless launchings took place in Kentucky, Connecticut, Washington, and California. Other states learned important lessons from these early innovators, as they did from other states whose exchanges encountered difficulties. Among the lessons learned were (1) to extensively beta-test the software and website; (2) to forgo fancy bells and whistles for a simple, straightforward website; (3) to enable users to browse the website without first logging in and setting up an account with personal data;[39] and (4) to hire a proven firm to oversee health exchange development and integrate it with Medicaid enrollment systems.[40]

A major concern, of course, is holding down Medicaid costs. Following are a few examples of specific approaches by state and local governments to rein in health care costs while providing quality services:

- Minnesota is a leader in Accountable Care Organizations (ACOs) (see Table 17.2). A network of physicians and health care facilities receive a fixed budget in return for accepting responsibility for providing care for a specified group of patients. If the goal of supplying coordinated, quality services for less cost is achieved, the ACO and the state share in the savings.[41] Primary, preventive care is emphasized to help avoid more expensive services—such as emergency room visits—down the road.
- Arkansas received federal permission under an ACA waiver to privatize its Medicaid program, paying health care insurance companies and other

providers based on quality of care instead of services rendered. The state has established standards for pricing specified services, from heart attacks to pregnancies, based on the total costs, from initial consultation and facility admission to discharge from the hospital or clinic. Each provider is evaluated annually with respect to its average costs; it may then receive a bonus, or it may have to return money to the state.[42]

- Several states, including California, Florida, and New Jersey, focused on Medicaid fraud prevention. California searched for unusual payments suggesting waste or fraud. Florida officials conducted unannounced visits to providers to audit payments and services; New Jersey used federal and state databases to identify repeated fraudulent practices by individuals.[43]

- Hennepin County, Minnesota, is experimenting with a holistic care program for chronic users of costly emergency services. A coordinator is assigned to such individuals to assist with ongoing, consistent health care attention and guidance, and with other related problems such as homelessness or alcoholism.[44]

State Health Care Reform Is Never Ending

Huge variations exist in state health care spending. The southeastern states present special health care problems because of the high prevalence of obesity, diabetes, and stroke. In the West and Southwest, especially Utah, teetotaling, nonsmoking Mormons enjoy good health and help keep costs down. Florida's large senior population is a heavy consumer of nursing homes and other health care facilities, driving these costs up. Figure 17.3 shows state health rankings. States that spend relatively high amounts per capita do not necessarily rank high on state health indicators.

State and local governments have always been concerned with the health of their citizens and indeed are delegated this responsibility in the U.S. Constitution. Colonial towns assumed responsibility for impoverished sick people in the 1600s, providing almshouses and primitive medical treatments involving leeches and native herbs. Cities and counties, along with private charities, built and operated public hospitals for the poor in the 1800s. Today, the states are hard at work dealing with the complexities of the ACA, including the decision of whether to keep or establish health benefits exchanges or to depend on the federal exchange.

Medicaid will continue to burden the states financially. This entitlement program, growing substantially as a result of the ACA, already comprises the largest portion of state expenditures. The most recent states to expand their Medicaid programs—Missouri, Nebraska, Oklahoma, and Virginia (2020)— are conservative and have opposed Medicaid expansion since the ACA passed in 2010. Lobbying by the health insurance and hospital industries and the lure of generous federal financial benefits figured in these states reversing course, as did the partisan turnover in the Virginia General Assembly in the 2019 state legislative election.

Medicaid costs are not the only serious problem. Prescription drug prices are escalating. A disturbing and deleterious nurse shortage threatens the quality of medical care. The nursing home industry is riddled with problems, as is care for the mentally disabled.

The COVID-19 pandemic turned a spotlight on many of these health care problems in the states. The early peaks in cases in states like New York, Massachusetts, and Illinois demonstrated how ill-equipped the country was to battle a major health crisis. Emergency rooms were flooded with patients as infections grew exponentially. Personal protective equipment (PPE) ran short as hospitals were required to treat much larger than expected numbers of severely ill patients. Doctors and nurses worked long hours and volunteer medical staff from other states attempted to help in areas experiencing peaks in infections. More than 90,000 health care workers (25,000 from outside the state) volunteered to help New York during its peak in infections in March and April 2020. But because of state licensing requirements, hospital bureaucracies, and other barriers, only 908 volunteers were actually deployed in New York City.[45] Many thought it was a lack of experience in dealing with a new pandemic that caused many of these problems. However, by the summer of 2020 similar problems were occurring in other states such as Florida, Arizona, and Texas that showed later peaking infections. Problems such as over taxed emergency rooms, overworked medical workers, not enough PPE, and insufficient testing capacity seem endemic in the U.S. health care sector.

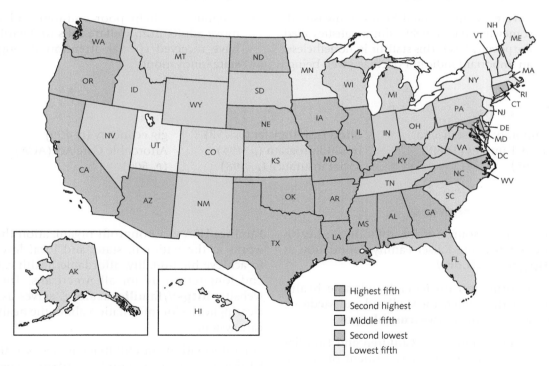

Figure 17.3 State Health Rankings, 2019
These rankings, from most healthy to least healthy, are based on various health indicators, including unemployment, poverty, smoking, availability of health services, obesity, and death rates. Low scores indicate the most healthy states, high scores the least healthy.

Source: "America's Health Rankings Annual Report 2019," United Health Foundation and American Public Health Association, https://assets.americashealthrankings.org/app/uploads/ahr_2019annualreport.pdf.

A national approach to health care has been a long time coming, but states—and their highly disparate preferences—will not be ignored. They will continue to act as service integrators, implementers, and innovators in their classic "middleman" role in U.S. federalism. Moreover, they continue clearing new trails that will inform and influence future federal policy making. The COVID-19 pandemic illustrates both the shortcomings and successes of a state-led health care sector in the United States.

 # Chapter Recap

- Social welfare and health care are major entrees on the federal–state policy menu. The national government may own the restaurant, but the cooks who turn out the policy dishes are the state and local governments.

- Poverty in the United States is measured, somewhat inaccurately, using a statistic called the poverty level. This statistic is, nonetheless, an important indicator of citizen well-being.

- The Affordable Care Act now serves as national health care policy, but the state and local governments are fully engaged in program design, experimentation, and administration.

- Programs to help poor children and to move adults from welfare rolls to payrolls have received special attention through state innovations.

Key Terms

Temporary Assistance for Needy Families (TANF) (*p. 491*)

direct cash transfer (*p. 492*)
in-kind program (*p. 494*)
social insurance (*p. 498*)

gig economy (*p. 499*)
Affordable Care Act (ACA) (*p. 506*)

Internet Resources

An excellent source of information on health care issues is the Kaiser Family Foundation at **http://www.kff.org/**.

For information on federal and state health care, see the Centers for Medicaid and Medicare Services at **https://www.cms.hhs.gov**.

The Administration for Children and Families (ACF), within the U.S. Department of Health and Human Services (DHHS), is responsible for federal programs that promote economic and social well-being. Information about their programs can be obtained from their website at **https://www.acf.hhs.gov**.

Families USA is a nonprofit organization that works at the national, state, and local levels to achieve high-quality, affordable health care and long-term care for all Americans. Their website, **https://familiesusa.org**, serves as a clearinghouse for information about the health care system.

For information on children's issues, see the Children's Defense Fund at **https://www .childrensdefense.org**.

For general information and links on welfare programs and initiatives, see **https://www .welfareinfo.org**.

18

Environmental Policy: Regulation and Innovation

WARNING

Possible Sewage Overflows During and Following Heavy Rain Questions? Call 206-205-1151 Regarding CSO# 124

Seattle - Department of Public Health | King County Public Health

A sign at a Seattle lake warns of potential pollution after heavy rainfalls.

Learning Objectives

LO 18-1 To articulate the relationship between environmental protection and economic growth.

LO 18-2 To discuss the concept of sustainability.

LO 18-3 To understand the intergovernmental relationships that define environmental policy.

LO 18-4 To differentiate among states and localities as to their eco-friendliness.

LO 18-5 To summarize the issues related to waste management.

LO 18-6 To assess the various environmental challenges facing states and localities.

LO 18-7 To explain how day-to-day decisions made by states and localities affect the global environment.

In the midst of the COVID-19 pandemic in spring and summer 2020, it may have been difficult for many to remember that a major environmental threat, global climate change, was still looming. Some reactions to the two crises seem eerily alike; for example, President Trump's oft-repeated tweet "We cannot let the cure be worse than the problem itself," could easily apply either to COVID-19 or to global climate change. The difference, however, is that although both threats are largely invisible—there aren't enemy soldiers or plumes of smoke or explosive blasts to indicate the existence of a problem—COVID-19 illnesses and deaths peaked in 2020, whereas the effects of climate change are just beginning to accumulate. One crisis will play out over a one- to two-year timeline whereas the other will play out over a fifty- to hundred-year timeline.

By 2050, the worst-case climate change scenario projections for some American cities are dramatic: Cleveland's projected 5.4 degree Fahrenheit increase in temperature will make it feel like St. Louis; St. Louis will feel like Tulsa; Amarillo will feel like central Texas rather than the panhandle.[1] Florida, New York, California, Virginia, New Jersey, Hawaii, and Louisiana, as measured by the percentage of population affected, will be dramatically affected by sea level rise.[2] Small changes can have big effects; just a two-degree average warmer temperature in the southwestern states has resulted in a fifteen-year drought.[3]

States shifting from fossil fuel-generating power plants to renewable energy sources such as solar, wind, hydropower, and so on have reduced the increase in greenhouse gasses and so may have reduced the probability of the worst-case scenario. In the 1980s, Iowa became the first state to mandate utility conversion to renewable energy production. By 2020, thirty states had developed renewable portfolio standards requiring a given percentage of electricity produced by utilities to come from renewable sources. In the process, these states have created a $64 billion market for renewable energy sources.[4] These state actions, and many others taken by government, private enterprise, and individual Americans, may have "flattened the curve" of the worst-case scenario of climate change effects, but it is unlikely that we will escape from such major climate changes unscathed.

When do environmental problems become so great that they threaten homeland security? Should New York City, Miami, Tampa, Virginia Beach, and New Orleans prepare evacuation plans for parts of the city that most likely will experience major flooding? How much of the responsibility for such actions falls on local governments, state governments, and the federal government? Government activity has tended to be regulatory, that is, making rules and setting standards that affect the private sector, monitoring compliance, and imposing penalties. Finally, solutions to environmental problems are moving beyond the more traditional approaches and are becoming increasingly innovative and fresh. As will be evident in this chapter, environmental policy tests the capacity of states and localities to make smart choices for the future.

The Political Economy of Environmental Protection

LO 18-1
To articulate the relationship between environmental protection and economic growth.

Although global climate change represents a major threat to many states and localities in the United States, most current environmental problems are much more localized and much more immediate. Where can a new landfill be located? How can a city guarantee safe drinking water to its residents when that water may be delivered by 100-year-old lead pipes? How do local policy makers trade off jobs created by a new firm against possible environmental damage that firm may cause? Should states encourage or discourage hydraulic fracturing (fracking) in a search for new oil and natural gas deposits?

Environmental policy choices are made especially difficult by their economic implications. Controlling pollution is a significant economic cost for many firms today. In the essentially nonregulatory era prior to the 1960s, this expense was either quite low or nonexistent. Increasing government regulatory intervention in industrial processes and outputs reflects the indisputable fact that market forces by themselves will not guarantee the protection of our health and the environment. Clean air and clean water are public goods that should be available to all of us, but polluters often have little economic incentive to stop polluting.

When left unregulated, most firms tend to maximize profits by minimizing costs—including the costs of environmental protection. Often, firms minimize costs by externalizing them on the public; environmental cleanup then becomes something the general public rather than the individual company is required to undertake. Determining exactly what constitutes pollution or environmental degradation and deciding how stringently to regulate polluting activities have tremendous economic implications for firms and governments. Too much regulation could depress economic growth at national, state, and local levels; reduce employment; and even force some companies into bankruptcy. These concerns are not simply conjecture. To some degree, states that imposed costlier regulatory burdens on the private sector experienced lower rates of new capital investment.[5] Obviously, the trade-offs between economic growth and environmental protection can spawn conflict.

Public Opinion

Research tells us that Americans generally support the goals of environmental protection. Public opinion polls indicate that most people are in favor of increased government spending for environmental protection and oppose efforts to weaken environmental standards.[6] This resounding endorsement lessens, however, when environmental protection is pitted against goals such as economic growth and adequate energy. When members of the environmental group Earth First! square off against loggers in the forests of the Pacific Northwest, environmentalism becomes more than an abstraction. Environmental protection does not occur in a vacuum; achievement of its goals comes at a cost to other valued objectives.

Although support among the public for protecting the environment was strong in the early part of the century, it eventually began to lose ground as the priority accorded economic growth increased. Figure 18.1 shows the fluctuation in national public opinion from 2000 to 2019, as reported by the Gallup Poll. The polling question requires the respondent to weigh environmental protection against economic development and was worded in this manner:

> With which one of these statements about the environment and the economy do you most agree—protection of the environment should be given priority, even at the risk of curbing economic growth (or) economic growth should be given priority, even if the environment suffers to some extent?[7]

As Figure 18.1 shows, the gap between the two priorities narrowed over time; and by 2009, the public preferred economic growth to environmental protection. The increased importance of economic growth can be attributed in part to the downturn in the nation's economy during the period. By 2014, with the economy back on track, support for environmental protection (50 percent) once again took precedence over economic growth (41 percent). And as the economy continued to improve from 2014 to 2019, support for the environment grew, reaching 65 percent by 2019—the highest level since 2000. Even when the economy is a greater priority, environmental protection continues to be valued because all of us are potential or actual victims of environmental problems. Polluted air, water, and land offend us aesthetically, but, more important, they threaten the health and safety of ourselves, our children, and our grandchildren. People who drink contaminated water and breathe polluted air experience the costs directly.

Environmental Protection vs. Economic Growth

With which one of these statements do you most agree—protection of the environment should be given priority, even at the risk of curbing economic growth (or) economic growth should be given priority, even if the environment suffers to some extent?

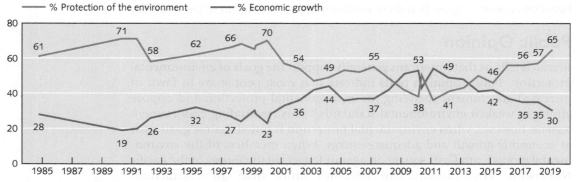

Figure 18.1 Changing Priorities in Public Opinion

Source: Lydia Saad, "Preference for Environment Over Economy Largest Since 2000," https://news.gallup.com/poll/248243/preference -environment-economy-largest-2000.aspx (April 4, 2019).

From a different perspective, all citizens must help pay the price of a safe and clean environment. We pay for a clean environment through the portion of our taxes that goes to government pollution-control efforts and through the prices we pay for goods, which include the cost of pollution control. The costs to consumers are especially heavy where the products of chemical companies, the auto industry, and coal-burning power plants are concerned. These industries have lobbied vigorously against what they perceive to be excessive regulation. One policy that is intended to improve relations between business and regulators is the **environmental self-audit**, which allows firms to self-report violations. If the firm then corrects the problem voluntarily, the penalty levied by the government is less than it would have been otherwise. Although proponents of this approach tout its promise, research shows that self-monitoring programs are often no better than traditional regulation in ensuring environmental performance.[8]

New Approaches: Moving Toward Sustainability

LO 18-2
To discuss the concept of sustainability.

Government's role is to balance economic growth with environmental protection by regulating polluters. The political economy of environmental protection argues strongly for national domination of policy making. Because states and local governments compete for industry, some jurisdictions might be tempted to relax environmental protection standards and thus influence a firm's decision about where to construct or expand a new manufacturing facility, a behavior that is often called a **race to the bottom**. Indeed, research indicates that state environmental agencies are influenced by other states' regulatory actions.[9] Moreover, state regulators pay attention to the effects of their regulatory decisions on industries' investment decisions. National policies and standards can prevent the sacrifice of environmental quality in jurisdictions that seek growth and development at almost any cost. But concern about the high costs of traditional regulatory approaches has spawned some creative thinking about alternatives. This new thinking has moved in four directions:

- Changing production processes to limit the amount of pollution produced in the first place,
- Reducing exposure to pollutants rather than trying to eliminate pollution altogether,
- Exploring the trade-offs between regulatory costs and environmental benefits to determine when an unacceptable imbalance exists, and
- Replacing traditional administrative procedures with economic incentives and other market strategies with the hope of achieving both environmental protection and economic efficiency.[10]

It is not clear whether these new approaches will achieve what some of their proponents intend, that is, the marrying of environmental protection and economic development. The word often used to describe this marriage is **sustainability**, that is, an approach to economic growth that prevents harm to the environment. These intertwined goals present continued challenges for policy makers.

environmental self-audit
A form of self-policing in which the regulated firm conducts its own review of its performance and voluntarily reports violations.

race to the bottom
Occurs when states alter their behaviors —relaxing regulations, lowering taxes, or reducing benefits— to gain an advantage over competing states.

sustainability
The simultaneous achievement of economic development and environmental protection.

LO 18-3
To understand the intergovernmental relationships that define environmental policy.

Clean Air, Clean Water, and Politics

In the early days of the United States, government involvement in environmental protection was minimal at best. Natural resources were abundant, the country was developing, and the future seemed limitless. The first government forays into the now-tangled jungle of environmental protection policy began in the early 1800s with local ordinances aimed at garbage; human and animal waste; contaminated drinking water; and other unsanitary, health-endangering conditions in American cities. Local failures to contain and control such problems were punctuated by cholera and typhoid epidemics throughout the nineteenth century and into the early twentieth century. In 1878, a yellow fever epidemic caused 5,000 deaths and the exodus of another 25,000 fearful residents from Memphis, Tennessee. Such episodes prompted the states to begin regulating conditions causing waterborne diseases, thereby redefining what had been a private problem into a problem for state government. By 1948, states had taken over responsibility for water pollution control. Their early regulatory efforts were rather weak, however. Even in modern times, waterborne diseases can be a problem. As late as 1993, more than 400,000 people in Milwaukee became ill (more than 100 died) after one of the two city water treatment plants became contaminated with cryptosporidium, a parasite that causes diarrhea, stomach cramps, fever, and dehydration. And disease is not the only problem; heavy metals—lead is the one most publicized—can contaminate drinking water and cause developmental problems in children. The problem in Flint, Michigan, was widely publicized in 2014 when 5 percent of the children in that city showed high levels of lead in their bloodstreams. But other cities have worse lead

A waterfall at Chewacia State Park near Auburn, Alabama.

problems. As a result of contaminated drinking water, lead exposure in Milwaukee, Newark, Pittsburgh, and Washington, D.C was much worse than in Flint.[11] Especially at risk are the more than 13.5 million Americans who use household wells for their water supply.

The Centralization of Environmental Policy

The issue of water pollution control shows the evolving centralization of federal government authority in environmental decision making. Although the federal government acted to protect natural resources by setting aside land for national parks in the late nineteenth century, it paid little attention to environmental problems until after World War II. At that point, the forces of urbanization and industrial production began to draw attention to the national dimensions of environmental dangers. The initial federal statutory step into the policy field was the Water Pollution Control Act of 1948. Under the original version of this act, the national government assumed limited enforcement authority for water pollution. Since then, seven other major federal statutes or amendments have been enacted to address the problem. Using this overall statutory framework, the federal government preempted existing state and local water quality standards and substituted national standards.

The reasons for this preemption are not difficult to understand. We have already noted that as states compete for economic development, they may be tempted to lower environmental standards to gain an edge over other states. In addition, because pollution problems are often cross-boundary (i.e., they extend beyond a single jurisdiction), solutions can be difficult to design. Toxins dumped into a river upstream have deleterious consequences for jurisdictions located downstream. The failure of states to work together to solve shared environmental problems led to more involvement by the federal government.

Increasingly strong federal statutes also addressed the problems of air pollution, pesticides, and hazardous waste. For example, the first national legislation on air quality, the Air Pollution Control Act of 1955, made funding available for research on the health effects of bad air. It was superseded by the Clean Air Act of 1963, which encouraged the development of emissions standards. The Clean Air Act of 1970, a massive overhaul of its predecessor, set air quality standards and strictly regulated emissions from factories and motor vehicles. By the late 1970s, the federal government had extended its authority to endangered species, strip mining, coastal zones, toxic substances, and many other areas. Thus, environmental protection was redefined as a national problem requiring national solutions. Since then, studies have found that the public prefers the federal government to take the lead on non local pollution matters.[12] The federal government does not operate alone, however; state and local governments play a significant role in implementing federal legislation.

States and localities speak with an important policy voice even in environmental fields that appear to be outside their sphere of influence. For example, one group of northeastern and mid-Atlantic states took on the issue of greenhouse gas emissions in a creative way by developing a regional cap-and-trade program. The Regional Greenhouse Gas Initiative (RGGI) sets an emissions cap for utilities and then auctions off emissions permits. The funds raised through the auctions are reinvested in programs related to energy efficiency, renewable energy, and other measures that help lower consumer electricity bills. RGGI has been quite successful. Even as the regional economy grew, by 2017 RGGI states experienced a 50 percent reduction in power-sector carbon dioxide pollution.[13]

Another example is public lands. Governed by Congress and managed by eight federal agencies, including the Bureau of Land Management, the U.S. Forest Service, and the National Park Service, the nation's 700 million acres of public lands make up 28 percent of the continental United States and more than 60 percent of the land area of four western states: Alaska, Idaho, Nevada, and Utah. (Table 18.1 displays federal land ownership figures for ten states.)

These lands contain vast timber, petroleum, coal, and mineral resources. The states have an enormous economic stake in the way these resources and their environmental implications are managed. In 2012, two Western state legislatures passed bills demanding that the federal government relinquish ownership of much of the land and if it failed to comply, giving states the right to seize the disputed land. In Utah, the governor signed the bill into law; in Arizona, the governor vetoed a similar bill. The primary complaint of the aggrieved state leaders was that federal policies toward the land are overly restrictive, making too much land off-limits to commercial activities, especially energy development.[14] The issue continues to percolate: In 2015, bills laying the groundwork for land transfers were introduced in the legislatures of seven western states—Alaska, Arizona, Colorado, Montana, New Mexico, Washington, and Wyoming. Several Republican members of Congress from

Table 18.1 Federal Land Ownership in the States

STATES WITH MOST FEDERAL LAND (AS % OF STATE LAND AREA)	FEDERAL ACREAGE (IN THOUSANDS OF ACRES)	PERCENTAGE OF THE STATE	STATES WITH LEAST FEDERAL LAND (AS % OF STATE LAND AREA)	FEDERAL ACREAGE (IN THOUSANDS OF ACRES)	PERCENTAGE OF THE STATE
Nevada	56,262	80.1	Connecticut	9	0.3
Utah	33,268	63.1	Iowa	98	0.3
Idaho	32,790	61.9	Kansas	254	0.5
Alaska	222,667	60.9	Rhode Island	5	0.7
Oregon	32,244	52.3	New York	231	0.8

Note: The figures include the lands of the four major federal land management agencies (U.S. Forest Service, National Park Service, Fish and Wildlife Service, and Bureau of Land Management) and the Department of Defense but exclude lands administered by other federal agencies such as the Agricultural Research Service, the Department of Energy, and NASA. Therefore, the percentages may be understated.

Source: Carol Hardy Vincent, Laura Hanson, and Lucas Bermejo, "Federal Land Ownership: Overview and Data," Congressional Research Service, R42346, https://fas.org/sgp/crs/misc/R42346.pdf (updated February 21, 2020).

western states have been receptive to the idea of large-scale land transfers; however, the full Congress is decidedly less enthusiastic. When Donald Trump became president in 2017 with Republican majorities in both the U.S. Senate and House of Representatives, many thought there would be a wholesale turnover of federal lands to the states.[15] The actual result was much more modest, amounting to only a small percentage of the acreage in states where the federal government owns the most land.

National Politics and the Environment

The lead agency in national environmental policy is the U.S. Environmental Protection Agency (EPA), which was created in 1970 as an independent regulatory body for pollution control. With its director appointed by the president, the EPA is faced with the task of coordinating and enforcing the broad array of environmental protection programs established by Congress. To help with this task, the agency has decentralized much of its operation to ten regional offices located in major cities throughout the country. The scope of the EPA's responsibility can be overwhelming, involving regular interaction and conflict with other federal agencies, powerful private interests, and state and local governments. Its job is complicated by the tendency of Congress to pass environmental legislation that sets unattainable program goals and unrealistic implementation dates. Many deadlines for compliance with federal laws have been missed by the EPA, which lends ammunition to its critics on all sides. Litigation brought by regulated industries and environmental groups has further ensnarled the agency, and a shortage of money and staff has plagued the EPA since the administration of President Reagan.

An example of the scope of the EPA's responsibilities is water pollution control. Every private and public facility that discharges wastes directly into water must obtain a permit from the EPA or, in some instances, from its state counterpart. The national government, through the EPA, establishes specific discharge standards. Day-to-day oversight and implementation, however, are performed by the states. In effect, the national government makes the rules and lets the states enforce them according to their own circumstances (a process known as **partial preemption**). The national government also disburses grants to state and local governments for the treatment and monitoring of water resources. Billions of federal dollars have been spent for the construction of wastewater treatment plants; millions more have gone for technical assistance and research and development.

One interesting attempt to build a more cooperative relationship between the EPA and state-level environmental protection agencies is the performance partnership agreement (PPA) that was promoted by the Clinton administration. PPAs allow a state to combine its EPA funding into block grants that can be used for comprehensive statewide environmental problems.[16] Basically, PPAs give states more power to set their own spending priorities. The idea was pilot tested in North Dakota, New Hampshire, and Massachusetts with sufficient success to warrant its extension to other interested states, and now nearly all states are engaged in PPAs.

partial preemption An approach common to federal environmental laws that requires states to apply federal standards.

During the presidency of George W. Bush, several states challenged the federal government, arguing that EPA should regulate greenhouse gases as pollutants under the Clean Air Act (CAA). In 2007, a U.S. Supreme Court ruling instructed the agency to study the issue and in 2009, after thorough scientific analysis, the EPA declared greenhouse gases pollutants that threaten public health. In 2014, the Court upheld the agency's plans to regulate greenhouse gas emissions from power plants and factories using the CAA but limited the agency's power to regulate smaller sources such as shopping centers and apartment buildings. Then in 2015, the Supreme Court decided that the EPA needed to consider the costs to the industry when developing rules to regulate emissions.[17] The current more conservative Supreme Court has not yet accepted a case directly concerning the Clean Air Act, but in 2019 it affirmed federal agency authority in how they use powers not directly delegated them by Congress.[18]

The Greening of States and Localities

State and local governments have taken on greater responsibility for financing and operating environmental protection programs and have become policy initiators. For example, Congress was gridlocked on acid rain legislation for years, but some states took unilateral actions to cut sulfur dioxide emissions within their borders (New Hampshire and New York were the first). Several states, including New Jersey and Ohio, passed legislation requiring firms to clean up hazardous wastes from industrial property before selling the property. Such legislation helps prevent companies from abandoning polluted sites that present health risks and leaving them for the states to clean up. California's far-reaching policies to improve the nation's worst air quality have become a model for other states and the national government. The Golden State also has led the way in its efforts to conserve water through, among other things, a statute requiring the use of water-efficient washing machines.

Today, states have ventured forth on several environmental fronts, notably climate change. More than half of the states have set goals for increased reliance on renewable energy sources for at least some of their utilities' power generation. For example, the state of Washington has created a series of financial incentives to spur the use of renewable energy sources. The state gives homeowners and small businesses with solar power and wind power systems a credit on their electric bills. Consumers get an even bigger break for using systems whose components were manufactured in Washington.[19] The bottom line is that states have become central actors in environmental protection through their innovative ideas.

States operate many of their pollution-control programs under the auspices of federal legislation and the EPA. They must develop and implement plans and standards under a host of federal laws. The Safe Drinking Water Act, for instance, requires local water systems to meet national standards for acceptable levels of contaminants such as coliform (a type of bacteria), asbestos, copper, and lead in their water supply. The Clean Air Act mandates the creation of vehicle inspection and maintenance programs for smog-stricken jurisdictions. States and localities are closer to pollution problems and hence are best situated to address them on a day-to-day basis. The problem with this approach, according to states and localities, is that they have to pay a large portion of the costs themselves. Approximately 77 percent of the money in state environmental budgets comes from state revenues. Even the EPA acknowledged that the cost of federally imposed environmental mandates on state and local governments could bust their budgets, requiring millions of dollars of new spending.

State Commitment to Environmental Protection

LO 18-4
To differentiate among states and localities as to their eco-friendliness.

During the Great Recession, environmental protection took a hit, with many states eliminating or cutting back programs and staff. Examples of programs affected by cutbacks included air quality inspections, water monitoring, environmental education, and recycling. Most reductions in environmental protection agency staff were accomplished through attrition, although furloughs and terminations did occur in some states. Even as the economy improved, states were slow to return to pre-recession spending levels.

The COVID-19 pandemic caused much industry around the world to shut down. Because of lower industrial activity and vehicle travel, many areas that had experienced severe air pollution problems saw their air begin to clear. In the San Francisco Bay Area, for example, the 2020 incidence of four of five key air pollution components—carbon monoxide, particulates, nitrogen dioxide and soot—were down by an average of 20 percent from the 2017–2018 average. Only one pollutant—ozone—was up.[20] In the Boston–Washington, D.C., metroplex, the air was cleaner in March 2020 than it had been since NASA first started measuring nitrogen dioxide in the atmosphere in 2005.[21] This is especially good news, because some evidence shows exposure to particulate matter—one component of air pollution—increases the lethality of COVID-19 dramatically.[22] During the pandemic, the federal government announced two major changes in environmental regulation. Fuel efficiency standards for new cars and trucks were reduced significantly. Obama-era rules would have required automakers to achieve an average 54 miles per gallon fuel efficiency for the vehicles they manufacture by 2025. The new rule reduces that to 40 miles per gallon by 2026. EPA also stopped enforcement of reporting and enforcement requirements on industries that could show a virus-related reason for noncompliance.[23]

State environmental protection agencies and natural resource departments vary in their structure and responsibilities. An example of the more comprehensive, single-agency structure is found in Delaware's Department of Natural Resources and Environmental Control, composed of five divisions: Air and Waste Management, Fish and Wildlife, Parks and Recreation, Soil and Water Conservation, and Water Resources. Arizona separates functions across a Department of Environmental Quality, a Game and Fish Department, and a Natural Resources Division within the State Land Department. Different still are states such as South Carolina, which combine environmental protection

Controversies in States and Localities

The Challenges of Regulating Polluters

When coal is burned to generate electricity, it creates a waste by-product called coal ash. In 2014, Duke Energy, the nation's largest utility, spilled 39,000 tons of coal ash into the Dan River in North Carolina, coating 70 miles of river bottom with a gray sludge containing toxic metals that threatened drinking water and aquatic life. Many environmentalists blamed not only Duke Energy but also the state's Department of Environment and Natural Resources (DENR) for failing to enforce federal and state regulations. The agency defended itself by noting that its budget for water pollution programs had been cut by 10 percent, and, furthermore, that former North Carolina Governor Pat McCrory had conveyed a preference for a more relaxed stance on regulatory enforcement. The head of DENR said that the governor had told him that "I want you to protect the environment and I want you to help us grow this economy." When Duke Energy fought demands from environmental groups that the utility relocate coal ash from unlined ponds to lined pits away from drinking water sources, the agency sided with the utility. However, the spill caused a critical reexamination of DENR's relationship with Duke Energy. Both the agency and the utility vowed to work together to establish an effective regulatory balance. In the meantime, the utility pleaded guilty to violating the Clean Water Act and negotiated an agreement with federal prosecutors to pay $102 million in fines and restitution. By 2019 the cleanup in the Dan River was almost complete, and in early 2020, Duke reached an agreement with the state of North Carolina to remove all of the nearly eighty million tons of coal ash it had stored at various facilities in the state.

Critical Thinking Questions

1. Some people view environmental regulations as a yoke on the neck of industry, and regulatory agencies as roadblocks to economic progress. Others see environmental regulations as a necessary protection of the health and quality of life for people in a given area and regulatory agencies as the authority that ensures public and environmental health and safety. Which of these philosophies more closely reflects your personal views? Why?

2. Regulatory agencies can either be preventive by ensuring that industries adhere to rules and regulations or reactive by fining companies after an event requiring cleanup. Preventive measures are often seen as "red tape" that makes doing business more difficult. However, reactive measures take place after the environmental damage has already been done. How can regulatory agencies find a happy medium between these two perspectives?

3. A state environmental protection agency ends up working closely with the industries it regulates. What are some of the consequences of working closely together?

Source: Trip Gabriel, "Ash Spill Shows How Watchdog Was Defanged," *New York Times*, https://www.nytimes.com/2014/03/01/us/coal-ash-spill-reveals-transformation-of-north-carolina-agency.html (March 1, 2014); "Duke Energy Fined $102 Million in Coal Ash Spill," CBS News, www.cbsnews.com/news/duke-energy-fined-102-million-in-coal-ash-spill/ (May 14, 2015); Associated Press, "Duke Energy Agrees to Remove Coal Ash in North Carolina," https://apnews.com/802d92f2b11a3838f60c899031b014af (January 2, 2020).

and public health in the same department. Clearly, there is no "one best way" to organize. In 2011, Connecticut merged its departments of Environmental Protection and Public Utility Control to form a Department of Energy and Environmental Protection. The same year, Michigan split its Department of Natural Resources and Environment into two separate agencies just eighteen months after its creation.[24] The Controversies in States and Localities box considers the relationship of state environmental protection agencies to powerful utility companies.

As noted earlier, states often face pressure from economic interests to weaken environmental regulations. Despite this pressure, at least some states have exceeded the guidelines set by the EPA to ensure better air quality. A survey of states found that nearly 30 percent had ambient air standards that went beyond the requirements of federal law.[25] What causes states to adopt more stringent regulations than the EPA requires? The answer seems to lie in the strength of green interest groups, supportive public opinion, and the ability to convert this pro-environment political climate into legislative action.

States are often ranked on their environmental conditions, policies, and programs. One recent rating by the financial products information website wallethub.com used fourteen key indicators of environmental quality and eco-friendly behaviors to evaluate the states. The criteria included air, water, and soil quality, carbon dioxide emissions, number of green-certified buildings, energy efficiency actions, green transportation, and recycling rates, among others. The analysis utilized data from independent scientific organizations and government sources, and it controlled for population differences among states. In 2019, the five greenest states were Vermont, New York, Oregon, Connecticut, and Minnesota; at the bottom of the list was Louisiana. Figure 18.2 categorizes the states into five groups, based on the

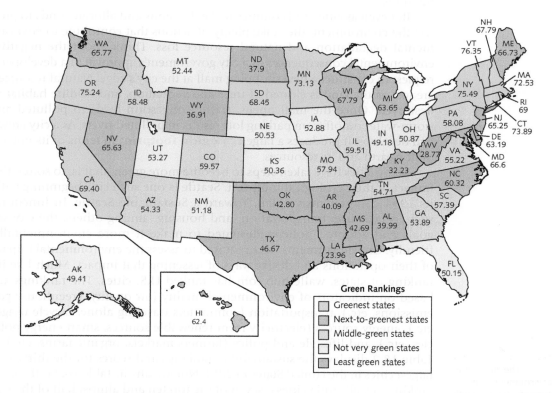

Figure 18.2 How Green Are the States?

Source: John Kiernan, "Greenest States," https://wallethub.com/edu/greenest-states/11987/#main-findings (April 15, 2019).

wallethub.com ratings. Among the southern states, only North Carolina shows up in either of the top two groupings. In general, research has shown that support for environmental protection tends to be strong among Democrats, liberals, the affluent, and the educated.[26]

Green Localities

Local governments regularly take action to protect the environment and conserve natural resources. For instance, Atlanta has sponsored a tree-planting project for National Arbor Day; Kansas City, Missouri, promoted its Keep Kansas City Beautiful anti-litter campaign; the green power program in Riverside, California, offered classes on recycling and composting; Spokane, Washington, adopted a special tax in support of open-space conservation. Meanwhile, New York City developed plans to convert its nearly 4,500 public buses to all-electric use by 2040, and Atlanta now requires all new residential homes and public parking facilities to be built ready to accommodate electric vehicles. More than 1,000 cities joined the Cities for Climate Protection campaign to reduce the emissions of greenhouse gases. Others have adopted green building codes to spur the construction of buildings that are substantially more energy efficient and less resource intensive than regular buildings.

But even as cities and counties make decisions and allocate funds to protect the environment, they take plenty of actions that contribute to environmental degradation and natural resource loss. Think about the negative environmental consequences of a city government's approval of a developer's request to construct a new shopping mall at the city's edge. Natural resources are lost as the land is cleared of trees and vegetation, and wildlife habitat is destroyed. Once the mall opens, traffic congestion leads to polluted air; storm-water runoff from parking lots results in polluted rivers. As a city grows and develops, it produces a large **ecological footprint** in terms of its impact on the earth and its resources.

Many cities have taken steps to become more green, that is, to soften the impact of their ecological footprint. Seattle is one such city, beginning with its 1994 comprehensive plan, Toward a Sustainable Seattle. In functions such as land use, transportation, and housing, among others, the city set goals and adopted policies designed to make it more environmentally friendly. City departments were required to assess the environmental impact of their operations and devise ways of lessening that impact. Much like its ranking of states, wallethub.com has ranked U.S. cities. The rankings are based on indicators of environmental quality (air quality, greenhouse gas emissions, etc.), transportation (commuters traveling alone, bicycle usage, etc.), energy sources (electricity from renewable sources, smart energy policies, etc.), and lifestyle and policy (farmers markets, organic farms, etc.).[27] Table 18.2 displays the sustainability rankings and scores for the thirty-five largest cities in the United States in 2019. Noteworthy in Table 18.2 is the high ranking of California cities—seven of the top ten and almost half of the top thirty-five overall.

ecological footprint The size of the environmental impact imposed on the earth and its resources.

The approach taken by San Francisco is especially interesting: The city's sustainability plan identified several areas of concern, such as air quality, biodiversity, climate change, and open spaces. For these areas of concern, specific indicators were developed to gauge the progress that the city has or has not made. For instance, the number of native plant species in parks is one indicator of biodiversity, as is the number of different bird species sighted. Given the city's propensity, it was not a surprise when, in 2007, it became the first jurisdiction in the country to ban the use of plastic checkout bags at supermarkets. And then, in 2009, San Francisco began requiring households and businesses to compost food scraps; those who do not comply can be fined. The city's goal is zero waste by 2020, meaning that it intends to reduce, reuse, and recycle such that the city sends no waste to landfills or incinerators. Success in achieving this goal is uncertain since the last bits of waste are items such as electronic equipment and furniture and clothing that may have been treated with flame retardants.[28]

Table 18.2 Thirty-Five Largest U.S. Cities and Their "Green" Scores

RANK	CITY	TOTAL SCORE
1	San Francisco CA	72.48
2	San Diego CA	72.04
3	Irvine CA	69.83
4	Washington, D.C.	68.84
5	San Jose CA	68.42
6	Seattle WA	68.05
7	Fremont CA	67.13
8	Sacramento CA	65.90
9	Portland OR	65.87
10	Oakland CA	65.32
11	Minneapolis MN	65.10
12	Honolulu HI	63.78
13	Buffalo NY	62.31
14	Chula Vista CA	61.20
15	Boston MA	60.73
16	San Bernardino CA	60.59
17	Saint Paul MN	60.55
18	Madison WI	60.39
19	Los Angeles	60.22
20	Austin TX	60.03
21	New York NY	59.64
22	Long Beach CA	58.79
23	Riverside CA	58.68

(continued)

Table 18.2 Thirty-Five Largest U.S. Cities and Their "Green" Scores (*continued*)

RANK	CITY	TOTAL SCORE
24	Fresno CA	57.49
25	Stockton CA	56.89
26	Anchorage AK	56.41
27	Santa Ana CA	56.09
28	Anaheim CA	55.79
29	Denver CO	55.64
30	Orlando FL	54.37
31	Boise ID	53.96
32	Cincinnati OH	53.72
33	Albuquerque NM	53.41
34	Bakersfield CA	52.72
35	Scottsdale AZ	52.29

Source: Adam McCann, "Greenest Cities in America," https://wallethub.com/edu/most-least-green
-cities/16246/ (October 8, 2019).

LO 18-5
To summarize the issues related to waste management.

Dealing with Waste

One of the by-products of modern life is waste of all varieties. Households, schools, hospitals, businesses, and factories produce massive quantities of waste daily. When garbage collectors in New York City went on strike several years ago, the towers of smelly refuse that piled up on city streets reminded New Yorkers how important this particular city service was. More threatening to public health and the environment are the toxic wastes generated by certain industrial processes and the wastes associated with nuclear power. One of the challenges for government is finding better ways to manage all this waste.

Recycling Solid Waste

Vast quantities of household and commercial refuse are generated daily in the United States. Americans produce about 267.8 million tons of trash annually, or 4.51 pounds per person per day.[29] In general, states with more commercial and industrial activity tend to generate more solid waste than those with a more agricultural economy. Of the solid waste generated in a year, 13 percent is combusted in waste-to-energy plants and another 35 percent is recycled or composted, leaving about 52 percent destined for landfills. Thousands of landfills were in operation in the 1980s; today there are about 2,000. Many of them are so-called super dumps, where more than 500 tons of waste is disposed of daily.

NIMBY
Not in my backyard; the public desire to keep an unwanted facility out of a neighborhood.

Like nuclear and hazardous waste, solid waste often brings out the not-in-my-backyard (**NIMBY**) syndrome. Everyone generates garbage, and lots of it, but no one wants to have it smelling over the back fence or threatening the well water. (There are some exceptions, of course, which have given rise to the term **PIMBY,** or put-in-my-backyard.) The shortage of disposal sites has naturally driven up the price of land disposal in the dumps that still operate, and disposal fees have tripled in many localities during the past few years. Many cities must ship their waste hundreds of miles and across state lines to find an open dump site. For example, household garbage from suburban New York City communities may be transported to a dump in central Illinois or rural Virginia. More than 20 percent of the trash dumped in Michigan's landfills comes from other states or from Canada.[30] Burning trash in waste-to-energy plants once seemed the perfect solution: disposing of solid waste and creating electrical power. But the high cost of building and operating these incinerators, especially as air-quality standards increased, has lessened their promise.

Recycling is a waste management solution that makes good sense. Approximately 25 percent of municipal solid waste is paper, 13 percent is plastic, and another 13 percent is yard trimmings. Most of these waste streams could be recycled.[31] Figure 18.3 shows the types of materials that make up municipal solid waste. Many states have aggressively tackled the mounting garbage problem by adopting statewide recycling laws, and a growing number of cities and counties have begun their own recycling efforts. Curbside recycling programs are available to some 69.8 million households in the United States, about 54 percent of all U.S. households. On average, we recycle or compost approximately 1.5 pounds of the waste we generate daily for a recycling rate of about 33 percent.

Recycling is not a panacea for the solid waste problem, however. It requires citizen cooperation if it is to be affordable, and some people simply will not cooperate. Recycling rates for aluminum cans and plastic soft drink bottles peaked a few years ago at 63 percent and 41 percent, respectively. But

PIMBY
Put in my backyard; a willingness to accept what others do not want, usually because of the economic benefit.

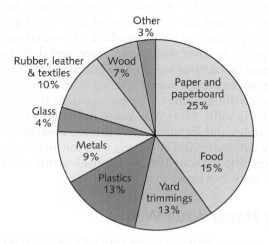

Figure 18.3 Materials in Municipal Solid Waste

Source: U.S. Environmental Protection Agency, "National Overview: Facts and Figures on Materials, Wastes and Recycling," https://www.epa.gov/facts-and-figures-about-materials-waste-and-recycling/national -overview-facts-and-figures-materials (accessed April 23, 2020).

a city cannot refuse to collect nonparticipants' garbage without creating a public health problem. Another dilemma is the shortage of markets for recycled paper, aluminum cans, plastics, and other materials.

For some states, glutted markets and low prices for recyclables make it difficult to reach their recycling goals. During the recession of 2008 through 2011, the demand for recycled materials such as cardboard, newspaper, plastic, and metals dropped dramatically. Many states had enacted laws and adopted policies aimed at stimulating demand for recycled goods, including sanctions (such as taxes on manufacturers based on their use of virgin materials), incentives (such as the provision of rebates to manufacturers using recovered materials), and exhortations (such as buy-recycled programs). And most state governments have adopted rules requiring or encouraging their agencies to purchase recycled paper products. But even with these market-priming mechanisms in place, when the economy slowed, many localities that once made money selling recyclables were forced to pay waste haulers to take the bottles, cans, and newspapers off their hands.[32] On top of this, in 2018, China said it would stop accepting most recycled plastics. This action by the largest purchaser of such plastics dried up that market and made it more difficult for cities in the United States to dispose of such materials in any other way than sending them to an area landfill.[33]

As noted, about one-third of the nation's solid waste is recycled, but the figures are substantially higher in some jurisdictions than in others. The explanation for why some states recycle at a greater rate than others is fairly straightforward: access and economics. In other words, recycling rates are higher in states that offer comprehensive curbside recycling programs and impose unit charges for refuse disposal. Making recycling convenient for consumers and creating an economic disincentive not to recycle stimulates behavior. For instance, Michigan, which has a bottle deposit law for certain beverage containers, can boast that upward of 90 percent of those beverage bottles and cans are returned. The program is so successful that lawmakers are considering expanding the policy to cover wine, water, juice, and dairy product bottles.[34] Managing the vast quantity of solid waste generated in our mass consumption, throwaway society is not easy. Recycling is an appealing option, but we cannot recycle everything. Some of the garbage must therefore be incinerated or deposited in a landfill. Every new waste technology has its own difficult issues, and the states and localities, with limited assistance from the federal government, are striving to deal effectively with the huge task of managing the country's garbage. The It's Your Turn box considers one way some cities have tried to address the waste issue.

Managing Hazardous Waste

The image of garbage mountains rising above the horizon is disconcerting, to say the least. But solid waste is just one of several contributors to environmental destruction. Another insidious public health threat comes from hazardous waste—the poisonous by-products of industrial processes. If these by-products are toxic, corrosive, flammable, or reactive, they are considered hazardous.

? It's Your Turn

Should Cities Enact Plastic Bag Bans?

Several major cities—San Francisco, Los Angeles, Chicago, and Seattle among them—have banned the use of plastic bags in supermarkets and stores; other cities such as Washington, D.C., and Boulder, Colorado, require stores to charge fees (usually five or ten cents) to consumers who opt for plastic bags at checkout. (Dallas repealed its plastic bag fee in June 2015; it had raised $500,000 in the five months it was in effect.) What do you think: Should cities ban the use of plastic bags by grocery stores and other retail outlets?

PROS	CONS
Most plastic bags do not biodegrade; discarded plastic bags harm wildlife on land and in the water for years to come.	Plastic bags are reusable and recyclable. Rather than banning bags, cities should educate consumers about reuse and recycling.
Many plastic bags end up as litter, an eyesore that can have negative effects on city tourism and require cities to conduct cleanups.	Letting cities ban bags means that in a single state, there will be different ordinances in different cities. This lack of uniformity across a state will create confusion.
Most plastic bags are manufactured from petroleum products and natural gas, thereby depleting natural resources.	Bag bans are an example of overzealous regulation, limiting the choices of retailers and consumers.

The industries that generate 90 percent of the hazardous waste in the United States are chemical and allied products, primary metals, petroleum and coal products, fabricated metal products, and rubber and plastic products. Table 18.3 lists the five states where the largest amounts of toxic chemicals were released into the air, water, and ground in 2018. Alaska's toxic waste is generated in a fairly small number (thirty) of large facilities whereas Texas's is generated in a relatively large number (1,796) of smaller facilities.

Hazardous waste is more ubiquitous than most people realize. Pesticide residues, used motor oil, discarded cadmium batteries, used refrigerants, and paint sludge are hazardous leftovers that are frequently found in households

Table 18.3 State Leaders in Toxic Releases, 2018

STATES LEADING IN TOTAL ON-AND-OFF SITE RELEASES (ALL INDUSTRIES, ALL CHEMICALS)	AMOUNT (IN THOUSANDS OF POUNDS)
Alaska	971,996
Nevada	339,147
Utah	291,315
Texas	225,215
Arizona	170,539

Source: U.S. Environmental Protection Agency, "Supporting Data Files for the TRI National Analysis: Where You Live," https://www.epa.gov/trinationalanalysis/supporting-data-files-tri-national-analysis (February 2020).

and in so-called nonpolluting industries. It is no exaggeration to say that hazardous waste is all around us.

The primary dilemma concerning hazardous waste is what to do with it. The discovery that wastes were not being properly or safely disposed of triggered government involvement; when hazardous liquids began seeping into people's basements from long-buried barrels, children playing in fields uncovered rotting drums of toxic waste, and motorists developed unusual skin rashes from pesticides sprayed along the roadway, government was called in. Some states feared that imposing tough new hazardous waste regulations would make them less attractive to industry. Others were concerned that tightening the laws for waste disposal would have the perverse effect of increasing the incidence of illegal dumping. A national policy initiative seemed preferable to state attempts at solving the problems.

The national government responded to the mounting crisis with two pieces of legislation: the Resource Conservation and Recovery Act (RCRA) of 1976 and the Comprehensive Environmental Response, Compensation, and Liability Act of 1980 (also known as Superfund). RCRA provides for cradle-to-grave tracking of waste and establishes standards for its treatment, storage, and disposal. Any firm that generates 220 pounds of hazardous waste per month (an amount that typically fills a 55-gallon barrel about halfway) is covered by the law. RCRA is considered partially preemptive because states have a degree of discretion and flexibility in implementation. Once the EPA is satisfied that a state program meets its standards and possesses adequate enforcement mechanisms, the agency authorizes the state to operate its own hazardous waste management program. Under RCRA, states can impose fines and hold individuals criminally liable for violating its provisions.

Superfund was passed in recognition of the fact that no matter how comprehensive and cautious hazardous waste management will be in the future, the pollution of the past remains with us. Under Superfund, the national government can intervene to clean up a dangerous hazardous waste site and later seek reimbursement from responsible parties. Originally, the law contained a provision dubbed "polluter pays," which created a cleanup fund from fees levied on chemical manufacturers and the petroleum industry. These fees, which generated between $1 and $2 billion annually, allowed government to step in and begin the cleanup before all the complex legal issues were resolved. The cleanup fund provision expired in 1995, however, and affected industries have been successful in blocking its renewal. Thus, Superfund has become a program funded by taxpayers.[35] In fact, federal stimulus money was used in 2010 to help accelerate the cleanup of fifty Superfund sites in twenty-eight states.[36]

One of the first actions taken under Superfund was the identification of particularly troublesome sites in need of immediate cleanup, the National Priorities List (NPL). New Jersey was the state with the most sites on the list; Nevada had the fewest. One factor confounding the Superfund program is determining which parties—waste generators, waste transporters, site owners—are responsible for paying for the cleanup. Some of the firms that dumped toxic waste at these sites have gone out of business, and the hope of recovering any of the cleanup costs is remote. As time passed, frustration grew over the slow pace of remediation. Subsequent amendments to the law increased funding levels for the program (although Superfund expenditures peaked in 2001) and expanded the role for state governments in selecting cleanup remedies. In addition, the EPA launched a new initiative to clean up and redevelop contaminated industrial sites, or **brownfields**. Many states have adopted their own mini-Superfund statutes that authorize them to conduct site assessments and initiate remedial cleanup actions or force a responsible party to do so. Some states have also passed laws making it easier to redevelop brownfields, adopted community right-to-know (about hazardous wastes in the area) statutes, and conducted household hazardous waste collection drives.

An issue that has bedeviled the states is disposing of hazardous waste. Disposal sites are locally unwanted land uses (**LULUs**). When efforts to find new disposal facilities are thwarted, states look beyond their borders for solutions. Some states and tribal governments have been willing to accept other states' hazardous waste for disposal—the PIMBY phenomenon—seeing it as a way to generate revenue. But even waste-importing states have their limits. At one point, Alabama banned hazardous waste importation from twenty-two states, an action that was struck down eventually by the federal courts. Alabama lawmakers responded with a fee schedule that taxed out-of-state waste at three times the rate of in-state-generated waste. The effect was dramatic: The quantity of out-of-state waste dropped by one-half, but the business still generated $30 million for the state treasury. Unfortunately for Alabama, the U.S. Supreme Court ruled that the surcharge on out-of-state waste violated the interstate commerce clause. Regardless, efforts to block out-of-state waste will continue until solutions to the hazardous waste disposal problem are found. One eminently plausible, if partial, solution to waste-disposal dilemmas is to reduce the amount of waste generated in the first place. Less waste produced means less waste to dispose of.

Storing Nuclear Waste

Nuclear power is thought by some to be a solution to the nation's energy problems, but it carries a heavy price: deadly, radioactive waste. Until 2009, the federal government had planned to bury high-level nuclear waste, which retains its toxicity for hundreds of thousands of years, at Yucca Mountain, an isolated spot 100 miles northwest of Las Vegas. This plan generated a firestorm of protest from environmentalists and Nevada officials and became an issue in the 2008 presidential election. One concern was the rate of corrosion for the canisters in which the waste would be stored; another was the possibility of earthquakes in the area, and still another was the safety of shipping the waste to the site.

In 2009, President Obama, making good on a campaign promise, terminated the Yucca Mountain waste disposal project and, with the support of Congress, allocated funds to convene a blue-ribbon commission to come up with an alternative plan. The commission delivered its final report in 2012

brownfields
Abandoned industrial sites with real or perceived environmental contamination.

LULU
Locally unwanted land use; a broad category of undesirable facilities such as landfills and prisons.

recommending an independent non political organization with a dedicated source of funding that would develop a facility, most likely at Yucca Mountain. The report met heavy political opposition, much of it from former Senator Harry Reid of Nevada who was majority leader of the U.S. Senate. President Trump has said that he is opposed to the Yucca Mountain site but research on other sites is not seriously being pursued. Currently, high-level nuclear waste is stored on-site at nuclear power plants around the United States, while the Hanford, Washington, facility—where the world's first large nuclear reactor began operation in the 1940s—still houses the remnants of plutonium production that occurred at that site over forty years. Some 54 tons of plutonium is also stored at a nuclear weapons facility near Amarillo, Texas.[37]

Low-level radioactive wastes (LLWs) are much less toxic in a relative sense because they break down to safe levels of radioactivity in anywhere from a few weeks or months to 300 years. LLWs are produced by commercial nuclear power installations (46 percent), nuclear-related industries (39 percent), and medical and research institutions (15 percent). The waste, much of it stored in 55-gallon steel drums, includes items such as contaminated laboratory clothes, tools, equipment, and leftover bomb materials, as well as bulk wastes.

The Low-Level Radioactive Waste Policy Act of 1980 made each state responsible for the disposal of the waste generated within its borders. States have the choice of managing LLWs within their own jurisdictions (i.e., developing their own disposal sites) or entering into an interstate compact for out-of-state disposal. As expected, a few states have opted to handle the problem alone, but most have joined with their neighbors to forge a regional answer to the disposal question.

The use of **interstate compacts** to address the LLW problem was particularly inventive because nuclear waste disposal has historically been considered a federal responsibility. When interstate compacts are successful, they are a shining example of what the states can accomplish when left to their own devices.[38] Potential member states have to negotiate a draft compact that must be ratified by their legislatures and by Congress. Negotiations often break down as each state tries to get the best deal for itself, precisely the goal of each of the other participating states. As of 2019, ten interstate LLW compacts had been formed; eight states remained unaligned, preferring to go it alone. As shown in Figure 18.4, several of the compacts are decidedly nonregional in their composition. For example, the two Dakotas joined Arizona and California to form the Southwestern Compact; Texas teamed up with Vermont to create the Texas Compact; and South Carolina joined with Connecticut and New Jersey to form the Atlantic Compact.

The case of the Midwest Compact demonstrates the hard decisions faced by all the compacts. The Midwest Compact was one of the first to win congressional consent. Seven states were members; each agreed that it would take its turn to host a disposal facility for the entire compact. Weighing three factors for each state—the volume of LLW produced, the radioactivity of that waste, and transportation modes and routes—compact members selected Michigan as the first host state. Michigan spent several years evaluating the suitability of three possible disposal locations only to reject all of them.

interstate compacts
Formal agreements among a subset of states, usually to solve a problem that affects each of the member states.

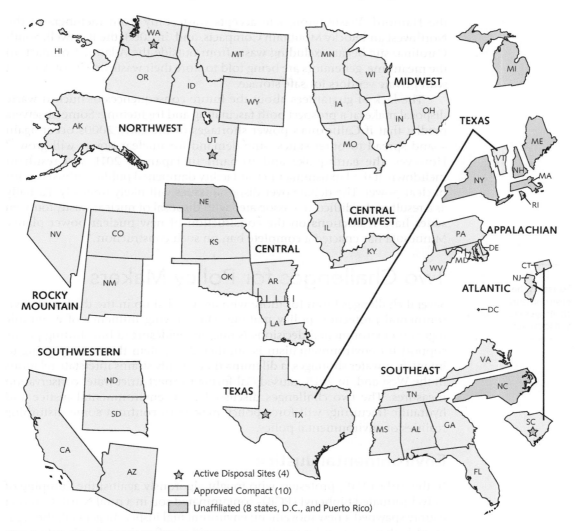

Figure 18.4 Low-Level Radioactive Waste Compacts

Note: Data as of May 2014. Alaska and Hawaii belong to the Northwest Compact. Puerto Rico is unaffiliated.

Source: U.S. Nuclear Regulatory Commission, "Low Level Waste Compacts," http://www.nrc.gov/waste/llw-disposal/licensing/compacts.html (accessed April 13, 2015).

The compact was no closer to a regional disposal site than it had been at the outset. In reaction, the other states booted Michigan out of the Midwest Compact (Michigan is currently unaligned). Ohio, the runner-up to Michigan in the earlier state-selection process, became the host state.

    With compacts in place and host states selected, the next challenge is the actual construction of new disposal facilities. This step can be difficult because of the **NIMTOO** (not in my term of office) phenomenon. But time is of the essence because existing sites have begun to restrict access. For example,

NIMTOO
Not in my term of office; the desire by elected officials to avoid accepting LULUs while they are in office.

the Hanford, Washington, site accepts waste only from members of the Northwest and Rocky Mountain Compacts, and, in 2008, the Barnwell, South Carolina, site began excluding waste from outside the Atlantic Compact. In the meantime, generators are being told to store their waste on site or contract with private vendors for safe storage.

The lack of guarantees about the future consequences of nuclear waste disposal makes it a prospect both fascinating and frightening. Some observers predict that if California's power shortages of the early 2000s occur again —and spread to other states—the demand for nuclear power will grow.[39] However, the earthquake and tsunami in Japan in 2011 and resultant meltdown at the Fukushima nuclear facility dampened public enthusiasm for nuclear power. The debate over disposal issues will likely intensify. Partially as a result of the difficulties associated with disposal of nuclear waste, fourteen states have restrictions on the construction of new nuclear power plants. Minnesota has enacted a complete ban on such construction.[40]

LO 18-6
To assess the various environmental challenges facing states and localities.

Two Challenges for Policy Makers

Several challenges loom for those who are tangled up in the thicket of environmental protection policy making. The growing influence of economic logic on environmental decisions is one; the widespread but shifting public support for environmentalism is another. A problem that is only going to intensify is water shortages, a dilemma that already strains interstate relations in the West and, in 2015, caused California to enact strict water conservation measures. The two challenges discussed next, environmental justice and hydraulic fracturing, will force policy makers to confront some disturbing realities of environmental policy.

Environmental Justice

In the early 1980s, protesters who fought vigorously against the dumping of polychlorinated biphenyl (PCB)–contaminated soil in a rural North Carolina county spawned a new movement: environmental justice. In general, the argument is that poor and minority communities suffer disproportionate exposure to environmental health risks. An example of environmental injustice is the area referred to as "Cancer Alley," an 85-mile strip along the Mississippi River in Louisiana that is home to more than 100 chemical, petrochemical, refining, and industrial plants. The households located within harm's way of these plants are disproportionately minority and low-income.[41] Two law school professors put the matter this way:

> People of color throughout the United States are receiving more than their fair share of the poisonous fruits of industrial production. They live cheek by jowl with waste dumps, incinerators, landfills, smelters, factories, chemical plants, and oil refineries whose operations make them sick and kill them young. They are poisoned by the air they breathe, the water they drink, the fish they catch, the vegetables they grow, and in the case of children, the very ground they play on.[42]

Research has found inequities in environmental policy. For instance, one study of the relationship between race and the enforcement of environmental laws by the EPA showed that white communities received faster action and more satisfactory results than did minority communities; other research uncovered race-based disparities in state inspections of hazardous waste generating facilities.[43] One of the distinctive differences between areas that contain commercial hazardous waste facilities and those that do not is the proportion of minority residents.[44] Communities with these facilities tend to have double the proportion of minority residents than those without them. Another study found that single-mother families are overrepresented in environmentally hazardous areas.[45] Other research, however, takes issue with contentions of environmental inequities. Statewide studies of Superfund site locations in New Jersey and hazardous waste facilities in South Carolina did not find statistically significant links to race or ethnicity.[46] Why are polluting facilities located where they are? The answer is multifaceted:

- Scientific rationality (e.g., the geologic characteristics of the site)
- Market factors (e.g., land prices, available labor pool)
- Neighborhood transition (e.g., changing demographics in the area over time)
- Political power (e.g., whether the residents in the area are politically active)
- Intentional discrimination (e.g., targeting poor and minority neighborhoods)[47]

Concern over environmental justice has led more than thirty states to take some sort of policy action. For example, Arkansas passed legislation that discourages the location of high-impact solid waste management facilities within 12 miles of each other. Exemptions may be granted if specific benefits are provided to the host community in the form of jobs, fees, and improvements to infrastructure. In Louisiana, the Department of Environmental Quality was instructed to hold public hearings and make policy recommendations on environmental equity issues. Pennsylvania added an Environmental Justice Advisory Board to its environmental protection agency. The federal government and EPA took up the issue as well, establishing a National Environmental Justice Advisory Council charged with ensuring that environmental justice be addressed in the agency's policies, programs, and activities. Clearly, environmental justice will continue to be a salient topic for policy makers well into the future.[48]

Hydraulic Fracturing

The nation has long sought a clean domestic energy source, one that is in plentiful supply and will reduce the country's dependence on foreign sources of energy. Natural gas has been touted by many as the answer. There are vast deposits of natural gas in the United States; and as an energy source, natural gas produces fewer greenhouse gases than conventional sources such as petroleum or coal.

Anti-fracking protestors gather in New York City to express their views on the state's fracking ban.

At issue is hydraulic fracturing, or "fracking," a process in which a mixture of water, sand, and chemicals is injected at high pressure into the ground to break up dense rock and release the gas. Technological advances have led to horizontal fracking, thereby allowing drillers to reach more distant rock formations that previously had been considered impractical and uneconomical to pursue. Now that these extensive natural gas deposits are more accessible, more drilling is occurring in more places. According to the U.S. Department of Energy, by 2018, there were more than 523,000 producing gas wells operating in thirty-four states and in the Gulf of Mexico.[49]

Enthusiasm for fracking is far from universal, however. Fracking comes with questions about the degree to which the process pollutes ground and surface waters. In 2005, Congress, relying on a 2004 study by the U.S. Environmental Protection Agency that concluded that fracking posed a minimal threat to drinking water, exempted fracking from regulation under the federal Safe Drinking Water Act (SDWA). The study's conclusion was criticized by many environmentalists because the research involved no direct monitoring of water wells but instead relied on scientific literature and interviews with industry and state and local government officials.[50]

States with natural gas resources have found themselves caught in the crossfire between the industry seeking permits to drill and environmentalists seeking bans on drilling. At the community level, disputes between neighbors have arisen, with some landowners wanting to lease their land for drilling whereas others want nothing to do with it.[51] Public awareness of the fracking issue increased with the release of a 2010 documentary film *Gasland* and the follow-up documentary in 2014 *Gasland II*. The films offered a very critical look at fracking and were denounced by many in the oil and gas industry. One of the most riveting scenes in *Gasland* was one in which a man lit water from his faucet on fire, claiming that natural gas drilling was responsible for the situation. Although most experts were skeptical of that particular scene, in 2011, EPA announced that compounds likely associated with fracking chemicals had been detected in the groundwater beneath a central Wyoming town where residents had complained their well water reeked of chemicals. This announcement put more pressure on states to take action.

Maryland and New York were among the states that placed a moratorium on fracking, awaiting further study and scientific review of the issue; in 2015, both states decided to let the fracking bans stay in place. Vermont, in 2012, was the first state to ban the practice of fracking altogether; that same year, the New Jersey legislature enacted a new law banning the disposal of fracking wastewater in the Garden State. The North Carolina legislature lifted its moratorium on fracking in 2012; but the governor vetoed the bill stating, "Our drinking water and the health and safety of North Carolina's families are too important. We can't put them in jeopardy by rushing to allow fracking without proper safeguards."[52] The North Carolina legislature later overrode her veto and by 2015, the state had rules in place to allow fracking. By 2020, there were yet to be any operating fracking wells in the state.[53] Texas, a state in which the oil and gas industry is a powerful player, surprised many when it enacted a law requiring drillers to publicly disclose the chemicals they use in the fracking process. However, when the voters in the Texas city of Denton approved a ban on fracking within the city's limits, the Texas legislature responded by overturning the ban.

Meanwhile, back in the nation's capital, bills to make fracking subject to the dictates of the SDWA and to require drillers to disclose the chemicals they use in their injection process have not been acted upon in Congress. In 2010, Congress did, however, request EPA to conduct a multiyear, comprehensive study to better understand any potential impacts of hydraulic fracturing on drinking water and ground water. In the meantime, the agency developed rules intended to reduce air pollution, primarily volatile organic compounds and air toxics, by requiring drillers to capture natural gas that escapes into the air.[54] The EPA report that Congress requested was released in 2015 and caused a furor with its finding that no conclusive evidence existed linking fracking to widespread, systemic pollution of drinking water.[55] The report did raise concerns about the amount of water used in fracking and the potential for poorly designed injection wells that store fracking fluids to leak into groundwater. It seems reasonable to conclude that fracking will remain on the governmental agenda for some time to come.

Another issue connected to fracking is the increase in small earthquakes that seem to be associated with fracking activity. Fracking was first used in Oklahoma in 1968. Before 2011, there were only four earthquakes in the entire state in recorded history. Between 2011 and 2016, Oklahoma experienced four earthquakes above magnitude 5.0 (considered moderate by seismologists).[56] Smaller earthquakes have become much more common—several hundred per year in the 2014 to 2019 time period, more than seismically active California.[57] When the state tightened rules on oil and gas drilling in 2015, the number of earthquakes per year began to drop, but it may be ten years before fracking-induced earthquakes stop in Oklahoma.[58] Similar incidences of small earthquakes occurred in Ohio, Pennsylvania, Texas, and West Virginia after fracking operations began in those states.

LO 18-7
To explain how day-to-day decisions made by states and localities affect the global environment.

From Short Term to Long Term

Much of environmental policy making by state and local governments involves day-to-day decisions such as managing automobile traffic or designing a recycling system. Others are longer term, like siting a landfill or a major economic development project. Each of these activities is often considered singularly with only small positive or negative effects on the global environment. However, when you sum up all those small actions, they cause a major impact on global climate change. Carbon dioxide composes 75 percent of the greenhouse gases generated in the United States. Carbon dioxide is a product of burning fossil fuels such as coal, gasoline, diesel fuel, and natural gas. Most carbon dioxide in the United States comes from automobile emissions.

Another greenhouse gas is methane, which composes about 10 percent of all emissions. Large landfills generate significant amounts of methane from the decomposition of garbage. If allowed to escape into the atmosphere, methane contributes to global warming. Many landfills around the country attempt to compensate for this by capturing the methane they produce and using it to generate electricity. For example, the Puente Hills landfill outside of Los Angeles was the largest landfill in the United States before it closed in 2014. Methane from the landfill generated 50 megawatts of electricity, enough to power some 70,000 homes in the Los Angeles area.

Other greenhouse gases include nitrous oxide (6 percent), a product mainly of nitrogen-based fertilizers and some industrial gases.[59] Single large stationary producers of pollution—like landfills or factories—are called point source producers. Nonpoint source producers are the opposite; they produce smaller amounts of pollution and are moveable. Automobiles are the best example. Reducing greenhouse gases and air pollution means regulating both point source and nonpoint sources of pollution.

If the direst predictions of climate change analysts described at the beginning of this chapter come true, state and local governments will need to cope with severe consequences. Abandoning large sections of low-lying cities is not something anybody wants to seriously entertain, but building levees and seawalls as New Orleans and other cities have had to do is an expensive proposition both in construction and long-term maintenance. New York and New Jersey, for example, have considered building a retractable 6-mile barrier that could be raised if a hurricane storm surge, like that generated by Hurricane Sandy in 2012, threatens the area. Such a barrier could also provide protection against sea level rise, one of the major consequences of global climate change. The cost—a mere $119 billion to build the barrier, with expensive annual maintenance costs to make sure it works when it's needed.[60] In other parts of the country, land is actually sinking, a phenomenon known as subsidence, causing waterfronts to be even more vulnerable to flooding. Charleston, South Carolina is subsiding at a rate of 5 inches per century as a result of development in the city and the depletion of groundwater. Coupling subsidence with sea level rise, the number of "nuisance floods" in Charleston increased from 4.6 days a year between 1957 and 1963 to 23.2 days a year from 2007 to 2013, a 409 percent increase.[61] Eight projects either underway or soon commencing to address flooding in Charleston are expected to cost nearly $550 million.[62] Plans by the U.S Army Corps of Engineers are even more ambitious—construction of an 8-mile sea wall surrounding Charleston's peninsula. The cost: more than $1 billion in federal funds with an additional $600 million (two and a half times the city's annual budget) coming from local government.[63] New Orleans is subsiding much faster than Charleston— up to 2 inches *per year*. The cost to address flooding in New Orleans: nearly $2 billion in 2020 alone![64] In 2017, residents of Miami approved a $400 million bond referendum; $192 million of this was to mitigate the effects of sea level rise. Estimates of sea wall construction in Hillsborough County, Florida (Tampa area), run to $2.7 billion over the next twenty years. The examples could go on.

These types of projects cannot be termed community improvement; rather than bettering the community, they are designed simply to keep things from getting worse. The federal government funds a large percentage of many of the projects, but the state and local match is still a staggering amount of money. To be sure, short-sighted local development decisions contribute to the problem. San Francisco's airport, for example, built on marshlands, now needs to have its seawall rebuilt at a cost of nearly $600 million. All three New York City–area airports—LaGuardia, Kennedy, and Newark—were similarly built on marshland, as were many other big city airports in the country. All will need expensive seawall construction to keep them operating over the next fifty years, or they will be forced to close or be relocated. Constructing housing, siting landfills, building subway systems and roadways—all decisions made using relative short-term economic considerations—now require solutions to keep them viable in the long run. As we have seen throughout this book, state and local governments are not nearly as good at long-term planning as they are at short-term decision making. Addressing the localized effects of global climate change will require a major change in state and local decision making.

Chapter Recap

- Public opinion shows support for environmental protection and economic growth; however, achieving one goal often comes at the expense of the other. After several years of preferring economic growth, public opinion has recently shifted in favor of environmental protection. Government's role is to balance the two objectives.

- The national government has been an important force in environmental protection. Performance partnership agreements and grants give states more power to set their own spending priorities.

- Environmental conditions and state programs vary from one state to another. A recent study found Vermont and New York to be the greenest states, and Louisiana to be the least green.

- Many cities, such as Portland, Oregon, San Francisco, and Seattle have embraced sustainability and have adopted green policies.

- A tremendous amount of solid waste is generated daily in the United States. Although most of it is disposed of in landfills, recycling continues to be a promising approach.

- Two major federal programs, RCRA and Superfund, have set the hazardous waste management agenda. States play a major part in implementing RCRA, and they partner with the federal government in Superfund cleanups.

- Interstate compacts (there are ten) are used for the disposal of low-level radioactive waste.

- Two challenges facing contemporary policy makers are environmental justice and hydraulic fracturing.

- Routine day-to-day development decisions made by local governments may have long-term environmental consequences.

Key Terms

environmental self-audit *(p. 517)*
race to the bottom *(p. 517)*
sustainability *(p. 517)*
partial preemption *(p. 521)*
ecological footprint *(p. 526)*
NIMBY *(p. 528)*
PIMBY *(p. 529)*
brownfields *(p. 533)*
LULU *(p. 533)*
interstate compacts *(p. 534)*
NIMTOO *(p. 535)*

Internet Resources

The official website of the Environmental Protection Agency (EPA) is **https://www.epa.gov**. It is packed with information about the EPA's programs and initiatives.

The official website of the Department of the Interior is **https://www.doi.gov**. It contains a wealth of information about the various activities of the agency.

All states have agencies devoted to environmental protection and natural resource conservation. See, for example, Oregon at **https://www.oregon.gov/deq/** and Ohio at **https://epa.state.oh.us**.

A good place to track environmental protection policies, laws, and regulations is at **https://**

www.envir.blr.com. This site is maintained by Business and Legal Reports, a firm that advertises itself as "making state environmental compliance easier."

For more information about environmental issues, contact the Sierra Club at **https://www.sierraclub.org**, the National Wildlife Federation at **https://www.nwf.org**, and the Nature Conservancy at **www.nature.org**.

To learn about the impact of pollution on the public, explore the website of the Environmental Justice Foundation at **https//ejfoundation.org**.

References

Chapter 01 State and Local Governments: New Directions

1. Governor Doug Burgum, "2019 State of the State Address" (January 3, 2019).
2. Bruce Wallin, "State and Local Governments Are American, Too," *Political Science Teacher* 1 (Fall 1988): 1–3.
3. Asa Hutchinson, quoted in "Governor Hutchinson Announces Formation of Transition Team to Aid with State Government Transformation," *Arkansas Governor's Office Press Releases* (April 11, 2019).
4. Mark Murphy, "Elimination and Consolidation of State Entities," National Conference of State Legislatures (August 1, 2011).
5. Council of State Governments, "Capitol Ideas" (April 4, 2015).
6. Bloomberg Philanthropies, "Government Innovation," https://www.bloomberg.org/ (accessed January 13, 2020).
7. Harvard Kennedy School Ash Center for Democratic Governance and Innovation, "Innovations in Government," https://ash.harvard.edu/innovations-government (accessed June 3, 2020).
8. Beth Walter Honadle, "Defining and Doing Capacity Building: Perspective and Experiences," in Beth Walter Honadle and Arnold M. Howitt, eds., *Perspectives on Management Capacity Building* (Albany, NY: SUNY Press, 1986), pp. 9–23.
9. Katherine Barrett and Richard Greene, "Grading the States '08," *Governing* 21 (March 2008): 24–95.
10. Julie Bundt and Gene M. Lutz, "Connecting State Government Reform with Public Priorities: The Iowa Test Case," *State and Local Government Review* 31 (Spring 1999): 73–90.
11. David M. Hedge, *Governance and the Changing American States* (Boulder, CO: Westview Press, 1998).
12. U.S. Department of Homeland Security, "REAL ID," https://www.dhs.gov/ (accessed June 4, 2020).
13. Terry Sanford, *The Storm Over the States* (New York: McGraw-Hill, 1967), p. 21.
14. Quoted in Sanford, *The Storm Over the States*, p. 21.
15. John Herbers, "The New Federalism: Unplanned, Innovative, and Here to Stay," *Governing* 1 (October 1987): 28.
16. Aaron Mak, "The Big Change Coming to Just About Every Website on New Year's Day: Thank You California!" www.slate.com (December 30, 2019).
17. Ann O'M. Bowman and Richard C. Kearney, *The Resurgence of the States* (Englewood Cliffs, NJ: Prentice-Hall, 1986).
18. Sanford, *The Storm Over the States*.
19. Ann O'M. Bowman and Richard C. Kearney, "Dimensions of State Government Capability," *Western Political Quarterly* 41 (June 1988): 341–62; David R. Morgan and Kenneth Kickham, "Modernization Among the U.S. States: Change and Continuity from 1960 to 1990," *Publius* 27 (Summer 1997): 23–39.
20. Michael Martz, "Virginia ABC Tops $1 Billion in Sales as New Authority Updates Old Monopoly," *Richmond Times-Dispatch* (August 13, 2019); Associated Press, "NC Lawmakers Look at Privatizing Liquor Business, Allowing ABC Store to Open on Sunday and Delivery" (February 11, 2019); Steve Wilson, "Will Mississippi Privatize Wine and Liquor Sales?" *Mississippi Center for Public Policy* (October 10, 2019).
21. Niall McCarthy, "Which States Made the Most Tax Revenue from Marijuana in 2018?" *Forbes* (March 26, 2019).
22. Dees Stribling, "Cities Push Back Against Dollar Stores in Food Deserts," www.bisnews.com (August 15, 2019).
23. Andrew Karch, *Democratic Laboratories: Policy Diffusion Among the American States* (Ann Arbor: University of Michigan Press, 2010).
24. Craig Savoye, "States Spare Residents from Telemarketers," *Christian Science Monitor* (December 22, 2000): 8.
25. U.S. Conference of Mayors Climate Protection Center, "Mayors Climate Protection Center" (November 13, 2019).
26. Lawrence J. Grossbeck, Sean Nicholson-Crotty, and David A. M. Peterson, "Ideology and Learning in Policy Diffusion," *American Politics Research* 32 (September 2004): 521–45; David M. Glick and Zoe Friedland, "How Often Do States Study Each Other? Evidence of Policy Knowledge Diffusion," *American Politics Research* 42 (November 2014): 956–85.
27. David W. Winder and James T. LaPlant, "State Lawsuits Against Big Tobacco: A Test of Diffusion Theory," *State and Local Government Review* 32 (Spring 2000): 132–41.
28. Mary Williams Walsh, "Judge Orders Pause in Opioid Litigation Against Purdue Pharma and Sacklers," *New York Times* (October 11, 2019).
29. Ann O'M. Bowman, "Horizontal Federalism: Exploring Interstate Interactions," *Journal of Public Administration Research and Theory* 14 (October 2004): 535–46.
30. Governor George Voinovich, quoted in "Reassessing Mandates," *State Policy Reports* 11 (October 1993): 16.
31. Brad Knickerbocker, "States Take Clean Air Measures into Their Own Hands," *Christian Science Monitor* (April 19, 2005): 1, 12; N. C. Aizenman, "Opponents Present Case Against Obama's Health-Care Law in 20-State Lawsuit," *Washington Post* (September 14, 2010).
32. Sarah Lunch and Dan Levine, "U.S. Justice Department Sues California Over Sanctuary Policies," *Reuters* (March 6, 2018).
33. Jeffrey M. Jones, "Illinois Residents Least Confident in Their State Government" (February 17, 2016), https://news.gallup.com.
34. As quoted in "It's Scary: State of the States 2009," *State News* 52 (May 2009): 9.
35. National Conference of State Legislatures, *State Budget Update: Summer 2011*. Denver, CO: NCSL.
36. Pamela M. Prah, "Reports: State Income Levels Plunge," www.stateline.org (June 19, 2009).
37. Rudolph Bush, "Dallas City Council Knows 'Brutal' Budget Cuts Coming," *Dallas Morning News* (June 18, 2009).
38. Lawrence L. Martin, Richard Levey, and Jenna Cawley, "The 'New Normal' for Local Government," *State and Local Government Review* 44 (August 2012): 17S–28S.
39. Scott Cohn, "Amazon Reveals the Truth on Why It Nixed New York and Chose Virginia for Its HQ2," www.cnbc.com (July 19, 2019).
40. Cindy Widner, "How Austin Landed the Apple Deal: It Takes a Village to Build a Tech Hub," *Austin Development News* (December 14, 2018).
41. Ralph Vartebedian, "The Race to Steal Bases Heats Up," *Los Angeles Times* (November 29, 2004).
42. Michael Johnston, "Right and Wrong in American Politics: Popular Conceptions of Corruption," in Arnold J. Heidenheimer and Michael Johnston, eds., *Political Corruption: Concepts and Contexts* (New Brunswick, NJ: Transaction, 2002), pp. 173–91; see also Richard T. Boylan and Cheryl X. Long, "Measuring Public Corruption in the American States," *State Politics and Policy Quarterly* (Winter 2003): 420–38.
43. Steven P. Lanza, *The Economics of Ethics: The Cost of Political Corruption* (Storrs, CT: Connecticut Center for Economic Analysis, 2004).
44. Boylan and Long, "Measuring Public Corruption in the American States."

45. Dick Simpson et al., "Chicago and Illinois, Leading the Pack in Corruption," Chicago: University of Illinois at Chicago (February 15, 2012).

46. U.S. Census Bureau, "Overview of Race and Hispanic Origin: 2010," www.census.gov/ (accessed February 20, 2012).

47. U.S. Census Bureau, "Foreign-Born Population—Selected Characteristics by Region of Origin: 2010," www.census.gov/ (accessed February 20, 2012).

48. Mark Mather, Linda Jacobsen, Beth Jarosz, Lillian Kilduff, Amanda Lee, Kevin Pollard, Paola Scommegna, and Alicia Vanorman, "America's Changing Population: What to Expect in the 2020 Census" (Washington, DC: Population Reference Bureau, 2019).

49. Bryan Baker, "Estimates of the Illegal Alien Population in the United States: January 2015," https://www.dhs.gov (accessed January 6, 2019).

50. Gary Reich, "Hitting the Wall? The Trump Administration Meets Immigration Federalism," *Publius: The Journal of Federalism* 48:3 (Summer 2018): 372–95.

51. Department of Homeland Security v. Regents of the University of California 591 U.S. _____ (2020).

52. Rodney E. Hero and Caroline J. Tolbert, "A Racial/Ethnic Diversity Interpretation of Politics and Policy in the States of the U.S.," *American Journal of Political Science* 40 (August 1996): 851–71.

53. Rodney Hero, *Racial Diversity and Social Capital: Equality and Community in America* (New York: Cambridge University Press, 2007); Ling Zhu and Jennifer Clark, "'Rights Without Access': The Political Context of Inequality in Health Care Coverage in the U.S. States," *State Politics and Policy Quarterly* 15 (February 2015): 239–62.

54. Sandra Colby and Jennifer Ortman, "Projections of the Size and Composition of the U.S. Population: 2014 to 2060," U.S. Census Bureau Current Population Reports (March 2015), https://www.census.gov/.

55. U.S. Census Bureau, "State Population Totals and Components of Change: 2010–2019," https://www.census.gov/.

56. U.S. Census Bureau, "Annual Estimates of Resident Population for Incorporated Places of 50,000 or more, Ranked by July 1, 2018 Population: April 1, 2010 to July 1, 2018," https://factfinder.census.gov/.

57. Frank Newport, ed., *The Gallup Poll: Public Opinion 2014* (Lanham, MD: Rowman & Littlefield, 2016).

58. Aaron Blake, "Census 2010 Shows Red States Gaining Congressional Seats," *Washington Post* (December 21, 2010).

59. Gregory Wallace, "Projection Shows Florida and North Carolina Among States That Could Gain Congressional Seats After Census" (December 31, 2019).

60. Daniel J. Elazar, *American Federalism: A View from the States*, 3rd ed. (New York: Harper & Row, 1984).

61. Jody L. Fitzpatrick and Rodney E. Hero, "Political Culture and Political Characteristics of the American States: A Consideration of Some Old and New Questions," *Western Political Quarterly* 41 (March 1988): 145–53.

62. Keith Boeckelman, "Political Culture and State Development Policy," *Publius* 21 (Spring 1991): 49–92; Russell L. Hanson, "Political Culture Variations in State Economic Development Policy," *Publius* 21 (Spring 1991): 63–81.

63. James P. Lester, "A New Federalism: Environmental Policy in the States," in Norman Vig and Michael Kraft, eds., *Environmental Policy in the 1990s* (Washington, DC: Congressional Quarterly Press, 1994), pp. 51–68; Lawrence M. Mead, "State Political Culture and Welfare Reform," *Policy Studies Journal* 32 (May 2004): 271–96.

64. Joel Lieske, "The Changing Regional Subcultures of the American States and the Utility of a New Cultural Measure," *Political Research Quarterly* 63 (September 2010): 538–52.

65. Emily Van Dunk, "Public Opinion, Gender and Handgun Safety Policy Across the States," paper presented at the annual meeting of the Midwest Political Science Association, Chicago, April 2000.

66. Elaine B. Sharp, "Introduction," in Elaine B. Sharp, ed., *Culture Wars and Local Politics* (Lawrence, KS: University Press of Kansas, 1999), pp. 1–20.

67. William G. Jacoby, "Is There a Culture War? Conflicting Value Structures in American Public Opinion," *American Political Science Review* 108 (November 2014): 754–71.

68. Shanna Rose and Cynthia Bowling, "The State of American Federalism 2014–15," *Publius: The Journal of Federalism* 45 (Summer 2015): 351–79.

69. WRAL.com, "Court: NC Magistrates Can Refuse to Perform Same-Sex Marriages" (June 28, 2017).

70. Matt Stevens, "Kentucky Must Pay $224,000 After Dispute Over Same-Sex Marriage Licenses," *New York Times* (July 21, 2017); Julie Moreau, "Oregon Supreme Court Suspends Judge Who Refused to Marry Gay Couples," *NBC News* (March 18, 2018).

71. John Shannon, "The Return to Fend-for-Yourself Federalism: The Reagan Mark," *Intergovernmental Perspective* 13 (Summer/Fall 1987): 34–37.

72. Alan Ehrenhalt, "The Increasing Irrelevance of Congress," *Governing* 11 (January 1998): 6–7; see also J. Mitchell Pickerill and Cynthia Bowling, "The State of American Federalism 2013–2014," *Publius: The Journal of Federalism* 44 (Summer 2014): 369–98.

Chapter 02 Federalism and the States: Sorting Out Roles and Responsibilities

1. Blas Nuñez-Neto, "Broken Border or Policy? The Nature of Illegal Immigration Is Changing, and So Must the U.S. Government's Response to It," *US News and World Report* (November 13, 2017)

2. Simon Romero, "All Over U.S., Local Officials Cancel Deals to Detain Immigrants," *New York Times* (June 28, 2018).

3. Julia Preston, "States Are Divided by the Lines They Draw on Immigration," *New York Times* (March 29, 2015).

4. Arizona v. United States, 567 U.S. 387 (2012).

5. Quoted in Richard Hofstadter, *The American Political Tradition* (New York: Vintage Books, 1948), p. 5.

6. Hofstadter, *Tradition*, pp. 9–10.

7. Richard H. Leach, *American Federalism* (New York: W. W. Norton, 1970), p. 1.

8. David C. Hendrickson, *Peace Pact: The Lost World of the American Founding* (Lawrence, KS: University Press of Kansas, 2003).

9. Charles S. McCoy, "Federalism: The Lost Tradition?" *Publius: The Journal of Federalism* 31 (Spring 2001): 1–14.

10. Walter Berns, "The Meaning of the Tenth Amendment," in Robert A. Goldwin, ed., *A Nation of States* (Chicago: Rand McNally, 1961), p. 130.

11. Forrest McDonald, *States' Rights and the Union: Imperium in Imperio* (Lawrence, KS: University Press of Kansas, 2000); David B. Walker, *The Rebirth of Federalism*, 2nd ed. (New York: Chatham House, 2000), pp. 39–64.

12. Hofstadter, *The American Political Tradition*, p. 72.

13. McCulloch v. Maryland, 17 U.S. (4 Wheat.) 316 (1819).

14. Gibbons v. Ogden, 22 U.S. (9 Wheat.) 1 (1824).

15. Joseph Story, *Commentaries on the Constitution of the United States* (Boston: Hilliard, Gray and Company, 1833).

16. Barron v. Baltimore, 32 U.S. (7 Pet.) 243 (1833).

17. Gitlow v. New York, 268 U.S. 652 (1925).

18. McDonald v. Chicago, 561 U.S. 742 (2010).

19. Mapp v. Ohio, 367 U.S. 643 (1961).

20. Clayton LaForge, "Ripe for Incorporation: The Seventh Amendment and the Civil Jury Trial," American Bar Association (December 16, 2015).

21. Thaddeus R. Lightfoot, "Bring on the Drones: Legal and Regulatory Issues in Using Unmanned Aircraft Systems," *Natural Resources & Environment* 32:4 (Spring 2018): 41–45.

22. National League of Cities v. Usery, 426 U.S. 833 (1976).

23. Garcia v. San Antonio Metropolitan Transit Authority, 469 U.S. 528 (1985).

24. *Garcia*, 469 U.S. 528 at p. 109 (O'Connor, J., dissenting).

25. John C. Pittenger, "Garcia and the Political Safeguards of Federalism: Is There a Better Solution to the Conundrum of the Tenth Amendment?" *Publius: The Journal of Federalism* 22:1 (Winter 1992): 1–19.

26. U.S. v. Lopez, 514 U.S. 549 (1995). See Kenneth T. Palmer and Edward B. Laverty, "The Impact of *U.S. v. Lopez* on Intergovernmental Relations: A Preliminary Assessment," *Publius: The Journal of Federalism* 26:3 (Summer 1996): 109–26.

27. Kansas v. Hendricks, 117 S. Ct. 2072 (1997).

28. Printz v. U.S., 521 U.S. 898 (1997).

29. Kelo v. New London, 545 U.S. 469 (2005).

30. DaimlerChrysler Corp. v. Cuno, 547 U.S. 332 (2006).

31. Murphy v. National Collegiate Athletic Association 584 U.S. _____ (2018).

32. Seminole Tribe of Florida v. Florida, 517 U.S. 44 (1996).

33. Nevada Department of Human Resources v. Hibbs, 538 U.S. 721 (2003).

34. Federal Maritime Commission v. South Carolina Ports Authority, 535 U.S. 743 (2002).

35. Nevada Department of Human Resources v. Hibbs, S. Ct.149 (1999).

36. Franchise Tax Board v. Hyatt, 587 U.S. _____ (2019); Nevada v. Hall, 440 U.S. 410 (1979).

37. Lorillard Tobacco Co. v. Reilly, 533 U.S. 525 (2001).

38. J. Mitchell Pickerill and Cynthia J. Bowling, "Polarized Parties, Politics, and Policies: Fragmented Federalism in 2013–2014," *Publius: The Journal of Federalism* 44:3 (Summer 2014): 369–98.

39. American Electric Power Co. v. U.S. 564 U.S. 410 (2011).

40. Christopher Shortell, "The End of the Federalism Five? Statutory Interpretation and the Roberts Court," *Publius: The Journal of Federalism* 42:3 (Summer 2012): 516–37.

41. John Kincaid, "State-Federal Relations: Civil War Redux?," in *The Book of the States*, (Lexington, KY: Council of State Governments, 2011): 21–28; American Tradition Partnership, Inc. v. Steve Bullock, Attorney General for the State of Montana (2012), 567 U.S. 516; Arizona v. Inter Tribal Council of Arizona, Inc. 570 U.S. 1 (2013); McCullen v. Coakley 573 U.S. 464 (2014).

42. National Federation of Independent Business v. Sebelius, 567 U.S. 519 (2012).

43. Martha Derthick, "American Federalism: Half-Full or Half-Empty?" *Brookings Review* 1:1 (Winter 2000): 24.

44. Graham Vyse, "What Brett Kavanaugh Means for States," *Governing* (September 24, 2018).

45. Robert Barnes, "They're Not 'Wonder Twins': Gorsuch, Kavanaugh Shift the Supreme Court, but Their Differences Are Striking," *Washington Post* (June 28, 2019).

46. Greg Goelzhauser and David M. Konisky, "The State of American Federalism 2018–2019: Litigation, Partisan Polarization, and the Administrative Presidency," *Publius: The Journal of Federalism* 49:3 (Summer 2019): 379–406.

47. Jake Grovum, "States Air Their Differences at Supreme Court," *Stateline*, an initiative of The Pew Charitable Trusts (January 15, 2014).

48. William H. Stewart, "Metaphors, Models and the Development of Federal Theory," *Publius: The Journal of Federalism* 12:2 (Spring 1982): 5–24.

49. Deil S. Wright, *Understanding Intergovernmental Relations*, 3rd ed. (Pacific Grove, CA: Brooks/Cole, 1988), pp. 40–42.

50. Walker, *Rebirth*, pp. 89–120.

51. Timothy J. Conlan, "Federalism and Competing Values in the Reagan Administration," *Publius: The Journal of Federalism* 16:1 (Winter 1986): 29–47.

52. Jennifer Wolak and Christine Kelleher Palus, "The Dynamics of Public Confidence in U.S. State and Local Government," *State Politics and Policy Quarterly* 10:4 (December 2010): 421–45.

53. John Kincaid and Richard L. Cole, "Changing Public Attitudes on Power and Taxation in the American Federal System," *Publius: The Journal of Federalism* 31:3 (Summer 2001): 205–14.

54. Alan Greenblatt, "The Washington Offensive," *Governing* (January 2005): 26–29.

55. Don Borut, executive director of the National League of Cities, cited in Peter Harkness, "What Brand of Federalism Is Next?" *Governing* (January 2012): 16–17.

56. Harkness, "What Brand of Federalism Is Next?"

57. Timothy J. Conlan and Paul L. Posner, "Inflection Point? Federalism and the Obama Administration," *Publius: The Journal of Federalism* 41:3 (Summer 2011): 421–46.

58. Donald Kettl, "'Jenga Federalism': Trump's Method for Undoing Obama's Policies," *Governing* (December 2018).

59. Pickerill and Bowling, "Fragmented Federalism."

60. Tivas Gupta, "The Future of Federalism," *Harvard Political Review* (September 24, 2019).

61. W. Dale Mason, *Indian Gaming: Tribal Sovereignty and American Politics* (Norman, OK: University of Oklahoma Press, 2000).

62. Erich Steinman, "American Federalism and Intergovernmental Innovation in State-Tribal Relations," *Publius: The Journal of Federalism* 34:2 (Spring 2004): 95–114.

63. Laura E. Evans, *Power from Powerlessness: Tribal Governments, Institutional Niches, and American Federalism* (New York: Oxford University Press, 2011); Laura E. Evans, "Expertise and Scale of Conflict: Governments as Advocates in American Indian Politics," *American Political Science Review* 105:4 (November 2011): 663–82.

64. McGirt v. Oklahoma 591 U.S. _____ (2020).

65. Lisa Rab, "What Makes Someone Native American? One Tribe's Long Struggle for Full Recognition," *Washington Post* (August 20, 2018).

66. Jim Morrill "Vegas Coming to Charlotte Area: Catawbas Plan Casino Groundbreaking for Wednesday," *Charlotte Observer* (July 17, 2020).

67. Joseph F. Zimmerman, *Horizontal Federalism: Interstate Relations* (Albany: State University of New York Press, 2011); Ann O'M. Bowman and Neal D. Woods, "Strength in Numbers: Why States Join Interstate Compacts," *State Politics and Policy Quarterly* 7:4 (Winter 2007): 347–68.

68. Zimmerman, *Horizontal Federalism*.

69. Edella Schlager, Tanya Heikkila, and Carl Case, "The Costs of Compliance with Interstate Compacts: Lessons from Water Compacts in the Western United States," *Publius: The Journal of Federalism* 42:3 (Summer 2012): 494–515.

70. Schlager, Heikkila, and Case, "Costs of Compliance."

71. Mark Niesse, "Georgia Renews Old Quest to Retake Tennessee Border," *The Atlanta Journal-Constitution* (March 23, 2018).

72. Melissa Breyer, "Missouri Files Suit Against California Egg Law" (February 5, 2014), https://www.mnn.com.

73. David Lieb, "U.S. Supreme Court Declines Involvement in State Egg Law Cases" *Associated Press* (January 8, 2019).

74. Robert Dilger and Michael Cecire, *Federal Grants to State and Local Governments: A Historical Perspective on Contemporary Issues* (Washington, DC: Congressional Research Service, 2019).

75. U.S. Office of Management and Budget, "Table 11.1— Summary Comparison of Outlays for Payments for Individuals, 1940–2025 (In Current Dollars, as Percentages of Total Outlays, as Percentages of GDP, and in Constant (FY 2012) Dollars)," Washington, DC.

76. Sean Nicholson-Crotty, "Leaving Money on the Table: Learning from Recent Refusals of Federal Grants in the American States," *Publius: The Journal of Federalism* 42:3 (Summer 2012): 449–66.

77. National Conference of State Legislatures Standing Committee on Budgets and Review, "Mandate Monitor," https://www.ncsl.org/ (accessed August 26, 2020).

78. "A Year-End Summary of Recent Railroad Preemption Cases," Lane Powell LLC (November 6, 2017).

79. Tony Barboza and Anna Phillips, "California Sues Trump Again for Revoking State's Authority to Limit Auto Emissions," *Los Angeles Times* (November 15, 2019).
80. U.S. Government Accountability Office, *Unfunded Mandates: Views Vary about Reform Act's Strengths, Weaknesses, and Options for Improvement*, GAO-05-454 (March 31, 2005).
81. Justin McCarthy, "American Still More Trusting of Local than State Government," *Gallup* (October 8, 2018).
82. Susan Milligan, "A Guide to Abortion Laws by State: State Laws Passed in 2019 Highlight One of the Nation's Most Divisive Issues," *U.S. News and World Report* (June 27, 2019).
83. Martha Derthick, "American Federalism: Half-Full or Half-Empty?" *Brookings Review* 18:1 (Winter 2000): 24.
84. J. B. Wogan, "States and Localities Are Losing Their Influence in Washington," *Governing* (June 2014).
85. Alan Greenblatt, "Recipe for Respect," *Governing* (February 2008): 22–26.
86. Samuel H. Beer, "The Future of the States in the Federal System," in Peter Woll, ed., *American Government: Readings and Cases* (Boston: Little, Brown, 1981), p. 92.
87. Richard P. Nathan, "Updating Theories of American Federalism," in Timothy Conlan, Paul Posner, and Alice Rivlin, eds., *Intergovernmental Management in the 21 Century* (Washington, DC: The Brookings Institution, 2008), pp. 13–25.

Chapter 03 State Constitutions: The Fundamental Rules of State Government

1. G. Alan Tarr, *Understanding State Constitutions* (Princeton, NJ: Princeton University Press, 1998).
2. U.S. Advisory Commission on Intergovernmental Relations (ACIR), *State Constitutions in the Federal System*, A-113 (Washington, DC: ACIR, 1989), p. 2.
3. Donald S. Lutz, "The United States Constitution as an Incomplete Text," *Annals of the American Academy of Political and Social Science* 496 (March 1989): 23–32.
4. Quoting James Quayle Dealey, *Growth of American State Constitutions* (1915), in Robert F. Williams, ed., *The Law of American State Constitutions* (New York: Oxford University Press, 2009); G. Alan Tarr, "Constitutional Theory and State Constitutional Interpretation," *Rutgers Law Journal* 22: 841, 848–56 (1991).
5. Donald S. Lutz, "Toward a Theory of Constitutional Amendment," *American Political Science Review* 88 (June 1994): 356, in G. Alan Tarr, ed., *Constitutional Politics in the States* (Westport, CT: Greenwood Press, 1996), p. xv.
6. Donald S. Lutz, "The Iroquois Confederation Constitution: An Analysis," *Publius* 22 (Spring 1998): 99–127.
7. Daniel J. Elazar, "The Principles and Traditions Underlying State Constitutions," *Publius* 12 (Winter 1982): 11.
8. Quoted in Perry Gilbert Miller, "Thomas Hooker and the Democracy of Early Connecticut," *New England Quarterly* 4 (1931): 695.
9. Bruce Fraser, *The Land of Steady Habits: A Brief History of Connecticut* (Hartford, CT: Connecticut Historical Commission, 1986), p. 10.
10. Willi Paul Adams, *The First American Constitutions* (Lanham, MD: Madison House, 2000), p. 61.
11. John Estill Reeves, *Kentucky Government* (Lexington, KY: University of Kentucky, 1966), p. 7. As quoted in Penny M. Miller, *Kentucky Government and Politics* (Lincoln: University of Nebraska Press, 1994), p. 82.
12. Albert L. Sturm, "The Development of American State Constitutions," *Publius* 12 (Winter 1982): 61.
13. Ibid., pp. 62–63.
14. Paul G. Reardon, "The Massachusetts Constitution Makes a Milestone," *Publius* 12 (Winter 1982): 45–55.
15. David McCullough, *John Adams* (New York: Touchstone Books, 2001).
16. Quoted in James Bryce, "Nature of the American State," in Bruce Stinebrickner, ed., *State and Local Government*, 3rd ed. (Guilford, CT: Dushkin, 1987), pp. 20–23.
17. Quoted in Thomas Parrish, "Kentucky's Fourth Constitution Is a Product of Its 1980 Times," in Thad L. Beyle, ed., *State Government: CQ's Guide to Current Issues and Activities 1991–92* (Washington, DC: Congressional Quarterly Press, 1991), p. 46.
18. Pamela M. Prah, "Alabama's Past, Future on Ballot," www.pewstates.org (August 13, 2012).
19. David Fellman, "What Should a State Constitution Contain?" in W. Brooke Graves, ed., *Major Problems in State Constitutional Revision* (Chicago, IL: Public Administration Service, 1960), p. 146.
20. Sturm, "The Development of American State Constitutions," p. 64; see Christopher W. Hammons, "Was James Madison Wrong? Rethinking the American Preference for Short, Framework-Oriented Constitutions," *American Political Science Review* 93 (December 1999): 837–49.
21. Josh Goodman, "Seizing the Initiative," *Governing* (October 2008): 32.
22. David C. Nice, "Interest Groups and State Constitutions: Another Look," *State and Local Government Review* 20 (Winter 1988): 22.
23. Donald S. Lutz, "Patterns in the Amending of American State Constitutions," in G. Alan Tarr, ed., *Constitutional Politics in the States* (Westport, CT: Greenwood Press, 1996), pp. 24–27.
24. National Municipal League, *Model State Constitution*, 6th ed., rev. (New York: National Municipal League, 1968).
25. U.S. Advisory Commission on Intergovernmental Relations (ACIR), *A Report to the President for Transmittal to the Congress* (Washington, DC: U.S. Government Printing Office, 1955).
26. John J. Carroll and Arthur English, "Traditions of State Constitution Making," *State and Local Government Review* 23 (Fall 1991): 103–109.
27. *Gitlow v. New York*, 268 U.S. 652 (1925).
28. Thomas C. Marks, Jr. and John F. Cooper, *State Constitutional Law* (St. Paul, MN: West, 1988), p. 38.
29. Ibid., pp. 38–42.
30. Thomas Jefferson to James Madison, "Popular Basis of Political Authority," in Philip B. Kurland and Ralph Lerner, eds., *The Founders' Constitution* Web Edition, press-pubs.uchicago.edu/founders, 1987.
31. Michael Besso, "Constitutional Amendment Procedures and the Informal Political Construction of Constitutions," *The Journal of Politics* 67 (February 2005): 6987.
32. Marks and Cooper, *State Constitutional Law*, p. 47.
33. Tarr and Porter, "Introduction," p. 9.
34. Stanley H. Friedelbaum, "The Complementary Role of Federal and State Courts," *Publius* 17 (Winter 1987): 48.
35. Goodman, "Seizing the Initiative," 2008.
36. Vladimir Kogan, "Lessons from Recent State Constitutional Conventions," *California Journal of Politics and Policy* 2 (2010): 1–24.
37. The Ohio Constitutional Modernization Commission, ocmc.ohio.gov/ocmc/home.
38. Quoted in U.S. Advisory Commission on Intergovernmental Relations, *State Constitutions in the Federal System* (Washington, DC: ACIR, 1989), p. 37.
39. Albert L. Sturm, "The Development of American State Constitutions," *Publius* 12 (Winter 1982): 104.
40. W. Brooke Graves, "State Constitutional Law: A Twenty-five Year Summary," *William and Mary Law Review* 8 (Fall 1966): 12.
41. ACIR, *The Question of State Government Capability*, p. 60.
42. Richard H. Leach, "A Quiet Revolution: 1933–1976," in *The Book of the States 1975–76* (Lexington, KY: Council of State Governments, 1976), p. 25.
43. Terry Sanford, *Storm Over the States* (New York: McGraw-Hill, 1967), p. 1983.

Chapter 04 Citizen Participation and Elections: Engaging the Public in Government

1. Lindsay A. Powers, "Takoma Park Grants 16-Year-Olds Right to Vote," *Washington Post* (May 14, 2013).
2. National Youth Rights Association, "Current Campaigns to Lower the Voting Age," https://youthrights.org (accessed December 27, 2019).
3. Robert D. Putnam, *Bowling Alone: The Collapse and Revival of American Community* (New York: Simon & Schuster, 2000); see also Nojin Kwak, Dhavan V. Shah, and R. Lance Holbrook, "Connecting, Trusting, and Participating: The Direct and Interactive Effects of Social Associations," *Political Research Quarterly* 57 (December 2004): 643–52.
4. John D. Griffin and Brian Newman, "Are Voters Better Represented?" *Journal of Politics* 67 (November 2005): 1206–27.
5. Jennifer Oser, Jan E. Leighley, and Kenneth M. Winneg, "Participation, Online and Otherwise: What's the Difference for Policy Preferences?" *Social Science Quarterly* 95 (December 2014): 1259–77.
6. William E. Lyons, David Lowery, and Ruth Hoogland De Hoog, *The Politics of Dissatisfaction* (Armonk, NY: M. E. Sharpe, 1992); Albert O. Hirschman, *Exit, Voice and Loyalty: Responses to Decline in Firms, Organizations, and States* (Cambridge, MA: Harvard University Press, 1972).
7. Nicholas A. Valentino et al., "Election Night's Alright for Fighting: The Role of Emotions in Political Participation," *Journal of Politics* 73 (January 2011): 156–70.
8. Zoltan Hajnal and Jessica Trounstine, "Identifying and Understanding Perceived Inequities in Local Politics," *Political Research Quarterly* 67 (2013): 56–70.
9. Lapo Salucci and Kenneth Bickers, "Exit, Voice, and Electoral Turnover," *Urban Affairs Review* 47 (March 2011): 155–82.
10. Henry E. Brady, Sidney Verba, and Kay Lehman Schlozman, "Beyond SES: A Resource Model of Political Participation," *American Political Science Review* 89 (June 1995): 271–94; see also Jennifer Jerit, Jason Barabas, and Toby Bolsen, "Citizens, Knowledge, and the Information Environment," *American Journal of Political Science* 50 (April 2006): 266–82.
11. Richard Murray and Arnold Vedlitz, "Race, Socioeconomic Status, and Voting Participation in Large Southern Cities," *Journal of Politics* 39 (November 1977): 1064–72; Fredrick C. Harris, Valeria Sinclair-Chapman, and Brian D. McKenzie, "Macrodynamics of Black Political Participation in the Post-Civil Rights Era," *Journal of Politics* 67 (November 2005): 1143–63.
12. Virginia Sapiro, *The Political Integration of Women* (Urbana, IL: University of Illinois Press, 1983).
13. Thom File, "Voting in America: A Look at the 2016 Presidential Election," https://www.census.gov (accessed January 21, 2019).
14. Center for Information and Research on Civic Learning and Engagement (CIRCLE), "Election Night 2018: Historically High Youth Turnout, Support for Democrats," https://civicyouth.org (accessed January 21, 2019).
15. J. Eric Oliver, "City Size and Civic Involvement in Metropolitan America," *American Political Science Review* 94 (June 2000): 361–73.
16. Anthony Downs, *An Economic Theory of Democracy* (New York: Harper & Row, 1957); see also Moshe Haspel and H. Gibbs Knotts, "Location, Location, Location: Precinct Placement and the Costs of Voting," *Journal of Politics* 67 (May 2005): 560–73.
17. Jan E. Leighley and Arnold Vedlitz, "Race, Ethnicity, and Political Participation," *Journal of Politics* 61 (November 1999): 1092–1114; Debra Horner, "Critiquing Measures of Political Interest," paper presented at the annual meeting of the Midwest Political Science Association, Chicago, IL, 2000.
18. Shelby County v. Holder, 570 U.S 529 (2013).
19. Kim Quaile Hill and Jan E. Leighley, "Party Ideology, Organization, and Competitiveness as Mobilizing Forces in Gubernatorial Elections," *American Journal of Political Science* 37 (November 1993): 1158–78.
20. Alan S. Gerber and Todd Rogers, "Descriptive Social Norms and Motivation to Vote: Everybody's Voting and So Should You," *Journal of Politics* 71 (January 2009): 178–91.
21. Michael McDonald, "2016 November General Election Turnout Rates," United States Elections Project, http://www.electproject.org/2016g (accessed January 19, 2019).
22. Peter L. Francia and Paul S. Herrnson, "The Synergistic Effect of Campaign Effort and Election Reform on Voter Turnout in State Legislative Elections," *State Politics and Policy Quarterly* 4 (Spring 2004): 74–93.
23. National Council of State Legislatures, "Same Day Voter Registration" (June 28, 2019).
24. Barry C. Burden et al., "Election Laws, Mobilization, and Turnout: The Unanticipated Consequences of Election Reform," *American Journal of Political Science* 58 (January 2014): 95–109.
25. Michael McDonald, "2018 November General Election Turnout Rates," United States Election Project (December 14, 2018).
26. Andrea McAtee and Jennifer Wolak, "Why People Decide to Participate in State Politics," *Political Research Quarterly* 64 (March 2011): 45–58.
27. Neil Malhotra et al., "Text Messages as Mobilization Tools: The Conditional Effect of Habitual Voting and Election Salience," *American Politics Research* 39 (July 2011): 664–81.
28. Henry E. Brady and John E. McNulty, "Turning Out to Vote: The Costs of Finding and Getting to the Polling Place," *American Political Science Review* 105 (February 2011): 115–34.
29. Michael Cooper, "New State Laws Raising Hurdles at Voting Booth," *The New York Times* (October 3, 2011).
30. "Absentee and Early Voting," National Conference on State Legislatures (accessed January 3, 2019), http://www.ncsl.org/research/.
31. National Conference of State Legislatures, "Voting Outside the Polling Place: Absentee, All-Mail and Other Voting at Home Options" (May 19, 2020).
32. Matt Vasilogambros, "Postal Service's Struggles Could Hurt Mail-In Election," *Pew Stateline* (May 8, 2020).
33. Yelena Dzhanova, "Trump Slams Mail-In Voting, Says It 'Doesn't Work Out Well for Republicans'" *CNBC* (April 8, 2020).
34. Nicholas Riccardi, "Democrats Try Again with Sweeping Mail Voting Requirements," *U.S. News and World Report* (May 16, 2020).
35. Lindsay Wise and Alexa Corse, "Partisan Fight Looms Over Voting by Mail: Democrats, Republicans in Congress Sharply Differ Over Expanding Mail Balloting in November to Ease Coronavirus Fears at Polls," *Wall Street Journal* (April 29, 2020).
36. Catherine Lucey, "Trump Upbraids Michigan, Nevada for Easing Vote by Mail; President Threatens to Withhold Funding from the States for Plans to Mail Out Absentee-Ballot Applications, *Wall Street Journal* (May 20, 2020).
37. Robert M. Stein and Greg Vonnahme, "Engaging the Unengaged Voter: Vote Centers and Voter Turnout," *Journal of Politics* 70 (April 2008): 487–97.
38. Priscilla L. Southwell, "Voting Behavior in Vote-by-Mail Elections," *Analyses of Social Issues and Public Policy* 10 (December 2010): 106–15; see also Cynthia Rugeley and Robert A. Jackson, "Getting on the Rolls: Analyzing the Effects of Lowered Barriers on Voter Registration," *State Politics and Policy Quarterly* 9 (Spring 2009): 56–78.
39. Michael McDonald, "2018 November General Election Early Voting," United States Elections Project (November 6, 2018), http://www.electproject.org/early_2018.
40. Michael J. Hanmer et al., "Losing Fewer Votes: The Impact of Changing Voting Systems on Residual Votes," *Political Research Quarterly* 63 (March 2010): 129–42.

41. "Methods of Nominating Candidates for State Offices," in *The Book of the States 2018, Table 6.3* (August 24, 2018), http://knowledgecenter.csg.org/kc/system/files/6.3.2018.pdf.
42. "State Primary Elections Types," National Conference of State Legislatures (June 26, 2018).
43. Calvin Blackwell and Peter Calcagno, "Party-Crashers or Wallflowers? The Lack of Strategic Voting in Experimental Primaries," *Applied Economic Letters* 26 (March 2019): 1641–48.
44. Charles S. Bullock, III, Ronald Keith Gaddie, and Anders Ferrington, "System Structure, Campaign Stimuli, and Voter Falloff in Runoff Primaries," *Journal of Politics* 64 (November 2002): 1210–24.
45. Kentucky Legislative Research Commission, "Election Filing Dates and Runoff Primary" (July 1, 2009).
46. Randall W. Partin, "Economic Conditions and Gubernatorial Elections," *American Politics Quarterly* 23 (January 1995): 81–95.
47. John Bacon, "And the Winner Is . . . Republican Wins After Name Drawn from a Bowl in Virginia House Race," *USA Today* (January 4, 2018).
48. StateVote 2014: Election Results, National Conference of State Legislatures, http://www.ncsl.org/ (accessed January 28, 2019).
49. Kimberly L. Nelson, *Elected Municipal Councils: Special Data Issue* (Washington, DC: International City/County Management Association, 2002).
50. Brian F. Schaffner, Gerald Wright, and Matthew Streb, "Teams Without Uniforms: The Nonpartisan Ballot in State and Local Elections," *Political Research Quarterly* 54 (March 2001): 7–30.
51. Zoltan Hajnal and Jessica Trounstine, "Where Turnout Matters: The Consequences of Uneven Turnout in City Elections," *Journal of Politics* 67 (May 2005): 515–36.
52. Gerald Wright, "Charles Adrian and the Study of Nonpartisan Elections," *Political Research Quarterly* 61 (March 2008): 13–16.
53. Arnold Fleischmann and Lana Stein, "Campaign Contributions in Local Elections," *Political Research Quarterly* 51 (September 1998): 673–89.
54. Luis Ricardo Fraga, "Domination through Democratic Means: Nonpartisan Slating Groups in City Electoral Politics," *Urban Affairs Quarterly* 23 (June 1988): 528–55; Christopher A. Cooper and Anthony J. Nownes, "Citizen Groups in Big City Politics," *State and Local Government Review* 35 (Spring 2003): 102–11.
55. Elizabeth R. Gerber, ed., *Stealing the Initiative* (Upper Saddle River, NJ: Prentice-Hall, 2001).
56. "November 2018 Election Results," *Ballotwatch* (January 3, 2019).
57. Jeff Hastings and Damon Cann, "Ballot Titles and Voter Decision Making on Ballot Questions," *State and Local Government Review* 46 (June 2014): 118–27.
58. Sierra Hatfield, "Unclear Ballot Language Comes Under Fire" (November 2, 2018).
59. Whitney Quesenbery and Dana Chisnell, "Ballot Measures Need to Be Written in Plain Language," *New York Times* (November 3, 2016).
60. Mark A Smith, "The Contingent Effects of Ballot Initiatives and Candidate Races on Turnout," *American Journal of Political Science* 45 (July 2001): 700–06; Caroline J. Tolbert, Ramona S. McNeal, and Daniel A. Smith, "Enhancing Civic Engagement: The Effect of Direct Democracy on Political Participation and Knowledge," *State Politics and Policy Quarterly* 3 (Spring 2003): 23–41; John A. Grummel, "Morality Politics, Direct Democracy, and Turnout," *State Politics and Policy Quarterly* 8 (Fall 2008): 282–92; Frederick J. Boehmke and R. Michael Alvarez, "The Influence of Initiative Signature-Gathering Campaigns on Political Participation," *Social Science Quarterly* 95 (March 2014): 165–83.
61. Joshua J. Dyck, "Initiated Distrust: Direct Democracy and Trust in Government," *American Politics Research* 37 (July 2009): 539–68; see also Justin H. Phillips, "Does the Citizen Initiative Weaken Party Government in the U.S. States?" *State Politics and Policy Quarterly* 8 (Summer 2008): 127–49.
62. John Myers, "New Law Brings Big Changes to California's Initiative Process," KQED (September 27, 2014).
63. Alana S. Jeydel and Brent S. Steel, "Public Attitudes Toward the Initiative Process in Oregon," *State and Local Government Review* 34 (Fall 2002): 173–82.
64. Elisabeth R. Gerber, Arthur Lupia, and Mathew D. McCubbins, "When Does Government Limit the Impact of Voter Initiatives? The Politics of Implementation and Enforcement," *Journal of Politics* 66 (February 2004): 43–68.
65. Valentina A. Bali, "Implementing Popular Initiatives: What Matters for Compliance?" *Journal of Politics* 65 (November 2003): 1130–46.
66. Joseph Choi, "13,000 Florida Felons Could Be Eligible Voters After Celebrities Paid Fines, Fees: Analysis," *The Hill* (November 2, 2020) https://the hill.com.
67. Alan Greenblatt, "Lawmakers Eye Changes to Ballot Measures—Passed and Future," *Governing* (January 16, 2019).
68. "Scott Walker Recall Elections Cost Taxpayers $13.5 Million," TwinCities.com (August 14, 2012).
69. Nathan Dickerson, "Electronic Communications and Public Records," Council of State Governments (February 2012): 3.
70. "New Report Ranks All Fifty States on Government Spending Transparency," U.S. PIRG (March 18, 2015).
71. Neal D. Woods, "Promoting Participation: An Examination of Rulemaking Notification and Access Procedures," *Public Administration Review* 69 (May/June 2009): 518–30.
72. Jonathan Walters, "Polling the Populace," *Governing* 20 (April 2007): 66–68.
73. Allen Kim, "In the Past 10 Months, 140 Local Governments, Police Stations and Hospitals Have Been Held Hostage by Ransomware Attacks," *CNN Business* (October 8, 2019).
74. Stephen Knack, "Social Capital and the Quality of Government: Evidence from the States," *American Journal of Political Science* 46 (October 2002): 772–85.
75. Ericka Harney, "State of Volunteers," *State News* 52 (May 2009): 16–18.
76. Sarah Breitenbach, "Nonprofits Poised for Bigger Role in Disaster Recovery," *Pew Stateline*, (June 23, 2017).
77. Markus Prior, "News vs. Entertainment: How Increasing Media Choice Widens Gap in Political Knowledge and Turnout," *American Journal of Political Science* 49 (July 2005): 577–92.
78. Evan J. Ringquist et al., "Lower-Class Mobilization and Policy Linkage in the U.S. States: A Correction," *American Journal of Political Science* 41 (January 1997): 339–44.
79. Coffee with Council 2015 (March 3, 2015), https://www.youtube.com/watch?v=imv3sRxL4eE.

Chapter 05 Political Parties, Interest Groups, and Campaigns: Influencing Public Policy

1. Reid Wilson, "Where Your Ideology Says You Should Live," *Washington Post* (June 17, 2014), "What Town Matches My Politics?" (March 31, 2015), http://www.claritycampaigns.com/townrank.
2. David Doherty and E. Scott Adler, "The Persuasive Effects of Partisan Campaign Mailers," *Political Research Quarterly* 67 (September 2014): 562–73.
3. Jeffrey Jones, "Americans Continue to Embrace Political Independence" (January 7, 2019).
4. Marjorie Randon Hershey, *Party Politics in America,* 11th ed. (New York: Pearson Longman, 2005).
5. Gallup, "Party Affiliation," https://news.gallup.com (accessed June 14, 2020).
6. David Von Drehle, "Culture Clash: Geography, Technology, and Strategy Have Nurtured a Political Split," *Washington Post National Weekly Edition* (May 24–30, 2004): 6–7.
7. Dante Scalia and Kenneth Johnson, "Political Polarization along the Rural-Urban Continuum? The Geography of the Presidential Vote, 2000–2016," *The Annals of the American Academy of Political and Social Science* (June 2017): 162–84.
8. Hershey, *Party Politics in America.*

9. Malcolm E. Jewell and Sarah M. Morehouse, *Political Parties and Elections in American States*, 4th ed. (Washington, DC: Congressional Quarterly Press, 2001).

10. John H. Aldrich, "Southern Parties in State and Nation," *Journal of Politics* 62 (August 2000): 643–70.

11. Robert E. Hogan, "Candidate Perceptions of Political Party Campaign Activity in State Legislative Elections," *State Politics and Policy Quarterly* 2 (Spring 2002): 66–85.

12. Ibid.

13. Shanna Pearson-Merkowitz and John Michael McTigue, "Partisan Mountains and Molehills: The Geography of U.S. State Intraparty Factionalism," *State Politics and Policy Quarterly* 8 (Spring 2008): 7–31.

14. Gary Jacobson, "The Triumph of Polarized Partisanship in 2016: Donald Trump's Improbable Victory," *Political Science Quarterly* 132 (March 2017): 9–42.

15. Alan Ware, "Donald Trump's Hijacking of the Republican Party in Historical Perspective," *The Political Quarterly* 87 (July 2016): 406–14.

16. Amy Davidson Sorkin, "How Doug Jones Beat Roy Moore," *The New Yorker* (December 13, 2017).

17. Gary Jacobson, quoted in Michael Hirsch, "Who Will Speak for the Democrats?" *New York Review of Books* (November 8, 2018).

18. Alan Abramowitz, "The Trump Effect: The 2018 Midterm Election as a Referendum on a Polarizing President," in Larry Sabato and Kyle Kondik, eds., *The Blue Wave: The 2018 Midterms and What They Mean for the 2020 Elections* (Lanham, MD: Rowman and Littlefield, 2019), p. 44.

19. John Fritze, "Trump Campaign Pledges 10 More Rallies Before Midterm Election," *USA Today* (October 23, 2018).

20. Elaine Kamarck, "Trump Endorsed 75 Candidates in the Midterms. How Did They Fare on Election Day?" (November 7, 2018).

21. Real Clear Politics, "Polls: 2020 Democratic Presidential Nomination," www.realclearpolitics.com (accessed February 9, 2020).

22. Peter Buisseret and Richard Van Wheelan, "Crashing the Party? Elites, Outsiders, and Elections," *American Journal of Political Science* 64 (September 2019).

23. "Party Composition of State Legislatures," Ballotpedia.org (assessed January 8, 2020).

24. R. J. Reinhart, "Majority in U.S. Still Say a Third Party Is Needed" (October 26, 2018).

25. "Elected Officials," www.lp.org/candidates/elected-officials; "Green Officeholders," www.gp.org/green-officeholders (accessed January 8, 2020).

26. Charles Barrilleaux, "A Test of the Independent Influence of Electoral Competition and Party Strength in a Model of State Policymaking," *American Journal of Political Science* 41 (October 1997): 1462–66.

27. Thomas M. Holbrook and Raymond J. La Raja, "Parties and Elections," in Virginia Gray, Russell L. Hanson, and Thad Kousser, eds., *Politics in the American States: A Comparative Analysis*, 11th ed. (Washington, DC: Congressional Quarterly Press, 2017), pp. 57–98.

28. John Fund, "Hawaii Republicans, One Near Extinction, Prepare a Comeback," *National Review* (July 28, 2018); Nick Reynolds, "Wyoming's Democrats Have a Vision. Now They Just Need Someone to Listen to Them," *Casper Star Tribune* (May 5, 2019).

29. Everett Ehrlich, "Virtual Political Reality," *Washington Post National Weekly Edition* (December 22, 2003–January 4, 2004): 22.

30. Frank Newport, "Party Identification Varies Widely Across the Age Spectrum," (July 10, 2014).

31. Corwin Smidt, "Polarization and the Decline of the American Floating Voter," *American Journal of Political Science* 61 (April 2017): 365–81.

32. J. P. Monroe, *The Political Party Matrix: The Persistence of Organization* (Albany, NY: SUNY Press, 2001).

33. Adam Newkirk and Anthony Nownes, "Interest Groups in the States," in Virginia Gray, Russell Hanson, and Thad Kousser,

eds., *Politics in the American States: A Comparative Analysis*, 11th ed. (Thousand Oaks, CA: CQ Press, 2018), p. 118.

34. Sarah M. Morehouse, "Interest Groups, Parties, and Policies in the American States," paper presented at the annual meeting of the American Political Science Association, Washington, DC, 1997.

35. Virginia Gray and David Lowery, *The Population Ecology of Interest Representation: Lobbying Communities in the American States* (Ann Arbor: University of Michigan Press, 1996).

36. Virginia Gray and David Lowery, "A Niche Theory of Interest Representation," *Journal of Politics* 58 (February 1996): 91–111; Michael T. Heaney, "Issue Networks, Information, and Interest Group Alliances, The Case of Wisconsin Welfare Politics, 1993–99," *State Politics and Policy Quarterly* 4 (Fall 2004): 237–70.

37. Donald P. Haider-Markel, "Interest Group Survival: Shared Interests versus Competition for Resources," *Journal of Politics* 59 (August 1997): 903–12.

38. Clive S. Thomas, Ronald J. Hrebenar, and Anthony J. Nownes, "Interest Group Politics in the States," in *The Book of the States 2008* (Lexington, KY: Council of State Governments, 2008), p. 327.

39. Peter L. Francia, "Interest Groups and Their Influence," in Richard G. Niemi and Joshua J. Dyck, eds., *State Politics and Policy* (Washington, DC: Congressional Quarterly Press, 2014).

40. Donald Kettl, *Politics of the Administrative Process*, 8th ed. (Washington, DC: Congressional Quarterly Press, 2019).

41. Chris Joyner, "Lobbyist Spending Jumps While Lawmakers Dine," *Atlanta Journal Constitution* (February 8, 2012).

42. James Salzer, "Lobbyists Spend More than $500K Wining and Dining Georgia Lawmakers, www.ajc.com (April 23, 2019).

43. Anthony Nownes, "Interest Groups and State Politics," in Burdett Loomis, ed., *Interest Groups and Lobbying in the United States* (Washington, DC: Congressional Quarterly Press, 2012), p. 450.

44. Anthony J. Nownes and Krissy Walker DeAlejandro, "Lobbying in the New Millennium: Evidence of Continuity and Change in Three States," *State Politics and Policy Quarterly* 9 (Winter 2009): 429–55.

45. Anthony J. Nownes and Patricia Freeman, "Interest Group Activity in the States," *Journal of Politics* 60 (February 1998): 86–112.

46. Daniel E. Bergan, "Does Grassroots Lobbying Work?" *American Politics Research* 37 (March 2009): 327–52.

47. John Cluverius, "How Flattened Costs of Grassroots Lobbying Affect Legislator Responsiveness," *Political Research Quarterly* 20 (January 2017): 279.

48. Linda Moss, "Common Cause Takes on 'Turf,'" *Multichannel News* (March 29, 2018).

49. National Conference of State Legislatures, "Legislator Gift Restrictions Overview" (December 17, 2019).

50. Joshua Ozymy, "Assessing the Impact of Legislative Lobbying Regulations on Interest Group Influence in U.S. State Legislatures," *State Politics and Policy Quarterly* 10 (Winter 2010): 397–420; Joshua Ozymy, "Keepin' on the Sunny Side: Scandals, Organized Interests, and the Passage of Legislative Lobbying Laws in the American States," *American Politics Review* 41 (January 2013): 3–23; Adam Newmark, "Lobbying Regulation in the States Revisited: What Are We Trying to Measure, and How Do We Measure It?" *Interest Groups and Advocacy* 6 (July 2017).

51. Patrick Flavin, "Lobbying Regulations and Political Equality in the American States," *American Politics Research* 43 (March 2015): 304–26.

52. William P. Browne and Delbert J. Ringquist, "Michigan Interests: The Politics of Diversification," paper presented at the annual meeting of the Midwest Political Science Association, Chicago, IL, 1987, p. 24.

53. Fred Monardi and Stanton A. Glantz, "Tobacco Industry Campaign Contributions and Legislative Behavior at the State Level," paper presented at the annual meeting of the American Political Science Association, San Francisco, CA, 1996, p. 8.

54. Louay M. Constant, "When Money Matters: Campaign Contributions, Roll Call Votes, and School Choice in Florida," *State Politics and Policy Quarterly* 6 (Summer 2006): 195–219.

55. National Conference of State Legislatures, "State Limits on Contributions to Candidates," (June 2019).

56. Craig Mauger, "Outside Groups' Spending More than Doubled Candidates' Spending in Governor's Race This Fall," *Michigan Campaign Finance Network* (December 10, 2018).

57. Center for Responsive Politics, "527s, Advocacy Group Spending 2012," https://www.opensecrets.org/527s/ (accessed January 13, 2020).

58. David H. Folz and P. Edward French, *Managing America's Small Communities* (Lanham, MD: Rowman & Littlefield, 2005).

59. Christopher A. Cooper and Anthony J. Nownes, "Perceptions of Power: Interest Groups in Local Politics," *State and Local Government Review* 37 (2005): 206–16; Paul Schumaker, "Group Involvements in City Politics and Pluralist Theory," *Urban Affairs Review* 49 (March 2013): 254–81.

60. Brian E. Adams, *Citizen Lobbyists: Local Efforts to Influence Public Policy* (Philadelphia, PA: Temple University Press, 2007).

61. Juliet Musso, Christopher Weare, and Kyu-Nahm Jun, "Democracy by Design: The Institutionalization of Community Participation Networks in Los Angeles," paper presented at the Tenth National Public Management Research Conference, Columbus, OH, 2009.

62. Christopher A. Cooper and Anthony J. Nownes, "Citizen Groups in Big City Politics," *State and Local Government Review* 35 (Spring 2003): 102–11.

63. Taylor Borden, "Black Lives Matter Is a Case Study in a New Kind of Leadership—Here's How the Movement Grew to International Prominence in Just 7 Years," *Business Insider* (June 6, 2020).

64. Mark Bray, *Antifa: The Anti-Fascist Handbook* (Brooklyn: Melville House, 2017).

65. Stanislav Vysotsky, *American Antifa: The Tactics, Culture, and Practice of Militant Antifascism* (New York: Routledge, 2020).

66. Daniel M. Shea and Michael John Burton, *Campaign Craft: The Strategies, Tactics, and Art of Political Campaign Management* (Westport, CT: Praeger, 2001), pp. 75–98.

67. R. Michael Alvarez, Asa Hopkins, and Betsy Sinclair, "Mobilizing Pasadena Democrats: Measuring the Effects of Partisan Campaign Contacts," *Journal of Politics* 72 (January 2010): 31–44.

68. Jerry Hagstrom and Robert Guskind, "Selling the Candidate," *National Journal* 18 (November 1, 1986): 2619–26.

69. Alan S. Gerber et al., "How Large and Long-lasting Are the Persuasive Effects of Televised Campaign Ads? Results from a Randomized Field Experiment," *American Political Science Review* 105 (February 2011): 135–50.

70. Laura Packard, "Making Your Campaign Site Work for Mobile," *Campaigns & Elections* (April 9, 2015).

71. Patrick McGreevy, "New California Rules Aim for Transparency in Online Campaign Material," *Los Angeles Times* (September 19, 2013).

72. Hunt Allcott and Mathew Gentzkow, "Social Media and Fake News in the 2016 Election," *Journal of Economic Perspectives* 31 (Spring 2017): 211–36.

73. Kate Conger, "Twitter Will Ban All Political Ads, C.E.O. Jack Dorsey Says," *New York Times* (October 30, 2019); Daisuke Wakabayashi and Shane Goldmacher, "Google Policy Upends Online Plans for 2020 Campaigns," *New York Times* (November 20, 2019); Mike Isaac and Cecilia Kang, "Facebook Says It Won't Back Down from Allowing Lies in Political Ads," *New York Times* (January 9, 2020).

74. Carol Thompson, "Dozens of New Websites Appear to Be Michigan Local News Outlets. But with Political Bent," *Lansing State Journal* (October 22, 2019).

75. Cleveland Ferguson, III, "The Politics of Ethics and Elections," *Florida State University Law Review* 25 (Fall 1997): 463–503.

76. Mandy Locke, "Attorney General Roy Cooper Ends 14-Year Feud with an Apology," *Charlotte Observer* (April 17, 2014).

77. Ted Braden, "Striking a Responsive Chord: How Political Ads Motivate and Persuade Voters by Appealing to Emotions," *American Journal of Political Science* 49 (April 2005): 388–405.

78. L. Marvin Overby and Jay Barth, "Radio Advertising in American Political Campaigns," *American Politics Research* 34 (July 2006): 451–78.

79. Owen G. Abbe and Paul S. Herrnson, "Campaign Professionalism in State Legislative Elections," *State Politics and Policy Quarterly* (Fall 2003): 223–45.

80. National Institute on Money in State Politics, "State Overviews," http://www.followthemoney.org (accessed January 14, 2020).

81. Donald A. Gross and Robert K. Goidel, "The Impact of State Campaign Finance Laws," *State Politics and Policy Quarterly* 1 (Summer 2001): 180–95; see also Nicholas R. Seabrook, "Money and State Legislative Elections: The Conditional Impact of Political Context," *American Politics Research* 38 (May 2010): 399–424.

82. Robert E. Hogan, "Campaign and Contextual Influences on Voter Participation in State Legislative Elections," *American Politics Quarterly* 27 (October 1999): 403–33; Robert E. Hogan, "Campaign Spending and Voter Participation in State Legislative Elections," *Social Science Quarterly* 94 (September 2013): 840–64.

83. Chad Day and Julie Bykowicz, "Small Donors Get Creative to Give Over and Over and Over to 2020 Candidates," *Wall Street Journal* (October 25, 2019).

84. National Conference of State Legislatures, "State Limits on Contributions to Candidates" (June 2019).

85. National Conference of State Legislatures, "Public Financing of Campaigns: An Overview" (February 8, 2019).

86. Neil Malhotra, "The Impact of Public Financing on Electoral Competition: Evidence from Arizona and Maine," *State Politics and Policy Quarterly* 8 (Fall 2008): 263–81.

87. Arizona Free Enterprise Clun's Freedom Club PAC v. Bennett 564 U.S. 721 (2011).

88. Kedron Bardwell, "Campaign Finance Laws and the Competition for Spending in Gubernatorial Elections," *Social Science Quarterly* 84 (December 2003): 811–25.

Chapter 06 State Legislatures: The People's Representatives

1. Jayme Fraser, "New Montana Lawmaker Will Be the Youngest Serving State Legislator in America," *Billings Gazette* (December 5, 2016).

2. Karl T. Kurtz et al., "Full-Time, Part-Time, and Real Time: Explaining State Legislators' Perceptions of Time on the Job," *State Politics and Policy Quarterly* 6 (Fall 2006): 322–38.

3. Ellen Perlman, "The 'Gold-plated' Legislature," *Governing* 11 (February 1998): 36–40.

4. Justin H. Kirkland, "Chamber Size Effects on the Collaborative Structure of Legislatures," *Legislative Studies Quarterly* 39 (May 2014): 169–98.

5. Beth Reingold, "Gender, Race/Ethnicity, and Representation in State Legislatures," *PS* 52 (July 2019): 426–29.

6. David E. Broockman, "Distorted Communication, Unequal Representation: Constituents Communicate Less to Representatives Not of Their Race," *American Journal of Political Science* 58 (April 2014): 307–21; Micah Gell-Redman, Neil Visalvanich, and Charles Crabtree, "It's All about Race: How State Legislators Respond to Immigrant Constituents," *Political Research Quarterly* 71 (January 2018): 517–31.

7. National Conference of State Legislatures, "NCSL Releases In-Depth Report on State Legislator Demographics" (December 8, 2015).

8. Lilliard E. Richardson, Jr., Brian E. Russell, and Christopher A. Cooper, "Legislative Representation in Single-Member versus Multiple-Member District System: The Arizona State Legislature," *Political Research Quarterly* 57 (June 2004): 337–44.

9. *Reynolds v. Sims*, 84 S. Ct. 1362 (1964).

10. Michael P. McDonald, "A Comparative Analysis of Redistricting Institutions in the U.S.," *State Politics and Policy Quarterly* 4 (Winter 2004): 371–95.

11. Andrew Karch, Corrine M. McConnaughy, and Sean M. Theriault, "The Legislative Politics of Congressional Redistricting Commission Proposals," *American Politics Research* 35 (November 2007): 808–25.

12. Michael A. Smith, "One Piece at a Time: The Role of Timing and Sequencing in Pivotal Politics," *Perspectives on Politics* 2 (March 2004): 85–89; see also Todd Makse, "Strategic Constituency Manipulation in State Legislative Redistricting," *Legislative Studies Quarterly* 37 (May 2012): 225–50.

13. William March, "Black Voters Win, Lose with Districting," *Tampa Tribune* (April 6, 1998), pp. B-1, B-5; see also Michael C. Herron and Alan E. Wiseman, "Gerrymanders and Theories of Law Making: A Study of Legislative Redistricting in Illinois," *Journal of Politics* 70 (January 2008): 151–67.

14. Rucho v. Common Cause, 588 U.S. _____ (2019).

15. Ronald E. Weber, "Emerging Trends in State Legislative Redistricting," *Spectrum* 75 (Winter 2002): 13.

16. Council of State Governments, "Table 3.9: Legislative Compensation and Living Expense Allowances During Sessions, 2019," *Book of the States: 2019*.

17. Peverill Squire and Gary Moncrief, *State Legislatures Today: Politics under the Domes*, 3rd ed. (Lanham, MD: Rowman & Littlefiled, 2020).

18. Ibid.

19. "Women in State Legislative Leadership Positions 2019," Center for American Women and Politics, https://www.cawp .rutgers.edu (accessed January 18, 2020).

20. Christopher Keating, "Democrats, Republicans Reach Senate Power Sharing Deal That Averts GOP Lawsuit," *Hartford Courant* (December 22, 2016).

21. Henry A. Kim and Justin H. Phillips, "Dividing the Spoils of Power: How Are the Benefits of Majority Party Status Distributed in U.S. State Legislatures?" *State Politics and Policy Quarterly* 9 (Summer 2009): 125–50; see also Kristin Kanthak, "U.S. State Legislative Committee Assignments and Encouragement of Party Loyalty: An Exploratory Analysis," *State Politics and Policy Quarterly* 9 (Fall 2009): 284–303.

22. Keith E. Hamm, Ronald D. Hedlund, and Stephanie S. Post, "Committee Specialization in State Legislatures During the Twentieth Century: Do Legislatures Tap the Talents of Their Members?" *State Politics and Policy Quarterly* 11 (September 2011): 299–325.

23. Ralph G. Wright, *Inside the Statehouse: Lessons from the Speaker* (Washington, DC: Congressional Quarterly Press, 2005).

24. L. Marvin Overby, Thomas A. Kazee, and David W. Prince, "Committee Outliers in State Legislatures," *Legislative Studies Quarterly* 29 (February 2004): 81–107; David W. Prince and L. Marvin Overby, "Legislative Organization Theory and Committee Preference Outliers in State Senates," *State Politics and Policy Quarterly* 5 (Spring 2005): 68–87.

25. Molly Jackman, "Parties, Median Legislators, and Agenda Setting: How Legislative Institutions Matter," *Journal of Politics* 76 (January 2014): 259–72.

26. Allen Ehrenhalt, "Putting Practice into Theory," *Governing* 14 (November 2000): 6, 8.

27. Roy Brasfield Herron, "Diary of a Legislator," *Southern Magazine* 2 (May 1988).

28. Christopher A. Cooper and Lilliard E. Richardson, Jr., "Institutions and Representational Roles in American State Legislatures," *State Politics and Policy Quarterly* 6 (Summer 2006): 174–94; see also Shannon Jenkins, "The Impact of Party and Ideology on Roll-Call Voting in State Legislatures," *Legislative Studies Quarterly* 31 (May 2006): 205–34.

29. Eric M. Uslaner and Ronald E. Weber, "U.S. State Legislators' Opinions and Perceptions of Constituency Attitudes," *Legislative Studies Quarterly* 4 (November 1979): 582.

30. "Table 3.19: Bill and Resolution Introductions and Enactments, 2018 Regular Sessions," *The Book of the States 2019* (accessed January 19, 2020).

31. Smith, "One Piece at a Time."

32. Alan Rosenthal, "The Legislature as Sausage Factory," *State Legislatures* 27 (September 2001): 12–15.

33. Tom Loftus, *The Art of Legislative Politics* (Washington, DC: Congressional Quarterly Press, 1994), p. 76.

34. Ibid., p. 77.

35. David C. Saffell, "School Funding in Ohio: Courts, Politicians, and Newspapers," *Comparative State Politics* 18 (October 1997): 9–25.

36. Citizens' Conference on State Legislatures, *The Sometimes Governments: A Critical Study of the 50 American Legislatures,* 2nd ed. (Kansas City, MO: CCSL, 1973), pp. 41–42.

37. Karl Kurtz and Brian Weberg, "What Legislatures Need Now," *State Legislatures* 36 (July/August 2010): 47–50.

38. Alan Rosenthal, "The New Legislature: Better or Worse and for Whom?" *State Legislatures* 12 (July 1986): 5.

39. Charles W. Wiggins, as quoted in Andrea Patterson, "Is the Citizen Legislator Becoming Extinct?" *State Legislatures* 12 (July 1986): 24.

40. Representative Vic Krouse, as quoted in Patterson, "Is the Citizen Legislator Becoming Extinct?" p. 24.

41. Peverill Squire, *The Evolution of American Legislatures: Colonies, Territories, and States, 1619–2009* (Ann Arbor: University of Michigan Press, 2012); see also Daniel C. Bowen and Zachary Greene, "Should We Measure Professionalism with an Index? A Note on Theory and Practice in State Legislative Professionalism Research," *State Politics and Policy Quarterly* 14 (September 2014): 277–96.

42. Alan Rosenthal, "The State Legislature," paper presented at the Vanderbilt Institute for Public Policy Studies, November 1987; James D. King, "Changes in Professionalism in U.S. State Legislatures," *Legislative Studies Quarterly* 25 (May 2000): 327–43.

43. National Conference of State Legislatures, "Full and Part-Time Legislatures" (June 14, 2017).

44. Richard Nathan, as cited in Kathe Callahan and Marc Holzer, "Rethinking Governmental Change," *Public Productivity Management & Review* 17 (Spring 1994): 202.

45. Brad Bumsted, "Rendell Jumps on Reform Bandwagon," *Pittsburgh Tribune-Review*, www.pittsburghlive.com (accessed March 22, 2007).

46. Stuart Rothenberg, "How Term Limits Became a National Phenomenon," *State Legislatures* 18 (January 1992): 35–39.

47. Joel A. Thompson and Gary F. Moncrief, "The Implications of Term Limits for Women and Minorities: Some Evidence from the States," *Social Science Quarterly* 74 (June 1993): 300–309.

48. Karen Hansen, "The Third Revolution," *State Legislatures* 23 (September 1997): 20–26; Thad Kousser, "The Limited Impact of Term Limits Contingent Effects on the Complexity and Breadth of Laws," *State Politics and Policy Quarterly* 6 (Winter 2006): 10–29.

49. Gary Moncrief and Joel A. Thompson, "On the Outside Looking In: Lobbyists' Perspectives on the Effects of State Legislative Term Limits," *State and Local Government Review* 1 (Winter 2001): 394–411; Joel Thompson and Gary Moncrief, "Lobbying Under Limits: Interest Group Perspectives on the Effects of Term Limits in State Legislatures," in Farmer, Rausch, and Green, eds., *The Test of Time: Coping with Legislative Term Limits*, pp. 211–24; Thad Kousser, *Term Limits and the Dismantling of State Legislative Professionalism* (New York: Cambridge University Press, 2005).

50. Robert A. Bernstein and Anita Chadha, "The Effects of Term Limits on Representation: Why So Few Women?" in Rick Farmer, John David Rausch, Jr., and John C. Green, eds., *The Test of Time: Coping with Legislative Term Limits* (Lanham, MD: Lexington Books, 2003), pp. 147–58; Stanley M. Caress et al., "Effect of Term Limits on the Election of Minority State Legislators," *State and Local Government Review* 35 (Fall 2003): 183–95; Liz Farmer, "Term Limits Don't Lead to More Women in Politics," *Governing* (April 22, 2016).

51. John M. Carey, Richard G. Niemi, Lynda W. Powell, and Gary F. Moncrief, "The Effects of Term Limits on State Legislatures: A New Survey of the 50 States," *Legislative Studies Quarterly* 31 (February 2006): 105–34; Susan A. Miller, Jill Nicholson-Crotty, and Sean Nicholson-Crotty, "Reexamining the Institutional Effects of Term Limits in U.S. State Legislatures," *Legislative Studies Quarterly* 36 (February 2011): 71–97.

52. Daniel C. Lewis, "Legislative Term Limits and Fiscal Policy Performance," *Legislative Studies Quarterly* 37 (August 2012): 305–28. For a different view, see Luke Keele, Neil Malhotra, and Colin H. McCubbins, "Do Term Limits Restrain State Fiscal Policy?" *Legislative Studies Quarterly* 38 (August 2013): 291–326.

53. Andrew B. Hall, "Partisan Effects of Legislative Term Limits," *Legislative Studies Quarterly* 39 (August 2014): 407–29.

54. Carol S. Weissert and Karen Halperin, "The Paradox of Term Limit Support: To Know Them Is Not to Love Them," *Political Research Quarterly* 60 (September 2007): 516–30.

55. David Eggers, "Ex-Lawmakers Sue to Block Michigan's Legislative Term Limits," *Associated Press* (November 20, 2019).

56. Daniel A. Smith, "Overturning Term Limits: The Legislature's Own Private Idaho?" *PS: Political Science and Politics* 36 (April 2003): 215–20.

57. Governor Haley Barbour, State of the State Address, January 26, 2004.

58. Madeleine Kunin, as quoted in Sharon Randall, "From Big Shot to Boss," *State Legislatures* 14 (June 1988): 348.

59. Travis J. Baker and David M. Hedge, "Term Limits and Legislative Executive-Conflict in the American States," *Legislative Studies Quarterly* 38 (May 2013): 237–58.

60. Thad Kousser and Justin H. Phillips, "Who Blinks First? Legislative Patience and Bargaining with Governors," *Legislative Studies Quarterly* 34 (February 2009): 55–86.

61. Brian J. Gerber, Cherie Maestas, and Nelson C. Dometrius, "State Legislative Influence over Agency Rulemaking," *State Politics and Policy Quarterly* 5 (Spring 2005): 24–46.

62. Missouri Coalition for the Environment v. Joint Committee on Administrative Rules, 948 S.W.2d 125 (1997); Mead v. Arnell 791 P.2d 410 (Idaho 1990).

63. "Summary of Sunset Legislation," *The Book of the States 2006* (Lexington, KY: Council of State Governments, 2006), pp. 132–34.

64. William M. Pearson and Van A. Wigginton, "Effectiveness of Administrative Controls: Some Perceptions of State Legislators," *Public Administration Review* 46 (July/August 1986): 328–31.

65. Alan Rosenthal, *Heavy Lifting: The Job of the American Legislature* (Washington, DC: Congressional Quarterly Press, 2004), p. 85; see also Alan Rosenthal, *Engines of Democracy: Politics and Policymaking in State Legislatures* (Washington, DC: Congressional Quarterly Press, 2009).

66. Lilliard E. Richardson, Jr., David M. Konisky, and Jeffrey Milyo, "Public Approval of U.S. State Legislatures," *Legislative Studies Quarterly* 37 (February 2012): 99–116.

67. Kurtz and Weberg, "What Legislatures Need Now," p. 47.

Chapter 07 Governors: Power, Politics, and Executive Leadership

1. Pew Research Center, "Most States Have Religious Exemptions to COVID-19 Social Distancing Rules" (April 28, 2020).

2. Adam Liptak, "Supreme Court, in 5-4 Decision, Rejects Church's Challenge to Shutdown Order," *New York Times* (May 30, 2020).

3. Christine Wilkie and Kevin Breuninger, "Trump Unloads on Governors over George Floyd Protests: 'Most of You Are Weak,'" *CNBC* (June 1, 2020).

4. "The Counted: People Killed by Police in the U.S., Recorded by the Guardian—with Your Help," *The Guardian*.

5. Centers for Disease Control, "COVID-19 Racial and Ethnic Minority Groups" (April 22, 2020).

6. Charisse Jones, "Historic Layoffs Take Biggest Toll on Blacks, Latinos, Women and the Young, *USA TODAY* (May 8, 2020).

7. Christopher Rugaber, "Jobless Rate Unexpectedly Falls to 13.3%, U.S. Adds 2.5 Million Jobs," *Wall Street Journal* (June 4, 2020); Ben Casselman, "What to Make of the Rebound in the U.S. Jobs Report," *The New York Times* (June 4, 2020).

8. Margaret Ferguson, "Governors and the Executive Branch," in Virginia Gray and Russell L. Hanson, eds., *Politics in the American States: A Comparative Analysis*, 11th ed. (Washington, DC: Congressional Quarterly Press, 2018), pp. 235–74.

9. Larry Sabato, *Goodbye to Goodtime Charles: The American Governorship Transformed* (Lexington, MA: Lexington Books, 1978), p. 13.

10. Alan Rosenthal, *The Best Job in State Politics* (Washington, DC: Congressional Quarterly Press, 2012).

11. Daniel Vock, "Gina Raimondo Confronts Rhode Island's Uncertain Future," *Governing* (April 2015).

12. Jonathan Bernstein, "Kinky Friedman Comes Home," *Rolling Stone* (November 3, 2018).

13. Ben Jacobs, "Who Voted for Idaho's Weirdo Candidates for Governor?" www.thedailybeast.com (May 21, 2014).

14. AP/Salon, "Final Meg Whitman Tally: $178.5M," www.salong.com (February 1, 2011).

15. Ted Cox, "Most Expensive Governor Race in U.S. History?" www.oneillinois.com (November 13, 2018).

16. Jennifer Jensen, "Gubernatorial Campaign Expenditures Database," https://jmj313.web.lehigh.edu/node/9 (accessed January 23, 2020).

17. Thad Beyle, "High Costs of Winning and Losing," *Southern Cultures* 4 (Spring 1998): 71.

18. John R. Wright, "Unemployment and the Democratic Electoral Advantage," *American Political Science Review* 106:4 (2012): 685–702.

19. Peveril Squire, "Challenger Profile and Gubernatorial Elections," *Western Politics Quarterly* 45 (1992): 125–42.

20. Elliott Fullmer and Rebecca Daniel, "Invisible Coattails: Presidential Approval and Gubernatorial Elections, 1994–2014," *The Forum* 16 (August 2018): 269–87.

21. Associated Press, "Campaigns Spent Record $93 Million in Wisconsin Gubernatorial Race," *Wisconsin Public Radio*, www.wpr.org (January 24, 2019).

22. Sharon Sherman, "Powersplit: When Legislatures and Governors Are of Opposing Parties," *State Legislatures* 10 (May/June 1984): 9–12.

23. Sander M. Polster, "Maine's King Makes Independence a Virtue," www.stateline.org (November 30, 1999).

24. Gabriel DeBenedetti, "Steve Bullock and the Lost Art of Persuasion," *Politico* (October 11, 2017).

25. Ron Cassie, "Likable Larry: Improbably Larry Hogan Is the Second-Most Popular Governor in the Country. But Is It Good for Baltimore?" *Baltimore Magazine*, www.baltimoremagazine.com (October 2018).

26. Michael Dukakis, as quoted in Thad Beyle and Linda Muchmore, *Reflections on Being Governor* (Washington, DC: National Governor's Association, 1978), p. 45.

27. National Academy for State Health Policy Staff, "The State of the States: How Governors Plan to Address Health-Related Social and Economic Factors in 2019" (February 25, 2019).

28. Cynthia Sewell, "Governor Little Vetoes Bill That Would Have Tightened Requirements for Citizen Initiatives," *Idaho Statesman* (April 5, 2019).

29. Josh Goodman, "Politics, Kentucky Style," *Governing* (December 2009): 15.

30. Laura Vozzella, "At Executive Mansion, McAuliffe Puts Out the Welcome Mat," *Washington Post* (February 5, 2014).

31. Jon Kamp, "Florida Judge Rules Against Emergency Nursing-Home Generator Measures," *Wall Street Journal* (October 27, 2017).

32. WBUR, "New Maine Governor Faces Slew of Pending Lawsuits from LePage Era," www.wbur.org (January 5, 2019).

33. Heather Perkins, "The Governors: Compensation, Staff Travel and Residence," *Book of the States*, 2019 (Washington, DC: Council of State Governments, 2019), Table 4.3.
34. Samuel Stebbing, "Best and Worst Run States in America: A Survey of All 50," *24/7 Wall Street*, (November 12, 2019).
35. Thad Beyle and Lynn Muchmore, "The Governor and the Public," in Thad Beyle and Lynn Muchmore, eds., *Being Governor: The View from the Office* (Durham, NC: Duke University Press, 1983) pp. 52–66.
36. J. B. Wogan, "Losing Their Voice," *Governing* (June 2014): 52–55; J. Wesley Leckrone, "Trying Not to Lose Ground: State and Local Government Advocacy during Passage of the 2017 Tax Cuts and Jobs Act," *Publius* 49 (July 2019): 407–36.
37. Adam R. Brown, "Are Governors Responsible for the State Economy? Partisanship, Blame, and Divided Federalism," *The Journal of Politics* 72 (July 2010): 605–15; Jeffrey E. Cohen and James D. King, "Relative Unemployment and Gubernatorial Popularity," *Journal of Politics* 66 (November 2004): 1267–82.
38. This exchange is cited in Rosenthal, *Governors and Legislators*, p. 18.
39. Thad L. Beyle and Lynn R. Muchmore, "The Governor as Party Leader," in Beyle and Muchmore, eds., *Being Governor*, pp. 44–51; Morehouse, *Governor as Party Leader*, pp. 45–51.
40. E. Lee Bernick, "Studying Governors over Five Decades: What We Know and Where We Need to Go?" *State and Local Government Review* 48 (June 2016): 132–46.
41. Louis Jacobson, "6 Months In, Most Rookie Governors Are Thriving: Following Years of Turmoil and Gridlock in Many States, Newly Elected Governors Are Getting a Lot Done," *Governing* (July 23, 2019).
42. Updates to Tables 8.3 and 8.4 in Ferguson "Governors and the Executive Branch."
43. Alfred E. Smith, as quoted in George Weeks, "Statehouse Hall of Fame, Ten Outstanding Governors of the 20th Century," paper presented at the annual meeting of the Southern Political Science Association, Memphis, Tennessee, November 1981.
44. Charles N. Wheeler III, "Gov. James R. Thompson, 1977–1991: The Complete Campaigner, The Pragmatic Centrist," *Illinois Issues* 16 (December 1990): 12–16.
45. Thad Beyle, "The Governors," in Virginia Gray and Russell Hanson, eds., *Politics in the American States* (Washington, DC: Congressional Quarterly Press, 2004), p. 216.
46. Alan Ehrenhalt, "The Veto Gambit," *Governing* (August 2006): 11–12.
47. John Buntin, "Dr. Yes," *Governing* (December 2013): 29.
48. Christopher Cousins, "Legislature Revives 9 of 10 Bills LePage Vetoed," *Bangor Daily News*, (June 9, 2015).
49. Glenn Blain, "Governor Paterson: Here Are Those 6,700 Vetoes I Promised," *New York Daily News*, (July 8, 2010).
50. Nelson C. Dometrius and Deil S. Wright, "Governors, Legislatures, and State Budgets across Time," *Political Research Quarterly* 63:4 (2010): 783–95.
51. Avery Wilks, "SC Legislature Overrides McMaster's Veto of 15 Percent SCE&G Rate Cut," *The State* (June 28, 2018).
52. Bryan Anderson, "What You Missed from Jerry Brown's Busy Weekend + Veto Rates, *Sacramento Bee* (October 1, 2018); Disability Rights California, "Signed and Vetoed Bills of Note—2018," www.disabilityrightsca.org (accessed January 28, 2020).
53. Matthew Yi, "Governor Sets Record for Vetoing Bills," www.wfgate.com (October 2, 2008).
54. Charles Barrilleaux and Michael Berkman, "Do Governors Matter? Budgeting Rules and the Politics of State Policymaking," *Political Research Quarterly* 56 (December 2003): 409–17.
55. Dan Durning, "Governors and Administrative Reform in the 1990s," *State and Local Government Review* 27 (Winter 1995): 36–54.
56. James K. Conant, "State Reorganization: A New Model?" *State Government* 58 (April 1985): 130–38.
57. Michael Berkman and Christopher Reenock, "Incremental Consolidation and Comprehensive Reorganization of American State Executive Branches," *American Journal of Political Science* 48 (October 2004): 796–812.
58. Robert F. Bennett, as quoted in H. Edward Flentje, "The Political Nature of the Governor as Manager," p.70, in Beyle and Muchmore, 1983.
59. *Book of the States*, 2019, Table 4.3.
60. National Governors Association, "The Many Roles of the Governors' Chief of Staff: 2018 Edition," https://www.nga.org/ (accessed January 29, 2020).
61. David Eggert, "GOP Legislatures Try to Curb Democratic Governors' Power," Associated Press, (November 17, 2018).
62. Thomas M. Holbrook, "Institutional Strength and Gubernatorial Elections: An Exploratory Analysis," *American Politics Quarterly* 21 (July 1993): 261–71.
63. Tom Ferrick, Jr., "Alienating a State from East to West," www.nyti.ms/1onKbCO (October 20, 2014).
64. Colin Woodard, "Maine's Governor Is in Trouble Again," *Governing* (July 8, 2014).
65. Thad L. Beyle, "Enhancing Executive Leadership in the States," *State and Local Government Review* 27 (Winter 1995): 18–35.
66. Alan Greenblat, "The Job of a Lifetime," *Governing* (June 2009): 24–30.
67. Rob Gurwitt, "The Ordeal of David Paterson," *Governing* (March 2009): 26–33.
68. Coleman Ransome, *The American Governorship* (Westport, CT: Greenwood Press, 1982).
69. Scott M. Matheson, with James Edwin Kee, *Out of Balance* (Salt Lake City: Peregrine Smith Books, 1986), p. 186.
70. Paul West, "They're Everywhere! For Today's Governors, Life Is a Never-Ending Campaign," *Governing* 3 (March 1990): 51–55.
71. A. G. Sulzberger, "Jokes and Secret Hopes for Lieutenant Governors," www.nytimes.com (December 3, 2010).
72. Josh Goodman, "The Second Best Job in the State," *Governing* (April 2009).
73. *The Book of the States* (2019): Table 4.14.
74. Eric Lipton, "Energy Firms in Secretive Alliance with Attorneys General," www.nytimes.com (December 6, 2014); Lipton, "Lobbyists, Bearing Gifts, Pursue Attorneys General" (October 28, 2014).
75. Rob Moritz, "Former Treasurer Convicted of Bribery, Extortion," www.ualrpublicradio.org (March 11, 2014).
76. National Association of Secretaries of State, "NASS Business Identify Theft Task Force Findings and Suggestions for States," www.nass.org (February 2017); Kay Stimson, "Secretaries of State Confront the Growing Problem of Business Identity Theft," *The Book of the States*, vol. 43 (2011): 167–69.

Chapter 08 Public Administration: Budgeting and Service Delivery

1. H. George Frederickson, "Can Bureaucracy Be Beautiful?" *Public Administration Review* 60 (January/February 2000): 47–53.
2. Judith Rayner et al., "Public Service Ethos: Developing a Generic Measure," *Journal of Public Administration Research and Theory* 21(1) (2011): 27–51; Ari Salminem and Venya Mantysalo, "Exploring the Public Service Ethos," *Public Integrity* 15 (April, 2013): 167–86.
3. See, for example, Theodore H. Poister and Gary T. Henry, "Citizen Ratings of Public and Private Service Quality: A Comparative Perspective," *Public Administration Review* 54 (March/April 1994): 155–59.
4. Mary E. Guy, Meredity A. Newman, and Sharon H. Mastracci, *Emotional Labor: Putting the Service in Public Service* (Armonk, NY: M. E. Sharpe, 2008).
5. U.S. Census, *Annual Survey of Public Employment and Payroll Summary Report: 2018*, www.census.gov (August 13, 2019).

6. Steven Maynard-Moody and Michael Musheno, *Cops, Teachers, Counselors: Stories from the Front Lines of Public Service* (Ann Arbor: University of Michigan Press, 2003).

7. Harold D. Laswell, *Politics: Who Gets What, When, Where, How?* (Cleveland, OH: World, 1958).

8. Rashawn Ray, "What Does 'Defund the Police' Mean and Does It Have Merit?" *Brookings Institution* (June 19, 2020).

9. Ellen Perlman, "Stat Fever," *Governing* (January 2007): 48–49.

10. Katherine Barrett and Richard Greene, "The Big Picture on Budgeting," *Governing* (November 2010): 60–62; Zach Patton, "Culture Change," *Governing* (January 2008): 68–69.

11. Aaron Wildavsky, "Toward a Radical Incrementalism," in Alfred De Grazia, ed., *Congress: The First Branch of Government* (Washington, DC: American Enterprise Institute, 1966).

12. Nelson C. Dometrius and Deil S. Wright, "Governors, Legislatures, and State Budgets across Time," *Political Research Quarterly* 63 (December 4, 2010): 783–95; Christian Breunig and Chris Koski, "Punctuated Budgets and Governors' Institutional Powers," *American Politics Research* 37:6 (2009): 1116–38; Tianfeng Li and Richard Feiock, "Explaining State Budget Punctuations: Policy Transparency, Political Institutions, and Electoral Incentives," *Policy Studies Journal* (June 17, 2019).

13. Dave McKinney, "Court Strikes Down State's $31 Billion Capital Program," www.suntimes.com (January 27, 2011).

14. John M. Kamensky, "When Citizens Decide How Public Money Is Spent," www.governing.com (September 15, 2014); Participatory Budgeting Project, "PB by the Numbers," www.participatorybudgeting.org (accessed January 31, 2020).

15. Charles E. Lindblom, "The Science of Muddling Through," *Public Administrative Review* 19 (Spring 1959): 79–88.

16. Elaine S. Povitch, "State Budgeting with an Eye on Results," www.stateline.org (August 28, 2014); Janet M. Kelly and William C. Rivenbark, *Performance Budgeting for State and Local Government* (Armonk, NY: M. E. Sharpe, 2003).

17. "Mayor's Plan for Zero-Based Budgeting" (November 19, 2019), https://urbanreform.org/ "Zero-Base Budgeting Concepts and Examples" (June 28, 2016), https://www.sandiego.gov/

18. Jon Seidel, "Watchdog Alleges 'Illegal Patronage' in Cook County Clerk's Office," *Chicago Sun-Times* (September 11, 2019); Brendan Lyons, "Government Workers' Campaign Duties Under Scrutiny," *Albany Times Union* (June 16, 2019).

19. David K. Hamilton, "The Staffing Function in Illinois State Government after Rutan," *Public Administration Review* 53 (July/August 1993): 381–86.

20. H. George Fredrickson and Todd LaPorte, "Airport Security, High Reliability, and the Problem of Rationality," *Public Administration Review* 62 (September 2002): 32–43.

21. J. Edward Kellough and Sally Coleman Selden, "The Reinvention of Public Personnel Administration: An Analysis of the Diffusion of Personnel Management Reforms in the States," *Public Administration Review* 63 (November/December 2003): 165–76.

22. Jerrell D. Coggburn, "Deregulating the Public Personnel Function," in Steven W. Hays and Richard C. Kearney, eds., *Public Personnel Administration: Problems and Prospects*, 4th ed. (Upper Saddle River, NJ: Prentice-Hall, 2003), pp. 75–79.

23. Robert J. McGrath, The Rise and Fall of Radical Civil Service Reform in the States," *Public Administration Review* 73 (July/August, 2013): 638–49.

24. Lael R. Keiser et al., "Lipstick and Logarithms: Gender, Institutional Context, and Representative Bureaucracy," *American Political Science Review* 96(3) (2002): 553–64; Vicky M. Wilkins and Lael R. Keiser, "Linking Passive and Active Representation by Gender: The Case of Child Support Agencies," *Journal of Public Administration Research and Theory* 16 (Winter 2005): 87–102; Vicky M. Wilkins "Exploring the Causal Story: Gender, Active Representation, and Bureaucratic Priorities," *Journal of Public Administration Research and Theory* 17 (Winter 2006): 77–94.

25. Wilkins, "Exploring the Causal Story."

26. David E. Brockman, "Black Politicians Are Intrinsically Motivated to Advance Blacks' Interests: A Field Experiment Manipulating Political Incentives," *American Journal of Political Science* 57 (July 2013): 521–36.

27. Nick A. Theobald and Donald P. Haider-Markel, "Race, Bureaucracy, and Symbolic Representation: Interactions between Citizens and Police," *Journal of Public Administration Research and Theory* 19:2 (2008): 409–26.

28. Ibid.

29. Mark D. Bradbury and J. Edward Kellough, "Representative Bureaucracy: Exploring the Potential for Active Representation in Local Government," *Journal of Public Administration Research and Theory* 18 (2011): 697–714.

30. See Ricci v. DeStefano (No. 07-1428, 2009); J. Edward Kellough, "Affirmative Action and Diversity in the Public Sector," in Steven W. Hays, Richard C. Kearney, and Jerrell D. Coggburn, eds., *Public Human Resource Management: Problems and Prospects*, 5th ed. (New York: Pearson Education, 2009), pp. 219–35.

31. Schuette v. Coalition to Defend Affirmative Action, No. 12-682 (April 22, 2014).

32. Gretz v. Bollinger, No. 02-241 F.3d732 (June 23, 2003).

33. Fisher v. University of Texas, 57 U.S. 297 (2013); Fisher v. University of Texas 579 U.S. ____ (2016).

34. Jared J. Llorens, Jeffrey B. Wenger, and J. Edward Kellough, "Choosing Public Sector Employment: The Impact of Wages on the Representation of Women and Minorities in State Bureaucracies," *Journal of Public Administration Research and Theory* 18:3 (2008): 397–413.

35. Mary E. Guy, "The Difference That Gender Makes," in Hays and Kearney (2003), pp. 256–70; Norma M. Riccucci, *Managing Diversity in Public Sector Workforces* (Boulder, CO: Westview Press, 2002).

36. Mary E. Guy, "Three Steps Forward, Two Steps Backward: The Status of Women's Integration into Public Management," *Public Administration Review* 53 (July/August 1993): 285–91.

37. M. G. Alkadry and L. E. Tower, *Women in Public Service: Barriers, Challenges, and Opportunities* (Armonk, NY: M. E. Sharpe, 2009); Heidi Voorhees and Rachel Lange-Skaggs, "Women Leading Government," www.icma.org/en/press/pm_magazine/article/105323.

38. Cynthia J. Bowling et al., "Cracked Ceilings, Firmer Floors, and Weakening Walls: Trends and Patterns in Gender Representation among Executives Leading American State Agencies, 1970–2000," *Public Administration Review* 66 (November/December 2006): 823–36.

39. Jennifer Laird, "Public Sector Employment Inequality in the United States and the Great Recession," *Demography* 54 (January 2017): 409.

40. Barb Rosewicz and Mike Maclag, "How COVID-19 Is Driving Big Job Losses in State and Local Government," *Pew Trust* (June 16, 2020),.

41. Rey Mashayekhi, "Everything You Need to Know about Furloughs—and What They Mean for Workers during the Coronavirus Pandemic," *Fortune* (March 30, 2020).

42. J. Edward Kellough, *Understanding Affirmative Action* (Washington, DC: Georgetown University Press, 2006); Daniel N. Lipson, "Where's the Justice? Affirmative Action's Severed Roots in the Age of Diversity," *Perspectives on Politics* 6 (December 2008): 691–705.

43. Sonia Ospina and James F. O'Sullivan, "Working Together: Meeting the Challenge of Workplace Diversity," in Hays and Kearney (2003), pp. 238–55; Norma Riccucci, *Managing Diversity in Public Sector Workforces*, 9th ed. (New York: Pearson, 2013).

44. Meritor Savings Bank v. Vinson, 1986, 477 U.S. 57; Teresa Haris v. Forklift Systems, Inc., S. Ct., 92-1168 (November 9, 1993).

45. Steve Miletich, "County to Pay $1 Million to 3 Detectives in Sex-Harassment Case," www.seattletimes.com (December 18, 2013).

46. Lilia Cortina and Jennifer L. Berdahl, "Sexual Harassment in Organizations: A Decade of Research in Review," in Julian Barling and Cary L. Cooper, eds., *The SAGE Handbook of Organizational Behavior Vol. I: Micro Perspectives* (Thousand Oaks, CA: SAGE, 2008), pp. 469–97; James Quick and M. Ann McFadyen, "Sexual Harassment: Have We Made Any Progress?" *Journal of Occupational Health Psychology* 22 (October 2016): 286–98.

47. Holly Kearl, *The Facts Behind the #MeToo Movement: A National Study on Sexual Harassment and Assault* (Reston, VA: Stop Street Harassment, 2018).

48. Jocelyn Frye, "Not Just the Rich and Famous: The Pervasiveness of Sexual Harassment Across Industries Affects All Workers," *Center for American Progress*, (November 20, 2017).

49. Bureau of Labor Statistics, "Union Members—2019" (January 22, 2020).

50. Richard C. Kearney and Patrice M. Mareschal, *Labor Relations in the Public Sector*, 5th ed. (New York: CRC Press, 2014).

51. Janus v. AFSCME, 585 U.S. _____ (2018).

52. Bureau of Labor Statistics, "Union Members—2019"; also see Daniel DiSalvo, "Janus Barely Dents Public-Sector Union Membership," *Wall Street Journal* (February 13, 2019).

53. Andrew Van Dam, "Teacher Strikes Made 2018 the Biggest Year for Worker Protest in a Generation," *The Washington Post* (February 14, 2019); Zachary B. Wolf, "Why Teacher Strikes Are Touching Every Part of America," *CNN* (February 23, 2019); Grace Hauck, "Chicago Teachers Approve 'Historic' Contract That Ended 11-Day Strike," *USA Today* (November 16, 2019); Holly Yan, "The LA Teachers' Strike Ends After Union Approves Deal with School District," *CNN* (January 22, 2019).

54. Erin Richards, "Strikes, Pay Raises and Charter Protests: American's Teachers' Exhausting, Exhilarating Year," *USA Today* (June 18, 2019).

55. Tracey Amick-Peer, "Atlanta Police Sickout Calls Continue for Third Day," *WXIA-TV* (June 19, 2020)

56. Dana Kozlov, "Text Message Urges Chicago Police Officers to Call in Sick, Limit Arrests in 'Blue Flu,'" *WBBM-TV* (June 22, 2020).

57. Kearney and Mareschal, 2014: Chapter 6; Eric Brunner and Andrew Ju, "State Collective Bargaining Laws and Public-Sector Pay," *ILR Review* 72 (March 2019): 480–508; Brigham Frandsen and Michael Webb, "Public Employee Pensions and Collective Bargaining Rights: Evidence from State and Local Government Finances," Hutchins Center Working Paper #35, www.brookings.edu (October 2019).

58. Kearney and Mareschal, *Labor Relations in the Public Sector*, 5th ed. (New York: CRC Press, 2009), pp. 194–96.

59. Eric M. Patashinik, *Reforms at Risk: What Happens after Major Policy Changes Are Enacted* (Princeton, N.J. Princeton University Press, 2008), p. 161.

60. Michael Lipsky, *Street-Level Bureaucrats: The Dilemmas of the Individual in Public Service* (New York: Sage, 1980).

61. U.S. Census, "Annual Survey of Public Employment and Payroll Summary Report: 2018," https://www.census.gov/ (accessed March 17, 2020).

62. Erin Huffer and Aravind Boddupalli, "COVID-19's Effect on Employment Varies Across States, Except in One Sector: Government Jobs," *The Urban Institute* (May 22, 2020).

63. David Osborne and Ted Gaebler, *Reinventing Government* (New York: Penguin Books, 1993).

64. John M. Bryson, Barbara C. Crosby, and Laura Bloomberg, "Public Value Governance: Moving Beyond Traditional Public Administration and the New Public Management," *Public Administration Review* 74:4 (2014): 445–56.

65. Robert Mohr and Steven C. Deller, "Alternative Methods of Service Delivery in Small and Rural Municipalities," *Public Administration Review* (November/December 2010): 894–904.

66. "Intergovernmental Cooperation: The Growing Reform," in ICMA, The Municipal Year Book, 2014 (Washington, DC: ICMA Press, 2014).

67. Morten Jakobsen and Simon Calmar Andersen, "Coproduction and Equity in Public Service Delivery," *Public Administration Review* 73:5 (2013): 704–13.

68. David Segal, "A Georgia Town Takes the People's Business Private," www.nytimes.com (August 23, 2012).

69. John Ruch, "Is the 'Sandy Springs Model' of Government Changing?" *Reporter Newspapers* (July 8, 2016); see also Jack Feldman, "Extreme Privatization: A Performance Analysis of the 'Sandy Springs Model,'" *Graduate Theses and Dissertations*, https://lib.dr.iastate.edu/etd/13870 (2014).

70. Stephen C. Fehr, "Study: Why Pa. Turnpike Plan Failed," www.stateline.org (March 24, 2009).

71. Ryan Holeywell, "Public-Private Practical?" *Governing* (November 2013): 34–41; Gerald T. Gabris and Douglas M. Ihrke, "Unanticipated Failures of Well-Intentional Reforms: Some Lessons Learned from Federal and Local Governments," *International Journal of Organization Theory and Behavior* 6 (February 2003): 195–225.

72. Tony Cook, "Indiana Gov. Mitch Daniels' Legacy: Privatization," www.indystar.com (January 1, 2013).

73. M. Ernita Joaquin and Thomas J. Greitens, "Contract Management Capacity Breakdown? An Analysis of U.S. Local Governments," *Public Administration Review* 72:6 (2012): 807–16.

74. E. S. Savas, *Privatization: The Key to Better Government* (Chatham, NJ: Chatham House, 1987), p. 233.

75. Mildred E. Warner and Austin M. Aldag, "Re-municipalization in the US: A Pragmatic Response to Contracting," *Journal of Economic Policy Reform* (September 2019); Judith Clifton, Mildred E. Warner, Raymond Gradus, and Germà Bel, "Re-municipalization of Public Services: Trend or Hype?" *Journal of Economic Policy Reform* (September 2019).

76. Melissa Maynard, "Why States Need Social Media Policies," www.stateline.org (October 29, 2013); "IBM Survey: Too Much Data in Public Sector Stymies Effective Analysis," www.govtech.com (May 16, 2011); Sharon S. Dawes, "The Evolution and Continuing Challenges of E-Governance," *Public Administration Review* 68 (December 2008): S86–S102.

77. Insurance Institute for Highway Safety, "New Guidelines for Automated Enforcement Programs Emphasize Safety Amid Rise in Red-Light Running Crash Deaths" (July 24, 2018).

78. Jillian D'Onfro, "This Map Shows Which Cities Are Using Facial Recognition Technology—and Which Have Banned It," *Forbes* (July 18, 2019).

79. Mass Transit, "The Connected Reality of a Smart City" (December 17, 2018), https://www.masstransitmag.com /technology/article/12412867/the-connected-reality-of -a-smart-city.

80. John Carroll, "Pros and Cons of San Diego's Gunshot Detection System," *KPBS* (June 19, 2019)

81. Kari Paul, "Amazon to Ban Police Use of Facial Recognition Software for a Year," *The Guardian* (June 10, 2020).

Chapter 09 The Judiciary: Independence vs Accountability

1. California v. Hodari D, 499 U.S. 621 (1991).

2. State v. Young, 957 P.2d 681 (1998).

3. People v. Bora, 634 N.E.2d 168 (NY 1994).

4. State v. Tucker, 136 N.J. 158 (1994).

5. LaKeith Faulkner and Christopher R. Green, "State-Constitutional Departures from the Supreme Court: The Fourth Amendment," *Mississippi Law Journal* 89, (September 2019).

6. Melinda Gann Hall, "State Courts: Politics and the Judicial Process," in Virginia Gray, Russell Hanson, and Thad Kousser, eds., *Politics in the American States: A Comparative Analysis*, 11th ed. (Thousand Oaks, CA: CQ Press, 2018), p. 277.

7. National Center for State Courts, "The State of State Courts: A 2018 NCSC Public Opinion Survey," https://www.ncsc.org/ (accessed February 10, 2020).

8. Henry Robert Glick and Kenneth N. Vines, *State Court Systems* (Englewood Cliffs, NJ: Prentice-Hall, 1973), p. 19.
9. Ibid., p. 21.
10. Caroline Cournoyer, "'Neighborhood' Courts to Reduce Crowding, Cut Costs," *www.governing.com* (May 2, 2011).
11. Torsten Ove, "Robert Bowers, Accused in Tree of Life Synagogue Shootings, Arraigned," *Pittsburgh Post-Gazette* (February 22, 2019).
12. National Center for State Courts, "Court Unification," www.ncsc.org (accessed February 20, 2020).
13. American Bar Association, "Standards on State Judicial Selection," www.americanbar.org (July 2000); G. Alan Tarr, *Without Fear or Favor: Judicial Independence and Judicial Accountability in the States* (Stanford: Stanford University Press, 2012).
14. Charles Gardner Geyh, *Who Is to Judge? The Perennial Debate over Whether to Elect or Appoint America's Judges* (New York: Oxford University Press, 2019).
15. National Center for State Courts, "Judicial Selection in the States: South Carolina," http://www.judicialselection.us/ (accessed February 11, 2020).
16. "State Judicial Elections, 2019," https://ballotpedia.org/State_judicial_elections,_2019 (accessed February 11, 2020).
17. Brandice Canes-Wrones, Tom S. Clark, and Jason P. Kelly, "Judicial Selection and Death Penalty Decisions," *American Political Science Review* 108 (February 2014): 23–39; Paul Brace and Brent D. Boyea, "State Public Opinion, the Death Penalty, and the Practice of Electing Judges," *American Journal of Political Science* 52(2) (April 2008): 360–72; Republican Party of Minnesota v. White, 536 U.S. 765 (2002); Citizens United v. Federal Election Commission, 558 U.S. 310 (2010).
18. Brandice Canes-Wrone, Tom Clark, and Amy Semet, "Judicial Elections, Public Opinion, and Decisions on Lower-Salience Issues," *Journal of Empirical Legal Studies* 15 (December 2018): 672–707.
19. Alicia Bannon, Cathleen Lisk, and Peter Hardin, "Who Pays for Judicial Races? The Politics of Judicial Elections: 2015–16" (December 14, 2017), www.brennancenter.org; Benjamin Woodson, "The Two Opposing Effects of Judicial Elections on Legitimacy Perceptions," *State Politics and Policy Quarterly* 17 (May 2016): 24–46.
20. Williams-Yulee v. The Florida Bar, 575 U.S. _____ (2015); Aman McLeod, "Understanding *Williams-Yulee v. The Florida Bar* and Its Implications for Freedom of Speech in Judicial Elections," *First Amendment Studies* 57 (March 2018): 61–79; Billy Corriher, "Supreme Court: Judges Aren't Politicians, and States Can Bar Them from Soliciting Cash," *Center for American Progress*, (April 30, 2015).
21. Richard Neely, *The Product Liability Mess: How Business Can Be Rescued from State Court Politics* (Boston: The Free Press, 1988), p. 4.
22. MetroNews Staff, "Former Justice Richard Neely Launches Run for 2020 Court Seat," www.metronews.com (October 9, 2019).
23. Adam Liptak and Janet Roberts, "Campaign Cash Mirrors a High Courts' Rulings," *The New York Times* (October 1, 2006): 1–10.
24. James P. Gibson and Gregory A. Caldeira, "Campaign Support, Conflicts of Interest, and Judicial Impartiality: Can Recusals Rescue the Legitimacy of Courts?" *The Journal of Politics* 74 (January 2012): 18–34; Stephen Ware, "Money, Politics, and Judicial Decisions: A Case Study of Arbitration Law in Alabama," *Journal of Law and Politics* 15 (Fall 1999): 645–86; Madhavi McCall, "The Politics of Judicial Elections: The Influence of Campaign Contributions on the Voting Patterns of Texas Supreme Court Justices," *Politics and Policy* 31 (June 2003): 314–33.
25. Justice Paul Pfeifer, quoted in Liptak and Roberts, 2006; "The Best Judges Business Can Buy," *The New York Times* editorial, www.nytimes.com (October 1, 2006).
26. Bannon, Lisk, and Hardin, 2017; Douglas Keith with Patrick Berry and Eric Velasco, "The Politics of Judicial Elections, 2017–18," *Brennan Center for Justice* (December 11, 2019).
27. See Carrie Johnson, "Report: Too Much Money Going to State Court Races," www.npr.org (August 16, 2010); David B. Rottman and Roy A. Schotland, "2004 Judicial Elections," in *The Book of the States 2005* (Lexington, KY: Council of State Governments, 2005), pp. 305–308.
28. Keith, Berry, and Velasco, 2019.
29. Ibid.
30. Adam Liptak, "Motion Ties W. Virginia Justice to Coal Executive," *New York Times*, (January 15, 2008); Adam Liptak, "Justices Tell Judges Not to Rule on Major Backers," *New York Times* (June 8, 2009); Len Boselovic, "W. Va. Chief Justice Accused of Bias" *Pittsburg Post-Gazette* (January 15, 2008).
31. Brennan Center for Justice, "New Poll: Vast Majority of Voters Fear Campaign Cash Skews Judges' Decisions" (October 29, 2013).
32. As quoted in Sheila Kaplan, "Justice for Sale," *State Government: CQ's Guide to Current Issues and Activities, 1986–87* (Washington, DC: Congressional Quarterly Press, 1987), pp. 51–57.
33. Melinda Gann Hall, "State Supreme Courts in American Democracy: Probing the Myths of Judicial Reform," *American Political Science Review* 95 (June 2001): 315–30.
34. William Glaberson, "States Take Steps to Rein in Excesses of Judicial Politicking," *The New York Times* (June 15, 2001): 1–4.
35. Caperton v. A.T. Massey Coal Co., No. 08–22, U.S. Supreme Court, 2009.
36. David Hughes, "New-Style Campaigns in State Supreme Court Retention Elections," *State Politics and Policy Quarterly* 19 (October 2018): 127–54.
37. John Culver, "California Supreme Court Election: 'Rose Bird and the Supremes,'" *Comparative State Politics Newsletter* (February 1987): 13.
38. Steven D. Williams, "The 1996 Retention Election of Justice White," *Comparative State Politics* 17 (October 1996): 28–30.
39. Melinda Gann Hall, "Electoral Politics and Strategic Voting in State Supreme Courts," *Journal of Politics* 54 (1992): 427–46.
40. Jan Biles, "State Supreme Court Justices Stave Off Ousting Campaign," *Topeka Capital-Journal* (November 10, 2014); Mary Ellen Klas, "Fla. Supreme Court Justices Fight Back to Retain Seats," *Miami Herald* (October 6, 2012).
41. Malia Reddick, "Judging the Quality of Judicial Selection Methods: Merit Selection, Elections, and Judicial Discipline" (April 1, 2010), https://ssrn.com/abstract=2731018.
42. Todd Curry and Mark Hurwitz, "Strategic Retirements of Elected and Appointed Justices: A Hazard Model Approach," *Journal of Politics* 78 (October 2016): 1061–75.
43. Kathleen Bratton and Rorie Spill, "Existing Diversity and Judicial Selection: The Role of Appointment Method in Establishing Gender Diversity in State Supreme Courts," *Social Science Quarterly* 83 (June 2002): 504–18.
44. Melinda Gann Hall and Chris W. Bonneau, "Attack Advertising, the *White* Decision, and Voter Participation in State Supreme Court Elections," *Political Research Quarterly* 66:1 (2013): 115–26.
45. Laila Robbins and Alicia Bannon, "State Supreme Court Diversity: Across the Country, Courts Fail to Reflect the Racial, Ethnic, and Gender Diversity of the Communities They Serve," Brennan Center for Justice (July 23, 2019).
46. Melinda Gann Hall, "Representation in State Supreme Courts: Evidence from the Terminal Term," *Political Research Quarterly* 67:2 (2014): 335–46; Melinda Gann Hall, "Electoral Politics and Strategic Voting in State Supreme Courts," *Journal of Politics* 54 (1992): 427–46; Melinda Gann Hall, "Toward an Integrated Model of Judicial Voting Behavior," *American Politics Quarterly* 20 (1992): 147–68.
47. Canes-Wrone, Clark, and Semet, 2018. Todd Justice, "Supreme Court Flap Between Justice Ann Bradley and Justice David Prosser Leads to Investigation," www.postcrescent.com (June 28, 2011).

48. John Ismay, "Booze, Gunshots and White Castle: Three Judges Are Suspended for Brawl," *New York Times* (November 15, 2019).

49. Frank Fernandez, "Supreme Court Suspends Former Flagler Judge Scott DuPont," *Daytona Beach News-Journal* (October 10, 2019).

50. Jim Rosica, "Caught on Camera: Florida Judge Stands Accused of Choking Court Worker" (July 19, 2019), https://floridapolitics.com

51. "New Questions about Rhode Island Chief Justice," *The New York Times* (October 3, 1993), section 1, p. 22; "Ex-Top Judge Ends Rhode Island Appeal with a Guilty Plea," *The New York Times* (April 30, 1994), section 1, p. 12; "Justice in Impeachment Inquiry Quits in Rhode Island," *The New York Times* (May 29, 1986), p. A14. Brent D. Boyea, "Does Seniority Matter? The Conditional Influences of State Methods of Judicial Retention," *Social Science Quarterly* 91:1 (2010): 209–27.

52. Bill Chappell, "Alabama Chief Justice Roy Moore Suspended for Rest of Term Over Gay Marriage Stance" *National Public Radio* (September 30, 2016).

53. Jeffrey Smith and Grant MacQueen, "Going, Going, But Not Quite Gone: Trials Continue to Decline in Federal and State Courts. Does it Matter?" *Judicature* 101 (Winter 2017).

54. Matt Reynolds, "Could Zoom Jury Trials Become the Norm During the Coronavirus Pandemic?" *ABA Journal* (May 11, 2020).

55. Associated Press, "Texas Court Holds First U.S. Jury Trial via Videoconferencing," *Fortune* (May 23, 2020).

56. Walter V. Schaefer, "Precedent and Policy," *The University of Chicago Law Review* 34 (Autumn 1966): 8.

57. Jennifer Barnes Bowie, Donald Songer, and John Szmer, *The View from the Bench and Chambers* (Charlottesville, University of Virginia Press, 2014).

58. Hall, "Electoral Politics and Strategic Voting."

59. Kate Berry, "How Judicial Elections Impact Criminal Cases," *Brennan Center for Justice* (December 2, 2015): 7.

60. Jake Dear and Edward Jessen, "'Followed Rates' and Leading State Cases, 1940–2005," *UC Davis Law Review* 41 (April 2007): 683–718.

61. Chris W. Bonneau and Heather Marie Rice, "Impartial Judges? Institutional Context and U.S. State Supreme Courts," *State Politics and Policy Quarterly* 9:4 (2009): 381–403; Rodriguez, Curry, and Lee, "Gender Differences in Criminal Sentencing."

62. Gerald S. Gryski, Eleanor C. Main, and William J. Dixon, "Models of State High Court Decision Making in Sex Discrimination Cases," *Journal of Politics* 48 (February 1986): 143–55; Donald R. Songer and Kelley A. Crews-Meyer, "Does Judge Gender Matter? Decision Making in State Supreme Courts," *Social Science Quarterly* 81 (September 2000): 750–62.

63. Darrell Steffensmeier and Chester Britt, "Judges' Race and Judicial Decision Making: Do Black Judges Sentence Differently?" *Social Science Quarterly* 82 (December 2001): 749–64; Laura Langer and Paul Brace, "The Preemptive Power of State Supreme Courts: Adoption of Abortion and Death Penalty Legislation," *Policy Studies Journal* 33 (2005): 317–39.

64. Stephanie A. Lindquist and Frank B. Cross, *Measuring Judicial Activism* (New York: Oxford University Press, 2010); John J. Scheb, III, Terry Bowen, and Gary Anderson, "Ideology, Role Orientations, and Behavior in the State Courts of Last Resort," *American Politics Quarterly* 19 (July 1991): 324–35.

65. Alan B. Morrison, "The Right and Wrong Kinds of Judicial Activism," *American Constitution Society for Law and Policy* (May 2010).

66. Michael Cooper, "Courts Upend Budgets as States Look for Savings," *New York Times* (June 6, 2011).

67. See Adam Skaggs and Maria da Silva, "America's Judiciary: Courting Disaster," *Los Angeles Times* (July 8, 2011), citing study by the National Center for State Courts.

68. Diego Zambrano, "Federal Expansion and the Decay of State Courts," *University of Chicago Law Review* 86 (July 2019).

69. "Nichols Case Weighs on Public Defender System," www.augustachronicle.com (March 11, 2010).

70. "State Courts at the Tipping Point," *New York Times* (November 24, 2009).

71. National Center for State Courts, "Budget Resource Center," https://www.ncsc.org/(accessed February 17, 2020).

72. Zambrano, "Federal Expansion and the Decay of State Courts."

73. Conference on State Court Administrators, "State Court Caseload Digest: 2017 Data," http://www.courtstatistics.org/ (accessed February 17, 2020).

74. Stephanie Francis Ward, "First-Year Class Sizes for ABA-Accredited Law Schools Are Slightly Smaller in 2019," *ABA Journal* (December 12, 2019); Ian Pisarcik, "Women Outnumber Men in Law School Classrooms for Third Year in a Row, but Statistics Don't Tell the Full Story," *Jurist* (March 5, 2019).

75. Debra Cassens Weiss, "Lawyer Count in US Increases 14.5% From Decade Ago; These 5 States Have High Number of Active Attorneys," *ABA Journal*, (June 3, 2019); Debra Cassens Weiss, "Lawyer Population 15% Higher than 10 Years Ago, New ABA Data Shows," *ABA Journal* (May 3, 2018).

76. National Center for State Courts, "Performance Measurement," https://www.ncsc.org/ (accessed June 20, 2020).

77. Council of State Governments, *Book of the States: 2019*, Table 5.4.

78. Institute for the Advancement of the American Legal System, "Judicial Performance Evaluation in the States," https://iaals.du.edu/ (accessed June 22, 2020).

79. Sharon Paynter and Richard Kearney, "Who Watches the Watchmen? Evaluating Judicial Performance in the American States," *Administration and Society* 41 (January 2010): 923–53.

Chapter 10 Local Government: Types and Functions

1. Illinois Government News Network, "Governor Names Members of Local Government and Unfunded Mandates Task Force" (March 13, 2015), www3.illinois.gov/

2. The Civic Federation, "Update on Illinois Government Consolidation and Unfunded Mandates Task Force Recommendations" (January 23, 2019).

3. John Nalbandian et al., "Contemporary Challenges in Local Government," *Public Administration Review* 73 (July/August 2013): 567–74.

4. John Kincaid, "Municipal Perspectives on Federalism," unpublished manuscript, 1987.

5. Dennis Hale, "The City as Polity and Economy," *Polity* 17 (Winter 1984): 205–24.

6. Kincaid, "Municipal Perspectives," p. 56.

7. Justin M. Ross, Joshua C. Hall, and William G. Resh, "Frictions in Polycentric Administration with Noncongruent Borders: Evidence from Ohio School District Class Sizes," *Journal of Public Administration Research and Theory* 24 (July 2014): 623–49.

8. U.S. Census Bureau, "2017 Census of Governments, Table 2: Local Governments by Type and State" (accessed March 3, 2020).

9. American National Election Study, "User's Guide and Codebook for the ANES 2016 Time Series Study" (September 4, 2019).

10. Christopher Hoene, Mark Baldassare, and Michael Shires, "The Development of Counties as Municipal Governments," *Urban Affairs Review* 37 (March 2002): 575–91.

11. Dale Krane, Platon N. Rigos, and Melvin B. Hill Jr., *Home Rule in America: A Fifty State Handbook* (Washington, DC: Congressional Quarterly Press, 2001).

12. Alan Greenblatt, "New Clout in a Big County," *Governing* 20 (May 2007): 22–23.

13. J. Edwin Benton, "The Impact of Structural Reform on County Government Service Provision," *Social Science Quarterly* 84 (December 2003): 858–74.

14. Jayce Farmer, "County Government Choices for Redistributive Services," *Urban Affairs Review* 47 (January 2011): 60–83.

15. Chris Tausanovitch and Christopher Warshaw, "Representation in Municipal Government," *American Political Science Review* 108 (August 2014): 605–41.

16. "Counties Out of Date," *State Legislatures* 17 (March 1991): 17.

17. Jerome Sherman, "6 Elected Row Officers Become 3 Appointed," *Pittsburgh Post–Gazette* (May 18, 2005).

18. See Olesva Tkacheva, "New Cities, Local Officials, and Municipal Incorporation Laws: A Supply-Side Model of City Formation," *Journal of Urban Affairs* 30 (2008): 155–74.

19. Edward McClelland, "Rahm Emanuel Could Be Chicago's Last Boss: The City Council Is Getting Stronger—and with a Weak Mayor, It Could Regain Control of Chicago's Purse Strings," *Chicago Politics & City Life* (September 12, 2018), https://www.chicagomag.com/city-life/September-2018/Rahm-Emanuel-Could-Be-Chicagos-Last-Boss/.

20. Kimberly L. Nelson and James H. Svara, "Adaptation of Models versus Variations in Form: Classifying Structures of City Government," *Urban Affairs Review* 45 (March 2010): 544–62.

21. Rebecca DeSantis, "Annual Update on CAO Salary and Compensation Survey Available to Members," *ICMA* (July 9, 2019), https://icma.org/

22. City Club of Portland, "New Government for Today's Portland: Rethinking 100 Years of the Commission System," *City Club of Portland Bulletin* 101 (February 10, 2017).

23. Kimberly L. Nelson and Karl Nollenberger, "Conflict and Cooperation in Municipalities: Do Variations in Form of Government Have an Effect?" *Urban Affairs Review* 47 (September 2011): 696–720.

24. Victor S. DeSantis and Tari Renner, "City Government Structures: An Attempt at Clarification," *State and Local Government Review* 34 (Spring 2002): 95–104; H. George Frederickson, Gary A. Johnson, and Curtis H. Wood, *The Adapted City: Institutional Dynamics and Structural Change* (Armonk, NY: M. E. Sharpe, 2004); Megan Mullin, Gillian Peele, and Bruce E. Cain, "City Caesars? Institutional Structure and Mayoral Success in Three California Cities," *Urban Affairs Review* 40 (September 2004): 19–43; Cheon Geun Choi, Richard C. Feiock, and Jungah Bae, "The Adoption and Abandonment of Council-Manager Government," *Public Administration Review* (September/October 2013): 727–36.

25. Jered Carr and Shanthi Karuppusamy, "Beyond Ideal Types of Municipal Structure," *American Review of Public Administration*, 39 (2009): 304–21.

26. Lawrence Toppman, "Magic Glows in the Night in Cincinnati's Gaslight District," *Duke Energy* (May 7, 2018).

27. Brian M. Green and Yda Schreuder, "Growth, Zoning and Neighborhood Organizations," *Journal of Urban Affairs* 13:1 (1991): 97–110.

28. Arnold Fleischmann and Carol A. Pierannunzi, "Citizens, Development Interests, and Local Land-Use Regulation," *Journal of Politics* 52 (August 1990): 838–53; Abigail York et al., "Zoning and Land Use: A Tale of Incompatibility and Environmental Injustice in Early Phoenix," *Journal of Urban Affairs* 36 (December 2014): 833–53.

29. Jonathan T. Rothwell and Douglas A. Massey, "Density Zoning and Class Segregation in U.S. Metropolitan Areas," *Social Science Quarterly* 91 (December 2010): 1123–43.

30. Mary Edwards, "Annexation: A Winner-Take-All Process?" *State and Local Government Review* 31 (Fall 1999): 221–31; Bev Wilson and Mary M. Edwards, "Annexation and Ethnicity in the American Midwest," *Urban Affairs Review* 50 (May 2014): 417–47.

31. Rex L. Facer II, "Annexation Activity and State Law in the United States," *Urban Affairs Review* 41 (May 2006): 697–709; see also David Rusk, "Annexation and the Fiscal Fate of Cities," *Brookings Institution Survey Series* (August 2006).

32. Ely Portillo, "Charlotte Is Growing—Literally—as the City Annexes More Land," *UNC Charlotte Urban Institute* (September 4, 2019).

33. Rob Gurwitt, "Not-So-Smart Growth," *Governing* 14 (October 2000): 34–38.

34. Mike Maciag, "Population Density for U.S. Cities Statistics," *Governing* (November 29, 2017).

35. Christopher W. Hoene and Michael A. Pagano, *City Fiscal Conditions in 2009* (Washington, DC: National League of Cities, 2009).

36. National League of Cities, "City Fiscal Conditions 2019," https://www.nlc.org/ (accessed February 22, 2020).

37. Jeanna Smialek, "The U.S. Entered a Recession in February," *New York Times* (June 8, 2020).

38. Jeanna Smialek, "Fed Leaves Rates Unchanged and Projects Years of High Unemployment," *New York Times* (June 10, 2020).

39. Susan Welch and Timothy Bledsoe, *Urban Reform and Its Consequences: A Study in Representation* (Chicago: University of Chicago Press, 1988).

40. Chandler Davidson and Bernard Grofman, "The Effect of Municipal Election Structure on Black Representation in Eight Southern States," in Davidson and Grofman, eds., *Quiet Revolution in the South* (Princeton, NJ: Princeton University Press, 1994), pp. 301–21.

41. Curtis Wood, "Voter Turnout in City Elections," *Urban Affairs Review* 39 (November 2002): 209–31.

42. Welch and Bledsoe, *Urban Reform and Its Consequences*; Jeffrey D. Greene, "Reformism and Public Policies in American Cities Revisited," paper presented at the annual meeting of the Southern Political Science Association, Atlanta, Georgia, 2000.

43. Kenneth J. Meier et al., "Structural Choices and Representational Biases: The Post-Election Color of Representation," *American Journal of Political Science* 49 (October 2005): 758–68.

44. Richard L. Cole and Delbert A. Taebel, "Cumulative Voting in Local Elections: Lessons from the Alamogordo Experience," *Social Science Quarterly* 73 (March 1992): 194–201.

45. FairVote, "Jurisdictions Using Fair Representation Voting," https://www.fairvote.org/ (accessed March 5, 2020).

46. William Keith, "What Are Those Tall Kiosks That Have Replaced Pay Phones in New York?" *New York Times* (January 14, 2018).

47. Nancy Torres, "How Columbus Is Accomplishing Its Smart City Vision," *Data-Smart City Solutions: Harvard University Kennedy School Ash Center for Democratic Governance and Innovation* (March 29, 2018).

48. Aneri Pattani, "Building the City of the Future—at a $41 Trillion Price Tag," *CNBC* (October 25, 2016).

49. Peter Cohan, "How Chattanooga Created $1.8B in Startup Exits in Under 5 Years," *Inc.*, https://www.inc.com/ (accessed March 10, 2020).

50. Daniel T. O'Brien, *The Urban Commons: How Data and Technology Can Rebuild Our Communities* (Cambridge, MA: Harvard University Press, 2019).

51. "311 Sets New Record with 44 Million Customer Interactions in 2018" (February 19, 2019), https://www1.nyc.gov/

52. Kerry Mulligan, Celina Cuevas, Edwin Grimsley, Preeti Chauhan, and Erica Bond, "Understanding New York City's 311 Data," *Data Collaborative for Justice at John Jay College* (March 2019).

53. Benjamin Clark, Jeffrey Brudney, Sung-Gheel Jang, and Bradford Davy, "Do Advanced Information Technologies Produce Equitable Government Responses in Coproduction" An Examination of 311 Systems in 15 U.S. Cities," *The American Review of Public Administration* 50 (April 2020): 315–27.

54. "Town (Village, City): What Is a Town? A Town (Geographer's Definition) Is a Place Where People Live Close Together and Where Services Are at Hand, and Bigger Than a Village, but Not Big Enough to Be Called a City," https://www.curriculumvisions.com/ (accessed March 5, 2020).

55. Victor S. DeSantis and David Hill, "Citizen Participation in Local Politics: Evidence from New England Town Meetings," *State and Local Government Review* 36 (Fall 2004): 172.

56. Melissa Conradi, "But Definitely Not St. Ventura," *Governing* 14 (January 2001): 16.

57. Dave Drury, "Town Meetings: An Enduring Image Changes," *Hartford Courant* (September 22, 1991), pp. A1, A10–A11; see also David K. Hamilton. "Township Government: A Tale of One State," *National Civic Review* (2008): 37–49.

58. Scott Bolejack, "Should Cary Call Itself a City or a Town? Does It Even Matter?" *The News and Observer,* (April 2, 2018).

59. Kathryn A. Foster, *The Political Economy of Special Purpose Government* (Washington, DC: Georgetown University Press, 1997).

60. U.S. Census Bureau, "2017 Census of Governments—Organization: Table 4. Special Purpose Local Governments by State: Census Years 1942 to 2017," https://www.census.gov/ (accessed February 12, 2020).

61. John C. Bollens, *Special District Governments in the United States* (Berkeley: University of California Press, 1957).

62. Larita Killian and Dagney Faulk, "Policy Brief: Special Districts and Local Government Reform," Center for Business and Economic Research, Ball State University (March 2012).

63. Christopher Goodman and Suzanne Leland, "Do Cities and Counties Attempt to Circumvent Changes in Their Autonomy by Creating Special Districts?" *American Review of Public Administration* 49 (February 2019): 203–17.

64. Barbara Coyle McCabe, "Special District Formation among the States," *State and Local Government Review* 32 (Spring 2000): 121–31.

65. Michael A. Molloy, "Local Special Districts and Public Accountability," paper presented at the annual meeting of the Midwest Political Science Association, Chicago, Illinois, 2000; see also Nicholas Bauroth, "The Effect of Limiting Participation in Special District Elections to Property Owners: A Research Note," *Public Budgeting & Finance* 27 (2007): 71–88.

66. Nancy Burns, *The Formation of American Local Governments* (New York: Oxford University Press, 1994).

67. Christopher R. Berry, *Imperfect Union: Representation and Taxation in Multilevel Governments* (New York: Cambridge, 2009).

68. Foster, *The Political Economy of Special Purpose Government.*

69. Jason A. Grissom and James R. Harrington, "Local Legislative Professionalism," *American Politics Research* 41 (January 2013): 76–98.

70. Robert S. McCord and Leslie A. Finnan, "2018–19 AASA Superintendent Salary & Benefits Study," *AASA-The School Superintendents Association* (January 2019).

71. Tausanovitch and Warshaw, "Representation in Municipal Government."

72. Frank Hendriks, "Understanding Good Urban Governance: Essentials, Shifts, and Values," *Urban Affairs Review* 50 (July 2014): 553–76.

73. "National Civic League, "The All-America City Award Recognizes Communities that Leverage Civic Engagement, Collaboration, Inclusiveness and Innovation to Successfully Address Local Issues" https://www.nationalcivicleague.org (accessed November 3, 2020).

Chapter 11 Local Leadership and Governance: Continuity and Change

1. Mike Kanin, "What's Left," *The Texas Observer* (December 2, 2013), http://www.texasobserver.org /whats-left/; "Districts Would Better Serve Austin's Diverse Voices," *Austin American Statesman* (November 3, 2012).

2. Andra Lim, "Should Austin Switch to a 'Strong-Mayor' System?" *Austin Statesman* (September 24, 2016).

3. Susan E. Howell and William P. McLean, "Performance and Race in Evaluating Minority Mayors," *Public Opinion Quarterly* 65 (2001): 321–43.

4. Mark Schneider, "Public Entrepreneurs as Agents of Change in American Government," *Urban News* 9 (Spring 1995): 1.

5. Deserai Anderson Crow, "Local Media and Experts: Sources of Environmental Policy Initiation?" *Policy Studies Journal* 38 (February 2010): 143–64.

6. Ryan Holeywell, "Indy's Clean and Green Fleet," *Governing* (March 2013): 19.

7. Chris Tausanovitch and Christopher Warshaw, "Representation in Municipal Government," *American Political Science Review* 108 (August 2014): 605–41.

8. Gaetano Mosca, *The Ruling Class* (New York: McGraw-Hill, 1939).

9. Robert S. Lynd and Helen M. Lynd, *Middletown* (New York: Harcourt Brace and World, 1929); Robert S. Lynd and Helen M. Lynd, *Middletown in Transition* (New York: Harcourt Brace and World, 1937).

10. Floyd Hunter, *Community Power Structure* (Chapel Hill, NC: University of North Carolina Press, 1953); Floyd Hunter, *Community Power Succession* (Chapel Hill: University of North Carolina Press, 1980).

11. Harvey Molotch, "Strategies and Constraints of Growth Elites," in Scott Cummings, ed., *Business Elites and Urban Development* (Albany, NY: SUNY Press, 1988), pp. 25–47.

12. Robert Dahl, *Who Governs?* (New Haven, CT: Yale University Press, 1961).

13. Paul Schumaker, "Group Involvements in City Politics and Pluralist Theory," *Urban Affairs Review* 49 (March 2013): 254–81; see also Eric Heberlig, Suzanne Leland, and Dustin Read, "Local Politics, Organized Interests, and Land-Use Policy," *Urban Affairs Review* 50 (November 2014): 890–903.

14. G. William Domhoff, *Who Really Rules?* (Santa Monica, CA: Goodyear, 1978). For a different perspective, see Douglas W. Rae, *City: Urbanism and Its End* (New Haven, CT: Yale University Press, 2003).

15. Juliet Gainsborough, "A Tale of Two Cities: Civic Culture and Public Policy in Miami," *Journal of Urban Affairs* 30 (2008): 431.

16. Curt Nickisch, "WBUR Poll: Deadline Looming, Public Support of Boston's Olympic Bid Largely Unchanged," WBUR (July 10, 2015).

17. Clarence N. Stone, *Regime Politics: Governing Atlanta, 1948–1988* (Lawrence: University Press of Kansas, 1989), p. 3.

18. Clarence N. Stone, "Systemic Power in Community Decision Making," *American Political Science Review* 74 (December 1980): 978–90.

19. Ibid., p. 989.

20. Peter Burns and Matthew O. Thomas, "The Failure of the Nonregime: How Katrina Exposed New Orleans as a Regimeless City," *Urban Affairs Review* 41 (March 2006): 517–27.

21. J. M. Ferris, "The Role of the Nonprofit Sector in a Self-Governing Society," *Voluntas* 9 (1998): 137–51.

22. Richard C. Hula and Cynthia Jackson-Elmoore, "Governing Nonprofits and Local Political Processes," *Urban Affairs Review* 36 (January 2001): 324–58.

23. Ibid., p. 326; see also Kelly LeRoux, "Nonprofits as Civic Intermediaries," *Urban Affairs Review* 42 (January 2007): 410–22.

24. Christopher A. Cooper, Anthony J. Nownes, and Steven Roberts, "Perceptions of Power: Interest Groups in Local Politics," *State and Local Government Review* 37:3 (2005): 206–16.

25. William Yardley, "After Eminent Domain Victory, Dispute Project Goes Nowhere," *The New York Times* (November 21, 2005).

26. Sandra Day O'Connor, dissenting, Kelo et al. v. City of New London et al., No. 04-108, (June 23, 2005).

27. Janice Nadler, Shari Seidman Diamond, and Matthew Patton, "Government Takings of Private Property" in Nathaniel Persily, Jack Citrin, and Patrick J. Egan, eds., *Public Opinion and Constitutional Controversy* (New York: Oxford University Press, 2008), pp. 286–309.

28. Elizabeth Kolbert, "The Un-Communicator," *The New Yorker* (March 1, 2004): 38–42.

29. Jessica Garrison and Patrick McGreevy, "Parks to File for Mayoral Race," *Los Angeles Times* (April 7, 2004).

30. Rob Gurwitt, "The Lure of the Strong Mayor," *Governing* 6 (July 1993): 36–41; Terrell Blodgett, "Beware the Lure of the 'Strong' Mayor," *Public Management* 76 (January 1994): 6–11. See also Tod Newcombe, "The Rise of Cities and the Strong Mayors Who Run Them," *Governing* (September 2013): 23.

31. David R. Morgan and Sheilah S. Watson, "The Effects of Mayoral Power on Urban Fiscal Policy," paper presented at the annual meeting of the American Political Science Association, New York City, 1994; see also R. Douglas Arnold and Nicholas Carnes, "Holding Mayors Accountable: New York's Executives from Koch to Bloomberg," *American Journal of Political Science* 56 (October 2012): 949–63.

32. W. John Moore, "From Dreamers to Doers," *National Journal* (February 13, 1988): 372–77; Daniel J. Hopkins and Katherine T. McCabe, "After It's Too Later: Estimating the Policy Impacts of Black Mayoralties in U.S. Cities," *American Politics Research* 40 (July 2012): 665–700.

33. "Mayor Harry LaRosiliere," https://www.plano.gov (accessed March 7, 2020).

34. Huey L. Perry, "Deracialization as an Analytical Construct in American Urban Politics," *Urban Affairs Quarterly* 27 (December 1991): 181–91; Nicholas O. Alonzie, "The Promise of Urban Democracy: Big City Black Mayoral Service in the Early 1990s," *Urban Affairs Review* 35 (January 2000): 422–34.

35. Mary E. Summers and Philip A. Klinkner, "The Daniels Election in New Haven and the Failure of the Deracialization Hypothesis," *Urban Affairs Quarterly* 27 (December 1991): 202–15.

36. Edward-Isaac Dovere, "How Detroit's Mayor Became Unbeatable: Mike Duggan Pulled a Symbol of American Decline Back from the Brink. Now He Wants to Finish What He Started," *Politico Magazine* (August 29, 2017).

37. Robert M. Stein, Stacy G. Ulbig, and Stephanie Shirley Post, "Voting for Minority Candidates in Multiracial/Multiethnic Communities," *Urban Affairs Review* 41 (November 2005): 157–81.

38. John A. Powell, "Blog: All Lives Can't Matter Until Black Lives Matter Too," *University of California at Berkeley Othering and Belonging Institute* (June 16, 2020).

39. Nina Feldman, "Meet the 2 Black Women Vying to Be the Next New Orleans Mayor," *NEXTCITY* (November 2, 2017; Ballotpedia.org, "Mayoral Election in New Orleans, Louisiana (2017)," https://ballotpedia.org (accessed March 7, 2020).

40. Several of these studies are summarized in Susan A. MacManus and Charles S. Bullock III, "Women and Racial/Ethnic Minorities in Mayoral and Council Positions," *The Municipal Year Book 1993* (Washington, DC: ICMA, 1993), pp. 70–84.

41. Mirya R. Holman, "Sex and the City: Female Leaders and Spending on Social Welfare Programs in U.S. Municipalities," *Journal of Urban Affairs* 36 (October 2014): 701–15.

42. Sue Thomas, Rebekah Herrick, Lori Franklin, Marcia Godwin, Eveline Gnabasik, and Jean Schroedel, "Not for the Faint of Heart: Assessing Physical Violence and Psychological Abuse against U.S. Mayors," *State and Local Government Review* 51 (June 2019): 57–67; Adeel Hassan, "'Worthless. Gutless. Loser.' Online Attacks Escalate When the Mayor Is a Woman," *New York Times* (December 23, 2019).

43. Michael Finnegan, "Eric Garcetti Invokes Latino-Jewish Ancestry in Mayor's Race," *Los Angeles Times* (January 2, 2013).

44. Kenneth Miller, "Mayor Jackson Continues Unprecedented Leadership Journey," *Cleveland Call and Post* (July 3, 2017).

45. Sanford Nowlin, "Bloc Party: Forget the Issues. Race and Ethnicity Could Play the Key Role in San Antonio's Mayoral Election," *San Antonio Current* (March 27, 2019).

46. "What Makes a Great Mayor?" *Talk of the Nation*, www.npr.org (December 10, 2003).

47. "From Vision to Reality: How City Administrations Succeed in the Long Haul," www.civic-strategies.com (September 30, 2003).

48. John Buntin, "Does Eric Garcetti Have a Big Enough Vision for L.A.?" *Governing* (August 2014).

49. Clifford J. Wirth and Michael L. Vasu, "Ideology and Decision Making for American City Managers," *Urban Affairs Quarterly* 22 (March 1987): 454–74.

50. Martin Vanacour, "Promoting the Community's Future," in Charldean Newell, ed., *The Effective Local Government Manager*, 3rd ed. (Washington, DC: International City/County Management Association, 2004), pp. 84–85; see also Timothy B. Krebs and John P. Pelissero, "Urban Managers and Public Policy: Do Institutional Arrangements Influence Decisions to Initiate Policy?" *Urban Affairs Review* 45 (January 2010): 391–411.

51. James H. Svara, "Conflict and Cooperation in Elected-Administrative Relations in Large Council-Manager Cities," *State and Local Government Review* 31 (Fall 1999): 173–89; see also James H. Svara, "Exploring Structures and Institutions in City Government," *Public Administration Review* 65 (2005): 500–06.

52. Tansu Demir and Christopher G. Reddick, "Understanding Shared Roles in Policy and Administration: An Empirical Study of Council-Manager Relations," *Public Administration Review* 72 (July/August 2012): 526–36.

53. Douglas J. Watson and Wendy L. Hassett, "Career Paths of City Managers in America's Largest Council-Manager Cities," *Public Administration Review* 64 (March 2004): 192–99.

54. Mark M. Levin, "How to Work with Elected Officials," *Public Management* (December 2008): 4–5.

55. H. George Frederickson, Gary A. Johnson, and Curtis H. Wood, *The Adapted City: Institutional Dynamics and Structural Change* (Armonk, NY: M. E. Sharpe, 2004); see also Alan Ehrenhalt, "The Mayor-Manager Merger," *Governing* 20 (October 2006): 9–10.

56. Douglas Hanks, "An End to Term Limits? A Route to Pay Increases? Miami-Dade Debates Charter Changes," *Miami Herald* (June 25, 2018).

57. Larry Azevedo, as quoted in Alan Ehrenhalt, "How a Liberal Government Came to Power in a Conservative Suburb," *Governing* 1 (March 1988): 51–56.

58. Kenneth Prewitt, *The Recruitment of Political Leaders: A Study of Citizen-Politicians* (Indianapolis, IN: Bobbs-Merrill, 1970).

59. Melissa Marschall, Anirudh V. Ruhil, and Paru Shah, "The New Racial Calculus: Electoral Institutions and Black Representation in Local Legislatures," *American Journal of Political Science* 54 (January 2010): 107–24.

60. "List of Current City Council Officials of the Top 100 Cities in the United States," https://ballotpedia.org/ (accessed March 9, 2020).

61. "State and Local Officials of Color," *Gender and Multicultural Leadership Project*, www.gmcl.org (August 10, 2009).

62. National Association of Latino Elected and Appointed Officials, *National Directory of Latino Elected Officials: 2018* (Washington, DC: NALEO Educational Fund, 2019).

63. Joshua G. Behr, *Race, Ethnicity and the Politics of Redistricting* (Albany, NY: SUNY Press, 2004); Jessica Trounstine and Melody D. Valdini, "The Context Matters: The Effects of Single-Member versus At-Large Districts on City Council Diversity," *American Journal of Political Science* 52 (July 2008): 554–69; Melissa J. Marschall, Anirudh V.S. Ruhil, and Paru R. Shah, "The New Racial Calculus: Electoral Institutions and Black Representation in Local Legislatures," *American Journal of Political Science* 54 (January 2010): 107–24.

64. Bari Anhalt, "Minority Representation and the Substantive Representation of Interests," paper presented at the annual meeting of the American Political Science Association, San Francisco, California, 1996; James H. Svara, "Two Decades of Continuity and Change in American City Councils" (National League of Cities, 2003).

65. Manning Marable, "Building Coalitions among Communities of Color," in James Jennings, ed., *Blacks, Latinos, and Asians in Urban America* (Westport, CT: Praeger, 1994), pp. 29–43.

66. Paula D. McClain and Steven C. Tauber, "Racial Minority Group Relations in a Multiracial Society," in Michael Jones-Correa, ed., *Governing American Cities: Immigrants and Inter-Ethnic Coalitions, Competition, and Conflict* (New York: Russell Sage Foundation, 2001).

67. Christian Collett, "Bloc Voting, Polarization, and the Panethnic Hypothesis: The Case of Little Saigon," *Political Research Quarterly* 67 (August 2005): 907–33.

68. James Svara, "Council Profile: More Diversity, Demands, Frustration," *Nation's Cities Weekly* 14 (November 18, 1991).

69. Susan Adams Beck, "Rethinking Municipal Governance: Gender Distinctions on Local Councils," in Debra L. Dodson, ed., *Gender and Policymaking: Studies of Women in Office* (New Brunswick, NJ: Center for the American Woman and Politics, 1991), p. 103.

70. Juliana Menasce Horowitz, Ruth Igielnik, and Kim Parker, "Women and Leadership 2018," *Pew Research Center Social and Demographic Trends* (September 20, 2018).

71. "Out for America," *Gay and Lesbian Victory Institute*, https://outforamerica.org/ (accessed March 10, 2020).

72. Julie Moreau, "LGBTQ Political Candidates Score Historic Victories Across U.S.," *NBC News* (November 8, 2017); Christine Caron, "In 'Rainbow Wave,' LGBT Candidates are Elected in Record Numbers," *New York Times* (November 7, 2018); Tim Fitzsimons, "Rainbow Wave 2.0: Nearly 100 LGBTQ Candidates Claim Victory in Tuesday's Elections," *NBC News* (November 6, 2019).

73. James W. Button, Kenneth D. Wald, and Barbara A. Rienzo, "The Election of Openly Gay Public Officials in American Communities," *Urban Affairs Review* 35 (November 1999): 188–209.

74. Jessica Trounstine, "Evidence of a Local Incumbency Advantage," *Legislative Studies Quarterly* 36 (May 2011): 255–80.

75. Kimberly L. Nelson and Karl Nollenberger, "Conflict and Cooperation in Municipalities: Do Variations in Form of Government Have an Effect?" *Urban Affairs Review* 47 (September 2011): 696–720; see also Brianne Heidbreder et al., "Determinants of Policy Conflict in Michigan Municipalities," *State and Local Government Review* 43 (April 2011): 32–45.

76. Craig M. Burnett and Vladimir Kogan, "Local Logrolling? Assessing the Impact of Legislative Districting in Los Angeles," *Urban Affairs Review* 50 (September 2014): 648–71.

77. Rob Gurwitt, "Are City Councils a Relic of the Past?" *Governing* 16 (April 2003): 20–24.

78. Meghan E. Irons, "Honeymoon Over for Walsh, Council," *Boston Globe* (November 9, 2014).

79. Jack E. White, "Bright City Lights," *Time* (November 1, 1993): 32.

80. Michael Bloomberg, as quoted in "Observer," *Governing* 19 (July 2006): 18.

81. Ian Duncan, "Now Officially Baltimore Mayor, Jack Young Inherits City's Problems—Particularly Violent Crime," *Baltimore Sun* (May 2, 2019).

82. Kate Amara, "Mayor Aims to Clean Up Baltimore's Trash Problem with Technology," *WBAl-TV* (January 29, 2020).

Chapter 12 State-Local Relations: Fifty Different Systems

1. Greg Lacour and Emma Way, "HB2: How North Carolina Got Here (Updated)," *Charlotte Magazine* (March 30, 2017).

2. Michael Gordon, Mark S. Price, and Katie Peralta, "Understanding HB2: North Carolina's Newest Law Solidifies State's Role in Defining Discrimination," *The Charlotte Observer* (March 26, 2016).

3. Steven D. Gold, "NCSL State-Local Task Force: The First Year," *Intergovernmental Perspective* 13 (Winter 1987): 11.

4. Merriam v. Moody's Executors, 25 Iowa 163, 170 (1868). Dillon's rule was first written in the case of *City of Clinton v. Cedar Rapids and Missouri Railroad Co.* (1868).

5. Jeffrey I. Chapman, "Local Government Autonomy and Fiscal Stress: The Case of California Counties," *State and Local Government Review* 35 (Winter 2003): 15–25.

6. U.S. Advisory Commission on Intergovernmental Relations, *The Organization of Local Public Economies* (Washington, DC: ACIR, December 1987), p. 54; see also Jesse J. Richardson, Jr., "Dillon's Rule Is from Mars, Home Rule Is from Venus: Local Government Autonomy and the Rules of Statutory Construction," *Publius: The Journal of Federalism* 41 (Fall 2011): 662–85.

7. Peter J. May, "State Regulatory Roles: Choices in the Regulation of Building Safety," *State and Local Government Review* 29 (Spring 1997): 70–80.

8. Dale Krane, Platon N. Rigos, and Melvin B. Hill, Jr., *Home Rule in America: A Fifty-State Handbook* (Washington, DC: Congressional Quarterly Press, 2001).

9. As quoted in Laura Vozzella and David Nitkin, "City Rejects State Plan, Offers Own School Loan," *Baltimore Sun* (March 9, 2004): 1.

10. Ann O'M. Bowman and Richard C. Kearney, "Second Order Devolution: Who's Got the Power," paper presented at the annual meeting of the Midwest Political Science Association, Chicago, 2010.

11. Kim Haddrow, Anthony Gad, and Katy Fleury, "The Growing Shadow of State Interference: Preemption in the 2019 State Legislative Sessions," *Local Solutions Support Center* (July 29, 2019).

12. Christopher Swope, "States Go for the Biotech Gold," *Governing* 17 (March 2004): 46.

13. David K. Hamilton, David Y. Miller, and Jerry Paytas, "Exploring Horizontal and Vertical Dimensions of the Governing of Metropolitan Regions," *Urban Affairs Review* 40 (November 2004): 147–82.

14. David Kocieniewski and Eric Lipton, "Two States Get High Marks for Five-Day Antiterrorism Exercise," *The New York Times* (April 9, 2005).

15. "National Response Framework, 4th ed.," *U.S. Department of Homeland Security,* www.fema.gov (October 28, 2019): 6.

16. Katy Moeller, "How You Can Access Idaho's Court Is About to Change," *Idaho Statesman* (July 16, 2016).

17. Office of Performance Evaluations, Idaho State Legislature, "Impact of State Mandates on County Governments," https://legislature.idaho.gov/wp-content/uploads/OPE/Reports/r1904.pdf (January 2019).

18. Ann O'M. Bowman and Richard C. Kearney, "Second-Order Devolution: Data and Doubt," *Publius: The Journal of Federalism* 41 (Fall 2011): 563–85.

19. Lawrence J. Grossback, "The Problem of State-Imposed Mandates: Lessons from Minnesota's Local Governments," *State and Local Government Review* 34 (Fall 2002): 191.

20. Colleen O'Dea, "Changes in Vote-by-Mail Ruled Null and Void, Unfunded Mandates," *NJSpotlight* (November 19, 2019); Colleen O'Dea, "Explainer: Little Known, Council on Local Mandates Wields Big Stick," *NJSpotlight* (November 27, 2019).

21. Richard L. Cole, "The Current Status and Roles of State Advisory Commissions on Intergovernmental Relations in the U.S. Federal System," *Public Administration Review* 71 (March/April 2011): 190–95.

22. Bruce Katz, *Smart Growth: The Future of the American Metropolis?* (Washington, DC: The Brookings Institution, 2002), p. 2.

23. William Fulton and Paul Shigley, "Operation Desert Sprawl," *Governing* 12 (August 1999): 16.

24. Christina McCarroll, "Measuring the Cost of Growth," *Christian Science Monitor* (February 6, 2002): 13.

25. Moon-Gi Jeong, "Local Choices for Development Impact Fees," *Urban Affairs Review* 41 (2006): 338–57.

26. Jon E. Keeley and Alexandra D. Syphard, "Twenty-First Century California, USA, Wildfires: Fuel-Dominated vs. Wind-Dominated Fires," *Fire Ecology* (July 2019).

27. "2018 Ballot Measures Results," The Trust for Public Land, https://www.tpl.org/2018 (accessed March 14, 2020).

28. Jayson T. Blair, "Maryland Draws Line against Sprawl," *Boston Globe* (December 7, 1997): A26.

29. Christopher Swope, "McGreevey's Magic Map," *Governing* 16 (May 2003): 45–48.

30. Christopher R. Conte, "The Boys of Sprawl," *Governing* 13 (May 2000): 28–33; see also Christopher Hawkins, "Electoral Support for Community Growth Management Policy," *Social Science Quarterly* 92 (March 2011): 268–84.

31. Alan Ehrenhalt, "Breaking the Density Deadlock," *Governing* 20 (March 2007): 11–12.

32. Randal O'Toole, "The New Feudalism: Why States Must Repeal Growth-Management Laws," *Cato Institute* (October 19, 2016).

33. Robert Jay Dilger, "Residential Community Associations: Issues, Impacts, and Relevance for Local Government," *State and Local Government Review* 23 (Winter 1991): 17–23; Barbara Coyle McCabe, "Homeowners Associations as Private Governments: What We Know, What We Don't Know, and Why It Matters," *Public Administration Review* 71 (August 2011): 535–42; Jill L. Tao and Barbara C. McCabe, "Where a Hollow State Casts No Shadow: Homeowner Associations in Local Governments," *American Review of Public Administration* 42 (November 2012): 678–94.

34. U.S. Census Bureau, "American Housing Survey: 2017 National Neighborhoods, All Occupied Units," https://www.census.gov (accessed March 14, 2020).

35. Evan McKenzie, *Privatopia: Homeowners' Associations and the Rise of Residential Private Government* (New Haven, CT: Yale University Press, 1996).

36. Jered B. Carr and Richard C. Feiock, "Who Becomes Involved in City-County Consolidation?" *State and Local Government Review* 34 (Spring 2002): 78–94.

37. H. V. Savitch and Ronald K. Vogel, "Suburbs without a City: Power and City-County Consolidation," *Urban Affairs Review* 39 (July 2004): 758–90; Benedict Jimenez and Rebecca Hendrick, "Is Government Consolidation the Answer?" *State and Local Government Review* 42 (December 2010): 258–70.

38. Alan Greenblatt, "Anatomy of a Merger," *Governing* 16 (December 2002): 20–25.

39. Ronald J. Oakerson, *Governing Local Political Economies: Creating the Civic Metropolis* (Oakland, CA: Institute for Contemporary Studies, 1999).

40. David Rusk, *Cities without Suburbs* (Washington, DC: Woodrow Wilson Center Press, 1993), p. 5.

41. Daniel Kemmis, as quoted in Neal R. Peirce, "Missoula's 'Citistate' Claim Marks a New Way to Define Regions," *The News & Observer* (July 1, 1993): 14A

42. "Portland Plan," https://www.portlandonline.com (accessed March 15, 2020).

43. Metropolitan Council, https://metrocouncil.org (accessed March 15, 2020); Derek Thompson, "The Miracle of Minneapolis," *The Atlantic* (March 2015).

44. Margaret Weir, Harold Wolman, and Todd Swanstrom, "The Calculus of Coalitions: Cities, Suburbs, and the Metropolitan Agenda," *Urban Affairs Review* 40 (July 2005): 730–60.

45. James F. Wolf and Tara Kolar Bryan, "Identifying the Capacities of Regional Councils of Government," *State and Local Government Review* 41 (2009): 61–68.

46. Keystone Policy Center, "Colorado Water and Growth Dialogue Final Report" (September 2018), http://www.keystone.org.

47. "Gulf Regional Planning Commission Scenario Planning Workshop" (March 15–16, 2016), http://www.grpc.com.

48. Bill Hanna, "What if a Major Tornado Strikes Dallas-Fort Worth?" (March 15, 2019), https://www.govtech.com.

49. James F. Wolf and Margaret Fenwick, "How Metropolitan Planning Organizations Incorporate Land Use Issues in Regional Transportation Planning," *State and Local Government Review* 35 (Spring 2003): 123–31; see also Alan Ehrenhalt, "Ready-To-Go Regionalism," *Governing* 22 (May 2009): 11–12.

50. David S. T. Matkin and George Frederickson, "Metropolitan Governance: Institutional Roles and Interjurisdictional Cooperation," *Journal of Urban Affairs* 31 (2009): 45–66.

51. Sung-Wook Kwon and Richard Feiock, "Overcoming the Barriers to Cooperation: Intergovernmental Service Agreements," *Public Administration Review* 70 (November/December 2010): 876–84.

52. Mara S. Sidney, *Unfair Housing: How National Policy Shapes Community Action* (Lawrence: University Press of Kansas, 2003).

53. *Beyond Shelter: Building Communities of Opportunity* (Washington, DC: U.S. Department of Housing and Urban Development, 1996).

54. Zach Patton, "Thinking Small," *Governing* (May 2011): 36–41.

55. Kol Peterson, *Backdoor Revolution: The Definitive Guide to ADU Development* (Portland, Oregon: Accessory Dwelling Strategies, 2018).

56. Jason Richardson, Bruce Mitchell, and Juan Franco, "Shifting Neighborhoods: Gentrification and Cultural Displacement in American Cities," *National Community Reinvestment Coalition* (March 19, 2019).

57. Chris Glynn and Alexander Casey, "Priced Out: Homelessness Rises Faster Where Rent Exceeds a Third of Income" (December 11, 2018), https://www.zillow.com.

58. Jack Steward and Amy Scott, "Is It OK Not To Pay Rent during the COVID-19 Pandemic?" (May 8, 2020), https://www.marketplace.org.

59. Ann O'Connell, "Emergency Bans on Evictions and Other Tenant Protections Related to Coronavirus," https://www.nolo.com (accessed June 28, 2020).

60. National Low Income Housing Coalition, "Federal Eviction Moratoriums" (June 22, 2020), https://nlihc.org/federal-moratoriums.

61. American Society of Civil Engineers, "America's Infrastructure Report Card: 2017," https://www.infrastructurereportcard.org/ (accessed March 15, 2020).

62. "Municipalities Need $300B in Sewer, Water Work," *Governing* (February 9, 2012).

63. ASCE, "Funding and Future Need," https://www.infrastructurereportcard.org/ (accessed March 15, 2020).

64. Ryan Felton, "Fixing Flint's Contaminated Water System Could Cost $216M, Report Says," *The Guardian* (June 6, 2016); Monica Eng, "Flint's Water Crisis Spurs Other Cities to Remove Lead Pipes," *National Public Radio* (December 23, 2019).

65. Donald F. Kettl, "Trump's Failed Infrastructure Plan Is a Wasted Opportunity," *Governing* (October 2018).

66. Jeff Mason and David Shepardson, "Trump Team Prepares $1 Trillion Infrastructure Plan to Spur Economy," *Reuters* (June 15, 2020).

67. Liz Farmer, "Obama Proposed P3 Tool to Help States Finance Infrastructure," *Governing* (January 21, 2015).

68. Stephen Goldsmith, "Creative Mayors and the Infrastructure Puzzle," *Governing* (October 9, 2011).

69. Anna Clark, "How $500 Million Turned Car-Centric Indianapolis into a More Walkable City," *Next City* (August 6, 2015).

70. "Minneapolis 2040: The City's Comprehensive Plan," https://minneapolis2040.com (accessed March 15, 2020).

71. Hugh Bartling, "Private Governance and Public Opinion in a Company Town: The Case of Celebration, Florida," paper presented at the annual meeting of the Midwest Political Science Association, Chicago, Illinois, 2000; see also Bruce Podobnik, "Assessing the Social and Environmental Achievements of New Urbanism: Evidence from Portland, Oregon," *Journal of Urbanism* 4 (July 2011): 105–26.

72. U.S. Department of Agriculture, "Rural Economy," https://www.ers.usda.gov/ (accessed March 16, 2020).

73. John Cromartie, "Rural American at a Glance," *U.S. Department of Agriculture Economic Research Service* (November 2019).

74. John Cromartie and Dennis Vilorio, "Rural Population Trends," *U.S. Department of Agriculture Economic Research Service* (February 15, 2019).

75. Anita Regmi, "Retaliatory Tariffs and U.S. Agriculture," *Congressional Research Service* (September 13, 2019).

76. Jim Seroka, "Community Growth and Administrative Capacity," *National Civic Review* 77 (January/February 1988): 45.

77. "Welcome to the City of Marquette," www.marquettekansas.com (accessed March 16, 2020).

78. Patrik Jonsson, "North Carolina's Gambit to Bring Internet Age to Rural Areas," *Christian Science Monitor* (July 1, 2004).

79. Sierra Dawn McClain, "Wind Energy Projects Pose Conflicts; Rural Areas Weigh Impacts," *National Wind Watch* (July 24, 2019).

80. David Loomis, "Economic Impact Analysis of the Badger State Solar Project," *Strategic Economic Research* (February 2019).

81. Richard Wilson, "Massive Solar Farms Divide Neighbors in Rural Areas," *Dayton Daily News* (June 23, 2019); McClain "Wind Energy Projects Pose Conflicts."

82. Eduardo Porter, "The Hard Truths of Trying to 'Save' the Rural Economy," *The Washington Post* (December 14, 2018); also see Rachel Harris and Lisa Tarchak, "Small Town American Is Dying: How Can We Save It?" *New York Times* (December 22, 2018).

83. Arthur Holst, "Review of Local Government and the States: Autonomy, Politics, and Policy," *Publius* 35 (Fall 2005): 644–45.

84. Alan Greenblatt, "'It Should Be on HBO Boxing': Cuomo vs. de Blasio," *Governing* (March 2016).

85. Amanda Eisenberg, "Cuomo, de Blasio Urge Calm in Wake of New York's First Confirmed Coronavirus Case," *Politico* (March 2, 2020).

86. Center for Health Care Strategies, Inc., "Combating Opioid Abuse through a Unified State and Local Response: The Ohio Governor's Cabinet Opioid Action" (May 2018), https://www.chcs.org/; Ohio Department of Health, "Drug Overdose" (January 10, 2020), https://odh.ohio.gov/.

87. George Pataki, "Governor Pataki Offers $1 Billion Plan to Help Local Governments," Press Release, January 10, 1997.

88. Phillip Reese, "California Government Lobbying Rose Again Last Year. Who Spent the Most?" *The Sacramento Bee* (February 12, 2019).

Chapter 13 Taxing and Spending: Where the Money Comes from and Where It Goes

1. Monica Davey and Mary Williams Walsh, "Billions in Debt, Detroit Tumbles into Insolvency," www.nytimes.com (July 18, 2013).

2. Monica Davey and Mary Williams Walsh, "Plan to Exit Bankruptcy Is Approved for Detroit," www.nytimes.com (November 7, 2014).

3. Pete Saunders, "Detroit, Five Years after Bankruptcy," *Forbes* (July 19, 2018).

4. U.S. Census Bureau, "State and Local Government Finances by Level of Government and by State: 2017," www.census.gov (accessed February 28, 2020).

5. Erin Huffer, John Iselin, Frank Sammartino, and David Weiner, "Effects of the Tax Cuts and Jobs Act on State Individual Income Taxes," *Washington University Journal of Law and Policy* 58 (2019): 205–29.

6. Lance Lambert, "Over 42.6 Million Americans Have Filed for Unemployment during the Coronavirus Pandemic," *Fortune* (June 4, 2020).

7. Rebecca Rainey, "Record-Breaking Unemployment Claims May Be Vast Undercount," *Politico* (March 26, 2020).

8. www.taxfoundation.org, *Facts and Figures: How Does Your State Compare?* 2020. Data are from 2012.

9. Binyamin Applebaum and Robert Gebeloff, "Tax Burden for Most Americans Is Lower than in the 1980s," nytimes.com (November 29, 2012).

10. Tax Policy Center, "State and Local General Revenue, Percentage Distribution," https://www.taxpolicycenter.org (December 15, 2017).

11. Mike Machiag, "Tax Exempt Properties Rise as Cities Cope with Shrinking Tax Bases," *Governing* (November 2012): 54–58.

12. Mark Schneider, "Local Budgets and the Maximization of Local Property Wealth in the System of Suburban Government," *Journal of Politics* 49 (November 1987): 11–14.

13. *The Book of the States: State Finance,* "Table 7.16a: State Sales Tax Rates and Food and Drug Exemptions (as of January 1, 2019)," knowledgecenter.csg.org (September 24, 2019).

14. "Sales Tax Holidays," *Sales Tax Institute,* www.salestaxinstitute.com (accessed March 1, 2020).

15. Neal R. Peirce, "Service Tax May Rise Again," *Public Administration Times* 11 (August 12, 1996): 2.

16. Kirk Davis and Evan Davis, "The Coming Wave of Federal and State Tax Zapper Prosecutions: Prosecuting Zapper Salespersons and Restaurant Owners While the Masterminds Go Free" (December–January 2018), https://www.taxlitigator.com.

17. Quill v. North Dakota, 504 U.S. 298 (1992).

18. South Dakota v. Wayfair, 585 U.S. _____ (2018); Joseph Bishop Henchman, "Supreme Court Decides Wayfair Online Sales Case," *Tax Foundation* (June 21, 2018).

19. Chris Isidore, "Amazon to Start Collecting State Sales Taxes Everywhere," *CNN Business* (March 29, 2017); Jessica Gresko, "Online Shoppers Can Be Forced to Pay Sales Tax, Supreme Court Rules," *Daily Herald* (June 21, 2018).

20. U.S. Census Bureau, "2018 Annual Survey of State Government Finances," www.census.gov (accessed March 2, 2020).

21. Jared Walczak, "Local Income Taxes in 2019," *Tax Foundation* (July 2019).

22. Kil Huh, "States Face Increasingly Uncertain Revenue Forecasts," *Pew Trusts* (October 24, 2019).

23. Scott Drenkard, "Cigarette Taxes and Cigarette Smuggling by State, 2015," *Tax Foundation Fiscal Fact, No. 565* (November, 2017).

24. Michael LaFaive, Scott Drenkard, and Todd Nesbit, "Strong Link between Cigarette Tax and Illegal Smuggling Rates," *Mackinac Center for Public Policy* (April 13, 2018).

25. Jim Estes, "How the Big Tobacco Deal Went Bad," www.nytimes.com (October 6, 2014).

26. Quoted in Lenny Bernstein, "Oklahoma Files Suit Against Three Major Opioid Distributors," *Washington Post* (January 13, 2020).

27. Jared Hopkins, "21 States Rejects $18 Billion Offer from Drug Wholesalers to Settle Opioid Litigation," *Wall Street Journal* (February 14, 2020).

28. Ryan Prete, "NBA Superstars Face Tax Bills in the Millions," *Bloomberg Tax* (October 30, 2018).

29. *The Book of the States,* Table 7.20 (2019).

30. Alaska Permanent Fund, www.apfc.org (accessed March 22, 2015).

31. U.S. Census Bureau, "2018 Annual Survey of State Government Finances: Income and Apportionment of State-Administered Lottery Funds," https://www.census.gov/ (accessed March 20, 2020).

32. Elizabeth A. Freund and Irwin L. Morris, "The Lottery and Income Inequality in the States," *Social Science Quarterly* 86 (2005): 996–1012; Riley Griffin and Katia Dmitrieva, "Lotteries Are Doing More Damage to Those Who Can Least Afford It," *Bloomberg Business* (September 12, 2018).

33. Pamela M. Prah, "Nevada Has Head Start as States React to Federal Gambling Decision," https://pewtrusts.org (January 6, 2012).

34. Legal Sports Report, "U.S. Sports Betting Revenue and Handle" (February 6, 2020), https://www.legalsportsreport.com/sports-betting/revenue/.

35. Legal Sports Report, "Legislative Tracker: Sports Betting" (January 11, 2020), https://www.legalsportsreport.com/sportsbetting-bill-tracker/.

36. National Association of State Budget Officers, "2019 State Expenditure Report, Table 5: State Spending by Function as a Percent of Total State Expenditures, Fiscal 2019," www.nasbo.org (accessed March 20, 2020).

37. Center on Budget and Policy Priorities, www.cbpp.org (accessed July 15, 2009).

38. Christine R. Martell and Paul Teske, "Fiscal Management Implications of the TABOR Bind," *Public Administration Review* (July/August, 2007): 673–86.

39. Changhoon Jung and Suho Bae, "Changing Revenue and Expenditure Structure and the Reliance on User Charges and Fees in American Counties, 1972–2002," *American Review of Public Administration* (Spring 2010): 1–19.

40. Judith Stallmann, Craig Maher, Steven Deller, and Sungho Park, "Survey the Effects of Limitations on Taxes and Expenditures: What Do/Don't We Know?" *Journal of Public and Nonprofit Affairs* 3 (July 2017): 197–222.

41. Jennifer Kates, Jennifer Tolbert, Kendal Orgera, Jose Michaud, and Larry Levitt, "Where Are the COVID-19 Hotspots? Tracking State Outbreaks," *Kaiser Family Foundation* (June 30, 2020); also see Jeffrey Kluger and Chris Wilson, "America Is Done with COVID-19. COVID-19 Isn't Done with America," *Time* (June 15, 2020).

42. Eli Rosenberg and Abha Bhattarai, "Workers Are Getting Laid Off for a Second Time, as the Virus's Surge Puts Reopenings on Hold," *Washington Post* (June 30, 2020).

43. Leigh Ann Caldwell and Rebecca Shabad, "Corona Virus: Trump Administration Warns of 20 Percent Unemployment Rate," *NBC News* (March 18, 2020).

44. American Society of Civil Engineers, "America's Infrastructure Grades Remain Near Failing," https://www.asce.org/ (March 9, 2017).

45. Matt Bittman, "A Cappuccino for Public Safety," *New York Times* (April 9, 2014).

46. Michael A. Pagano and Jocelyn M. Johnston, "Life at the Bottom of the Fiscal Food Chain: Examining City and Council Revenue Decisions," *Publius* 30 (Winter 2000): 159–70.

47. Janelle Cammenga, "How Well-Funded Are Pension Plans in Your State," *Tax Foundation* (July 17, 2019), https://taxfoundation.org; Hal Dardick and Juan Perez, Jr., "Despite Rahm Emanuel's Tax Hikes, City Pension Debt Grew by $7 Billion since 2015. Here's Why," *Chicago Tribune* (October 3, 2019).

48. Center for State and Local Government Excellence, "Other Post-Employment Benefits by State: FY 2017 Snapshot" (July 2019), https://www.slge.org.

49. Daniel DiSalvo, "North Carolina's OPEB Experiment: Defusing the State Debt Bomb," *Manhattan Institute* (February 2020).

50. Stephen C. Fehr, "States Get Off Revenue Roller Coaster," www.stateline.org (March 1, 2011).

51. Kil Huh, "States Face Increasingly Uncertain Revenue Forecasts: Possibility of Recession and Greater Volatility Add Complexity," *Pew Fiscal and Economic Policy and U.S. State Policy* (October 24, 2019).

52. John Gramlich, "As State Budgets, Payroll Shrink, So Do Ambitions," www.stateline.org (January 10, 2011).

53. Sallie Hofmeister, "Fund Head Resigns in California" and "Many Questions, but Too Late," *The New York Times* (December 6, 1994): D1, D2.

54. Mary Williams Walsh and Louise Story, "A Stealth Tax Subsidy for Business Faces New Scrutiny," *The New York Times* (March 4, 2013).

55. Clayton P. Gillette and David A. Skeel, Jr., "Governance Reform and the Judicial Role in Municipal Bankruptcy," *The Yale Law Journal* (March 2016).

Chapter 14 Economic Development: Competing for Growth

1. "Amazon HQ2 RFP," https://images-na.ssl-images-amazon.com/ (accessed March 21, 2020).

2. Bryce Covert, "Cities Should Stop Playing the Amazon HQ2 Bidding Game, " *New York Times* (November 13, 2018).

3. Robert McCartney, "Amazon HQ2 to Receive More Than $2.8 Billion in Incentives from Virginia, New York, and Tennessee," *Washington Post* (November 13, 2018).

4. Laura Stevens, Jimmy Vielkind, and Katie Honan, "Amazon Cancels HQ2 Plans in New York City," *Wall Street Journal* (February 14, 2019).

5. Andrew Schwartz, "The Realities of Economic Development Subsidies," *Center for American Progress* (November 1, 2018).

6. Nathan M. Jensen, "Amazon Will Move into New York City After All. Did It Really Need Public Investments?" *Washington Post* (December 11, 2019).

7. As quoted in "Washington State Gov. Chris Gregoire Says That Washington Has Consistently Ranked in the Top Five of Forbes' Best States for Business, Ahead of Texas," www.polifact.com (November 5, 2010).

8. Dana Feldman, "Southern California City Drops Bill Against Sriracha Hot Sauce Plant," *Reuters* (May 29, 2014).

9. W. Mark Crain, *Volatile States: Institutions, Policy, and the Performance of American State Economies* (Ann Arbor: University of Michigan Press, 2003).

10. Yolanda K. Kodrzycki and Ana Patricia Muñoz "Economic Distress and Resurgence in U.S. Central Cities: Concepts, Causes, and Policy Levers," *Economic Development Quarterly* 29 (May 2015): 113–34.

11. "America's Top States for Business in 2019," *CNBC* (January 27, 2020), https://www.cnbc.com.

12. State Policy Reports, "Index of State Economic Momentum," *Federal Funds Information for States* 37: 23–24 (December 2019). The authors thank Marcia Howard of Federal Funds Information for States for making these data available.

13. State Policy Reports, "Index of State Economic Momentum," *Federal Funds Information for States* 38: 12 (June 2020). The authors thank Marcia Howard of Federal Funds Information for States for making these data available.

14. Maryann P. Feldman and Johanna L. Francis, "Homegrown Solutions: Fostering Cluster Formation," *Economic Development Quarterly* 18 (May 2004): 127–37; Harold (Hal) Wolman and Diana Hincapie, "Clusters and Cluster-Based Development Policy," *Economic Development Quarterly* 29 (May 2015): 135–49.

15. Mary Jo Waits, "Building an Economic Future," *State Government News* 38 (September 1995): 6–10.

16. Ross Gittell, Jeffrey Sohl, and Edinaldo Tebaldi, "Do Entrepreneurship and High-Tech Concentration Create Jobs? Exploring the Growth in Employment in U.S. Metropolitan Areas From 1991 to 2007," *Economic Development Quarterly* 28 (August 2014): 244–53.

17. Susan E. Clarke and Gary L. Gaile, *The Work of Cities* (Minneapolis: University of Minnesota Press, 1998).

18. J. Mac Holladay, "Trends That Strengthen Economies," *State Government News* 40 (August 1997): 6–7; see also Edwin Melendez et al., "The Restructured Landscape of Economic Development: Challenges and Opportunities for Regional Workforce Development Collaborations," *Economic Development Quarterly* 29 (May 2015): 150–66.

19. Robert D. Atkinson and Scott Andes, "The 2010 State New Economy Index," http://www.itif.org/ (accessed June 15, 2012).

20. Caroline Hanley and Michael T. Douglass, "High Road, Low Road, or Off Road? Economic Development Strategies in the American States," *Economic Development Quarterly* 28 (August 2014): 220–29.

21. Governor's Office of Economic Development, www.goed.utah.gov (July 5, 2006).

22. Quoted in Alan Greenblatt, "Welcome to Jobs Inc., Where States Have Little Say in Economic Development," *Governing* (November 2015).

23. As quoted in Richard Reeves, *American Journey* (New York: Simon & Schuster, 1982), p. 46.

24. Barbara Soderlin, "To Move Its HQ to Chicago, ConAgra Settled for Less than Half the $28.5M in Incentives That Nebraska Was Willing to Offer," *Omaha World-Herald* (September 27, 2016)

25. Committee for Economic Development, *Leadership for Dynamic State Economies* (Washington, DC: Committee for Economic Development, 1986), pp. 73–77; see also Maryann P. Feldman, Lauren Lanahan, and Iryna V. Lendel, "Experiments in the Laboratories of Democracy: State Scientific Capacity Building," *Economic Development Quarterly* 28 (May 2014): 107–31.

26. As quoted in Laurie Clewett, "State of the States," *State Government News* (March 2004): 20.

27. Zachary Brown, "A Bulwark Against Trump's Stem Cell Ban: California's Institute for Regenerative Medicine, a Kind of Mini-NIH, Does Crucial Basic Research without Federal Funding," *Scientific American* (July 2, 2019).

28. National Association of State Development Agencies, *The NASDA Newsletter* (January 21, 1987), p. 5.

29. Missouri Department of Economic Development, "Executive Summary: Missouri Strategic Initiative for Economic Growth," http://ded.mo.gov/ (April 11, 2011).

30. Missouri Department of Economic Development, "FACT SHEET: Five Years Since the Strategic Plan Initiative for Economic Growth, Transforming Missouri's Economy for the 21st Century" (April 11, 2016), https://ded.mo.gov.

31. U.S. Travel Association, "Travel Answer Sheet" (March 2020), https://www.ustravel.org.

32. David Reynolds, as quoted in Charles Mahtesian, "How States Get People to (Love) Them," *Governing* 7 (January 1994): 47.

33. Travel Oregon, "Oregon Coast," https://traveloregon.com/ (accessed March 23, 2020).

34. Paul Egan and Kathleen Gray, "Whitmer Budget Revives Pure Michigan, Boosts Schools and Environment," *Detroit Free Press* (February 7, 2020).

35. William Yardley, "A Tourism Office Falls Victim to Hard Times," *The New York Times* (July 11, 2011).

36. Patrick McGeehan, "NYC Is On Pace to Draw a Record 67 Million Tourists This Year," *New York Times* (August 19, 2019); ""Broadway Is Dark. Liberty Island Is Empty. Will the Tourists Come Back?" *New York Times* (July 24, 2020); Curtis Tate, "In Sign of COVID-19's Impact on New York Tourism, Hilton to Close Times Square Hotel," *USA Today* (September 7, 2020).

37. Richard Bilbao, "Millions Lost: The Daily Pandemic Cost for Disney and the Rest of the Tourism Industry," *Orlando Business Journal* (April 2, 2020); Ryan Lynch, "Local Unemployment Rate Skyrockets in April," *Orlando Business Journal* (May 22, 2020); Brooks Barnes, "Disney World Is Reopening, But You Won't Be Able to Hug Mickey," *New York Times* (May 27, 2020).

38. J. Allen Whitt, "The Arts Coalition in Strategies of Urban Development," in Clarence N. Stone and Heywood T. Sanders, eds., *The Politics of Urban Development* (Lawrence: University Press of Kansas, 1987), pp. 144–56; Elizabeth Strom, "Revisiting the Arts as a Socially Innovative Urban Development Strategy," *European Planning Studies* 28 (March 2020): 475–95.

39. "If You Build It," *Governing* 19 (January 2006): 18.

40. Richard Sandomir, "A Texas-Size Stadium," *The New York Times* (July 17, 2009).

41. Conrad Defiebre and Jay Weiner, "Pawlenty Unveils Plans for Stadiums," *Minneapolis Star Tribune* (March 16, 2004).

42. Nick Sibilla, "Over Thirty Years Ago, Maryland Tried to Seize an NLF Team," *Forbes* (May 28, 2014).

43. Rodd Zolkos, "Cities Blast Stadium Study," *City & State* 4 (April 1987): 3, 53; see also Kevin G. Quinn, Christopher P. Borick, and Paul B. Bursick, "The Stadium Game: An Empirical Analysis," paper presented at the annual meeting of the Midwest Political Science Association, Chicago, Illinois, 2000.

44. Gary Enos and Rodd Zolkos, "Stadiums Ding Home Runs," *City & State* 8 (September 23–October 6, 1991): 1, 24.

45. Natalie Gochnour, Juliette Tennert, Jennifer Leaver, and Meredith King, "Utah's Olympic Economic Legacy," *University of Utah Kem C. Gardner Policy Institute* (February 2018).

46. John Larkin, "States Spark Foreign Relations of Their Own," *PA Times* (June 1, 1992): 1, 20; see also Jeffrey A. Finkle, "State Economic Development Strategies: Trends and Issues," in *The Book of the States 2006* (Lexington, KY: Council of State Governments, 2006), pp. 511–14.

47. U.S. Census Bureau, "U.S. Exports of Goods by State, Based on Origin of Movement, by NAICS-Based Product" (December 2019), https://www.census.gov.

48. U.S. Bureau of Economic Analysis, "Foreign Direct Investment in the United States (FDIUS): Employment by State and Country," https://www.bea.gov (accessed August 25, 2020).

49. Global Business Alliance, "New State Data Show Importance of International Companies" (January 16, 2019), https://globalbusiness.org.

50. Quoted in John Fritze, "Trump Will Formally Cancel NAFTA to Press Congress to Approve New Trade Deal," *USA Today* (December 2, 2018).

51. Jeff Mason and Andrea Shalal, "Trump Signs USMCA, 'Ending the NAFTA Nightmare'; Key Democrats Not Invited," *Reuters* (January 29, 2020).

52. Nordea, "Foreign Direct Investment (FDI) in the United States: FDI in Figures" (March 2020), https://www.nordeatrade.com.

53. Adrian Seric and Jostein Hauge, "Foreign Direct Investment Could Contract By 40% This Year, Hitting Developing Countries Hardest," *World Economic Forum* (June 2, 2020).

54. Richard S. Krannich and Craig R. Humphrey, "Local Mobilization and Community Growth: Toward an Assessment of the 'Growth Machine' Hypothesis," *Rural Sociology* 48 (Spring 1983): 60–81; John M. Levy, *Urban and Metropolitan Economics* (New York: McGraw-Hill, 1985); G. Jason Jolley, Mandee Foushee Lancaster, and Jiang Gao, "Tax Incentives and Business Climate: Executive Perceptions From Incented and Nonincented Firms," *Economic Development Quarterly* 29 (May 2015): 180–86.

55. Roger Schmenner, "Location Decisions of Large Firms: Implications for Public Policy," *Commentary* 5 (January 1981): 307.

56. Paul Brace, *State Government and Economic Performance* (Baltimore, MD: Johns Hopkins University Press, 1993); Laura A. Reese, "The Alchemy of Local Economic Development," *Economic Development Quarterly* 28 (August 2014): 206–19.

57. Michael A. Pagano and Ann O'M. Bowman, *Cityscapes and Capital* (Baltimore, MD: Johns Hopkins University Press, 1995).

58. Tim Flach, "Amazon Furor Already Taking Economic Toll," *The State*, (April 30, 2011).

59. Parris Glendening, "Smart Growth Tops Governors' Agenda," *Washington Post* (July 12, 2000): A14.

60. Craig Jenkins, Kevin T. Leicht, and Arthur Jaynes, "Creating High-Technology Growth: High-Tech Employment Growth in U.S. Metropolitan Areas, 1988–1998," *Social Science Quarterly* 89: 2 (2009): 456–81.

61. J. Norman Baldwin, Stephen A. Borrelli, and Michael J. New, "State Educational Investments and Economic Growth in the United States: A Path Analysis," *Social Science Quarterly* 92 (March 2011): 226–45.

62. Jay S. Baron, "At 25, Toyota Plan Still Lean, Flexible, World-Famous," www.kentucky.com (November 13, 2011).

63. Cassie Cope and Andrew Shain, "S.C. Offered More than $200 Million to Win Volvo," *The State* (May 11, 2015); *Business Facilities*, "Volvo Investing Another $520 Million in South Carolina" (October 3, 2017).

64. David Wren, "Volvo to Build Charleston-Area Battery Plant to Power SC-Made Vehicles," *The Post and Courier* (January 13, 2020).
65. Mac R. Holmes, as quoted in Peter Applebome, "States Raise Stakes in Fight for Jobs," *The New York Times* (October 4, 1993): A10.
66. Jim Malewitz, "Report: Few States Study Impact of Costly Tax Breaks," www.stateline.org (April 12, 2012).
67. Susan K. Urahn, "Showing the Way on Tax Incentives," *Governing* (June 13, 2012).
68. William Fulton, "The Clawback Clause," *Governing* 16 (October 2002): 72.
69. Ann O'M. Bowman, *The Visible Hand: Major Issues in City Economic Policy* (Washington, DC: National League of Cities, 1987).
70. Darrene Hackler and Heike Mayer, "Diversity, Entrepreneurship, and the Urban Environment," *Journal of Urban Affairs* 30 (2008): 273–307.
71. Peter Waldman, "Cities Are Pressured to Make Developers Share Their Wealth," *The Wall Street Journal* (March 10, 1987): 1.
72. Carol Steinbach, "Tapping Private Resources," *National Journal* (April 26, 1986): 993.
73. "Taking Care of Business," *The Economist* (February 18, 1989): 28.
74. Neal Peirce, "Cities Must Learn When to Say No," *Houston Chronicle* (February 13, 1989): A12.
75. Melissa Wylie, "Best Places for New Small Businesses" (February 20, 2020), https://www.lendingtree.com.
76. Charles J. Spindler, "Winners and Losers in Industrial Recruitment: Mercedes-Benz and Alabama," *State and Local Government Review* 26 (Fall 1994): 192–204.
77. Daniel C. Vock, "Court Allows Smokestack Chasing—For Now," www.stateline.org (May 16, 2006).
78. Charles Mahtesian, "A Non-Poaching Peace Pact Is Under Fire in Florida," *Governing* 13 (May 2000): 88; see also Christopher W. Hawkins, "Competition and Cooperation: Local Government Joint Ventures for Economic Development," *Journal of Urban Affairs* 32:2 (2010): 253–75.

Chapter 15 Education Policy: Reading, Writing, and Reform

1. National Commission on Excellence in Education, *A Nation at Risk: The Imperative for Educational Reform* (Washington, DC: U.S. Government Printing Office, 1983), p. 1.
2. "PISA 2018 U.S. Results," https://nces.ed.gov/ (accessed June 27, 2020).
3. Lyndsey Layton, "Majority of U.S. Public School Students in Poverty," www.washingtonpost.com (January 15, 2015); Michael J. Petrilli, "No, Half of American Schoolchildren Are Not 'Low-Income'" (October 4, 2017), https://fordhaminstitute.org/
4. U.S. Census Bureau, "Annual Survey of School System Finances: 2017—Table 1 Summary of Public Elementary-Secondary School System Finances by State, Fiscal Year 2017" (May 21, 2019), https://www.census.gov.
5. National Center for Education Statistics, "The Condition of Education 2019" (May 2019), https://nces.ed.gov.
6. National Center for Education Statistics, "Fast Facts: What Are the Dropout Rates of High School Students?" https://nces.ed.gov/ (accessed March 29, 2020).
7. College Board, "2019 SAT Suite of Assessments Annual Report: Total Group," https://reports.collegeboard.org (accessed March 28, 2020).
8. Diane Rado, "Should Teachers Stay in the Classroom if They Can't Pass the State's General Knowledge Test?" *Florida Phoenix* (March 15, 2019).
9. *The Condition of Education*, U.S. Department of Education, www.nces.ed.gov (accessed April 7, 2015).
10. John Bohte, "School Bureaucracy and Student Performance at the Local Level," *Public Administration Review* 61 (January/February 2001): 92–99; John E. Chubb and Terry Moe, *Politics, Markets, and America's Schools* (Washington, DC: The Brookings Institution, 1990).
11. Kevin B. Smith and Christopher W. Larimer, "A Mixed Relationship: Bureaucracy and School Performance," *Public Administration Review* 64 (November/December 2004): 728–36; Kevin B. Smith and Kenneth J. Meier, *The Case Against School Choice: Politics, Markets, and Fools* (Armonk, NY: M. E. Sharpe, 1995); Kevin B. Smith and Christopher W. Larimer, "A Mixed Relationship: Bureaucracy and School Performance," *Public Administration Review* 64 (November/December 2004): 728–36; see also Robert Maranto, Scott Milliman, and Scott Stevens, "Does Private School Competition Harm Public Schools?" *Political Research Quarterly* 53 (March 2000): 177–92.
12. Dirk F. Zuschlag and Kristine L. Bowman, "States' Intervention in School Districts' Finances," National Education Policy Center (September 5, 2019).
13. Richard Welsh, "Recovery, Achievement, and Opportunity: A Comparative Analysis of State Takeover Districts in Louisiana, Tennessee, and Georgia," *Urban Education* 54 (March 2019): 311–38.
14. Patrick McGuinn, "The National Schoolmarm: No Child Left Behind and the New Educational Federalism," *Publius* 35 (Winter 2005): 41–69.
15. Wayne Riddle, *Major Accountability Themes of Second-Round State Applications for NCLB Waivers* (Washington, DC: Center on Education Policy, May 2012).
16. Andrew Schultz, Lance Fusarelli, and Andrew McEachin, "The Every Student Succeeds Act, the Decline of the Federal Role in Education, and the Curbing of Executive Authority," *Publius: The Journal of Federalism* 47 (Summer 2017): 426–44.
17. Serrano v. Priest, 5 Cal. 3d 584 (1971).
18. San Antonio Independent School District v. Rodriguez, 411 U.S. 1 (1973).
19. New Jersey School Boards Association, "School Finance 101," https://www.njsba.org/ (accessed March 30, 2020).
20. Kenneth Saltman, *The Politics of Education: A Critical Introduction*, 2nd ed. (New York: Routledge, 2018).
21. Douglas S. Reed, *On Equal Terms: The Constitutional Politics of Educational Opportunity* (Princeton, NJ: Princeton University Press, 2001).
22. See Eric A. Hanushek and Alfred A. Lindseth, *Schoolhouses, Courthouses, and Statehouses: Solving the Funding-Achievement Puzzle in America's Public Schools* (Princeton: Princeton University Press, 2009).
23. James S. Coleman, *Equality of Educational Opportunity* (Washington, DC: U.S. Government Printing Office, 1966).
24. Michael A. Gottfried, "Peer Effects in Urban Schools: Assessing the Impact of Classroom Composition on Student Achievement," *Educational Policy* 28:5 (2014): 607–47; Eric A. Hanushek, John F. Kain, Jacob M. Markman, and Steven G. Rivkin, "Does Peer Ability Affect Student Achievement?" *Journal of Applied Econometrics* 18 (September/October 2003): 527–44, www.edpro.stanford.edueahpaperspeersaug01.pdf/.
25. Eric A. Hanushek, "The Economics of Schooling: Production and Efficiency in Public Schools," *Journal of Economic Literature* 24 (September 1986): 1141–77.
26. Michael T. Hartney and Patrick Flavin, "The Political Foundations of the Black-White Achievement Gap," *American Politics Research* 42:1 (2014): 3–33; Nathan Glazer, *We Are All Multiculturalists Now* (Cambridge, MA: Harvard University Press, 1997).
27. R. L. Linn and K. G. Welner, eds., *Race-Conscious Policies for Assigning Students to Schools: Social Science Research and the Court Cases* (Washington, DC: National Academy of Education, 2007).
28. Roland G. Fryer, Jr. and Steven D. Levitt, "Testing for Racial Differences in the Mental Ability of Young Children," *American Economic Review* 103:2 (2013): 981–1005.
29. Eric A. Hanushek and Steven G. Rivkin, "Harming the Best: How Schools Affect the Black-White Achievement Gap," *Journal of Policy Analysis and Management* 28:3 (2009): 366–93.
30. Meredith v. Jefferson County Board of Education, U.S. Sup. Ct. No. 05-915 (2007).
31. Hanushek and Rifkin, "Harming the Best"; Hanushek and Lindseth, *Schoolhouses*.

32. Karl L. Alexander, Doris R. Entwisle, and Linda Steffel Olson, "Lasting Consequences of the Summer Learning Gap," *American Sociological Review* 72 (April 2007): 167–80.

33. See, for example, Fryer G. Roland, "'Acting White': The Social Price Paid by the Best and Brightest Minority Students," *Education Next* 6:1 (2006): 52–59.

34. Hartney and Flavin, 2014.

35. Michael B. Berkman and Eric Plutzner, *Ten Thousand Democracies: Politics and Public Opinion in America's School Districts* (Washington, DC: Georgetown University Press, 2005).

36. Brown v. Board of Education of Topeka, 347 U.S. 483 (1954).

37. Swann v. Charlotte-Mecklenberg County Schools, 402 U.S. 1 (1971).

38. Chase Billingham, "Within-District Racial Segregation and the Elusiveness of White Students Return to Urban Public Schools," *Urban Education* 54 (February 2019): 151–81; Sean Reardon and Ann Owens, "60 Years after *Brown*: Trends and Consequences of School Segregation," *Annual Review of Sociology* 40 (June 2014): 199–218.

39. Reed, *On Equal Terms*.

40. Charles T. Clotfelter, "Public School Segregation in Metropolitan Areas," *Land Economics* 75 (December 1999): 487–504.

41. Sarah Reckhow, *Follow the Money: How Foundation Dollars Change Public School Politics* (New York: Oxford University Press, 2013); also see Alan Greenblatt, "Billionaires in the Classroom," *Governing* (October 2011): 27–35; and Natasha Singer, "The Silicon Valley Billionaires Remaking America's Schools," *New York Times* (June 6, 2017).

42. Ray Hart, Michael Casserly, Renata Uzzell, Moses Palacios, Amanda Corcoran, and Liz Spurgeon, "Student Testing in America's Great Schools: An Inventory and Preliminary Analysis," *Council of Great City Schools* (October 2015).

43. Lisette Alvarez, "States Listen as Parents Give Rampant Testing an F," www.nytimes.com (November 9, 2014).

44. Sam Dillon, "Federal Researchers Find Lower Standards in Schools," www.nytimes.com (October 30, 2009).

45. Heather Vogell, John Pery, Alan Judd, and M. B. Pell, "Cheating Our Children: Suspicious School Test Scores across the Nation," www.ajc.com (January 26, 2012); Trip Gabriel, "Under Pressure, Teachers Tamper with Test Scores," www.nytimes.com (June 10, 2010).

46. Alan Wong and Terrence F. Ross, "When Teachers Cheat," *The Atlantic* (April 2, 2015).

47. Dylan Scott, "States Begin Implementing Common Core Standards," *Governing* (February 7, 2012).

48. Cited in Gregory Korte, "The Every Student Succeeds Act vs. No Child Left Behind: What's Changed?" *USA Today* (December 10, 2015).

49. David L. Kirp, *The Sandbox Investment: The Preschool Movement and Kids-First Politics* (Cambridge, MA: Harvard University Press, 2007).

50. The National Institute of Early Education Research, "The State of Preschool 2018" (2019), http://nieer.org.

51. Center for Effective Discipline, www.gundersonhealth.org (accessed April 14, 2015).

52. Sam Dillon, "High Schools to Offer Plan to Graduate 2 Years Early," www.nytimes.com (February 18, 2010).

53. Education Commission of the States, "Advanced Placement: State Financial Support for AP Course Offerings/AP Success," http://ecs.force.com (accessed April 2, 2020).

54. Raj Chetty, John N. Friedman, and Jonah E. Rockoff, "The Long-Term Impacts of Teachers: Teacher Value-Added and Student Outcomes in Adulthood" (Washington, DC: National Bureau of Economic Research Paper No. 17699, December 2011).

55. Lauren Camera, "Teacher Salaries Fell 4.5% Over the Last Decade," *U.S. News and World Report* (April 29, 2019).

56. National Education Association, "Rankings of the States 2018 and Estimates of School Statistics 2019" (April 2019), https://www.nea.org/.

57. Daarel Burnette II and Madeline Will, "See Where Teachers Got Pay Raises This Year: Protests Across the Country Swayed Governors to Push for Salary Bumps," *Education Week* (June 18, 2019).

58. Talia Milgrom-Elcott, "There's a Nationwide STEM Teacher Shortage. Will It Cost Us the Next Einstein?" *Forbes* (May 30, 2019).

59. William H. Marinell and Susan Moore Johnson, "Midcareer Entrants to Teaching: Who They Are and How They May, or May Not, Change Teaching," *Educational Policy* 28:6 (2014): 743–79.

60. Phi Delta Kappa, "Frustration in the Schools: Teachers Speak Out on Pay, Funding, and Feeling Valued, 51st Annual PDK Poll of the Public's Attitudes Toward the Public Schools" (September 2019), https://pdkpoll.org.

61. Dan Wieder, "Charter-School Debate Takes Different Turns in Georgia, New Jersey," *Governing* (March 29, 2012); Diana Jean Schemo, "Study of Test Scores Finds Charter Schools Lagging," *The New York Times* (August 23, 2006): 1–3 (citing a federal study).

62. National Center for Education Statistics, "School Choice in the United States: 2019," https://nces.ed.gov (accessed April 2, 2020).

63. Zelman et al. v. Simmons-Harris et al. (No. 001751, June 27, 2002).

64. Sam Dillon, "Florida Court Strikes Down School Voucher Program," *The New York Times* (January 5, 2006).

65. Erin Richards, "Wisconsin Voucher Programs March Toward 30,000 Student Threshold," *The Journal Sentinel* (December 8, 2014), www.edchoice.org (accessed June 14, 2015).

66. Stacy Teicher Khadaroo, "Nevada's Groundbreaking School Choice Law: Help or Hindrance to Public System?, www.csmonitor.com (June 3, 2015).

67. Lauren McDonald, "Think Tanks and the Media: How the Conservative Movement Gained Entry into the Education Policy Arena," *Educational Policy* 28:6 (2013): 845–80; Associated Press, "School Vouchers Spark Legal and Political Fights," *Governing* (April 9, 2012).

68. Michelle Rindels, "School Choice Battle Returns, This Time Over Coming Drop-Off of Opportunity Scholarships," *Nevada Independent* (January 25, 2019).

69. Patrick Wolf, "The Comparative Longitudinal Evaluation of the Milwaukee Parental Choice Program: Summary of Final Reports," SCDP Milwaukee Evaluation, Report No. 36, www.uaedreform.org (February 2012); Borsh and Wolf; "Study Finds Academic Gains Not Superior among Students Enrolled in Privately-Run Schools," www.rand.org (February 1, 2007).

70. Jacques Steinberg, "At 42 Newly Privatized Philadelphia Schools, Uncertainty Abounds," *The New York Times* (April 19, 2002): 1–3.

71. Andrea Gabor, "Betsy Devos's Voucher Boondoggle: Look No Further than Trump's Education Budget for Billions in Government Waste," *Bloomberg Opinion,* (February 18, 2020).

72. Espinoza v. Montana Department of Revenue 591 U.S. _____ (2020).

73. Kristen A. Graham, "Philadelphia Taking Back 6 Privatized Schools," www.philly.com (June 19, 2008).

74. Brian Gill, Michael Timpane, and Dominic Brewer, *Rhetoric versus Reality: What We Know and What We Need to Know about School Vouchers and Charter Schools* (Santa Monica, CA: Rand Corporation, 2001).

75. www.nces.gov (accessed April 14, 2015).

76. Arianna Prothero, "Is There a Growing Political Backlash to For-Profit Charter Schools?" *Education Week* (September 17, 2018).

77. Brian D. Ray, "A Systematic Review of the Empirical Research on Selected Aspects of Homeschooling as a School Choice," *Journal of School Choice* 11 (November 2017): 604–21.

78. Lyndsey Layton, "Study Raises Questions about Virtual Schools," www.washingtonpost.com (October 24, 2011).
79. Dana Goldstein, "Coronavirus Is Shutting Schools. Is America Ready for Virtual Learning?" *New York Times* (March 13, 2020).
80. Cecilia Kang, Davey Alba, and Adam Satariano, "Surging Traffic Is Slowing Down Our Internet," *New York Times* (March 26, 2020).
81. Valerie Strauss, "Returning To School This Fall May Be 'Extremely Difficult' with COVID-19 Still Raging, South Carolina Official Says," *Washington Post* (June 23, 2020).
82. Denise Grady, "The Fear of Coronavirus and Flu Colliding in the Fall," *New York Times* (April 22, 2020).
83. Diane Ravitch, *Reign of Error: The Hoax of the Privatization Movement and the Danger to America's Public Schools* (New York: Random House, 2014).
84. Bryan Shelley, *Money, Mandates, and Control in American Public Education* (Ann Arbor: University of Michigan Press, 2011).

Chapter 16 Criminal Justice: Cops and Corrections

1. *KTAR News* (July 1, 2020), https://ktar.com/.
2. Tim Harlow and Shannon Prather, "Authorities: Suspect Who Shot at Coon Rapids Police After Traffic Stop Is Killed by Officer," *Minneapolis Star-Tribune* (April 19, 2019).
3. Cristina Carrega, "Veteran Oklahoma Police Officer Killed, Rookie in Critical Condition, After Suspect Shoots Both in the Head," *ABC News* (July 1, 2020).
4. Associated Press, "Phoenix Police Commander Killed, 2 Others Wounded in Shooting," https://www.nbcnews.com (March 30, 2020).
5. Lynne Peeples, "What the Data Say about Police Shootings," *Nature* (September 4, 2019); Rich Morin, Kim Parker, Renee Stepler, and Andrew Mercer, "Police Views, Public Views," *Pew Research Center: Social and Demographic Trends* (January 11, 2017).
6. Lindsey Van Ness, "Body Cameras May Not Be the Easy Answer Everyone Was Looking For," *Pew Stateline* (January 14, 2020).
7. Rachel Morgan and Barbara Oudekerk, "Criminal Victimization, 2018," *Bureau of Justice Statistics* (September 2019).
8. *Criminal Justice 2000*, vol. 4, National Criminal Justice Reference Service, www.ncjrs.gov (accessed December 7, 2011).
9. SafeHome.org, "Criminal Confessions: Over 2,000 People Reveal Their Criminal Rap Sheets" (January 27, 2017), https://www.safehome.org.
10. Wesley Marshall, quoted in Robert Boos, "Survey Finds Bicyclists and Motorists Ignore Traffic Laws at Similar Rates," *Science Friday*, PRI (July 18, 2015).
11. William J. Wilem, *When Work Disappears: The World of the New Urban Poor* (New York: Alfred A. Knopf, 1996); Alex Piquero, John MacDonald, and Karen F. Parker, "Race, Local Life Circumstances, and Criminal Activity," *Social Science Quarterly* 83 (September 2002): 654–70.
12. "Chart of the Week: the Black-White Gap in Incarceration Rates," www.pewresearch.org (July 18, 2014); Bruce Western, *Punishment and Inequality in America* (New York: Russell Sage Press, 2006).
13. Wendy Sawyer and Peter Wagner, "Mass Incarceration: The Whole Pie 2020," *Prison Policy Initiative* (March 24, 2020).
14. Federal Bureau of Investigation, "Crime in the United States, 2018," https://ucr.fbi.gov/ (accessed April 8, 2020).
15. Gary Cordner, "Community Policing," in Michael D. Reisig and Robert J. Kane, eds., *The Oxford Handbook of Police and Policing* (New York: Oxford University Press, 2014), pp. 148–71; Mark A. Glaser and Janet Denhardt, "Community Policing and Community Building: A Case of Officer Perception," *American Review of Public Administration* 40:3 (2009): 309–25.
16. James Q. Wilson and George L. Kelling, "Broken Windows: The Police and Neighborhood Safety," *Atlantic Monthly* (March 1982): 29–38; see also Rob Gurwitt, "Not by Cops Alone," *Governing* 8 (May 1995): 16–26.

17. Justin Fox, "'Broken Windows' Theory Was Right About the Windows: Addressing Physical Signs of Disorder Really Does Fight Crime," *Bloomberg Politics & Policy* (October 16, 2019); Bench Ansfield, "How a 50-Year-Old Study Was Misconstrued to Create Destructive Broken Windows Policing," *Washington Post* (December 27, 2019); Center for Evidence-Based Crime Policy, "What Works in Policing?," https://cebcp.org/ (accessed July 5, 2020).
18. Terry v. Ohio, 392 U.S. 1 (1968).
19. New York Civil Liberties Union, "Stop-and-Frisk in the DeBlasio Era (2019)," (March 14, 2019), https://www.nyclu.org/.
20. Nigel Fielding, Karren Bullock, and Simon Holdaway, eds., *Critical Reflections on Evidence-Based Policing* (London: Routledge, 2019).
21. Los Angeles Police Department, "Crime Mapping and COMPSTAT," http://www.lapdonline.org/crime_mapping_and_compstat (accessed April 8, 2019).
22. U.S. Census Bureau, "2018 ASPEP Datasets & Tables: State and Local Government Employment Data," https://www.census.gov/data (accessed April 8, 2020).
23. Brian Barrett, "The Pentagon's Hand-Me-Downs Helped Militarize Police. Here's How," *Wired* (June 2, 2020); see also Aaron Davenport, Jonathan William Wilburn, Andrew Lauland, Annelise Pietenpol, Marc Robbins, Erin Rebhan, Patricia Boren, and E. Jack Riley, *An Evaluation of the Department of Defense's Excess Property Program: Law Enforcement Agency Equipment Acquisition Policies, Findings, and Options* (Santa Monica, CA: RAND Corporation, 2018).
24. U.S. Census Bureau, "2018 ASPEP Datasets & Tables,"
25. Jeremy Carter, David Carter, Steve Chermak, and Edmund McGarrell, "Law Enforcement Fusion Centers: Cultivating an Information Sharing Environment While Safeguarding Privacy," *Journal of Police and Criminal Psychology* 32 (March 2017): 11–27.
26. Miranda v. Arizona, 384 U.S. 486 (1966).
27. Mapp v. Ohio, 307 U.S. 643 (1961).
28. "Free at Last, Free at Last," *Time* (November 2, 1987): 55.
29. Adam Pasick, "The Bizarre Tale of the 'Indict a Ham Sandwich' Judge Who Became a Felon" (November 26, 2014), https://qz.com/.
30. Steve Helber and Denise Lavoie, "Richmond Removes Statue of Confederate General J.E.B. Stuart," *ABC News* (July 7, 2020).
31. Ivan Pereira, "Here's Where Confederate Statues and Memorials Have Been Removed in the U.S.," *ABC News* (June 19, 2020).
32. Jeanine Santucci, "Trump Says He Won't Consider Renaming Military Bases Named for Confederate Generals," *USA Today* (June 10, 2020).
33. Summer Lin, "What Are Chokeholds and Can Police Use Them? It Depends on What Kind and Where You Live," *Miami Herald* (June 3, 2020); Kaveh Waddell, "Why Many Large Police Departments Tolerate Their Officers Using Neck Holds," *The Atlantic* (December 10, 2014).
34. National Association of Crime Victims Compensation Board, www.nacvb.org (accessed May 14, 2015).
35. Klaas Kids Foundation, http://klaaskids.org/pg-legmeg2.htm.
36. Renee Scherlen, "The Never-Ending Drug War: Obstacles to Drug War Policy Termination," *PS* (January 2012): 67–74.
37. Furman v. Georgia, 408 U.S. 239 (1972).
38. Roper v. Simmons, 543 U.S. 551 (2005).
39. Singleton v. Norris, 124 S. Ct. 74 (2003).
40. Kennedy v. Louisiana, 554 U.S. 407 (2008).
41. Baze v. Rees, 553 U.S. 35 (2008).
42. Death Penalty Information Center, https://deathpenaltyinfo.org (accessed March 15, 2020).
43. "Death Penalty," https://news.gallup.com/ (accessed April 9, 2020).
44. NAACP Legal Defense and Education Fund, "Death Row USA" (Winter 2020), https://www.naacpldf.org/; Death

Penalty Information Center, "Executions of Women," https://deathpenaltyinfo.org/ (accessed April 9, 2020).

45. Death Penalty Information Center, www.deathpenaltyinfo.org (2020).

46. Melinda Gann Hall and Paul Brace, "The Vicissitudes of Death by Decree: Forces Influencing Capital Punishment Decision Making in State Supreme Courts," *Social Science Quarterly* 75 (March 1999): 1368.

47. Erin Dunne, "Drug Companies Opposed to Death Penalty Have Changed Executions," *Washington Examiner* (August 14, 2018).

48. Lee Black and Robert Sade, "Lethal Injection and Physicians: State Law vs Medical Ethics," *Journal of the American Medical Association* 23 (December 19, 2007): 2779–881.

49. Frank Baumgartner, Suzanne L. DeBoef, and Amber E. Boydstun, *The Decline of the Death Penalty and the Discovery of Innocence* (Cambridge: Cambridge University Press, 2008).

50. Death Penalty Information Center, "Execution Database," https://deathpenaltyinfo.org/executions/execution-database; "Death Sentences in the United States Since 1977," https://deathpenaltyinfo.org/ (accessed April 9, 2020).

51. Death Penalty Focus, "1,500 Executions; 166 Exonerations" (July 11, 2019), https://deathpenalty.org.

52. David C. May, Brandon K. Applegate, Rick Ruddell, and Peter B. Wood, "Going to Jail Sucks (And It Really Doesn't Matter Who You Ask," *American Journal of Criminal Justice* 39 (2014): 250–66.

53. See Oliver Roeder, Lauren Brooke-Eisen, and Julia Bowling, "What Caused the Crime Decline?" Report of Brennan Center for Law and Justice, 2015.

54. Danielle Kaeble and Mary Cowhig, "Correctional Populations in the United States, 2016," *Bureau of Justice Statistics Bulletin* (April 2018).

55. Jeff Yates and Richard Fording, "Politics and State Punitiveness in Black and White," *Journal of Politics* 67 (November 2005): 1118.

56. Jon Hurwitz and Mark Peffley, "Explaining the Great Racial Divide: Perceptions of Fairness in the U.S. Criminal Justice System," *Journal of Politics* 67 (August 2005): 762–83.

57. Stephen Demuth and Darrell Steffensmeier, "Ethnicity Effects on Sentence Outcomes in Large Urban Courts: Comparisons among White, Black, and Hispanic Defendants," *Social Science Quarterly* 85 (December 2004): 994–1011.

58. Sawyer and Wagner, 2020.

59. Sintia Radu, "Countries with the Highest Incarceration Rates," *U.S. News and World Reports* (May 13, 2019).

60. Marie Gottschalk, *The Prison and the Gallows: The Politics of Mass Incarceration in America* (New York: Cambridge University Press, 2006).

61. Erica Goode, "U.S. Prison Populations Decline, Reflecting New Approach to Crime," www.nytimes.com (July 25, 2013); John Buntin, "Game Changers," *Governing* (February 2012): 35–38.

62. Christine Vestal, "For Aging Inmates, Care Outside Prison Walls," www.pewtrusts.org (August 12, 2014); David Levine, "Jailhouse Shock," *Governing* (March 2012): 18.

63. D. Walsh, "Judges Order California to Cut Prison Population by 40,591," *Sacramento Bee* (August 5, 2009).

64. Ryan Holeywell, "Crowded Out," *Governing* (February 2014): 31–35.

65. U.S. Census Bureau, "Annual Survey of State Government Finances, 1992–2018," https://www.census.gov.

66. The Sentencing Project, "The Facts of Life Sentences: 1 in 7 People in Prisons Is Serving a Life Sentence," https://www.sentencingproject.org/ (accessed April 10, 2020).

67. Sawyer and Wagner, 2020.

68. Bernadette Rabuy and Daniel Kopf, "Detaining the Poor," *Prison Policy Initiative* (May 10, 2016).

69. C. J. Ciaramella, "8 of the Top 10 Biggest U.S. Coronavirus Hotspots Are Prisons and Jails," *Reason: Free Minds and Free Markets* (April 29, 2020).

70. Kenya Evelyn, "Prison Uprising Put Down as U.S. Inmates Demand Protection from Coronavirus," *The Guardian* (April 10, 2020).

71. Timothy Williams and Danielle Ivory, "Chicago's Jail Is Top Hot Spot as Virus Spreads Behind Bars," *New York Times* (April 23, 2020).

72. University of Michigan Criminal Law Professor Sonja Starr, quoted in Catherine Kim, "Why People Are Being Released from Jails and Prisons During the Pandemic," *Vox* (April 3, 2020).

73. Timothy Williams, Benjamin Weiser, and William Rashbaum, " 'Jails Are Petri Dishes': Inmates Freed as the Virus Spreads Behind Bars," *New York Times* (March 31, 2020).

74. Pew Center on the States, *One in 31: The Long Reach of American Corrections* (Washington, DC: Pew Center on the States, 2009), p. 12.

75. Pew Center, *One in 31*, p. 13.

76. Kaeble and Cowhig (2018).

77. Buntin, "Game Changers"; Keith B. Richburg, "States Seek Less Costly Substitutes for Prison," *The Washington Post* (July 13, 2009).

78. Beth Schwartzapfel, "Want to Shrink the Prison Population? Look at Parole," *The Marshall Project* (February 11, 2019).

79. Pew Center on the States, *One in 31*, p. 80.

80. Avdi S. Avdija and JiHee Lee, "Does Electronic Detention Home Detention Program Work? Evaluating Program Suitability Based on Offenders' Post-Program Recidivism Status," *Justice Policy Journal* 11 (Fall 2014): 1–15.

81. Rand Corporation, "Education and Vocational Training in Prison Reduces Recidivism, Improves Job Outlook," www.rand.org (August 22, 2013).

82. Jenny Gold, "A National Model for Decrowding Jails and Helping the Mentally Ill," www.governing.com (August 20, 2014).

83. Olim v. Wakinekona, 461 U.S. 238 (1983).

84. See Justice Policy Institute, www.justicepolicy.org (accessed July 12, 2012).

85. Rebecca Boone, "Otter: State to Take Over Privately Run Prison," www.idahostatesman.com (January 4, 2014).

86. Carl Hulse, "Unlikely Cause Unites the Left and the Right: Justice Reform," *New York Times* (February 15, 2015); Arthur Rizer and Lars Trautman, "The Conservative Case for Criminal Justice Reform," *The Guardian* (August 5, 2018).

Chapter 17 Social Welfare and Health Care Policy: Addressing Poverty and Sickness

1. World Bank, *Poverty and Shared Prosperity 2018: Piecing Together the Poverty Puzzle* (Washington DC: World Bank, 2018).

2. Philip Alston, "Statement on Visit to the USA by Professor Philip Alston, United Nations Special Rapporteur on Extreme Poverty and Human Rights," *United Nations Office of the High Commissioner for Human Rights* (December 15, 2017).

3. Jamie Bryan Hall and Robert Rector, "Don't Believe the UN's Propaganda about 'Extreme Poverty' in the US," *The Heritage Foundation* (July 17, 2018).

4. U.S. Census Bureau, "Poverty Thresholds: 2019," http://www.census.gov (accessed April 13, 2020).

5. Jessica Semega, Melissa Kollar, John Creamer, and Abinash Mohanty, "Income and Poverty in the United States: 2018," Table B-5 (September 2019), https://www.census.gov/.

6. Thomas B. Edsall, "How Poor Are the Poor?" www.nytimes.com (March 25, 2015).

7. Semega et al. (2018), Table B-6.

8. Semega et al. (2018), Table B-7.

9. Fred Block, Richard A. Cloward, Barbara Ehrenreich, and Francis Fox Piven, *The Mean Season: The Attack on the Welfare State* (New York: Pantheon Books, 1987), p. 92.

10. See Charles Murray, *Coming Apart: The State of White America, 1960–2010* (New York: Crown Forum, 2012); *In Our Hands: A Plan to Replace the Welfare State* (Washington, DC: American Enterprise Institute, 2006).

11. Martin Gilens, *Why Americans Hate Welfare: Race, Media, and the Politics of Antipoverty Policy* (Chicago, IL: University of Chicago Press, 1999).

12. Jake Grovum, "In Some States, Low Poverty Rate Obscures Deeper Despair," www.stateline.org (September 24, 2014).
13. Inequality.org "Income Inequality in the United States," www.inequality.org (accessed May 30, 2015).
14. Matthew C. Fellowes and Gretchen Rowe, "Politics and the New American Welfare States," *American Journal of Political Science* 48 (April 2004): 362–73.
15. Pamela M. Prah, "Why Are Welfare Rolls Flat, While the Food Stamp Program Grows Rapidly?" www.stateline.org (July 1, 2012); Jason DeParle, "Welfare Limits Left Poor Adrift as Recession Hit," www.nytimes.com (April 7, 2012).
16. Liz Schott, "State General Assistance Programs Very Limited in Half the States and Nonexistent in Others, Despite Need," *Center on Budget and Policy Priorities* (July 2, 2020), https://www.cbpp.org/.
17. Medicaid and CHIP Payment and Access Commission [MACPAC], "Report to Congress on Medicaid and CHIP" (March 2020), https://www.macpac.gov/.
18. T. J. McCue, "57 Million U.S. Workers Are Part of the Gig Economy," *Forbes* (August 31, 2018).
19. Council of Economic Advisors, "Jobs Report Shows Booming Labor Force Is Bringing Americans Off the Sidelines" (January 10, 2020), https://www.whitehouse.gov/.
20. Lance Lambert, "22 Million Have Lost Their Jobs Over the Past Month—Real Unemployment Rate Likely Nearing 18%," *Fortune* (April 16, 2020).
21. U.S. Department of Labor, "Unemployment Insurance Weekly Claims" (April 16, 2020), https://www.dol.gov/ui/data.pdf.
22. Juliet F. Gainsborough, *Scandalous Politics: Child Welfare Policy in the States* (Washington, DC: Georgetown University Press, 2010).
23. Jennifer Wolf, "Single Parent Statistics Based on Census Data," *Very Well Family* (May 1, 2020), https://www.verywellfamily.com/.
24. United Health Foundation, "America's Health Rankings: 2018 Annual Report—Infant Mortality," https://www.americashealthrankings.org/ (accessed July 9, 2020).
25. Gretchen Livingston and Deja Thomas, "Why Is the Teen Birth Rate Falling?" *Pew Research Center* (August 2, 2019), https://www.pewresearch.org/.
26. Ibid.
27. Francesca Jaroz et al., "Rollout of Indiana Welfare Changes Halted," www.indystar.com (July 31, 2008).
28. Jonathan Walters, "Is Welfare Working?" *Governing* (February 2008): 28–34.
29. National Conference of State Legislatures, "State Minimum Wages: 2020 Minimum Wage by State" (January 6, 2020), https://www.ncsl.org/.
30. Colleen Grogan, Michael Gusmano, and Richard Fording, "State Health and Welfare Programs," in Virginia Gray, Russell L. Hanson, and Thad Kousser, eds., *Politics in the American States*, 11th ed. (Los Angeles: Sage/CQ Press, 2018).
31. Roosa Tikkanen and Melinda Abrams, "U.S. Health Care from a Global Perspective, 2019: Higher Spending, Worse Outcomes?" *The Commonwealth Fund* (January 30, 2020), https://www.commonwealthfund.org/.
32. Health Management Associates, "COVID-19 Impact on Medicaid, Marketplace, and the Uninsured, by State" (April 3, 2020), https://www.healthmanagement.com.
33. Marilyn Werber Serafini, "Medicare Crooks," *National Journal* 29 (July 19, 1997): 1458–60; Malcolm Sparran, *License to Steal: Why Fraud Plagues America's Health Care System* (Boulder, CO: Westview Press, 1996).
34. United Health Foundation, *America's Health Rankings: A Call to Action for Individuals and Their Communities* (United Health Foundation, 2008).
35. American Medical Association, www.ama-assn.org (accessed July 11, 2012).
36. National Federation of Independent Business v. Sebelius et al., 567 U.S. _____ (2012).

37. Center for Medicaid and Medicare Services, "National Health Expenditures Projections 2018–2027," https://www.cms.gov/ (accessed July 9, 2020).
38. Robin Rudowitz and Elizabeth Hinton, "Early Look at Medicaid Spending and Enrollment Trends Amid COVID-19," *Kaiser Family Foundation* (May 15, 2020).
39. Sarah Kliff, "Healthcare.Gov Is Busted: These Four State Exchanges Aren't," www.washingtonpost.com (October 25, 2013).
40. Christine Vestal, "Why Some State-Run Health Exchanges Worked," www.pewstates.org (December 10, 2013).
41. Chris Kardish, "By Changing How They Pay for Them," *Governing* (September, 2014): 47–49.
42. Dylan Scott, "Could Arkansas Crack the Cost-Containment Code?," *Governing* (August 2013): 11.
43. David Levine, "Fraud Prevention's ROI," *Governing* (May 2013): 22.
44. Chris Kardish, "Creating Connections," *Governing* (February 2014): 48–51.
45. Nicole Hong, "Volunteers Rushed to Help New York Hospitals. They Found a Bottleneck," *New York Times* (April 8, 2020), https://www.nytimes.com.

Chapter 18 Environmental Policy: Regulation and Innovation

1. Umair Irfan and Kavya Sukumar, "Watch How the Climate Could Change These U.S. Cities by 2050" (May 24, 2019), https://www.vox.com/.
2. Doyle Rice, "New Visualizations Show Worst-Case Scenario for Sea Levels by 2100," *USA Today* (April 27, 2017).
3. U.S. Environmental Protection Agency, "A Closer Look: Temperature and Drought in the Southwest," https://www.epa.gov (accessed January 13, 2020).
4. National Conference on State Legislatures, "State Renewable Portfolio Standards and Goals" (April 17, 2020), https://www.ncsl.org/
5. Richard C. Feiock and Christopher Stream, "Environmental Protection versus Economic Development: A False Trade-Off?" *Public Administration Review* 61 (May/June 2001): 313–21.
6. Deborah Lynn Guber, *The Grassroots of a Green Revolution* (Cambridge, MA: MIT Press, 2003).
7. Art Swift, "Americans Again Pick Environment over Economic Growth," http://www.gallup.com/ (accessed June 5, 2015); see also Steven E. Barkan, "Explaining Public Support for the Environmental Movement: A Civic Voluntarism Model," *Social Science Quarterly* 85 (December 2004): 913–37.
8. Svetlana Flankova, Peter Tashman, Marc Van Essen, and Valentina Marano, "A Meta-Analysis of the Effectiveness of Voluntary Environmental Programs," *Academy of Management Annual Meeting Proceedings* (July 2018), https://journals.aom.org/.
9. David M. Konisky, "Regulator Attitudes and the Environmental Race to the Bottom Argument," *Journal of Public Administration Research and Theory* 18 (2008): 321–44.
10. Walter A. Rosenbaum, *Environmental Politics and Policy*, 5th ed. (Washington, DC: Congressional Quarterly Press, 2002), pp. 12–13.
11. Aria Bendix, "12 Cities with the Worst Tap Water in the US," *Business Insider* (March 17, 2020).
12. David M. Konisky, "Public Preferences for Environmental Policy Responsibility," *Publius: The Journal of Federalism* 41 (Winter 2011): 76–100.
13. Regional Greenhouse Gas Initiative, "The Investment of RGGI Proceeds in 2017" (October 2019), https://www.rggi.org/.
14. John M. Glionna, "Western Land War: 5 States Fight D.C. for Control of Federal Areas," *Los Angeles Times* (April 26, 2012), http://articles.latimes.com; Brian Calvert, "Western States Eye Federal Lands—Again," *High Country News* (October 27, 2014), www.hcn.org/issues/.

15. "The Next Great Western Land War Has Begun: An In-Depth Look at the GOP's Full-Scale Assault on our 640 Million Acres of Public Land," www.outsideonline.com (December 4, 2017).

16. "Performance Partnership Agreements," www.epa.gov (July 24, 2006).

17. Utility Air Regulatory Group v. Environmental Protection Agency, 573 U.S. 302 (2014); Michigan v. Environmental Protection Agency, 576 U.S. _____ (2015).

18. Gundy v. United States, 588 U.S. _____ (2019).

19. "National Model for Renewable Energy," *State Legislatures* (February 2006), p. 9.

20. Melissa Lunden and Meghan Thurlow, "The Stunning Impact of COVID-19 Social Distancing on Air Pollution," *GreenBiz* (March 31, 2020).

21. Seth Borenstein, "As People Stay Home, Earth Turns Wilder and Cleaner," *Associated Press* (April 22, 2020); also see Jesse Berman and Keita Ebisu, "Changes in U.S. Air Pollution During the COVID-19 Pandemic," *Science of The Total Environment* (October 2020).

22. Xiao Wu, Rachel Nethery, M. Benjamin Sabath, Danielle Braun, and Francesca Dominici, "Exposure to Air Pollution and COVID-19 Mortality in the United States" (April 24, 2020).

23. Anna Phillips and Russ Mitchell, "Trump Weakens Fuel Economy Standards, Rolling Back Key U.S. Effort Against Climate Change," *Los Angeles Times* (March 31, 2020); Nishan Degnarain, "Ten Areas Where COVID-19 Responses Have Increased Environmental Risks," *Forbes* (April 16, 2020).

24. Elizabeth Daigneau, "Consolidating 'Green' Departments," *Governing*, www.governing.com (accessed June 26, 2012).

25. Matthew Potoski, "Clean Air Federalism: Do States Race to the Bottom?" *Public Administration Review* 61 (May/June 2001): 335–42.

26. Travis Coan and Mirya R. Holman, "Voting Green," *Social Science Quarterly* 89 (2008): 1121–35; David M. Konisky, Jeffrey Milyo, and Lilliard E. Richardson, "Environmental Policy Attitudes: Issues, Geographical Scale, and Political Trust," *Social Science Quarterly* 89 (2008): 1066–85.

27. Adam McCann, "Greenest Cities in America" (October 8, 2019), https://wallethub.com.

28. Ellen Airhart, "San Francisco's Dream of 'Zero Waste' Lands in the Dumpster," *Wired* (September 28, 2018).

29. U.S. Environmental Protection Agency, "National Overview: Facts and Figures on Materials, Wastes and Recycling," https://www.epa.gov/ (accessed April 23, 2020).

30. Paula Gardner, "See Which States (and Country) Send Trash to Michigan Landfills" (February 19, 2020), https://www.mlive.com/.

31. "National Overview: Facts and Figures on Materials, Wastes and Recycling."

32. Christopher Swope and Brendan Schlauch, "Recycling Recession," *Governing* (June 2009): 20.

33. Alana Semuels, "Is This the End of Recycling?" *The Atlantic* (March 5, 2019).

34. Genevieve Grippo, "An Effort to Dramatically Expand Michigan's Bottle Deposit Law Is Back," *WWMT* (December 29, 2019).

35. Katherine N. Probst and David M. Konisky, *Superfund's Future: What Will It Cost?* (Washington, DC: Resources for the Future, 2001).

36. John M. Broder, "Without Superfund Tax, Stimulus Aids Cleanups," *The New York Times* (April 26, 2009).

37. Fred Pearce, "Awash in Radioactive Waste," *New York Times* (May 24, 2018).

38. Anthony L. Dodson, "Interstate Compacts to Bury Radioactive Waste: A Useful Tool for Environmental Policy?" *State and Local Government Review* 30 (Spring 1998): 118–28.

39. Josh Goodman, "The Nuclear Option," *Governing* 20 (November 2006): 43–45.

40. "State Restrictions on New Nuclear Power Facility Construction," *National Conference of State Legislatures* (May 2017).

41. Abigail D. Blodgett, "An Analysis of Pollution and Community Advocacy in 'Cancer Alley': Setting an Example for the Environmental Justice Movement in St James Parish, Louisiana," *Local Environment* 11 (2006): 647–61.

42. Regina Austin and Michael Schill, "Black, Brown, Red, and Poisoned," in Robert D. Bullard, ed., *Unequal Protection* (San Francisco, CA: Sierra Club Books, 1994), p. 53.

43. Deb Starkey, "Environmental Justice: Win, Lose, or Draw?" *State Legislatures* 20 (March 1994): 28; Francesca Spina, "Environmental Justice and Patterns of State Inspections," *Social Science Quarterly* 96 (June 2015): 417–29.

44. United Church of Christ Commission for Racial Justice, *Toxic Waste and Race* (New York: United Church of Christ, 1987).

45. Liam Downey and Brian Hawkins, "Single-Mother Families and Air Pollution: A National Study," *Social Science Quarterly* 89 (2008): 523–36.

46. Susan Cutter, "Race, Class, and Environmental Justice," *Progress in Human Geography* 19 (March 1995): 111–22.

47. Evan J. Ringquist, "Environmental Justice: Normative Concerns, Empirical Evidence, and Government Action," in Norman J. Vig and Michael E. Kraft, eds., *Environmental Policy: New Directions for the Twenty-First Century* (Washington, DC: Congressional Quarterly Press, 2006).

48. Evan J. Ringquist and David H. Clark, "Issue Definition and the Politics of State Environmental Justice Policy Adoption," *International Journal of Public Administration* 25 (February/March 2002): 351–89.

49. U.S. Department of Energy, "Number of Producing Gas Wells" (March 31, 2020), https://www.eia.gov/.

50. John Manuel, "Mining: EPA Tackles Fracking," *Environmental Health Perspectives* (May 2010).

51. See, for example, Tanya Heikkila et al., "Understanding a Period of Policy Change: The Case of Hydraulic Fracturing Disclosure Policy in Colorado," *Review of Policy Research* 31 (March 2014): 65–87.

52. Wade Rawlins, "North Carolina Governor Rejects Fracking Law," www.Reuters.com (July 1, 2012).

53. Kirk Ross, "The North Carolina Fracking Boom That Didn't Happen," *Carolina Public Press* (March 14, 2018).

54. U.S. Environmental Protection Agency, "EPA Issues Final Air Rules for the Oil and Natural Gas Industry" (April 17, 2012), www.epa.gov/.

55. U.S. Environmental Protection Agency, "Assessment of the Potential Impacts of Hydraulic Fracturing for Oil and Gas on Drinking Water Resources (External Review Draft)" (June 4, 2015), http://cfpub.epa.gov/.

56. United States Geological Survey, "Does the Production of Natural Gas from Shales Cause Earthquakes? If So, How Are the Earthquakes Related to These Operations?" https://www.usgs.gov/ (accessed April 24, 2020).

57. Oklahoma Secretary of Energy and Environment, "Earthquakes in Oklahoma," https://earthquakes.ok.gov/ (accessed April 24, 2020).

58. Anna Kuchment, "Even if Injection of Fracking Wastewater Stops, Quakes Won't," *Scientific American* (September 9, 2019)

59. U.S. Environmental Protection Agency, "Where Greenhouse Gases Come From" (June 19, 2019), https://www.eia.gov/.

60. Anne Barnard, "The $119 Billion Sea Wall That Could Defend New York ... or Not," *New York Times* (January 19, 2020).

61. John H. Tibbetts, "Water Cities: Can We Climate-Proof the Coast?" *Coastal Heritage Magazine*, 28 (Fall 2014): 3–11.

62. Mikaela Porter, "The Latest on Charleston Flooding Infrastructure Projects After Years of Planning and Work," *The Post and Courier* (February 19, 2020).

63. Chloe Johnson and Mikaela Porter, "Charleston's Peninsula Could Be Walled In Under New $1.75 Billion Flood Prevention Plan," *The Post and Courier* (April 20, 2020).

64. Mark Schleifstein, "$2 Billion in Restoration, Levee Projects to be Put Out to Bid by Louisiana Coastal Authority in 2020," NOLA.COM (January 15, 2020).

Index